ALTERNATIVE METHODS
OF
DISPUTE RESOLUTION

DELMAR CENGAGE Learning

Options.
Over 300 products in every area of the law: textbooks, online courses, CD-ROMs, reference books, companion websites, and more – helping you succeed in the classroom and on the job.

Support.
We offer unparalleled, practical support: robust instructor and student supplements to ensure the best learning experience, custom publishing to meet your unique needs, and other benefits such as Delmar Cengage Learning's Student Achievement Award. And our sales representatives are always ready to provide you with dependable service.

Feedback.
As always, we want to hear from you! Your feedback is our best resource for improving the quality of our products. Contact your sales representative or write us at the address below if you have any comments about our materials or if you have a product proposal.

Accounting and Financials for the Law Office • Administrative Law • Alternative Dispute Resolution • Bankruptcy Business Organizations/Corporations • Careers and Employment • Civil Litigation and Procedure • CLA Exam Preparation • Computer Applications in the Law Office • Constitutional Law • Contract Law • Court Reporting Criminal Law and Procedure • Document Preparation • Elder Law • Employment Law • Environmental Law • Ethics Evidence Law • Family Law • Health Care Law • Immigration Law • Intellectual Property • Internships Interviewing and Investigation • Introduction to Law • Introduction to Paralegalism • Juvenile Law • Law Office Management • Law Office Procedures • Legal Nurse Consulting • Legal Research, Writing, and Analysis • Legal Terminology • Legal Transcription • Media and Entertainment Law • Medical Malpractice Law Product Liability • Real Estate Law • Reference Materials • Social Security • Sports Law • Torts and Personal Injury Law • Wills, Trusts, and Estate Administration • Workers' Compensation Law

DELMAR CENGAGE Learning
5 Maxwell Drive
Clifton Park, New York 12065-2919

For additional information, find us online at:
www.cengage.com/delmar

ALTERNATIVE METHODS
OF
DISPUTE RESOLUTION

MARTIN A. FREY

Professor Emeritus
The University of Tulsa College of Law

DELMAR
CENGAGE Learning

Australia • Brazil • Japan • Korea • Mexico • Singapore • Spain • United Kingdom • United States

DELMAR
CENGAGE Learning™

Alternative Methods of Dispute Resolution
Martin A. Frey

Business Unit Executive Director: Susan L.
    Simpfenderfer

Senior Acquisitions Editor: Joan M. Gill

Developmental Editor: Alexis Breen Ferraro

Editorial Assistant: Lisa Flatley

Executive Production Manager: Wendy A. Troeger

Production Manager: Carolyn Miller

Production Editor: Matthew J. Williams

Executive Marketing Manager: Donna J. Lewis

Channel Manager: Nigar Hale

Cover Design: Dutton & Sherman Design

For product information and technology assistance, contact us at
Cengage Learning Customer & Sales Support, 1-800-354-9706

For permission to use material from this text or product,
submit all requests online at **www.cengage.com/permissions**
Further permissions questions can be emailed to
permissionrequest@cengage.com

Library of Congress Control Number: 2002019276

ISBN-13: 978-0-7668-2110-1

ISBN-10: 0-7668-2110-2

Delmar
Executive Woods
5 Maxwell Drive
Clifton Park, NY 12065
USA

Cengage Learning is a leading provider of customized learning solutions with office
locations around the globe, including Singapore, the United Kingdom, Australia,
Mexico, Brazil, and Japan. Locate your local office at
www.cengage.com/global

Cengage Learning products are represented in Canada by Nelson Education, Ltd.

To learn more about Delmar, visit **www.cengage.com/delmar**

Purchase any of our products at your local bookstore or at our preferred online
store **www.CengageBrain.com**

Printed in the United States of America
4 5 6 7 8   14 13 12 11 10

ED004

In memory of my brother-in-law
Kenneth Huey Riddle

Contents

Table of Cases

Preface

Who needs to know about ADR? Is it just attorneys, judges, and paralegals, or is knowledge about the alternative methods of dispute resolution (ADR) essential for business and everyday life?

Knowledge of ADR is fundamental to the practice of law. ADR has become so much a part of the practice of law some judges believe that attorneys who fail to discuss alternative methods of dispute resolution with their clients have committed malpractice. Attorneys may also serve as neutral third parties (ombuds, early neutral evaluators, mediators, arbitrators, and private judges) and not represent either party. Therefore, attorneys must be knowledgeable about ADR.

Paralegals must be knowledgeable about the alternatives to litigation since their attorneys may involve them in the planning and preparation that are necessary for selecting and executing the dispute resolution strategy. Paralegals may also represent parties in ADR proceedings before some administrative agencies. Paralegals may, at times, also serve as third-party neutrals (ombuds, mediators, and arbitrators).

Third parties must be well versed in ADR because as clients they are the parties with the ultimate decision-making authority as to the dispute resolution strategy, and they must participate in an appropriate way in the execution of this strategy. When not a client, they may also, at times, represent parties in ADR proceedings before some administrative agencies and may serve as third-party neutrals.

The discussion up to this point, however, has focused on disputants and their disputes. But even beyond disputes, knowledge of ADR is important for making knowledgeable decisions in everyday life. ADR relates to problem solving and not just to dispute resolution.

A dispute involves conflict; a problem does not. A problem could exist without conflict or could be elevated to the level of a dispute by adding conflict. ADR may focus on whether a party with a problem wants to elevate that problem to the level of a dispute. A number of ADR processes involve this threshold question. Does a person with a problem want to elevate that problem to a dispute or does he or she merely want to select unilaterally the "dispute" resolution process of *inaction* (Chapter 3) or *acquiescence* (Chapter 4)? Or does the party want to be a bit more aggressive and select unilaterally the "dispute" resolution process of *self-help* (Chapter 5)? Or a person with a problem could visit an *ombuds* (Chapter 9), if one is available, and have the ombuds attempt to work out a solution without raising the problem to the level of a dispute. Or a person with a problem arising out of contract may find that he or she has agreed to *private arbitration* (Chapter 13) when the contract was created and long before the problem arose.

Some problems either are inherently disputes or must be elevated to the level of a dispute. For these disputes, a party must make the decision of whether to allow the dispute to remain a dispute or to deescalate the conflict by selecting the unilateral dispute resolution process of *inaction* (Chapter 3) or *acquiescence* (Chapter 4).

But not all disputes should be deescalated. For some, the appropriate decision is to seek resolution by *negotiation* (Chapter 6) or *private mediation* (Chapter 10). In other instances, the courts must be involved and the filing of a complaint appears necessary. Most complaints never reach trial. The parties resolve their dispute through *negotiation* (Chapter 6) or *private mediation* (Chapter 10). In other cases, the parties use court-sponsored ADR programs such as *court-sponsored mediation* (Chapter 11), *court-annexed arbitration* (Chapter 14), or *private judging* (court referred) (Chapter 17).

This text explores a broad range of problem-solving and dispute resolution processes. It begins with an overview and ends with a discussion of dispute resolution strategies.

A Well-Organized, Functional Approach to Dispute Resolution

Alternative Methods of Dispute Resolution provides students with a well-organized, functional approach to dispute resolution processes. Students learn about dispute resolution as an interrelated array of processes since ADR offers a party a continuum of choices ranging from where a party has total control over the process and the outcome to where a party loses control over the process once the process has been initiated and has no control over the outcome. Students learn to distinguish one process from another, who participates in each process, how they participate, and the advantages and disadvantages of each process. They explore why a party would select one process over another and how a party can create a dispute resolution strategy that consists of a series of dispute resolution processes. This knowledge can be readily transferred from this text and accompanying classroom experience into a student's professional life.

Organization of the Textbook

Alternative Methods of Dispute Resolution is divided into seven parts. Part I introduces the student to the various methods of dispute resolution and to the participants. Parts II through VI group the various methods of dispute resolution by who participates in the process (i.e., one party, two parties, or two parties and a neutral third party) and the purpose of the process (i.e., to provide the parties with an opportunity to resolve the dispute or to the resolution of the dispute by a third party). Each chapter within Parts II through VI considers a different dispute resolution process. The chapters begin with the least technical process that can be implemented unilaterally and progress through the most technical process that requires a third party to adjudicate the dispute for the parties. Part VII explores the planning of a dispute resolution strategy.

It should be noted that one chapter has been devoted to litigation. Although litigation is not considered ADR, it is a dispute resolution process. The "A" in ADR stands for "alternative." To compare a process that is an alternative to litigation requires some knowledge of litigation. The initiation of litigation may also be a necessary step in reaching a court-sponsored process such as court-sponsored mediation or court-annexed arbitration. For these reasons, litigation is included.

Primary Pedagogical Feature

The primary pedagogical feature of this text is the active involvement of students in learning the broad array of dispute resolution processes, when a process might be applicable to a situation, how a process is initiated, and the relative advantages and disadvantages.

Concepts are presented in three stages. Students first read about the rule in the abstract. Thus students acquire the "black letter" of the process. The concept may be followed by a clearly designated Example. The Example demonstrates how the concept relates to a concrete set of facts. The concept is no longer merely an abstraction but becomes a tool for selecting a dispute resolution process. Finally, students may be asked to actively participate in the solution of a Problem by relating a given set of facts to the concept. The Problem enables students to develop their reasoning skills as they apply the concept. By actively participating in analyzing the Problem, students gain an understanding of the dynamics of the concepts and how they relate to one another. The concept-example, concept-problem, and concept-example-problem approach provides students with a practical method of immediately reinforcing newly acquired knowledge.

Other Pedagogical Features

A handful of judicial opinions have been included in the text. They explore concepts in a way that exceeds the capability of a simple example or problem. They show how the courts grapple with dispute resolution issues when, at times, the outcome is not certain.

A few ethical provisions, some relating to attorneys, some to paralegals, and some to neutral third parties, have been included in the text and appendices. Some are included to make an ethical point. Others are included to call attention to their existence and the degree of detail that has been included in their drafting. The ethical provisions are included as illustrations and are not intended to be exhaustive of the subject matter.

A number of websites have been cited throughout the text. Not only will these sites provide students with a wealth of information about dispute resolution, they also encourage students to explore the Web for other sites that could be equally valuable.

Review and Role-Play Materials

Each dispute resolution process chapter ends with a Chart outlining the attributes of that process. The Chart provides students with a brief, but detailed review of the chapter and is an effective method of summarizing what was learned in the chapter.

Following the Chart is a test bank of review questions. The review questions include five different formats: defining new terms, true/false, fill-in-the-blank, multiple choice, and short answer. These questions are designed to test the student's knowledge of the basic concepts discussed in the chapter. The answers are found in the Instructor's Manual.

In five chapters (Chapter 6, "Negotiation;" Chapter 10, "Private Mediation;" Chapter 11, "Court-Sponsored Mediation;" Chapter 13, "Private Arbitration;" and Chapter 19, "Selecting a Strategy"), several role-play exercises follow the review questions. The role play may be conducted during or out of class. The role-play exercises give students an opportunity to participate in the various dispute resolution processes. Some fact patterns are revisited under several different dispute resolution processes. This gives students an opportunity to compare the impact of the process on the resolution of a dispute.

Back Matter

The back matter consists of a number of appendices, a glossary, and an index. The appendices include several model acts, court rules, statutes, and ethical guidelines. The glossary includes the key terms bolded in the text. The glossary provides a quick reference for defining terms and a source for review prior to tests. The extensive index that concludes the book assists students in quickly finding the location of materials within the text.

Supplemental Teaching Materials

- The **Instructor's Manual** is available both in print and on-line at *www.paralegalstudies. com* in the Instructor's Lounge under Resource. Written by the author of the text, the *Instructor's Manual* contains the following:
  - Suggestions for developing a course syllabus for courses of varying credit hours
  - Answers to the Problems within the text
  - Answers to the Review Questions within the text
  - Additional role-play problems with confidential facts
  - Synopses of the cases presented in the text
- **On-line Resource™**—the On-line Resource™ is a protected area that requires a username and password to gain access. You will find your username and password information below. You will need these to enter the protected area, and you must enter the username and password exactly as they appear below. The On-line Resource™ can be found at *www.paralegalstudies.com* in the On-line Resource™ section of the Web Site.

  Username: freyolc
  Password: frey1

- **Web page**—Come visit our website at *www.paralegalstudies.com,* where you will find valuable information such as hot links and sample materials to download, as well as other Delmar, Cengage Learning products.
- **WESTLAW®**—Delmar's on-line computerized legal research system offers students "hands-on" experience with a system commonly used in law offices. Qualified adopters can receive ten free hours of WESTLAW®. WESTLAW® can be accessed with Macintosh and IBM PC and compatibles. A modem is required.
- **Strategies and Tips for Paralegal Educators,** a pamphlet by Anita Tebbe of Johnson County Community College, provides teaching strategies specifically designed for paralegal educators. A copy of this pamphlet is available to each adopter. Quantities for distribution to adjunct instructors are available for purchase at a minimal price. A coupon on the pamphlet provides ordering information.
- **Survival Guide for Paralegal Students,** a pamphlet by Kathleen Mercer Reed and Bradene Moore covers practical and basic information to help students make the most of their paralegal courses. Topics covered include choosing courses of study and note-taking skills.
- **Delmar's Paralegal Video Library**—Delmar, Cengage Learning is pleased to offer the following videos at no charge to qualified adopters:
  - *The Drama of the Law II: Paralegal Issues Video*
    ISBN: 0-314-07088-5

- *"I Never Said I Was a Lawyer"*
  Paralegal Ethics Video
  ISBN: 0-314-08049-x
- *The Making of a Case Video*
  ISBN: 0-314-07300-0
- *ABA Mock Trial Video-Anatomy of a Trail: A Contracts Case*
  ISBN: 0-314-07343-4
- *ABA Mock Trial Video-Product Liability*
  ISBN: 0-314-07342-6
- *Arguments to the United States Supreme Court Video*
  ISBN: 0-314-07070-2

Acknowledgments

My involvement in the field of ADR did not come about by design but rather by happenstance. I was encouraged to become a mediator by Terry J. Simonson, the creator of Project Early Settlement—a community mediation program in Tulsa, and I received my initial training for that program from Dr. Bob Helm of Oklahoma State University. Several years later, I was invited by Magistrate Judge John Leo Wagner, the creator of the Adjunct Settlement Judge Program for the United States District Court for the Northern District of Oklahoma, to join the court's newly formed ASJ panel. One case led to another and I found myself being the mediator in a superfund case and in the bankruptcy court. My work as an ASJ led to my appointment as the Reporter for the Civil Justice Reform Act Advisory Group for the Northern District of Oklahoma. Ultimately, we created a Center for Dispute Resolution at The University of Tulsa College of Law and one of my colleagues, Vicki J. Limas, became my codirector.

Along the way I had the opportunity to work with Magistrate Judge Claire V. Eagan, who succeeded Judge Wagner as the ADR coordinator in the Northern District; Chief Judges H. Dale Cook, James O. Ellison, Thomas R. Brett, and Terry C. Kern; Bankruptcy Judges Steven Covey, Mickey D. Wilson, Dana L. Rasure, and Terrence L. Michael; and Magistrate Judges Jeffrey S. Wolfe, Sam A. Joyner, and Frank H. McCarthy. I have learned from each and all have been great supporters of ADR.

I would also like to thank Kara L. Horton of St. Louis, Missouri, Class of 1998, my former research assistant, and Melissa Stewart of West Plains, Missouri, Class of 2000, my reader and critiquer, and my former ADR students at The University of Tulsa and at Washington University who used various versions of this text.

I would like to express my thanks to my wife, Phyllis Hurley Frey, who has been my coauthor in several Delmar Series texts and who volunteered to read and critique the manuscript and page proofs as they were produced. I appreciate her encouragement throughout this and other projects and her willing assistance in the editorial process.

Special thanks to Joan Gill, my acquisitions editor; Rhonda Dearborn and Alexis Ferraro, my developmental editors; Matthew Williams, my production editor; Lisa Flatley, my editorial assistant; Jeff J. Stiles, Production Service Coordinator; and to all my friends at Delmar, Cengage Learning and Shepherd Inc., whose efforts have made this book possible. I would also like to thank Dr. Mary P. Rowe, Ombudsperson, at MIT for her comments on the Ombuds chapter.

And thanks to the following who reviewed an earlier manuscript of this book. I appreciate your comments.

Bernhard Behrend
Duquesne University
Pittsburgh, PA

Leigh Anne Chavez
Albuquerque TVI
Albuquerque, NM

Robert Diotalevi
Mountain State University/College of
West Virginia
Beckley, WV

Wendy Edson
Hilbert College
Hamburg, NY

Les Sturdivant Ennis, J.D.
Samford University
Birmingham, AL

Elizabeth Mann
Greenville Technical College
Greenville, SC

Bruce Hamm
Syracuse University
Syracuse, NY

Judith Sturgill
North Central State College
Mansfield, OH

Penny Lorenzo
Rhodes College
Phoenix, AZ

Chris Whaley
Roane State Community College
Harriman, TN

Introduction

The ADR Movement

The 1970s and 1980s mark the beginning of the movement around the country when judges, court administrators, legal and nonlegal educators, legislators, attorneys, paralegals, clients, and others became interested in thinking about and developing a broad array of dispute resolution processes. The acronym "ADR" was chosen. It stands for "alternative dispute resolution."

The driving force for this ADR movement was the mounting costs and delays inherent in the judicial system. It was not uncommon to hear about litigants waiting years before coming to trial. Other litigants were caught in a time warp as they bounced around from trial court, to appellate court, back to trial court, and back again to appellate court.

At the same time statistical data from the courts revealed that less than 10 percent of the civil cases filed ever went to trial, and, of those cases that went to trial, a number were settled by the parties before the court rendered a judgment. And even in those in which a judgment was rendered, a number of cases were settled by the parties while their case was pending on appeal. Based on these statistics, those interested in the judicial system began to wonder what it would take to have these cases settle earlier, thus saving not only judicial time in the pretrial and trial process but also saving time and expense for the parties. Better yet, are there ways to divert some of these cases so the parties resolve their disputes without involving the judicial system at all?

Another stimulus for the ADR movement was the escalating confrontational nature of society. Protracted litigation merely heightened the conflict. At judgment, the court would declare a "winner" and a "loser." Certainly the loser did not go away believing that justice was done and often after the winner deducted transaction costs (including attorney's fees, court costs, expert witness fees, time, effort, and mental stress) from the judgment, the winner often wondered who really won and whether justice was served. Is there a better way to resolve disputes so parties would feel better about the process and about the outcome?

Even receiving a judgment might prove a hollow victory. Defendants generally do not come to trial with their checkbooks. The plaintiffs who waited patiently for their judgments often found it difficult to convert their judgments into hard cash. They would find many defendants would not pay unless pursued. At times the "winner" would find the "loser" to be without the assets necessary to satisfy the judgment. Furthermore, the losing parties did not even say they were sorry. Are there dispute resolution processes that foster performance of the resolution?

The litigants also found that the courts were limited as to what they could grant in their judgments. Judgments were generally limited to monetary damages. The courts had no latitude to tailor their judgments to the interests or needs of the parties. Could ADR encourage creativity in designing dispute outcomes that meet at least some of the interests or needs of both parties?

As the ADR movement gained momentum, it became obvious that many ADR processes already existed in one form or another. Processes such as negotiation, ombuds, private mediation, private arbitration, and private judging were not new. These methods of dispute resolution were available to the parties but existed in isolation. The ADR movement created the environment that allowed bringing these processes to the forefront. The ADR movement brought these processes together as a coherent and interrelated set of processes, thus empowering the parties to design dispute resolution strategies. Negotiation, in one form or another, for example, has been around since the beginning of civilization. It took the national best-seller, *Getting to Yes,* to focus attention on how to negotiate effectively. Ombuds has been used in the Scandinavian countries since the early 1800s but did not appear in the United States until the 1920s. By 1977, the number of public sector ombuds in the United States was sufficient to support the creation of the United States Ombudsman Association (USOA). Church-sponsored conciliation and mediation has been used since colonial days. The National Mediation Board was created in 1934 to deal with labor-management relations issues in the transportation field, specifically railroads and airlines. A limited number of private mediation providers have been around for years. Now private mediation providers (international, national, regional, and local), community mediation services, and court-sponsored mediation (settlement conferences) are numerous. Mediation has become so popular that even students in grades K–12 are being taught mediation skills and formally mediate disputes between their peers. Private arbitration has been used internationally for centuries and has found legal support in American jurisdictions for over 70 years. The number of private arbitration providers (international, national, regional, and local) has increased dramatically over the past decade. And although some states have had private judging or temporary judge statutes (referral to a private judge by a state trial court) for a hundred years, it is only recently that litigants have requested court referral to private judging in any significant numbers.

The ADR movement focused attention on these processes, thereby creating more interest in alternatives to litigation. Rather than viewing each dispute resolution process in isolation, the processes began to be thought of as an array of processes. A party with a dispute could map out a dispute resolution strategy.

The movement led to experimentation so ADR processes that had been private in nature were used in a public forum. This led to court-sponsored mediation, court-annexed arbitration, and ombuds in governmental agencies. The movement also led to public processes being used in private forums, thus leading to the growth of private judging.

As ADR processes grew in visibility, experimentation increased. Arbitration was expanded to include final offer arbitration where an arbitrator's award could be no more than nor no less than a predetermined amount and high/low, or baseball arbitration, where the arbitrator's award was limited to a choice between the parties' last offer. Mediation was joined with arbitration to form a new process called med-arb. The parties would begin with mediation and if they could not resolve their dispute with the help of a mediator, the process would change to arbitration where an arbitrator would resolve the dispute for them. Through this combination of processes, the parties would be assured that their dispute would be resolved by the end of the process. Other processes such as early neutral evaluation, the mini-trial, and the summary jury trial were created as well.

As the use of ADR processes increased, so did the number of ADR providers. Browsing the web for such topics as mediation, ombuds, arbitration, or private judging reveals that ADR is in fact a growth industry.

As the 20th century drew to a close, the ADR movement shifted its interest from experimentation to institutionalization. The National Conference of Commissioners on Uniform State Laws drafted the Uniform Arbitration Act and the Uniform Mediation Act. They can be found on the Web at *http://www.law.upenn.edu/bll/ulc/ulc_frame.htm.* Various other groups drafted Codes of Conduct and Ethical Rules. Legislatures drafted statutes and courts enacted local rules. Federal district courts were ordered by Congress to offer an ADR program. One can explore the various federal court ADR programs by visiting The Federal Judiciary Homepage at *http://www.uscourts.gov.* Often a district will list its ADR program on its Web page. Browsing the Web also leads to a number of the state court programs. For example, the National Center for State Courts (NCSC) maintains a state court website at *http://www.ncsconline.org.* Congress also required each federal executive agency to adopt a policy on the use of alternative dispute resolution and to encourage its use.

As ADR grew in acceptance and the number of ADR providers grew proportionally, those involved in ADR began forming educational and support groups. The American Bar Association created a Section on Dispute Resolution. Its website is *http:www.abanet.org/dispute/home.html.* Other support groups include the United States Ombudsman Association (USOA) at *http://www.usombudsman.org* and the Association of Conflict Resolution (a merged organization of AFM, CREnet, and SPIDR) at *http://www.acresolution.org.*

The vast majority of disputes are resolved through the traditional methods of dispute resolution—inaction, acquiescence, self-help, negotiation, mediation, arbitration, and litigation. Very little is heard about inaction, acquiescence, and self-help, where a party uses unilateral action to resolve the dispute. The only time self-help draws interest is when it is used improperly. Negotiation, a process where two parties come together to resolve their dispute, is commonplace since daily interaction requires negotiation, although the negotiation may not necessarily be used to resolve a dispute. All cooperative problem solving requires some give and take, i.e., negotiation. Mediation, a process that involves a neutral third party to help the parties negotiate an agreement has gained popularity in recent years since it empowers the parties to resolve their own dispute. Arbitration and litigation, the two adjudication processes, while making for good TV (certainly much better than watching inaction), may act more as a catalyst for the parties to resolve their own dispute rather than a process that resolves a vast number of disputes.

One aspect of the institutionalization of ADR is the concept of a multidoor dispute resolution center. The concept of a multidoor dispute resolution center envisions a location where a party with a dispute can seek advice that tailors the array of dispute resolution processes to his or her dispute. Often the multidoor dispute resolution center is incorporated into the courthouse so the courthouse becomes a multidoor courthouse.

A multidoor courthouse offers an array of dispute resolution options. Some courts provide personnel who screen cases and channel them to the appropriate dispute resolution process. Others simply offer litigants a choice of dispute resolution processes.

Multidoor courthouses have been established on the federal level in most districts.

Example I-1

The United States District Court for the Northern District of California provides four ADR processes:

> **Court-Annexed Arbitration**
> **Early Neutral Evaluation**
> **Mediation**
> **Court-Sponsored Settlement Conference**

See *http://www.adr.cand.uscourt.gov/* and use links to this court.

The United States District Court for the Western District of Oklahoma lists five ADR processes:

> **Mediation**
> **Early Neutral Evaluation**
> **Court-Annexed Arbitration**
> **Judicial Settlement Conferences**
> **Summary/Advisory Trials**

See *http://www.okwd.uscourts.gov/adr.htm*

The United States District Court for the District of Utah offers two ADR processes:

> **Mediation**
> **Court-Annexed Arbitration**

See *http://www.utd.uscourts.gov/documents/adrpage.html.*

Problem I-1

Does your federal district court list its ADR programs on its homepage on the Web? To check, visit *http://www.uscourts.gov* and follow the links to your federal district.

Multidoor courthouses have also been established in a number of state trial courts.

Problem I-2

Does the state trial court for your jurisdiction have a homepage on the Web? If it does, does it list its ADR programs?

ADR has found its way onto the Internet. A quick search will reveal a number of online dispute resolution services.

Problem I-3

Find three online dispute resolution services. You might try "online mediation," "online arbitration," or "online ADR" as search terms.

Compare these services as to the following:

1.   Do they all purport to cover the same types of disputes?
2.   Do they offer a variety of ADR processes or a single process?
3.   How do their online ADR programs work?
4.   What are their fees?

This text explores the array of ADR processes produced by the ADR movement. What are these processes? How are they similar and how are they different? Who has control over selecting the dispute resolution strategy? Who controls the outcome and what is the range of outcomes? What are the costs? What are the advantages and disadvantages inherent in each process? What factors should be considered when selecting a dispute resolution strategy? The answers to these questions is what this text is all about.

PART ONE

Introduction

Part One of *Alternative Methods of Dispute Resolution* presents an overview of dispute resolution processes.

Chapter 1, "The Methods of Dispute Resolution," introduces the broad array of dispute resolution processes currently being used both in the public and private sectors, identifies the basic characteristics of each process, and distinguishes one process from another. Chapter 1 describes the dispute resolution processes as a spectrum, beginning with the least interfering (unilateral action) and ending with the most interfering (third-party adjudication).

Chapter 2, "The Participants," discusses who participates in each dispute resolution process and what their role is in the process. Understanding who participates and their role provides a clear contrast among processes.

CHAPTER 1

The Methods of Dispute Resolution

The range of dispute resolution processes or dispute resolution methods forms a continuum, beginning with the least interfering where one disputant resolves the dispute through inaction, acquiescence, or self-help, to the most interfering where one or both parties invite a third party to resolve the dispute for them through arbitration or litigation. The continuum includes:

> unilateral action in dispute resolution
>> inaction
>> acquiescence
>> self-help
> bilateral action in dispute resolution
>> negotiation
> third-party evaluation as a prelude to dispute resolution
>> early neutral evaluation
>> summary jury trial
> third-party assistance in dispute resolution
>> ombuds
>> private mediation
>> court-sponsored mediation
>> mini-trial
> third-party adjudication in dispute resolution
>> private arbitration including high/low and final offer arbitration
>>> court-annexed arbitration
>>> mediation/arbitration
>>> litigation
>>> private judging

Unilateral Action

Only one party is involved in the selection of the process, has an active role in the process, and determines the resolution of the dispute.

Bilateral Action

The two parties to the dispute are involved in the process and both, together, resolve the dispute.

Third-Party Evaluation

Three parties are involved in the process (the two disputing parties [and their attorneys] and a neutral third party). The third party listens to the attorneys' discussion of the case and then provides the parties with an evaluation as to the strengths and weaknesses of the case.

Third-Party Assistance

Three parties are involved in the process (the two disputing parties and a neutral third party), and the disputants, not the neutral third party, resolve the dispute.

Third-Party Adjudication

Three parties are involved in the process (the two disputing parties and a neutral third party), not the disputing parties, resolve the dispute.

This continuum can be subdivided into five categories: unilateral action, bilateral action, third-party evaluation, third-party assistance, and third-party adjudication. These categories are based on who is involved in the process and who resolves the dispute. In a **unilateral action,** only one party is involved in the selection of the process, has an active role in the process, and determines the resolution of the dispute. In a **bilateral action,** the two parties to the dispute are involved in the process and both, together, resolve the dispute. Negotiation is a bilateral action. In a **third-party evaluation,** three parties are involved in the process, the two disputing parties (and their attorneys) and a neutral third party. The third party listens to the attorneys' discussion of the case and then provides the parties with an evaluation as to the strengths and weaknesses of the case. The third party neither resolves the dispute nor assists the parties in resolving their dispute. Third-party evaluation includes early neutral evaluation and summary jury trial. In a **third-party assistance,** three parties are involved in the process, the two disputing parties and a neutral third party. The disputing parties, and not the neutral third party, resolve the dispute. Third-party assistance includes ombuds, mediation, and mini-trial. In a **third-party adjudication,** three parties are involved in the process, the two disputing parties and a neutral third party. The neutral third party, and not the disputing parties, resolves the dispute. Adjudication includes arbitration, mediation-arbitration, litigation, and private judging.

Historically, the various methods of dispute resolution were either private or public processes. Unilateral action (inaction, acquiescence, and self-help), negotiation, mediation, and arbitration were all private processes. Litigation was a public process. The ADR movement led to experimentation. Mediation, a traditionally private process, was adopted by some courts in the public sector and labeled *court-sponsored mediation, court-annexed mediation,* or *settlement conference.* Arbitration, a traditionally private process, was taken up by some courts in the public sector and labeled *court-annexed, court-ordered,* or *court-sponsored arbitration.* Litigation, a traditionally public process, expanded into the private sector and is called *private judging* or *rent-a-judge.*

Often an aggrieved party can create a dispute resolution strategy that incorporates several methods of dispute resolution. A party may decide to try negotiation and if a favorable solution cannot be reached, then move to mediation, and then to litigation. Or a party could decide to file a complaint to begin the litigation process to capture the other party's attention and then seek to negotiate a settlement.

Several methods have been more formally linked. Mediation and arbitration have been linked to form a process called mediation-arbitration or med-arb. In med-arb, the parties begin with mediation and if they cannot reach an agreement, the process morphs into arbitration. Trial and negotiation have been linked to form a summary jury trial and a mini-trial. In a summary jury trial, an abbreviated nonbinding trial is held before a judge and mock jury and is followed by the parties negotiating a settlement. In a mini-trial, an abbreviated nonbinding trial is held before a three-person panel (one corporate officer with settlement authority from each corporation and a neutral third party) and is followed by the corporate officers negotiating a settlement. If the corporate officers invite the neutral third party to participate, the process becomes a mediation.

As you study the following materials, distinguish the dispute resolution process from the solution of the dispute. This text is about selecting the process for resolving a dispute. It is not about resolving the dispute itself. The process selected, however, may well dictate how the dispute will be resolved.

Example 1-1

Parties who select inaction as their method of dispute resolution will simply walk away from the problem and neither give something to nor receive something from the other side.

Parties who select negotiation as their method of dispute resolution will most likely need to compromise to reach an agreement and therefore either give more than they had expected to give or receive less than what they had hoped to receive.

Parties who select litigation as their method of dispute resolution may receive everything they had asked for, not as much as they had asked for, or nothing at all.

Unilateral Action in Dispute Resolution

Unilateral action is a method of dispute resolution that does not require the other party's cooperation. One party just does it. Since a dispute requires at least two participants, removing one party resolves the dispute. Unilateral action may take the form of inaction, acquiescence, or self-help.

Inaction

Inaction

One party voluntarily withdraws from the dispute and since a dispute requires at least two participants, the dispute is resolved.

Inaction is the most common form of dispute resolution. **Inaction** is one party's voluntary withdrawal from the dispute. Since a dispute requires at least two participants, if one party does not pursue the other, the dispute is resolved.

When a party selects inaction as the method of dispute resolution, he or she also selects the substantive resolution of the dispute.

Example 1-2

Kathleen purchased a used Buick from Friendly Motors. Friendly told Kathleen that the car had been inspected and was in "fine shape." Within two weeks after receiving delivery of the car, the brakes failed and needed to be replaced. Rather than complain to Friendly Motors, Kathleen took the car to Eddie's Brake Shop and had the brakes replaced. Kathleen has chosen inaction as her method of dispute resolution.

Problem 1-1

1. Why would Kathleen decide to pay Eddie's Brake Shop to have her brakes replaced rather than go back to Friendly Motors and try to have her brakes replaced for free?
2. If Kathleen takes her car back to Friendly Motors and they refuse to replace her brakes on the grounds that she had purchased the car "as is" (i.e., without any express or implied warranties), should she take her problem to an attorney?
3. What would you do?

Problem 1-2

Have you ever used inaction as a method of dispute resolution? Identify three such situations, and state why you chose this method of dispute resolution.

In order to select inaction as the method of dispute resolution, a party must have the power to walk away from a problem. Not all disputing parties have this power. Some disputes require a neutral third party to impose a resolution.

Example 1-3

After 15 years of marriage, Reginald decided that he was bored being married to Edwina and would rather be married to his secretary, Priscilla. Reginald and Edwina have a legal relationship that requires a judicially imposed disassociation known as divorce. Reginald cannot marry Priscilla until he has been granted a divorce by the court from Edwina. Merely walking away from the marriage will not terminate his relationship with Edwina.

In other disputes, one party will have the power to refuse to let the other just walk away. These disputes require a negotiated agreement or, if the parties are unable to reach such an agreement, a resolution imposed by a neutral third party.

Example 1-4

Maria was driving her BMW down San Mateo Boulevard when a Ford Mustang driven by Julio sped through a red light and broadsided her car. As a result of the accident, Maria spent a week in the hospital and two months in rehabilitation. Her vehicle sustained $15,000 worth of damage. Maria will not let Julio just walk away from the accident without holding him accountable. This dispute will require either a negotiated agreement or a resolution imposed by the courts.

Another aspect of inaction is wait and see. Wait and see requires patience. Rather than do something such as acquiescence, the disputant merely waits to see what develops. The other party may consciously or unconsciously select inaction (walk away from the dispute), thus resolving the dispute. Or the other party may pursue a method of dispute resolution that could produce a resolution more in his or her favor. At times, action may be premature because all the facts are not known, the problem appears greater than it turns out to be, or the problem resolves itself.

Problem 1-3

After Ryan and Samantha moved into their new home in the Wicker Park area of Chicago, they noticed that the house next door was looking a little shabby. The grass had not been cut, exterior repairs had not been completed, and the truck parked in the driveway had not been moved for several weeks. All were violations of city ordinances.

Should Ryan and Samantha report these violations to the police or wait to see what happens?

Problem 1-4

Jason was involved in an automobile accident that was his fault. Christine, the driver of the other car, was driving without a valid driver's license. Her license had been revoked for driving under the influence of drugs. Jason's car had $2,000 in damage. Christine's car had $3,000 in damage. Jason does not want to report this accident to his insurance company because this is his third accident. Jason and Christine have exchanged names and telephone numbers. They have not exchanged insurance information. A week has passed and Jason has not heard from Christine. Neither has suffered personal injury.

Should Jason choose wait and see as his method of dispute resolution?

Problem 1-5

Have you ever used the wait and see version of inaction as a method of dispute resolution? Identify one such situation, and state why you chose this method of dispute resolution.

Acquiescence

Acquiescence
One party gives up and accedes to the demands of the other.

Acquiescence, another common form of dispute resolution, is the opposite of inaction and occurs when one party gives up and accedes to the demands of the other. When parties select acquiescence as their method of dispute resolution, they also select the substantive resolution of their dispute.

Example 1-5

Ryan and Samantha rented an apartment near Watertower Plaza in Chicago. They signed a one-year lease that included a provision requiring a one-month rent payment in the event they terminate the lease before the expiration of the lease term.

When Samantha became pregnant, they decided to purchase a home in the Wicker Park area of Chicago. Samantha and Ryan decided to pay the one-month rent penalty rather than pursue the matter with the apartment manager.

Problem 1-6

1. Why would Samatha and Ryan pay the penalty rather than pursue the matter with the apartment manager?
2. If Samatha and Ryan had spoken to the apartment manager and the manager had refused to waive the penalty, should they have taken their problem to an attorney rather than pay? What would you have done?

Problem 1-7

Have you ever used acquiescence as a method of dispute resolution? Identify one such situation, and state why you chose this method of dispute resolution.

Self-Help

Self-Help
An aggrieved party pursues relief without the assistance of the courts.

Self-help, another form of the unilateral method of dispute resolution, is the opposite of inaction. Inaction is passive; self-help is active. Inaction abandons rights; self-help asserts rights. Under self-help an aggrieved party may pursue relief without the assistance of the courts. Often, the self-help relief occurs when a contract has been breached.

Example 1-6

Multiplex, Inc., hired the High Plains Construction Company to build a 24-screen theater at a contract price of $12 million. The contract called for the following payment schedule:

$1 million	at signing of the contract
$2 million	upon completion of the foundation
$3 million	upon completion of the building shell
$2 million	upon completion of heating and air conditioning, electrical, and plumbing
$2 million	upon completion of all construction and landscaping
$2 million	90 days after completion of all construction and landscaping

Shortly after the theater was complete, Multiplex discovered significant problems with the heating and air conditioning, electrical, and plumbing, which made only 18 theaters fully operational. When High Plains refused to promptly fulfill its obligations under the contract, Multiplex exercised its common law self-help right to withhold the final $2 million payment, claiming a lack of substantial performance on the part of High Plains.

Problem 1-8

1. Why would Multiplex withhold the final payment to High Plains rather than make the final payment under the contract and pursue the matter in court?
2. What would you have done?

Example 1-7

Sara and Jon Edwards purchased a new Lexus from Gotham Lexus of Metropolis. They paid $10,000 down and borrowed the balance from Friendly Bank. Sara and Jon gave Friendly Bank a security interest in their Lexus. After making 10 monthly payments, Jon lost his job when his company downsized. With monthly income now less than monthly expenditures, Sara and Jon defaulted on their payments to Friendly Bank. Friendly Bank exercised its self-help right under state law (i.e., the state's version of Article 9 of the Uniform Commercial Code) and repossessed the Lexus.

Under state law, Friendly Bank must resell the Lexus in a commercially reasonable manner. The proceeds from the sale are then deducted from the balance owed by Sara and Jon. If the proceeds from the resale exceed the balance due, Sara and Jon are due a refund. If the proceeds from the resale are less than the balance due, Sara and Jon remain liable to Friendly Bank for the deficiency.

Problem 1-9

Have you ever used self-help as a method of dispute resolution? List one such situation, and state why you chose this method of dispute resolution.

Bilateral Action in Dispute Resolution

Bilateral action requires the cooperation of both disputing parties. Negotiation is a bilateral action.

Negotiation

Negotiation
This private, voluntary, consensual dispute resolution process involves only the two disputing parties (or their representatives) as they attempt to resolve their dispute.

Negotiation is a private, voluntary, consensual process involving the two disputing parties (or their representatives) as they attempt to resolve their dispute. Unlike inaction, acquiescence, and self-help where a party acts unilaterally, the parties in negotiation must work together to resolve their dispute.

In a negotiation, the parties provide their own process and resolve their own dispute. They do not seek the help of a neutral third party either to direct the discussion or to resolve the dispute for them. When parties select negotiation as the method of dispute resolution, they participate in a process that may well require compromise.

Example 1-8

When Roberto and Isabella became engaged, Roberto gave Isabella a 1.5 carat emerald-cut diamond ring and a sporty BMW. After a long engagement, Isabella decided not to marry Roberto. They discussed whether Isabella should keep the ring and the BMW, whether Isabella should give the ring and the BMW back to Roberto, or whether Isabella should sell both the ring and the BMW and divide the proceeds from the sale with Roberto. After much discussion, they decided that Isabella would keep the ring but would return the car. This substantive decision was the product of a negotiation. The process was voluntary, consensual, and involved only the two disputing parties.

Problem 1-10

1. Why would Isabella and Roberto select negotiation as their method of dispute resolution?
2. Should Isabella have refused to negotiate and instead unilaterally selected either inaction or acquiescence?
3. What would Isabella have done had she chosen inaction? What would Roberto have done?
4. What would Isabella have done had she chosen acquiescence? What would Roberto have done?

Problem 1-11

Have you ever used negotiation as a method of dispute resolution? Identify three such situations, and state why you chose negotiation.

Third-Party Evaluation as a Prelude to Dispute Resolution

Third-party evaluation of a dispute is not a dispute resolution process in and of itself. Third-party evaluation prepares the parties for another dispute resolution process. Third-party evaluation includes early neutral evaluation (ENE) and summary jury trial.

Early Neutral Evaluation

Early Neutral Evaluation (ENE)
An early case assessment by a member of the bar provides the parties and their attorneys with the opportunity to visualize the case from a third party's perspective.

Early neutral evaluation (ENE) is a relatively new form of court-sponsored ADR that involves an early case assessment by a member of the bar who has experience in the substantive area of the dispute. This evaluation by a neutral third party provides the parties and their attorneys with the opportunity to visualize the case from a third party's perspective. By having this preview of what might happen at trial, the parties have a clearer understanding of the settlement value of their dispute.

Summary Jury Trial

Summary Jury Trial
An abbreviated trial, usually before a mock jury, gives the litigants and their attorneys an opportunity to preview what might be the result if the case proceeds to trial.

A **summary jury trial** is an abbreviated trial, usually before a mock jury. The evidentiary presentations are shortened so the jury receives enough of the flavor of the case to render a mock verdict. The summary jury trial gives the litigants and their attorneys an opportunity to preview what the result might be if the case proceeds to trial. The parties and their attorneys can use this information to pursue settlement discussions.

Third-Party Assistance in Dispute Resolution

Third-party assistance in dispute resolution involves a neutral third party as a facilitator and not as the decision maker. Although a third party is involved, the dispute is still resolved by the disputing parties. Third-party assistance may take the form of ombuds, mediation, or mini-trial.

Ombuds

Ombuds
A neutral third party who listens to complaints, counsels as to governmental or organizational rules and procedures, and informally investigates the facts.

An **ombuds,** a neutral third party, comes in several forms including the classical ombuds, the organizational ombuds, and the advocate ombuds. The classical ombuds involves a public official appointed to address issues raised by members of the general public or by members of a governmental entity, usually concerning actions or policies of the governmental entity or individuals within those entities.

The organizational ombuds may be in either the public or private section of the community and ordinarily addresses problems presented by members, employees, or contractors of the organization concerning the actions of individuals within the organization or policies of the organization. The organizational ombuds listens to the aggrieved party, explains organizational rules and procedures, and informally investigates the aggrieved party's complaint. The ombuds neither represents the aggrieved party nor the organization. The ombuds, however, through informal investigation and counseling, helps resolve organizational-related disputes confidentially and before they develop into lawsuits. The ombuds can also alert upper management to major problems as they are arising. Management may then gain insight into ways to resolve these problems and take corrective action before these problems reach the litigation stage and become much more difficult to address.

Unlike either the classical or organization ombuds who is not an advocate, the advocate ombuds advocates on behalf of those who seek the advocate ombuds' services. The advocate ombuds may be found in either the public or private sector of the community.

Example 1-9

When Stephanie was in her final semester at State University, she received a letter from the registrar stating that she could not graduate because her cumulative grade point average was slightly below that required for graduation. Stephanie went to her advisor, and they discovered that Stephanie's transcript carried a grade of "F" in a course that Stephanie thought she had dropped during her junior year. Stephanie spoke to the registrar but the registrar told Stephanie that she could not change the grade to "W" without a letter from the course professor. Unfortunately, the professor had left the university and was teaching somewhere in England.

Stephanie discovered that State University had an Office of the Ombuds. She visited the ombuds and explained her dilemma. The ombuds discussed the matter with Stephanie's advisor, the registrar, and the vice president for academic affairs and a process was created whereby Stephanie could petition the vice president for academic affairs to have her grade of "F" changed to "W."

Problem 1-12

1. If you are enrolled in a university, college, or other academic program, check whether your educational institution has an ombuds office. What services does the ombuds provide?
2. If you are employed, check whether your employer has an ombuds office. What services does the ombuds provide?
3. Check whether your city or county government has an ombuds office. What services does the ombuds provide?
4. Check whether any of your state administrative agencies, such as your state taxing authority, has an ombuds office. What services does the ombuds provide?

Private Mediation

Mediation
A neutral third party is invited to direct the process.

Private Mediation
The parties hire a neutral third party to facilitate their discussion in an attempt to help them resolve their dispute.

If the parties are unable to resolve their own dispute through negotiation, they may turn to mediation. **Mediation,** like ombuds, adds a third party to the dispute resolution process. In mediation, the third party is neutral and is invited to direct the process.

Mediation has traditionally been a private consensual process. This means that the parties decide to pursue **private mediation** in an effort to resolve their dispute. Since mediation is private, the procedural and evidentiary rules of the process are those agreed to by the parties. Rather than fashion their own rules, the parties may agree to have the mediator determine the rules for them.

In private mediation, a neutral third party facilitates the discussion between the parties in an attempt to help the parties resolve their dispute. The mediator controls the process, and the parties negotiate through the mediator. The mediator does not resolve the dispute. The parties must agree on the resolution of the dispute. When parties select mediation as the method of dispute resolution, they become involved in a process that will most likely require compromise.

Facilitative mediation
The mediator refrains from suggesting solutions, but does assist the parties in focusing on the nature of their problem, their interests, and an array of resolutions they suggest for their dispute.

In **facilitative mediation,** the mediator refrains from suggesting solutions, but does assist the parties in focusing on the nature of their problem, their interests, and an array of resolutions they suggest for their dispute. Not all mediators are facilitative mediators. Some mediators evaluate the problem and suggest solutions as they assist the parties in working through the process. Even if the mediator suggests solutions, the parties ultimately must resolve their own dispute.

Example 1-10

For the last year the Pilots' Union for Coast-to-Coast Airlines and management have attempted to negotiate a new five-year contract. They have met on numerous occasions but could never resolve the sticking points of overtime compensation, maternity leave, health benefits, and mandatory retirement. When the contract expired last month, the parties agreed to hire a mediator to help them work through these issues. The parties agreed to permit the mediator to design the process although the decisions on the issues would remain theirs. Thus the parties have selected private mediation as their method of dispute resolution.

Problem 1-13
Why would the Pilots' Union and management select private mediation as their method of dispute resolution?

Problem 1-14
Have you used private mediation as a method of dispute resolution? Identify three situations in which private mediation could be used.

Court-Sponsored Mediation

Although traditionally mediation has been a private process (i.e., the parties hire and pay the mediator), in recent years a number of courts have added mediation to the litigation process. If the mediator is a judge, magistrate judge, or adjunct settlement judge, the process may be called a court-sponsored mediation, a court-ordered mediation, or a settlement conference.

Court-Sponsored Mediation
The litigants participate in mediation before they have an opportunity to try their dispute in court.

In a **court-sponsored mediation,** the litigants participate in mediation before they have an opportunity to appear in court to litigate their dispute. The mediation is conducted by a neutral third party (judge, magistrate judge, or court-appointed settlement judge) and is held in private at the courthouse. The neutral third party may or may not have been selected because of his or her specialized subject expertise.

The mediation is informal but structured by the settlement judge. The proceedings give the settlement judge and the parties an opportunity to explore the factors that might lead to settlement. These factors include: the legal aspects of the dispute; the probability of success at trial; the likelihood of appeal; the fairness of a litigated result; the extent of the injury (and how sympathetic the injured party will look at trial); a defendant's ability to pay a judgment or settlement; the cost of litigation; the hometown aspects of the case (i.e., whether a local litigant will have an advantage over an out-of-towner); the attractiveness of the parties and the witnesses to the jury; the individual concerns and needs of the parties; and creative solutions.

If settlement is not reached, the mediation can be used to refine timetables, resolve discovery issues, and streamline the issues for trial. If settlement is achieved, a mutually acceptable agreement is attained. The agreement is the litigants' agreement and not a resolution imposed by the settlement judge. The agreement need not parallel the "legal" resolution of the dispute. If settlement is reached, it usually is based on personal or business needs and interests rather than on the law, although a projected legal decision will influence the personal or business decision.

Some appellate courts also sponsor mediations. The appellate courts provide the process and the mediators. The mediation takes place while the appeal is pending.

The mediation can be privatized by the parties so the conference is not sponsored by the court. The litigants could select their own mediator and decide on the place, the time, and the fee for the mediator. The fact that a private mediation was held would not be a matter of court record. Parties could participate in a noncourt-sponsored mediation at any time: before filing a complaint, after filing but before discovery, during discovery, after discovery, on the eve of trial, during trial, after trial, during appeal, or after appeal.

Mini-Trial

A **mini-trial** is designed for disputes between large corporations where the dispute takes place on a level below upper management.

The mini-trial is not a trial before a judge. Rather the mini-trial is a presentation of evidence before a three-person panel. Two of the three members of the panel are not neutral, but are members of the two corporations that are the parties to the dispute. Each has settlement authority. The third member of the panel is neutral and directs the proceedings.

At the mini-trial, the attorneys representing the corporations make their abbreviated presentation of evidence to the panel. The members of the panel have an opportunity to question the presenters. By the time the evidentiary phase of the mini-trial is concluded, the members of the panel have developed a good working knowledge about the dispute and the legal positions of both sides.

After both sides have presented their evidence, the corporate representatives on the panel will attempt to negotiate a settlement. If the neutral third party is invited to participate, the conference may become a mediation with the neutral third party presiding.

Third-Party Adjudication in Dispute Resolution

Adjudication is used in this text to describe a process whereby a neutral third party makes the decision for the parties. In **adjudication,** the disputing parties come before a neutral third party, they relate the nature of their dispute to the third party, and the adjudicator resolves the dispute. The parties do not resolve their own dispute. The third party adjudicates or judges the dispute. Adjudication processes include arbitration, mediation-arbitration, litigation, and private judging.

Mini-Trial
An abbreviated nonbinding trial is held before a three-person panel (one corporate officer with settlement authority from each corporation and a neutral third party), rather than before a judge and jury. After the evidence has been presented, the corporate officers attempt to negotiate a settlement.

Adjudication
The disputing parties come before a neutral third party, they relate the nature of their dispute to the third party, and the adjudicator resolves the dispute.

Arbitration
The disputing parties come before a neutral third party (an arbitrator) or a panel of neutral third parties (an arbitration panel), they relate the nature of their dispute to the arbitrator or the arbitration panel, and the arbitrator or arbitration panel resolves the dispute.

Private Arbitration
The parties select the arbitrator or arbitration panel or the arbitration service provider and pay for the process. The arbitrator or arbitration panel hears the evidence and then resolves the dispute for the parties.

Private Arbitration Including High/Low and Final Offer Arbitration

Arbitration is at the interfering end of the dispute resolution spectrum. In **arbitration,** the arbitrator or arbitration panel resolves the dispute and the parties lose control over the outcome of their dispute. In **private arbitration,** the parties agree to arbitrate their dispute either before the dispute arises or after the dispute has arisen.

Problem 1-15

Alice purchased a jet ski from Aqua Marine. The sales contract contained the following boiler plate provision:

> Any dispute between the parties shall be resolved through arbitration under the rules of the American Arbitration Association.

Several weeks after delivery, Alice discovered that her jet ski had developed a crack along its entire underside. When Alice attempted to return the ski to Aqua Marine, Aqua Marine refused to replace it. Aqua Marine did, however, offer to repair it. Alice rejected Aqua Marine's offer to repair since she thought she was entitled to a new jet ski.

Alice filed a complaint in state court claiming breach of an implied warranty of merchantability under state law (i.e., the state's version of Article 2 of the Uniform Commercial Code). Aqua Marine moved to dismiss the complaint on the ground that the court lacked jurisdiction. The trial court granted Aqua Marine's motion on the ground that the provision in the sales contract mandates that Alice arbitrate her dispute with Aqua Marine using the process established by the American Arbitration Association.

1. Could Alice refuse to arbitrate?
2. Could she select another method of dispute resolution?
3. Would another method of dispute resolution have been a better method for Alice?
4. Would another method of dispute resolution have been a better method for Aqua Marine?

Not all private arbitration is provided for by contract before the dispute arises. The parties may agree upon arbitration after the dispute has arisen.

Problem 1-16

Return to Alice and the jet ski in Problem 1-15. Change the facts so the contract is silent as to the method of dispute resolution in the event of a dispute.

If Aqua Marine offers to arbitrate its dispute with Alice, should Alice accept Aqua Marine's offer? What are your reasons?

Since arbitration is private, the procedural and evidentiary rules of the process are those agreed to by the parties. Rather than fashion their own rules, the parties may agree to have the arbitrator determine the rules for them.

Example 1-11

The Firefighters' Union and the City of Richmond were having a dispute over whether the firefighters were entitled to additional compensation for extra hazardous service. The union claimed the firefighters' contract provided for such compensation. The city claimed the contract did not provide for such compensation. The parties agreed to hire the American Arbitration Association (AAA), a private arbitration service.

The AAA provided the parties with a list of potential arbitrators. The parties reviewed the list and selected one arbitrator. The AAA then outlined the arbitration process for the parties. The arbitrator conducted a hearing where both parties made opening and closing statements and presented evidence. At the conclusion of the hearing, the arbitrator issued her decision, thus resolving the issue for the parties.

Regardless of who fashions the rules for the arbitration, the arbitrator resolves the dispute for the parties. The arbitrator resolves both issues of fact and issues of law. In arbitration, there is no jury to resolve issues of fact. In arbitration, the arbitrator's decision is generally final and can be appealed to the courts only on very limited grounds.

Problem 1-17

1. Why would the Firefighters' Union and the city select arbitration as their method of dispute resolution?
2. Why would the union and the city agree to have an organization such as the American Arbitration Association provide the process and the arbitrator?
3. Should either the union or the city have refused to arbitrate?
4. Should either have selected inaction, acquiescence, negotiation, or mediation?

Problem 1-18

1. Have you ever used arbitration as a method of dispute resolution?
2. If you have not used arbitration, can you list a dispute where arbitration has been used? Why was arbitration chosen?

When parties select arbitration as the method of dispute resolution, they become involved in a process that will result in a winner and a loser. The parties may achieve all, some, or none of their goals. Since in arbitration the dispute is decided by a third party, arbitration does not foster compromise. The parties have lost their power to determine the outcome.

High/Low or **bounded arbitration** is a variation of private arbitration. High/low arbitration follows the private arbitration process with the exception that in high/low arbitration, the parties agree on the range of the outcome. The arbitrator's award must be in the range established by the parties. The arbitrator's award may neither be more than nor less than this preagreed amount.

Final offer or **baseball arbitration** is another variation of private arbitration. Final offer arbitration follows the private arbitration process with the exception that in final offer arbitration, the parties agree that the arbitrator must select one of the parties' last offer. The arbitrator has no leeway and may not make an award more than, less than, or in between the parties' last offers.

Court-Annexed Arbitration

Arbitration has traditionally been a private consensual process. This means that either prior to or during the dispute, the parties decide that the dispute should be resolved by an arbitrator. Since arbitration is private, the procedural and evidentiary rules of the process are those agreed to by the parties. Rather than fashion their own rules, the parties may agree to have the arbitrator determine the rules for them.

Some federal district courts and some state trial courts offer **court-annexed arbitration** as part of the litigation process. If a case came within the local court rules for arbitration, the litigants would be required to arbitrate their dispute in front of a court-appointed arbitrator or arbitration panel before they would have the opportunity to present their case to a judge. The parties could accept the award or proceed to a trial de novo before the court. A **trial de novo** is a "trial from the beginning" and proceeds as if the arbitration never took place.

High/Low (Bounded) Arbitration
In high/low arbitration, the arbitrator's award must be in the range of the outcome established by the parties.

Final Offer (Last Offer or Baseball) Arbitration
The parties agree that the arbitrator must select one of the parties' last offer and has no leeway and may not make an award more than, less than, or in between the parties' last offers.

Court-Annexed Arbitration
If a case came within the local court rules for arbitration, the litigants are required to arbitrate their dispute before a court-appointed arbitrator before they would have the opportunity to present their case to a judge.

Trial de novo
A trial from the beginning that takes place as if no court-annexed arbitration had taken place.

Example 1-12

Esther Chen purchased a Ford Explorer from Garden State Motors in Newark, New Jersey. When she was traveling through the Blue Ridge Mountains, her Explorer blew a tire and her vehicle left the highway and rolled over several times. Fortunately for Esther, she was wearing her seat belt and she received only minor physical injuries, although her vehicle was a complete loss.

Esther sued Garden State Motors, the Ford Motor Company, and Firestone tires in the United States District Court for New Jersey. She sued on several theories (strict liability, breach of an implied warranty of merchantability, and breach of an implied warranty of fitness for a particular purpose). She claimed $100,000 damages.

Under the court's local court rules, the court ordered Esther's case to proceed through court-sponsored arbitration before it could proceed to litigation. After the arbitration hearing, the arbitrator awarded Esther $75,000. Neither Esther Chen nor the three defendants requested a trial de novo. The arbitrator's award was entered as a judgment.

Problem 1-19

1. Based on the material in the paragraph preceding Example 1-12, was the hypothetical case of *Chen v. Garden State Motors,* a proper case for court-annexed arbitration?
2. After the arbitrator issued his award, should any of the parties have requested a trial de novo?

Mediation-Arbitration

Mediation-Arbitration (Med-Arb) begins with private mediation and, if the parties cannot resolve their own dispute, the process evolves into private arbitration. By the end of the process, the dispute is resolved either by the parties or by a neutral third party.

Litigation

Litigation is at the most-interfering end of the dispute resolution spectrum. Traditionally, litigation has been a governmentally sponsored process involving federal, state, and municipal courts. The magistrates, judges, or justices are either elected or appointed and serve for a term of years or, in the case of federal district court and court of appeals judges and United States Supreme Court justices, appointed and serve for life. The court staff serves the public, the facilities are maintained by the government, and the rules of evidence and procedure are created by the legislature and the court.

Litigation is initiated by one of the parties before a public forum (i.e., the governmentally created, managed, and financed court). The party who initiates the process becomes the plaintiff. The other party involuntarily becomes the defendant. The procedural and evidentiary rules of the court apply to this dispute and to these parties as well as to all disputes and all parties coming before this court. The parties have no say in the applicable rules of procedure, the rules of evidence, the scheduling of a trial, or the selection of the judge.

Mediation-Arbitration (Med-Arb)
The parties agree that the process will begin as a private mediation and, if they are unable to reach a mediated agreement, the process shifts to private arbitration.

Litigation
Litigation is initiated by one of the parties before a public forum (i.e., the governmentally created, managed, and financed court).

Example 1-13

If the complaint is filed in the United States District Court, the parties are subject to the Federal Rules of Civil Procedure, the court's local rules, and the Federal Rules of Evidence.

If the complaint is filed in a state court, the parties are subject to the state's rules of civil procedure, the court's local rules, and the state's rules of evidence.

In litigation, the litigants' attorneys choreograph the presentation of facts and law. If the case is before a jury, the jury will resolve questions of fact and the judge will resolve issues of law. If no jury is present, the judge will resolve both questions of fact and issues of law. The dispute is resolved according to "the law" and not according to the needs or interests of the parties. The parties have a right to appeal the trial court's judgment (or decree if an equitable proceeding) to a higher court.

Example 1-14

The Great Mountain Railroad and the resort village of Sleepyhaven were having a dispute over whether the trains were required to blow their whistles at every crossing within the village. The railroad read the state statute as requiring a whistle at every street crossing. The village read the statute as requiring a whistle only when approaching the village. The village brought action against the railroad in state district court to enjoin the railroad from blowing its whistle at every street crossing. The village, by selecting litigation as its method of dispute resolution became the plaintiff. The railroad involuntarily became the defendant.

After discovery, the parties proceeded to trial before the judge. After both sides made their opening statements, they presented their evidence (through witnesses and exhibits) and made their closing arguments. The judge, after considering the questions of fact and the issues of law, ruled for the village granting its request for an injunction. The railroad moved for a new trial. The judge rejected the railroad's motion. The railroad appealed the judge's decision to the state's court of appeals.

Problem 1-20

1. Why would the village select litigation as its method of dispute resolution?
2. Should the village have selected inaction, acquiescence, negotiation, mediation, or arbitration?
3. Did the railroad have a say in the choice of dispute resolution process?

Problem 1-21

1. Can you list three disputes where litigation has been used?
2. Why was litigation chosen?

When a party selects litigation as the method of dispute resolution, it becomes involved in a process that will result in a winner and a loser. A litigant may achieve all, some, or none of his or her goals. Litigation does not produce a compromise. Since a third party (or third parties) resolves the dispute, the litigants lose control over the outcome of their dispute.

Private Judging

Private Judging ("Rent-a-Judge")
A neutral third party who is not a sitting judge is selected to conduct a private trial between the parties.

Recent experimentation has led to an increase in private litigation known as private judging. **Private judging,** loosely referred to as "**rent-a-judge,**" is consensual and takes two forms. In one, the parties contract to have private judging as their method of dispute resolution. In the other, litigation has been instituted by one of the parties, and both parties apply to the court to appoint a private judge.

Private Judging by Contract

Private Judging by Contract
Both parties agree on the process and they negotiate the rules for the process.

Unlike public litigation where one party files a complaint to initiate the process and the other involuntarily becomes a defendant, in **private judging by contract** both parties agree on the process. The parties must negotiate the procedural and evidentiary rules as well as the extent of pretrial discovery, whether the trial will be before a judge and jury or only a judge, who will be the judge (and jurors), who will pay the judge (and jurors) and how much, where and when the trial will be held, how long the trial will last, and whether the decision will be advisory (merely an opinion) or binding (obligatory). In private judging, the parties' attorneys choreograph the presentation of facts and law and the third party or parties (the judge or the jury and judge) resolve the dispute. The dispute is resolved according to the law and the decision is binding unless the parties have decided otherwise. If binding, the decision may not be appealed to a public tribunal.

Example 1-15

Return to Great Mountain Railroad and the facts of Example 1-14. In an effort to save some of the costs associated with litigation and to accelerate the timetable for a decision, the village and the railroad agreed to proceed to private judging with the village being the plaintiff and the railroad being the defendant.

The parties hired a retired trial court judge to adjudicate the dispute. The parties met with the private judge and agreed to an abbreviated discovery and trial schedule. The parties also agreed that the judge's ruling would be binding and not advisory.

After discovery, the parties proceeded to trial before the private judge. After both sides made their opening statements, they presented their evidence (including witnesses and exhibits) and made their closing arguments. The judge, after considering the questions of fact and the issues of law, ruled for the village.

Problem 1-22

1. Why would the village select private judging as its method of dispute resolution?
2. Should the village have selected inaction, acquiescence, negotiation, mediation, or arbitration?
3. Did the railroad have a say in the choice of dispute resolution process?

Problem 1-23

Identify a dispute where private judging by contract, rather than litigation before a court, should be used.

Private Judging by Court Referral

After one of the parties has initiated litigation by filing a complaint before a court, the litigants ask the judge to refer the case to a private judge.

Private Judging by Court Referral

Private judging by court referral takes place after one of the parties has initiated litigation by filing a complaint before a court. As the case is proceeding down the litigation track, the litigants decide that they may not want to wait for trial before the court. Rather

ADR Process	Availability	Who selects the process?
Unilateral Action		
inaction	depends on the facts	one party
acquiescence	depends on the facts	the aggrieved party
self-help	depends on the facts and the law	the aggrieved party
Bilateral Action		
negotiation	always	the parties
Third-Party Evaluation		
early neutral evaluation	depends on whether the court has a program	the court
summary jury trial	depends on whether the court has a program	the parties and the judge
Third-Party Assistance		
ombuds	depends on whether an ombuds office exists	the aggrieved party
private mediation	always	the parties
court-sponsored mediation	limited to those courts with a program	the judge with parties' consent
mini-trial	requires a corporate dispute	the parties
Third-Party Adjudication		
private arbitration	always	the parties
court-annexed arbitration	limited to those courts with a program	automatic if case comes with subject matter and monetary limits of the court's rule
mediation–arbitration	always	the parties
litigation	always, but must be within the jurisdiction of the court	the aggrieved party
private judging (by contract)	always	the parties
private judging (by court referral)	limited to those courts with a program	the parties request and the judge consents

FIGURE 1-1 Comparison of Dispute Resolution Processes

Who participates in the process?	Who decides the outcome?	On what is the outcome based?
Unilateral Action		
one party	one party	primarily nonlegal
the aggrieved party	the aggrieved party	primarily nonlegal
the aggrieved party	the aggrieved party	the law
Bilateral Action		
the parties	the parties	primarily nonlegal
Third-PartyEvaluation		
the parties, their attorneys, and a neutral third party	neutral third party gives evaluation	process not designed to resolve the dispute
the parties, their attorneys, a judge, a mock jury, and a few witnesses	judge or judge and mock jury evaluate	process not designed to resolve the dispute
Third-Party Assistance		
the aggrieved party, the ombuds and whomever the ombuds consults	one party	primarily nonlegal
the parties and a mediator	the parties	primarily nonlegal
the parties, their attorneys, and settlement judge	the parties	primarily nonlegal
corporate reps, a neutral third party, attorneys, and a few witnesses	the corporate representatives	primarily nonlegal
Third-Party Adjudication		
the parties, their attorneys, the arbitrator, and a few witnesses	the arbitrator	the law
the parties, their attorneys, a court-appointed arbitrator, and a few witnesses	the arbitrator	the law
the parties, their attorneys, a mediator, an arbitrator, and a few witnesses	the parties if settled during mediation; the arbitrator if resolved by arbitration	primarily nonlegal if settled during mediation; the law if resolved by arbitration
the parties, their attorneys, a judge, a jury if one is seated, and witnesses	if a jury trial, the judge on the law and the jury on the facts; if no jury, then the judge on both the law and the facts	the law
the parties, their attorneys, the private judge, possibly a jury, and witnesses	if a jury trial, the judge on the law and the jury on the facts; if no jury, then the judge on both the law and the facts	the law
the parties, their attorneys, the private judge, possibly a jury, and witnesses	if a jury trial, the judge on the law and the jury on the facts; if no jury, then the judge on both the law and the facts	the law

than wait, they may ask the judge to refer the case to a private judge. About half of the states have laws that permit the courts to appoint a private judge if requested by the parties.

The parties work with the judge in the selection of the private judge (i.e., a retired or former judge, a law professor, or another attorney). The procedural and evidentiary rules of the court apply to private judging, although the parties may work with the private judge to modify some of the rules. The trial may be before the private judge or before the private judge and a private jury. At the end of the trial, the ruling may be appealed to a public court as specified by law.

Comparing Dispute Resolution Processes

Figure 1-1 uses five features to compare the 16 dispute resolution processes discussed in this text: availability, who selects the process, who participates in the process, who decides the outcome, and on what is the outcome based.

Key Terms and Phrases

acquiescence	negotiation
adjudication	ombuds
arbitration	private arbitration
bilateral action	private judging
court-annexed arbitration	private judging by contract
court-sponsored mediation	private judging by court referral
early neutral evaluation	private mediation
facilitative mediation	rent-a-judge
final offer or baseball arbitration	self-help
high/low or bounded arbitration	summary jury trial
inaction	third-party adjudication
litigation	third-party assistance
mediation	third-party evaluation
mediation-arbitration (med-arb)	trial de novo
mini-trial	unilateral action

Review Questions

True/False Questions

1. T F In arbitration, the jury is the finder of fact and the judge is the finder of law.

2. T F Litigation is the slowest and most costly form of dispute resolution.

3. T F A mini-trial is an abbreviated trial that results in a binding judgment.

4. T F The safety valve in court-annexed arbitration is the opportunity for a trial de novo.

5. T F   Trials result in judgments or decrees while arbitration results in awards.

6. T F   A summary jury trial is a mini-trial.

7. T F   The party who selects inaction as his or her dispute resolution process also controls the outcome of the dispute.

8. T F   One advantage of private judging is the fact that the parties need not wait for the court to set a trial date.

9. T F   Private arbitration awards and litigation judgments may be appealed to a higher tribunal.

10. T F   An ombuds works for and is paid by the institution or organization that is involved in the grievance and not for or paid by the party bringing the grievance.

Fill-in-the-blank Questions

1. _____   The process in which a judge decides the outcome of the dispute for the parties.

2. _____   The process in which the parties receive an advisory decision by a jury.

3. _____   The process in which one party selects the process and the outcome.

4. _____   The process in which high-level corporate representatives hear the evidence presented in summary fashion that may include witnesses.

5. _____   The process in which the parties work together without the assistance of a third party to reach an agreement.

6. _____   The process in which a trial de novo is available.

7. _____   The process in which the parties have no right to appeal a judgment.

8. _____   The process in which the parties have a very limited right to appeal a decision of a neutral third party.

9. _____   The process in which one party gives in to the demands of the other.

10. _____   Three processes in which there can be a win/win
_____   outcome.
_____

Multiple-Choice Questions

1. Which of the following dispute resolution processes are forms of unilateral action?
   (a) inaction
   (b) negotiation
   (c) self-help
   (d) ombuds
   (e) acquiescence

2. Which of the following dispute resolution processes are forms of bilateral action?
   (a) private mediation
   (b) ombuds
   (c) private judging
   (d) court-sponsored mediation
   (e) negotiation

3. Which of the following dispute resolution processes are forms of third-party evaluation in dispute resolution?
   (a) summary jury trial
   (b) private judging
   (c) self-help
   (d) early neutral evaluation
   (e) settlement conference

4. Which of the following dispute resolution processes are forms of third-party assistance in dispute resolution?
   (a) summary jury trial
   (b) self-help
   (c) early neutral evaluation
   (d) private judging
   (e) settlement conference

5. Which of the following dispute resolution processes are forms of third-party adjudication?
   (a) private arbitration
   (b) summary jury trial
   (c) private judging
   (d) ombuds
   (e) mediation-arbitration

6. In which of the following dispute resolution processes do one or both disputing parties control the outcome?
   (a) acquiescence
   (b) ombuds
   (c) court-sponsored mediation
   (d) court-annexed arbitration
   (e) private judging

7. In which of the following dispute resolution processes do both disputing parties, together, control the selection of the process?
   (a) self-help
   (b) ombuds
   (c) court-annexed arbitration
   (d) litigation
   (e) private judging
   (f) negotiation

8. In which of the following dispute resolution processes is the outcome determined for the parties by a third party?

   (a) private mediation
   (b) court-annexed arbitration
   (c) litigation
   (d) negotiation
   (e) summary jury trial
 9. Which of the following dispute resolution processes requires compromise?
   (a) court-annexed arbitration
   (b) acquiescence
   (c) negotiation
   (d) private mediation
   (e) private judging
10. Which of the following dispute resolution processes will result in a winner and a loser?
   (a) court-annexed arbitration
   (b) litigation
   (c) inaction
   (d) private mediation
   (e) ombuds

Short-Answer Questions

1. Discuss the underlying reasons for the emergence of the ADR movement.
2. Identify the five categories of dispute resolution processes and distinguish one from another.
3. Of the 16 dispute resolution processes discussed in this chapter, which do you think is the most commonly used and why?
4. Of the 16 dispute resolution processes discussed in this chapter, which do you think is the least commonly used and why?
5. Litigation is an adjudication process. Should arbitration also be considered an adjudication process? Why?
6. As a dispute resolution process, do you find court-annexed arbitration more appealing than court-sponsored mediation or court-sponsored mediation more appealing than court-annexed arbitration? What features of each do you like or dislike, and why?

CHAPTER 2

The Participants

Who participates in the dispute resolution process depends on which process is selected. Beyond the question of who participates is the question of to what degree they participate. The degree of participation depends on the process and their role in determining the outcome.

The Party or Parties

As the methods of dispute resolution sweep from the least interfering (unilateral action) to the most interfering (adjudication), a party's power to select the method of dispute resolution, participate in the process, and determine the outcome varies.

Unilateral Action

On one end of the spectrum, unilateral action (inaction, acquiescence, and self-help), only one party selects and actively participates in the process. By selecting the process, this party dictates the outcome of the dispute. If inaction is selected as the process, the problem is resolved unless inaction has been selected as a wait and see tactic. If the other party takes no action the dispute is resolved; if the other party takes action, the dispute resolution process will no longer remain one of inaction.

If acquiescence is selected as the process, the problem is resolved unless the party who selected acquiescence does not fully surrender to the other party's demands.

If self-help is selected, the dispute is resolved unless self-help does not fully satisfy the other party's obligations or self-help has been exercised improperly. If the latter, the party who was the subject of self-help may have a claim against the party who exercised self-help.

Bilateral Action

Both parties participate in the selection of negotiation as a method of dispute resolution. Both parties participate in the process unless they have delegated their participation to a third party, such as their attorney. Both parties also control the outcome because a negotiated agreement requires assent by both parties.

Third-Party Evaluation

Generally a third-party evaluation (early neutral evaluation and summary jury trial) occurs after one party has sought the assistance of a court in resolving the dispute. The court may offer early neutral evaluation or a summary jury trial as one of its ADR processes. If the case comes within the parameters of the court's early neutral evaluation program, a court administrator may assign the case for ENE without consulting the parties. Authorizing a summary jury trial, on the other hand, is less administrative. The judge assigned to resolve pretrial issues in the case may suggest a summary jury trial to the parties, and the parties may accept or reject the judge's suggestion.

If the case is assigned to early neutral evaluation, the parties will accompany their attorneys to the evaluation and will defer to their attorneys to interact with the early neutral evaluator. If the case proceeds to a summary jury trial, the parties will consult with their attorneys during the trial but will participate as witnesses only if called to testify.

Since both early neutral evaluation and summary jury trial are evaluative procedures, the parties are not called upon to tender or to accept an offer.

Third-Party Assistance

Third-party assistance (ombuds, private mediation, court-sponsored mediation, and mini-trial) involves the neutral third party as a go-between and not as an evaluator or decision maker.

In ombuds, an aggrieved party will consult an ombuds and the ombuds will listen to the aggrieved party, explain organizational rules and procedures, and informally investigate the grievance. Although only one party initiates the ombuds process and the ombuds may discuss the grievance with a number of people, the aggrieved must decide on the outcome.

Both parties must agree to pursue private mediation. At a mediation, the parties may be present without attorneys, may be present with attorneys, or may not be present and be represented by attorneys. Even when the parties and their attorneys are present, their participation may vary depending on the process. The parties may have the active role and their attorneys only act as advisors. Or the attorneys may have the active role and their clients participate in only limited ways, although the clients make the ultimate decision whether to make or accept a settlement offer. In the end, however, it is the parties who must assent to the outcome.

Generally a court-sponsored mediation occurs after one party has filed a complaint seeking the assistance of a court in resolving the dispute. The judge assigned to resolve discovery disputes will recommend the court-sponsored mediation to the parties, or the judge may assign the case to court-sponsored mediation and the parties have the option of requesting the mediation be canceled. During the mediation the parties will be represented by their attorneys and will actively participate in the mediation process. As with private mediation, it is the parties who must assent to the outcome.

In a mini-trial, the parties, who are generally corporations, must agree to the process. Each corporation is represented by a high-level official with decision-making authority. The two corporate officials, along with the neutral, form a three-person panel that listens to the opening statements, the presentation of evidence, and the closing arguments. They have an opportunity to question the attorneys as they present the evidence. At the end of the trial phase of the mini-trial, the corporate officials and the neutral (if the officials wish the neutral to participate) discuss what they have observed and attempt to resolve the dispute.

Third-Party Adjudication

Third-party adjudication (private arbitration, court-annexed arbitration, mediation-arbitration, litigation, and private judging) involves the neutral third party as a decision maker.

Both parties must agree to pursue private arbitration and must agree upon the rules of the arbitration unless they have selected an arbitration service that will provide both the rules and the arbitrator or arbitration panel. Both parties actively participate in the arbitration unless they are represented by attorneys. If represented, their participation is reduced to consulting with their attorneys and testifying, if called as witnesses. By selecting arbitration, the parties have delegated their power to resolve the dispute to the arbitrator or the arbitration panel. The parties no longer have the power to accept or reject the outcome.

Court-annexed arbitration may occur after one party has filed a complaint seeking the assistance of a court in resolving the dispute. If the case comes within the parameters of the court's arbitration process, the case will be referred to arbitration. In some courts, the parties have the option of requesting the arbitration be canceled. During the arbitration the parties will be represented by their attorneys and will not actively participate. Their participation is reduced to consulting with their attorneys and testifying, if called as witnesses. By being in court-annexed arbitration, the arbitrator or arbitration panel, not the parties, has the power to resolve the dispute. A party has the power to reject the award and request a trial de novo.

If the parties agree upon mediation-arbitration (med-arb) as their method of dispute resolution, their participation will change depending on whether the process is mediation or arbitration. In the mediation phase of med-arb, the parties actively participate in discussing the facts, their needs and interests, and possible solutions. They will make the ultimate decision whether to make or accept a settlement offer. If the parties can not resolve their dispute during the mediation, the process becomes arbitration where the parties' participation is greatly reduced and the outcome is determined by the arbitrator. In the arbitration phase of med-arb, the parties have a passive role since their attorneys will make the opening statements, orchestrate the presentation of evidence, and make the closing arguments. The parties may sit at the counsel table and may be called as witnesses. If called, they will perform the same role as any other witness by responding to the questions asked by his or her attorney during direct examination and by responding to the questions asked by the other party's attorney during cross-examination.

When one party initiates the litigation, the other party participates involuntarily. During the litigation process, the parties will be represented by their attorneys (unless they represent themselves and appear *pro se*) and will not actively participate. Their participation is reduced to consulting with their attorneys and testifying, if called as witnesses. By being in litigation, the trial judge and the jury, if one is present, have the power to resolve the dispute. After the judgment has been rendered, a party may request a new trial. The party making the motion for a new trial, however, must demonstrate that reversible error occurred during the trial. If the motion for a new trial is overruled by the trial judge, a party may appeal the trial court's judgment to a higher court, but must demonstrate that reversible error occurred during the trial in order to gain a new trial. By being within the judicial system, the parties have lost their power to design their own outcome.

Some courts by statute or court rule permit the parties to request the court to refer (or reference) the case to a private judge. This requires the parties to agree on private judging as their method of dispute resolution and on the private judge. Once the case is referred to a private judge and the parties and the private judge have agreed upon a procedure, the parties assume a greatly reduced role and the private judging proceeds as if the case were being tried in a public courtroom. If one of the parties is dissatisfied with the judgment, he or she may appeal within the judicial system. The appeal, however, must be based on reversible error.

The Attorney

Attorneys may participate in all dispute resolution processes. The attorney's initial role will be during the interview and counseling sessions with the client. The attorney must gather information from the client, develop this information through investigation, evaluate the facts in light of the law, and develop with the client a dispute resolution strategy.

If the client selects unilateral action, the attorney may still have a role. If the client selects inaction, the attorney must be prepared to advise the client in the event the other party takes action when the client has used inaction as a wait and see tactic. If the client selects acquiescence, the attorney may act on behalf of the client in executing the acquiescence. For example, the attorney could draft a letter that accompanies the client's check. If the client selects self-help, the attorney may act on behalf of the client by writing a letter to the other party explaining his or her client's actions or may assist his or her client in finding a third party to perform the act of self-help, such as repossession.

If the client selects bilateral action, the attorney could advise the client on how to negotiate, could negotiate on behalf of the client, and could participate in the drafting and execution of the agreement.

If the client selects a process that involves a neutral third party, the attorney may have little or no role, as in the case of ombuds, to a shared role with the client, as in the case of mediation, to a dominant role, as in the case of an early neutral evaluation, summary jury trial, mini-trial, arbitration, litigation, and private judging. In an early neutral evaluation, the attorney presents the client's case to the evaluator. In summary jury trial, mini-trial, arbitration, litigation, and private judging, the attorney must prepare the case for the trial or hearing (including gathering the facts through discovery and researching the law) and present the case through opening statement, presentation of evidence including the examination of witnesses, and closing argument to the neutral third party (judge or judge and jury, arbitrator or arbitration panel, or corporate officials and neutral). The attorney must prepare all written motions, exhibits, and briefs essential to the case. If the process permits an appeal, the attorney must prepare all appellate briefs and participate in the oral argument before the appellate court, if an oral argument is scheduled.

Problem 2-1

What are the respective roles of client and attorney? Read the following ABA Model Rules of Professional Conduct.

RULE 1.1 COMPETENCE

A lawyer shall provide competent representation to a client. Competent representation requires the legal knowledge, skill, thoroughness and preparation reasonably necessary for the representation.

RULE 1.2 SCOPE OF REPRESENTATION

(a) A lawyer shall abide by a client's decisions concerning the objectives of representation, subject to paragraphs (c), (d), and (e), and shall consult with the client as to the means by which they are to be pursued. A lawyer shall abide by a client's decision whether to accept an offer of settlement of a matter. In a criminal case, the lawyer shall abide by the client's decision, after consultation with the lawyer, as to a plea to be entered, whether to waive jury trial and whether the client will testify.

(b) A lawyer's representation of a client, including representation by appointment, does not constitute an endorsement of the client's political, economic, social or moral views or activities.

(c) A lawyer may limit the objectives of the representation if the client consents after consultation.

(d) A lawyer shall not counsel a client to engage, or assist a client, in conduct that the lawyer knows is criminal or fraudulent, but a lawyer may discuss the legal consequences of any proposed course of conduct with a client and may counsel or assist a client to make a good faith effort to determine the validity, scope, meaning or application of the law.

(e) When a lawyer knows that a client expects assistance not permitted by the rules of professional conduct or other law, the lawyer shall consult with the client regarding the relevant limitations on the lawyer's conduct.

RULE 1.3 DILIGENCE

A lawyer shall act with reasonable diligence and promptness in representing a client.

RULE 1.4 COMMUNICATION

(a) A lawyer shall keep a client reasonably informed about the status of a matter and promptly comply with reasonable requests for information.

(b) A lawyer shall explain a matter to the extent reasonably necessary to permit the client to make informed decisions regarding the representation.

RULE 2.1 ADVISOR

In representing a client, a lawyer shall exercise independent professional judgment and render candid advice. In rendering advice, a lawyer may refer not only to law but to other considerations such as moral, economic, social and political factors, that may be relevant to the client's situation.

The Paralegal

In addition to a number of state bar associations that define the terms paralegal and legal assistant (see *http://paralegals.org/development/pl_defin.html*), the terms are defined by a number of national organizations. The following are four definitions—some more expansive, some more limiting.

The National Association of Legal Assistants (NALA):

Legal assistants, also known as paralegals, are a distinguishable group of persons who assist attorneys in the delivery of legal services. Through formal education, training and experience, legal assistants [paralegals] have knowledge and expertise regarding the legal system and substantive and procedural law which qualify them to do work of a legal nature under the supervision of an attorney.
http://www.nala.org/whatis.htm

The National Federation of Paralegal Associations (NFPA):

A paralegal/legal assistant is a person qualified through education, training or work experience to perform substantive legal work that requires knowledge of legal concepts and is customarily, but not exclusively, performed by a lawyer. This person may be retained or employed by a lawyer, law office, governmental agency or other entity or may be authorized by administrative, statutory or court authority to perform the work.
http://www.paralegals.org/Development/pl_defin.htm

The American Association for Paralegal Education (AAfPE):

Paralegals perform substantive and procedural legal work as authorized by law, which work, in the absence of the paralegal, would be performed by an attorney. Paralegals have knowledge of the law gained through education, or education and work experience, which qualifies them to perform legal work. Paralegals adhere to recognized ethical standards and rules of professional responsibility.

http://www.aafpe.org

The American Bar Association's Standing Committee on Legal Assistants:

A legal assistant or paralegal is a person, qualified by education, training or work experience who is employed or retained by a lawyer, law office, corporation, governmental agency or other entity who performs specifically designated substantive legal work for which a lawyer is responsible.

http://www.abanet.org/legal.assts

Problem 2-2
How are these definitions similar and how are they different?

The paralegal is not licensed to practice law and therefore cannot advise the attorney's clients. The paralegal, however, plays a critical role in assisting the attorney in duties assigned and supervised by the attorney. For example, the attorney may ask the paralegal to gather preliminary information from the client before the interview. The paralegal may prepare the attorney for the interview by gathering additional facts and researching what might be applicable law. The paralegal could participate at the interview by taking notes. After the interview the paralegal could work with the attorney in developing the facts and the law and in creating dispute resolution options for the client. During the counseling session, the paralegal may assist the attorney but cannot advise the client.

Once the client, with the advise of the attorney, has formulated a dispute resolution strategy, the paralegal could assist the attorney in preparing for mediation, arbitration, litigation, summary jury trial, mini-trial, or private judging by further developing the facts and researching the law. The paralegal could prepare drafts of letters, memoranda, and other documents that might prove necessary in the case. If the case comes before an arbitrator or judge, the paralegal could prepare and arrange all necessary exhibits. During the trial or hearing, the paralegal could assist the attorney by being the document and exhibit manager.

The following are the canons of the National Association of Legal Assistants (NALA) Code of Ethics and Professional Responsibility (*http://www.nala.org*).

Canon 1.
A legal assistant must not perform any of the duties that attorneys only may perform nor take any actions that attorneys may not take.

Canon 2.
A legal assistant may perform any task which is properly delegated and supervised by an attorney, as long as the attorney is ultimately responsible to the client, maintains a direct relationship with the client, and assumes professional responsibility for the work product.

Canon 3.
A legal assistant must not: (a) engage in, encourage, or contribute to any act which could constitute the unauthorized practice of law; and (b) establish attorney-client

relationships, set fees, give legal opinions or advice or represent a client before a court or agency unless so authorized by that court or agency; and (c) engage in conduct or take any action which would assist or involve the attorney in a violation of professional ethics or give the appearance of professional impropriety.

Canon 4.

A legal assistant must use discretion and professional judgment commensurate with knowledge and experience but must not render independent legal judgment in place of an attorney. The services of an attorney are essential in the public interest whenever such legal judgment is required.

Canon 5.

A legal assistant must disclose his or her status as a legal assistant at the outset of any professional relationship with a client, attorney, a court or administrative agency or personnel thereof, or a member of the general public. A legal assistant must act prudently in determining the extent to which a client may be assisted without the presence of an attorney.

Canon 6.

A legal assistant must strive to maintain integrity and a high degree of competency through education and training with respect to professional responsibility, local rules and practice, and through continuing education in substantive areas of law to better assist the legal profession in fulfilling its duty to provide legal service.

Canon 7.

A legal assistant must protect the confidences of a client and must not violate any rule or statute now in effect or hereafter enacted controlling the doctrine of privileged communications between a client and an attorney.

Canon 8.

A legal assistant must do all other things incidental, necessary, or expedient for the attainment of the ethics and responsibilities as defined by statute or rule of court.

Canon 9.

A legal assistant's conduct is guided by bar associations' codes of professional responsibility and rules of professional conduct.

Problem 2-3

Based on the NALA canons, is there a difference in what a paralegal can do when working for an attorney who represents clients in litigation and what a paralegal can do when working for an attorney who represents clients in another dispute resolution process?

Although paralegals are primarily support staff to attorneys who use various methods of dispute resolution to resolve their clients' disputes, paralegals also assist attorneys and nonattorneys who function as neutral third parties such as mediators, arbitrators, early neutral evaluators, or private judges.

Paralegals may also function as client advocates in administrative hearings, ADR processes, and other nonjudicial forums that permit the use of nonattorney advocates. This is especially true in most federal agencies that provide services directly to individuals. For example, a nonattorney may represent a claimant at a hearing before an administrative law judge when the claimant has been denied Social Security benefits.

Problem 2-4
As a client advocate, can a paralegal give a client legal advice?

Paralegals also may serve as neutral third parties, such as mediators, ombuds, and arbitrators, provided they have the requisite expertise and training.

Problem 2-5
As a third party neutral, such as a mediator, ombuds, or arbitrator, can a paralegal give one or both disputing parties legal advice?

The Neutral Third Party

The neutral third party may be an evaluator, an ombuds, a mediator, an arbitrator, or a judge.

The evaluator in ENE is a court-appointed local attorney who practices in the field of the dispute. The evaluator is appointed early in the litigation process. He or she listens to the parties and their attorneys discuss the case and provides them with an objective evaluation. Early neutral evaluation is not, in and of itself, a process designed to settle disputes. The parties, however, may participate in another dispute resolution process after ENE that will produce a resolution of their dispute.

The ombuds is employed by the organization or governmental agency that will be investigated. The ombuds, however, is independent of the politics of the organization. An ombuds may or may not be an attorney. The ombuds' role is to listen to grievances, explain organizational rules and procedures and informally investigate but not to legally advise or represent those who seek the assistance of the ombuds.

The mediator is appointed by the parties or by the court, depending on whether the mediation is a private mediation or a court-sponsored mediation. The mediator may or may not be a member of the bench, if the mediation is court sponsored. A court-appointed mediator generally is an attorney, although being an attorney is not a prerequisite for appointment. Regardless of whether the mediator is or is not an attorney, the mediator should have expertise in the field of the mediation. The mediator, by being a neutral third party, does not represent either party. If the mediator is an attorney, neither party is the mediator's client. Mediators may conduct mediations alone or may team with another mediator so the mediation becomes a co-mediation.

An arbitrator is appointed by the parties or by the court, depending on whether the mediation is a private arbitration or a court-annexed arbitration. An arbitrator may or may not be an attorney. The arbitrator, however, should have expertise in the field of the arbitration. The arbitrator, by being a neutral third party, does not represent either party. If the arbitrator is an attorney, neither party is the arbitrator's client. Arbitrators generally conduct arbitrations alone or in panels of three. In rare cases, the panel may exceed three, although the number of arbitrators will always be an odd number.

A judge may be appointed or elected, depending on the jurisdiction. Generally, the judge will be an attorney. Unless the judge's court is a specialized one such as bankruptcy or worker's compensation, the trial court judge will have general expertise. The trial judge is assigned to the case under a system developed by the court. The judge, by being a neutral third party, does not represent either party. Neither party is his or her client. The judge presides alone and is the only judge conducting the trial. The trial may be conducted as a binding trial or as an advisory trial known as a summary jury trial.

A private judge, in a private judging under contract, is selected by the parties. A private judge, in a private judging referenced by the court, is selected by the parties but appointed by the trial judge or by the court. The private judge, by being a neutral third party, does not represent either party. Neither party is his or her client. The private judge presides alone and is the only judge conducting the trial.

The Jury

Juries may participate in litigation, private judging, and summary jury trials. When the litigation is at the courthouse, whether it be by a traditional trial or by a summary jury trial, the jury will be selected from the jury pool assembled by the clerk of the court. When the litigation is conducted by private judging, the jury is selected by the parties. In some instances when the private judging is by court reference, the court may permit the parties to select the jury from the court's jury pool.

When a jury participates in the trial, the judge will instruct the jury as to the law and the jury, as the trier of fact, and will render a verdict. After the jury has returned its verdict and before the judge has entered the judgment, the party who has suffered an adverse verdict may move for a judgment notwithstanding the verdict or judgment n.o.v. (judgment *non obstante veredicto*). A judgment n.o.v. reverses the jury verdict on the ground that the jury's verdict was not justified by the facts. Once the judge has entered the judgment, issues of fact are seldom appealable.

A jury that participates in a summary jury trial acts as a mock jury. Its verdict is advisory only. After the jury has returned its verdict, the attorneys may question the jurors to gain an objective understanding of the strengths and weaknesses of their case. This information may assist the parties as they participate in settlement discussions.

Figure 2-1 lists the participants for each dispute resolution process.

THE PROCESS	THE PARTICIPANTS
Unilateral Action	
Inaction	the aggrieved party
Acquiescence	the aggrieved party
Self-Help	the aggrieved party
Bilateral Action	
Negotiation	the parties
Third Party Evaluation	
Early Neutral Evaluation	the parties
	their attorneys
	court-appointed evaluator
Summary Jury Trial	the parties
	their attorneys
	judge
	mock jury
	several witnesses
Third Party Assistance	
Ombuds	the aggrieved party
	ombuds
	any parties the ombuds wishes to consult
Private Mediation	the parties
	sometimes their attorneys
	mediator
Court-Sponsored Mediation	the parties
	their attorneys
	court-appointed mediator or settlement judge
Mini-Trial	upper level official with settlement authority for each corporation
	neutral third party who may also act as a mediator
	attorneys for each corporation
	several witnesses
Third Party Adjudication	
Private Arbitration	the parties
	generally their attorneys
	one or three arbitrators
	numerous witnesses
Court-Annexed Arbitration	the parties
	their attorneys
	one or three court-appointed arbitrators
	several witnesses
Mediation-Arbitration	the parties
	their attorneys
	mediator (for the mediation)
	arbitrator (for the arbitration) (may or may not be the same person as the mediator depending on what the parties decided)
	several witnesses for the arbitration
Litigation	the parties
	their attorneys
	trial judge
	6–12 jurors when appropriate
	numerous witnesses
Private Judging	the parties
	their attorneys
	private judge
	6–12 jurors when appropriate
	a number of witnesses

FIGURE 2-1   Who Are the Participants in the Various Dispute Resolution Processes?

Review Questions

True/False Questions

1. T F   In arbitration, the jury is the finder of fact and the judge is the finder of law.
2. T F   When a party is represented by an attorney, the attorney and not the client resolves the dispute.
3. T F   A paralegal who is employed by an attorney may provide the attorney's client with legal advice.
4. T F   All neutral third parties must be sitting judges, former judges, or practicing attorneys.
5. T F   An ombuds must be a member of the state's bar association.
6. T F   The role of the aggrieved party will vary depending on which dispute resolution process he or she has selected.
7. T F   The neutral third party resolves the dispute for the parties in mediation.
8. T F   The award of an arbitrator is more final than the judgment of a judge.
9. T F   An arbitrator may sit alone or as a member of an arbitration panel; a trial judge always sits alone.
10. T F   The mediator in a court-sponsored mediation, the arbitrator in a court-annexed arbitration, and the trial judge in a private judging by court referral must all be active, retired, or former judges.

Fill-in-the-Blank Questions

1. _____   Name six processes where witnesses may participate.
_____
_____
_____
_____
_____

2. _____   Name three processes where only one party actively participates.
_____
_____

3. _____   Name the process where a neutral third party resolves the dispute for the parties and there is either no right to appeal or only a very limited right to appeal to a higher tribunal.

4. _____   Name two processes where the parties ultimately resolve the dispute together.
_____

5. _____   Name the process where a party decides to surrender to the demands of another.

6. _____ Name the process where high-level corporate representatives listen to testimony and then resolve their own dispute.

7. _____ Name the process where one party chooses to simply walk away from the dispute.

8. _____
   _____
   _____
   _____
   Name four processes where the filing of a complaint with the clerk of the court may be a prerequisite for entering into the process.

9. _____
   _____
   _____
   _____
   _____
   _____
   _____
   _____
   Name eight processes in which the attorneys may more actively participate than their clients.

10. _____
    _____
    _____
    _____
    _____
    _____
    _____
    Name seven processes in which the party or parties have an active role, even if they have retained counsel.

Multiple-Choice Questions

1. Which of the following may actively participate in inaction?
   (a) the aggrieved party only
   (b) both parties
   (c) the parties' attorneys
   (d) the attorneys' paralegals, if they employ paralegals
   (e) a neutral third party or parties
   (f) a jury
2. Which of the following may actively participate in acquiescence?
   (a) the aggrieved party only
   (b) both parties
   (c) the parties' attorneys
   (d) the attorneys' paralegals, if they employ paralegals
   (e) a neutral third party or parties
   (f) a jury

3. Which of the following may actively participate in self-help?
    (a) the aggrieved party only
    (b) both parties
    (c) the parties' attorneys
    (d) the attorneys' paralegals, if they employ paralegals
    (e) a neutral third party or parties
    (f) a jury

4. Which of the following may actively participate in negotiation?
    (a) the aggrieved party only
    (b) both parties
    (c) the parties' attorneys
    (d) the attorneys' paralegals, if they employ paralegals
    (e) a neutral third party or parties
    (f) a jury

5. Which of the following may actively participate in early neutral evaluation?
    (a) the aggrieved party only
    (b) both parties
    (c) the parties' attorneys
    (d) the attorneys' paralegals, if they employ paralegals
    (e) a neutral third party or parties
    (f) a jury

6. Which of the following may actively participate in summary jury trial?
    (a) the aggrieved party only
    (b) both parties
    (c) the parties' attorneys
    (d) the attorneys' paralegals, if they employ paralegals
    (e) a neutral third party or parties
    (f) a jury

7. Which of the following may actively participate in ombuds?
    (a) the aggrieved party only
    (b) both parties
    (c) the parties' attorneys
    (d) the attorneys' paralegals, if they employ paralegals
    (e) a neutral third party or parties
    (f) a jury

8. Which of the following may actively participate in mediation?
    (a) the aggrieved party only
    (b) both parties
    (c) the parties' attorneys
    (d) the attorneys' paralegals, if they employ paralegals
    (e) a neutral third party or parties
    (f) a jury

9. Which of the following may actively participate in mini-trial?
    (a) the aggrieved party only
    (b) both parties

(c) the parties' attorneys
(d) the attorneys' paralegals, if they employ paralegals
(e) a neutral third party or parties
(f) a jury

10. Which of the following may actively participate in arbitration?
    (a) the aggrieved party only
    (b) both parties
    (c) the parties' attorneys
    (d) the attorneys' paralegals, if they employ paralegals
    (e) a neutral third party or parties
    (f) a jury

11. Which of the following may actively participate in mediation-arbitration?
    (a) the aggrieved party only
    (b) both parties
    (c) the parties' attorneys
    (d) the attorneys' paralegals, if they employ paralegals
    (e) a neutral third party or parties
    (f) a jury

12. Which of the following may actively participate in litigation?
    (a) the aggrieved party only
    (b) both parties
    (c) the parties' attorneys
    (d) the attorneys' paralegals, if they employ paralegals
    (e) a neutral third party or parties
    (f) a jury

13. Which of the following may actively participate in private judging?
    (a) the aggrieved party only
    (b) both parties
    (c) the parties' attorneys
    (d) the attorneys' paralegals, if they employ paralegals
    (e) a neutral third party or parties
    (f) a jury

Short-Answer Questions

1. The litigation process begins when one party files a complaint with the clerk of the court, thus making the other party the defendant. Once the litigation process has been initiated, the parties may become involved in one or more of a number of other court-related dispute resolution processes, such as early neutral evaluation, court-sponsored mediation, court-annexed arbitration, and private judging by court referral.

   Some courts do not offer any dispute resolution process other than litigation. Most, however, offer at least one additional process. Some offer more. From the ADR processes that a court could offer, select two. Discuss how the defendant's participation is different depending upon which of the three processes (the third process is litigation) the defendant is participating in at the time.

2. If you are the landlord involved in a landlord/tenant dispute, would you want your dispute resolved by private mediation or private arbitration? Discuss how your participation changes from process to process.

3. How would a paralegal's participation change depending on whether the paralegal's employer were acting as an arbitrator or as a mediator? Would the paralegal's participation change depending upon whether the arbitration were private or court annexed?

4. You are the director of a human resources department of a major corporation. Your CEO has decided that your corporation should have an ombuds office and has asked you to advertise for the position. What qualifications should you require for the position of ombuds?

5. You are a paralegal. Would you find more job satisfaction being employed by an attorney as a paralegal, being an ombuds, being a mediator in a community mediations center, or being an arbitrator?

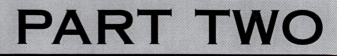

PART TWO

Introduction

Part Two presents unilateral action in dispute resolution. In a *unilateral action,* only one party is involved in the selection of the process, actively participates in the process, and determines the resolution of the dispute. Unilateral action includes inaction, acquiescence, and self-help.

Chapter 3 introduces *inaction,* the most commonly used form of dispute resolution. Inaction may be used by the aggrieved party and by the party who has caused the grievance. For the aggrieved party, inaction takes the form of walking away from the problem or dispute. For the party who is the source of the problem, inaction takes the form of waiting and seeing what the aggrieved party will or will not do.

Chapter 4 discusses *acquiescence,* another common form of dispute resolution. If one party surrenders to the other's demand, he or she acquiesces and the dispute is resolved. Acquiescence may take the form of an act (i.e., doing what the other party has asked to be done) or an omission (i.e., forbearing from doing what the other party has asked not to be done).

Chapter 5 develops the concept of *self-help* as a dispute resolution process. Parties who pursue self-help select a more active method of dispute resolution than the passive methods of inaction or acquiescence. Parties who select inaction walk away from confrontation or take a wait-and-see stance. Parties who select acquiescence give in to the other parties' demands. Self-help is more aggressive and requires affirmative action. Rather than abandoning potential rights, the party using self-help exercises those rights. Self-help may be authorized by statute, common law, or contract.

CHAPTER 3

Inaction

Inaction as a Dispute Resolution Process

Inaction
One party voluntarily withdraws from the dispute and since a dispute requires at least two participants, the dispute is resolved.

Inaction is the most common form of dispute resolution. It applies to everyday problems where the stakes are very low and to problems where the stakes are much greater. Inaction may be used by the party who claims to be aggrieved and by the party who is alleged to have created the grievance.

Inaction by the Aggrieved Party

An aggrieved party may use inaction as a dispute resolution process when only he or she knows of the grievance or when both the aggrieved and the party who has created the grievance know of the grievance.

When Only the Aggrieved Party Knows of the Grievance

The fact that one party has a grievance with another does not necessarily mean that the other party is even aware that a potential dispute was brewing. In these situations, if the aggrieved party merely "walks away" from the grievance, the grievance is resolved.

Example 3-1

When Randy McMillian proposed marriage to Lara LaRue, he gave her a one-carat diamond ring. A week before the wedding, Lara sent Randy an e-mail canceling the wedding. One would think that Randy would have been upset by the e-mail, but in fact he was relieved because he had met Stephanie Goodfortune and was passionately in love with her. Lara's e-mail gave Randy an easy way out of his relationship with her. Randy sent a reply e-mail to Lara stating that he was sorry that their relationship did not work out and he wished her well.

Since all the wedding gifts were sent to Lara, Randy assumed that Lara would be the one to return them to their senders. His only interest was the diamond ring. He thought Lara should return the ring to him because she was the one who canceled the wedding. Randy found himself in a quandary. Should he ask her to return the ring, or should he not say a word? If he asks Lara for the ring, she could refuse and then what would he do?

Randy decided not to ask Lara for the ring, but rather to keep his grievance to himself. By doing so, Randy chose inaction as his method of dispute resolution.

Example 3-2

Cassandra Symthe was having dinner with her friend Amy Andrews in a three-star restaurant by the harbor. When the waiter delivered the check, Cassandra discovered that she did not have enough money to pay, so she borrowed $30 from Amy, and Amy put the tab on her credit card.

Several weeks later Cassandra met Amy for lunch. All through lunch Amy waited for Cassandra to repay her the $30. Even when the check was delivered, Cassandra made no effort to repay Amy.

Although Amy was annoyed with Cassandra because Cassandra did not volunteer to repay her, she decided not to raise the issue. Amy chose inaction as her method of dispute resolution.

Problem 3-1
What would be another illustration of a grievance where the aggrieved party does not come forward and confront the other party with the existence of the grievance?

When Both Parties Know of the Grievance
Even when both parties know of the grievance, inaction may become the method of dispute resolution. The aggrieved party may walk away from the dispute without pressing the issue. Since a dispute requires two participants, if one party does not pursue the other, the dispute is resolved.

Example 3-3

In Example 3-1, change the facts by adding Cassie, Lara's cousin and Randy's friend. Cassie has told Lara that she should return the ring to Randy and has told Randy that he is entitled to the ring since Lara canceled the wedding. In her e-mail, however, Lara has told Randy that she will keep the diamond engagement ring because she has seen Randy with Stephanie.

Both Randy and Lara know there is a dispute over the ring. Randy, not wanting to discuss his relationship with Stephanie, decides not to press the issue and drops the matter. He has chosen inaction as his method of dispute resolution.

Some situations may go one step further. Both parties know of the dispute, and they have begun to negotiate. The aggrieved party has made a demand and the other party has rejected the demand. The aggrieved party now must decide whether to press the issue or walk away. If the aggrieved party merely walks away, inaction has been selected as the method of dispute resolution.

Problem 3-2
Justin Koch and his wife Josephine cared for Justin's elderly mother, Mary, a widow. Justin was Mary's only child. In early September, Mary suffered a stroke and died a few days later. Shortly after Mary's funeral, Justin was killed in a boating accident.

When Josephine was preparing Mary's house for sale, she discovered an old insurance policy with a stated death benefit of $500. Mary's husband, Charles, was listed as Mary's beneficiary.

Josephine wrote the insurance company explaining that she had found the policy and that Charles, Mary, and Justin were dead and that she was Justin's widow. She asked the insurance company pay her the $500.

Several weeks later, Josephine received a letter from the insurance company rejecting her claim on the grounds that it would only pay the named beneficiary, Charles, or if he had predeceased Mary, then Mary's surviving son.

Should Josephine ask her lawyer, who is probating both Mary's and Justin's estates, to pursue the insurance company or should she chose inaction as her method of dispute resolution?

Inaction by the Party Who Caused the Grievance

An aggrieved party is not the only party who may use inaction as a dispute resolution method. The party who is alleged to have caused the grievance may also use inaction. In these situations, inaction takes the form of wait and see.

Example 3-4

Geraldine and Roger Foltz were married for five years and have two children, Alice, age three and Roger, Jr., age one. Throughout their marriage, both Geraldine and Roger have held full-time jobs outside the home. Recently Geraldine's company filed for bankruptcy under Chapter 11 of the United States Bankruptcy Code, and Geraldine received notice that she was being laid off. Geraldine's loss of income created tension within the Foltz household, and this tension led to a separation. Geraldine took the children and moved in with her parents, who live across town.

Roger wrote a letter to Geraldine asking for shared custody of the children. Geraldine did not respond. Geraldine has chosen inaction as her method of dispute resolution.

Inaction by the party who caused the grievance may or may not be an effective strategy. If the aggrieved party also decides to take no further action, the dispute is resolved. The party who caused the grievance has effectively called the aggrieved party's bluff. The aggrieved party may, however, not select inaction and may decide upon a more active method of dispute resolution.

Example 3-5

Return to Example 3-4. Roger could decide to take no further action and not press his demand for shared custody. Or Roger could hire an attorney and file a petition with the court seeking shared or even full custody of the children.

The Advantages and Disadvantages of Inaction as a Dispute Resolution Process

The decision whether or not to take further action is based on personal and business needs and interests as well as an assessment of what might be the law. The party who decides to take no further action weighs the known gains (and losses) attributable to inaction against the hypothetical gains (and losses) that another process might produce. What does a party gain or lose by selecting inaction as a dispute resolution process?

Inaction is quick, producing in many situations an immediate resolution of the dispute. Inaction may not produce an immediate resolution of the dispute in situations in which the party against whom inaction is used has the reason and opportunity to employ another form of dispute resolution so that inaction will not end the dispute. Example 3-5 illustrates this point where Geraldine attempts to use inaction to thwart Roger's efforts to secure custody, and Roger may refuse to accept Geraldine's inaction as the end of the dispute.

When selecting inaction, the party weighs the need to resolve the dispute now against what might happen if the dispute is resolved later. The party may have a need to resolve the dispute now, put the problem behind him or her, and move on. Selecting a dispute resolution process other than inaction does not guarantee that the dispute will be resolved more favorably to the party who decides against selecting inaction.

When inaction is a dispute resolution process, the outcome of the dispute is known to the party who selects inaction, even though that party would rather have a different and more favorable outcome. Uncertainty as to the outcome is at least eliminated. Example 3-3 illustrates this point because Randy knows that by selecting inaction, he will not receive the engagement ring.

Selecting inaction guarantees that transaction costs will be dramatically reduced since there will be no further discovery, no attorneys, and no filing fees. The party who decides to take no further action decides that the dispute is simply not worth the additional personal and business time. Devoting this time to something else may be more important and have greater value than a possible but uncertain gain that could be achieved by continuing the dispute.

The successful pursuit of the grievance by another dispute resolution process may yield a monetary gain and a psychological victory. Pursuing a grievance, however, does not come without risks and costs. Transaction costs (time, money) accumulate and worse yet, the pursuit may prove to be unsuccessful. This effort may involve conflict that spawns psychological trauma. Even when a successful result is achieved, the transaction costs must be factored into the outcome to produce a net gain.

Controlling the process and the outcome may be very important to a party. If a party elects to take no further action, it is that party alone who makes the selection and who controls his or her own destiny. The decision to take no further action is one party's decision and one party's only. Neither the other party nor a neutral third party must acquiesce or consent to the decision.

The party selecting inaction selects a process that is private with no public airing of the dispute.

Unless the party selecting inaction later decides to pursue a remedy or unless the other party has a pursuable claim, the resolution of the dispute is final.

By electing not to take further action, a party may feel that he or she has given away a legal right and the other party has received a windfall, something that he or she has no legal right to retain. A party electing to take no further action knows, however, that he or she is saving transaction costs and is eliminating the risk of receiving little or nothing under a different process. Although the party electing to take no further action may believe that the outcome is less than fair, he or she knows that the decision makes sense under the circumstances. Figures 3-1 and 3-2 present an overview of inaction.

AVAILABILITY	depends on the facts
PROCESS SELECTION	by one party (the aggrieved party)
THE PARTICIPANTS	the aggrieved party with no interaction between the parties
PREPARATION	requires minimal fact gathering although inaction may occur without adequate information
THE PROCESS	preserves the aggrieved party's personal privacy and the confidentiality of records and documents doing nothing
FAIRNESS	process necessitates the aggrieved party to abandon possible legal rights
THE OUTCOME	determined by the party selecting the process primarily on non-legal factors resolves the dispute immediately (although the aggrieved party could change his or her mind up to the expiration of the statute of limitations) eliminates all uncertainties as to outcome (so long as the other party does not believe he or she is aggrieved and does something)
COSTS	costs nothing for the process although the aggrieved party may be giving up the possibility of receiving something may save the aggrieved party the need to give the other party something (provided the other party does not believe that he or she is aggrieved and does something) saves the aggrieved party discovery and discovery costs saves the aggrieved party transaction costs saves the aggrieved party attorney's fees
PRECEDENTIAL VALUE	establishes no binding precedent
IMPACT ON FUTURE RELATIONSHIP	neither encourages nor discourages future cooperation or confrontation between the parties

FIGURE 3-1   Inaction (Walk Away)

AVAILABILITY	depends on the facts
PROCESS SELECTION	by one party (the party who created the grievance)
THE PARTICIPANTS	the party who created the grievance with no interaction between the parties
PREPARATION	requires minimal fact gathering although waiting may occur without adequate information presents an opportunity to gather additional information
THE PROCESS	temporarily preserves personal privacy and the confidentiality of records and documents of the party who waits the party who created the grievance does nothing
FAIRNESS	no unfairness to the aggrieved party because the aggrieved party may act
THE OUTCOME	if the aggrieved party does not act, the outcome is determined by the party electing to wait primarily on non-legal factors if the aggrieved party does not act, the dispute is resolved eliminates all uncertainties as to outcome so long as the aggrieved party does not act
COSTS	costs nothing to the party who waits may save the party who waits the need to give the aggrieved party something may or may not ultimately save the party who waits discovery and discovery costs may or may not ultimately save the party who waits transaction costs may or may not ultimately save the party who waits attorney's fees
PRECEDENTIAL VALUE	establishes no binding precedent
IMPACT ON FUTURE RELATIONSHIP	neither encourages nor discourages future cooperation or confrontation between the parties

FIGURE 3-2   Inaction (Waiting)

Key Terms and Phrases

inaction

Review Questions

True/False Questions

1. T   F   An aggrieved party may use inaction as a dispute resolution process when only he or she knows of the grievance or when both the aggrieved and the party who has created the grievance know of the grievance.

2. T   F   Inaction establishes binding precedent.

3. T   F   Inaction may be used by an aggrieved party but not by the party who has caused the grievance.

4. T   F   Inaction may save the aggrieved party transaction costs.

5. T   F   An aggrieved party who selects inaction trades receiving nothing for the possibility of receiving something in the future.

6. T   F   The decision to select inaction is based on the law and not on the party's needs or interests.

7. T   F   Inaction requires little, if any, discovery.

8. T   F   Parties waive potential legal rights when they select inaction.

9. T   F   Inaction is two-sided—the aggrieved party may walk away and the party who created the grievance may wait and see.

10. T   F   The decision to select inaction may be based on inadequate information.

Fill-in-the-Blank Questions

1. _____ Who selects inaction as a dispute resolution process?

2. _____ When an aggrieved party selects inaction, what is the _____ other party's response?

3. _____ How much time expires between the time the aggrieved party selects inaction and the outcome of the dispute becomes known?

4. _____ What does the aggrieved party gain by selecting _____ inaction?

5. _____ What does the party who created the grievance gain by inaction?

Multiple-Choice Questions

1. Which of the following may actively participate in inaction as a dispute resolution process?
   (a) the aggrieved party
   (b) the other party to the dispute
   (c) a neutral third party
   (d) a jury
   (e) the attorney for the aggrieved party

2. Inaction is classified as:
   (a) unilateral action in dispute resolution
   (b) bilateral action in dispute resolution
   (c) third-party evaluation as a prelude to dispute resolution
   (d) third-party assistance in dispute resolution
   (e) third-party adjudication in dispute resolution

3. In inaction:
   (a) the aggrieved party selects the process and the outcome
   (b) the aggrieved party selects the process but does not select the outcome
   (c) the aggrieved party selects neither the process nor the outcome
   (d) the party who caused the grievance selects the process and the outcome
   (e) the party who caused the grievance selects the process but not the outcome

4. Inaction may be used by the party who created the grievance:
   (a) as a tactical ploy to see whether the aggrieved party will pursue the grievance
   (b) as a tactical ploy to lower the aggrieved party's expectations before beginning another form of dispute resolution
   (c) will not serve any useful purpose but only postpone the inevitable
   (d) as a way to create good will with the aggrieved party
   (e) as a tactic for taking advantage of the aggrieved party

5. Inaction may:
   (a) save attorney's fees
   (b) establish precedent
   (c) require the parties to interact
   (d) result in an immediate resolution
   (e) encourage future cooperation between the parties

Short-Answer Questions

1. Why would an aggrieved party simply walk away from a dispute rather than pursuing a more favorable solution?
2. Why would a party take a wait-and-see attitude when facing a dispute? What can be gained? Can anything be lost?
3. Do you believe that more people should use inaction as a method of dispute resolution rather than seek some other solution through another dispute resolution process?
4. Create a scenario where an aggrieved party selects inaction as his or her dispute resolution process. Then discuss whether the choice of inaction was appropriate and why.
5. Discuss the advantages and disadvantages of inaction as a dispute resolution process.

CHAPTER 4

Acquiescence

Acquiescence as a Dispute Resolution Process

Acquiescence
One party gives up and accedes to the demands of the other.

Acquiescence is another common form of dispute resolution. **Acquiescence,** as a dispute resolution process, occurs when one party gives in to the other's demand and the dispute is resolved. Acquiescence may take the form of an act (i.e., doing something) or an omission (i.e., refraining from doing something).

Acquiescence as an Act

Acquiescence may take the form of an act. One party may demand that the other do something. The latter may believe that he or she has no obligation to do it and in fact may not want to do it. If the party upon whom the demand is made performs anyway, he or she has chosen acquiescence as his or her method of dispute resolution.

Example 4-1

Steven leased an apartment from Buena Vista Apartments for one year. The lease stated that in the event Steven terminated his lease before its expiration, he would be required to pay three months' rent as a penalty. Six months into his lease, Steven received a promotion at work that required him to move to another city. He gave Buena Vista written notice of his intent to terminate at the end of the following month. Buena Vista notified Steven that as per the lease, he would be required to pay three months' rent. Although Steven knew that the apartment occupancy rate was over 90 percent and that Buena Vista would have little trouble renting his apartment, he had neither the time nor the inclination to challenge Buena Vista's demand for the extra payment. Rather than confront Buena Vista, Steven vacated the apartment as planned and gave Buena Vista a check for three months' rent. By not confronting Buena Vista, Steven chose acquiescence as his dispute resolution process.

Acquiescence as an Omission

Acquiescence can also take the form of an omission. An omission is a refraining from acting.

Example 4-2

Randolph McCoy told Johnson Hatfield that he did not want him to date his daughter, Roseanna. If Johnson does not date Randolph's daughter, Johnson has chosen acquiescence as his method of dispute resolution. The acquiescence is in the form of not doing something, dating. Not dating is a negative act, that is, an omission.

Differentiating Acquiescence from Negotiation

Although acquiescence and negotiation as methods of dispute resolution may appear similar, they differ significantly. When parties negotiate, they may or may not reach agreement. If they do not reach a negotiated agreement, they must then decide what to do next. Should they use inaction as their method of dispute resolution and merely walk away from the problem, or should they select another form of dispute resolution that might produce a less-passive result?

If the parties do reach a negotiated agreement, their agreement is a contract. Who made the offer and who made the acceptance becomes unimportant because a contract has

Quid pro quo
The exchange of one thing for another.

been formed. The basis of the contract is an exchange. One party promises to do something (or not to do something) in exchange for the other party's promise to do something (or not to do something). A contract provides a **quid pro quo**.

Example 4-3

Jacklyn Jones was walking in front of Ryan Wang's theater when she was struck on the head by a falling object and rendered unconscious. Jacklyn was taken to a nearby hospital where she spent a week before being discharged. Jacklyn hired an attorney to investigate the incident, and she discovered that the theater was being remodeled and the workers on the roof had negligently released some scrap materials that fell to the sidewalk below. It appears that Jacklyn was struck by some of these discarded materials.

When Jacklyn's attorney contacted Ryan, he gave her the name of his insurance company, United Insurance. Jacklyn's attorney then contacted United and negotiated the following agreement. United promised to pay Jacklyn $250,000 in exchange for Jacklyn's promise to accept the $250,000 as full payment for her claim and not to sue either Ryan or United. Jacklyn's promise to accept $250,000 in full payment of her claim is the quid pro quo for United's promise to pay. United's promise to pay is the quid pro quo for Jacklyn's promise to accept $250,000 in full payment of her claim that was uncertain as to the amount.

If acquiescence is the method of dispute resolution, there is no quid pro quo. There is no exchange of promises. One party demands that the other either do or not do something. The party demanding promises nothing in exchange for the other's actions.

Example 4-4

Grandpa Stover promised to give his granddaughter Tina $1,500 on her 16th birthday. When Tina turned 16, she asked her grandfather for the money and he refused. Several days later Tina asked him for the money again.

If Grandpa Stover pays Tina, he has chosen acquiescence as his method of dispute resolution. His promise to pay was a gift promise and not an offer. Without an offer, there can be no acceptance and no contract. Without a contract Grandpa Stover's promise is unenforceable and he has no obligation to pay. There was no exchange of promises and therefore no quid pro quo. The negotiation between Tina and her grandfather has not ended in a negotiated agreement but rather in acquiescence.

The Advantages and Disadvantages of Acquiescence as a Dispute Resolution Process

As with inaction, the decision whether to acquiesce in the demands of the other party is based on personal and business needs and interests as well as on what is perceived to be the law. The party who decides to acquiesce weighs the gains and losses attributable to acquiescence against the hypothetical gains and losses that another process might produce. What does a party gain or lose by selecting acquiescence as the method of dispute resolution?

Acquiescence is quick and the resolution of the dispute is immediate. When selecting acquiescence, the party weighs the need to resolve the dispute now against what might happen if the dispute is resolved later. The party may have a need to resolve the dispute now, put the problem behind himself or herself, and move on. Delaying the resolution of the dispute does not guarantee that the dispute will be resolved favorably to the party who decides against acquiescence.

Control of the process may be very important to a party. If a party elects to acquiesce, it is he or she alone who makes the decision, and it is he or she who controls his or her own destiny. The decision to take action is that party's and that party's only. Neither the other party nor a neutral third party must give acquiescence or consent to the decision.

The party selecting acquiescence controls not only the process but also the outcome, and the outcome is known when the process is selected. Acquiescence most likely will have up-front costs. Acquiescence may involve payment to the other side. If payment is involved, the amount of the payment is known when acquiescence is decided upon. The risk that the amount will change over time has been eliminated. Also the risk of having to pay the other party's transaction costs has been eliminated.

As with inaction, the party who decides to acquiesce decides that continuing the dispute is simply not worth the costs. Continuing the dispute will mean that he or she will be required to devote additional personal time to this dispute. Saving this time may be more important and have greater value than a possible but uncertain gain that could be achieved by continuing the dispute. Additional time will include the additional effort on the part of the party that will need to be committed to the dispute. This effort may involve conflict that spawns psychological trauma. Selecting acquiescence will guarantee that transaction costs will be dramatically reduced since there will be no discovery, no attorneys, and no filing fees.

Acquiescence is a private process with no public airing of the dispute unless the parties themselves go public.

When a party selects acquiescence as the method of dispute resolution, he or she may not be foregoing the opportunity to pursue the dispute. Opportunities may be present for the acquiescing party to pursue another form of dispute resolution. If he or she does not pursue another method, the resolution of the dispute is final.

Example 4-5

Sally took her car to the local garage for a new transmission, and when the work was done, she refused to pay claiming that the work was not done in a workmanlike manner. When Sally refused to pay, the garage refused to return her car claiming a mechanics lien under state statute. To get her car back, Sally paid and then sued the garage for breach of contract. Sally elected to use acquiescence to get her car back, followed by litigation to get her money back.

As is the case with inaction, although the party electing to acquiesce feels that he or she has given away a legal right, the decision is his or her own. The party who decides to acquiesce may feel forced into making this decision by the circumstances (transaction costs, the risks of an unfavorable outcome, need for an immediate resolution that is final, and a greater need to use time and money in other endeavors), but without coercion or duress, the outcome is to that party, at that moment, a correct decision. Figure 4-1 presents an overview of acquiescence as a dispute resolution process.

Problem 4-1

Gretchen and Helmut Schoenfeld met in college, fell in love, and were married. Within three years, they had two children. Meanwhile, Gretchen left college to raise the children, and Helmut was on his way up the corporate ladder. Within five years, they were divorced and the court awarded them shared custody of the children.

Gretchen returned to college, finished her degree, and now is also climbing the corporate ladder at a local bank. Also in the interim, Gretchen's parents have retired and moved to town. Now that they have the time and the money, they have spent a substantial amount of their time with the grandchildren. This has given Gretchen the freedom to pursue her career.

Gretchen has asked Helmut to informally change the custody arrangement so she will be the custodial parent.

1. Should Helmut acquiesce to Gretchen's demands?
2. What does Helmut gain by acquiescing?
3. What does he lose?

AVAILABILITY	depends on the facts
PROCESS SELECTION	by one party (the party being told to do or not do something)
THE PARTICIPANTS	the party who does the act or omission with minimal interaction between the parties
PREPARATION	requires minimal fact gathering although acquiescence may occur without adequate information
THE PROCESS	preserves personal privacy and the confidentiality of records and documents of the person who acquiesces
	the party who was told to do or not do something, does or does not do it
	generally, requires limited interaction between the parties
FAIRNESS	permits the party with dominant power to take advantage of the party who acquiesced
THE OUTCOME	determined by the party who acquiesced although dictated by the other party
	based primarily on non-legal factors
	resolves the dispute immediately although the party who acquiesces may pursue another form of dispute resolution
	eliminates all uncertainties as to outcome if the party who acquiesces does not pursue another form of dispute resolution
COSTS	costs nothing for the process although the party who acquiesces gives up all that the other party has demanded
	saves the party who acquiesces discovery and discovery costs
	saves the party who acquiesces transaction costs
	saves the party who acquiesces attorney's fees
PRECEDENTIAL VALUE	establishes no binding precedent although nonbinding precedent by performance may be created between the parties
IMPACT ON FUTURE RELATIONSHIP	neither encourages nor discourages future cooperation or confrontation between the parties

FIGURE 4-1   Acquiescence

Key Terms and Phrases

acquiescence
quid pro quo

Review Questions

True/False Questions

1. T   F   Acquiescence must be an act; it cannot be an omission.
2. T   F   Acquiescence requires a quid pro quo.
3. T   F   Acquiescence forms a contract.
4. T   F   A person who acquiesces may give up a legal right in return for nothing.
5. T   F   The decision to acquiesce is generally based on the law and not on the needs and interests of the party who acquiesces.
6. T   F   Acquiescence adds finality to the dispute.
7. T   F   Acquiescence reduces transaction costs, although there may be a cost associated with acquiescence.
8. T   F   Acquiescence is a public process and exposes private records to public scrutiny.
9. T   F   Acquiescence is a seldom-used and antiquated form of dispute resolution.
10. T   F   Acquiescence may be used as a tactical dispute resolution process.

Fill-in-the-Blank Questions

1. _____ When one party gives in to the other's demands without there being a quid pro quo.

2. _____ Doing something that another person has demanded be done.

3. _____ Forbearing from doing something that another person has demanded not be done.

4. _____ The category that includes inaction, acquiescence, and self-help.

5. _____ When one party promises to do something (or not to do something) in exchange for the other party's promise to do something (or not to do something).

Multiple-Choice Questions

1. Which of the following may actively participate in acquiescence as a dispute resolution process:
   (a) the party who acquiesces
   (b) the other party to the dispute
   (c) a neutral third party
   (d) a jury
   (e) the attorney for the party who acquiesces

2. Acquiescence is classified as:
   (a) unilateral action in dispute resolution
   (b) bilateral action in dispute resolution
   (c) third-party evaluation as a prelude to dispute resolution
   (d) third-party assistance in dispute resolution
   (e) third-party adjudication in dispute resolution

3. Some of the advantages of acquiescence are that it:
   (a) reduces transaction costs for the party who acquiesces
   (b) preserves legal rights
   (c) provides finality to the dispute
   (d) generally costs the party who acquiesces nothing
   (e) builds respect and fosters cooperation between the parties

4. Some of the disadvantages of acquiescence are that it:
   (a) may provide only a temporary resolution of the dispute
   (b) may require the party who acquiesces to abandon legal rights
   (c) requires the intervention of a neutral third party
   (d) may prey upon an imbalance of power
   (e) could have significant costs associated with performance

Short-Answer Questions

1. Abby and Andrew signed a one-year lease and moved into the Rio Vista Towers apartment complex. After living at Rio Vista Towers for five months, Abby heard rumors at work that she was to be promoted to a regional vice presidency, which would require relocation to another city. Andrew, meanwhile, was thinking about leaving his job and returning to school for an MBA.

   Abby and Andrew have reread their lease and have discovered that they cannot sublease their apartment. They have also discovered a provision that would require them to pay three months' rent in the event they terminated their lease before the lease term had been completed. Abby and Andrew found these lease provisions puzzling since the apartment across the hall had been subleased and another couple had only forfeited their deposit (equivalent to one month's rent) when they terminated their lease early. Andrew believes that the landlord will have no problem rerenting their apartment.

Abby has already had a run-in with the landlord, so neither Abby nor Andrew wants to discuss the matter with him.

Should Abby and Andrew select inaction or acquiescence, and why?

2. As seen in Example 4-5, acquiescence can be used tactically. A price may be associated with this tactic. In Example 4-5, Sally acquiesced by paying out money to get her car back from the local garage. She then used another dispute resolution process to get her money back.

Should dispute resolution processes be used as tactical weapons?

3. In a dispute both parties may perceive that they are right. Is this what happened in Example 4-5? In such a dispute, is there an advantage to being the plaintiff rather than the defendant or the defendant rather than the plaintiff?

Can acquiescence help at least one of the parties select his or her side of the case if litigation is on the horizon?

CHAPTER 5

Self-Help

Self-Help as a Dispute Resolution Process

Self-Help
An aggrieved party may pursue relief without the assistance of the courts.

Self-help is another unilateral dispute resolution process. **Self-help** is taking care of one-self without judicial assistance. Parties who pursue self-help select a more active method of dispute resolution than the passive methods of inaction or acquiescence. Parties who select inaction walk away from confrontation or take a wait-and-see approach. Parties who select acquiescence surrender to the other parties' demands. Self-help is more aggressive and requires affirmative action. Rather than abandon potential rights, parties pursuing self-help exercise those rights.

Unlike the decision to select inaction or acquiescence, a decision based on personal or business needs and interests and not so much on the law, the decision to exercise self-help must be based on the law. Self-help is a legally based process created by statute, by the common law, or by contract. Therefore, whether self-help is available and whether self-help is pursued properly involves technical legal analysis. Exercising self-help when it does not exist or when it exists but is implemented improperly will place the party pursuing self-help in a legally vulnerable position.

Self-Help under Statute

Statutes provide a number of self-help opportunities. To exercise the right of self-help requires technical knowledge of the law. For example, a statute may give the buyer of goods the right to reject goods if they do not conform to the contract.

Example 5-1

Ernie contracts to purchase a 52-inch TV from Lone Star Appliance Company. After the TV is delivered and as it is being uncrated, Ernie discovers that the TV cabinet is scratched. Ernie may exercise his statutory right of self-help by rejecting the delivery of the TV. See Uniform Commercial Code (UCC) § 2-601.

Problem 5-1

1. What is Ernie's next step after he rejects the TV delivery?
2. What would his next step have been had he accepted the delivery?
3. Is he in a better position by exercising self-help in rejecting the delivery rather than by accepting the delivery?

The buyer's statutory right to reject delivery becomes more complicated if the contract for the sale of the goods authorizes delivery in installments. The buyer's right to reject nonconforming goods of an installment is more limited than the buyer's right to reject nonconforming goods to be delivered in a single shipment. The buyer who receives an installment may reject the installment if the nonconformity "substantially impairs the value of the installment and cannot be cured. . . ." UCC § 2-612(2).

Problem 5-2

The Boston Zoo purchased two white female tiger cubs from the Cincinnati Zoo. Under the contract, one cub was to be shipped on Monday and the other on Wednesday. The first cub arrived at the Boston Zoo in excellent condition. The second cub arrived ill.

Could the Boston Zoo reject the second cub? Had the contract been for the sale of only the second cub, the Zoo could have rejected that shipment. The contract, however, was for two cubs to be delivered separately. Remember, the buyer who receives an installment may reject the installment if the nonconformity "substantially impairs the value of the installment and cannot be cured. . . ." UCC § 2-612(2).

Could the Zoo also reject the first cub since the zoo needs two tiger cubs for its exhibit?

Another section of the Uniform Commercial Code authorizes a buyer, who has accepted delivery of goods, to pursue self-help by revoking the acceptance of delivered goods and by returning them to the seller if the "non-conformity substantially impairs its value to him." UCC § 2-608.

Example 5-2

Maryanne purchased a new minivan from Quality Motors. As soon as Maryanne drove the minivan out of the dealership, she began to experience problems. At first, she had transmission problems. Then she had engine problems and finally electrical problems. Each time there was a problem, Maryanne would return the minivan to the dealership and they would spend several days making the necessary repairs. Over the first three months, Maryanne's minivan was at the dealership being repaired for over 50 days. Finally, Maryanne had enough. She returned the minivan to the dealership along with the keys and the title. Maryanne has pursued self-help by revoking her acceptance of the minivan. See UCC § 2-608.

Another section of the UCC gives the buyer the right to deduct the damages from any part of the contract price still due when the seller breaches the contract for the sale of goods and the buyer still owes the seller a part of the contract price. See UCC § 2-717.

Problem 5-3

Sunshine Food Mart contracted to purchase 52 tons of Idaho potatoes from United Wholesale Grocers at $500 a ton. The contract provided that United would deliver one ton of potatoes every Monday for a year. The contract also provided that Sunshine would pay on Friday for the delivery that was made the previous Monday. After three months United notified Sunshine that it could only deliver one-half ton of potatoes a week. Sunshine then found another wholesaler who would deliver one-half ton of Idaho potatoes a week for the remaining nine months of the contract. The new wholesaler charged $600 a ton or $300 for a half ton.

So, for every week of the remaining nine months of the contract United delivered one-half ton of potatoes on Monday and was paid $200 on Friday.

How did Sunshine calculate the Friday payment?

In labor-management disputes, self-help may take the form of a strike, a walkout, or a lockout. Often, they are regulated by statute. Note in these situations, self-help is a step in the dispute resolution process and not the final method of dispute resolution.

Self-Help under Common Law

Self-help under common law often appears in a contract setting. If the transaction is governed by a contract, one party may in some circumstances withhold performance if the other party breaches the contract. Self-help is under common law and not governed by contract because the contract is silent as to what the nonbreaching party may do in the event of breach. Had the contract provided, the self-help would have been stated in the contract. Self-help under common law involves the doctrines of substantial performance (construction contracts) and material/immaterial breach (employment and other contracts). These doctrines recognize the difficulty of fully performing a contract without any breach. Under these doctrines, self-help in the form of withholding performance is not available if a construction contract has been substantially performed or an employment or another type of contract has been performed to the point that any breach is less than material (immaterial breach). When a construction contract is breached after substantial performance or an employment or another type of contract has been breached, but the breach is less than material, the nonbreaching party's remedy is limited to money damages and not withholding performance.

Although the exercise of self-help under common law is not as technical as the exercise of self-help under statute, the law is still unforgiving if self-help is not exercised properly. The following two cases illustrate this point.

The first is *Rose v. Ditto,* a case dealing with child support. After the former husband was in arrears in his child support payments, he and his former wife contracted for a new payment schedule, thus reducing his obligation for payments that were in arrears. The contract provided that in the event he did not pay, he would again be obligated for all payments in arrears. He was two days late in a payment and his former wife exercised what she believed to be her common law right to reject the payment and reassert her right to all payments in arrears. Did she have a common law right to exercise self-help and reject the late payment?

Rose v. Ditto
District Court of Appeal of Florida, Fourth District
804 So.2d 351 (2001)

POLEN, C.J.

Former Husband, Joseph Rose, timely appeals from a final judgment entered post-divorce which awarded Former Wife, Kelley Ditto, $62,788.75 in child support arrearages and prejudgment interest thereon, and $18,000 in attorney's fees and costs. Of the many issues raised in this appeal, one is dispositive. We hold that Former Husband's two-day delay in tendering Former Wife a $10,000 installment payment was not a material breach which triggered default of the parties' mediation agreement and, thus, reverse the awards.

In 1991, after eight years of marriage, the parties divorced. Their marital settlement agreement, incorporated into the final judgment of dissolution of marriage, obligated Former Husband to pay Former Wife $3,000 per

(continued)

month in child support for their two minor children. In 1992, the trial court modified Former Husband's obligation to $1,000 per month, established that he owed $31,700 in arrearages as of March 31, 1992, and required him to pay $200 per month on the arrearages.

In 1997, the parties entered into an addendum to their marital settlement agreement. In this addendum, they agreed, among other issues, that Former Husband had paid down his prior child support arrearages to $22,395.86; that his monthly child support would be increased to $1,200; that $200 of the monthly child support payment would be applied toward his arrearages for the purpose of reducing such arrearages; and that Former Wife would abate the interest accruing on the child support arrearages so long as Former Husband complied with his obligations under the addendum. The addendum provided that in the event of Former Husband's default, Former Wife could seek payment of the $31,700 principal plus interest for unpaid child support.

In 1999, following a series of disputes, the parties attended mediation which culminated in an agreement between them. The agreement increased Former Husband's support obligation retroactively to $1,900 per month. As a compromise of Former Wife's claims, the parties also agreed to limit Former Husband's total arrearages to $20,000.[1] Former Husband agreed to pay this amount in two equal monthly installments, the first by July 1, 1999, and the second by August 1, 1999. The agreement provided that if payment was not made in accordance with this schedule, Former Wife could seek recovery of the "full amount of arrears plus interest."

Former Husband tendered the first $10,000 installment to Former Wife on July 3, 1999, two days late. She rejected the payment. He also tendered her the second installment on July 31, 1999. She also rejected this payment.

---

[1]The $20,000 amount represented a compromise of what the Former Wife claimed the Former Husband owed on the agreed-upon retroactive increase in his current monthly support obligation as well as the balance of his existing arrearage as determined in 1992.

On August 25, 1999, Former Wife filed suit to recoup the original $31,700 in arrearages based on Former Husband's default in tendering the first installment two days late. Following an evidentiary hearing, the court determined that Former Husband's two-day delay in making the first installment payment constituted a material breach of the 1999 mediation agreement. It determined that the interest he owed accrued on the original arrearage ($31,700) and could not be waived. It awarded Former Wife this amount plus prejudgment interest thereon, and attorney's fees as well. This appeal followed.

In *National Exhibition Co. v. Ball*, 139 So.2d 489 (Fla. 2d DCA 1962), the second district observed,

> The modern trend of decisions concerning brief delays by one party in performance of a contract or conditions thereunder, in the absence of an express stipulation in the contract that time is of the essence, is not to treat such delays as a failure of a constructive condition discharging the other party unless performance on time was clearly an essential and vital part of the bargain.

Id. at 492. In *Blaustein v. Weiss*, 409 So.2d 103 (Fla. 4th DCA 1982), this court held that time should be considered of the essence in three circumstances: (1) where there has been an express recital by the parties; (2) where the treating of time as a non-essential would produce a hardship, and delay by one party in completing or in complying with a term would necessarily subject the other party to a serious injury or loss; and (3) where there has been an express notice given to the defaulting party requiring the contract to be performed within a stated time, which must be a reasonable time according to the circumstances of the case. *Id.* at 105 (citations omitted); *accord Edward Waters College, Inc. v. Johnson*, 707 So.2d 801, 802 (Fla. 1st DCA 1998)(applying the *Blaustein* factors to hold that without any express recital, time was not of the essence in the parties' settlement agreement).

Notwithstanding that none of the *Blaustein* factors are present in this case, Former Wife argues that this court's recent decision in *Treasure Coast, Inc. v. Ludlum Construction Company*, 760 So.2d 232 (Fla. 4th DCA 2000) is controlling and compels affirmance. In that case, the parties entered into a settlement agreement requiring the appellee construction party to make payments by a specific date. The agreement provided that "[i]f payment is more than ten days late then the Plaintiff will be entitled to a judgment upon Affidavit against the Defendant for $65,000.00 less payments made." The company was seven days late after the ten-day grace period had expired in making payment. This court held that even though the settlement agreement did not contain language specifying that time was of the essence, the untimely payment constituted a material breach of the agreement. *Id.* at 235. It explained,

> When commercial parties agree that the debtor shall pay the creditor on or before a specific date, time being of the essence, they mean exactly that. The debtor shall deliver money to the creditor on or before the due date. There is almost always no such thing as "substantial performance" of payment between commercial parties when the duty is simply the general one to pay. Payment is either made in the amount and on the due date, or it is not. Although the agreement in this case did not contain a "time is of the essence" clause, the terms in this agreement clearly contained the express provision for payment of a sum certain on a specific date. In providing appellant with a

specific remedy, judgment for the entire amount due and owing in the event of nonpayment, the parties essentially agreed that time was of the essence.

Id. at 234–35 (internal citations omitted). Based on our *de novo* review of the parties' 1999 mediation agreement, we hold *Treasure Coast* is distinguishable. Unlike that case, the case at bar did not involve a commercial transaction nor did the mediation agreement specify that time was of the essence. Moreover, and unlike *Treasure Coast*, there was no grace period provided that would have put Former Husband on notice that any brief delay in payment would accelerate payments due or otherwise trigger total default. As such, we conclude the July 1, 1999 deadline was not absolute and, accordingly, we hold Former Husband's breach was not material.

Our reversal in this regard similarly requires reversal of the award of prejudgment interest as well. As far as Former Wife's award of attorney's fees, because we are reversing on the other points on appeal, we also reverse this award and remand it for reconsideration under *Rosen v. Rosen*, 696 So.2d 697 (Fla. 1997).

REVERSED and REMANDED for further proceedings consistent with this opinion.

STONE, J., and MARRA, KENNETH A., Associate Judge, concur.

The second case is *Teramo & Co., Inc. v. O'Brien-Sheipe Funeral Home, Inc.*, a case involving an addition to a funeral home. The funeral home sought to exercise its common law right to withhold payment for incomplete work. The contractor brought a breach of contract action against the funeral home seeking to recover the outstanding balance owed for the construction. The funeral home counterclaimed for breach of contract seeking damages for business lost due to the delays in completing the addition and for the costs of hiring other contractors to correct problems caused by the contractor's poor workmanship. The following is what happened.

Teramo & Co., Inc. v. O'Brien-Sheipe Funeral Home, Inc.
Supreme Court, Appellate Division, Second Department, New York
725 N.Y.S.3d 87 (2001)

GABRIEL M. KRAUSMAN, J.P., HOWARD MILLER, ROBERT W. SCHMIDT and STEPHEN G. CRANE, JJ.

In an action, *inter alia,* to recover damages for breach of contract, the plaintiff appeals from a judgment of the Supreme Court, Nassau County (DiNoto, J.), dated February 28, 2000, which, after a nonjury trial, is in favor of the defendant on the counterclaims and against it in the principal sum of $27,180.

ORDERED that the judgment is reversed, on the law, with costs, and the matter is remitted to the Supreme Court, Nassau County, for the entry of a judgment in favor of the plaintiff and against the defendant in the principal sum of $11,770.

On May 6, 1996, the defendant hired the plaintiff to construct an addition to its funeral home. The parties' contract did not specify a date for completion of the proposed work. A building permit for the project was issued by the Town of Hempstead on June 14, 1996, and work commenced about two weeks later. The project was substantially completed by late March 1997, and a Certificate of Completion was issued by the Town on April 15, 1997. Although the defendant made periodic payments to the plaintiff during the course of construction, the defendant failed to make full payment of the plaintiff's final bill, leaving a balance due of $17,950. The plaintiff subsequently commenced this action to recover the outstanding balance, and the defendant asserted counterclaims seeking damages for business allegedly lost due to delays in construction, and for the cost of hiring other contractors to correct problems caused by poor workmanship. At the conclusion of a nonjury trial, the Supreme Court dismissed the complaint, finding, *inter alia,* that the plaintiff's performance was "unsatisfactory from both a timely and skillful manner." The court also awarded the defendant judgment on its counterclaims, finding that it had lost $21,000 in profits due to construction delay, and suffered damages in the sum of $6,180 due to the plaintiff's faulty workmanship. We reverse.

Where a contract fails to state a date for the completion of a construction project, a reasonable time is implied (*see Young v. Whitney,* 111 A.D.2d 1013, 490 N.Y.S.2d 330; *Lake Steel Erection v. Egan,* 61 A.D.2d 1125, 403 N.Y.S.2d 387; *see also Savasta v. 470 Newport Assocs.,* 82 N.Y.2d 763, 603 N.Y.S.2d 821, 623 N.E.2d 1171). What constitutes a reasonable time for performance of a contract depends upon the facts and circumstances of the particular case (*see, Savasta v. 470 Newport Assocs., supra*), including the subject matter of the contract, the situation of the parties, their intention, what they contemplated at the time the contract was made, and the circumstances surrounding performance (*see Young v. Whitney, supra; Lake Steel Erection v. Egan, supra; Hills v. Melenbacher,* 23 A.D.2d 803, 258 N.Y.S.2d 243).

Taking these factors into account, we find that the court's determination that the plaintiff's performance was untimely is not supported by a fair interpretation of the evidence, and exercise our authority, in reviewing a bench trial, to render a judgment we find warranted by the facts (*see Northern Westchester Professional Park Assocs. v. Town of Bedford,* 60 N.Y.2d 492, 499, 470 N.Y.S.2d 350, 458 N.E.2d 809; *Terranova v. Secured Capital Corp. of New York,* 275 A.D.2d 743, 713 N.Y.S.2d 486; *Krol v. Eckman,* 256 A.D.2d 945, 681 N.Y.S.2d 885). Significantly, there was no clause in the parties' contract which made time of the essence (*cf. Bilotto v. Webber,* 172 A.D.2d 639, 568 N.Y.S.2d 438), and the defendant continued to make periodic payments to the plaintiff through February 1997. The evidence presented at trial reveals that some delay in construction was attributable to the defendant's request that no work at the premises be performed while funeral services were in progress.

While the evidence presented in support of the defendant's counterclaims established that the defendant expended $6,180 to repair certain items which had not been properly completed in a workmanlike manner, this constituted only a small portion of the project, and does not preclude the plaintiff contractor from recovering on the theory of substantial performance (*see A-1 Gen. Contr. v. River Mkt. Commodities,* 212 A.D.2d 897, 900, 622 N.Y.S.2d 378; *Lyon v. Belosky Constr.,* 247 A.D.2d 730, 669 N.Y.S.2d 400). In such circumstances, the appropriate measure of damages is the contract price less the cost of repairing the work improperly done (*see Frank v. Feiss,* 266 A.D.2d 825, 698 N.Y.S.2d 363; *Lyon v. Belosky Constr., supra; Sherman v. Hanu,* 195 A.D.2d 810, 600 N.Y.S.2d 371).

Accordingly, we find that the plaintiff should be permitted to recover on its first cause of action which seeks the outstanding balance due on the contract price, a sum of $17,950. However, the principal sum of the plaintiff's recovery should be reduced by $6,180, representing the damages sustained by the defendant for the cost of repairing work found to be unacceptable.

We further find that the Trial Court improperly awarded the defendant judgment on its first counterclaim seeking damages for lost profits. The defendant's unsubstantiated claim that it lost business due to the delay in completing construction of the extension to the funeral home is too speculative to allow recovery (*see Lehigh Constr. Group v. Almquist,* 262 A.D.2d 943, 692 N.Y.S.2d 551; *Ecker v. Zwaik & Bernstein,* 240 A.D.2d 360, 658 N.Y.S.2d 113; *Gazzola Bldg. Corp. v. Shapiro,* 181 A.D.2d 718, 719, 580 N.Y.S.2d 477).

Problem 5-4

Erin Kelly hired Century Builders to build her a new house for $250,000. After the house was 80 percent complete and $200,000 had been paid, Century left the job site to work on another house. What remained to be done was the installation of the fixtures and appliances in the bathrooms and the kitchen, the installation of the heating and air conditioning unit, the completion of the stone fireplace in the living room, and the installation of the sidewalks, driveway, and irrigation system.

When Century asks for the final payment, should Erin refuse, claiming a common law right of self-help?

Problem 5-5

Roland Reynolds was employed as an Assistant Professor at Gotham University. Although Roland was on a tenure track, his contract was for one year. He was paid one-ninth of his annual salary on the first of every month of the academic year. Roland taught August through February, but did not return after spring recess. When Roland did not return to complete the spring semester, the university declared that Roland had committed a material breach of the contract and the university exercised its right to self-help thereby withholding Roland's pay for the months that he did not work. Roland, meanwhile, has demanded payment for the months he did not work.

Should the university have paid Roland and then sued him for its damages for his breach of contract? The university's damages would have been what it had paid a replacement less what it would have paid Roland plus any costs incurred in finding a replacement.

Self-Help as Provided by Contract

Parties may contract and include a self-help provision in the contract in the event of breach. Such a provision will tell the nonbreaching party how he or she may respond without judicial assistance.

Example 5-3

The Incredible Carpet Cleaning Co. purchased a new commercial carpet cleaning vacuum from the Leisure World Cleaning Supply Co. The contract provides:

Leisure World warrants that your product is free from defect in material and workmanship for a period of one year. Leisure World will replace any product defective in materials and workmanship without charge if you return the product either in person or by mail, postpaid, to a Leisure World Authorized Service Dealer or Company-Owned Service Center within one year of the date of purchase.

Leisure World also guarantees your satisfaction with our product. If you are not personally satisfied with this product, return the product either in person or by mail, postpaid, to a Leisure World Authorized Service Dealer or Company-Owned Service Center within 30 days of the date of purchase and Leisure World will refund your purchase price.

Incredible Carpet Cleaning used the vacuum for two weeks and found the vacuum was not as good as advertised. Incredible exercised its right to self-help under the contract and returned the vacuum to Leisure World. Incredible is entitled to a refund.

Often a self-help provision found in a contract will carry limited relief.

Problem 5-6

Return to Example 5-3.
1. What is the limitation on the one-year warranty?
2. How does this impact the buyer's right of self-help?

Seldom does a buyer of a motor vehicle pay cash. Rather the purchase is financed by the seller or by a third party lender. As part of the transaction, the buyer contracts to repay the lender and to give the lender a security interest in the vehicle until the loan has been repaid. This security interest gives the lender the right to repossess the vehicle in the event the buyer (now known as the debtor) breaches (defaults) on the loan. This repossession, which must be done without "breach of the peace," may be accomplished without judicial process. Upon default and repossession, the lender may sell the vehicle and use the proceeds from the sale to pay down the loan. This transaction is known as a *secured transaction* and is authorized by Article 9 of the Uniform Commercial Code. The District of Columbia and all states have enacted Article 9, although each has made its own revisions.

Example 5-4

Tia purchased a new Ford 150 truck from Rocky Mountain Ford and paid $3,000 down. She then went to the Friendly Credit Union and borrowed $22,000 for the balance. The Credit Union paid Rocky Mountain, and Tia signed a security agreement giving the credit union a security interest in the truck. After making six monthly payments, Tia ceased making payments, thus defaulting on her obligation to the Credit Union. The Credit Union then exercised self-help as provided in its contract and repossessed the truck.

The following case, *Jennings v. American Honda Finance Corp.*, demonstrates the legal complexities when self-help is exercised. In this case, Monica Jennings purchased an automobile from a dealership and financed the purchase with a loan from American Honda Finance Corporation. As a condition to receiving the loan, Monica was required to give American Honda Finance a security interest in the automobile. By doing so, Monica gave American Honda Finance the right to repossess the automobile if she did not pay as she had promised. The right to repossess allowed American Honda Finance to take Monica's automobile, to sell it, and to use the proceeds from the sale to pay as much of Monica's loan as it would cover.

As you read this case, develop an understanding of where American Honda Finance went wrong as it tried to exercise its right to self-help.

Jennings v. American Honda Finance Corp.
Superior Court of Connecticut
2001 WL 477443

Memorandum of Decision on Motion to Strike Counts Two and Three

Hodgson.

The defendant, American Honda Finance Corporation ("American Honda"), has moved to strike the counts of the second amended complaint in which the plaintiff, Monica Jennings, alleges a violation of the Uniform Commercial Code, Conn. Gen. Stat. §§ 42a-9-501 and 504 (Count Two) and the Connecticut Unfair Trade Practices Act, Conn. Gen. Stat. § 42a-110 et seq. ("CUTPA") (Count Three). The defendant does not challenge the first count of the complaint, in which the plaintiff alleges that the defendant violated the Retail Installment Sales Financing Act ("RISFA") (Conn. Gen. Stat. § 36a-770 et seq.) in connection with the repossession of an automobile in which the defendant had a security interest.

. . . .

Accordingly, the grounds to be decided are as follows:

1. Plaintiff fails to state a valid claim under the UCC in Count II because she relies solely on her RISFA claim to support her UCC claim.
2. The plaintiff fails to state a valid claim under CUTPA because the plaintiff relies solely on her RISFA allegations to support her CUTPA claim.

. . . .

UCC Claim

The plaintiff alleges in the first count of her second amended complaint that when she missed two car payments, the defendant sent her a notice that failed to state

(continued)

that she would have a right to redeem her vehicle in the event that the defendant repossessed it. She further alleges that after the defendant repossessed the car, it informed her that in order to redeem she would have to pay the accelerated total amount due under the financing agreement. The plaintiff alleges that these notices were not in conformity with the requirements of the Connecticut RISFA, specifically, Conn. Gen. Stat. § 36a-785(c). The plaintiff alleges that the defendant used the same forms containing the same alleged non-conformities in a large number of transactions, and she has alleged the existence of a class of similarly situated plaintiffs. The issue of class certification is not before the court at this time.

In the second count of her complaint, the plaintiff incorporates by reference the factual allegations of the first count and alleges that:

22. The security agreements executed by plaintiff and class members and subsequently assigned to AHFC provided that plaintiff and class members had the right to redeem their vehicles after repossession in accordance with Connecticut law.
23. AHFC failed to provide the plaintiff and the class members with all of their rights under their security agreements as required by Conn. Gen. Stat. § 42a-9-501. Specifically, AHFC improperly accelerated their contract balances and improperly imposed repossession and storage charges.
24. AHFC failed to conduct the repossession of plaintiffs and the class members' motor vehicles in a commercially reasonable manner as required by Conn. Gen. Stat. § 42a-9-504, by having improperly accelerated the amounts due on their contracts or loan agreements and by having included inaccurate and false information concerning the rights of plaintiff and the class members in its notices.

Connecticut's Retail Installment Sales Financing Act, at Conn. Gen. Stat. § 36a-770(a) specifically provides that "a transaction subject to sections 36a-770 to 36a-788, inclusive . . . , is also subject to the Uniform Commercial Code, title 42a" except in case of

conflict. The movant has not identified any conflicting terms with respect to the violations alleged by the plaintiff.

The Connecticut Supreme Court has ruled in *Jacobs v. Healy Ford-Subaru, Inc.*, 231 Conn. 707, 722, 652 A.2d 496 (1995), that a party may seek remedies under both RISFA and the UCC, and that neither statute's remedies are exclusive of remedies under other statutes. Other trial courts have ruled that claims under RISFA and 42a-9-501 et seq. may be maintained in the same action and that the remedies are cumulative. *Condor Capital Corp. v. Michaud*, Docket No. 9905889115 (Judicial District of Hartford) (July 25, 2000) (Peck, J.) (27 Conn. L. Rptr. 697); *Hunter v. American Honda Finance Corp.*, Docket No. CV 990587409 (Judicial District of Hartford, April 4, 2000) (27 Conn. L. Rptr. 35).

Conn. Gen. Stat. § 42a-9-501(2) provides in pertinent part that "(a)fter default, the debtor has the rights and remedies . . . provided in the security agreement." The plaintiff has not set forth the actual text of the security agreement, but alleges that it entitles her to "the right to redeem (her) vehicle(s) after repossession in accordance with Connecticut law." She takes the position that Connecticut law required that she be able to redeem by paying only the amounts due as of the date of default, not the accelerated total amount due under the contract. She also alleges that under the security agreement, she was entitled to cure the default without paying repossession and storage charges.

Contrary to American Honda's contention, the plaintiff does not claim that American Honda violated the cited UCC section by violating RISFA; rather, she alleges that it violated the cited provisions by exercising rights and remedies not permitted under the security agreement, in violation of her right to be subjected only to rights and remedies provided in the agreement or by Part 5 of Article 9 of the UCC. The plaintiff's allegations concerning violation of 42a-9-504 in repossession must be read to include the whole process of repossession, including disposition. *Bohan v. Last, supra*, 236 Conn. 670, 675, 674 A.2d 839.

The court finds that American Honda has not established grounds for striking the second count.

CUTPA Claim

The defendant asserts that the plaintiff's claim of violation of CUTPA should be stricken because it is based on the same facts that are the basis for the plaintiff's RISFA claim. By its terms, RISFA is not the exclusive remedy for alleged misfeasance in consumer financing transactions.

Though a violation of RISFA is not an automatic or per se violation of CUTPA, no provision of either statute prohibits a finding that the same conduct violates both statutes.

The third count of the plaintiff's complaint, read in the manner required in the context of a motion to strike, alleges that the defendant did not merely violate RISFA and the UCC with regard to the single transaction involving the plaintiff, but that it engaged in a pattern and practice of failing to implement repossession procedures designed reasonably to ensure compliance with the rights secured by those statutes. The plaintiff also alleges that the defendant engaged in an unfair practice by making reports that the defendant is "not entitled to report," and that these reports damaged her credit worthiness.

The standard for determining whether an act or practice constitutes a CUTPA violation is the test, known as the "cigarette rule" recognized by the Federal Trade Commission in enforcing the federal statute on which CUTPA is modeled:

Whether the practice, without necessarily having been considered unlawful, offends public policy as it has been established by statutes, the common law, or otherwise—whether, in other words, it is within at least the penumbra of some common law, statutory, or other established concept of unfairness; (2) whether it is immoral, unethical, oppressive or unscrupulous; (3) whether it causes substantial injury to consumers.

A-G Foods, Inc. v. Pepperidge Farms, Inc., 216 Conn. 200, 215, 579 A.2d 69 (1990).

In *Jacobs v. Healey Ford-Subaru, Inc., supra,* 231 Conn. 729, the Supreme Court found that the RISFA and UCC violations in the particular transaction were inadvertent. Contrary to the defendant's position, the court did not hold in *Jacobs* that RISFA or UCC violations that are not isolated and inadvertent likewise cannot form the basis for a CUTPA violation. In fact, the Supreme Court approved the approach taken by the attorney trial referee, who, after determining that a RISFA or UCC violation was not a *per se* violation of CUTPA as well, considered the facts in light of the test set forth above. In *Jacobs v. Healey Ford-Subaru, Inc.,* the referee found that a temporary loss of records and sloppy accounting, not a business policy or practice, caused the noncompliances at issue.

The plaintiff in the case before this court has alleged no such inadvertence or isolated lapse, but rather a practice of ignoring or violating consumer protection provisions.

The court finds that the plaintiff has stated a claim under CUTPA.

Conclusion

The motion to strike is denied.

The Advantages and Disadvantages of Self-Help as a Dispute Resolution Process

The party who decides to pursue self-help must weigh the gains and losses attributable to self-help against the hypothetical gains and losses another process might produce. What does a party gain or lose by selecting self-help as a dispute resolution process?

Self-help resolves the dispute quickly and immediately. Self-help, however, may resolve a part but not the entire dispute.

Example 5-5

If a debtor defaults on a secured loan with an outstanding balance of $100,000, and the collateral after repossession and resale brings only $75,000, the debtor still owes the creditor a deficiency of $25,000, even though the creditor has pursued self-help.

The party who decides to pursue self-help seeks to maximize his or her recovery while minimizing transaction costs.

Example 5-6

A lender (secured party) loans $150,000 to a debtor and takes a security interest in all of the borrower's (debtor's) inventory. After repaying $50,000 on the loan, the debtor defaults. If the secured party pursues its right to repossess the debtor's inventory and resells it for $110,000, the secured party has satisfied the debtor's outstanding loan and has $10,000 to return to the debtor. The secured party has no transaction costs except for the costs incurred from repossessing and reselling the inventory.

If the resale brought only $75,000, the secured party has satisfied $75,000 of the debtor's outstanding loan and has a claim against the debtor for the remaining $25,000.

If the secured party had decided to seek a judgment rather than use self-help (repossession), the debtor could have disposed of all of its inventory (and all of its other assets) before the sheriff was able to execute the judgment. The secured party then would have a claim against the debtor for $100,000 and would need to get in line with the debtor's other creditors. The secured party would also face the transaction costs inherent in converting its claim to dollars (assuming that full or partial recovery is even possible).

The self-help process is private with no public airing of the dispute. The telltale signs of exercising self-help, however, may be in the public domain.

Example 5-7

The act of repossession of a motor vehicle may occur where members of the general public may witness the event.

Control of the process may be very important to a party. If a party elects to pursue self-help, it is that party's decision alone and it is that party who controls his or her own destiny. Neither the other party nor a neutral third party must give acquiescence or consent to this decision.

The party selecting self-help controls not only the process but also the outcome, and the outcome is known when the process is selected and implemented. For example, the buyer of goods who deducts damages for breach of contract from the price still due knows the amount that he or she is deducting. The secured party knows the amount of the outstanding balance of the loan that will be satisfied with the resale of repossessed collateral after the collateral has been resold. In either case, the pursuit of self-help may lead to additional problems between the buyer and seller and the secured party and the debtor since the seller may claim that the buyer did not give appropriate notice or miscalculated the damages and the debtor may claim that the repossession was wrongful or the resale was not conducted in a commercially reasonable manner.

The party selecting self-help gives away nothing and gains the full measure of his or her right at the expense of the other party. The party selecting self-help precludes the other party from receiving a windfall because the decision to pursue self-help prevents the other party from retaining what he or she has no legal right to retain. So the party selecting self-help believes that the outcome is legal, fair, and makes good sense.

Is the outcome correct? Legally, a person pursuing self-help exercises his or her rights to the extent provided by law, as he or she perceives the law to be. The outstanding question is whether the legal right to self-help did in fact exist and whether the pursuit of self-help conforms with the law. The pursuit of self-help may not end the dispute if the party against whom self-help was exercised challenges the existence of the legal right to self-help under the circumstances or the manner in which that right was carried out.

Finally, can the other party to the dispute claim to be treated unfairly by the first party's election of self-help? As long as the right to self-help exists and the exercise of self-help does not exceed what is authorized by statute, common law, or contract, the party who is the subject of self-help cannot be heard to complain. Figure 5-1 illustrates self-help as a dispute resolution process.

AVAILABILITY	depends on the facts and the law
PROCESS SELECTION	by one party (the aggrieved party)
THE PARTICIPANTS	the party selecting self-help with minimal interaction between the parties
PREPARATION	requires minimal fact gathering, although self-help may occur without adequate information
THE PROCESS	may or may not be private depending on the facts the aggrieved party acts without outside assistance does not require the parties to meet requires limited interaction between the parties
FAIRNESS	permits the aggrieved party to exercise dominant power over the other
THE OUTCOME	determined by the party electing to exercise self-help based on the law (statute, common law or contract) produces immediate results and resolves the dispute immediately, unless self-help only partially resolves the dispute eliminates all uncertainties as to outcome, unless self-help was improper or improperly exercised may subject the party who pursued self-help to a legal action if self-help was unjustifiably pursued or pursued in an overly zealous manner
COSTS	costs the aggrieved party very little for the process, although may require some technical or legal expertise saves the aggrieved party discovery and discovery costs saves the aggrieved party transaction costs saves the aggrieved party attorney's fees
PRECEDENTIAL VALUE	establishes no binding precedent, although nonbinding precedent by performance may be created between the parties
IMPACT ON FUTURE RELATIONSHIP	discourages future cooperation between the parties may encourage confrontation between the parties

FIGURE 5-1   Self-Help

Key Terms and Phrases

self-help

Review Questions

True/False Questions

1. T F   Self-help requires affirmative action rather than the passiveness of inaction and acquiescence.
2. T F   Self-help is based on needs and interests and not on the law.
3. T F   Self-help may be authorized by statute, common law, or contract.
4. T F   Self-help is technical in nature and should not be undertaken without a thorough understanding of what may and what may not be done.
5. T F   Self-help does not necessarily resolve the whole dispute.
6. T F   Self-help may save the aggrieved party transaction costs, discovery costs, and substantial attorney's fees.
7. T F   Self-help may increase the confrontational relationship between the parties, rather than decrease it.
8. T F   Self-help produces immediate results.
9. T F   Acts of self-help require judicial authorization.
10. T F   Self-help is a rarely used form of dispute resolution.

Fill-in-the-Blank Questions

1. _____ The three sources of authority for self-help.
   _____
   _____

2. _____ Taking care of oneself without judicial assistance.

3. _____ The buyer's statutory right to reject the delivery of an installment of goods that substantially impairs the value of the installment and cannot be cured.

4. _____ The buyer's statutory right to revoke his or her acceptance of goods when the nonconformity of the goods substantially impairs the value of the goods.

5. _____ The buyer's statutory right to deduct the damages to goods received from any part of the contract price that is still due.

6. _____ The common law doctrine that authorizes the owner of a home to exercise self-help by withholding payment from the contractor when the contractor has not completed the work according to the contract.

7. _____ The self-help right that a lender has when a debtor has defaulted on his or her loan and collateral has been pledged to ensure the loan will be paid.

8. _____ The name of the transaction where a borrower pledges collateral to ensure the payment of the loan.

Multiple-Choice Questions

1. Which of the following actively participates in self-help as a dispute resolution process?
   (a) the aggrieved party
   (b) the other party to the dispute
   (c) a neutral third party
   (d) a jury
   (e) the attorney for the aggrieved party

2. Self-help is classified as:
   (a) unilateral action in dispute resolution
   (b) bilateral action in dispute resolution
   (c) third-party evaluation as a prelude to dispute resolution
   (d) third-party assistance in dispute resolution
   (e) third-party adjudication in dispute resolution

3. Self-help may be authorized by:
   (a) contract
   (b) a judge
   (c) statute
   (d) an arbitrator
   (e) common law

4. Which of the following are advantages of self-help?
   (a) reduces transaction costs and attorney's fees
   (b) eliminates attorney's fees
   (c) can be appealed within the judicial system
   (d) is always available
   (e) can be done without judicial assistance

5. Which of the following are disadvantages of self-help?
   (a) may subject the party who pursues self-help to a legal action if self-help was unjustifiably pursued or pursued in an overly zealous manner
   (b) requires substantial discovery
   (c) may only partially resolve the dispute
   (d) may encourage confrontation between the parties
   (e) does not encourage future cooperation between the parties

Short-Answer Questions

1. Describe some of the pitfalls a party may face when attempting to exercise his or her right to self-help.
2. Compare the outcomes that result from inaction, acquiescence, and self-help.
3. Compare the costs of using inaction, acquiescence, and self-help as dispute resolution processes.
4. Create a brief fact situation (one paragraph) describing a dispute. Would inaction, acquiescence, and self-help all be applicable to resolve the dispute? Which one or ones would be applicable and why? Which one or ones would be inapplicable and why?
5. What tactical advantage (or advantages) does a party gain when using self-help as a dispute resolution process?

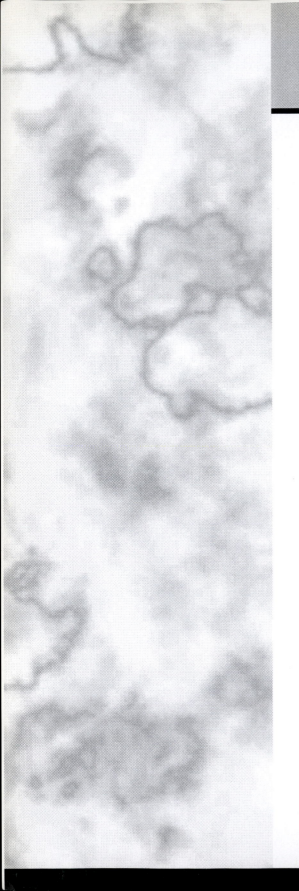

PART THREE

Bilateral Action in Dispute Resolution

INTRODUCTION

Negotiation, a bilateral dispute resolution process, is designed to facilitate discussion between the parties. Because no third party is involved, the parties must provide their own process and must resolve their own problem. If the parties are unable to resolve their own problem, their problem will remain unresolved and the parties must consider another process for resolution.

In the previous paragraph, the word *problem* rather than *dispute* is used. Negotiation, as a resolution process, is not limited to resolving disputes. *Dispute* connotes argument or controversy. *Problem* relates more to a question or a situation. *Dispute* implies greater conflict than does *problem*. The techniques and strategies that apply to negotiating the resolution of a dispute also apply to negotiating the solution of a problem.

CHAPTER 6

Negotiation

Negotiation
Negotiation, a private, voluntary, consensual dispute resolution process, involves the two disputing parties (or their representatives) as they attempt to resolve their dispute.

Negotiation is a private, voluntary, consensual process involving the two disputants (or their representatives) as they attempt to resolve their dispute. Unlike inaction, acquiescence, and self-help where a party acts unilaterally, the parties in negotiation must work together to resolve their dispute.

In a negotiation, the parties provide their own process and resolve their own dispute. They do not seek the help of a neutral third party either to direct the discussion or to resolve the dispute for them. By providing their own process, the parties create their own rules. Generally the rules of the negotiation are unstated but are implicitly created as the process unfolds.

When parties select negotiation as the method of dispute resolution, they become involved in a process that will require compromise. Seldom will a party receive everything that he or she wants and seldom will a party give everything that the other side demands. If position-based negotiation is used, the parties distribute the "fixed pie." If interest-based negotiation is used, the parties can be creative as they distribute an "expanded pie." These strategies will be discussed later in this chapter.

Preparing for Negotiation

A negotiation, by its very name, is two sided. Therefore, a party preparing for a negotiation should visualize both his or her side and the other side.

Evaluating the Dispute
Evaluating the dispute requires the problem be defined, the facts investigated and the law researched, the facts applied to the law, the legal and nonlegal issues evaluated, the parties' interests identified, a range of solutions identified and evaluated against those interests, and a plan developed in the event a negotiated resolution cannot be achieved.

Define the Problem
Defining the problem requires the problem be defined both from one party's perspective and from the other party's perspective. As the problem is defined, a party may discover not one but two problems—his or her perception of the problem and the other party's perception of the problem.

Example 6-1

In the real estate market, the owner of a house may view her problem as selling her home quickly for the maximum price that could be realized. On the other hand, a potential buyer may view his problem as buying a house to satisfy specific needs.

Example 6-2

An employer may view her problem as needing a employee to perform unique and essential services for the company. A prospective employee may view his problem as finding a position that accommodates his lifestyle.

Not all problems are disputes. The previous examples describe problems that are not disputes. The parties are attempting to create new relationships. The analysis for resolving disputes through negotiation also applies to resolving problems that are not disputes. The following is an example that *does* take the form of a dispute.

Example 6-3

Stephanie Emerson, a teller at First Bank, claims that she was approached by the branch manager who told her that if she would provide him with sexual favors, he would see that she would be promoted to head teller. Stephanie responded by filing a sexual harassment claim against the branch manager and the bank. The branch manager asserts that he never made the statement.

Investigate the Facts and Research the Law

The facts available at the time must be investigated for accuracy and completeness. The law associated with these facts must then be researched.

Investigating the facts requires more than reviewing the facts given during an interview. An investigator must be creative and search for additional facts. A good, quick source of information is the Internet. If the problem deals with solar panels, an Internet search on solar panels may provide background information about solar panels. A check for judicial opinions on Westlaw or Lexis may reveal whether the party on the other side has been involved in litigation and, if so, with what result. An investigation of the facts also requires consideration of the parties' feelings. Often, a party's feelings drive a dispute.

Depending on the problem, the degree to which the law needs to be researched may depend on whether the central problem is nonlegal or legal. If the central problem is legal, substantial legal research may be necessary. If the central problem is nonlegal, some legal research is required but substantial research may be necessary as to the nonlegal issues. Nonlegal research may be important as to the setting of the problem in addition to the specific issue. For example, in a neighborhood dispute, knowledge of the social, ethnic, or religious customs of the residents of that neighborhood might prove useful. Neither the legal nor the nonlegal issues can be ignored.

Example 6-4

The Century, Inc., designs and manufactures solar-powered automobiles. Century is negotiating with Maria Figarro, an internationally known automobile designer, to be its chief designer. The negotiation between Century and Figarro for her services (i.e., an employment contract) will include the topic of a covenant not to compete. Although most issues of the negotiation are nonlegal (e.g., scope of duties, salary, retirement, medical, vacations, and bonuses), the covenant not to compete must be drafted so it can be legally enforceable. Century must be seeking to protect its legitimate interests and in doing so must not place an unreasonable restriction on Figarro as to scope, geography, and duration.

Researching the law requires the determination of possible causes of action. These actions may be those that one party could initiate and those that the other party might initiate. Could the facts present an action, for example, for negligence, strict liability, defamation, breach of contract, or sexual harassment? Or could the facts present an action based on statute, such as, implied warranty of merchantability, an unfair labor practice, or an antitrust violation? For each possibility, the existing precedent must be found, assuming existing precedent does exist.

Apply the Facts to the Law and Evaluate the Legal Issues of the Dispute

Once the facts are developed and the applicable law researched, the question becomes how does the law apply to the facts. For each cause of action, its component parts (i.e., elements, factors, or prongs) must be isolated and each component of the law applied to the facts. If a problem were to be litigated, what would be the strengths and weaknesses in the plaintiff's position as to each component part of each cause of action? Once this analysis has been concluded, a party has a pretty good idea of what the respective legal positions will be.

Understanding the legal positions is important in understanding the backdrop for the dispute. The law will not be a central issue of the negotiations. The parties will attempt to resolve their dispute by making a good decision based on needs and interests rather than by resolving the legal issues. Although the parties may want to talk about the law, little is gained by an extensive discussion of the legal issues. When both parties attempt to convince each other of the merits of their respective legal positions, neither will make much headway because neither is an objective decision maker. Documents and other evidence, however, will be helpful when attempting to stake out a position that a claim has some merit or lacks merit, and this discussion may then lead to a discussion of the needs and interests of the parties.

Evaluate the Nonlegal Issues of the Dispute

Once the legal issues are evaluated, the nonlegal issues must be addressed. The fact that the dispute involves a nonlegal rather than a legal issue does not make it any less a dispute. The methods of dispute resolution, however, will be limited. Those dispute resolution processes that deal exclusively with legal issues, such as arbitration, litigation, and private judging, will not be available.

Example 6-5

The First Baptist Church of Springfield was located in a neighborhood that once had been basically residential but now was a mix of residential and commercial. A strip shopping center was located about a thousand feet from the church. One storefront had become vacant and the Great Plains Microbrewery took a lease to open a brew pub. Although the local zoning ordinance only required establishments selling beer to be 760 feet from a church, the local residents and church members protested the location of the brew pub. This dispute centered around a nonlegal rather than a legal issue.

Problem 6-1

Design an environmental problem that has a nonlegal rather than legal focus. For example, your problem could involve the competing interests of a logging company and an environmental group. You may find the internet a source of ideas.

Identify the Interests of the Parties

Identify the parties' interests. *Why* does one party want a certain outcome and the other party want a different outcome? The interests of both parties must be identified and organized as to priority. A party will never agree to a settlement if the settlement does not satisfy the majority of his or her interests. The other party will also never agree if the settlement does not satisfy the majority of his or her interests. Therefore, the key interests of both parties must be satisfied for there to be a negotiated agreement.

Problem 6-2

Joanne and Tom McPherson, the parents of two children (Megan, age 6, and William, age 3) were married for eight years when Joanne filed for divorce. Joanne claimed that Tom was having an affair with one of his coworkers and therefore their marriage had developed irreconcilable differences. Joanne has sought custody of the children and has requested child support of $1,000 a month for each child. Tom has also requested custody of the children and has requested child support of $800 a month for each child. Both Joanne and Tom hold executive positions with major corporations.

The judge has instructed the parties to negotiate their issues on child custody and child support.

1. What are Joanne's interests as to the custody and support issues? If you have doubt as to what Joanne's interests are as to custody, ask yourself "Why does Joanne want custody?"
2. What are Tom's interests as to the custody and support issues? If you have doubt as to what Tom's interests are as to custody, ask yourself "Why does Tom want custody?"
3. Which interests do they share and which interests do they not share?

Identify a Range of Solutions and Evaluate the Solutions against the Parties' Interests

A list of hypothetical solutions should be created and these solutions should be committed to paper. The list could begin by articulating a solution that would be the most favorable to one party. Then the list could state a solution that would be the most favorable to the other party. It should be readily apparent that one party will not accept the solution that is most favorable to the other because it would not meet his or her interests (although it would possibly satisfy all of the other party's interests). It should also be readily apparent that the other party will not accept the solution that is most favorable to the first party because it would not meet his or her interests (although it would possibly satisfy all of the first party's interests). This approach establishes the two extreme or polar positions for the negotiation. An agreement, however, will not be reached if only one party has his or her interests met. Both parties must come away from the bargaining table feeling that at least some of their interests have been met. Therefore, a party should create a range of possible solutions between these two extreme positions. A party should try to develop solutions that will meet not only his or her interests but also those of the other party.

Figure 6-1 is a work sheet that will help a party define the problem(s), interests, and possible solutions.

Defining the Problem(s)

Defining the Problem from Your Perspective

Defining the Problem from the Other Party's Perspective

Identifying Interests

Your Interest

The Other Party's Interests

Range of Solutions and Evaluation against Interests

Solution Most Favorable to You

Meets the Following of Your Interests

Does Not Meet the Following of Your Interests

Meets the Following Interests of the Other Side

Does Not Meet the Following Interests of the Other Side

(continued)

FIGURE 6-1 Work Sheet for Dissecting the Content of a Negotiation

Solution Most Favorable to the Other Side	Meets the Following of Your Interests
	Does Not Meet the Following of Your Interests
	Meets the Following Interests of the Other Side
	Does Not Meet the Following Interests of the Other Side
Another Solution	Meets the Following of Your Interests
	Does Not Meet the Following of Your Interests
	Meets the Following Interests of the Other Side
	Does Not Meet the Following Interests of the Other Side
Another Solution	Meets the Following of Your Interests
	Does Not Meet the Following of Your Interests
	Meets the Following Interests of the Other Side
	Does Not Meet the Following Interests of the Other Side

FIGURE 6-1 *(continued)*

Develop a Plan in the Event a Negotiated Resolution of the Dispute Cannot Be Achieved at This Time

Not all disputes end in a negotiated agreement. Some are resolved by the unilateral action of one of the parties (inaction, acquiescence, or self-help); others require the intervention of a neutral third party (ombuds, mediation, arbitration, or litigation).

Since a negotiation does not guarantee an agreement, it is important to understanding what the situation will be if the negotiation does not produce an agreement. Do alternatives exist? As the last step in the planning process, list solutions that do not require the other party's agreement.

Example 6-6

Mary Ethel leased an apartment for a year at $1200 a month from Buena Siesta, an apartment conglomerate that owned 260,000 units nationwide. Shortly after Mary Ethel moved into her apartment, Buena Siesta sold the building to Quick Buck Realty. Quick Buck did not provide the services (including prompt maintenance and custodial care) that had been provided by Buena Siesta. Mary Ethel thought about moving out, but she still had six months remaining on her lease, she liked the location, and she liked her apartment.

Mary Ethel has an appointment with Quick Buck to discuss her situation. Prior to this meeting, Mary Ethel has prepared by completing the Work Sheet for Dissecting the Content of a Negotiation (Figure 6-1). When considering her options if she cannot reach an agreement with Quick Buck, Mary Ethel has listed the following:

1. Find another apartment (or a house) and break the lease.
2. Stay for the remainder of the lease and then find another apartment (or a house).
3. Find another apartment (or a house) and sublease her apartment.
4. File a complaint with the local housing authority.
5. File a complaint with the Better Business Bureau.
6. Organize the other tenants against Quick Buck.

If a solution is based on incomplete information, complete the missing information, if possible.

Example 6-7

The fourth item on the list (file a complaint with the local housing authority) in Example 6-6 is based on incomplete information. Does a local housing authority exist? What is its jurisdiction? Can it put pressure on Quick Buck to correct its behavior?

Acquiring this information requires a telephone call to city hall or the reference desk of the local library. If there is a local housing authority, a telephone call to that agency could prove helpful.

Problem 6-3

1. What additional information is needed in Example 6-6?
2. How would you find this information?

Preparing the Parties for Their Roles in the Negotiation Process

The roles of the parties in a negotiation will vary depending on the design of the process. The parties may not hire attorneys and represent themselves at a negotiation. The parties may hire attorneys and not accompany their attorneys to the negotiation. The parties may hire attorneys and accompany them to the negotiation where the clients may or may not actively participate in the negotiation or where the attorneys may or may not actively participate in the negotiation but merely be present to advise their clients.

If the parties have not hired attorneys, they must consciously or subconsciously design the process, develop their negotiation plan, and execute that plan when negotiating. They must be prepared to articulate the facts as they see them, their feelings, and their interests. The parties must be able to evaluate offers and counteroffers and understand when they need professional assistance to do so. Finally, if an agreement is reached, they must be able to draft the agreement so each party knows what he or she must do and what to expect the other party to do and when. They must also be able to draft an agreement to minimize the problems that could arise when the agreement is being performed.

In negotiations where the parties are represented by legal counsel, the attorneys, working with their clients, prepare for the negotiation. The clients must understand the negotiation process, the fact that not all negotiations end in settlement, the necessity to keep an open mind and expect to compromise, and what they will do if the negotiations fail to produce a settlement. If the clients are present, they may or may not actively participate in the negotiation. If the clients have an active role, they must be prepared for that role. What will their attorneys expect them to say? What will their attorneys expect them *not* to say? What will the clients hear their attorneys say? The clients must develop a comfort level with their role. The attorneys may or may not be accompanied by their paralegal. Since only the attorney can represent the client, the paralegal will be present to assist his or her attorney and will not have an active role in the negotiation. If the paralegals will be present, they must know what their attorneys will want them to do.

The attorneys must help their clients and paralegals understand how they should conduct themselves during the negotiations. This includes what they should wear, how long they should expect to be there, where they should sit, what they should be prepared to say, what questions they should answer, if any, and how they should communicate with their attorneys.

In still other negotiations, the attorneys represent their clients and the clients are not present. The attorneys must be prepared to articulate their client's facts, feelings, and interests. The attorneys must know whether they have authority to evaluate an offer and act upon it or have only limited authority that requires communication with their clients so the clients can evaluate the offer and act upon it.

Selecting a Negotiating Strategy

Position-Based Negotiation
The parties in position-based negotiation begin by stating their positions and then negotiate from those positions.

Once the problems, interests, and possible solutions have been identified and the possible solutions have been evaluated against the interests of both parties, it is time to decide upon a negotiating strategy. The following discussion focuses on two negotiation strategies: position-based negotiation and interest-based negotiation.

Traditionally, negotiations have been position (outcome) based. In **position-based negotiation** the parties state their positions and negotiate from those positions.

Example 6-8

The following are positions:

"I offer you $60,000 for Photo Finish, a thoroughbred yearling."

"I will take no less than $26,000 for my father's stamp collection."

"I will work for you for one year and will not accept a covenant not to compete."

Interest-Based Negotiation
The parties in interest-based negotiation begin by identifying the problem from their respective perspectives, then discussing their respective interests, followed by mutually developing a range of solutions.

In position-based negotiation, each party tries to back the other away from his or her preconceived solution. As the negotiation evolves, the parties focus on "distributing a fixed pie" rather than seeing creative solutions that result in "expanding the pie." Both parties cannot have their interests equally met and thus solution-based negotiation results in an outcome whereby what one party *wins* the other party *loses*.

Interest-based negotiation focuses on the parties' interests and a range of solutions. It is not constructed around the single position (or solution) offered by each party. In this way, the parties create new solutions to meet their similar and different interests.

Example 6-9

The following are interests:

"I need a place to live that will be within my budget."

"I need a place to live where I will feel safe."

"I need a place to live where I can have peace and quiet."

As a part of the interest-based negotiation process, the parties focus on creative solutions for "expanding the pie" rather than considering only the original preconceived solutions for distributing a "fixed pie." Both parties can have their primary interests met, and thus interest-based negotiation leads to a solution whereby both parties *win*. This approach moves the parties from a "win/lose" to a "win/win" philosophy.

Problem 6-4

Which of the following are positions and which are interests? Interests can be distinguished from positions by asking *why*. If the statement is a position, *why* leads to an interest. Some statements contain both positions and interests.

"Lend me $600."
"I will sell you my house for $240,000 in cash or $280,000 paid over five years."
"I will work for you this fall but not next spring."
"I need a week off to visit my grandmother."
"I need a working environment where I feel appreciated."

Interests are absolute and cannot be negotiated away. Interests may be prioritized so some interests are perceived as more important than others. Each party to a negotiation will have a set of interests. Some interests may coincide but others will not.

A position is a solution or outcome that satisfies a party's interests. An interest may be satisfied in more than one way. Therefore, a number of positions can satisfy an interest. Discovering an array of positions (solutions) that will accomplish the task of satisfying an interest is an exercise in creativity.

Example 6-10

Marianne would like to find a clean, quiet place to live that would cost her no more than $760 a month. Marianne could satisfy her interests by leasing or subleasing an apartment, a condominium, or a house or by buying a condominium or a house. If buying, she could consider a single family house or a duplex that could give her extra monthly income. Depending on how long she needs the accommodations, she might think about housesitting or renting a room in a house. Depending on Marianne's financial situation, the $760 could be increased if she purchased and calculated tax deductions for property tax and mortgage interest and equity accumulated (forced savings). She could live alone or with a roommate who would share expenses.

Problem 6-5

Richard and Georgette were married for six years when they decided to divorce. Both have jobs that are demanding, require long and at times uncertain hours, and some travel. Richard is an accountant and Georgette is a physician's assistant. They have been living in an upper middle class neighborhood with their two children, Richard, Jr., age 5, and Jennifer, age 4. Both would like to participate in raising their children and would like to spend as much time as possible with them. There is some animosity between Richard and Georgette. Both have parents who live in town and have taken turns caring for the children.

1. List Richard's interests as to custody and support of the children. Prioritize Richard's interests.
2. List Georgette's interests as to custody and support of the children. Prioritize Georgette's interests.

3. Do they share any interests?
4. List a solution that will meet all of Richard's primary interests and none of Georgette's primary interests.
5. List a solution that will meet all of Georgette's primary interests and none of Richard's interests.
6. List several solutions that will meet both Richard's and Georgette's primary interests.

Negotiating from a Preconceived Position

Position-based (distributive) negotiation, as its name denotes, requires a party to begin by stating his or her position or solution. For planning purposes, position-based negotiators should know three positions rather than just one. Assuming that the negotiation deals with money, the parties should know their opening position, their most extreme position (e.g., the highest they would pay if they are the buyer or the lowest they would accept if they are the seller), and their target position (i.e., what they really want).

Example 6-11

Tom and Misty Montoya own a house that they would like to sell. Before they advertise their house, they should know three figures. The first is their target price. This is the amount they would like to receive for their house. To arrive at this figure, they have investigated what other comparable houses in their neighborhood have sold for over the past year. The second is the minimum amount they would take for their house. This depends on their financial situation, the market, and the urgency with which they need to sell their house. The third figure is their opening price. They can calculate this by comparing what other sellers in their neighborhood have opened with, how long their houses were on the market, and the actual selling price. If the Montoyas had opened at their target price, it would be unlikely that they could sell their house without dropping some amount off their price. Therefore, they gave themselves little opportunity to receive their target price.

Figure 6-2 is a planning tool for position-based negotiation.

In a position-based negotiation, a negotiated agreement cannot be reached until there is some overlap between the opening offer and bottom line on the part of one party and the opening counteroffer and maximum of the other. This overlap creates a settlement zone. That is, the parties will negotiate an agreement somewhere in this overlap area. When the negotiations first open, generally the parties will have no settlement zone. As the parties tug and push each other, one party's bottom line (i.e., the seller's price) will descend and the other party's maximum (i.e., the buyer's purchase price) will ascend. If enough movement occurs, a settlement zone will be created and the parties will arrive at an agreement.

Identify your own opening offer, target, and bottom line or opening counteroffer, target, maximum.

Can you predict the other side's three points?

one side	scale	other side
opening offer ___	___	___
___	___	___
___	___	___
___	___	___
target ___	___	___
___	___	___
___	___	___
___	___	___
___	___	___
bottom line ___	___	___
___	___	___
___	___	___
___	___	___ maximum
___	___	___
___	___	___
___	___	___
___	___	___ target
___	___	___
___	___	___
___	___	___ opening counteroffer

Reasons why the other side should change their position	Their response to your reasons
(1)	
(2)	
(3)	
(4)	
(5)	
(6)	

Reasons posed by the other side why you should change your position	Your response to their reasons
(1)	
(2)	
(3)	
(4)	
(5)	
(6)	

FIGURE 6-2 Position-Based Negotiation Work Sheet

Example 6-12

Tom and Misty Montoya own a house that they would like to sell. Before they advertise their house, they know three figures. They have investigated the sale price of other comparable houses in their neighborhood and have calculated their target price to be $225,000. The second is the minimum amount they would take for their house, $200,000. The third figure is their opening price, $250,000.

Richard and Mary O'Connor have been looking for a house in the school district in which the Montoya house is located. Their realtor has shown them the Montoya house. The O'Connors open with an offer of $185,000. Although the Montoyas do not know it, the O'Connors have a target of $210,000 and are willing to go as high as $235,000.

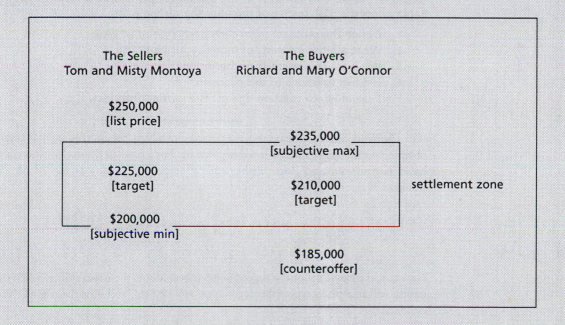

The settlement zone is between $200,000 and $235,000. The house should sell to the O'Connors at somewhere between these two figures. The settlement zone is dynamic because the parties may change their numbers as the negotiation continues. Often there is no settlement zone when the negotiation begins, but one develops as the negotiation continues.

Not all problems merely distribute money for property or services. Can the Position-Based Negotiation Work Sheet (Figure 6-2) be adopted for a nonmoney problem?

Negotiating from Interests

An interest-based negotiation can be structured in five segments—defining the problem(s) to be negotiated, identifying the parties' interests, creating a range of solutions, evaluating these solutions against the parties' interests, and drafting the agreement.

Problem 6-6

The Blue Sky Airlines Pilots have been working for a number of years without a contract. Recently, the Union threatened to strike if the company would not offer them a contract which had the following:

1. pay increase of 11 percent over four years;
2. guarantee that Blue Sky Eagle Jets would not be flown by non-Blue Sky Airlines pilots; and
3. more stock options.

Blue Sky offered the Union a 5.5 percent pay increase over the next four years and more stock options up front. Blue Sky refused to agree to guarantee that the Blue Sky Eagle jets would only be flown by Blue Sky Airlines pilots because it would not be able to compete in the commuter plane area if it had to pay the Eagle pilots the high wages of the Blue Sky Airline pilots.

1. Define the problem from each party's point of view.
2. What are the interests of Blue Sky Airlines?
3. What are the interests of the Union?
4. List five solutions to this problem.
5. Evaluate each solution against the parties' interests.

The Work Sheet for Dissecting the Content of a Negotiation (Figure 6-1) provides the planning document for interest-based negotiation. For a more in depth discussion of interest-based negotiation, read Roger Fisher and William Ury, *Getting to Yes,* 2d ed. (Penguin Books, 1991).

Executing the Negotiation Strategy: When, Where, and How

Now that the planning for the negotiation has been done, the issues shift to when the negotiation will take place, where the negotiation will be held, and how the negotiation will be conducted.

The Timing

Inaction, acquiescence, and self-help are unilateral in nature. Only one of the disputing parties selects the process of dispute resolution. The selection is made independent of input from the other party. Negotiation, on the other hand, requires the participation by both parties. They must agree to negotiate. This agreement to negotiate may be the result of an active decision to negotiate ("Let's negotiate"), or negotiations may just happen. The parties often begin substantive discussions without discussing whether they will begin discussions.

The decision of whether to negotiate is based on needs and interests and not on the law. The parties weigh the gains attributable through negotiation against the hypothetical gains that another process might produce.

The timing for a negotiation is up to the parties. Some parties prefer to negotiate as soon as a problem arises and thus control the problem before it can grow. Others take a wait-and-see approach. They may want to gather more facts or give the problem time to solve itself.

When selecting negotiation, the parties weigh the need to resolve the dispute now against what might happen if the dispute is resolved later. The parties may have a need to resolve the dispute now so they can put the problem behind them and move on. Delaying the resolution of the dispute does not guarantee that the dispute will be resolved more favorably to the party who decides against negotiation.

Negotiation can be an ongoing process. The parties may begin to negotiate early in the life of the dispute. The negotiation may continue sporadically. As the dispute remains unresolved, the relative relationship between the parties will change. New facts may be discovered, a party may fall into poor health or die, a corporation may become financially insolvent, and a party's needs and interests may change. Any change will have an impact on the negotiations.

Example 6-13

Barry Kwan suffered an on-the-job injury when the tool he was using broke. Barry sued the retailer, the tool wholesaler, and the tool manufacturer in actions of product liability, negligence, implied warranty of fitness for a particular purpose, and implied warranty of merchantability.

The insurance company representing the manufacturer made an offer to Barry through Barry's attorney for $600,000. Although Barry's attorney had counseled Barry to wait, Barry was very excited about the offer since he had mounting medical bills and his workers' compensation was about ready to run out. As Berry was on the verge of accepting the offer, he discovered that he was holding the winning lottery ticket in the New Jersey lottery. The ticket was worth $26,000,000. Barry no longer has the need for an immediate settlement.

The fact that a negotiation is conducted that fails to produce an agreement does not mean that a second and a third negotiation cannot be held. Often negotiation has periods of activity and periods of inactivity. Disputes must be ripe for settlement, so what may appear to be a false start may really be a step leading toward a negotiated agreement.

The Setting

Unlike some processes such as litigation, negotiation does not require a specific setting. Negotiations can be conducted face to face, by telephone, by e-mail, by telegram, and by letter. Negotiations can be conducted directly by the parties or through an intermediary such as an attorney.

Problem 6-7
What are some of the advantages and disadvantages of negotiating face to face when compared to negotiating by telephone, e-mail, FAX, telegram, or letter?

If the parties are negotiating face to face, the setting can be used to create a tactical advantage for one party over the other.

Problem 6-8

Mary Fireside, the managing partner of a large shopping mall invited Jason Winters to her office to negotiate a contract for lease space that Jason was seeking for his retail candy store. Jason arrived at Mary's office at the appointed time and was kept waiting for half an hour before he was ushered into Mary's very expansive and well furnished office. He found Mary sitting behind a large desk. He was shown to a rather low, overstuffed chair on the other side of Mary's desk. Mary's receptionist brought Jason a glass of water and he balanced the glass in one hand while holding his notebook in the other.

At the beginning of the meeting, Mary informed Jason that she had only 46 minutes to spend with him since she had a plane to catch for Paris. As they discussed the lease and the lease space, Mary kept receiving telephone calls or hand-delivered messages from her secretary. At times, Mary left Jason sitting alone in her office while she met with someone else.

After 40 minutes, Mary gave Jason a copy of the lease and told him to read it over and if he agreed to the terms, he should sign and return it by 9:00 A.M. the next day. When Jason attempted to ask questions about the lease, Mary told him to call her secretary and she would answer his questions. Mary then buzzed for her receptionist to usher Jason out.

How did Mary use her office to gain a tactical advantage over Jason?

The parties can negotiate at a distance, for example, through letters.

Example 6-14

The Johnsons contracted with Rio Rancho Cabinet Makers, Inc. for the remodeling of their kitchen. The contract price was $12,000. The work was completed but not to the Johnsons' satisfaction. The Johnsons wanted some of the work redone, but Rio Rancho said it could not schedule the work for six months. The Johnsons told Rio Rancho that they needed the work done within the month. When Rio Rancho demanded payment of the contract price, the Johnsons refused. After thinking it over and finding another company that could satisfactorily complete the work within a month for $3,000, the Johnsons sent Rio Rancho a check for $9,000 with the notation "the acceptance of this check constitutes payment in full." By sending the check with the "payment in full" notation, the Johnsons were making Rio Rancho an offer. When Rio Rancho deposited the Johnsons' check, it accepted the offer and formed a contract. Even though the parties did not discuss the Johnsons' offer, they negotiated a settlement of the dispute.

Executing the Strategy

A party should feel free to bring a step-by-step outline of his or her plan to the negotiation. The plan helps the party keep with his or her format. If the plan follows the previously discussed format, the first step in the execution of the plan, regardless of whether a position-based or interest-based strategy will be followed, requires defining the problem or problems that will be discussed at the negotiation. Do the parties share the same problem or do they have different problems to resolve? Each party must listen carefully to what the other has to say about the problem.

Position-Based Negotiation

If a position-based negotiation strategy is selected, one party will open with his or her initial offer. By making the first offer, this party becomes the offeror. Now the other party (offeree) knows four points: its initial counteroffer, its target, its highest counteroffer, and the offeror's initial offer. The offeree will counteroffer. Now the offeror knows four points as well: its initial offer, its target, its lowest counteroffer, and the offeree's initial counteroffer. The offeror will then counteroffer and begin moving toward its target. The offeree will then counteroffer and begin moving toward its target. As the negotiations progress, the parties may pass their targets and move toward their minimum and maximum, respectively. Also as the negotiations progress, the parties will readjust their minimum and maximum. Although a party may purport that this is as high or as low as it will go ("take it or leave it"), the other party will not know whether that statement is a bluff. Each side will justify why its position should prevail. The counteroffers will continue until the parties either reach the settlement range or do not. The settlement range is the overlap between the offeror's and offeree's minimum and maximum. If the settlement range is not reached, the parties will not reach an agreement.

Example 6-15

The seller has her house on the market. She has listed it at $250,000, would like to get $200,000, but would take $175,000. A potential buyer likes the house and is prepared to make an offer for $140,000, would like to get it for $150,000, and is prepared to go as high as $185,000. The difference between the seller's $175,000 and the buyer's $185,000 is the settlement range.

Seller	scale	Buyer
seller's opening offer	$250,000	
	$225,000	
seller's target	$200,000	
	$185,000	buyer's maximum
settlement range	$180,000	settlement range
seller's bottom line	$175,000	
	$155,000	
	$150,000	buyer's target
	$145,000	
	$140,000	buyer's opening counteroffer

(continued)

During the negotiation, the buyer may be able to get the seller to lower her minimum to $170,000 or the seller may be able to get the buyer to raise his maximum to $190,000. Thus the settlement range floats as the negotiations progress.

 ## Problem 6-9

If the buyer's maximum was $170,000 while the seller's minimum was $175,000, the parties have no settlement range and the negotiations will not produce an agreement, unless the buyer were to increase his maximum to $175,000 or the seller were to reduce her minimum to $170,000, or some combination were to occur.

1. If you were the seller, what could the buyer say that could cause you to lower your bottom line?
2. If you were the buyer, what could the seller say that could cause you to raise your maximum?

Use the Position-Based Negotiation Work Sheet (Figure 6-2) to organize your answers.

Interest-Based Negotiation

If an interest-based negotiation strategy is selected, the parties after discussing the problem will move toward a discussion of interests. This will be followed by listing a range of solutions and the evaluation of each solution against the interests. After the solution or combination of solutions that best meets the parties' interests has been selected, the agreement is reduced to a writing. The writing should be as complete as possible. Details omitted from the writing will cause the contract to unravel.

Example 6-16

Bridget and George Knutson had three children before their divorce. Prior to their divorce, the parties agreed upon custody and visitation. Bridget was to have custody of the children, George would have unlimited visitation rights, and the children were to visit their father on two holidays a year. All went well until the first Christmas after the divorce. George wanted the children to visit him so he could take them to Disney World. Bridget wanted the children to stay with her so they would be with her parents on Christmas Day. Although Bridget and George had agreed on two holidays a year, the writing did not designate which holidays were under the visitation plan or how the holiday determination was to be made.

Several technical rules of contract law come into play when agreements are reduced to writing. Under the parol evidence rule, a substantive rule of contract law, a contract may have two components: a written component (i.e., the integration or final writing) and a parol component (i.e., the nonintegrated writings and oral terms). A writing (i.e., final writing or integration) that includes all the terms in detail will diminish a subsequent challenge that the writing is not a total integration and that terms not in this writing are a part of the contract.

After the agreement has been reduced to writing, both sides should read and correct the writing before either signs. If the writing is written by one party and signed before the other party has read and consented to it, the party who did not participate in producing the physical writing may have corrections, additions, or deletions that will need to be initialed by the parties. By waiting to sign until both parties have read and agreed upon the accuracy and completeness of the writing, one signature per party (without the need for initialing changes) will be sufficient. If the agreement extends to multiple pages, each page must be initialed by each party, numbered (i.e., 1 of 3, 2 of 3, 3 of 3), and dated.

If an attorney negotiating on behalf of his or her client does not have the authority to accept the agreement, the terms of the agreement cannot be finalized without the client's assent. The attorney must, in good faith, present the tentative agreement to his or her client and recommend the client's acceptance. Before the attorney leaves the negotiation, however, he or she should initial the agreement with the understanding that the agreement will be presented to the client for acceptance by a date certain.

Before the negotiation has concluded, both sides should have a copy of the signed agreement. Only one version of the agreement should be signed and dated. If each attorney makes a draft of the agreement, the versions may differ, however slightly, and this may lead to a subsequent dispute.

The following tips contribute to a better contract.

1. Create an outline for the contract and draft from this outline. An outline will help organize the terms of the contract in a logical, orderly fashion. An outline prevents duplication or the omission of essential terms.
2. Define the purpose of the contract.
3. Organize the contract by grouping similar items together (e.g., group the duties of one party and then group the duties of the other party).
4. Be brief, omitting surplus words, sentences, and paragraphs.
5. Draft concisely. Wordiness creates opportunity for ambiguity and confusion.
6. Use concise terms, avoiding synonyms. Using different words to refer to the same thing adds ambiguity and confusion.
7. Avoid legalese since legalese only makes a writing pompous and confusing. Minimize confusion by referring to the parties by name rather than "the party of the first part."
8. Avoid indefinite pronouns, such as "it, they, this, who, and which," since indefinite pronouns only add confusion. When possible substitute a noun for a pronoun.
9. Avoid "etc." for etc. adds no new content.
10. Avoid sexist language.

Enforcing a Negotiated Agreement

If the parties negotiate an agreement, their agreement is a contract. Who made the offer and who made the acceptance becomes unimportant because a contract has been formed. The basis of the contract is an exchange. Actually, the basis of a contract is two exchanges. The first party promises to do something (or not to do something) in exchange for the second party's promise to do something (or not to do something). The second party promises to do something (or not to do something) in exchange for the first party's promise to do something (or not to do something). A contract provides a quid pro quo.

Example 6-17

Gary McLean, a part-time buildings code enforcement officer in the Village of Sleepy Hollow, New York, was fired after a new mayor took office. McLean sued the village under 42 U.S.C. § 1983, contending that he had been fired in retaliation for his vocal support of the previous administration. McLean's attorney met with the attorney for the village, and they negotiated the following agreement. The village promised to reinstate McLean, pay him back pay in the full amount he had lost during the period he was unemployed, and pay his attorney's fees in exchange for McLean's promise to dismiss his lawsuit with prejudice. McLean's promise to dismiss his lawsuit with prejudice is the quid pro quo for the village's promise to reinstate, pay back pay in the full amount McLean had lost during the period he was unemployed, and pay his attorney's fees. The village's promise to reinstate, pay back pay in the full amount McLean had lost during the period he was unemployed, and pay his attorney's fees is the quid pro quo for McLean's promise to dismiss his lawsuit with prejudice.

Because a negotiated agreement is a contract, it is enforceable in the courts through a breach of contract action. Generally, breach of contract actions yield monetary damages that place the nonbreaching party in the position he or she would have been in had the contract been fully performed. Thus the nonbreaching party receives his or her contract expectations. In some instances, a nonbreaching party may seek an injunction that requires the breaching party to desist from doing something or that requires specific performance that compels the breaching party to do something.

If litigation is pending when an agreement is negotiated, the parties may agree to mutually dismiss the litigation. At the same time, the parties can agree to have the court enter the negotiated agreement as a consent judgment so the agreement could be enforced by the courts.

Negotiating in Bad Faith

Negotiation is a voluntary, consensual, private dispute resolution process. Unlike inaction, acquiescence, and self-help, where a party acts unilaterally, the parties in negotiation must work together to resolve their dispute. The parties, however, are not mandated to work together. Each may try to get the other to do something that is not in his or her best interest. Since the process is voluntary, each party has the power to terminate the negotiation at any time, so each has a vehicle by which to protect himself or herself during the negotiations. Furthermore, neither party has a duty to negotiate in good faith. The duty of good faith only arises after the agreement has been created.

Example 6-18

Section 1-203 of the Uniform Commercial Code states:

Every contract or duty within this Act imposes an obligation of good faith in its performance or enforcement.

This section mandates good faith in the performance of an agreement subject to the Uniform Commercial Code but does not mandate good faith in the negotiation of that agreement.

This is not to say that there are no standards of conduct for the negotiation process. Some conduct such as fraud, coercion, duress, and undue influence exceeds what is permissible. Unless such conduct has been present, neither party can claim that the process is unfair. The fairness claim will arise out of the negotiated agreement. The agreement may be challenged based on how it was negotiated.

McLean v. Village of Sleepy Hollow
United States District Court, S.D. New York
166 F.Supp.2d 898 (2001)

MEMORANDUM DECISION AND ORDER DENYING PLAINTIFF'S MOTION TO ENFORCE SETTLEMENT

MCMAHON, District Judge.

Plaintiff Gary McLean was for some time a part-time Buildings Code Enforcement Officer in the Village of Sleepy Hollow (formerly North Tarrytown), New York. Shortly after a new mayor took office in 1999, McLean lost that position. He sued the Village under 42 U.S.C. § 1983, contending that he had been fired in retaliation for his vocal support of the previous administration.

In March 2000, the Village agreed to settle the case by consenting to reinstate McLean, pay him back pay in the full amount he had lost during the period he was unemployed, and pay his attorney's fees—in other words, all the relief he would have been entitled to had he prevailed in the action. Settlement documents memorializing the deal were signed, and the Court "so ordered" the Stipulation and Order of Settlement and Discontinuance on April 3, 2000. That document contained the following provision: "IT IS FURTHER AGREED that the plaintiff will be re-employed by the Village of Sleepy Hollow at the annual salary of $10,000 per annum as a part-time Code Enforcement Officer subject to all terms and conditions of employment attendant to that position." At its meeting on June 13, 2000, the Village Board voted to reinstate plaintiff. McLean was notified that he could return to work by letter dated June 14, 2000.

At some point prior to the settlement's being reached, but no later than January 2000, the new Mayor of Sleepy Hollow began a review of Village practices regarding part-time workers. This review culminated in the naming of one Robert Stilowski (who had replaced McLean when he was fired) to fill the newly-created position of Director of Fire and Life Safety. On May 24, 2000, the Mayor endorsed Srilowski's May 24, 2000 recommendation that Building Code Inspectors be required to work between the hours of 9 A.M. and 12 P.M. Mondays through Fridays. Prior to that time, part-time employees (like McLean) could work whenever they wished. McLean, a master plumber who held a full-time job between the hours of 7:30 A.M. and 3:30 P.M., had always performed his duties in the evening and on weekends. The possibility of a new policy's being adopted was not mentioned to McLean during the settlement negotiations.

When McLean called Stilowski to set his schedule, he learned of the new policy. Understandably, he was unable to work between the hours of 9 and 12 on weekdays, as compliance with that schedule would require him to give up his full-time job. The Village offered McLean the option of working any three successive hours between 8:30 A.M. and 4:30 P.M. on weekdays, but this accommodation did not solve the plaintiff's problem. So he never started back on the job as contemplated by the settlement.

Because he did not report for work "as scheduled," the Village commenced disciplinary proceedings against McLean in September 2000.[1] A hearing officer found that

---

[1] The Village could not simply fire McLean because of his civil service status.

(continued)

the Village had acted within its authority by changing McLean's work schedule, and recommended that McLean be fired for failing to report for work. On April 10, 2001, the Village Board adopted the hearing officer's findings and recommendations, and McLean was officially terminated. McLean's appeal from that determination, brought pursuant to C.P.L.R. Article 78, is currently *sub judice* in the Westchester County Supreme Court.

On July 12, 2001, McLean filed a motion to enforce the settlement in this Court. He argues that he would never have settled the case if he had known that he would have to give up his full-time job in order to go back to work as a Building Code Examiner (a proposition that seems indisputable, and that the Village does not dispute). He contends that the use of the phrase "subject to all the terms and conditions of employment attendant to that position" in the Stipulation and Order means that the Village had to reemploy him on the terms that were in effect at the time he agreed to settle the case. And he alleges that the Village's subsequent adoption of the new "policy" supposedly affecting all part-time employees was a sham that was specifically designed to keep him from resuming his job—a conclusion he buttresses by pointing to other Village employees who perform their duties on nights and weekends.

The Village contends that there is nothing for this Court to enforce. It notes that, as a matter of law, a municipality enjoys relatively unfettered discretion in setting the working hours of its employees. *Ostaseki v. Board of Trustees*, 119 Misc.2d 113, 118, 462 N.Y.S.2d 564, 568 (Sup. Ct. Nassau Co. 1983), *aff'd*, 111 A.D.2d 239, 489 N.Y.S.2d 273 (2d Dep't. 1985); *Maineri v. Syosset Central School District*, 276 A.D.2d 793 (2d Dep't. 2000). It admits that certain employees work after hours or on weekends but contends that they are doing so (1) because they are performing extra duties in addition to their regular employment; or (2) because they are doing work that must be done after hours or on weekends (garbage pick-up in parks, for example). It argues that the language of the Stipulation and Order does not bind the Village to maintain the terms and conditions of McLean's employment as they were in April 2000. And it observes that this matter is more properly determined by

the Supreme Court in the Article 78 appeal from the hearing officer's determination that the Village's position is correct.

This situation is extremely unfortunate. Mr. McLean certainly has not gotten what he thought he was getting out of the settlement to which he agreed. However, I agree with the Village that his motion must be denied.

That the Court has subject matter jurisdiction to enforce the settlement is clear. A federal court has jurisdiction to enforce a settlement agreement if the dismissal order specifically reserves such authority or if the order embodies the terms of the settlement. *Scelsa v. City University of New York*, 76 F.3d 37, 40 (2d Cir. 1996) (citing *Kokkonen v. Guardian Life Ins. Co.*, 511 U.S. 375, 381, 114 S.Ct. 1673, 1677 (1994)). Here, the settlement terms were incorporated into a stipulation that was so-ordered by this Court, thus giving rise to jurisdiction. *Thanning v. Nassau County Medical Examiner's Office*, 187 F.R.D. 69, 71 (E.D.N.Y. 1999).

In this case, however, subject matter jurisdiction is only the first hurdle to adjudication. Plaintiff participated in a civil service disciplinary hearing, where he litigated and lost the issue of the Village's right to dismiss him in view of the settlement agreement. That administrative judgment is currently on appeal in an Article 78 proceeding. Whether the hearing examiner's finding against McLean precludes him from obtaining in this court a different interpretation of the meaning of the relevant language in the settlement Stipulation is a complicated question.

Ordinarily, any decision by the New York State Supreme Court in the Article 78 proceeding would be entitled to preclusive effect under the Full Faith & Credit Clause, regardless of whether the Supreme Court ruled on questions of fact or of law. *Leather v. Eyck*, 180 F.3d 420, 424 (2d Cir. 1999). There is at present no such decision from the State Supreme Court. There is only the administrative determination. Whether the hearing officer's unreviewed findings are entitled to preclusive effect depends on whether they constitute findings of fact (where preclusive effect is accorded, *see University of Tennessee v. Elliott*, 478 U.S. 788, 106 S.Ct. 3220 (1986) and

(continued)

Doe v. Pfrommer, 148 F.3d 73, 79 (2d Cir.1998)) or of law (an issue on which the Circuits are split and on which the Second Circuit has yet to speak).[2] Further complicating the issue is the fact that the application before me involves a court's power to enforce the terms of its own decree. Whether blind application of the usual rules of issue preclusion, whatever they be, is appropriate in such a situation presents its own fascinating set of issues (although McLean did elect to go forward with the hearing rather than come to this Court for relief).

But I do not need to decide any of these questions. Assuming, without deciding, that plaintiff is entitled to relitigate the meaning of the settlement agreement before me, I reach the same conclusion as the hearing officer.

[2]The Ninth Circuit has held that unreviewed administrative adjudications are entitled to collateral estoppel effect on questions of law as well as questions of fact. *Eilrich v. Remas*, 839 F.2d 630, 632–33 (9th Cir. 1988). The Third, Fourth, Eighth and Eleventh Circuits have gone the other way. *Edmundson v. Borough of Kennett Square*, 4 F.3d 186, 192–93 (3rd Cir. 1993); *Dionne v. Mayor and City Council of Baltimore*, 40 F.3d 677, 685 (4th Cir. 1994); *Peery v. Brakke*, 826 F.2d 740 (8th Cir. 1987); *Gjellum v. City of Birmingham*, 820 F.2d 1056 (11th Cir. 1987). Our own Court of Appeals has expressly refused to reach this issue in the past (see most recently *Doe*, 148 F.3d at 80), but there is currently pending before the Second Circuit a case that raises the question. (*See Pappas v. Giuliani*, No. 00-0487, to be argued Nov. 16, 2001).

McLean's motion turns on the construction of a contract, which, in the absence of some ambiguity, presents only a question of law. *Ark Bryant Park Corp. v. Bryant Park Restoration Corp.*, 730 N.Y.S.2d 48 (1st Dep't. 2001) ("[I]nterpretation of an unambiguous contract is a question of law for the court."). I find no ambiguity in the contract. Thus, to decide whether the hearing officer's findings are preclusive, I would have to stake out a position on the issue that is currently on appeal in *Pappas*. Ordinarily I would not hesitate to develop a point of view on the issue and add it to the mix of opinion available to the Court of Appeals. However, by sheer coincidence, I am sitting by designation on the *Pappas* panel. I am, therefore, uncomfortable about reaching this issue at this time. Fortunately, I can dispose of the motion without addressing it.

McLean acknowledges that the Village does indeed have the right to set the terms and conditions (including the hours) of employment for its employees. The Village is of course free to waive its rights in this regard, but any such waiver must be apparent from the face of the contract between McLean and Sleepy Hollow. The terms of the Stipulation and Order are artless (at least from McLean's perspective), but the relevant sentence is not ambiguous and cannot be read as a waiver by the Village of its right to alter the terms and conditions of its employees' jobs. The Stipulation does not require the Village to maintain the terms and conditions of McLean's employment as they were at the time the settlement was negotiated. It says only that McLean will be reemployed on the terms and conditions that are "attendant to his position." While the words "from time to time" do not appear after the word "position," they do not have to, because the usual rule is that job terms can be changed. McLean's reading of the Stipulation, not the Village's, is the one that departs from the usual rule; thus McLean's reading cannot be adopted unless it is clearly spelled out in the contract. It is not. End of discussion.

This leads to a harsh result. McLean contends that he would never have settled the case if he had known, in the Spring of last year, that the rules for part-time employees were about to change in Sleepy Hollow. I am sure that is correct. But there is nothing in the language of the Stipulation and Order, and nothing in the record before me, from which I can infer that plaintiff ever explicitly conditioned his acceptance of a settlement on his continued ability to work nights and weekends. Indeed, I very much doubt that it ever occurred to McLean or to his lawyer that the rules might change. However, the fact that plaintiff and his counsel assumed that everything would go back to the way it was (i.e., that they *subjectively intended* the settlement would restore the status quo ante) is insufficient to bind the Village when that subjective intention is not clear from the *objective manifestation* of McLean's intent—the words of the Stipulation and Order. *See Brown Bros. Elec. Contrs. v. Beam Constr. Corp.*, 41 N.Y.2d 397, 399, 393 N.Y.2d 350 (1977) (stating that the "existence of a binding

(continued)

contract is not dependent on the subjective intent of either [party]," but rather on "the objective manifestations of the intent of the parties as gathered by their expressed words and deeds."); *Cutter v. Peterson*, 203 A.D.2d 812, 611 N.Y.S.2d 368 (3d Dep't. 1994).

While I cannot grant the motion to enforce the settlement, there remains an issue that I raised with counsel at conference—whether, in view of the foregoing, McLean wishes (or is able) either to make a motion or commence an action to set aside the settlement on the ground that he was fraudulently induced to enter into it. The papers opposing the instant motion were filed in August 2001. To those papers the Village attached documents from which it is possible to infer that Village officials might well have known, prior to offering McLean his job back, that the terms and conditions of part-time employment in Sleepy Hollow would change in a way unfavorable to McLean. McLean had no way of knowing about these documents prior to the time they were presented to this Court; counsel for McLean represents, and the Village does not deny, that they were not produced to the hearing examiner at the disciplinary hearing which is currently on appeal in the State Supreme Court. I do not mean to suggest that the Village improperly concealed documents at the disciplinary hearing; these documents were undoubtedly not material to the Village's case.

However, the fact remains that McLean's counsel had no good faith basis, until August of this year, to assert that the Village withheld material information about the terms and conditions of McLean's job from him during the settlement negotiations. My review of the transcript of the hearing reveals that this issue was not actually litigated, so it cannot be precluded. Of course, if the settlement were fraudulently induced, it would, at McLean's option, be voidable.

It is not for the Court to direct McLean's next move, if indeed there is to be another move in this Court. Setting aside the settlement may not be a palatable option for plaintiff, since he would have to tender back the financial benefits he has already accepted. McLean's desire to follow such a course may be affected by the outcome of the Article 78 proceeding. And it is not clear whether such a motion, even if made immediately, would be timely—if, indeed, Fed. R. Civ. P. 60(b)(3) applies to such a motion at all (a question that depends on whether the Stipulation and Order are a "judgment" within the meaning of Fed. R. Civ. P. 54(a))—or whether McLean has grounds to commence an independent action in reliance on the third sentence of Rule 60(b). These matters are best left to plaintiff and his counsel.

The motion to enforce the settlement is denied. This constitutes the decision and order of the Court.

The Advantages and Disadvantages of Negotiation as a Dispute Resolution Process

Negotiation requires active participation by both parties. They must agree to negotiate. This agreement to negotiate may be the result of an active decision to negotiate ("Let's negotiate") or negotiations may just happen. The parties often begin substantive discussions without discussing whether they will begin discussions. Without the cooperation of both parties, there can be no negotiation.

The decision whether to negotiate is based on a party's needs and interests and not on the law. The parties weigh the gains attributable through negotiation against the hypothetical gains that another process might produce. What does a party gain by selecting negotiation as the method of dispute resolution?

Negotiation as a method of dispute resolution offers the parties complete flexibility. They can negotiate themselves or through their attorneys. They can begin when they want to begin. If they are so minded, negotiations may begin immediately and the dispute can be resolved by the end of the process. The parties can establish their own timetable and are not bound by the artificial constraints established by someone else. The parties by their conduct establish their own procedural and substantive rules for the negotiation. The parties can be creative in formulating a solution, and their creativity is not limited by legal principles. A negotiated agreement generally accommodates at least some of the interests of both parties. Negotiating an agreement will guarantee that transaction costs will be dramatically reduced since a negotiated solution will reduce or eliminate the need for discovery and may eliminate filing fees.

The parties are not required to reach an agreement. When a party believes that his or her interests are not being addressed, he or she may end the negotiation and proceed to another form of dispute resolution. Continuing the dispute will mean that he or she will be required to expend additional personal time on this dispute and incur the costs associated with the newly selected process. Spending this time and money to seek an uncertain gain may have greater value to the party than the certain gain that the negotiation could produce.

When selecting negotiation, the parties weigh the need to resolve the dispute now against what might happen if the dispute is resolved later. The parties may have a need to resolve the dispute now so they can put the problem behind them and move on. Delaying the resolution of the dispute does not guarantee that the dispute will be resolved more favorably to the party who decides against negotiation.

Control of the process and the outcome may be very important to a party. If a party elects to negotiate and the other party agrees, it is the parties who control their own destinies. No neutral third party must acquiesce or consent to the decision.

The parties selecting negotiation control not only the process but also the outcome, and the outcome is known when the process has been completed. The process is private with no public airing of the dispute. Unless a party later decides to breach the negotiated agreement, the resolution of the dispute is final.

Parties who select negotiation as their method of dispute resolution do not forgo the opportunity to pursue the dispute if the negotiation does not produce an agreement. The successful pursuit of the dispute by another dispute resolution process may yield a monetary gain and a psychological victory. The opportunity to pursue the dispute, however, does not come without costs and risks. Transaction costs (time, money, psychological trauma) accumulate and worse yet, the end result may not be favorable. Even when a successful outcome is achieved, the transaction costs must be factored into the outcome to produce a net gain. Figure 6-3 summarizes negotiation as a dispute resolution process.

AVAILABILITY	always available
PROCESS SELECTION	by both parties the parties control the scheduling
THE PARTICIPANTS	both parties (or their representatives)
PREPARATION	requires minimal fact gathering, although negotiation may occur without adequate information
THE PROCESS	takes place in a private setting informal provides an opportunity to discuss feelings, perception of the dispute, interests, and array of settlement options preserves the privacy of records and documents
FAIRNESS	the parties may not have equal power and therefore one party may take advantage of the other
THE OUTCOME	determined by the parties based on the parties' needs and interests and less on the law may encourage creative solutions a negotiated agreement produces immediate results and resolves the dispute immediately eliminates all uncertainties as to outcome agreement may be based on inadequate information negotiated agreement is enforceable as a contract and the disputing parties will more than likely fulfill their promises the parties may not be able to agree; as a result, there will be no negotiated agreement
COSTS	inexpensive process, although may require some technical or legal expertise reduces discovery and discovery costs through early resolution saves litigation and appeal costs if an agreement is reached saves or reduces attorney's fees
PRECEDENTIAL VALUE	establishes no binding precedent, although nonbinding precedent by performance may be created between the parties
IMPACT ON FUTURE RELATIONSHIP	may encourage future cooperation or reduce confrontation between the parties

FIGURE 6-3   Negotiation

Key Terms and Phrases

interest-based negotiation
negotiation
position-based negotiation

Review Questions

True/False Questions

1. T   F   In negotiation, the jury is the finder of fact and the judge is the finder of law.
2. T   F   In negotiation, the court requires the parties be represented by legal counsel.

3. T F In negotiation, the outcome is more based on the needs and interests of the parties rather than the law.
4. T F In negotiation, the parties negotiate the rules.
5. T F Position-based negotiation leads to a win/win solution.
6. T F Negotiations may be conducted before or after a complaint is filed with the court.
7. T F Negotiation may take place over a period of time and may start and stop.
8. T F Negotiations may involve a dispute or a problem that is not a dispute.
9. T F An effective negotiation is based on preparation.
10. T F Negotiation is consensual and can be terminated by either party at any time.
11. T F A negotiated agreement is enforceable as a contract.
12. T F During a negotiation, a dominant party may take advantage of a weaker party through psychological gamesmanship.
13. T F As a general rule, a party need not negotiate in good faith, although a court may find a contract unenforceable if, at the time of contract formation, one of the parties took an unconscionable advantage over the other, committed fraud or duress, or misrepresented material facts.
14. T F Negotiation gives the parties control over the outcome.

Fill-in-the-Blank Questions

1. _____ Another name for a bargained-for exchange.
2. _____ The type of negotiation where the parties distribute a fixed pie.
3. _____ The type of negotiation where the parties attempt to expand the pie.
4. _____ The overlap area in a position-based negotiation between the settlement range of one party and the settlement range of the other.
5. _____ The substantive rule of contract law that relates to which terms are and which terms are not in the contract.
6. _____ One reason why a court will not enforce a negotiated agreement.

Multiple-Choice Questions

1. Which of the following always participate in negotiation as a dispute resolution process:
    (a) the aggrieved party
    (b) the other party to the dispute
    (c) a neutral third party
    (d) a jury
    (e) the attorney for the aggrieved party

2. Negotiation is classified as:
   (a) unilateral action in dispute resolution
   (b) bilateral action in dispute resolution
   (c) third-party evaluation as a prelude to dispute resolution
   (d) third-party assistance in dispute resolution
   (e) third-party adjudication in dispute resolution

3. Identify the settlement zone in the following situation.
   Kelly was in the market for a new car when she visited the showroom of Friendly Motors. She saw a car that she liked that had a sticker price of $18,900. Kelly had done her homework before she visited Friendly Motors and determined that she could only pay $2,000 down and $300 to $350 a month for three years (although she would be willing to pay over four years). Friendly expects to sell its vehicles for about 5 percent below the sticker price ($17,955), although they could go down another 5 percent off the sticker price ($17,010).
   (a) between $14,600 and $18,900
   (b) between $16,400 and $18,900
   (c) between $17,010 and $17,955
   (d) between $17,010 and $18,800
   (e) between $14,600 and $17,955

Short-Answer Questions

1. Brenda McTavish was involved in an automobile accident with Jerry Kim. Brenda suffered extensive injuries and was partially paralyzed. Clearly the accident was Jerry's fault. Brenda would like a quick resolution and payment because she cannot work, has a family to support, and has medical bills to pay. The Gotham Insurance Company, Jerry's insurer and the party who will ultimately pay, would like the process to be as slow as possible.

   Gotham has offered Brenda $100,000. Brenda believes her injuries are worth $1,000,000.

   Should Brenda accept Gotham's settlement offer? Why?

2. The Great Northwest Cannery Company entered into an installment contract with the Quality Can Company for all the cans that Great Northwest would need in order to process this year's salmon harvest. The contract provided that shipments would be weekly and the quantity would fluctuate depending on Great Northwest's order. An order placed on Monday would be delivered the following Monday.

   When Great Northwest received its first shipment, it noticed that 12 percent of the cans were dented and could not be used. It is not unusual in the trade for 5 to 8 percent of shipped cans to be dented. Should Great Northwest select inaction (wait and see what happens with the next shipment), acquiescence (pay for the shipment), self-help (return the shipment and cancel the contract), or negotiation (speak with Quality about the problem and possibly seek replacement cans or a price adjustment)?

   Can you think of other possible solutions?

Since the law is the backdrop for all methods of dispute resolution, you have researched the problem and have discovered the following:

(a) Article 2 of the Uniform Commercial Code applies to the problem since the sale of cans is a sale of goods.

(b) The contract is an installment contract under UCC § 2-612(1) since delivery was to be in separate lots.

(c) The first shipment cannot be rejected under UCC §§ 2-612(2) and (3) since it does substantially impair the value of the shipment and does not substantially impair the value of the contract.

(d) UCC § 2-507 provides an opportunity for the seller to cure a defective shipment.

(e) UCC § 2-717 provides the buyer with an opportunity to deduct its damages from the price owed under the contract.

(f) UCC § 2-711(1)(a) permits the buyer to buy substitute goods.

(g) UCC § 2-714(1) authorizes the recovery of damages for the nonconformity.

3. Explain how the parol evidence rule plays a role in a negotiation.

4. Describe the difference between position-based negotiation and interest-based negotiation.

5. Using Figure 6-1, Work Sheet for Dissecting the Content of a Negotiation, create a plan for the following factual situation. The plan is being created for Geraldine Green, a professional entertainer.

   Geraldine Green went to Dr. O'Connor, a plastic surgeon, who promised to improve the looks of her nose. Geraldine's nose had been straight, but long and prominent. Dr. O'Connor undertook by two operations to reduce its prominence and to shorten it, thus making it more pleasing in relation to Geraldine's other features. Geraldine was obliged to undergo three operations, and her appearance was worsened. Geraldine's nose now has a concave line to about the midpoint, at which it became bulbous; viewed frontally, the nose from bridge to midpoint is flattened and broadened, and the two sides of the tip have lost symmetry. This configuration evidently could not be improved by further surgery.

   Payments by Geraldine covering the doctor's fee and hospital expenses were $5,622.65. She complains of pain and suffering during the three operations and for a substantial recovery period after the operations. She also complains of continuing mental distress.

6. Jackie Johnson had been working for the Big Bread Bakery for three years earning $10 an hour. Shortly before Christmas, Jackie wants to speak with Sarah Murphy, the CEO at Big Bread, to ask for a raise to $11 a hour.

   The fact that Jackie will be asking Sarah for a raise is a negotiation. Sarah's position as CEO has dictated some of the ground rules for the negotiation. One is that the employee must meet with the CEO at the place designated by the CEO. Thus the relative positions of the two employees within the corporation dictate where the negotiations will take place.

   What impact does the implicit rule as to place in this example have on a negotiation? Does the CEO gain a home court advantage by holding the negotiations, were the negotiation to take place?

   In addition to the implicit rule dictating the place of the negotiation, are there other implicit rules in this example?

7. Several months ago, Jerome Smith was involved in an automobile accident with Rachel O'Roark. The accident happened at 2:30 A.M., and Jerome had been drinking at a local tavern. Rachel, a registered nurse, had just finished her shift at a nearby hospital. The roads were slick due to a thundershower that had recently passed through the area. Although Jerome was uninjured, Rachel received a dislocated shoulder that could impact her work as a nurse.

Jerome did not want the civil side of the accident to be litigated. He had the money to make Rachel a nice settlement. When Jerome telephoned Rachel, she refused to talk to him. He then hired Cynthia Chang to represent him.

Cynthia telephoned Rachel to try to set up a meeting. Rachel informed Cynthia that she had turned her case over to Roland White, an attorney.

Cynthia then telephoned Roland. His secretary informed Cynthia that Roland was "out of the office" and would not be back for several days. Cynthia left a message for Roland to call her about the O'Roark/Smith case. A week passed and no call from Roland. Another week passed and no call from Roland. Cynthia called again and this time was able to speak with Roland who informed her that he was in the middle of a big trial and could not meet with her for another three weeks. Roland proposed a time and place for the meeting and Cynthia agreed.

What rules of negotiation are being negotiated? Are the rules being explicitly or implicitly negotiated?

What impact can these rules have on the outcome of the negotiation?

When did the negotiation begin?

Role-Play Exercises

Role-Play Exercise 6-1   Drug Testing

The Players: Several members of the school board
Several union officials

Before beginning your negotiation, use Figure 6-1, Work Sheet for Dissecting the Content of a Negotiation, to create your negotiation plan. Then negotiate the following. If you negotiate an agreement, it should be in writing.

The Buena Vista School Board has been concerned about the drug problem in their school system. Recently, a teacher at one of the high schools was arrested and charged with selling cocaine to students. Naturally, the schools in the district received bad press, and the story even made national news. The board would like to impose a mandatory drug testing program for all teachers, and they would like to impose it now.

The teachers at the school system are members of a union. The union opposed mandatory drug testing of teachers.

The board is concerned with what the teachers' union might do if they impose a mandatory drug testing program, at least without first speaking with the union's representatives. A meeting has been arranged between representatives from the board and representatives from the Union.

Before the negotiations begin, it is important for each side to plan its strategy. As a part of your preparation, complete the Work Sheet for Dissecting the Content of a Negotiation,

Figure 6-1. You may also find it helpful to check the Web and Westlaw or Lexis for information on drug testing of teachers in public schools.

Once both parties have completed their preparation, negotiate the drug testing issue.

Role-Play Exercise 6-2   Sports Law

The Players: Agent for Darrell James, a pitcher for a major league baseball team
The general manager for the baseball team

Before beginning your negotiation, use Figure 6-1, Work Sheet for Dissecting the Content of a Negotiation, to create your negotiation plan. Then negotiate the following. If you negotiate an agreement, it should be in writing.

Darrell James is a pitcher for a major league baseball team. The team is owned by a brewing company and is governed by the rules of major league baseball.

Darrell, 28 years old, has played in the major leagues for six years and will be in the fifth year of his five-year contract. Because of the length of his service, he will become a free agent at the end of this baseball season and is eligible for baseball arbitration.

Darrell, a relief pitcher for the team, specializes in coming into the game in the eighth or ninth inning and closing out the game. This season he has pitched in 89 games. His pitching statistics over the course of his major league career are:

Season	G	W	L	Saves	ERA
1st	20	3	1	0	5.81
2d	26	1	3	0	6.15
3d	78	3	6	1	2.76
4th	82	7	4	0	3.75
5th	83	1	5	14	3.50
6th	89	3	3	9	1.80
Career total	378	18	22	24	3.41

His record indicates that he is successful when entering the game with runners on base, can pitch for one or two innings and keep the team in the game, and has a very good strike out-to-walk ratio. Darrell is moody, is sometimes not a team player, dyes his hair various colors as his mood swings, and cannot keep control of his tongue when speaking with the press. Recently Darrell was arrested in a domestic dispute and pleaded no contest. The fans either love or hate him. To say the least, Darrell is a good pitcher but flamboyant.

Darrell has been making $1,750,000 a year for the past five years. He would like to make $3,000,000 next year and would like a three-year contract. He may have some marketability although not at the $3,000,000 figure. The general manager has indicated that the team would pay him $2,000,000 next year and would not give him a three-year contract.

Before the negotiations begin, it is important for each side to plan its strategy. As a part of your preparation, complete the Work Sheet for Dissecting the Content of a Negotiation, Figure 6-1. You may also find it helpful to check the Major League Baseball website: *http://www.mlb.com*. You may find other websites helpful as well.

Once both parties have completed their preparation, negotiate a new contract for Darrell.

Role-Play Exercise 6-3   Racial Discrimination

Jessie Jefferson, a probationary employee, was discharged by the Big Sky Soup Company. He filed an EEOC complaint.

The Players: Mr. Jefferson's attorney
               A vice president for Big Sky

Before beginning your negotiation, use Figure 6-1, Work Sheet for Dissecting the Content of a Negotiation, to create your negotiation plan. Then negotiate the following. If you negotiate an agreement, it should be in writing.

The parties are seeking a negotiated settlement to this dispute. The vice president has settlement authority and Mr. Jefferson's attorney has been given the authority to negotiate, but the final agreement must be approved by the client.

The Big Sky Soup Company manufactures and distributes canned soup and related food products. Two organizational units at Big Sky's Springfield plant where Jessie Jefferson worked are pertinent to this case: (1) the production area where soups are manufactured, run by Manager of Production Walter Ward, a white; and (2) the warehouse area where finished product is stored and sorted for shipment, run by Manager Richard Brown, a white.

JEFFERSON'S DEPOSITION
1. I am black and 38 years old. I was hired by Big Sky on June 18, of last year, as an hourly paid laborer assigned to the warehouse under the supervision of Otis Newsome, also black.
2. Although I had previously worked for Big Sky for seven years, I had voluntarily terminated my employment after being laid off for six months.
3. I understood when I was rehired that I would be a probationary employee, and probationary employees work for Big Sky on a trial basis.
4. To permit uninterrupted production each day, employees take their breaks (two each day) and lunch in a staggered manner so "relief" persons may fill in for them.
5. If an employee returns late from a break or lunch, the relief person is delayed in relieving the next individual scheduled to leave production, and all later breaks and lunches are delayed in a kind of domino effect.
6. During my initial employment with Big Sky, I overstayed my breaks at least two times and was given written warnings.
7. I remember working for Carson during my earlier employment with Big Sky.
8. Although I was assigned to work for Newsome in the warehouse when I was rehired by Big Sky, I was temporarily reassigned to various production departments when the need arose.
9. One production department to which I was transferred 10 to 15 times was Department 3-C ("Filling"), where I was under the supervision of Carson as well as Group Leader James Watson, a black.
10. On the first day that I worked in Department 3-C, Carson said to me, "How are you?" I said, "Pretty good. How about yourself?" He then shook my hand. He asked, "What are you doing back in the plant?" I replied, "I came back in the plant, you know, to work." While he was still holding my hand, he said, "Glad to have you back, but if you don't watch yourself, and watch your lunch and breaks, I am going to get rid of all you blacks that were here before, just as I got rid of your friend Mr. Spoon."

11. Later that same day I told Watson what Carson had said, but Watson just laughed.

12. I also told Newsome, in the presence of Shop Steward Miller, what Carson had said but Newsome simply smiled and went back to his office. Miller advised me to watch my step.

13. When I returned from my first break that day, Carson told me, in the presence of Watson (who was laughing) and the relief person, "Rose," that I was 10 minutes late. I told him I was early rather than late and Rose agreed that I was early. Carson then walked away.

14. Carson claims that I was back late from lunch on that first day, but I was back early and he never spoke to me about that.

15. I do remember Carson falsely accusing me of returning late from lunch on another day in June.

16. I complained to Newsome three or four times that Carson was picking on me.

17. Carson harassed me in other ways as well. He would come by and like if the machine is down that I am working on, he would pick the nastiest or the worst thing it is to do and he'd point me out to do it. And he and Watson would stand back and laugh while I would do it. And I'd do it.

18. I complained to the union steward about Carson harassing me and I asked the steward: "Please ask Mr. Carson what the problem is? Why he's harassing me all the time." The steward said there as nothing he could do. I was a probationary employee and he was allowed to do that.

19. On July 31 of last year, I was assigned to work in Department 3-A ("Blending") under Supervisor Jack Wright, a white.

20. I was told by both Newsome and Miller that Carson "had set down the order for me to be terminated."

21. I filed a grievance with the union. On August 7 of last year, the Union requested that I be reinstated because the union felt the dismissal was unjust.

22. On May 29 of the next year, I filed a charge of discrimination with the Equal Employment Opportunity Commission (EEOC) alleging Big Sky has discriminated against me by harassing me with warnings and terminating me because of my race. The EEOC action is still pending.

BECHTOL'S DEPOSITION

1. I am Lew Bechtol. I am manager of human resources at Big Sky.

2. For the past two years there have been between 660 and 790 Big Sky employees.

3. About 85 to 88 percent of the hourly paid production and maintenance employees hired by Big Sky between August four years ago and August of last year (179, or 97.2 percent of whom were black), were classified as probationary employees during their first 50 working days.

4. Probationary employees are subject to dismissal without step-by-step progressive discipline if their work is unsatisfactory.

5. Like all Big Sky employees, probationary employees are required to adhere to the "Big Sky Soup Company Rules."

6. Jefferson was aware of Rule 4.

7. Following Jefferson's termination, I conducted my customary investigation of the circumstances surrounding the termination. I spoke with Wright, Newsome, and Carson and had Carson prepare a written report concerning Jefferson's failure to return from breaks on time.

8. After Jefferson's termination, a white employee was hired to replace Jefferson. Five of the seven new Big Sky employees hired in August of last year were white.

9. There have been complaints before from other workers concerning whether Carson was a racist, but the charges were never proven.

BROWN'S DEPOSITION

1. I am Richard Brown. I am the manager of the warehouse at Big Sky and I am white.

2. One of my supervisors is Otis Newsome.

3. On May 31, I received a telephone call from Ward telling me that Jefferson had overstayed his lunch that day and that he had evidence of his having done so twice before. Ward strongly recommended that Jefferson be terminated. I told Ward that I "wholeheartedly agreed" and I took steps to effectuate the termination. I did not ask Ward about the "evidence" of prior tardiness because, having worked with Ward for six years, I knew Ward to be very thorough in his investigation of employee relation–type activities, and I had total confidence in his judgment. I never saw any written documentation of Jefferson's tardiness.

4. In carrying out the termination, I followed my standard procedure of advising both the personnel manager and the employee's supervisor, in this case Newsome, of my termination decision.

5. On May 31, Newsome gave me Jefferson's dismissal notice which I initialed and returned to Newsome.

CARSON'S DEPOSITION

1. I am a supervisor and I am white.

2. I supervised Jefferson when he previously worked for Big Sky.

3. When he worked for me then, I orally counseled him two or three times for overstaying breaks.

4. When Jefferson was rehired by Big Sky, he was temporarily assigned to my department.

5. I was watching the clock the first day Jefferson worked in my department and Jefferson was not only 5 minutes late returning from his break, but he was also 10 minutes late returning from lunch. On both occasions I confronted Jefferson about his tardiness.

6. Jefferson claims that I picked on him, but that was all in his imagination. I never picked on Jefferson.

7. I remember orally advising Newsome each time Jefferson was late.

8. I had nothing to do with the decision to terminate Jefferson. I did not even know of the termination until one week later.

NEWSOME'S DEPOSITION

1. I am Otis Newsome, and I am a supervisor in the warehouse. I am black.

2. Although Big Sky's department heads continuously consult one another about the performance of probationary employees, it was my responsibility, as Jefferson's supervisor, to evaluate Jefferson and make a recommendation whether he should be a permanent hire.

3. I confronted Jefferson about Carson's reports of tardiness and Jefferson simply said "okay" without denying the truth of the reports.

4. On July 31, I prepared Jefferson's dismissal notice and took it to Brown for his initials. On August 1, I gave Jefferson his dismissal notice.

WRIGHT'S DEPOSITION

1. I am Jack Wright. I am the supervisor for Department 3-A, otherwise known as "blending." I am white.
2. On July 31, Mr. Jefferson was temporarily assigned to work in my department.
3. On July 31st, Jefferson requested a gate pass from me so he could leave the premises during lunch. His gate pass was time-stamped at the entrance to the plant when he left and when he returned. Later in the day the plant's entrance guard sent Jefferson's gate pass to Ward, who in turn called me into his office to advise me that Jefferson had returned from lunch two minutes late.
4. While I was in Ward's office, Ward telephoned Brown and told him Jefferson had overstayed his lunch that day and there was evidence of his having done so twice before. Ward strongly recommended Jefferson be terminated.
5. I socialize with Carson from time to time, and I do not believe him to be a racist. Carson does not have a reputation among blacks at Big Sky as being a racist.

BIG SKY SOUP COMPANY RULES

Rule 4. Watch your break and lunch times. 12 minutes for breaks and 1/2 hour for lunch.

JEFFERSON'S DISMISSAL NOTICE

Reason for Dismissal: Overstaying lunch or break period. Excessive (Rule #4)

EEOC COMPLAINT

Jefferson did not assert that Brown or Ward terminated him because of his race or even that they suspected Carson had falsely accused Jefferson of tardiness because of his race. Jefferson did contend that Carson, because Jefferson is black, intentionally caused Brown and Ward to terminate him by creating a record of tardiness on which they relied in making the termination decision.

Big Sky response to the EEOC complaint asserted:

1. Ward and Brown (not Carson) made the decision to terminate Jefferson. It is therefore irrelevant whether Carson intended to discriminate on the basis of race, so long as Ward and Brown did not.
2. Jefferson has not, in any event, met his burden of establishing a prima facie case of racial discrimination by Carson.
3. No evidence suggests Big Sky's articulated reason for terminating Jefferson is a pretext for racial discrimination.

PART FOUR

INTRODUCTION

Third-Party Evaluation as a Prelude to Dispute Resolution

INTRODUCTION

Part IV explores the role of third-party evaluation as a prelude to dispute resolution. The evaluator may be a member of the bar as in the case of early neutral evaluation or a judge and mock jury as in the case of a summary jury trial.

In neither process is the dispute resolved by the disputing parties or by the neutral party. The evaluator or the judge and jury only provide the disputing parties with an objective evaluation of their dispute. Part IV consists of two brief chapters: Chapter 7, "Early Neutral Evaluation" and Chapter 8, "Summary Jury Trial."

CHAPTER 7

Early Neutral Evaluation

Early neutral evaluation (ENE) traces its origins back to 1985 and the United States District Court for the Northern District of California. There the court experimented with providing the disputing parties with an early evaluation of the case by a neutral third party. Unlike ombuds, private mediation, and court-sponsored mediation, early neutral evaluation is not designed to provide the parties with an opportunity to resolve their dispute. Early neutral evaluation is intended to accomplish these specific goals:

1. to force the parties to confront the merits of their own case and that of the other side;
2. to identify at an early stage of the litigation the facts and the law that were and were not in dispute;
3. to streamline discovery; and
4. to provide an objective assessment of the case.

As a result, early neutral evaluation could promote future discussion between the parties that may lead to resolution of the dispute.

The Early Neutral Evaluation Process

Early Neutral Evaluation (ENE)
A member of the bar who has experience in the substantive area of the dispute provides the parties and their attorneys with an early case assessment.

Early neutral evaluation takes the following general form. After the complaint has been filed with the clerk of the court, the parties and their attorneys attend an evaluation session with a court-appointed attorney who has expertise in the substantive area of the dispute or a judge who will not have trial responsibility for the case. At the session each side makes an oral presentation of the facts and law involved in the dispute. The neutral third party asks questions and seeks to help the parties identify areas of agreement and disagreement. The neutral third party evaluates the key issues involving liability and gives an opinion on the damage range.

ENE may be structured as a process independent of other processes or may be incorporated in a court-sponsored mediation. If incorporated in a mediation, the mediator (settlement judge), in private caucus, would give his or her opinion to the parties and their attorneys as to the strengths and weaknesses of the case and would forecast the outcome of the dispute. By providing this information, the mediator can coax the parties toward settlement. This style of mediation with early neutral evaluation is in marked contrast to the facilitative mediation where the mediator merely encourages the disputing parties to discuss their needs and interests and possible solutions.

Early neutral evaluation may be better suited to some types of cases than to others. For example, ENE is well suited to cases involving contractual issues, personal injury, wrongful termination, and certain types of commercial litigation such as those involving securities and antitrust laws and civil RICO. ENE is less suited to cases where a party is proceeding *pro se,* the principal relief is equitable in nature (e.g., injunction or specific performance), the law is unsettled, or public policy demands the issues be litigated and precedent established. ENE is also less suited to areas of law where the number of attorneys who practice in that area is relatively small so the pool of evaluators is correspondingly small, thus increasing the potential for conflicts of interest.

A number of federal district courts offer ENE as one of their ADR processes.

Example 7-1

The United States District Court for the Northern District of California offers early neutral evaluation. Visit the court's website through links at *www.adr.cand.uscourts.gov/adr* or *www.uscourts.gov.*

Problem 7-1
Check the homepage for The Federal Judiciary at *http://www.uscourts.gov* for links to all the federal district courts. Does the homepage of your federal district court state that it offers early neutral evaluation as one of its ADR processes?

The Advantages and Disadvantages of Early Neutral Evaluation as a Dispute Resolution Process

Early neutral evaluation, a confidential process, occurs early in the litigation process, thus expediting the pretrial and trial process by narrowing and clarifying the issues, streamlining discovery, and positioning the litigants for meaningful settlement discussion before litigation costs escalate. Unlike mediation that favors a discussion of "what makes good sense," early neutral evaluation tends to focus on the legal issues. Early neutral evaluation provides the parties and their attorneys with a reality check so they may more objectively evaluate the strengths and weaknesses of their case and encourage realistic settlement discussion. Figure 7-1 summarizes early neutral evaluation as a dispute resolution process.

AVAILABILITY	depends on the court (more a process found in federal district courts than in state trial courts)
PROCESS SELECTION	scheduled by the court if the case comes within the parameters of its ENE program
THE PARTICIPANTS	the parties, their attorneys, and the court-appointed evaluator
PREPARATION	scheduled shortly after a case is filed with the court some discovery is required so the parties and their attorneys understand the case
THE PROCESS	takes place in a private setting informal and structured by the evaluator, with each side giving an overview of its case to the evaluator confidential and preserves the privacy of the parties' records and documents
FAIRNESS	does not address the power imbalances that may exist between the parties or their attorneys
THE OUTCOME	allows the parties to control the outcome because the evaluator's comments are advisory only, thus encouraging subsequent creative resolutions not intended as a resolution process, but can stimulate the parties in subsequent settlement discussions
COSTS	requires some discovery costs saves further discovery and discovery costs if settlement is reached during subsequent settlement discussions saves the costs of a trial and appeal if a settlement can be reached during subsequent settlement discussions can reduce attorney's fees by streamlining the issues and discovery will add another layer of costs to the dispute resolution process if the process does not contribute to the resolution of the dispute through subsequent settlement discussions may provide low-cost discovery due to the discussion of the evidence
PRECEDENTIAL VALUE	establishes no binding precedent
IMPACT ON FUTURE RELATIONSHIP	may encourage future cooperation or reduce confrontation between the parties

FIGURE 7-1 Early Neutral Evaluation

Key Terms and Phrases

early neutral evaluation

Review Questions

True/False Questions

1. T   F   In early neutral evaluation, the jury is the finder of fact and the judge is the finder of law.

2. T   F   Early neutral evaluation is more of a case management tool than a dispute resolution process.

3. T   F   The parties can streamline issues and discovery at an early neutral evaluation.

4. T   F   Early neutral evaluation should be conducted by the judge who will try the case.

5. T   F   Early neutral evaluation is a court-sponsored program and occurs after the complaint has been filed and before trial.

6. T   F   Early neutral evaluation is generally held after discovery has been completed.

7. T   F   An early neutral evaluation program requires a pool of attorneys who have expertise in the areas of the cases assigned to the program.

8. T   F   Early neutral evaluation is confidential and preserves the confidentiality of private records.

9. T   F   Early neutral evaluation is another name for court-sponsored settlement conference.

10. T   F   Only certain types of cases are well suited for ENE.

Fill-in-the-Blank Questions

1. _____   Name four types of cases that are well suited for ENE.
   _____
   _____
   _____

2. _____   Name four types of cases that are not well suited
   _____   for ENE.
   _____
   _____

Multiple-Choice Questions

1. Which of the following actively participates in early neutral evaluation?
   (a) the aggrieved party
   (b) the other party to the dispute
   (c) a neutral third party
   (d) a jury
   (e) the attorney for the aggrieved party

2. Early neutral evaluation is classified as:
   (a) unilateral action in dispute resolution
   (b) bilateral action in dispute resolution
   (c) third-party evaluation as a prelude to dispute resolution
   (d) third-party assistance in dispute resolution
   (e) third-party adjudication in dispute resolution

Short-Answer Questions

1. Discuss the advantages and disadvantages of early neutral evaluation.
2. Why is early neutral evaluation primarily an ADR process found in federal rather than state trial courts?

CHAPTER 8

Summary Jury Trial

The summary jury trial was developed in 1980 by Judge Thomas D. Lambros, a federal judge for the Northern District of Ohio. He first used this process in a products liability case after all other attempts at settlement had been exhausted.

A summary jury trial is a judicially ordered settlement process that provides a no-risk, nonbinding method for the parties to obtain the evaluation of jurors on the merits of the case.

Summary Jury Trial
An abbreviated trial before a mock jury that gives the litigants and their attorneys an opportunity to preview what might be the result if the case proceeds to trial.

The **summary jury trial** is a sophisticated settlement process involving a summary presentation of the evidence by the attorneys to a judge and a 6- to 12-person jury impaneled by the court. The summary jury trial has all of the trappings of a traditional jury trial except most of the evidence is presented by the attorneys, and the trial is substantially abbreviated.

Summary jury trials are designed principally for those cases where discovery has been completed, no motions are pending, and the case is substantially ready for trial. The summary jury trial gives the attorneys an opportunity to present their case to a jury and gain the jury's reaction without being bound by the jury's verdict. In effect, the attorneys see how their case will play to the jury. Summary jury trials also are well suited for cases where the parties or their attorneys have unrealistic expectations as to the outcomes: for example, cases where lawyer evaluations of probable damage awards are widely disparate or where litigants reach an impasse concerning their view of how the jury will perceive difficult legal concepts such as "reasonableness" and "ordinary care." Other cases that can benefit from summary jury trials are cases that do not settle due to emotional factors that require parties to have their day in court and cases that are technically complex, but involve an amount in controversy that does not exceed the cost of full-blown litigation.

The Summary Jury Trial Process

A summary jury trial is conducted by a judge or magistrate and starts with picking a jury. The jury selection may begin, for example, with 10 potential jurors. After a brief *voir dire* (questioning of the individual potential jurors), each side is given two strikes. After the strikes are exercised, the result is a 6-person jury. A greater number of potential jurors could be called to produce a 9- or 12-person jury.

After the jury is empaneled, each side gives an opening statement followed by a presentation of the evidence. Most, if not all, of the evidence is presented by the attorneys. Rather than call witnesses to testify, the attorneys may read from depositions. Some summary jury trials permit a limited number of witnesses to give abbreviated testimony. At the conclusion of the evidentiary presentation, the attorneys are given an opportunity to make closing arguments. The judge then instructs the jury and the jury is given a limited amount of time to deliberate. The jury may or may not be able to reach a verdict within this time. After the jury returns with or without its verdict, the litigants and their attorneys are permitted to talk at length with them. The proceedings are usually private, and the verdict is advisory and nonbinding. The entire process lasts no more than one or two days, and the summary jury trial is usually followed by settlement discussions between the parties and their attorneys.

Although a summary jury trial is often hosted by a court, disputants can agree to have a private summary jury trial. A private summary jury trial would require the parties to agree on the format and all the rules involved in the litigation of the case.

In some cases where the stakes are high, a party may design a private summary jury trial without the other party's participation. The other party would be a role-play party, and the summary jury trial would be confidential. Such a mock (imitation) trial would give a party the opportunity to test his or her case before a jury. Adjustments could then be made for the trial before the court.

The Advantages and Disadvantages of Summary Jury Trial as a Dispute Resolution Process

A summary jury trial permits the parties to view a realistic playing of the case. The jury's verdict is nonbinding, thus providing the parties with a dress rehearsal for the real jury trial. Presenting the case before a mock jury gives each attorney and his or her client a preview of how an actual jury may evaluate the dispute. The parties learn what evidence the jury accepts and what evidence it rejects. In a way, a summary jury trial provides the parties with a reality check. The verdict and comments of the jurors are considered as the settlement negotiations proceed. The preparation and presentation of a summary jury trial requires substantial effort and is not routinely used.

Once the parties have learned what a jury might do, they may intensify their efforts at settlement. The summary jury trial clarifies the issues for settlement or trial.

A summary jury trial is private and not open to the public. This provides the parties with an opportunity to keep the details of their dispute private unless the settlement discussions prove unproductive and the case goes to trial.

A summary jury trial is less expensive and less time consuming than a trial because it is an abbreviated procedure. If, however, the settlement discussions after a summary jury trial prove unproductive and the case goes to trial, the costs of a summary jury trial would be added to the costs of the trial in the courthouse.

The summary jury trial raises a few criticisms. Most have to do with the process as it relates to a future trial in the event the parties cannot negotiate a settlement. For example, in a summary jury trial, there is little opportunity for *voir dire*, and therefore the jury may not be representative of the jury if the case received a traditional trial.

Also, the summary jury trial provides the parties with an opportunity to discover the trial strategy of the other side. To diminish the effectiveness of this discovery, the parties may not fully present their case. They can withhold information that would normally be submitted at trial, thus skewing the jury's verdict. Even if all the evidence is presented, the individual members of the jury or the collective decision of the jury panel may not accurately predict the outcome of a real trial due to the absence of live testimony and the abbreviated nature of the parties' presentations. The jury's evaluation of the evidence may be distorted because there may be little or no opportunity for cross-examination or to observe the demeanor of the witnesses. In a summary jury trial, there may be little or no opportunity for impeachment of witnesses.

Finally, because a summary jury trial is nonbinding, the dispute is not resolved unless the parties negotiate a settlement. Without a negotiated settlement, the parties must proceed to trial, thus incurring an additional layer of costs to resolve the dispute. Figure 8-1 presents an overview of a summary jury trial as a dispute resolution process.

AVAILABILITY	always available, but best suited for disputes with factual issues
PROCESS SELECTION	by the parties, although could be recommended by the court
	if the parties create the process, they control the scheduling; if the court creates the process, the court controls the scheduling
THE PARTICIPANTS	the parties, their attorneys, the judge, a jury, and a limited number of witnesses
PREPARATION	if a private process, the parties fashion the rules and select the judge and jury; if court sponsored, the judge fashions the rules and selects the jury
	may involve less discovery than for a full trial
THE PROCESS	takes place in a private setting and involves two phases: the abbreviated imitation trial and the subsequent negotiation or mediation involving the parties and their attorneys
	formal and structured as a trial, although the attorneys may present most of the evidence by reading depositions and submitting exhibits; witnesses testify when credibility is in issue
	confidential and preserves the privacy of the parties' records and documents
FAIRNESS	does not address the power imbalances that may exist between the parties or their attorneys
THE OUTCOME	allows the parties to control the outcome because the jury's verdict is only advisory, thus encouraging creative resolutions
	can result in the immediate resolution of the dispute if the parties agree based on the parties' interests and needs in light of the jury's advisory verdict
	eliminates all uncertainties as to outcome if the parties agree
	agreement is enforceable as a contract
	if the parties are unable to agree, the dispute will continue
	the trial phase provides the parties and their attorney with a preview of the outcome if the case proceeds to trial
COSTS	the preparation for the trial phase includes many of the costs involved preparing for a trial, including discovery
	saves further discovery and discovery costs if settlement is reached during the negotiation or mediation phase
	the presentation of evidence in summary fashion reduces the costs when compared with the costs involved presenting evidence at a trial (including expert witnesses)
	if a private process, the parties pay the judge and the jury; if court-sponsored, the costs for the jury may come out of the court's funds
	saves the costs of a full trial and appeal if a settlement can be reached during the negotiation or mediation phase
	can reduce attorney's fees
	will add another layer of costs to the dispute resolution process if the process does not result in the resolution of the dispute
	may provide low-cost discovery due to the presentation of evidence at the abbreviated trial and openness of the settlement discussion
PRECEDENTIAL VALUE	establishes no binding precedent although nonbinding precedent by performance may be created between the parties
IMPACT ON FUTURE RELATIONSHIP	may encourage future cooperation or reduce confrontation between the parties

FIGURE 8-1   Summary Jury Trial

Key Terms and Phrases

summary jury trial

Review Questions

True/False Questions

1. T   F   In a summary jury trial, the jury is the finder of fact and the judge is the finder of law.
2. T   F   A summary jury trial is more of a case management tool than a dispute resolution process.
3. T   F   The parties can streamline issues and discovery at a summary jury trial.
4. T   F   A summary jury trial gives the parties an objective evaluation of the case.
5. T   F   A summary jury trial should be conducted by the judge who will try the case.
6. T   F   A summary jury trial is a court-sponsored program and occurs after the complaint has been filed and before trial.
7. T   F   A summary jury trial is generally held after discovery has been completed.
8. T   F   A summary jury trial is confidential and preserves the confidentiality of private records.
9. T   F   Summary jury trial is another name for a mini-trial.
10. T   F   A summary jury trial is better suited for issues of law than questions of fact.

Fill-in-the-Blank Questions

1. _____   List four advantages of summary jury trial.
   _____
   _____
   _____

2. _____   List four disadvantages of summary jury trial.
   _____
   _____
   _____

Multiple-Choice Questions

1. Which of the following actively participates in a summary jury trial?
   (a) the aggrieved party
   (b) the other party to the dispute
   (c) a neutral third party
   (d) a jury
   (e) the attorney for the aggrieved party

2. Summary jury trial is classified as:
   (a) unilateral action in dispute resolution
   (b) bilateral action in dispute resolution
   (c) third-party evaluation as a prelude to dispute resolution
   (d) third-party assistance in dispute resolution
   (e) third-party adjudication in dispute resolution

3. The primary function of a summary jury trial is:
   (a) to streamline discovery issues
   (b) to give the parties a forum in which to discuss settlement
   (c) to give the parties an objective evaluation of their case
   (d) to clear the court's docket
   (e) to have the case decided by a neutral third party (the judge and jury)

Short-Answer Questions

1. Loretta Baca was driving her SUV south on I-35 when a chunk of used building material became dislodged from the bed of a McMillian Construction Company truck that was traveling west on the overpass over I-35 and fell on Loretta's SUV. The building material came through Loretta's windshield. Loretta was killed in the ensuing accident. Loretta's family claims that the McMillian truck was overfilled and that its tarp was not securely fastened.

   Loretta's family has filed a complaint in state court seeking $50 million in damages. The trial court judge has suggested the parties consider a summary jury trial to gain a realistic understanding of what could happen at trial.

   Should McMillian accept the judge's suggestion?

   Should Loretta's family accept the judge's suggestion?

   If both accept the judge's suggestion, should they ask the judge to assist them in a court-sponsored summary jury trial or should they seek a private ADR group who would conduct a private summary jury trial?

2. Discuss the advantages and disadvantages of summary jury trial.

3. Why is summary jury trial primarily an ADR process found in federal rather than state trial courts?

PART FIVE

Third-Party Assistance in Dispute Resolution

Introduction

Part V explores the role of third party assistance in dispute resolution. The third party is a neutral who helps the parties resolve their dispute by assisting them through the dispute resolution process. The dispute is not resolved by the neutral third party but rather by the parties. Part V consists of four chapters: Chapter 9, "Ombuds;" Chapter 10, "Private Mediation;" Chapter 11, "Court-Sponsored Mediation;" and Chapter 12, "Mini-Trial."

Ombuds involves a neutral third party who receives complaints and investigates and counsels, but does not resolve the problem brought before him or her. A *classical ombuds* involves a public official appointed to address issues raised by members of the general public, usually concerning actions or policies of the governmental entity or individuals within those entities. An organizational ombuds may be in either the public or private sector of the community and ordinarily addresses problems presented by members, employees, or contractors of the entity, or students in an academic institution, concerning the actions of individuals within the entity or policies of the entity. An advocate ombuds advocates on behalf of those who seek the advocate ombuds's services and is not an ombuds in the traditional sense, since an ombuds is the designation for a neutral and impartial third party.

Mediation adds a third-party neutral to the process who brings the parties together and helps them discuss and resolve their dispute. Mediation may be either private or court sponsored.

Private mediation involves a mediator who is hired and paid by the parties. The mediator assists the parties to define the problem, identify their needs and interests, and create solutions to give the parties an opportunity to reach a resolution.

If the litigation process has been initiated by the filing of a complaint with the clerk of the court, the court, as a part of its dispute resolution process, may offer the parties the opportunity to mediate their dispute under the auspices of the court. The court provides the parties with the mediation process and the mediator, usually a judge, a magistrate, or an attorney who is trained as a settlement judge. The mediator assists the parties to discuss the problem, their interests, and possible solutions. The mediator or settlement judge also may suggest possible settlement arrangements. The court-sponsored mediation provides the parties with an opportunity to settle their own dispute.

The commonality among ombuds, private mediation, and court-sponsored mediation is the fact that the neutral third party assists the parties through a process, but makes no decisions for them. The outcome of the dispute remains in the hands of the parties.

In a mini-trial, a senior corporate executive who has full settlement authority and who has not been directly involved in the dispute joins a similarly situated senior corporate executive from the other side and a neutral third party to form a three-person panel. Attorneys for both corporations present a summary of the dispute to the panel. The executives, sometimes with and sometimes without the neutral, then meet to discuss what they have observed and how the problem may be resolved. Since the executives have not been personally involved in the dispute, they can evaluate the case objectively and design a solution that satisfies the interests of their corporations.

CHAPTER 9

Ombuds

Classical Ombuds
The classical ombuds involves a public official appointed to address issues raised by members of the general public, usually concerning actions or policies of the governmental entity or individuals within those entities.

Organizational Ombuds
An organizational ombuds may be in either the public or private sector of the community and ordinarily addresses problems presented by members, employees, or contractors of the entity, or students in an academic institution, concerning the actions of individuals within the entity or policies of the entity.

Advocate Ombuds
An advocate ombuds advocates on behalf of those who seek the advocate ombuds's services and is not an ombuds in the traditional sense since an ombuds is the designation for a neutral and impartial third party.

Ombuds adds a third party to the dispute resolution process. The first ombuds was appointed by the Swedish Parliament in 1809. This form of ombuds, commonly known as **classical ombuds,** involves a public official appointed to address issues raised by members of the general public, usually concerning actions or policies of the governmental entity or individuals within those entities. By 2001, over 110 countries around the globe had some form of classical ombuds.

Another form of ombuds, the **organizational ombuds,** was first developed in the United States in the late 1920s in the private business sector although the term organizational ombuds is a more recent creation. Unlike the classical ombuds who operates in the public sector and addresses issues raised by the general public that concern actions of governmental employees or policies of the governmental entities, the organizational ombuds may be in either the public or private sector of the community and ordinarily addresses problems presented by members, employees, or contractors of the entity, or students in an academic institution, concerning the actions of individuals within the entity or policies of the entity. In the late 1960s and early 1970s, ombuds offices began springing up on college and university campuses in the United States and Canada. By 2001, over 200 American and Canadian colleges and universities had institutional ombuds offices.

Today, an office of ombuds can be found in many areas of industry, education, and government. Although all are called ombuds, the office of ombuds varies greatly in structure and duties.

A third form of ombuds is the advocate ombuds. An **advocate ombuds** may be located in either the public or private sector of a community. Unlike either the classical or organizational ombuds, the advocate ombuds advocates on behalf of those who seek the advocate ombuds's services. This use of the term "ombuds" in "advocate ombuds" is problematic since an ombuds is the designation for a neutral and impartial third party.

The Ombuds (Ombudsman)

The ombuds does not represent any person. The ombuds acts as a neutral party who hears the concerns or disputes brought to the ombuds office. Parties who seek ombuds services may be referred to as clients, complainants, visitors, customers, or merely by name or name and title. The practice varies from office to office.

Regardless of whether the ombuds office is classical or organizational, they share three essential characteristics: independence, impartiality in all functions, and confidentiality.

The ombuds must be free and give the appearance of being free from the influence of the entity that appointed the ombuds. By being independent, the ombuds can perform their function without limits being imposed or fear of retaliation.

Inquiries and informal investigations must be conducted in an impartial manner, without conflicts or the appearance of conflicts of interest and without bias.

Information provided to the ombuds in confidence must remain in confidence, whether the source was the party who initially visited the ombuds office or the party who spoke to the ombuds during the inquiry or informal investigation.

Classical Ombuds

In government, the office of ombuds may be found attached to both federal and state administrative agencies. Their function is to assist the public through the maze of administrative regulations and procedures associated with their administrative agency.

Example 9-1

Ombuds offices at the federal level include:
   CDER (Center for Drug Evaluation and Research) Ombuds—*http://www.fda.gov/cder/ombud.htm*
   FDIC Office of the Ombuds—*http://www.fdic.gov/about/contact/office/index.html*

Example 9-2

Ombuds offices at the state level include:
   Kentucky—Office of Taxpayer Ombuds—*http://www.state.ky.us/agencies/revenue/ombudsman.htm*
   Oregon—Ombuds for Injured Workers—*http://www.cbs.state.or.us/external/wco/index.html*

Some states have created a general ombuds office that has authority to investigate complaints involving a broad array of government related problems.

Example 9-3

The Alaska State Ombuds—*http://www.state.ak.ujs/local/akpages/LEGISLATURE/ombud/home.htm*
   This office "investigates complaints against state government agencies and employees. If a problem is found, the Ombudsman may recommend a solution." "The Office of the Ombudsman is a non-partisan, neutral, fact-finding agency and takes no sides in a dispute. Our job is to determine whether state government actions are fair and reasonable."

Arizona's general ombuds is called Ombudsman-Citizens' Aide—
http://www.azleg.state.az.us/ombuds/about.htm
   This office has the authority to help Arizona citizens "when they feel they have been treated unfairly by a state administrator, agency, department, board, or commission."

Organizational Ombuds

The organizational ombuds is an employee of the organization who reports directly to a high ranking officer of the organization. The ombuds receives complaints from members of the organization and helps resolve these complaints informally and confidentially. The ombuds also acts as an early warning system, alerting upper management to major problems as they arise to allow management to take corrective action before these problems become more difficult to address in an informal setting.

In the private business sector, a number of corporations have an ombuds office.

Example 9-4

The following are a sampling of corporations using ombuds:

American Express	McDonald's
Anheuser-Busch	Shell
Chevron	TIAA/CREF

In educational institutions, the ombuds office is open to students, faculty, administrators, and staff who have concerns or problems arising from or affecting their studies or work at the institution. Concerns may include discrimination, ethics, favoritism, fear of retaliation, interpersonal conflicts, professional or scientific misconduct, sexual harassment, stress or anxiety, and working conditions. The ombuds office may:

- explain organization policies and procedures to a party and may help the party use the procedures
- advise a party as to his or her options and help the party pursue whichever option the party selects
- refer a party to the appropriate person who could address the party's concerns or problem and arrange a meeting
- recommend changes to the organization to correct problem areas
- function as a mediator or shuttle diplomat.

Example 9-5

The following is a sampling of colleges and universities using an ombuds:

Colorado State University—*http://www.sc.colostate.edu/ombudsman*
Columbia University—*http://www.columbia.edu/cu/ombuds*
Cornell University—*http://cuinfo.cornell.edu/Admin/Ombudsman/home.htm*
University of Florida—*http://www.ufl.edu/suggest.htm*
University of Illinois at Chicago—*http://www.uic.edu/depts/publ/yp/production/UNIT1-349.html*
Massachusetts Institute of Technology—*http://web.mit.edu/ombud*
Michigan State University—*http://www.msu.edu/unit.ombud*
Stanford University—*http://www.stanford.edu/dept/ocr/ombudsperson*
University of Texas at Austin—*http://www.utexas.edu/student/registrar/catalogs/gen-info/students2.html*
Washington State University—*http://www.wsu.edu/~ombuds*
University of Western Michigan—*http://www.wmich.edu/ombudsman/standards/htm*

Problem 9-1
Using the Internet, find three institutions of higher learning in your region of the country that have an ombuds.

Some graduate and professional schools have their own ombuds offices.

Example 9-6

The following is a sampling of a university using a separate ombuds office for graduate or professional students:

    University of Maryland (Ombuds Office for Graduate Students)—*http://www.gradschool. umd.edu/Ombuds/index.html*

    Harvard Medical School, School of Dental Medicine, and School of Public Health—*http://www. hms.harvard.edu/ombuds/ombbro.html*

Some K-12 school districts have their own ombuds.

Example 9-7

The Arlington, Texas, Independent School District has its own ombuds office (AISD Parent/School Ombudsman Service):—*http://www.arlington. k12.tx.us/information/conduct.shtml*

In prisons, the ombuds office reviews prisoner complaints and assists the prisoners in resolving their issues with their organization.

Advocate Ombuds

In the health care field, in hospitals and nursing homes, ombuds help patients and their families resolve complaints against caregivers and caregiving institutions. Licensing agencies, such as those that license nursing homes, also have ombuds offices.

Example 9-8

Arkansas—Long Term Care Ombuds—*http://www.arombudsman.com*
Minnesota—Ombuds for Mental Health and Mental Retardation—*http://www.ombudmhmr.state.mn.us*
Virginia—Northern Virginia Long-Term Care Ombuds Program—*http://www.co.fairfax.va.us/ service/aaa/html/Ombud_main.htm*

In the securities and insurance industries, ombuds help consumers resolve problems with industry members.

Example 9-9

> The National Association of Securities Dealers, Inc., has an Office of the Ombudsman.—*http://www.nasd.com/corpinfo/ombudsman.html*

The Ombuds Process

Although ombuds as a process moves beyond what one party can do by himself or herself, only one party is needed to initiate this process. The selection of ombuds is made independent of input from the other party whether it be an individual or entity and begins with the aggrieved party contacting the ombuds who may be located in his or her ombuds office. The ombuds process is only available in a limited number of settings. The ombuds office must have been created by a corporation, an industry, an educational institution, or a governmental entity and must have been authorized to address specific types of grievances. Therefore, an ombuds may not be an available option in a great number of disputes.

If the ombuds process is an option for dispute resolution, the party who seeks the assistance of the ombuds is seeking a nonlegal resolution of the dispute. A party who seeks the aid of an ombuds seeks a quick, inexpensive (generally free), and confidential process. Often the ombuds, after listening to the party and after making an informal investigation (gathering information), will help the party clarify the issues and develop and evaluate an array of alternatives for resolving the conflict.

Although the ombuds does not make the decision that resolves the problem for the party, at times the interaction of the ombuds with the party who is perceived to be the source of the problem may result in the resolution of the dispute. The party who seeks the assistance of an ombuds does not abandon his or her legal rights by selecting this process. The party faces the choice of which solution to use. This choice may or may not be based on the law. The decision at this point is the party's and his or her decision alone. If the intercession of the ombuds does not produce a resolution of the grievance, the party can proceed to another form of dispute resolution.

While the ombuds may benefit the party who seeks assistance, the interfacing of the ombuds with respondents or organizational managers may also benefit others who have not come forward with their complaints. The activities of the ombuds constitute an early warning to respondents and those in management that an organizational problem is brewing and needs to be addressed. In this fashion, the ombuds serves the greater good of both the individuals and the organization.

Ethical and Legal Issues

At its 2001 annual meeting, the House of Delegates of the American Bar Association approved "Standards for the Establishment and Operation of Ombuds Offices." The recommendation, standards, and report may be found at *http://www.abanet.org/adminlaw/ombuds*. In addition to the ABA's standards, several other organizations have formulated codes of ethics or standards of practice.

Example 9-10

The Ombudsman Association (TOA) Code of Ethics—*http://www.ombuds-toa.org/library.htm*
The Ombudsman Association (TOA) Standards of Practice—*http://www.ombuds-toa.org/library.htm*
University and College Ombuds Association (UCOA) Code of Ethics—*http://www.colorado.edu/Ombuds/UCOA*

These codes require independence, impartiality, and confidentiality. The person seeking the assistance of the ombuds must feel that seeking assistance will not lead to reprisals from management.

The Ombudsman Association (TOA), a nonprofit, international organization of professional organizational ombuds, has both a code of ethics and standards of practice. They are located in Appendix A. They may also be found on The Ombudsman Association website, *http://www.ombuds-toa.org/*. The United States Ombudsman Association, a national organization for public sector ombuds professionals also has a website, *http://www.usombudsman.org/AboutUSOA/association.htm*.

Conflict of Interest

Conflict of Interest
A conflict of interest exists when the neutral third party (ombuds, mediator, arbitrator, or judge) and one of the disputing parties have potentially incompatible interests.

A **conflict of interest** exists if the organizational ombuds and the party using the ombuds office have potentially incompatible interests. If a conflict or a perceived conflict exists, the ombuds is required to excuse himself or herself from further participation in the matter. Although the organizational ombuds is within the organization, he or she must be able to act outside the staff structure of the organization so there will be no real or perceived conflict of interest. When these ethical and procedural guidelines are violated, or are perceived to be violated, the impartiality and fairness of the ombuds process comes into question.

Problem 9-2

Robert Lovell is the ombuds for a major corporation. He received a complaint from Ava Greenstreet who claimed that she was being sexually harassed by her immediate supervisor, Charlie Rolands. On the same day, Robert also received a complaint from Alice Brownfield who claimed that she was being sexually harassed by a fellow employee by the name of Ava Greenstreet.

1. Can Robert act as the ombuds for both Ava and Alice?
2. Does he have a conflict of interest?
3. What should he do?
4. Do the Standards of Practice of The Ombudsman Association provide guidance? See Appendix A.

Impartiality

Impartiality
Impartiality is a lack of bias or prejudice on the part of the neutral third person (ombuds, mediator, arbitrator, or judge) in favor of one party over the other.

Impartiality is a lack of bias or prejudice in favor of one party over the other. The ombuds must function in an impartial fashion as he or she informally considers the problem and discusses various options with the party who initiated contact with the ombuds. Failure to act impartially destroys the credibility of the ombuds office and casts a shadow over ombuds in general.

Problem 9-3

Susan Aster, a student, sought the assistance of the ombuds office at her university concerning grading irregularities by Professor Amanda West. Unknown to Susan, Amanda West is the wife of the ombuds, Peter Marler.

1. How should Peter Marler handle this problem in light of the Standards of Practice of The Ombudsman Association? See Appendix A.
2. Does this problem also raise a conflict of interest?

Problem 9-4

Same facts as Problem 9-3 with the exception of the following. Amanda West is the wife of the provost.

1. How should Peter Marler handle this problem in light of the Standards of Practice of The Ombudsman Association? See Appendix A.
2. Does this problem also raise a conflict of interest?

Privileged Communication

Privileged Communication
A privileged communication is information given by one party to another that is not permitted by law to be divulged by the party receiving it.

In the lawyer/client, doctor/patient, priest/penitent, and husband/wife relationships, a **privileged communication** is information given by one party to another that is not permitted by law to be divulged by the party receiving it. The privilege is the privilege of the party conferring the information and not the party who receives it. In the case of an ombuds office, the privilege is deemed to belong to the ombuds, and not to the visitor.

Example 9-11

Tony Pizzaro hired Lucinda Goodpasture as his attorney to represent him in a work-related accident. During Tony's interview with Lucinda, he told her that he was on medication at the time of the accident and that he probably should not have been operating the equipment that caused his injury.

The law views the relationship between attorney and client as a fiduciary relationship and treats communications made by the client to his or her attorney as privileged. If Lucinda were asked whether Tony had been on medication during the time of the accident, she could not respond because the information was privileged communication and Lucinda did not have the power to waive Tony's privilege.

The Ombudsman Association and the United States Ombudsman Association seek to treat communications between the ombuds and all parties who provide the ombuds with information as privileged. The ombuds privilege, however, is differentiated from those of the lawyer/client, doctor/patient, priest/penitent, and husband/wife privilege. In these traditional privilege situations, the party who provided the information has the privilege. He or she can waive the privilege. The ombuds privilege is held by the ombuds office. The ombuds privilege cannot be waived by the party providing the information nor can it be waived by the ombuds office.

Problem 9-5

1. Should the ombuds have a privilege? Why or why not?
2. In most cases do other parties have the information that the ombuds has? Therefore, is this information available although not from the ombuds?

The Advantages and Disadvantages of Ombuds as a Dispute Resolution Process

The biggest drawback of the ombuds process is its lack of availability. Ombuds only functions when an individual has a grievance with an organization that has established an office of the ombuds to address that type of grievance. Therefore, ombuds may not be an available option in a great many disputes.

In those situations where an office of the ombuds does exist, the ombuds takes into account the interests of the party seeking assistance, any others involved in the dispute, and the organization that created the ombuds office. A party can initiate the process without the consent of the other party, and therefore can initiate the process without confronting the other party. A party may seek assistance unilaterally, quickly, and confidentially. Many problems can be resolved without the offending party even knowing who the complainant was (for example through a training program about safety or sexual harassment), thus reducing the complainant's fear of retribution.

Since the decision to visit the ombuds office is based on nonlegal factors, the complainant need not seek the assistance of an attorney to provide a legal analysis of the problem or to represent the complainant's interests. The resolution of the dispute is expedient and inexpensive, generally free to the complainant since the office of the ombuds is funded by the organization.

The organization benefits by having an inexpensive early warning system that alerts management to problems that are brewing. This gives management an opportunity to resolve problems before they become potentially expensive in terms of transaction costs, adverse awards, declining good will, and unfavorable publicity. Figure 9-1 presents an overview of organizational ombuds as a dispute resolution process.

AVAILABILITY	only available in certain settings (*e.g.*, within a corporation, educational institution, governmental agency, health field) where an ombuds office exists
PROCESS SELECTION	by the aggrieved party
THE PARTICIPANTS	the complainant, the ombuds, and anyone the ombuds wishes to talk to
PREPARATION	may require some informal fact gathering by the ombuds
THE PROCESS	takes place in a private setting
	informal and unstructured with each party having an opportunity to discuss the problem in private with the ombuds, a neutral third party
	preserves the confidentiality statements of all parties
	provides an opportunity to discuss feelings, perception of the dispute, interests, and array of settlement options
	the ombuds may be able to arrange a resolution
FAIRNESS	the ombuds may provide a balance of power between the complainant and the respondent
THE OUTCOME	chosen by the complainant
	based on the parties' interests and needs
	encourages creative solutions
	agreement produces immediate results and resolves the dispute immediately
	eliminates all uncertainties as to outcome
	agreement may be based on inadequate information
	the organization's party will more than likely fulfill its agreement because the process is sponsored by the organization
	the parties may not be able to agree; as a result, there will be no resolution
COSTS	ombuds services are offered as a no-cost service to the party bringing a complaint because the ombuds office is financed by the host (sponsoring) organization
	saves the complainant and the host organization discovery, litigation, and appeal costs if the dispute can be resolved
	saves or reduces attorney's fees
	if the ombuds process does not result in a resolution, the process will have added no costs to other dispute resolution processes
PRECEDENTIAL VALUE	establishes no binding precedent although nonbinding precedent by performance may be created between the parties
	the ombuds may, during an investigation, discover a problem within the host organization that if remedied, can save the host organization substantial time and money
IMPACT ON FUTURE RELATIONSHIP	may encourage future cooperation or reduce confrontation between the parties
	promotes goodwill within the host organization

FIGURE 9-1 Organizational Ombuds

Key Terms and Phrases

advocate ombuds
classical ombuds
conflict of interest
impartiality
organizational ombuds
privileged communication

Review Questions

True/False

1. T   F   In the ombuds process, the jury is the finder of fact and the judge is the finder of law.
2. T   F   Ombuds is a case management tool rather than a dispute resolution process.
3. T   F   The parties can work out an accommodation for the aggrieved party through the ombuds.
4. T   F   The ombuds gives the parties an objective evaluation of the case.
5. T   F   The ombuds process is conducted by the judge who will try the case.
6. T   F   The ombuds process is a court-sponsored program and occurs after the complaint has been filed and before trial.
7. T   F   The ombuds process is generally held after discovery has been completed.
8. T   F   The ombuds process is confidential and preserves the confidentiality of private records.
9. T   F   The ombuds process is another name for mediation.
10. T   F   The ombuds process is better suited for issues of law rather than questions of fact.

Fill-in-the-Blank questions

1. _____   List four advantages of ombuds.
   _____
   _____
   _____

2. _____   List four disadvantages of ombuds.
   _____
   _____
   _____

Multiple Choice

1. Which of the following actively participates in the ombuds process:
   (a) the aggrieved party
   (b) the other party to the dispute
   (c) a neutral third party
   (d) a jury
   (e) the attorney for the aggrieved party
2. Ombuds is classified as:
   (a) unilateral action in dispute resolution
   (b) bilateral action in dispute resolution
   (c) third-party evaluation as a prelude to dispute resolution
   (d) third-party assistance in dispute resolution
   (e) third-party adjudication in dispute resolution
3. The primary function of the ombuds process is:
   (a) to streamline discovery issues
   (b) to give the parties a setting to discuss settlement
   (c) to give the parties an objective evaluation of their case
   (d) to provide an aggrieved party the assistance of a neutral third party who can investigate the complaint and seek a resolution
   (e) to have the case decided by a neutral third party (the judge and jury)

Short Answer Questions

1. Anna Berryman has been a resident at the Golden Age Retirement and Nursing Center for three years. Her daughter, Sylvia, believes that her mother is not receiving her medications in a timely manner. Sylvia has complained to the director of the center, but her complaints have produced no results.

   The regional nursing home association has established an ombuds office for nursing home complaints. Should Sylvia take her complaint to the ombuds office?
2. Discuss the advantages and disadvantages of the organizational ombuds as a dispute resolution process.
3. Why is the ombuds limited in its use in the United States?
4. Where should ombuds be used where they are not currently used?

CHAPTER 10

Private Mediation

Private mediation is a consensual process. Parties who contract may select private mediation as their dispute resolution process and include it as a term in their contract. When, at a subsequent date, a dispute arises out of the contract, the parties need only implement the contract's private mediation provision.

If, however, the dispute does not arise out of contract or if the dispute does arise out of contract but the contract did not include a private mediation provision, the parties may select private mediation after a dispute arises. Private mediation may be selected before litigation is initiated. If the parties resolve their dispute, there will be no need to pursue litigation. If the mediation does not produce a settlement, a party can file a complaint and begin the litigation process.

If the parties have not preselected private mediation and a dispute arises, one party may file a complaint to begin the litigation process, thus using the pending litigation as an incentive to bring a reluctant party to the mediation table. This opens two avenues of dispute resolution and each will progress along its own timetable. If the parties resolve their dispute through private mediation, they will terminate the litigation process by filing motions to dismiss with prejudice.

The decision to mediate requires the participation by both parties. They must agree to mediate. Unlike negotiation that may just happen, the decision to mediate requires actual consent and planning by both parties because a neutral third party will participate in the process.

Unlike negotiation where the parties facilitate their own discussion, in **private mediation,** a neutral third party facilitates the discussion between the parties. The parties must still resolve their own dispute. If the parties are unable to reach an agreement, their dispute will go unresolved unless another dispute resolution process follows.

Private Mediation

In private mediation, a neutral third party facilitates the discussion between the parties in an attempt to help the parties resolve their dispute.

What Should a Party Expect at the Mediation

Parties who participate in private mediation must enter the process with reasonable expectations. Before the parties participate in a private mediation, they should understand that they will be asked to describe the dispute in detail. They should be prepared to discuss their needs and interests and to listen to the other party's needs and interests. They should be prepared to discuss and evaluate creative ways to resolve their dispute. They should expect the mediation to be a give-and-take process, and they should be prepared to reevaluate their position and make adjustments as the discussion evolves. They should be prepared to make concessions and take significantly less or give significantly more than their opening position. They must understand that they must arrive at their own agreement and that the mediator will not resolve the dispute for them.

Preparing for Private Mediation

The decision to mediate requires participation by both parties. They must agree to mediate. The parties may design the rules for their mediation and may select their own mediator.

Selecting the Rules for the Mediation

Since mediation is private, the parties can draft their own rules for the mediation. The procedural and evidentiary rules of the process are those agreed to by the parties.

Rather than fashion their own rules, the parties may agree to have the mediator or a mediation service design the rules for them. The American Arbitration Association, for example, is a service that provides both mediators and the rules for the mediation process. See American Arbitration Association at *http://www.adr.org/contents2/htm.* See also CPR Institute for Dispute Resolution at *http://www.cpradr.org/home1.htm;* United States Arbitration & Mediation (USA&M) at *http://www.usam.com;* and International Chamber of Commerce at *http://www.jus.uio.no/lm/icc.html.* See also National Association for Community Mediators, *http://www.nafcm.org,* for a partial list of community mediation centers. A number of other international, national, regional, and local mediation services exist.

Also, a number of specialized mediation services are available. Examples include the National Mediation Board (mediating collective bargaining disputes in the railroad and airline industries) at *http://www.nmb.gov;* the Federal Mediation and Conciliation Service (mediating disputes in contract negotiations between employers and unions representing employees in the private, public, and federal sectors) at *http://www.fmcs.gov/aboutfmcs.htm;* and the State Mediation & Conciliation Service (investigating and mediating labor disputes in both the public and private sectors) at *http://www.dir.ca.gov/csmcs/smcs.html.* A number of private local mediation services specialize in domestic disputes. These include mediation and conciliation services sponsored by religious institutions. A number of these services can be found by searching *mediation* on the Internet.

Selecting and Compensating the Mediator

The parties can select a mediator or a mediation service that will provide them with a list of mediators from which to choose. Mediators may be selected because they have expertise in the subject matter, because they have expertise in the mediation process, or both.

Problem 10-1

Your bank has wrongfully dishonored several large checks that you issued to your important clients. The bank has agreed to private mediation. You now must work with the bank on selecting a mediator. What factors would be important to you?

Selecting the Timing and the Setting for the Mediation

The timing of a mediation depends on the parties, their attorneys if they are represented by counsel, the availability of the mediator, and the nature of the dispute. Some parties believe it necessary to have the case fully prepared before beginning a mediation. Others prefer to participate in a mediation before much discovery has been conducted and before much has been spent on the case.

In some cases where both private mediation and litigation have been initiated, an attorney may find it helpful to begin the discovery process by completing a deposition or two or by interviewing several witnesses before he or she can effectively participate in the mediation. Certainly, all relevant documents should be reviewed. If a dispositive motion was filed with the court, some attorneys want the motion to be ruled upon before settlement offers are tendered. Others prefer the uncertainty created by a pending dispositive motion.

Preparing the Participants for Their Roles in the Mediation Process

Private mediations may have different participants. In some mediations, the parties (who may or may not have attorneys) appear without attorneys. In other mediations, attorneys participate without clients being present. In still other mediations, both attorneys and clients are present. In the last category, the roles of attorney and client vary. The attorney may be present but have no voice. The attorney only advises the client. In other mediations, the attorneys may have more active roles and the clients reduced roles.

Documents and other legal evidence are of limited importance in a mediation since the parties are attempting to resolve their own dispute with the mediator acting as facilitator. Although some reference to the law will be helpful in placing the dispute in context, the parties waste time by trying to convince the mediator of the merits of their respective positions because the mediator is not the decision maker. Documents and other evidence may help the other party understand the merit or lack of merit of a claim.

When the Attorney and Client Appear Together

When the attorney and client appear together at the mediation, the attorney must advise the client about what to wear, how to behave, what to say and when to say it, and how long the process may take. The attorney may want to advise the client that he or she may be left alone in a room while the attorney speaks with the mediator or with the mediator and the other attorney. Therefore, the client should be prepared to entertain himself or herself. The client may be advised to bring someone to act as his or her support team. This may be especially true where the client already feels the playing field is not level. The attorney also may advise the client that he or she may be asked to speak privately with the mediator, without the attorney being present.

The attorney who represents a client at a mediation or a party who appears without legal counsel at a mediation should consider the following as he or she prepares for the mediation.

1. Be prepared to spend time in the mediation exhausting all avenues of settlement.
2. Be civil to the other side and show respect for attorneys, clients, and the mediator. Do not belittle anyone.
3. Be candid with the mediator.
4. Be prepared to answer questions posed by the mediator.
5. Listen carefully without interrupting. Mediation is an opportunity to learn about the other side and their needs that must be met for a settlement to take place.
6. Speak directly to the other side in the presence of the mediator and not just to the mediator. Treating the opposing party as someone who has feelings and interests is an important step on the road to a settlement. Since a settlement requires the agreement between the parties, the opposing party cannot be ignored.
7. Be prepared to discuss with the mediator the strengths and weaknesses of your client's case.
8. Be prepared, if asked by the mediator, to give an opening statement that will present the salient facts and issues. An opening statement should not amount to a legal argument and should not be inflammatory.
9. Be prepared to discuss your client's needs and interests, and be prepared to work toward fashioning a settlement that achieves those interests or needs.
10. Avoid being positional, but rather emphasize your client's needs or interests.

11. Be prepared to discuss previous settlement offers and counteroffers.
12. Consider the costs of going to litigation, the costs of losing, and the costs of winning.
13. Consider the insurance aspects of the case as well as wanted and unwanted publicity.
14. Have at hand any necessary computations of costs and exhibits as well as relevant telephone numbers.
15. Avoid grandstanding.

A party who appears with or without legal counsel at a mediation should also consider the following.

1. You must attend and participate in the mediation in good faith. Participation in good faith does not mean that you must accept a proposed settlement. You must, however, consider a proposed settlement and have the authority to accept it if you believe it is in your best interest.
2. The mediator has no interest in the case and does not care if the case settles.
3. The mediator is experienced and knowledgable in the mediation process and is able to provide understanding and assistance.
4. Ask questions when you do not understand something.
5. Listen, learn, and work with the mediator and the other party. Be cooperative and polite.
6. All statements will be confidential and cannot be used for *any* purpose later.
7. All parties speak without being interrupted.
8. Mediation has a cathartic aspect (i.e., an opportunity to vent feelings by telling your story to the mediator—uninterrupted—and have the other party do the same).
9. Understand the logistics of the mediation: that is, that the parties may be in the same or different rooms, that there may be no snack breaks, and that the mediation may span a number of hours and extend into the evening.
10. Each party will have an opportunity to speak privately with the mediator and may choose to do so with or without your attorney being present.
11. You may be left alone in a room for an extended period when the mediator meets with your attorney privately.
12. Understand the sequencing of events at a mediation and what you will be asked to do during each phase of the mediation.
13. If asked by the mediator, be prepared to give an opening statement that presents the salient facts.
14. Think about and discuss your needs or interests and do not focus on an outcome.
15. Listen to the other party and understand that some of the other party's needs and interests must be satisfied for there to be a settlement.
16. Think about being flexible, as flexibility pertains to the outcome so long as the outcome satisfies your needs and interests.
17. Do not compromise your needs or interests but be flexible and creative on how these needs or interests can be satisfied.
18. Understand what will follow if the dispute does settle (i.e., written agreement and dismissal of the lawsuit, if one has been filed) and what will follow if the case does not settle (i.e., additional discovery, trial, and possibly an appeal, assuming a suit will be or has been filed).

If the attorney appears with his or her paralegal, the paralegal participates in the role assigned by his or her attorney. The paralegal may maintain the documents in the case, take notes, communicate and discuss strategy with his or her attorney, and interface with the client. The paralegal, however, may neither counsel nor represent the client.

When the Party Appears without an Attorney

In some mediations, a party represents himself or herself. In these situations, the party may or may not have employed counsel. If the party has counsel, the mediation rules may require him or her to appear without counsel.

If the party has employed an attorney, his or her attorney must carefully prepare the client for the mediation. If the party has not employed an attorney, then the party must prepare himself or herself for the mediation process. A party should not appear at a mediation without being fully prepared on both the mediation process and the substantive aspects of his or her problem.

A party who appears without an attorney must be prepared to articulate his or her facts, feelings, and needs and interests. The party must also be able to present and consider a wide range of solutions and must be able to evaluate offers and counteroffers and act upon them. A party must be able to recognize when he or she does not have the expertise to make a fully informed decision and must then be able to ask that the mediation be continued to a later date, a date after which the party can have outside experts advise him or her about the offer.

When the Attorney Appears without the Client

In some mediations, the client's attorney will appear without the client. The critical issue becomes whether the attorney has been given full or limited settlement authority by the client. If the attorney has full settlement authority, he or she may use discretion to settle the case for the client. If the attorney has limited settlement authority, the client will have given the attorney the settlement range.

Example 10-1

Leah Lancaster was involved in an automobile accident with Brian Von Trapp. The accident was clearly Leah's fault, and Brian sustained permanent physical injuries. Brian filed a complaint against Leah in state court seeking $2 million in damages. Leah's insurance has a maximum coverage of $500,000. Leah and Brian have agreed to try private mediation as the case progresses down the litigation track.

The mediation has been designed so only four people will be present: the mediator, Leah's attorney, Brian's attorney, and a representative from Leah's insurance company. Clients would not be present. Prior to the mediation, Leah has instructed her attorney that she would pay up to $250,000 above whatever her insurance company would pay, but payments would need to be structured over 25 years.

At the mediation, the representative from Leah's insurance company told Leah's attorney that the insurance company would be willing to pay the policy limit, $500,000, if necessary to settle the case. Leah's attorney now knows that she has settlement authority to agree to a settlement that would pay up to $750,000 with $500,000 to be paid immediately and the remaining $250,000 to be paid over 25 years.

If Brian's attorney will not settle for anything less than $1 million, Leah's attorney does not have the settlement authority to accept that offer. Leah's attorney must discuss Brian's $1 million offer with Leah, and she must decide whether to accept or reject it.

The Mediation Process

Private mediation may have different formats. The mediator is in some ways a negotiator but is negotiating with two parties at the same time. The mediator, however, lacks both a personal interest in the case and the settlement authority to settle the case. The mediator is not a party to the agreement. The mediator is and must remain neutral.

Regardless of whether the mediator follows an interest-based or a position-based negotiation strategy, the mediation should be thought of as a process. An effective mediator will have a plan. The mediator must proceed in an orderly fashion and prepare the parties to rationally discuss their problems and seek creative solutions. The following steps illustrate the mediator's plan:

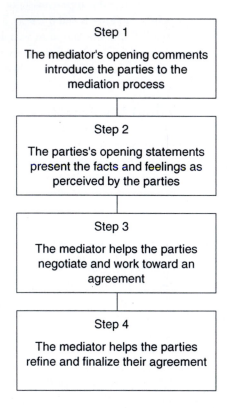

Step 1

The mediator's opening comments introduce the parties to the mediation process

Step 2

The parties's opening statements present the facts and feelings as perceived by the parties

Step 3

The mediator helps the parties negotiate and work toward an agreement

Step 4

The mediator helps the parties refine and finalize their agreement

To be effective, a mediator must feel at ease with the mediation process and must develop a mediation style within that process.

The following discussion uses the phrase "party" to include "attorney and client," "client without attorney," and "attorney without client." Naturally the dynamics change depending on who is present at the mediation and what their respective roles are. For example, when an attorney describes the client's perception of the facts and the client's feelings, this description will be very different from how the client describes his or her perception of the facts and his or her feelings. With this in mind, the following is a very general discussion of a mediation process.

Step 1. The Mediator's Opening Comments Introduce the Parties to the Mediation Process

A mediation begins when the mediator introduces the parties to the mediation process. The mediator uses this time as an opportunity to gain the parties' trust as a mediator and for the mediation process.

By greeting the parties, by showing them where to sit, and by being the only person who speaks during this time, the mediator takes control of the process. The mediator begins to establish his or her neutrality by investigating the existence of any conflict of interest and if no conflict exists, whether the parties will commit to the mediator as *their* mediator.

The mediator develops support for the mediation process by stating the purpose of the mediation and by describing the process that will unfold that day. The mediator assures the parties that the mediation is voluntary and that they can discontinue the mediation at anytime. The mediator assures the parties that if an agreement is reached, it will be their agreement and not the mediator's agreement.

The mediator establishes the ground rules for the mediation. The mediator also emphasizes that each party will have an opportunity to fully develop his or her story without interruption and that what is said during the mediation is confidential.

Step 2. The Parties' Opening Statements Present the Facts and Feelings as Perceived by the Parties

Once the process is introduced and some degree of comfort is established for the mediator and the process, the mediator begins to gather the facts and feelings as perceived by the parties. Both parties are asked to make statements about what happened. These statements will contain feelings as well as facts. The parties often express anger, make accusations, and show frustration. Ultimately the problem is revealed, in both its facts component and its feelings component.

If all parties are present when each party speaks, the parties may for the first time hear the other party's full rendition of the facts and his or her feelings. This may prove an enlightening experience that ultimately assists the parties in reaching an agreement.

Step 3. The Mediator Helps the Parties Negotiate and Work toward an Agreement

Once the parties have an opportunity to develop their respective perceptions of the facts and to express their feelings, the negotiating phase of the mediation begins. The mediator may use an interest-based or a position-based negotiation model. These models are described in Chapter 6. As the parties negotiate, the dynamics change. At times the mediator encourages the parties to negotiate and at other times the mediator acts as a messenger carrying ideas and offers between the parties.

Private Caucus
A meeting between the mediator and one party outside the presence of the other party.

During this phase of the mediation, the mediator may hold private caucuses with the parties. A **private caucus** is a meeting between the mediator and one party outside the presence of the other party. Normally if the mediator has a private caucus with one side, he or she will have a private caucus with the other side. This preserves the appearance of neutrality. Information received by the mediator at a private caucus is confidential and will not be revealed to the other party unless the party who has given this information waives its confidentiality.

Step 4. The Mediator Helps the Parties Refine and Finalize Their Agreement

If the parties reach an agreement, the mediator helps the parties refine and finalize that agreement. The agreement must be in writing, otherwise each party will have a different understanding of the terms of the agreement. All aspects of the agreement must be reduced to writing to avoid any misunderstanding about what was and what was not agreed upon. Also the writing must include all the whats, whens, and wheres. No detail should be left out. The parties should carefully reread the final writing before either party signs. The time before signatures are added to the writing is the time to ensure that the writing accurately and completely reflects the agreement.

Example 10-2

Clancy O'Shay is the leasing agent for Midtown Towers, a high-rise office building in downtown Gotham. Gina Lapino owns and operates a small delicatessen on the first floor of the building. Last March, Clancy and Gina negotiated a renewal of Gina's five-year lease. During the negotiations, the parties discussed whether Gina would have the exclusive right to sell cappuccino in her delicatessen. Six months later, Clancy leased another space on the first floor of Midtown Towers to the West Coast Coffee House. When West Coast opened, it served cappuccino. Gina's complaints to Clancy fell on deaf ears. Gina then hired an attorney and proceeded to seek an injunction in state court. Clancy offered to try to mediate the dispute.

At the mediation, Clancy produced the signed writing entitled "lease." Gina claimed that the actual lease included terms in addition to those in the signed writing. Clancy claimed that the lease included only those terms in the signed writing.

The parties have this dispute because the writing did not fully reflect their discussion. The parties should have stated what their agreement was as to cappuccino. If Gina had the exclusive right to sell cappuccino, this right should have been stated in the writing. If Gina did not have the exclusive right to sell cappuccino, the fact that she did not have the exclusive right also should have been in the writing.

Before the writing is signed, the mediator may ask whether the parties have other issues that need to be discussed. These issues may impact on the agreement.

At times, a mediation does not produce a resolution of all the issues the parties have with one another. A mediation, however, may resolve some of the issues, may simplify some of the issues, or may simplify some discovery issues. Also, mediation may encourage the parties to continue their dialogue to resolve their dispute after the mediation has formally ended.

Enforceability of the Mediated Agreement

The fact that the parties have mediated their agreement bodes well for the parties adhering to their promises. The parties have exchanged promises in an arrangement that they perceive to advance their best interests. Although they have found it necessary to compromise to reach the agreement, they have done so of their own volition.

The agreement is acceptable, although not what each may have expected. Because the parties have fashioned their own agreement and it was not imposed upon them by a third party means that the parties will, in the vast majority of cases, adhere to their agreement. Therefore, unless the agreement has not been artfully drafted (the writing contains ambiguities), a parol evidence rule problem arises (the writing may not include all the terms of the contract), or a mistake in integration occurs (the writing does not accurately reflect the agreement), enforceability of the agreement will not become an issue.

There are cases, however, where enforceability of the mediated agreement is placed in issue. The argument can be made that the agreement is enforceable as a contract. Classic contract law theory requires a "bargained-for exchange" or a quid pro quo. This exchange takes the form of a "promise for a promise" or a "promise for a performance." Since a "promise for a performance" rarely occurs, the following discussion focuses on a "promise for a promise." In a settlement, one party promises to do (or not to do) something in exchange for the other party's promise to do (or not to do) something.

Example 10-3

Roger and Augustine were involved in an automobile accident. Augustine was injured and sued Roger. As the case languished in the court, Roger and Augustine agreed to try to resolve their dispute through mediation.

At mediation Roger agrees to pay $50,000 and Augustine promises to dismiss his lawsuit with prejudice. In classic contract law language, the exchanges take the following form:

Roger promises to pay Augustine $50,000 in exchange for Augustine's promise to dismiss his lawsuit with prejudice.

Roger makes his promise to pay to receive Augustine's promise to dismiss. Augustine's promise is the quid pro quo for Roger's promise.

Augustine promises to dismiss his lawsuit with prejudice in exchange for Roger's promise to pay $50,000.

Augustine makes his promise to dismiss to receive Roger's promise to pay. Roger's promise is the quid pro quo for Augustine's promise.

Each party's promise has a quid pro quo and therefore the parties have formed a contract.

As a general rule, the nonbreaching party in a breach of contract action recovers damages based on his or her expectation under the contract. These damages place the nonbreaching party in the position he or she would have been had the contract been fully performed. Since a settlement agreement is a contract, these expectation damages would apply to breach of a settlement agreement as well.

Example 10-4

Holly, a tenant of the Athena Apartments, moved out of her apartment when the apartment manager refused to make repairs. When the manager refused to return Holly's deposit, they agreed to go to a community mediation center.

At the mediation, they entered a settlement agreement whereby the manager agreed to return Holly's deposit and to reimburse her for her moving expenses. The manager now refuses to honor the settlement agreement.

Holly could file a breach of contract action against the Athena Apartments and seek damages. She is entitled to a judgment for expectation damages which would be measured by the amount of her deposit and her moving expenses.

In some cases, the court may order specific performance of the mediated agreement. The court would order the breaching party to do what he or she agreed to do in the agreement.

Example 10-5

Raymond Cox and Thomas Hicks entered into a partnership to acquire and develop real property and to engage in residential and commercial development. As the partnership was being dissolved, the parties had a disagreement over the fair market value of one of their pieces of property. Cox and Hicks entered into a mediated agreement whereby each party would select an appraiser and these two appraisers would select a third. The three appraisers would appraise this piece of property and each would provide the mediator with his or her fair market value. The mediator would then average the two appraisals that were closest to one another. When this was done, Cox refused to follow the mediation formula.

The parties then went to litigation. The court ordered the mediation agreement specifically enforced. This ordered Cox to perform the agreement.

In some mediated agreements, a party promises not to do something. If that party breaches the agreement by beginning to do what he or she had promised not to do, the court could order the party to discontinue doing what he or she was doing. Thus the court could issue an injunction against the breaching party.

The parties to a mediation can take their mediated agreement one step further. If they were in litigation at the time they reached their mediated agreement, they could file mutual dismissals. At the same time, the mediated agreement can be entered as a consent judgment. This judgment would then be enforceable as any other judgment.

The parties may also enter mediation after a judgment has been rendered. The following is an except from *Gallagher v. Gallagher.* Susie Gallagher and Patrick Gallagher were divorced by final decree in 1992. The decree affirmed, ratified, and incorporated the parties' child custody, support, and property settlement agreement which required the father to pay child support for their two children.

In 1995, the parties in a mediation renegotiated child support and executed an agreement amending the 1992 divorce decree. This agreement was not filed, approved, or incorporated into any order of the court. Based on this agreement, Patrick began making the lower child support payments.

In 1999, Susie petitioned the court for child support arrearages against Patrick based on the difference between the court's original order in 1992 and what he had been paying under the mediation agreement. Patrick moved to incorporate the mediated agreement into the divorce decree and deny his former wife's petition. The following is the Virginia Court of Appeals's discussion of this issue.

Gallagher v. Gallagher
Court of Appeals of Virginia
32 Va.App. 714, 530 S.E.2d 913 (2000)

RETROACTIVE COURT RATIFICATION OF MODIFIED CHILD SUPPORT

The mother contends that the trial court erred by enforcing the provisions of the 1995 amendment, because it was not incorporated into the final decree when the parties entered into the amended agreement and because the amended agreement had expired when the trial court incorporated it. We agree that any modification of child support payments established by agreement of the parties must be reviewed and approved by the court. *See Kelley v. Kelley*, 248 Va. 295, 298, 449 S.E.2d 55, 56 (1994) ("Parents may not contract away their children's rights to support, nor may a court be precluded by agreement from exercising its power to decree child support."); *Wilderman v. Wilderman*, 25 Va.App. 500, 506, 489 S.E.2d 701, 704–05 (1997)("When changed circumstances dictate a modification of a support decree, the appropriate remedy is for the party to petition the court to modify the decree. The party or parties may not unilaterally or bilaterally vary its terms." (quoting *Commonwealth v. Skeens*, 18 Va.App. 154, 158, 442 S.E.2d 432, 434–35 (1994); *Scott v. Scott*, 12 Va.App. 1245, 1247, 408 S.E.2d 579, 581 (1991) ("Divorcing parents cannot by agreement divest a divorce court of its jurisdiction to award child support.")).

However, nothing in our previous holdings suggests that court approval may not be granted retroactively after an agreement has been performed, provided the modification does not adversely affect the child's interest. It follows that the evidence in cases in which such *ex post facto* court approval is sought must fully support the modification when viewed in light of the dictates of *Acree, i.e.,* the record must affirmatively show that the best interests of the child are served and the agreed modification "substantially satisfies the purpose and function of the support award and . . . does not vary [in effect] the support award." *Wilderman*, 25 Va.App. at 506, 489 S.E.2d at 704–05. Where the party seeking ratification of an agreement to modify child support fails to meet this burden of proof, the child support modification will be deemed invalid and arrearages may be awarded. *See Henderlite*, 3 Va.App. at 542, 351 S.E.2d at 914.

In sum, parties who enter into agreements for support and implement them without seeking and obtaining court approval, do so at their peril and may later be held liable for non-conforming payments, when measured against the court's ultimate determination of appropriate support levels, viewed in light of the best interests of the child standard. *See Watkinson v. Henley*, 13 Va.App. 151, 158–59, 409 S.E.2d 470, 474 (1991); *Alexander v. Alexander*, 12 Va.App. 691, 695, 406 S.E.2d 666, 668 (1991). However, as we made abundantly clear in *Goodpasture v. Goodpasture*, 7 Va.App. 55, 58, 371 S.E.2d 845, 847 (1988), any such modification by agreement implemented prior to court approval will be subject to scrutiny

(continued)

(continued from previous page)

by the court, and, in the absence of evidence proving the modification of support amount or mode of payment served the best interests of the child, will be disallowed. *See also Kelley,* 248 Va. at 298, 449 S.E.2d at 56 (a court cannot be precluded by agreement between the parties from exercising its power to decree child support).

The mother's claim that the trial court should not have incorporated the 1995 amendment into the parties' final decree is, therefore, without merit, because the evidence supports the trial court's findings that the amendment created a permanent alteration in the custody arrangements, not one of limited duration, and that under the amended agreement, the purpose and function of the support award, including the total amount of support the children were entitled to receive under the decree, were substantially satisfied. The trial court thus properly incorporated the 1995 amendment effective as of the date of the parties' agreement.

The mother also contends that, under established Virginia law, *ex post facto* approval of the parties' agreement constituted an improper retroactive modification of support. *See, e.g., Cofer v. Cofer,* 205 Va. 834, 839, 140 S.E.2d 663, 666 (1965); *Bennett v. Bennett,* 22 Va.App. 684, 696, 472 S.E.2d 668, 674 (1996). We conclude that the various authorities cited by the mother are not controlling, because they do not address the effect of an unequivocal agreement between the parties which, in effect, does not vary the total amount of support awarded to the children by decree but only the "method of payment," such as may occur concurrently with a permanent change of custody. *Acree, Skeens, Henderlite,* and *Wilderman* all stand for the proposition that non-conforming child support payments will be approved by the court *retroactively* where the purpose and function of the child support award have been substantially satisfied. Based on the evidence in this case, and the principles that apply, we find that the trial court did not improperly modify retroactively the child support decree.

Ethical and Legal Issues

Some of the current issues concerning mediation involve training, qualifications, and certification of mediators; ethical rules for mediators; impartiality, fairness, and imbalances in power and knowledge; conflict of interest; confidentiality; and mediator's liability and immunity.

Training, Qualifications, and Certification of Mediators

A number of private organizations, courts, and state legislatures are struggling with the issue of who should be a mediator. What skills, knowledge, and training are essential?

The Society of Professionals in Dispute Resolution (SPIDR) established a commission to study the qualifications of mediators (and arbitrators). The commission emphasized performance rather than paper credentials as the core qualification criteria. The SPIDR commission identified the following skills necessary for competent performance as a mediator:

1. ability to understand the negotiating process and the role of advocacy;
2. ability to earn trust and maintain acceptability;
3. ability to convert parties' positions into needs and interests;
4. ability to screen out nonmediable issues;
5. ability to help parties invent creative options;
6. ability to help the parties identify principles and criteria that will guide their decision making;

7. ability to help parties assess their nonsettlement alternatives;
8. ability to help the parties make their own informed choices;
9. ability to help parties assess whether their agreement can be implemented.

Problem 10-2

1. If these are the skills necessary for competent performance as a mediator, what training should be required and who should provide this training?
2. Should the training be certified and, if so, by whom?
3. Should training be a condition precedent to mediation?
4. If the training should be certified, then should mediators be certified, how, and by whom?
5. Should only lawyers or psychologists be mediators? Should paralegals be mediators?
6. Who has the authority to preclude a nonlawyer from mediating?

Ethical Rules for Mediators

The National Conference of Commissioners on Uniform State Laws is in the process of drafting a Uniform Mediation Act. Once the drafting process has been completed, the Uniform Act will be presented to the states through the Uniform State Laws committee of each state. These state committees will review the Uniform Act and make recommendations to their respective legislatures. If recommended, the Uniform Act must be passed by the state's legislature and signed by the governor. The Uniform Act will then become the law of that state. The various drafts of the Uniform Mediation Act are found on the Internet at *http://www.law.upenn.edu/bll/ula/mediat/*. The Uniform Mediation Act is found in Appendix B.

Problem 10-3

1. Should ethical rules be developed for mediators, who should draft these rules, and, if drafted, what should be included?
2. Who has the authority to regulate mediators?

Impartiality, Fairness, and Imbalances in Power and Knowledge

Mediation involves a neutral third party who directs the discussion. A mediator who is neutral does not side with either party. The mediator must remain neutral throughout the mediation.

There are situations where one party will agree to pay for the mediator or to pay more for the mediation than the other party will need to pay. If both parties do not pay equally, could the mediator be perceived to favor the party who pays more?

Problem 10-4

Kerry Amsterdam was driving his car on Interstate 40 when he was involved in an accident with a semitrailer owned by the Coast to Coast Trucking Company. Kerry suffered multiple injuries and was hospitalized for five weeks. As a result of the accident, Kerry has lost substantial income as a stock broker. Both Kerry and the trucker accuse the other of being at fault.

Coast to Coast Trucking Company and its insurer, Quaker Insurance, have offered to mediate the dispute. Quaker has also offered to pay for the mediation.

Should Kerry agree to mediate?

If a party frequently uses mediation, that party will have more expertise in selecting a mediator.

Problem 10-5

1. Will a party who uses mediation on a regular basis tend to favor the selection of a mediator who has participated in mediations where that party was able to negotiate favorable outcomes?
2. Would this party also tend to favor a mediator who has in the past favored this party's position or industry?
3. Should the parties select an environmentalist to mediate a dispute between an oil drilling company and the Sierra Club?
4. Who should not mediate a child custody, an employment discrimination, or a labor/management dispute?
5. Would a party tend to favor a mediator who is a member of his or her profession, trade, political party, country club, church, or civic organization?
6. Would a party tend to favor a mediator whom he or she knows personally rather than someone who is unknown?
7. Does one party to the mediation have an advantage because he or she knows more about the mediators being considered than does the other party? Is this an unfair advantage? What should be done about it?

If a mediator must remain neutral throughout the mediation, how should a mediator approach a power imbalance between the parties? Should the mediator attempt to correct the imbalance and, if so, how? Do mediators lose their impartiality when they attempt to correct power imbalances?

Problem 10-6

Perry is the mediator in a family dispute involving the custody of minor children. Jon, the father, wants full custody while Deborah, the mother, is willing to share custody. As the mediation progresses, Perry learns that the marriage has been an abusive one. While Jon has not physically assaulted Deborah, he has subjected her to psychological abuse. As Perry watches the parties interact, he finds that Jon dominates Deborah to the point that Deborah is having difficulty holding her own. What should Perry do?

1. Should he try to correct the power imbalance and, if so, how?
2. Should he hold a private caucus with Deborah and, if so, what should he talk to her about?
3. Should he end the mediation session because of the imbalance, or should he do something else?

————————

Although the outcome of the mediation remains the decision of the parties, the mediator's active participation certainly influences the direction of the discussion and leads the parties away from some outcomes and toward others. Therefore, at least hypothetically, the mediator in a private mediation may be less than impartial. A mediator who is impartial becomes less than impartial if one of the parties perceives the mediator to be either partial or hostile toward him or her personally or toward his or her performance or position at the mediation.

Problem 10-7

1. Are there situations where the conduct of one party pushes the mediator to the point where the mediator feels that he or she is no longer neutral? Describe such a situation?
2. What should a mediator do upon realizing that he or she is no longer neutral?

————————

As with negotiation, each party in a private mediation has the power to terminate the process. Therefore, each party has the power to terminate what he or she perceives to be an unfair process. The inequality of the parties, however, may cause a party to be reluctant to exercise this power. While a party may be perfectly comfortable walking out of a negotiation, he or she may be uncomfortable or even embarrassed to walk out of a mediation because of the presence of the mediator, the location of the mediation, the loss of control over the process, and the greater formality of the process.

Neither party can claim to be treated unfairly by the other party. As with a negotiation without a mediator, in mediation neither party has a duty to negotiate in good faith. If mediation produces an agreement, the dispute is settled on the terms agreed to by the parties. If one party feels the terms of the proposed agreement are unfair, he or she should not accept the proposed agreement. The playing field may not have begun as level with one party having little to offer and few options. Accepting the best offer under the circumstances does not mean that a party is treated unfairly.

Can the outcome be unfair? Although one party may try to entice the other to do something that is not consistent with his or her interests, fairness does not require that a party be protected from himself or herself. When a party agrees to a mediated solution, he or she feels that something has been given away, but something has been gained in return. What is gained is usually at the expense of the other party. Even if a party feels that the agreement is less than fair, he or she will agree because it makes good personal or business sense to do so.

Does the mediator have the duty to protect a party from making an unwise decision, especially when the mediator knows the playing field is not level?

Problem 10-8

The Model Standards of Conduct for Mediators of the American Arbitration Association states in the Comments after Standard I on *Self-determination:*

> A mediator cannot personally ensure that each party has made a fully informed choice to reach a particular agreement, but it is a good practice for the mediator to make the parties aware of the importance of consulting other professionals, where appropriate, to help them make informed decisions.

> See *http://www.adr.org/rules/ethics/standard.html.* Does this practice by the mediator reduce his or her impartiality?

Problem 10-9

1. What is the role of the mediator when the parties are on the verge of settling a dispute in which the proposed settlement has significant tax consequences and one of the parties is totally ignorant of these consequences?
2. Should the mediator give the party tax advice, should the mediator advise the party to consult a tax advisor before entering into the agreement, or should the mediator remain silent?

_____

Is the outcome correct? The parties in a mediated agreement may elect to give up their legal rights in exchange for an outcome that makes personal or business sense. The mediated agreement ends the dispute, establishes certainty as to the rights and duties of the parties, and permits the parties to move forward. At times, the parties have a continuing personal or business relationship that is enhanced by the mediated agreement.

Example 10-6

In 1990, Georgia Clays, Inc., sold its kaolin mining and processing company to Rutherford, Inc., but retained ownership in a number of clay properties in Georgia. Kaolin is a clay which, among its other uses, is needed in the paper industry. As part of the sales agreement, Georgia Clays leased various properties that it owned to Rutherford so Rutherford could mine the kaolin. Also as part of the sales agreement, Georgia Clays subleased its rights to mine other property to Rutherford. The sales agreement required a royalty payment of 1.5 percent of Rutherford's "net receipts" from kaolin derived from all the properties and sold by Rutherford during a given period. Since some of the properties were only leased to Georgia Clays, Rutherford was permitted under the sales agreement, to deduct royalties it had to pay to those landowners.

A dispute arose over how Rutherford was calculating the deduction to one of the landowners. Rutherford and Georgia Clays agreed to mediate their dispute. Although the dispute only involved one sublease, the mediation could help the parties resolve future disputes as to their other properties.

What might be considered the correct outcome for one party might not be the correct outcome for another. Since the outcome has been influenced more by personal or business factors and less by the law, there is no abstract standard by which to evaluate "correctness." Correctness depends on the perception of the party who accepts the mediated agreement.

Finally, does the mediator have a duty to represent the interests of third parties who are not present at the mediation? The Society of Professionals in Dispute Resolution (SPIDR) approaches this issue in its *Ethical Standards of Professional Responsibility* as follows:

> **Unrepresented Interests**
> The neutral must consider circumstances where interests are not represented in the process. The neutral has an obligation, where in his or or judgment the needs of parties dictate, to assure that such interests have been considered by the principal parties.

SPIDR's *Ethical Standards of Professional Responsibility* may be found on the Internet at *http://www.spidr.org/ethic.htm.*

Problem 10-10

In Problem 10-6, Perry was the mediator in a family dispute involving the custody of minor children. Jon, the father, wanted full custody while Deborah, the mother, was willing to share custody. The custody dispute involves the couple's four children: Jon, Jr., age 14, Deborah Ann, age 12, and the twins, Christopher and Mary Alice, age 2.

During the mediation, it appeared to Perry that Jon, Jr., would prefer to stay with his father, although he also wanted to stay with his mother and sisters. Deborah Ann would prefer to stay with her mother and the twins, although she also wanted to stay with her father and her brother.

During the mediation, it also appeared to Perry that Deborah's mother and father were interested in having custody of the children and could keep all the children together.

1. What is the role of the mediator when the parties are on the verge of settling the custody issue and they are more interested in their own interests than those of the children and grandparents?
2. Should the mediator represent these unrepresented parties?
3. Should the mediator merely raise the issue of third-party interests and leave it at that?
4. Should the mediator terminate the mediation if these interests are not addressed to the mediator's satisfaction?
5. What would the SPIDR *Ethical Standards* provide and do you agree with them?

Conflict of Interest
A conflict of interest exists when the neutral third party and one of the disputing parties have potentially incompatible interests.

Conflict of Interest

A **conflict of interest** arises when two or more duties or interests come into competition.

Example 10-7

Richard Wise, an attorney, is hired by Estella Gomez to represent her in her divorce action against her husband, Charles. After the divorce is granted, a custody issue arises between Estella and Charles. Charles hires Richard as his attorney in the custody matter.

Richard has a conflict of interest because he cannot represent opposing parties in related matters. Richard's representation of Charles would adversely affect Estella's interests. Richard has received confidential information when he represented Estella, and this confidential information would not be preserved if he represented Charles against Estella.

Problem 10-11

Rosy Kim, a paralegal, was working for Richard Wise when he was hired by Estella Gomez to pursue her divorce action against Charles. Rosy worked closely with Richard on the Gomez case. Several weeks later, Rosy left Richard's employ and went to work for Carmen Quay. Carmen has been hired by Charles to represent him in his custody action against his former wife, Estella Gomez.

1. Does Rosy have a conflict of interest?
2. What should she do?

If a mediator has a conflict of interest with either of the parties, his or her impartiality comes into issue. Although the mediator represents neither party at the mediation, he or she may not be fit to serve as the mediator.

The *Ethical Standards of Professional Responsibility* of the Society of Professionals in Dispute Resolution describes the mediator's responsibility as to conflict of interest:

> 4. **Conflict of Interest.** The neutral must refrain from entering or continuing in any dispute if he or she believes or perceives that participation as a neutral would be a clear conflict of interest and any circumstances that may reasonably raise a question as to the neutral's impartiality. The duty to disclose is a continuing obligation throughout the process.

See http://www.spidr.org/ethic.htm.

Attorney-mediators, because of their special relationship with clients, will have more conflict of interest problems than will nonattorney-mediators even though the attorney-mediator is not practicing law when he or she is a mediator.

Problem 10-12

1. Can a mediator, who happens to be an attorney, mediate a dispute when one of the parties to the dispute has been a client of the mediator's law firm?
2. Can a mediator, who happens to be a paralegal, mediate a dispute when one of the parties to the dispute has been a client of the paralegal's law firm?

3. Can an attorney represent a party who once was a party in a dispute that the attorney mediated?
4. Can a paralegal work on a case at his or her law firm when the party represented by the firm was a party in a dispute that the paralegal either mediated or assisted an attorney who mediated?

Confidentiality

Confidential Information

Information is confidential when it is secret, classified, concealed, hidden, off the record, privileged, private, or sentitive.

Confidential information is information that is secret, classified, concealed, hidden, off the record, privileged, private, or sensitive. Mediation promises the parties confidentiality. Confidentiality protects the parties and protects the mediator.

The *Ethical Standards of Professional Responsibility* of the Society of Professionals in Dispute Resolution describes the mediator's responsibility as to confidentiality:

> 3. **Confidentiality.** Maintaining confidentiality is critical to the dispute resolution process. Confidentiality encourages candor, a full exploration of the issues, and a neutral's acceptability. There may be some types of cases, however, in which confidentiality is not protected. In such cases, the neutral must advise the parties, when appropriate in the dispute resolution process, that the confidentiality of the proceedings cannot necessarily be maintained. Except in such instances, the neutral must resist all attempts to cause him or her to reveal any information outside the process. A commitment by the neutral to hold information in confidence within the process also must be honored.

See http://www.spidr.org/ethic.htm.

The Uniform Mediation Act, sections 4 and 6 of the National Conference of Commissioners on Uniform State Laws provide:

> **Section 4. Privilege Against Disclosure; Admissibility; Discovery**
> (a) Except as otherwise provided in Section 6, a mediation communication is privileged as provided in subsection (b) and is not subject to discovery or admissible in evidence in a proceeding unless waived or precluded as provided by Section 5.
> (b) In a proceeding, the following privileges apply:
>   (1) A mediation party may refuse to disclose, and may prevent any other person from disclosing, a mediation communication.
>   (2) A mediator may refuse to disclose a mediation communication, and may prevent any other person from disclosing a mediation communication of the mediator.
>   (3) A nonparty participant may refuse to disclose, and may prevent any other person from disclosing, a mediation communication of the nonparty participant.
> (c) Evidence or information that is otherwise admissible or subject to discovery does not become inadmissible or protected from discovery solely by reason of its disclosure or use in a mediation.

> **Section 6. Exceptions to Privilege**
> (a) There is no privilege under Section 4 for a mediation communication that is:
>   (1) in an agreement evidenced by a record signed by all parties to the agreement;

(2) available to the public under [insert statutory reference to open records act] or made during a session of a mediation which is open, or is required by law to be open, to the public;

(3) a threat or statement of a plan to inflict bodily injury or commit a crime of violence;

(4) intentionally used to plan a crime, attempt to commit or commit a crime, or to conceal an ongoing crime or ongoing criminal activity;

(5) sought or offered to prove or disprove a claim or complaint of professional misconduct or malpractice filed against a mediator;

(6) except as otherwise provided in subsection (c), sought or offered to prove or disprove a claim or complaint of professional misconduct or malpractice filed against a mediation party, nonparty participant, or representative of a party based on conduct occurring during a mediation; or

(7) sought or offered to prove or disprove abuse, neglect, abandonment, or exploitation in a proceeding in which a child or adult protective services agency is a party, unless the
[Alternative A: [State to insert, for example, child or adult protection] case is referred by a court to mediation and a public agency participates.]
[Alternative B: public agency participates in the [State to insert, for example, child or adult protection] mediation].

(b) There is no privilege under Section 4 if a court, administrative agency, or arbitrator finds, after a hearing in camera, that the party seeking discovery or the proponent of the evidence has shown that the evidence is not otherwise available, that there is a need for the evidence that substantially outweighs the interest in protecting confidentiality, and that the mediation communication is sought or offered in:

(1) a court proceeding involving a felony [or misdemeanor]; or

(2) except as otherwise provided in subsection (c), a proceeding to prove a claim to rescind or reform or a defense to avoid liability on a contract arising out of the mediation.

(c) A mediator may not be compelled to provide evidence of a mediation communication referred to in subsection (a)(6) or (b)(2).

(d) If a mediation communication is not privileged under subsection (a) or (b), only the portion of the communication necessary for the application of the exception from nondisclosure may be admitted. Admission of evidence under subsection (a) or (b) does not render the evidence, or any other mediation communication, discoverable or admissible for any other purpose.

Confidentiality That Protects the Parties

In mediation, the mediator leads the parties to believe that they may speak freely, that their statements are made off the record, and that their statements will not be quoted, published, or released at some future date. The expectation of confidentiality permits the parties to explore sensitive topics that they would otherwise not feel free to explore. At times, the parties may release this confidential information to each other. At other times, a party may release this confidential information only to the mediator in a private caucus.

In either case, the party who releases confidential information expects the information to remain confidential.

Confidentiality may be waived by the parties as illustrated by section 5 of the Uniform Mediation Act of the National Conference of Commissioners on Uniform State Laws:

Section 5. Waiver and Preclusion of Privilege

(a) A privilege under Section 4 may be waived in a record or orally during a proceeding if it is expressly waived by all parties to the mediation and:

    (1) in the case of the privilege of a mediator, it is expressly waived by the mediator; and

    (2) in the case of the privilege of a nonparty participant, it is expressly waived by the nonparty participant.

(b) A person that discloses or makes a representation about a mediation communication which prejudices another person in a proceeding is precluded from asserting a privilege under Section 4, but only to the extent necessary for the person prejudiced to respond to the representation or disclosure.

(c) A person that intentionally uses a mediation to plan, attempt to commit or commit a crime, or to conceal an ongoing crime or ongoing criminal activity is precluded from asserting a privilege under Section 4.

Confidentiality That Protects the Mediator

The mediator is a neutral third party. The mediator at the mediation sides with neither party. Mediators, however, who are called to testify in court as to what the parties said during the mediation lose their neutrality because the mediators' testimony will be perceived as favoring certain parties over the others.

When would a mediator be called to testify in court as to what the parties said during a mediation? The mediator's testimony may be requested when the terms of the mediated agreement come into issue.

The Uniform Mediation Act, section 7 of the National Conference of Commissioners on Uniform State Laws discusses when a mediator may and may not disclose communications from the mediation:

Section 7. Prohibited Mediator Reports

(a) Except as required in subsection (b), a mediator may not make a report, assessment, evaluation, recommendation, finding, or other communication regarding a mediation to a court, administrative agency, or other authority that may make a ruling on the dispute that is the subject of the mediation.

(b) A mediator may disclose:

    (1) whether the mediation occurred or has terminated, whether a settlement was reached, and attendance;

    (2) a mediation communication as permitted under Section 6; or

    (3) a mediation communication evidencing abuse, neglect, abandonment, or exploitation of an individual to a public agency responsible for protecting individuals against such mistreatment.

(c) A communication made in violation of subsection (a) may not be considered by a court, administrative agency, or arbitrator.

Example 10-8

Sally sued Benjamin for divorce and for custody of their daughter, Samantha. When Benjamin sought custody for himself, the judge told the parties to try to mediate an agreement on the custody issue. Sally and Benjamin proceeded to private mediation where they entered into a joint custody arrangement. The court approved the parties' agreement.

Six months later Sally and Benjamin were again before the judge. This time they were disputing what the mediated agreement meant in regard to who had custody on Thanksgiving, Christmas, and the Fourth of July. The parties requested that the mediator be subpoenaed to testify as to what was said during the mediation.

In *Vernon v. Acton,* Vernon was involved in an automobile accident with a car driven by Acton. The Vernons and Acton participated in a mediation that resulted in an oral settlement agreement. The Vernons then disregarded the mediated agreement and filed a complaint against Acton. Vernon sued in negligence to recover for injuries he sustained in the accident. Vernon's wife sued for loss of consortium.

Vernon v. Acton
Supreme Court of Indiana
732 N.E.2d 805 (2000)

DICKSON, Justice

The plaintiff-appellants, Kirk and Martha Vernon, are appealing from a judgment granting motions to enforce an oral pre-trial mediation settlement agreement and to impose attorney fees filed by the defendant-appellee, Adam Acton. Denying the existence of any agreement, the plaintiffs raised multiple issues on appeal. The Court of Appeals affirmed. *Vernon v. Acton,* 693 N.E.2d 1345 (Ind. Ct. App. 1998). We granted transfer and requested additional briefing regarding issues related to the Indiana Rules for Alternative Dispute Resolution (A.D.R. Rules). We now reverse the trial court, concluding that the mediator's testimony regarding the alleged oral settlement agreement was confidential and privileged and that it was not admissible pursuant to the A.D.R. Rules incorporated in the parties' written agreement to mediate.

This case arises from an automobile collision involving vehicles driven by plaintiff Kirk Vernon and defendant Adam Acton. Prior to filing a complaint for damages, the plaintiffs and the defendant engaged in a voluntary pre-suit mediation pursuant to a written agreement establishing the terms and conditions of the mediation process. The defendant contends that the session produced an oral agreement to settle the plaintiffs' claims for $29,500.00. A few days after the mediation session, the defendant's insurance company issued a check and a release form to the plaintiffs. The plaintiffs returned both unsigned and promptly filed a complaint against the defendant alleging negligence and seeking damages for physical injuries and loss of consortium. In his answer, the defendant asserted various affirmative defenses and a counterclaim seeking damages for breach of the settlement agreement and attorney fees. Both parties timely filed demands for jury trial. Two months later, the defendant filed a "Motion to Enforce Settlement Agreement," along with a "Motion for Attorney's Fees."

The trial court heard evidence on the defendant's pre-trial motions and made the following determinations: that the plaintiff had accepted the defendant's settlement offer; that there was an oral agreement that the plaintiffs would execute a release of all claims in exchange for $29,500.00; that the defendant did not breach the confidentiality provisions of the Agreement to Mediate or the A.D.R. Rules by disclosing statements made during the mediation process; and that the defendant was entitled to $8,000.00 in attorney fees from the plaintiffs because the lawsuit was a frivolous, unreasonable, and groundless action in light of the settlement agreement.

The plaintiffs contend that, during the hearing on the defendant's pre-trial motions to enforce settlement agreement and for attorney fees, the trial court erroneously admitted evidence regarding the alleged settlement in contravention of the parties' mediation agreement, A.D.R. Rule 2.12,[1] and Indiana Evidence Rule 408. The defendant asserts that only the statements made during the mediation process *before* settlement were confidential. He *argues that neither the* parties' agreement, the A.D.R. Rules, nor the Evidence Rules prohibit evidence of an oral settlement agreement reached in mediation.

At the trial court evidentiary hearing, David Young, a claims representative for Farmers Insurance, the defendant's insurance company, testified regarding events that occurred on October 23, 1995, at the Indianapolis offices of National Alternative Dispute Resolution Services, Inc. Young; the mediator, Paul S. Petticrew; the plaintiffs; their attorney, Kirk A. Knoll; and his investigator, Clifford Somers, attended the mediation, held pursuant to a signed Agreement to Mediate. The mediation session lasted about three and one-third hours on a single day. Over the plaintiffs' objection, the trial court permitted Young to testify that, at the conclusion of the mediation session and while at the mediator's offices, "We agreed to settle the claim at

$29,500." Record at 214. Young stated that he delivered the settlement check and release to Somers a few days after the mediation session. Over repeated objections by plaintiffs' counsel, the mediator, Petticrew, testified that the parties reached agreement in separate rooms, after which he brought them together for the purpose of summarizing the terms of the agreement. Petticrew stated that "[t]he parties had reached an agreement of $29,500 in full and final satisfaction of the claims" and that "the parties agreed that the adjustor was to deliver a check for $29,500 along with a release to the claimants' attorney's office." Record at 305–06. At no time did Petticrew prepare or submit a written version of the agreement to the parties to be signed. However, five months later, on March 18, 1996, in response to a request from Young, Petticrew issued a written report on the mediation, stating in part: "After three and one third hours of negotiation through the pre-litigation mediation process, the parties reached an agreement for a full and final settlement of claimants' claims for twenty-nine thousand five hundred dollars ($29,500.00)." Record at 276.

In response to the trial court overruling the plaintiffs' objections and admitting evidence of the existence of an alleged oral settlement agreement, plaintiff Kirk Vernon testified that, when he left the meeting with the mediator, he did not believe that he had entered into a binding agreement. Sowers, the investigator for the plaintiffs' attorney, testified that, at the time of leaving the mediator's office, an offer had been extended but the plaintiffs had unresolved questions regarding whether they had to pay back their medical insurance carrier. To establish their contention that there was no meeting of the minds, the plaintiffs also attempted to present testimony during the hearing regarding statements and events during the portion of the mediation session that preceded the mediator's summary, but the trial court sustained the defendant's objections to this testimony. The plaintiffs contend that the trial court's decision had the effect of allowing the parties to testify as to the legal conclusion that an agreement had been reached but excluded evidence of the facts relevant to whether the alleged agreement existed.

[1]Pursuant to amendment of December 23, 1996, effective March 1, 1997, the substance of this Rule 2.12 is now found in Rule 2.11 (1999).

(continued)

(continued from previous page)

The trial court ruled that it could hear evidence that an agreement was reached, but that A.D.R. Rule 2.12 prevented it from receiving evidence of "what went on during the mediation process."[2] Record at 228. The Court of Appeals upheld the trial court's judgment, based upon Indiana Evidence Rules 402 and 408 and its view that the confidentiality provisions in the parties' written agreement to mediate could not supersede the Rules of Evidence. Vernon, 693 N.E.2d at 1348–50.

This mediation was entered into pursuant to a written Agreement to Mediate.[3] The agreement required confidentiality in conformity with state law and Supreme

[2]The trial court explained its ruling as follows: "The Court may hear evidence that there was an agreement reached and I have received that. What negotiations and so on that went into it, I may not under these rules receive that evidence." Record at 226. Further, "[n]ow, under 2.12, I'm not permitted to receive information on what went on during the mediation process. So I've got the very difficult problem that I can see the footprint but I can't be told what happened when the footprint was being made." Record at 228.

[3]The Agreement to Mediate was not admitted into evidence at the trial court's hearing on the defendant's motions, but it is in the Record as Exhibit A to the Plaintiffs' Reply to Counterclaim; Demand for Jury Trial. Record at 30–37. This agreement included the following provisions regarding confidentiality:

2.1 The mediation process is confidential. All parties expressly understand and agree that any statements made during the mediation process by either party about any matter shall be considered confidential, in conformity with State law and Supreme Court Rules.

Further, all parties understand and agree that insofar as the mediation process is directed towards the settlement of issues which might otherwise be the subject of litigation, statements made by either party during the process are intended to be taken as being in furtherance of settlement and, therefore, not admissible as evidence in court. Further, in signing this Agreement, all parties understand and agree to be foreclosed and barred from: telling any statement made by the other party; requesting the production of any notes, documents, or tapes made in mediation; or, requesting the testimony of the mediator with regard to any part of the mediation process in Court or any other legal process.

Record at 36–37.

Court Rules.[4] Both parties claim that by their Agreement to Mediate they intended to be governed by the A.D.R. Rules. They dispute the scope, but not the applicability, of the A.D.R. mediation confidentiality rule. Each party presented arguments both to the trial court and to the Court of Appeals based on the A.D.R. Rules. The trial court's decision was grounded solely upon the A.D.R. Rules. We note that the A.D.R. Rules would not have otherwise applied to this pre-suit mediation,[5] *see Anderson v. Yorktown Classroom Teachers Ass'n*, 677 N.E.2d 540, 542 (Ind. Ct. App. 1997). However, because each of the parties intended to be governed by the A.D.R. mediation confidentiality rule, and to guide the bench and bar, we will analyze the mediation in this case as governed by the A.D.R. Rules.

At the time of the mediation in this case, the Indiana A.D.R. Rules provided in pertinent part:

RULE 2.12 CONFIDENTIALITY

Mediation shall be regarded as settlement negotiations. Evidence of (1) furnishing or offering or promising to furnish, or (2) accepting or offering or promising to accept, a valuable consideration in compromising or attempting to compromise a claim which was disputed as to either validity or amount, is not admissible to prove

[4]Supplemental Brief of Appellants at 3–4; Appellee's Supplemental Brief on A.D.R. Rules at 7.
[5]The A.D.R. Rules apply only to "all civil and domestic relations litigation filed" in Indiana trial courts, subject to certain exceptions not relevant to this case. A.D.R. 1.4. By their terms, they do not apply to a mediation not instituted pursuant to judicial action in a pending case. Although not in effect at the time of the mediation in the present case, this Court has since expressly recommended the Pre-Suit Mediation Guidelines developed by the Indiana State Bar Association. A.D.R. Guideline 8 (adopted Dec. 4, 1998, effective Jan. 1, 1999). The Pre-Suit Guideline suggests that the parties should, by private agreement, protect the confidentiality of the pre-suit mediation process in accordance with the A.D.R. Rules. A.D.R. Guideline 8.4 & Form B(5). Strongly favoring the amicable resolution of disputes without resort to litigation, this Court encourages the use of mediation and other amicable settlement techniques and procedures.

liability for or invalidity of the claim or its amount. *Evidence of conduct or statements made in the course of mediation is likewise not admissible.* This rule does not require the exclusion of any evidence otherwise discoverable merely because it is presented in the course of the mediation process. This rule also does not require exclusion when the evidence is offered for another purpose, such as proving bias or prejudice of a witness, or negating a contention of undue delay. Mediation meetings shall be closed to all persons other than the parties of record, their legal representatives, and other invited persons. *Mediators shall not be subject to process requiring the disclosure of any matter discussed during the mediation, but rather, such matter shall be considered confidential and privileged in nature. The confidentiality requirement may not be waived by the parties, and an objection to the obtaining of testimony or physical evidence from mediation may be made by any party or by the mediators.* A.D.R. 2.12 (1995) (emphasis added).

This rule provides for confidentiality in mediation to the extent provided for in other settlement negotiations. This remained so when we revised and renumbered the rule as A.D.R. Rule 2.11 in December of 1996 (effective March 1, 1997), modifying it to read: "Mediation shall be regarded as settlement negotiations as governed by Ind. Evidence Rule 408," the language of which we specifically set forth in this A.D.R. Rule. Likewise, this evidence rule has, from the time of its adoption in 1994, provided: "Compromise negotiations encompass alternative dispute resolution." Ind. Evid. R. 408. Although the mediation confidentiality rule declares that "[e]vidence of conduct or statements made in the course of mediation is likewise not admissible," the rule also provides:

> This rule does not require exclusion of any evidence otherwise discoverable merely because it is presented in the course of the mediation process. This rule does not require exclusion when the evidence is offered for another purpose, such as proving bias or prejudice of a witness, or negating a contention of undue delay.

A.D.R. 2.12 (1995). Evidence Rule 408 contains a parallel provision.

We note that, in general, settlement agreements need not be in writing to be enforceable. *Ind. Farmers*

Mut. Ins. Co. v. Walters, 221 Ind. 642, 646, 50 N.E.2d 868, 869 (1943); *Klebes v. Forest Lake Corp.,* 607 N.E.2d 978, 982 (Ind. Ct. App. 1993). However, when a settlement agreement is reached in mediation, the mediation rules required that "it shall be reduced to writing and signed." A.D.R. 2.7(E)(2).[6] In *Silkey v. Investors Diversified Serv., Inc.,* 690 N.E.2d 329 (Ind. Ct. App. 1997), the Court of Appeals confronted the issue of "what effect, if any, should be given to the oral agreement reached by the parties at the conclusion of a mediation." *Id.* at 331–32. Unlike the present case, the parties in *Silkey* agreed that an agreement was reached, and the claim presented was whether the agreement was enforceable even though it was not signed. Noting that the terms of the agreement were not in dispute, the Court of Appeals held that the trial court acted properly in ordering the parties to reduce their agreement to writing and to file it with the court. *Id.* at 334. The *Silkey* court did not address the admissibility of evidence to establish the existence and terms of an alleged oral mediation settlement agreement.

Because of the nature of the mediation process and its significant and increasing role, considerable attention has been given to whether claims of oral mediation settlement agreements should be enforceable. We note that the March 2000 discussion draft of a proposed Uniform Mediation Act under consideration by the National Conference of Commissioners on Uniform State Laws provides that "a record of an agreement between two or more disputants" shall not be protected by privilege or prohibition against

---

[6]At the time of the mediation, A.D.R. 2.7(E)(2) stated: "If an agreement is reached, it shall be reduced to writing and signed. The agreement shall then be filed with the court. If the agreement is complete on all issues, it shall be accompanied by a joint stipulation of disposition." Amendments to this subsection adopted December 23, 1996, effective March 1, 1997, added the phrase "and signed by the parties and their counsel" to the end of the first sentence and the phrase "In domestic relations matters" to the beginning of the second sentence. Similarly, A.D.R. Guideline 8.8 states: "If an agreement to settlement is reached, it should be reduced to writing promptly and a copy provided to all parties."

(continued)

(continued from previous page)
disclosure. Section 8(a)(1), and the Reporter's Notes provide the following thoughtful explanation:

> This exception is noteworthy only for what is not included: oral agreements. The disadvantage of exempting oral settlements is that nearly everything said during a mediation session could bear on either whether the disputants came to an agreement or the content of the agreement. In other words, an exception for oral agreements has the potential to swallow the rule. As a result, mediation participants might be less candid, not knowing whether a controversy later would erupt over an oral agreement. Unfortunately, excluding evidence of oral settlements reached during a mediation session would operate to the disadvantage of a less legally-sophisticated disputant who is accustomed to the enforcement of oral settlements reached in negotiations. Such a person might also mistakenly assume the admissibility of evidence of oral settlements reached in mediation as well. However, because the majority of courts and statutes limit the confidentiality exception to signed written agreements, one would expect that mediators and others will soon incorporate knowledge of a writing requirement into their practices. *See Ryan v. Garcia,* 27 Cal. App. 4th 1006, 33 Cal. Rptr. 2d 158 (1994) (privilege statute precluded evidence of oral agreement); *Hudson v. Hudson,* 600 So.2d 7 (Fla. App. 1992) (privilege statute precluded evidence of oral settlement); *Cohen v. Cohen,* 609 So.2d 783 [785] (Fla. App. 1992)(same); Ohio Rev. Code 2317.02–03 (Baldwin 1998).

Nat'l Conf. of Comm'rs on Unif. State Laws, Uniform Mediation Act, Draft Report, Section 8, Reporter's Note 2, Subsection 8(a)(1), Record of an Agreement (Mar. 2000) *http://www.law.upenn.edu/ bll/ulc/ulc_frame.htm.*

We agree with this approach. Notwithstanding the importance of ensuring the enforceability of agreements that result from mediation, other goals are also important, including: facilitating agreements that result from mutual assent, achieving complete resolution of disputes, and producing clear understandings that the parties are less likely to dispute or challenge. These objectives are fostered by disfavoring oral agreements, about which the parties are more likely to have misunderstandings and disagreements. Requiring written agreements, signed by the parties, is more likely to maintain mediation as a viable avenue for clear and enduring dispute resolution rather than one leading to further uncertainty and conflict. Once the full assent of the parties is memorialized in a signed written agreement, the important goal of enforceability is achieved. We decline to find that the enforcement of oral mediation agreements is a sufficient ground to satisfy the "offered for another purpose" exception to the confidentiality rule and Evidence Rule 408.

We therefore hold that the mediation confidentiality provisions of our A.D.R. Rules[7] extend to and include oral settlement agreements undertaken or reached in mediation. Until reduced to writing and signed by the parties, mediation settlement agreements must be considered as compromise settlement *negotiations under the* applicable A.D.R. Rules and Evidence Rule 408.[8]

Having previously granted transfer, thereby vacating the opinion of the Court of Appeals, we now reverse the judgment of the trial court and remand this cause for a jury trial.

SHEPARD, C.J., SULLIVAN, BOEHM, and RUCKER, JJ., concur.

---

[7]A.D.R. 2.12 (1995), and A.D.R. 2.11 (1997).

[8]To the extent that *Silkey,* 690 N.E.2d 329, holds to the contrary, it is disapproved.

Mediator's Liability and Immunity

In theory, a party to a mediation may hold a private mediator liable on theories of negligence and breach of contract. A successful negligence action requires proof of the existence of a duty the mediator owes to the party, the breach of that duty by the mediator, an injury suffered by the party, and causation between the mediator's breach of duty and the party's asserted injury. A successful breach of contract action requires establishing a contract between the mediator and the party, the enforceability of that contract, the mediator's breach of a contractual duty, and a remedy available to the party for the mediator's breach of the contractual duty.

The Uniform Mediation Act does not seek to protect a private mediator from liability. Sections 6(a)(5) and (6) of the Uniform Mediation Act provide:

Section 6. Exceptions to Privilege

(a)   There is no privilege against disclosure under Section 4 for a mediation communication that is:

. . .

(5)   sought or offered to prove or disprove a claim or complaint of professional misconduct or malpractice filed against a mediator;

(6)   except as otherwise provided in subsection (c), sought or offered to prove or disprove a claim or complaint of professional misconduct or malpractice filed against a mediation party, nonparty participant, or representative of a party based on conduct occurring during a mediation;

. . . .

Problem 10-13
Should private mediators have immunity and, if so, from what?

The Advantages and Disadvantages of Private Mediation as a Dispute Resolution Process

The decision to mediate is based on personal or business factors and not on legal principles. The parties weigh the gains and losses attributable to mediation against the hypothetical gains and losses that another process might produce. What does a party gain or lose by selecting mediation as the method of dispute resolution?

Private mediation, as does negotiation, offers the parties complete flexibility. They can arrange when the mediation will begin, who will be the mediator, how the mediator will be compensated, where the mediation will be held, and how the mediation will be conducted. They can also decide whether the mediator will act only as a facilitator or will play a more active role by providing evaluations, suggestions, and recommendations. In short, the parties can negotiate all the details about the mediation or they can leave the details to the mediator. If the mediator comes from a group such as the American Arbitration Association, that organization will provide the mediator, the rules for the mediation, and a fee structure. *See* American Arbitration Association at *http://www.adr.org/contents2.htm*. A number of international, national, regional, and local services provide mediation services, as well.

Although negotiation and mediation are both informal, mediation is more formal since the mediator, rather than the parties, controls the process and directs the discussion.

As is the case with negotiation, mediation does not guarantee that the dispute will be resolved by the end of the process. In mediation, since the mediator provides only the process, it is the parties who must agree on how the dispute will be resolved.

In private mediation, the parties can be creative in formulating a solution and their creativity is not limited by legal principles. A mediated agreement generally accommodates at least some of the needs and interests of both parties.

Mediating an agreement will guarantee that transaction costs will be dramatically reduced when compared to the transaction costs for arbitration or litigation. The reduction, however, is not as great as if the parties had negotiated their agreement without mediation. Before the mediation process has begun, the parties may have hired attorneys and their attorneys may have begun discovery. Also, the mediator must be paid.

How much information does an attorney need before a dispute can be mediated? Some attorneys feel they need significant discovery to have a full understanding of the case. Others like to mediate before much discovery has been done. The latter reduces the transaction costs and permits mediation to serve as a discovery tool.

If mediation is conducted after litigation has been filed, some attorneys would like to begin mediation only after all dispositive motions have been decided by the judge. Others like the uncertainty created by pending dispositive motions.

If the mediation begins after litigation has been initiated, filing fees have been incurred and motions and briefs may have been filed with the court, driving up the transaction costs.

When selecting mediation, as is the case with selecting negotiation, the parties weigh the need to try to resolve the dispute now against what might happen if the dispute is resolved later. The parties may have a need to resolve the dispute sooner rather than later so they can put the problem behind them and move on. Delaying the resolution of the dispute does not guarantee that the dispute will be resolved any more favorably for the party who decides against mediation.

If a party elects to mediate and the other party agrees, it is the parties who control their own destinies. No neutral third party must acquiesce or consent to this decision to mediate.

The parties control not only the selection of mediation as the process but they also control the outcome and the outcome is known when the process is completed. Control of the outcome is important to a number of parties.

The mediation process is private and confidential with no public airing of the dispute. Privacy and confidentiality impact on one's reputation and may affect personal relationships, prestige in the community, and business opportunities.

When parties mediate an agreement, they almost always perform the agreement because the mediation has been thorough and the agreement has been carefully drafted so each party knows what is expected of him or her under the agreement. In those cases where a party fails to perform, the mediated agreement may be the basis for a breach of contract action. Unless a party later decides to breach the mediated agreement, the resolution of the dispute is final.

The parties are not required to reach an agreement. When a party believes that his or her interests are not being addressed, he or she may end the mediation and proceed to another form of dispute resolution. Continuing the dispute will mean that he or she will be required to devote additional personal time to this dispute and incur the costs associated with the newly selected process. Spending this time and money to seek an uncertain gain may have greater value to the party than the certain gain that the mediation could produce.

Control of the process and the outcome may be very important to a party. If a party elects to mediate and the other party agrees, it is the parties who control their own destinies. No neutral third party must acquiesce or consent to this decision.

The parties selecting mediation control not only the process but also the outcome, and the outcome is known when the process has been completed. The process is private and confidential with no public airing of the dispute. Unless a party later decides to breach the mediated agreement, the resolution of the dispute is final. When parties mediate an agreement, they almost always perform the agreement because the mediation has been thorough and the agreement has been carefully drafted so each party knows what is expected of him or her under the agreement. In those cases where a party fails to perform, the mediated agreement may be the basis for a breach of contract action. Figure 10-1 illustrates private mediation as a dispute resolution process.

AVAILABILITY	always available
PROCESS SELECTION	by the parties
	the parties control the scheduling, and the mediation can be scheduled before a case is filed or at any time after filing
THE PARTICIPANTS	the parties, a mediator, and depending on the mediation, the parties' attorneys
PREPARATION	each party may be required to prepare a short position document summarizing the facts, the issues, and previous settlement discussions
THE PROCESS	takes place in a private setting
	informal, with each party having an opportunity to discuss his or her perception of the dispute, his or her feelings, interests, and proposed solutions
	confidential and preserves the privacy of the parties' records and documents
	if the mediation is only facilitative, the mediator will not suggest solutions; if evaluative, the mediator will suggest solutions
FAIRNESS	generally does not address the inequality of power between the parties, and therefore one party may try to take advantage of the other
THE OUTCOME	allows the parties to control the outcome of their dispute and encourages creative resolutions
	can result in the immediate resolution of the dispute if the parties agree
	based on the parties' interests and needs
	eliminates all uncertainties as to outcome
	agreement may be based on inadequate information
	agreement is enforceable as a contract, and its promises will most likely be performed because they meet some of the parties' needs and interests
	if the parties are unable to agree, there will be no agreement and the dispute will continue
COSTS	the parties pay the mediator and any costs involved, although less expensive than adjudication (i.e., arbitration and litigation)
	if the dispute is resolved through private mediation, the parties save on discovery, litigation, and appeal costs
	saves or reduces attorney's fees
	will add another layer of costs to the dispute resolution process if the mediation does not resolve the dispute
	may provide low-cost discovery due to the openness of the discussion
PRECEDENTIAL VALUE	establishes no binding precedent, although nonbinding precedent by performance may be created between the parties
IMPACT ON FUTURE RELATIONSHIP	may encourage future cooperation or reduce confrontation between the parties

FIGURE 10-1   Private Mediation

Key Terms and Phrases

confidential information
conflict of interest
private caucus
private mediation

Review Questions

True/False Questions

1. T F   In mediation, the jury is the finder of fact and the judge is the finder of law.
2. T F   In mediation, the parties must be represented by legal counsel.
3. T F   In mediation, the outcome is based more on the needs and interests of the parties than the law.
4. T F   In private mediation, the parties can negotiate the rules.
5. T F   Mediation leads to a win/win solution.
6. T F   Mediation may be conducted before or after a complaint is filed with the court.
7. T F   Mediation generally takes place over a period of time and may start and stop.
8. T F   An effective mediation is based on preparation.
9. T F   Private mediation is consensual and can be terminated by either party at any time.
10. T F   A mediated agreement is enforceable as a contract.
11. T F   During a mediation, a dominant party may take advantage of a weaker party through psychological gamesmanship.
12. T F   A court may find a mediated agreement unenforceable if at the time of mediation one of the parties took an unconscionable advantage over the other, committed fraud or duress, or misrepresented material facts.
13. T F   Mediation gives the parties control over the outcome.
14. T F   Mediation is designed so one party wins and the other loses.
15. T F   Oral mediation agreements are enforceable.
16. T F   A mediation agreement must be drafted with the same skill as a negotiated agreement.
17. T F   A mediation may never take place after the court has rendered a judgment in the dispute.

Fill-in-the Blank Questions

1. _private caucus_   When a party and the mediator meet together out of the presence of the other party.

2. _Opening comments_   The four phases of a mediation.
   Parties opening statements
   Negotiate + work to agree
   Refine + Finalize

3. _facilitative_   Two different mediation styles.
   evaluative

Multiple-Choice Questions

1. Which of the following may always participate in private mediation as a dispute resolution process:
   (a) the aggrieved party
   (b) the other party to the dispute
   (c) a neutral third party
   (d) a jury
   (e) the attorney for the aggrieved party
2. Private mediation is classified as:
   (a) unilateral action in dispute resolution
   (b) bilateral action in dispute resolution
   (c) third-party evaluation as a prelude to dispute resolution
   (d) third-party assistance in dispute resolution
   (e) third-party adjudication in dispute resolution

Short-Answer Questions

1. When Phillip Moffett went to work for the Aztec Pharmaceutical Company as a senior researcher, he signed a covenant that precluded him from working for another pharmaceutical company for five years after his employment with Aztec terminated. After working for Aztec for three years, Moffett was lured away by another pharmaceutical company. Moffett claims that the covenant he signed was unreasonable and therefore unenforceable. Aztec claims the covenant is a standard industry covenant and is enforceable.

   Discuss whether private mediation would provide the parties with an appropriate method of dispute resolution.
2. Discuss the advantages and disadvantages of private mediation as a dispute resolution process.
3. Why is private mediation so popular in the United States?
4. Discuss the need to have a signed mediation agreement.
5. Discuss the role of the mediator in a private mediation.
6. If the parties have received a divorce decree which contains a property settlement, custody, and child support, can the parties change the terms of the court's decree through private mediation and, if so, what steps must they take to change the court's decree?

Role-Play Exercises

Role-Play Exercise 10-1   Drug Testing

Return to Role-Play Exercise 6-1 concerning drug testing. Change the dispute resolution process from negotiation to private mediation by adding a mediator.

The Players: Several members of the school board
Several union officials
A mediator

Before beginning your mediation, use Figure 6-1, Work Sheet for Dissecting the Content of a Negotiation, to create your mediation plan. Then mediate. If you mediate to an agreement, the agreement should be in writing.

Role-Play Exercise 10-2   Sports Law

Return to Role-Play Exercise 6-2 concerning sports law. Change the dispute resolution process from negotiation to private mediation by adding a mediator.

The Players: Agent for Darrell James, a pitcher for a major league baseball team
The general manager for the baseball team
A mediator

Before beginning your mediation, use Figure 6-1, Work Sheet for Dissecting the Content of a Negotiation, to create your mediation plan. Then mediate. If you mediate to an agreement, the agreement should be in writing.

Role-Play Exercise 10-3   Racial Discrimination

Return to Role-Play Exercise 6-3 concerning racial discrimination. Change the dispute resolution process from negotiation to private mediation by adding a mediator.

The Players: Mr. Jefferson's attorney
A vice president for Big Sky
A mediator

Before beginning your mediation, use Figure 6-1, Work Sheet for Dissecting the Content of a Negotiation, to create your mediation plan. Then mediate. If you mediate to an agreement, the agreement should be in writing.

Role-Play Exercise 10-4   The Land Developer

The Players: A representative or representatives from Westpark Mall
A representative or representatives from Unicorn Enterprises, a building contractor
A mediator

Westpark has been in existence for 20 years. It has been very successful, and the mall now has 120 stores. The mall would like to expand by developing an adjoining 30 acres. The mall would like to use this area for extended parking, an addition that would include another 30 to 50 stores, and surrounding eating establishments.

The land is currently owned by a building developer, Unicorn Enterprises. Although currently undeveloped, this land is adjacent to a development (Oakwood Estates) that Unicorn has built over the past 15 years. Unicorn plans to begin building $200,000 to $300,000 homes in this area early next year. Unicorn also plans to use some of this land for a recreational center for the development that would include handball courts, indoor/outdoor pools, basketball courts, a baseball diamond, and a soccer field.

This is the only real estate adjacent to the mall that is undeveloped.

Unicorn is not interested in selling, but would sell if the deal is right.

Unicorn and the mall have tried to negotiate a contract for the sale of the land, but they were unsuccessful. They are now trying private mediation.

Role-Play Exercie 10-5   The Divorce

The Players: A wife
      A husband
      A mediator

The husband and wife were married in 1990 after meeting in the National Guard. The husband is a stock broker and the wife is the principal at a local high school. They have two children, a boy 6, and a girl 4. Both the husband and wife have parents who live in the same town and both sets of parents are very fond of their grandchildren. Both sets of parents have spent substantial time caring for their grandchilden.

Together the husband and wife have an annual income of $200,000. He makes $120,000 a year and she makes $80,000. Both have retirement plans. Together they have stocks valued at $100,000, bonds valued at $50,000, and savings of $10,000. In addition to their $225,000 home (which has a $150,000 mortgage), they own a $125,000 rental property (which has a $50,000 mortgage).

Both parents would like custody of the children and neither would like to pay child support. Both want the house and neither wants the rental property. The grandparents, who are unrepresented at the mediation, want to play an active role in raising the children. Neither spouse likes the other's parents. The children, however, are very attached to both sets of grandparents. Neither party has tax expertise.

Mediate a property settlement, custody, and child support agreement.

CHAPTER 11

Court-Sponsored Mediation

Historically, the vast majority of civil cases settle before trial. For example, in the 94 United States District Courts during the 12-month period ending September 30, 2000, the courts reported a total of 179,360 civil cases filed, 32,350 cases terminated without court action, 122,508 terminated before pretrial, 19,474 terminated during or after pretrial, and only 5,028 completed through trial. Although not all the cases resolved during this 12-month period were filed during the same 12-month period, the number of civil cases filed in 1999 and 2000 were comparable and assuming the fungibility of cases, a comparison could be made between cases filed and cases terminated. Of the roughly 180,000 civil cases filed a year, 18 percent were terminated without court action, 68 percent were terminated before pretrial, 11 percent were terminated during or after pretrial, leaving only 3 percent remaining at the end of trial. Therefore, it makes little sense to believe that all cases filed will be tried and less sense not to explore settlement early in the life of a dispute, before substantial costs and expenses are incurred.

To obtain earlier and more satisfactory results, a number of state and federal courts have made court-sponsored (court-ordered) mediation available. In those courts that have court-sponsored mediation, litigants are encouraged to seriously consider using the procedure. In some courts, the procedure is mandatory unless the parties persuade the court to permit them to opt out.

Mediation is the most commonly used, and most successful, ADR procedure offered by the courts. A number of federal district courts that had offered court-annexed arbitration now offer court-sponsored mediation in its place. Some courts refer to court-sponsored mediation as a settlement conference.

Court-sponsored mediations can be scheduled shortly after a complaint is filed, although a party may request the mediation at any time before, during, or after trial.

The **court-sponsored mediation** may be presided over by a judge, a magistrate, or mediator specially appointed by the court to mediate that particular case. Some courts refer to this court-appointed mediator as an adjunct settlement judge or ASJ. A court-appointed mediator generally is a lawyer who has been specially selected and trained by the court to conduct court-sponsored mediations. A mediator may have one or more areas of expertise and may be assigned to cases involving those areas of expertise. The courts often encourage court-sponsored mediations presided over by court-appointed mediators because the judges and magistrates have very limited availability for mediations.

Court-Sponsored Mediation (Settlement Conference)
In a court-sponsored mediation the litigants participate in mediation before they have an opportunity to try their dispute in court.

Court-Sponsored Mediation in the Federal Courts

Congress enacted the Civil Justice Reform Act (CJRA) of 1990, requiring each federal district court to develop a case management plan to reduce delay and litigation costs in its court. The CJRA also created a pilot program in 10 districts to test six principles of pretrial case management. One such principle was the use of alternative dispute resolution programs, and one ADR technique was court-sponsored mediation.

The Judicial Conference and the Administrative Office of the United States Courts asked RAND's Institute for Civil Justice to conduct an evaluation of the 10 pilot and 10 comparison districts. In 1996 the RAND Institute issued four reports. One report stated:

Mediation or neutral evaluation programs as implemented in the six districts studied, provided no strong statistical evidence that time to disposition, litigation costs, or attorney views of fairness or satisfaction with case management were significantly affected, either positively or negatively. The low completion rate for our litigant surveys does not allow us to confidently make statistical inferences from the litigant data. The only generally significant finding, however, is that these ADR programs appear to increase the fraction of cases with a monetary settlement.

Mediation and neutral evaluation programs as implemented in these six district do not appear to be a panacea for perceived problems of cost and delay, but neither do they appear to be detrimental. We have no justification for a strong policy recommendation because we found no major program effects, either positive or negative.

Participants in these ADR programs are generally supportive of them. Only a small percentage of participants in any district thought the referral to ADR was inappropriate or that the program should be dropped. Most of them felt that the programs were worthwhile both in general and for their individual cases. James S. Kakalik, Terence Dunworth, Laural A. Hill, Daniel McCaffrey, Marian Oshiro, Nikcholas M. Pace, & Mary E. Vaiana, *An Evaluation of Mediation and Early Neutral Evaluation under the Civil Justice Reform Act 6,* RAND Institute for Civil Justice (1996).

Although RAND did not report that ADR in general and court-sponsored mediation in particular were the panacea to reducing the costs and delay in the federal court system, ADR, including court-sponsored mediation, had developed its following. This led Congress to enact the Alternative Dispute Resolution Act of 1998.

The Alternative Dispute Resolution Act of 1998 requires each federal district court to authorize the use of ADR in all civil actions, including adversary proceedings in bankruptcy. By the turn of the century, all federal district courts developed an array of ADR processes, although court-sponsored mediation has the greatest following. For example, the United States District Court for the District of Massachusetts describes its mediation program as:

B. Mediation

Mediation is a process in which the parties meet with a designated mediator to isolate disputed issues, to develop options, and to consider settlement alternatives, in an effort to reach a consensual agreement that will accommodate the needs and interests of all parties. The mediator may be an impartial individual selected from the Panel established by the court, or a judicial officer of this court other than the one to whom the case is assigned. Entering the mediation process is ordinarily voluntary and reaching an agreement is always voluntary.

The mediator does not impose any terms or result upon the parties but rather seeks to facilitate the process of negotiation. This is accomplished by exploring alternatives in joint or separate meetings, and communicating options and alternatives, when authorized.

This court also distinguishes between court-sponsored mediations and settlement conferences.

F. Settlement Conferences Conducted by District Judge or Magistrate Judge

A settlement conference with a judicial officer, other than the one to whom the case is assigned, may be conducted at any stage of the litigation. The conference is usually requested by one or more of the parties, or by the judge to whom the case is assigned. The judicial officer acts as a facilitator at the conferences, meeting with the parties, promoting communications, offering an objective assessment of the case and suggesting settlement options.

Problem 11-1

Does your federal district court discuss its ADR plan on its website? Your federal district court's Web page may be found at *http://www.uscourts.gov/alllinks.html.*

———————

Mediation in federal court does not end on the trial level. A number of federal circuit courts (courts of appeals) also have mediation programs.

Problem 11-2

Does your federal circuit court discuss its ADR plan on its website? Your federal circuit court's Web page may also be found at *http://www.uscourts.gov/alllinks.html.*

Problem 11-3

Rosemary Baca was severely scalded when a cup of coffee she has just purchased at the drive-up window spilled on her lap. She sued the fast-food franchisor and franchisee in federal district court and received a judgment for $2.8 million. The defendants appealed to the federal court of appeals. Both sides filed briefs and the court took the case under advisement.

Why would Ms. Baca, who received a judgment in the trial court, want to settle her case before the circuit court has rendered its decision?

———————

Court-Sponsored Mediation in the State Courts

Article III of the United States Constitution created the federal courts as courts of limited jurisdiction. By doing so, the federal courts hear only cases emunerated in the Constitution as implemented by federal statute. The federal court system is relatively small when compared to the totality of the state court systems. In the federal system, there are 94 federal district courts, 13 courts of appeals (11 multistate circuits plus the District of Columbia Circuit and the Federal Circuit), and one Supreme Court. Congress legislates for the federal courts and the Administrative Office of the Court oversees the administration of the courts.

The state courts, in contrast, are courts of general jurisdiction. They hear all types of disputes. Each state has its own courts with trial courts and one or more appellate courts. Each state constitution creates the court system within that state, and each state legislature develops the court system within the state's constitutional framework. The courts within each state develop court rules to further implement the constitutional and legislative design. Therefore, unlike the federal system where Congress can direct the federal courts to develop ADR programs, each state must, through its own initiative, develop its own ADR programs. Many states have enacted legislation or created court rules providing for court-sponsored mediation. The court websites often tout their programs. For example, the website for the Florida State Courts states:

Alternative Dispute Resolution (ADR) has been utilized by the Florida Court System to resolve disputes for over 20 years, starting with the creation of the first citizen dispute settlement (CDS) center in Dade County in 1975. Since that time, the use of mediation and arbitration has grown as the Legislature and judiciary have created one of the most comprehensive court-connected mediation programs in the country.

See http://www.flcourts.org/osca/divisions/adr/index.html. The Florida Statute, entitled "Mediation Alternatives to Judicial Action" is located in Appendix C. The website for the Indiana Supreme Court, Division of State Court Administration, provides the alternative dispute resolution rules for the state. *See http://www.www.state.in.us/judicaiary/cle/button4/button4.html.* The website for the Wisconsin court system provides the background and history of ADR in Wisconsin. *See http://www.courts.state.wi/us/circuit/Alternative_Dispute_Resolution.htm.* An "ADR" query on the State of New York Unified Court System website produces over 200 links to ADR in New York. *See http://www.courts.state.ny.us/search/query.asp.*

Problem 11-4

Does your state have a court-sponsored mediation statute or court rules? Use the Internet to conduct your search.

Mediation has long been used in domestic relations matters to resolve disputes involving child custody, visitation rights, and support obligations. Mediation is well suited to resolving family conflict because it fosters joint decision making and promotes the continuing relationship between parents, a relationship that is essential when considering the children's best interest.

Problem 11-5

Consider §§ 44.101(2)(d) and 44.102(2)(d) of the Florida Mediation Alternatives to Judicial Action statute found in Appendix C. Is court-sponsored mediation limited to issues of child custody, visitation, and support?
1.   What else is included and why?
2.   What types of cases are excluded and why?

Preparing for Court-Sponsored Mediation

Unlike private mediation where the parties negotiate the rules for the mediation or defer to the mediator or mediation service to provide the rules, the court, in court-sponsored mediation, provides the rules. These rules are created by the court and apply to all mediations sponsored by that court.

The court's rules will provide the system for selecting the mediator. The parties may have an opportunity to select whether the mediator will be a judge or magistrate or whether the mediator will come from the court's panel of mediators. If a mediator is used, some courts permit the parties to select a mediator from the court's panel of mediators, while others will select the mediator for the parties without input from the parties.

The court rules will also provide whether the mediation is a free service of the court or whether a fee will be charged for the mediator's services.

The judge assigned to litigate the case may instruct the court's ADR administrator when to set the mediation, although some courts will permit the parties input as to when they believe mediation will be most effective. The ADR administrator and the appointed mediator will determine the location of the mediation.

In most court-sponsored mediations, the parties will be represented by their attorneys. The court rules may require attorney and client to participate in the mediation.

The court will select, train, and certify its own mediators for its panel.

The Litigation/Mediation Process

The following steps outline the litigation/mediation process in a federal district court–sponsored mediation program.

Step 1. Initiation of the Lawsuit

An aggrieved party files a complaint in the Office of the Clerk of the Court. The aggrieved party becomes the plaintiff and the other party involuntarily becomes the defendant. The defendant receives notice that a complaint has been filed and files a response to the complaint called an answer.

Step 2. Case Management Conference with the Trial Judge

Shortly after the case is filed, the federal district court judge assigned to the case meets with the parties at a case management conference. During the conference, the judge may suggest or order a court-sponsored mediation. If the parties agree to mediation or if the judge orders mediation, the parties are assigned a judge, magistrate judge, or mediator. The decision whether a judge, magistrate judge, or mediator will be assigned depends on the availability of a judge or magistrate judge and the preference of the parties. A mediator is not assigned if one of the parties objects.

Step 3. Selection of the Mediator

If a mediator will be assigned to the case, the administrator supervising the mediation program selects the mediator using a number of factors including the mediator's availability, the rotation of mediators so all mediators have mediation opportunities, and the type of case so mediators are matched to cases within their areas of expertise.

Step 4. Appointment of the Mediator

If the case is assigned to a mediator, the administrator sends the assigned mediator an appointment letter along with a copy of the docket sheet.

Upon receipt of the appointment letter, the assigned mediator checks the docket sheet for conflicts of interest. If a conflict or the appearance of a conflict exists, the mediator notifies the administrator so another mediator could be assigned to the case. The mediator checks his or her calendar for possible dates, times, and locations for the court-sponsored mediation. The appointment letter may suggest a range of dates for the mediation. The mediator contacts the administrator to arrange the date, place, and time of the court-sponsored mediation.

Step 5. Court-Sponsored Mediation Order

If the court has developed a court-sponsored mediation order, it could take the following form:

IN THE UNITED STATES DISTRICT COURT FOR THE
_____ **DISTRICT OF** _____

JANE DOE	)	
	)	
Plaintiff(s),	)	
	)	
v.	)	No. 01-C-000-B
	)	
JOHN SMITH	)	
	)	
Defendant(s).	)	
	)	

COURT-SPONSORED MEDIATION ORDER

PLEASE READ THIS ORDER CAREFULLY!
Judge _____ has referred this case for a court-sponsored mediation and directed the Clerk to enter this Order.   **MEDIATOR'S NAME**   will act as a mediator who will not be involved in the actual trial of the case and who will assist in an objective appraisal and evaluation of the lawsuit. The following are mandatory guidelines for the parties in preparing for the court-sponsored mediation.

1.   PURPOSE OF THE MEDIATION
The purpose of the court-sponsored mediation is to permit an informal discussion between the attorneys, parties, non-party indemnitors or insurers, and the mediator of every aspect of the lawsuit. This educational process provides the advantage of permitting the mediator to privately express his or her views concerning the parties' claims. The mediator may, in his or her discretion, converse with the lawyers, the parties, the insurance representatives or any one of them outside the hearing of the others. Ordinarily, the court-sponsored mediation provides the parties with an enhanced opportunity to settle the case, due to the assistance rendered by the mediator.

2.   FULL SETTLEMENT AUTHORITY REQUIRED
In addition to counsel who will try the case being present, a person with full settlement authority must likewise be present for the mediation. This requires the presence of your client or, if a corporate entity, an authorized non-lawyer representative of your client.

For a defendant, such representative must have final settlement authority to commit the company to pay, in the representative's discretion, a settlement amount recommended by the mediator up to the plaintiff's prayer (excluding punitive damage prayers in excess of $100,000.00) or up to the plaintiff's last demand, whichever is lower.

For a plaintiff, such representative must have final authority, in the representative's discretion, to authorize dismissal of the case with prejudice, or to accept a settlement amount recommended by the mediator down to the defendant's last offer.

The purpose of this requirement is to have representatives present who can settle the case during the course of the mediation without consulting a superior. A governmental entity may be granted permission to proceed with a representative with limited authority upon proper application pursuant to Local Court Rule _____.

3.   EXCEPTION WHERE BOARD APPROVAL REQUIRED
If Board approval is required to authorize settlement, attendance of the entire Board is requested. The attendance of a least one sitting member of the Board (preferably the Chair) is *absolutely required*.

(continued)

4.   APPEARANCE WITHOUT CLIENT PROHIBITED

Counsel appearing without their clients (whether or not you have been given settlement authority) will cause the mediation to be canceled and rescheduled. Counsel for a government entity may be excused from this requirement upon proper application under Local Court Rule _____.

5.   AUTHORIZED INSURANCE REPRESENTATIVE(S) REQUIRED

Any insurance company that (1) is a party, (2) can assert that it is contractually entitled to indemnity or subrogation proceeds, or (3) has received notice or a demand pursuant to an alleged contractual requirement that it defend or pay damages, if any, assessed within its policy limits in this case must have a fully authorized settlement representative present at the mediation. Such representative must have final settlement authority to commit the company to pay, in the representative's discretion, an amount recommended by the mediator within the policy limits.

The purpose of this requirement is to have an insurance representative present who can settle the outstanding claim or claims during the course of the mediation without consulting a superior. An insurance representative authorized to pay, in his or her discretion, up to the plaintiff's last demand will also satisfy this requirement.

6.   ADVICE TO NON-PARTY INSURANCE COMPANIES REQUIRED

Counsel of record will be responsible for timely advising any involved non-party insurance company of the requirements of this order.

7.   PRE-MEDIATION DISCUSSIONS REQUIRED

Prior to the court-sponsored mediation, the attorneys are directed to discuss settlement with their respective clients and insurance representatives, and opposing parties are directed to discuss settlement so the parameters of settlement have been explored well in advance of the court-sponsored mediation. This means the following:

> By 25 DAYS PRIOR TO MEDIATION, plaintiff must tender a written settlement offer to defendant and the assigned mediator.

> By 15 DAYS PRIOR TO MEDIATION, each defendant *must* make and deliver a written response to plaintiff and the assigned mediator. That response may either take the form of a written substantive offer, or a written communication that a Defendant declines to make any offer.

Silence or failure to communicate as required is not itself a form of communication which satisfies these requirements.

8.   COURT-SPONSORED MEDIATION STATEMENT REQUIRED

One copy of each party's court-sponsored mediation statement of each party must be submitted to the judge(s) listed below:

Magistrate Judge _____
U.S. Courthouse
_____Address_____

_____

___MEDIATOR___
___Address___

_____

(continued)

Court-Sponsored Mediation Statements must be directly submitted no later than _1 WEEK PRIOR TO MEDIATION._ They must NOT be filed with the Clerk of the Court.

Your statement should set forth the relevant positions of the parties concerning factual issues, issues of law, damages, and the settlement negotiation history of the case, including a recitation of any specific demands and offers that may have been conveyed. Copies of your court-sponsored mediation statement are to be promptly transmitted to all counsel of record.

The court-sponsored mediation statement may not exceed five (5) pages in length and will not be made a part of the case file. Lengthy appendices should not be submitted. Pertinent evidence to be offered at trial should be brought to the court-sponsored mediation for presentation to the mediator if thought particularly relevant.

9. CONFIDENTIALITY STRICTLY ENFORCED
Neither the court-sponsored mediation statements nor communications of any kind occurring during the court-sponsored mediation can be used by any party with regard to any aspect of the litigation or trial of the case. Strict confidentiality shall be maintained with regard to such communications by both the mediator and the parties.

10. CONTINUANCES
Applications for continuance of the court-sponsored mediation will not be entertained unless such application is submitted to the court-sponsored mediation judge in writing at least **seven (7)** days prior to the scheduled mediation. Any such application must contain both a statement setting forth good cause for a continuance and a recitation of whether or not the continuance is opposed by any other party.

11. SETTING
The court-sponsored mediation is set on _____, the _____ day of_____ , 20__, at _____ o'clock _____.m., in _____, Magistrate's Courtroom #2, on the _____ Floor of the Federal Courthouse.

12. NOTIFICATION OF PRIOR SETTLEMENT REQUIRED
In the event a settlement between the parties is reached before the court-sponsored mediation date, parties are to notify the mediator immediately.

13. CONSEQUENCES OF NON-COMPLIANCE
Upon certification by the mediator of circumstances showing non-compliance with this order, the assigned trial judge may take any corrective action permitted by law. Such action may include contempt proceedings, assessment of costs, expenses, and attorney's fees, together with any additional measures deemed by the court to be appropriate under the circumstances.

Dated the ____ day of _____, 20____.
_____, CLERK
        UNITED STATES DISTRICT COURT
        _____ DISTRICT OF _____
  By: _____
                        Deputy Clerk
cc: ALL COUNSEL OF RECORD

Prior to the mediation, one of several events may occur. A party may request the mediation be rescheduled, may request the mediation be canceled because the parties feel it would be unproductive, may request the mediation be canceled because the parties are near settlement, or may inform the ADR administrator that the case has settled.

Step 6. Court-Sponsored Mediation Statements

The court-sponsored mediation order may require each party to submit to the mediator, opposing counsel, and the ADR administrator a court-sponsored mediation statement. The order requires the parties to submit their statements in advance of the mediation. The order may limit the length of the statement. The statement should set forth the high points of the case and the pertinent settlement history. The statements, generally, have no fixed format. The following two samples illustrate a letter format and a more formal looking format. The more formal format runs the risk of being filed by mistake in the Office of the Clerk of the Court where it would become a part of the case record. Since the mediation statements are confidential documents to be used only by the parties participating in the mediation (and the ADR administrator), they should not become part of the case record and should not be available to the judge who conducts the trial in the event settlement is not achieved.

Sample 1: Plaintiff's Court-Sponsored Mediation Statement in Informal Letter Format

Roberta Raintree, Esq.
_____firm name_____
_____address_____

In re: Johnson v. Gotham Steel Company
01-C-495-K

Dear Ms _____:

Our firm has been advised that you have been appointed mediator in Johnson v. Gotham Steel Co. This letter is the Plaintiff's Court-Sponsored Mediation Statement, as required by the Court's Court-Sponsored Mediation Order dated _____.

[brief statement of the facts leading up to and including the filing of the complaint]

[brief statement of the nature of the complaint and the relief being sought from the court]

[brief statement of the issues]

[brief statement of the settlement discussions that have taken place to date]

Sincerely,

Horace McPherson, Esq.
Attorney for _____

cc: The ADR Administrator The United States District Court
for the _____ District of _____
_____address_____

_____

Charles M. Bright, Esq.
_____firm name_____
_____address_____

Sample 2: Defendant's Court-Sponsored Mediation Statement in a More Formal Format

NOT TO BE FILED WITH THE COURT CLERK
IN THE UNITED STATES DISTRICT COURT
FOR THE _____ DISTRICT OF _____

Johnson	)
v.	) 01-C-495-K
Gothan Steel Company	)

Defendant's Court-Sponsored Mediation Statement

Appearing for the defendant, Gotham Steel Company, will be attorney Charles M. Bright. Also appearing for defendant will be the representative from the Great Plains Insurance Company who will have full settlement authority in this case.

Statement of the Facts

[Brief statement of the facts from the Defendant's point of view]

Plaintiff's Causes of Action and Relief Sought

[Brief statement of what the plaintiff alleges as his or her causes of action and the relief being sought]

Defendant's Response to the Plaintiff's Allegation

[Brief statement with defendant's response to the plaintiff's alleged causes of action, element by element]

History of the Case after the Complaint Was Filed Including Counterclaims
and the History of Settlement Discussions

[Brief statement of what motions have been filed, the status of discovery, and the various settlement offers and counteroffers. Include any counterclaim]

Charles M. Bright, esq.
firm name
address

phone number

Step 7. The Court-Sponsored Mediation

Although the court-sponsored mediation has no mandatory format, it usually contains the sign-in, an opening statement by the mediator, an opening statement by each attorney, the settlement discussion including private caucuses, and a closing where the agreement, if any, is finalized and signed.

The Sign-In   If the mediation is held in the courthouse, a member of the ADR administrator's staff may sign-in the parties and their attorneys. The parties and their attorneys may be asked to provide the staff member with their names, official capacity in the mediation, addresses, and telephone numbers. The parties also may be asked to affirm whether they have settlement authority.

In a court-sponsored mediation, the court may or may not require both counsel and client to be present and participate in the mediation. The advantages of client participation include first-hand information gained by the client (the client can speak with and listen directly to the mediator and the other side) and the instantaneous exchange of information, offers, and counteroffers. By being present, the client, after being advised by counsel, can determine whether to accept an offer or propose a counteroffer.

If a client or a representative of the client is to attend the mediation, that person must have full settlement authority. Without full settlement authority, the representative acts only as a messenger and does not have the ability to fully participate in the process. In a corporate dispute, the corporate official with the greatest understanding of the corporation's interests involved in the dispute and its resolution should be selected as the corporate representative.

The Opening Remarks by the Mediator   The mediator's opening remarks create the foundation for establishing his or her fairness and credibility. The mediator may comment on having no interest in the case and not caring whether the case settles or who prevails at trial if the case does not settle. A mediator may comment on the fact that court-appointed mediators volunteer their time to do mediations for the court and are not being paid (if that is the case). The mediator may comment that court-appointed mediators provide a professional service to the parties and to the court by acting as the mediator. They are experienced, knowledgeable, and able to provide the parties with invaluable assistance if the parties elect to accept their assistance. The mediator may also note to the parties that mediators are selected by the judiciary to conduct these court-sponsored mediations, that they are especially trained to conduct effective mediations, and that they are in a unique position to view the merits of the case with *objective* fairness.

The mediator's opening statement may describe the ground rules for the process, thereby establishing trust and confidence in the procedure. He or she may note that the mediator is a *mediator* only and will not communicate with the trial judge about the case. The mediator will have no decision-making function in the case, and all statements made in the context of the mediation will be confidential and cannot be used for *any purpose* in connection with the litigation or trial.

Example 11-1

If an attempt is made by counsel to turn a statement made during a court-sponsored mediation into an "admission" or to quote a statement made during a court-sponsored mediation as support of his or her position in a motion or trial brief constitutes unprofessional conduct.

The mediator may emphasize that no statement or confidence shared privately with the mediator will be transmitted to the opposing party (or anyone else participating in the mediation).

The mediator may discuss the fact that he or she is present in good faith and may ask the parties to join him or her in a good faith effort. The mediator could emphasize that everyone will have the opportunity to speak without interruption.

During his or her opening statement, the mediator could explain the purpose of the mediation. He or she could emphasize that the mediation is taking place to help the parties and to provide them with an opportunity to settle. It will provide them with a candid evaluation of the case from a disinterested third party and a settlement recommendation that is objective.

The mediator may tell the parties that the court-sponsored mediation is not intended to deprive them of their day in court. The mediator, however, may use the court-sponsored mediation to convey the realities of continuing the litigation process and the ultimate trial as they will impact this case and the parties.

The mediator may emphasize that the mediation will be an educational process for all the parties. They will learn first-hand about their case and about their opponent's case. They will hear not only how their own attorney evaluates the case but also how the opposing attorney and client evaluate the case. Each party will have opportunities to listen and to speak. All the parties will learn first-hand what a disinterested third party thinks about the case.

The mediator may tell the parties that he or she will assist them in focusing and refining their interests and defining common ground.

The mediator may emphasize that the court-sponsored mediation is intended to *assist* parties in resolving their disputes. The court-sponsored mediation is not intended to force the parties into doing something they truly do not want to do.

The court-sponsored mediation will provide the parties with an opportunity to exchange offers and counteroffers without the delays and expenses that occur when the parties are communicating at a distance. The court-sponsored mediation will provide the parties with an opportunity to fashion a result that is unavailable as a result of trial.

The mediator may note that any recommendation made by him or her will be based on the *merits* of the case, as he or she ascertains the merits to be in light of the information given at the mediation by the attorneys and parties. Therefore, the more open and complete the parties are with the mediator, the more informed the mediator's recommendation will be.

Finally, during the opening statement, the mediator may explain his or her approach to the mediation.

After the Mediator's Opening Remarks   After the mediator has given his or her opening remarks, each attorney may be asked to make an opening statement. These statements provide the clients with an opportunity to hear the attorney for the other side since each client may have only heard his or her own side and has come to believe there is no other side. The mediator may pose questions to the attorneys and their clients to clarify the issues, the clients needs and interests, and the respective positions of the parties.

As the mediation progresses, the mediator may decide to hold private caucuses with a client and his or her attorney, with individual attorneys and with both attorneys, and with individual clients. During these caucuses, the mediator may explore topics that can only be productively explored in private. As the process evolves, the mediator will help the parties refine their interests and objectives.

As the mediation unfolds, the mediator may urge the parties to explore creative solutions. He or she will carry offers and counteroffers between the parties. The mediator may help the parties evaluate solutions against their stated interests. The mediator may even help the parties create solutions that better satisfy their interests.

The mediator may probe for the prior settlement efforts. Prior settlement offers and counteroffers may provide the parameters for the mediation.

Example 11-2

Vera Vandever was injured in a car crash involving a train. She alleged in her complaint that the railroad was negligent in failing to properly maintain the crossing gates at the crossing where she was injured. She claimed $1 million in damages.

The railroad's answer denied negligence alleging that the gates were in proper repair and that Vera was negligent in failing to heed the warning lights at the crossing.

The court-sponsored mediation statements reveal a series of offers and counteroffers. Vera's last offer was $250,000 and the railroad's counteroffer was $50,000. Even though Vera might win a $1 million judgment or the railroad might be held not liable at trial, the court-sponsored mediation begins with the parameters of $250,000 and $50,000.

The mediator will listen and clarify each party's *needs and interests*. The mediator may inquire as to what each party *needs* in the way of settlement. The lawsuit will be settled when each party realizes that his or her needs and interests are being accommodated insofar as possible.

The mediator will discuss some of the following concerns that the parties should or should not have. Some concerns are legitimate and others are spurious. Among the legitimate concerns of the parties are:

1. If the plaintiff loses the case—
   Must the plaintiff pay the attorney's fees?
   Must the plaintiff pay for the experts?
   Must the plaintiff pay court costs?
   Must the plaintiff pay for discovery?
   Has the plaintiff considered the cost of tying up key personnel during discovery and trial?
2. If the plaintiff wins the case—
   Are the attorney's fees recoverable by the plaintiff?
   Are experts' fees recoverable by the plaintiff?
   May the plaintiff recover court costs from the defendant?
   Must the plaintiff pay for discovery?
   Has the plaintiff considered the cost of tying up key personnel during discovery and trial and would this cost be recoverable?
   Does the cost outweigh probable gain?

3. If the defendant loses the case—

   Is the defendant prepared to pay his or her attorney's fees?

   Is this the type of case where the defendant will also be required to pay for the plaintiff's attorney's fees if the plaintiff prevails?

   Is the defendant prepared to pay for experts?

   Is the defendant prepared to bear the cost of tying up key personnel?

   Does the cost of litigation outweigh the savings if the defendant wins or outweigh the obligation to pay the judgment if the defendant loses?

4. When will there be finality (a final decision and payment of the judgment if plaintiff wins)?—

   Will the nonprevailing party appeal? Reversal of the judgment may require repeat of the process.

   Even if the plaintiff wins at trial, does the plaintiff understand that he or she may not see a dime until the process is over?

   Is it better for the plaintiff to receive something now (a certainty) rather than wait for something bigger later even though there may be nothing later (a possibility)?

5. If the plaintiff wins, will the judgment be paid?—

   Even if the plaintiff wins a judgment, does the defendant have the ability to pay the judgment?

   Is there a risk that the defendant will file for bankruptcy and the plaintiff will never be able to satisfy his or her judgment?

6. Who can prove his or her case?—

   Can the plaintiff prove the elements of the claim?

   Can the defendant prove the elements of a defense?

   Whose witnesses will be viewed as credible?

   Is the case dependent on testimony of parties, and which party will be viewed as credible?

   Will bad faith allegations be raised, and is there a reasonable chance to prove these allegations?

7. Is there insurance to pay the claim and possibly attorney's fees?—

   Is the claim covered by insurance or will the insurance company claim lack of coverage?

   Is the insurance adequate or will the defendant be personally liable on the judgment?

8. What are the damages, if any?—

   Can the plaintiff prove his or her damages?

   Are the damages significant enough to warrant trial?

   Are the damages intangible and thus present some difficulty to prove?

   Should the defendant consider a negotiated settlement to negate any risk of a much larger judgment?

9. Will the lawsuit create publicity?—

   Does the plaintiff or the defendant want publicity?

   Will the plaintiff get the publicity he or she seeks?

   Will the plaintiff or the defendant be able to cope with unwanted publicity (lack of privacy)?

   Will trial and accompanying publicity lead to a "litigation explosion"?

10. Will the lawsuit create precedents?—

    Will litigation create an unwanted precedent for the plaintiff or the defendant?

    Must the plaintiff or the defendant convince the court to overturn existing precedents?

    Does the lack of existing precedents make the outcome of this case difficult to predict?

11. Will the trial be totally impartial?—

    Will the case be tried by a new judge with no track record in this type of case?

    Is this the type of case where the jury will sympathize with one of the parties?

    Is there a chance that one of the parties will be "hometowned" by the other?

    Is the plaintiff or the defendant seeking the elusive "just result"? Will both litigants view a judgment as "just" or "fair"?

    Are the parties prepared for the uncertainty of trial?

The parties may raise concerns that are less than legitimate. For example, a party may contend that he or she should prevail "as a matter of principle" or a defendant may contend that it cannot settle because settlement will open the floodgates to a rash of litigation.

The mediator will encourage the parties to make settlement offers and counteroffers during the mediation. The mediation presents an excellent opportunity for the litigants to communicate settlement offers back and forth conveniently, expeditiously, and cost effectively. The mediator can assist the parties in focusing on their needs and interests so realistic offers and counteroffers can be presented. The mediator can communicate these offers for the parties and encourage the parties to respond. The mediator can assist the parties in clarifying their offers and counteroffers. The mediator can encourage and assist the parties in creating innovative settlement solutions (e.g., apologies, bartered settlement, structured settlement, modification of contract).

During the court-sponsored mediation, the mediator may make settlement recommendations privately to each party. A party may accept the recommendation and authorize the mediator to make the offer to the other side on his or her behalf. A party may accept the recommendation but only authorize the mediator to characterize the recommendation as the mediator's recommendation. The mediator may give each side an opportunity to accept or reject a recommendation without revealing whether the other side will accept or reject the recommendation. Naturally, if both sides accept, the case is settled.

If an impasse is reached, the mediator may recommend a settlement for the parties to consider and respond to by a date and time certain. Individual plaintiffs sometimes will accept a compromise suggestion once they have left the pressure of the mediation behind. A day or two may give a party a chance to talk over the settlement recommendation with his or her spouse, relatives, friends, business associates, and attorney. The time will give the plaintiff an opportunity to weigh the certainty of the settlement recommendation against the risks and costs involved by continuing the litigation. It also gives an individual plaintiff a chance to mentally spend the money to be received from the settlement.

The comfort level of a defendant corporate representative is often greatly enhanced if he or she can take the compromise proposal back to the office and have it approved by corporate superiors.

The mediator's settlement recommendation may be made on a take-it-or-leave-it basis. The mediator could use a blind call-in system. Under this system, the parties are instructed that each must call the ADR administrator by a specific date (usually from 1 to 10 days from the date of the mediation) and report whether they accept or reject the mediator's settlement recommendation. By using a blind call-in system, a party who rejects the settlement recommendation will not know whether the other party has accepted or rejected the recommendation.

If settlement is reached during the mediation, the mediator will have one of the parties memorialize the agreement prior to concluding the mediation and all parties will sign the memorial. The memorial will be as detailed as possible so disputes do not arise when the agreement is being implemented. For example, if the settlement requires the payment of money, the memorial should reference the date by which the settlement will be paid, the method of payment, where payment will be made, if by check, who will be the drawer, the drawee, and the payee, and whether the check will be certified.

The exercise of memorializing the agreement may prompt the parties to think of unresolved issues that can be resolved before the mediation is concluded. Leaving details to be resolved by the parties at a later date is a dangerous practice and may lead to the unraveling of the settlement agreement.

This hand-written document can serve as the foundation for a formal, typed settlement agreement that can be signed by the parties subsequent to the mediation. Many settlements can be implemented without a more formal document.

Step 8. Follow-up from the Mediation

After the mediation the mediator will file a report with the ADR administrator noting whether the case settled. The attorneys and their clients will then proceed to comply with the terms of their settlement agreement.

After the mediation has produced a settlement, the parties must address the litigation pending with the court. If the agreement results in immediate performance, the parties will file a stipulation for dismissal with prejudice. A stipulation for dismissal will be deemed a stipulation for dismissal without prejudice unless it states dismissal with prejudice. The stipulation is followed by a court order dismissing the litigation. If something remains to be done in the agreement, such as payments under a payout plan, the parties may ask the court to administratively close the case. The complaint is not technically dismissed but remains inactive until the settlement agreement has been performed. The mediator or the plaintiff's attorney may hold an executed "standby" judgment and an executed "standby" stipulation for dismissal with prejudice. If the defendant complies with the settlement agreement, the stipulation for dismissal with prejudice will be filed. If the defendant fails to comply with the settlement agreement, the judgment will be filed. Once the settlement agreement has been performed, the court will issue an order of dismissal with prejudice thus ending the litigation.

If the litigation concerned ongoing conduct, the settlement agreement could deal with the ending of this conduct. The parties could file a consent decree that would produce a court order prohibiting the conduct. Future conduct would be a violation of the court's order punishable by contempt.

If the case has not settled at the mediation, the parties can continue their settlement discussions, ask for another court-sponsored mediation, and at the same time proceed with preparations for trial.

Enforceability of the Mediated Agreement

When the parties come to an agreement in a court-sponsored mediation, the likelihood is that the parties will comply with the terms of the agreement. Often when the parties reach an agreement in a court-sponsored mediation, neither is totally pleased. Each feels that he or she has given up more than originally planned. Both, however, realize that unless they were to pursue litigation, neither could achieve all that they wanted.

By accommodating at least some of each party's needs and interests, the agreement is in the best interest of both parties, and by having something in it for everyone, the likelihood is that the parties will comply with the agreement.

Another factor that promotes the self-enforceability of the court-sponsored mediation agreement is the fact that it was made under the watchful eye of the court. The attorneys who represent clients in court-sponsored mediations are generally regulars in the court, and they do not want the reputation that their court-sponsored mediation agreements are not self-enforceable.

At times, however, a party to a court-sponsored mediation settlement will refuse to perform or may perform in a way that does not comport with the understanding of the other party. A follow-up court-sponsored mediation may be held to discuss the problem. If the subsequent mediation does not resolve the matter, the agreement may be enforceable as a contract.

One attribute of the court-sponsored mediation is that it is conducted in private and what is said at the mediation is confidential. This also means that the court-sponsored mediation agreement is a private document and its terms are confidential. The parties, however, may waive the confidentiality of the agreement and have it recorded as a consent judgment. If so recorded, the agreement may be enforced as any other judgment is enforced.

In *Vitakis-Valchine v. Valchine,* a husband and wife entered into a marital settlement agreement during a court-sponsored mediation. The settlement was incorporated into the judgment of divorce. Later the former wife moved to set aside the mediated agreement on the grounds of coercion and duress by her former husband, his attorney, and the mediator, and that the settlement agreement was unreasonable and unfair.

Vitakis-Valchine v. Valchine
**District Court of Appeal of Florida,
Fourth District
793 So.2d 1094 (2001)**

STEVENSON, J.

This is an appeal from a final judgment of dissolution which was entered pursuant to a mediated settlement agreement. The wife argues that the trial court erred in affirming the recommendations of the general master and in denying her request to set aside the settlement agreement on the grounds that it was entered into under duress and coercion. We affirm the order to the extent that the trial court concluded that the wife failed to meet her burden of establishing that the marital settlement agreement was reached by duress or coercion on the part of the husband and the husband's attorney. The wife also alleges that the mediator committed misconduct during the mediation session, including but not limited to coercion and improper influence, and that she entered into the settlement agreement as a direct result of this misconduct. For the reasons which follow, we hold that mediator misconduct can be the basis for a trial court refusing to enforce a settlement agreement reached at court-ordered mediation. Because neither the general master nor the trial court made any findings relative to the truth of the allegations of the mediator's alleged misconduct, we remand this case for further findings.

Procedural Background

By August of 1999, Kalliope and David Valchine's divorce proceedings to end their near twelve-year marriage had been going on for one and a half to two years. On August 17, 1999, the couple attended court-ordered mediation to attempt to resolve their dispute. At the mediation, both parties were represented by counsel. The mediation lasted seven to eight hours and resulted in a twenty-three page marital settlement agreement. The agreement was comprehensive and dealt with alimony, bank accounts, both parties' IRAs, and the husband's federal customs, postal, and military pensions. The agreement also addressed the disposition of embryos that the couple had frozen during *in vitro* fertilization attempts prior to the divorce. The agreement provided in this regard that "[t]he Wife has expressed her desire to have the frozen embryos, but has reluctantly agreed to provide them to the husband to dispose of."

A month later, the wife filed a *pro se* motion seeking to set aside the mediated settlement agreement, but by the time of the hearing, she was represented by new counsel. The wife's counsel argued two grounds for setting aside the agreement: (1) coercion and duress on the part of the husband, the husband's attorney and the mediator; and (2) the agreement was unfair and unreasonable on its face. The trial court accepted the general master's findings which rejected the wife's claim on both grounds. On appeal, the wife attacks only the trial court's refusal to set aside the couple's settlement agreement on the ground that it was reached through duress and coercion.

Third Party Coercion

As a general rule under Florida law, a contract or settlement may not be set aside on the basis of duress or coercion unless the improper influence emanated from one of the contracting parties—the actions of a third party will not suffice. *See Cronacher v. Cronacher,* 508 So.2d 1270, 1271 (Fla. 3d DCA 1987); *Bubenik v. Bubenik,* 392 So.2d 943, 944 (Fla. 3d DCA 1980); *see also Herald v. Hardin,* 95 Fla. 889, 116 So. 863 (1928). In this case, the record adequately supports the finding that neither the husband nor the husband's attorney was involved in any

duress or coercion and had no knowledge of any improper conduct on the part of the mediator.

Because there was no authority at the time holding that mediator misconduct, including the exertion of duress or coercion, could serve as a basis for overturning the agreement, the general master made no findings relative to the wife's allegations. The mediator's testimony was presented prior to that of the wife, and, consequently, her allegations of potential misconduct were not directly confronted. Here, we must decide whether the wife's claim that the mediator committed misconduct by improperly influencing her and coercing her to enter into the settlement agreement can be an exception to the general rule that coercion and duress by a third party will not suffice to invalidate an agreement between the principals.

The Former Wife's Claims

The wife testified that the eight-hour mediation, with Mark London as the mediator, began at approximately 10:45 A.M., that both her attorney and her brother attended, and that her husband was there with his counsel. Everyone initially gathered together, the mediator explained the process, and then the wife, her attorney and her brother were left in one room while the husband and his attorney went to another. The mediator then went back and forth between the two rooms during the course of the negotiations in what the mediator described as "Kissinger-style shuttle diplomacy."

With respect to the frozen embryos, which were in the custody of the Fertility Institute of Boca Raton, the wife explained that there were lengthy discussions concerning what was to become of them. The wife was concerned about destroying the embryos and wanted to retain them herself. The wife testified that the mediator told her that the embryos were not "lives in being" and that the court would not require the husband to pay child support if she were impregnated with the embryos after the divorce. According to the wife, the mediator told her that the judge would *never* give her custody of the embryos, but would order them destroyed. The wife said that at one point during the discussion of the frozen embryo issue, the mediator came in, threw the papers on

(continued)

(continued from previous page)

the table, and declared "that's it, I give up." Then, according to the wife, the mediator told her that if no agreement was reached, he (the mediator) would report to the trial judge that the settlement failed because of her. Additionally, the wife testified that the mediator told her that if she signed the agreement at the mediation, she could still protest any provisions she didn't agree with at the final hearing—including her objection to the husband "disposing" of the frozen embryos.

With respect to the distribution of assets, the wife alleges that the mediator told her that she was not entitled to any of the husband's federal pensions. She further testified that the mediator told her that the husband's pensions were only worth about $200 per month and that she would spend at least $70,000 in court litigating entitlement to this relatively modest sum. The wife states that the mediation was conducted with neither her nor the mediator knowing the present value of the husband's pensions or the marital estate itself. The wife testified that she and her new attorney had since constructed a list of assets and liabilities, and that she was shortchanged by approximately $34,000—not including the husband's pensions. When asked what she would have done if Mr. London had told her that the attorney's fees could have amounted to as little as $15,000, the wife stated, "I would have took [sic] it to trial."

Finally, the wife testified that she signed the agreement in part due to "time pressure" being placed on her by the mediator. She testified that while the final draft was being typed up, the mediator got a call and she heard him say "have a bottle of wine and a glass of drink, and a strong drink ready for me." The wife explained that the mediator had repeatedly stated that his daughter was leaving for law school, and finally said that "you guys have five minutes to hurry up and get out of here because that family is more important to me." The wife testified that she ultimately signed the agreement because

> [I] felt pressured. I felt that I had no other alternative but to accept the Agreement from the things that I was told by Mr. London. I believed everything that he said.

Court-Ordered Mediation

Mediation is a process whereby a neutral third party, the mediator, assists the principals of a dispute in reaching a complete or partial voluntary resolution of their issues of conflict. *See* 44.1011, Fla. Stat. (2000). Mandatory, court-ordered mediation was officially sanctioned by the Florida legislature in 1987, and since then, mediation has become institutionalized within Florida's court system. *See* Ch. 44, Fla. Stat. (2000).[1] All twenty judicial circuits in Florida utilize some form of court-connected mediation to assist with their caseloads.[2] The process is meant to be non-adversarial and informal, with the mediator essentially serving as a facilitator for communications between the parties and providing assistance in the identification of issues and the exploration of options to resolve the dispute. Ultimate authority to settle remains with the parties. *See* 44.1011(2), Fla. Stat. Mediation, as a method of alternative dispute resolution, potentially saves both the parties and the judicial system time and money while leaving the power to structure the terms of any resolution of the dispute in the hands of the parties themselves.

Mediation, pursuant to chapter 44, is mandatory when ordered by the court. Any court in which a civil action, including a family matter, is pending may refer the case to mediation, with or without the parties' consent. *See* 44.102(2), Fla. Stat. (2000). Communications during the mediation sessions are privileged and confidential. *See* 44.102(3)–(4), Fla. Stat. During court-ordered mediation conducted pursuant to the statute, the

---

[1.] For an excellent perspective on the development of mediation within the courts of Florida, see Sharon Press, Institutionalization: Savior or Saboteur of Mediation?, 24 FLA. ST. U.L. REV. 903 (1997), and articles cited therein.

[2.] *See* Press, *supra* note 1. Additionally, at the present time, the First District Court of Appeal has two court-annexed mediators on staff. The Fifth District Court of Appeal is currently engaged in a pilot project involving private mediators doing appellate mediation. This court presently has two appellate mediators on staff, but because of budgetary and other considerations, the Fourth District's appellate mediation program will be discontinued as of September 30, 2001.

mediator enjoys "judicial immunity in the same manner and to the same extent as a judge." 44.107, Fla. Stat. The mediation must be conducted in accordance with rules of practice and procedure adopted by the Florida Supreme Court. *See* 44.102(1).

Comprehensive procedures for conducting the mediation session and minimum standards for qualification, training, certification, professional conduct, and discipline of mediators have been set forth by the Florida Supreme Court in the Florida Rules for Certified and Court-Appointed Mediators, Rule 10. Predecessors to these rules initially took effect in 1987 and were amended in February 2000. *See In re* Amendments to the Fla. Rules for Certified & Court-Appointed Mediators, 762 So.2d 441 (Fla. 2000). One of the hallmarks of the process of mediation is the empowerment of the parties to resolve their dispute on their own, agreed-upon terms. While parties are required to attend mediation, no party is required to settle at mediation.

> (a) **Decision-making.** Decisions made during a mediation are to be made by the parties. A mediator shall not make substantive decisions for any party. A mediator is responsible for assisting the parties in reaching informed and voluntary decisions while protecting their right of self-determination.

Fla. R. Med. 10.310(a). The committee notes to the rule provide in part that

> While mediation techniques and practice styles may vary from mediator to mediator and mediation to mediation, a line is crossed and ethical standards are violated when any conduct of the mediator serves to compromise the parties' basic right to agree or not to agree. Special care should be taken to preserve the party's right to self-determination if the mediator provides input to the mediation process.

In keeping with the notion of self-determination and voluntary resolution of the dispute at court-ordered mediation, any improper influence such as coercion or duress on the part of the mediator is expressly prohibited:

> (b) **Coercion Prohibited.** A mediator shall not coerce or improperly influence any party to make a decision or unwillingly participate in a mediation.

Fla. R. Med. 10.310(b). Likewise, a mediator may not intentionally misrepresent any material fact in an effort to promote or encourage an agreement:

> (c) **Misrepresentation Prohibited.** A mediator shall not intentionally or knowingly misrepresent any material fact or circumstance in the course of conducting a mediation.

Fla. R. Med. 10.310(c).

Other sections of Rule 10 address the rendering of personal or professional opinions by the mediator, and one section specifically provides that

> A mediator shall not offer a personal or professional opinion as to how the court in which the case has been filed will resolve the dispute.

Fla. R. Med. 10.370(c). Under this section, the committee notes caution that

> While mediators may call upon their own qualifications and experience to supply information and options, the parties must be given the opportunity to freely decide upon any agreement. Mediators shall not utilize their opinions to decide any aspect of the dispute or to coerce the parties or their representatives to accept any resolution option.

The question we are confronted with in this case is whether a referring court may set aside an agreement reached in court-ordered mediation if the court finds that the agreement was reached as a direct result of the mediator's substantial violation of the rules of conduct for mediators. We believe that it would be unconscionable for a court to enforce a settlement agreement reached through coercion or any other improper tactics utilized by a court-appointed mediator.[3] When a court refers a

---

[3.]Most mediation is conducted by private mediators who are appointed by the court and paid by the parties. A few jurisdictions have mediators on staff who may be paid by the court or the parties, depending on the financial circumstances of the participants. In either event, "[a] mediator is accountable to the referring court with ultimate authority over the case." Fla. R. Med. 10.500.

(continued)

(continued from previous page)

case to mediation, the mediation must be conducted according to the practices and procedures outlined in the applicable statutes and rules. If the required practices and procedures are not substantially complied with, no party to the mediation can rightfully claim the benefits of an agreement reached in such a way. During a court-ordered mediation, the mediator is no ordinary third party, but is, for all intent and purposes, an agent of the court carrying out an official court-ordered function. We hold that the court may invoke its inherent power to maintain the integrity of the judicial system and its processes by invalidating a court-ordered mediation settlement agreement obtained through violation and abuse of the judicially-prescribed mediation procedures.

"Every court has inherent power to do all things that are reasonably necessary for the administration of justice within the scope of its jurisdiction, subject to valid existing laws and constitutional provisions." *Rose v. Palm Beach County*, 361 So.2d 135, 137 (Fla. 1978). In a variety of contexts, it has been held that the courts have the inherent power to protect the integrity of the judicial process from perversion and abuse. *See Attwood v. Singletary*, 661 So.2d 1216 (Fla. 1995) (invoking court's inherent authority to prevent "abusive filer" from filing additional cases and, thus, interfering with orderly process of judicial administration); *Tramel v. Bass*, 672 So.2d 78 (Fla. 1st DCA 1996) (invoking court's inherent authority to strike pleadings to sanction fraud perpetrated on the court). While the doctrine of inherent power should be invoked "cautiously" and "only in situations of clear necessity," we have little trouble deciding that the instant case presents a compelling occasion for its use. *See Rose*, 361 So.2d at 138.

We hasten to add that no findings were made as to whether the mediator actually committed the alleged misconduct. Nevertheless, at least some of the wife's claims clearly are sufficient to allege a violation of the applicable rules. On remand, the trial court must determine whether the mediator substantially violated the Rules for Mediators, and whether that misconduct led to the settlement agreement in this case.

AFFIRMED in part, REVERSED in part, and REMANDED.
GUNTHER and SHAHOOD, JJ., concur.

Legal and Ethical Issues

Many of the legal and ethical issues that could arise during a private mediation are less likely to arise in a court-sponsored mediation. If the mediation is conducted by a judge or magistrate, he or she is protected by judicial immunity. Those who receive special appointments by the court to mediate disputes for the court (court-appointed mediators), may receive protection from the court-sponsored mediation order issued by the court and by judicial immunity since they are court appointees. If a mediator is sued for breach of contract or negligence, the party bringing the action must prove the damages that were the result of the mediator's actions.

In *Lehrer v. Zwernemann*, an unhappy client sued his former attorneys for legal malpractice. The trial judge ordered mediation. Although the mediation produced a settlement agreement, the unhappy client then sued the mediator for negligence or legal malpractice, breach of contract, breach of fiduciary duty, Texas Deceptive Trade Practices Act violations, fraud, and conspiracy to commit fraud.

Lehrer v. Zwernemann

**Court of Appeals of Texas,
Houston (1st Dist.)
14 S.W.3d 775 (2000)**

Panel consists of Justices O'CONNOR, HEDGES, and PRICE.*

Opinion

ADELE HEDGES, Justice.

Appellant participated in a court-ordered mediation, but was dissatisfied with the result. He sued his attorney, the opposing counsel, and the mediator, Donald Zwernemann. In this appeal, we are asked to determine whether the trial court erred in rendering summary judgment for the mediator.[1] We affirm.

Background

Appellant hired two attorneys to represent him in a divorce action. Unhappy with the result, he hired James L. Supkis to sue the attorneys for legal malpractice. The trial judge ordered mediation. Supkis and the opposing counsel agreed to select Zwernemann as the mediator. The mediation resulted in a voluntary settlement agreement.

Supkis and the opposing counsel then filed a joint motion to dismiss the legal malpractice suit under the settlement agreement, and the trial judge signed the order. Shortly thereafter, Supkis filed a motion for new trial and motion to withdraw, informing the court that he had not had appellant's permission to file the motion to dismiss. After he fired Supkis, appellant filed a motion for new trial to rescind the dismissal. The trial judge denied the motion, and this Court affirmed that ruling in *Lehrer v. Garner*, No. 01-94-00537-CV, 1995 WL 241715 (Tex. App.—Houston [1st Dist.] 1995, no writ) (not designated for publication).

Subsequently, appellant sued Supkis. He later amended his petition to include the opposing counsel and Zwernemann. Appellant contended that the three defendants did not notify him or the court that (1) the opposing counsel had a pre-existing professional relationship with Zwernemann or (2) Supkis had not conducted any discovery in the case. Appellant pleaded causes of action against Zwernemann for negligence or legal malpractice, breach of contract, breach of fiduciary duty, Texas Deceptive Trade Practices Act violations, fraud, and conspiracy to commit fraud. He sought actual and exemplary damages plus attorney's fees. Zwernemann moved for summary judgment based on a lack of summary judgment evidence to support appellant's causes of actions. The trial judge rendered summary judgment for Zwernemann.[2]

In four points of error, appellant argues that the trial judge erred in rendering summary judgment because: (1) there was sufficient summary judgment proof to support his breach of contract cause of action; (2) there was sufficient summary judgment proof to support his fraud cause of action; (3) *res judicata* was an improper basis for the summary judgment; and (4) there was sufficient summary judgment proof that Zwernemann caused damages to appellant.

---

*The Honorable Frank C. Price, former Justice, Court of Appeals, First District of Texas at Houston, participating by assignment.

[1]On May 13, 1999, this Court affirmed the summary judgment in favor of the opposing counsel. *Lehrer v. Weinberg*, No. 01-98-00704-CV, 1999 WL 312327 (Tex. App.—Houston [1st Dist.] 1999, pet. denied (not designated for publication).

[2]Although Zwernemann's motion for summary judgment did not cite Texas Rule of Civil Procedure 166a(i), it is clear from the language in the motion, appellant's response to the motion, the trial judge's order, appellant's points of error on appeal, and Zwernemann's reply to the points of error that the trial judge granted the motion based on the lack of evidence to support appellant's causes of action. Therefore, we will review the order as though it is a no-evidence summary judgment. *See* Tex. R. Civ. P. 166a(i).

(continued)

(continued from previous page)
Summary Judgment Standard of Review

Under rule 166a(i), a party may move for summary judgment if there is no evidence of one or more essential elements of a claim or defense on which an adverse party would have the burden of proof at trial. Tex. R. Civ. P. 66a(i). The trial judge must grant the motion unless the non-movant produces more than a scintilla of evidence raising a genuine issue of material fact on the challenged elements. *Flameout Design & Fabrication, Inc. v. Pennzoil Caspian Corp.*, 994 S.W.2d 830, 834 (Tex. App.—Houston [1st Dist.] 1999, no pet.). Therefore, the party with the burden of proof at trial has the burden of proof in the summary judgment proceeding. *See id.* When reviewing a summary judgment, we must indulge every reasonable inference in favor of the non-movant and resolve any doubts in its favor. *Id.*

Legal Injury

In point of error four, appellant argues that the trial judge erred in rendering summary judgment because he adduced sufficient summary judgment evidence that he was damaged by Zwernemann's actions at the mediation.

As a general rule, a cause of action accrues when a wrongful act causes some legal injury. *See Hay v. Shell Oil Co.*, 986 S.W.2d 772, 776 (Tex. App.—Corpus Christi 1999, pet. denied). Therefore, in order to withstand a no-evidence summary judgment review, appellant was required to produce some evidence that he suffered a legal injury as a result of Zwernemann's actions at the mediation. Appellant has not produced any evidence of legal injury.

Appellant argues that he was injured by Zwernemann because he represented himself to be a "third-party neutral" mediator, but at the mediation acted contrary to appellant's best interests. Specifically, appellant alleges that Zwernemann and the opposing counsel had a prior professional relationship because they had worked together in the past. Additionally, appellant alleges that Zwernemann did not inform him that Supkis had not conducted discovery in the case. However, appellant has produced no evidence to support his allegations. To the contrary, the evidence proves that Zwernemann fulfilled his primary obligation as a mediator to facilitate a settlement. In fact, as a result of the mediation, appellant entered into a voluntary settlement agreement, in which he agreed to dismiss his legal malpractice claims against his attorneys. In return, his attorneys dismissed their counter-claims against him for unpaid attorneys' fees.

Additionally, in his affidavit attached to his response to Zwernemann's motion for summary judgment, appellant stated that, if he had known about the prior relationship between the opposing counsel and Zwernemann, he would not have agreed to permit Zwernemann to act as the mediator. However, appellant did not state that he would not have entered into the settlement agreement.

Further, it is apparent that appellant had, at a minimum, constructive knowledge of the prior professional relationship before the mediation took place. In his own case against appellant, the opposing counsel stated by affidavit that, before the mediation, he informed Supkis that he and Zwernemann had been involved in numerous legal matters. For example, "Zwernemann served as opposing counsel, co-counsel, mediator and, on occasion, as an expert witness for me."[3] Knowledge or notice to an attorney, acquired during the existence of the attorney-client relationship and while acting within the scope of his authority, is imputed to the client. *Gulf Atlantic Life Ins. v. Hurlbut*, 749 S.W.2d 96, 98 (Tex. App.—Dallas 1985), *rev'd on other grounds*, 749 S.W.2d 762, 768–69 (Tex. 1987). By virtue of Supkis's knowledge of the relationship, appellant was "on notice" of the relationship. *See id.* Appellant also stated in his affidavit that he was aware, before the mediation, that Zwernemann had acted as a mediator for the opposing counsel in the past.

Moreover, in his affidavit, appellant alleged specific economic injuries that resulted from the mediation. Specifically, he stated that he "suffered economic injuries as a result of the actions of Mr. Supkis, as outlined below . . . . " He did not, however, allege that any specific injuries or damages were caused by Zwernemann.

---

[3]We take judicial notice of this statement. *See Trevino v. Pemberton*, 918 S.W.2d 102, 103 n.2 (Tex. App.—Amarillo 1996, orig. proceeding).

Accordingly, because appellant has not produced any summary judgment evidence establishing a legal injury as a result of the actions of Zwernemann, summary judgment was appropriate.

We overrule point of error four.

Conclusion

Because we find that summary judgment was appropriate based on a lack of evidence of injury, we need not address appellant's remaining points of error.

We affirm the summary judgment of the trial court.

Ethical issues do, however, arise. Often these issues involve the attorneys who are representing clients at the court-sponsored mediation.

Problem 11-6

Jerry Malone, an attorney, represents Rachel Sanchez and Raphael Lopez, who jointly own a patent. Rachel and Raphael have sued the Milky Way Corporation for patent infringement, and the case has been sent to a court-sponsored mediation.

As the mediation progresses, the mediator discovers that Rachel and Raphael have competing interests. Each believes that she or he is entitled to more than the other if the case is settled for a reasonable sum of money.

1. Is Jerry, by representing both Rachel and Raphael, involved in a conflict of interest?
2. Should he be representing both clients?
3. What should the mediator do?

Problem 11-7

During a court-sponsored mediation, the mediator has asked one of the parties and her attorney to join her in another room so they could have a private caucus. When the attorney left the mediation room, he left his attaché case in the corner.

When the mediator came back to the mediation room to get something that she had left behind, she discovered the attorney rummaging through the other attorney's attaché case.

1. Has the attorney committed an ethical violation?
2. What should the mediator do?

Problem 11-8

During a court-sponsored mediation, the mediator has observed that the attorney for one of the parties has a lack of understanding of the law as it relates to his client's case.

What should the mediator do?

The Advantages and Disadvantages of Court-Sponsored Mediation

Although the parties have the luxury to select or not to select private mediation, they may not have the same luxury when it comes to court-sponsored mediation. When a judge recommends court-sponsored mediation to the litigants, few attorneys will advise their clients to refuse the judge's invitation. Once the litigants consent to mediation, the court's mediation procedure goes into effect. The court may schedule the time and the place for the mediation, select the mediator, and provide the parties (attorneys and clients) and the mediator with the rules for the mediation. Each court follows its own procedure.

Problem 11-9

Compare the procedure of the United States District Court for the Northern District of Oklahoma, N.D. Okla. R. 16.3 at *http://207.41.19.205/okndpub1/welcome.nsf/main/page,* with the procedure of the United States District Court for the Western District of Oklahoma, W.D. Okla. Guidelines for Mediators at *http://www.okwd.uscourts.gov/adr.htm.*

1. Do the courts differ on how a mediator is selected?
2. Do the courts differ on how the scheduling of the mediation is arranged?
3. Do the courts differ on whether the mediator will be paid and, if so, by whom?

As was the case with private mediation, court-sponsored mediation does not guarantee that the dispute will be resolved by the end of the process. Since the mediator only provides the process, the parties must agree on the resolution. The parties can be creative in formulating a solution, and their creativity is not limited by legal principles. A mediated agreement generally accommodates at least some of the needs and interests of both parties.

Mediating an agreement through a court-sponsored process will guarantee that transaction costs will be reduced. The reduction, however, is not as great as if the parties had negotiated or privately mediated their dispute without a complaint being filed. Since the case is before the court, the parties will have hired attorneys and their attorneys will have begun discovery and may have filed motions and briefs with the court, driving up the transaction costs.

Court-sponsored mediation provides the parties with an opportunity to weigh the need to try to resolve the dispute now against what might happen if the dispute is resolved later by the triers of fact and law. The parties may have a need to resolve the dispute quickly so they can put the problem behind them and move on. Delaying the resolution of the dispute does not guarantee that the dispute will be resolved more favorably to the party who decides against a mediated agreement.

Although the parties do not control the process, they do control the outcome and this control may be extremely important to a party. If a settlement agreement can be reached, the parties control their own destinies. No neutral third party must consent to the parties' agreement.

Although the litigants participating in a court-sponsored mediation do not control the process, they do control the outcome and the outcome is known if the mediation produces a written settlement agreement. The mediation is private and confidential with no public airing of the dispute. Unless a party later decides to breach the settlement agreement, the resolution of the dispute is final. When parties mediate an agreement, they almost always perform the agreement because the agreement incorporates their needs and interests and has been carefully drafted so each party knows what to expect. In those cases where a party fails to perform, a breach of contract action may be maintained. In some cases where the outcome of the dispute need not be kept confidential and the parties would like the settlement agreement to be treated as more than a contract, the settlement agreement could be entered as a consent judgment and would have the same effect as a court judgment.

Parties who participate in court-sponsored mediation do not forgo the opportunity to continue with the litigation of the dispute if the mediation does not produce an agreement. The opportunity to pursue the dispute, however, does not come without costs. Transaction costs (time, money, psychological trauma) accumulate, and worse yet, the end result may not be favorable to the party who could have chosen a mediated ADR process, and the transaction costs must be factored into the outcome to produce a net gain. Figure 11-1 presents an overview of court-sponsored mediation as a dispute resolution process.

AVAILABILITY	the litigation process must have been initiated and the court must have a court-sponsored mediation program
PROCESS SELECTION	generally recommended by the court although the parties may opt out the court controls the scheduling
THE PARTICIPANTS	the mediator, the parties, and their attorneys
PREPARATION	each party may be required to prepare a short position document summarizing the facts, the issues, and previous settlement discussions
THE PROCESS	takes place in a private setting informal and structured by the mediator, with each party having an opportunity to discuss his or her perception of the dispute, his or her feelings, interests, and proposed solutions confidential and preserves the privacy of the parties' records and documents if the mediation is only facilitative, the mediator will not suggest solutions; if evaluative, the mediator can provide the parties with a preview of the outcome if the case proceeds to trial
FAIRNESS	generally does not address the inequality of power between the parties and therefore one party may try to take advantage of the other the mediator will not participate in the discovery or trial aspects of the case if the case does not settle
THE OUTCOME	allows the parties to control the outcome of their dispute and encourages creative resolutions can result in the immediate resolution of the dispute if the parties agree based on the parties interests and needs eliminates all uncertainties as to outcome without sufficient discovery, an agreement may be based on inadequate information agreement is enforceable as a contract and may be entered as a judgment if the parties so desire if the parties are unable to agree, there will be no agreement and the dispute will continue
COSTS	unless the court provides otherwise, the court does not charge for the process if the dispute is resolved through court-sponsored mediation, the parties save some discovery and litigation costs reduces attorney's fees will add another layer of costs to the dispute resolution process if the mediation does not resolve the dispute may provide low cost discovery due to the openness of the discussion
PRECEDENTIAL VALUE	establishes no binding precedent although nonbinding precedent by performance may be created between the parties
IMPACT ON FUTURE RELATIONSHIP	may encourage future cooperation or reduce confrontation between the parties

FIGURE 11-1   Court-Sponsored Mediation

Key Terms and Phrases

court-sponsored mediation

Review Questions

True/False Questions

1. T F   In court-sponsored mediation, the jury is the finder of fact and the judge is the finder of law.

2. T F   In court-sponsored mediation, the parties will be represent by legal counsel unless a party is *pro se*.

3. T F   In court-sponsored mediation, the outcome is based more on the needs and interests of the parties than the law.

4. T (F) In court-sponsored mediation, the parties negotiate the rules.

5. T (F) Court-sponsored mediation leads to a win/win solution.

6. T F   Court-sponsored mediation may be conducted before or after a complaint is filed with the court.

7. T F   Court-sponsored mediation generally takes place over a period of time and may start and stop.

8. T F   An effective court-sponsored mediation is based on preparation.

9. T F   Court-sponsored mediation is consensual and can be terminated by either party at any time.

10. T F   A mediated agreement is enforceable as a contract and the court could enter a consent decree.

11. T F   During a court-sponsored mediation, a dominant party may take advantage of a weaker party through psychological gamesmanship.

12. T F   A court may find a court-sponsored mediated agreement unenforceable if at the time of mediation one of the parties took an unconscionable advantage over the other, committed fraud or duress, or misrepresented material facts.

13. T F   Court-sponsored mediation gives the parties control over the outcome.

14. T F   Court-sponsored mediation is designed so one party wins and the other loses.

15. T F   Oral mediation agreements run the risk of being unenforceable if they are made during a court-sponsored mediation.

16. T F   A court-sponsored mediation agreement must be drafted with the same skill as a negotiated agreement.

17. T F   A court-sponsored mediation may never take place after the court has rendered a judgment in the dispute.

18. T F The RAND study endorsed court-sponsored mediation as "the panacea for problems of cost and delay in the courts."

19. T F Most federal district courts and many state trial courts have a court-sponsored mediation program.

20. T F Of all the court-sponsored ADR programs, mediation is the most widely used.

Fill-in-the-Blank Questions

1. _Initiation of the lawsuit_ List the steps of the litigation/mediation process.
   Case mgmt Conference w/ trial judge
   Seletion of Mediation
   Appt of Mediator
   Court Sponsored Mediation order
   Court Sponsored Mediation Statements
   Court Sponsored Mediation
   Follow up from the mediation

2. _____ List 10 legitimate concerns that should be addressed
   _____ during a court-sponsored mediation.
   _____
   _____
   _____
   _____
   _____
   _____
   _____
   _____

Multiple-Choice Questions

1. Which of the following may always participate in court-sponsored mediation:
   (a) the aggrieved party
   (b) the other party to the dispute
   (c) a neutral third party
   (d) a jury
   (e) the attorney for the aggrieved party

2. Court-sponsored mediation is classified as:
   (a) unilateral action in dispute resolution
   (b) bilateral action in dispute resolution
   (c) third-party evaluation as a prelude to dispute resolution
   (d) third-party assistance in dispute resolution
   (e) third-party adjudication in dispute resolution

Short-Answer Questions

1. Dirk LaBlue was making his escape from a late-night burglary at a local pharmacy when he was shot by a police officer. The police report stated that the officer thought LaBlue was reaching for a gun. No gun was found at the scene. Although LaBlue has been convicted of the robbery, he has filed a civil complaint in federal court against the city alleging that the police officer used excessive force while attempting to make a lawful arrest.

    The court sponsors a mediation program. Should the court order this case to mediation?
2. Discuss the advantages and disadvantages of court-sponsored mediation as a dispute resolution process.
3. Why is court-sponsored mediation gaining popularity in the courts?
4. Should a court-appointed mediator limit his or her role to facilitative mediation?
5. Can a court-appointed mediator be sued by one of the parties to the mediation and, if so, on what basis?
6. Discuss the steps in a court-sponsored mediation.
7. Discuss the legitimate concerns that should be discussed during a court-sponsored mediation.

Role-Play Exercises

Role-Play Exercise 11-1   The Cost-of-Living Allowance

The Players: Alice Steuben
Alice's attorney
James Steuben
James's attorney
The court-appointed mediator

Alice and James Steuben were married for 24 years until their divorce in 1990. The judgment of dissolution that the trial court rendered provided for the payment of periodic alimony from James to Alice. The judgment also provided that James pay an annual cost-of-living allowance in addition to the amount of alimony provided in the judgment. The judgment provided in relevant part:

> Commencing this day and for a period of two (2) years thereafter, James shall pay to Alice, as periodic unallocated alimony, the sum of $26,000 per year payable $2166.66 per month. At the expiration of the two (2) years and for a period of eight (8) years thereafter, James shall pay to Alice, as unallocated alimony, the sum of $17,500 per year payable $1458.33 per month. After the expiration of said eight (8) year period, and thereafter, James shall pay to Alice as unallocated alimony, the sum of $15,000 per year payable $1250 per month. In addition to these payments, *if applicable as additional periodic alimony* . . . James shall pay to Alice as a cost of living allowance a sum to commence in February of 1992 with the first adjustment to be in February, 1993, as per Agreement on file.

The court found that the parties' separation agreement was fair and equitable and incorporated it by reference into the dissolution judgment. The judgment specifically referred to the parties' separation agreement for the method by which the cost-of-living allowance should be calculated. Article 2.1 of the separation agreement provides in relevant part:

> In addition to these payments, if applicable as additional periodic alimony or child support as the case may be, James shall pay to Alice as a cost of living allowance a sum to commence in February of 1992, with the first adjustment to be in February, 1993, and to be arrived at as follows:
>
> (a) The Consumer Price Index figure applicable to January, 1992, shall be the basis for further increases. On the second day of February, 1993, and on the same day of each year thereafter, an evaluation of the cost of living for the preceding calendar year shall be made and an average figure of the twelve months of the preceding calendar year of the Consumer Price Index shall be taken.
>
> (b) If the cost of living so computed shall be different from the present cost of living, then all monies paid by James to Alice for alimony and support during the preceding calendar year shall be adjusted in exact proportion as the cost of living figure of the preceding year is to the newly established figure. Any monies computed to be due in accordance with this formula shall be paid by James to Alice in twelve monthly payments for the next calendar year.

Three months ago, Alice filed a motion for contempt, alleging that James has failed to pay the cost-of-living adjustments provided for by the parties' separation agreement that was incorporated into the judgment dissolving their marriage for 1993 and all subsequent years. Alice also sought interest on the arrearage.

Since the petition was filed, both parties has taken the depositions of expert witnesses. If a trial were held, Alice's and James's certified public accountants would offer conflicting testimony as to the proper method for calculating the total amount of cost-of-living adjustments that James should have paid. Their disagreement revolved around the proper method for calculating the cost-of-living allowance provided for in the agreement. James' CPA would, when performing the necessary calculation for each year, use the original base amount of agreed alimony as the basis for determining that year's cost-of-living adjustment. Alice's CPA would use the adjusted base from the previous year to calculate the following year's cost-of-living adjustment.

The trial court judge has referred the case to the court's mediation program. In preparation for the mediation, the attorneys should prepare their court-sponsored mediation statements and submit them to opposing counsel and the mediator.

Role-Play Exercise 11-2   The Reluctant Insurers

The Players: Sylvia Garcia, the plaintiff
Julio Garcia, Sylvia's husband and co-plaintiff
The Garcias' attorney
Carolyn Marsten's husband, the executor of her estate and the beneficiary under her will

> The attorney for the Marsten estate
> General Counsel for the Health Care Authority
> Representative of Eastern
> Representative of Western
> Representative of Omega
> Court-appointed mediator

In August of last year, Carolyn Marsten was employed as a home health aide by the Avery State Medical Center Health Care Authority ("the Health Care Authority"). She traveled to patients' homes and provided in-home care to those patients. Carolyn's employment with the Health Care Authority was conditioned upon her providing her own transportation to perform her duties. As compensation for her employment, the Health Care Authority paid Carolyn an hourly rate. Additionally, the Health Care Authority paid her a sum for mileage, based upon the number of miles she drove in the performance of her duties.

In August of last year, Carolyn reported to the Health Care Authority to obtain her schedule of patient visits for the day. She then went about visiting her patients, driving her personal car. While en route to a patient's home, Carolyn entered U.S. Highway 62 in Jackson County and collided with a car driven by Sylvia Garcia. Sylvia was seriously injured in the accident, and Carolyn died as a result of the injuries she sustained in the accident.

Sylvia and her husband, Julio, sued Carolyn's estate, the Health Care Authority, and Omega Mutual Insurance Company ("Omega"). The Garcias claimed that Carolyn's negligence had caused the accident, that the Health Care Authority was vicariously liable for her misconduct, and that Sylvia was entitled to underinsured motorist benefits under the automobile liability insurance policy issued to Sylvia by Omega.

Carolyn's estate filed a counterclaim alleging that Sylvia's negligence caused the accident.

The police report is inconclusive as to negligence. It states that Carolyn may have been on her mobile phone at the time of the accident. It also reports that Sylvia may have had her pet poodle on her lap at the time of the accident. Each side has witnesses that support their side of the case.

At the time of the August accident, Carolyn was insured under a personal automobile liability insurance policy issued by Eastern Insurance Company ("Eastern"). Under that policy, the coverage for bodily injury was limited to $20,000. The Health Care Authority was insured under a automobile liability insurance policy issued by Western Fire and Casualty Insurance Company ("Western") that provided coverage for bodily injury, with a limit of $1,000,000. Sylvia was insured under an automobile liability policy issued by Omega that provided underinsured motorist benefits up to $320,000.

In an effort to dispose of the lawsuit before trial, the parties entered into settlement negotiations. On behalf of Carolyn's estate, Eastern tendered its policy limits of $20,000. A dispute arose between Omega and Western as to the amount Western should contribute to a settlement. Western took the position that the vicarious liability of the Health Care Authority was limited to $100,000 by state statute. State statute limits the recovery of damages under a judgment against a governmental entity to $100,000 for bodily injury to, or the death, of one person in any single occurrence. Western tendered $100,000 toward the settlement on behalf of the Health Care Authority. Western also took the position that Carolyn was not an insured under the Health Care Authority's policy and that Western was not otherwise obligated to contribute to the settlement on behalf of Carolyn. Omega contended that Carolyn was an insured under the policy Western issued to the Health Care Authority and that state statute did not limit Western's liability on behalf of the Health Care Authority. Omega also contends that Carolyn was an insured under the Health Care Authority's policy issued by Western. Omega contends that it was not obligated to pay any underinsured motorist benefits to Sylvia until Western's policy limits ($1,000,000) had been exhausted by payments on behalf of the Health Care Authority or Carolyn.

Since the parties could not negotiate a settlement, the court has ordered the case to mediation. In preparation for the court-sponsored mediation, all parties, or their counsel, should prepare and submit court-sponsored mediation statements to each other and the court-appointed mediator.

CHAPTER 12

Mini-Trial

The mini-trial was created in 1977 in a patent infringement case between Telecredit, Inc. and TRW, Inc. The mini-trial can be useful in resolving disputes between corporate parties. The term *mini-trial* is actually a misnomer because it is not a trial at all. In a **mini-trial,** a senior executive with full settlement authority from each disputing corporation joins a neutral third party to form a three-person panel. The corporate executives usually have had no personal involvement in the dispute. This allows them to evaluate the dispute more objectively than if they had been personally involved. The atmosphere of objectivity creates a climate conducive to settlement. The neutral third party may or may not have specialized subject matter expertise.

Mini-Trial

A mini-trial is an abbreviated nonbinding trial held before a three-person panel (one corporate officer with settlement authority from each corporation and a neutral third party) and is followed by the corporate officers negotiating a settlement.

The Mini-Trial Process

The mini-trial has two distinct stages. During the initial stage, the panel listens to a formal presentation of evidence and arguments by the attorneys representing the corporations. The evidence is presented in a summary fashion. The mini-trial is less formal than a traditional trial and the procedural rules are established by the parties. Some witnesses could be used along with summary proofs. Each corporate officer will hear not only the attorney representing his or her own corporation but also the attorney representing the other corporation. As the presentations unfold, the panel members have an opportunity to question the attorneys. In large corporations, often this is the first time that the senior executive will have heard the details of the dispute, and certainly this will be the first time that the senior executive will have heard the details of the dispute directly from the other side.

The final stage of the mini-trial takes place between the two corporate officers and away from the attorneys who made the presentations. The degree of involvement by the neutral will vary from mini-trial to mini-trial. Some neutrals have an active role; others are available as advisors in the event they are needed. If the neutral is present when the corporate officers meet, the neutral may act as a mediator. If the neutral is not present, the corporate officers negotiate directly with each other. In either event, the corporate officers discuss what they have heard and seen and attempt to resolve the dispute.

A mini-trial is a flexible procedure that allows the parties to structure an agreement that is tailored to their particular dispute. The parties can require that discovery proceed to a certain point before the mini-trial occurs. They can also require the attorneys to submit briefs to the panel members before the mini-trial. Additionally, the parties can alter the role of the neutral. Depending on the agreement of the parties the neutral can perform many roles: answering legal/technical questions from the corporate representatives and serving as a sounding board, questioning witnesses and the attorneys representing the corporations to clarify facts and legal theories, and actively presiding over the mini-trial to keep the attorneys on the mutually established schedule. The neutral could also be asked to prepare a written summary or analysis of the case for the other members of the panel.

Unlike the settlement conference where the neutral third party negotiates and mediates with the parties' attorneys and the parties, and unlike the summary jury trial where the mock jury renders an advisory decision, the officials representing the corporate disputants in the mini-trial resolve their own dispute. As was true of the settlement agreement, the agreement coming from a mini-trial is the parties' agreement and not that imposed by the neutral. If the corporate officers reach an agreement, it will be based on their corporate needs and interests as influenced by the projected legal outcome of the dispute. The agreement need not parallel the legal resolution of the dispute.

If a settlement does not occur, the parties may proceed to arbitration, litigation, or private judging.

Selecting the Mini-Trial as an Appropriate Dispute Resolution Process

A number of factors should be considered when determining if a particular case is suitable for a mini-trial. Cases in which the parties are on the same level financially are very good for mini-trials because this will create a sense of equality in the negotiation process and will prevent one side from feeling manipulated. Similarly, cases where an ongoing business relationship is involved will provide the trust and cooperation that is needed for a successful mini-trial. Also, cases that lend themselves to creative solutions and can be settled by something other than monetary damages are highly conducive to this sort of process.

Although a number of corporate/corporate disputes are appropriate for mini-trials, there are some that do not work very well with this informal format. Cases that involve significant issues of law and not questions of facts are better suited to conventional litigation. Also, cases where one of the parties is demanding punitive damages would be better handled by a jury.

The Advantages and Disadvantages of the Mini-Trial as a Dispute Resolution Process

The mini-trial is voluntary, flexible, and informal. The parties can establish their own schedule for the mini-trial rather than waiting in the queue for their trial date. They can control discovery and thereby control costs. They can formulate their own rules of evidence and their own rules of procedure in order to give the process maximum informality and efficiency.

The mini-trial is a confidential process. The information given at the mini-trial can not be used against the parties at trial. If the mini-trial does not result in a settlement, the parties risk revealing their trial strategy to the other side. This may encourage some parties to withhold information they may consider using at trial.

The mini-trial permits upper-level management an opportunity to listen to its case and the other side's case directly, without the information being processed by a third person for them. In this way, they can gain a clear understanding of the problem.

When the corporate officers meet after the presentation of evidence, they have an opportunity to formulate a solution that is based on their needs and interests rather than being hemmed in by "the law." They maintain full control over the resolution of the dispute. They can choose not to settle and proceed to another form of dispute resolution. If this occurs, the parties have had a dry run through the evidence and have a better understanding of the strengths and weaknesses of their case.

The corporate representatives have the opportunity to listen to a neutral third party who also has listened to all of the evidence. This party can provide the corporate representatives with an objective evaluation of the dispute. Figure 12-1 presents an overview of mini-trial as a dispute resolution process.

AVAILABILITY	always available but best suited for corporate disputes and may be court-sponsored
PROCESS SELECTION	by the parties, although could be recommended by the court the parties control the scheduling unless court sponsored
THE PARTICIPANTS	a corporate officer with settlement authority from each corporate party, a neutral third party, the attorneys representing the corporations, and several witnesses
PREPARATION	fashioning the rules for the process and selecting the neutral third party the normal discovery required for trial
THE PROCESS	takes place in a private setting the hearing phase is formal and structured and the negotiation or mediation phase is informal and unstructured, with each member of the panel having an opportunity to discuss his or her impressions of the case as presented at the hearing phase and his or her corporation's interests and range of solutions confidential and preserves the privacy of the parties' records and documents
FAIRNESS	a mini-trial does not address the power imbalances that may exist between the corporate officials
THE OUTCOME	allows the corporate officials to control the outcome of their corporate dispute, and encourages creative resolutions can result in the immediate resolution of the dispute if the parties agree based on the parties' interests and needs eliminates all uncertainties as to outcome agreement is enforceable as a contract if the parties are unable to agree, there will be no agreement and the dispute will continue the hearing phase and the neutral third-party's evaluation can provide the corporate officials with a preview of the outcome if the case proceeds to trial
COSTS	the preparation for the hearing phase includes many of the costs involved preparing for a trial, including discovery a mini-trial saves further discovery and discovery costs if settlement is reached during the negotiation or mediation phase the presentation of evidence at the hearing phase includes many of the costs involved presenting evidence at a trial (including expert witnesses) the parties pay the neutral third party (unless a sitting judge) and for other associated expenses saves the costs of a full trial and appeal if a settlement can be reached during the mediation phase reduces attorney's fees will add another layer of costs to the dispute resolution process if the mediation does not resolve the dispute may provide low-cost discovery due to the presentation of evidence at the abbreviated trial and openness of the settlement discussion
PRECEDENTIAL VALUE	establishes no binding precedent although nonbinding precedent by performance may be created between the parties
IMPACT ON FUTURE RELATIONSHIP	may encourage future cooperation or reduce confrontation between the parties

FIGURE 12-1   Mini-Trial

Key Terms and Phrases

mini-trial

Review Questions

True/False Questions

1. T F   In a mini-trial, the jury is the finder of fact and the judge is the finder of law.
2. T F   A mini-trial is more of a case management tool than a dispute resolution process.
3. T F   The parties can streamline issues and discovery at a mini-trial.
4. T F   A mini-trial gives the parties an objective evaluation of the case.
5. T F   A mini-trial is conducted by the judge who will try the case.
6. T F   A mini-trial is a court-sponsored program and occurs after the complaint has been filed and before trial.
7. T F   A mini-trial is generally held after discovery has been completed.
8. T F   A mini-trial is confidential and preserves the confidentiality of private records.
9. T F   A mini-trial is another name for a summary jury trial.
10. T F   A mini-trial is better suited for issues of law than questions of fact.

Fill-in-the-Blank Questions

1. _____ List four advantages of a mini-trial.
   _____
   _____
   _____

2. _____ List four disadvantages of a mini-trial.
   _____
   _____
   _____

Multiple-Choice Questions

1. Which of the following may actively participate in a mini-trial?
   (a) the aggrieved party
   (b) the other party to the dispute
   (c) a neutral third party
   (d) a jury
   (e) the attorney for the aggrieved party

2. Mini-trial is classified as:
   (a) unilateral action in dispute resolution
   (b) bilateral action in dispute resolution
   (c) third-party evaluation as a prelude to dispute resolution
   (d) third-party assistance in dispute resolution
   (e) third-party adjudication in dispute resolution
3. The primary function of a mini-trial is:
   (a) to streamline discovery issues
   (b) to give corporate officers an opportunity to hear both sides of the case so they may then negotiate a settlement
   (c) to give the parties an objective evaluation of their case
   (d) to clear the court's docket
   (e) to have the case decided by a neutral third party (the judge and jury)

Short-Answer Questions

1. The Apex Oil Company contracted with the United Transport Company to have United tow a drilling platform from the Gulf of Mexico to the North Sea where Apex was exploring for oil and gas. During the tow, the drilling platform capsized and sank to the bottom of the Atlantic Ocean. Each corporation blamed the other for the loss of the drilling platform. Apex would like to be paid for the loss of the drilling platform and for the economic loss it suffered while waiting for another drilling platform to be towed to the drilling site. United would like to be paid on the transport contract.

   Is this an appropriate case for a mini-trial?
2. Why is mini-trial primarily an ADR process involving corporate disputes?

PART SIX

Third-Party Adjudication in Dispute Resolution

Introduction

Part VI explores third-party adjudication in dispute resolution. The third party is a neutral party who directs the process and resolves the dispute. In an adjudication process the third party judges. The parties no longer have control over the outcome of their dispute. Part VI consists of five chapters: Chapter 13, "Private Arbitration"; Chapter 14, "Court-Annexed Arbitration"; Chapter 15, "Mediation-Arbitration"; Chapter 16, "Litigation"; and Chapter 17, "Private Judging."

Private arbitration may be selected by the parties as the method of dispute resolution either before or after the dispute arises. The predispute election occurs when the parties contract and the party who drafts the contract designates arbitration as the dispute resolution method for all subsequent disputes arising under the contract. The postdispute election occurs when the parties agree to proceed to private arbitration after the dispute arises. The agreement to arbitrate designates the arbitrator, arbitration panel, or arbitration service. An arbitration service provides the parties with the arbitration process and with a list of arbitrators from which to make their selection. If the parties select an arbitrator or arbitration panel rather than an arbitration service, either the parties or the arbitrator or panel create the arbitration process. Regardless of whether an arbitration service or an arbitrator or arbitration panel is chosen, the parties pay for the process and for the arbitrator or arbitrators.

Court-annexed arbitration is a court-created and court-administered process. Although once more popular than it currently is, court-annexed arbitration is offered in only a limited number of state and federal jurisdictions. The process begins when a party files a complaint in a jurisdiction that offers court-annexed arbitration as a matter of statute or court rule. If the case comes within the subject matter and monetary limits of the program, the court clerk will refer the case to the court's ADR administrator. The administrator will schedule the case for arbitration. The court provides the arbitrator or panel, usually a member or members of the local bar association. The arbitrator or panel conducts the arbitration using the procedural and evidentiary rules established by the court for its court-annexed arbitration program. Upon the conclusion of the arbitra-

tion, the arbitrator or arbitrators issue an award and a dissatisfied party may seek a trial de novo before the court.

Mediation-arbitration (med-arb) is a combination of mediation and arbitration. The process begins as private mediation which gives the parties an opportunity to resolve their own dispute. If by the end of the mediation process, the dispute is not resolved, the mediation process ends and the arbitration begins. The parties present their respective cases to an arbitrator or arbitration panel for resolution of the dispute.

Litigation, although not considered ADR (an *alternative* method of dispute resolution), is a traditional method of dispute resolution. The process begins when a party files a complaint in the office of the clerk of the court. The case proceeds through discovery and ultimately is tried before a judge or a judge and jury, if the case is one where a jury may be seated. At the conclusion of the trial, a judgment is rendered and a dissatisfied party may appeal alleged error to an appellate court.

Private judging has both a broad and a more narrow meaning. In the broad sense, private judging includes temporary judges, referees and special masters. The role of these private judges may vary depending the needs of the particular case. Some may serve as trial judges, some discovery referees, and others as special fact finders. In the more narrow sense and in the sense that they will be discussed in Chapter 17, the private judge will assume the duties of a trial judge and conduct the trial of the case.

After a dispute arises, the parties may contract for private judging rather than have the aggrieved party file a complaint initiating the litigation process. Or the aggrieved party may file a complaint initiating the litigation process and the parties can ask the court to refer the case to a private judge. In the former, the rules of the process are those established by the parties. In the latter, the rules of the process are those established for the court by the legislature (i.e., the court's evidentiary and procedural rules) and by local court rules unless modified by the parties and the private judge. The parties pay the private judge for his or her services.

Private judging by contract is available to all parties to a dispute. Private judging as a court-referred process is available in about half the states and is most popular in California and New York.

CHAPTER 13

Private Arbitration

Private Arbitration
The parties agree to arbitrate their dispute either before the dispute arises or after the dispute has arisen and they select the arbitrator, arbitration panel, or arbitration service provider and pay for the process.

Private arbitration involves the submission of a dispute to a neutral third party or a neutral third party panel who hears the evidence and renders a decision on the law as it applies to the facts.

A private arbitration proceeding is less formal than a trial. Since private arbitration is consensual, the parties have an opportunity to fashion the procedural rules for their arbitration. They may negotiate the rules or they may delegate the formulation of rules to the arbitration service, the arbitrator, or the arbitration panel. Unless the parties in a private arbitration specify otherwise, decision or award of the arbitrator or arbitration panel is binding. An arbitration award may not be appealed to a court unless the appeal alleges the unconstitutionality of the process or an abuse of arbitrator's discretion.

Private Arbitration as a Dispute Resolution Process

As a general rule a party in a private arbitration will be represented by an attorney. At times a party will appear in private arbitration *pro se;* that is, the party appears without an attorney and represents himself or herself. The effectiveness of the advocate, whether an attorney or the party, depends on the advocate's knowledge of the purpose of arbitration, the best timing for arbitration, the rules of arbitration, what is prepared for the arbitration hearing, and the conduct of the advocate during the arbitration.

The Purpose of Private Arbitration

Private arbitration provides the disputants with an opportunity to present their case to a neutral third party or a neutral panel (generally three) who will resolve the dispute for them. Arbitration guarantees the parties that their dispute will be resolved at the end of the process.

Unlike litigation where trials are open to the public, arbitration hearings are private and confidential unless stipulated otherwise by the parties to the dispute.

The Rules of Private Arbitration

Although early American courts did not look favorably upon arbitration, by the early twentieth century, attitudes toward arbitration began to change with the enactment of state and federal legislation. In 1920, New York enacted the first statute giving parties the right to settle disputes through arbitration. The New York statute provided the model for the **Uniform Arbitration Act** of 1955. The validity of arbitration agreements is provided in section 1 of the UAA.

Uniform Arbitration Act
The Uniform Arbitration Act is a model act originally drafted in 1955 by the Conference of Commissioners on Uniform State Laws.

> A written agreement to submit any existing controversy to arbitration or a provision in a written contract to submit to arbitration any controversy thereafter arising between the parties is valid, enforceable and irrevocable, save upon such grounds as exist at law or in equity for the revocation of any contract. This act also applies to arbitration agreements between employers and employees or between their respective representatives (unless otherwise provided in the agreement).

The Uniform Arbitration Act may be found in Appendix E. Today, a majority of states have enacted arbitration statutes modeled after the Uniform Arbitration Act.

Problem 13-1
Has your state enacted a version of the Uniform Arbitration Act?

Federal Arbitration Act
The Federal Arbitration Act was enacted by Congress in 1925 to validate agreements to arbitrate and to encourage the use of commercial arbitration as an alternative to litigation.

In 1925, Congress enacted the **Federal Arbitration Act (FAA)** (originally known as the United States Arbitration Act). The FAA, 9 U.S.C., validates agreements to arbitrate and encourages the use of commercial arbitration as an alternative to litigation. Section 2 of the FAA provides for the validity, irrevocability, and enforcement of agreements to arbitrate.

> A written provision in any maritime transaction or a contract evidencing a transaction involving commerce to settle by arbitration a controversy thereafter arising out of such contract or transaction, or the refusal to perform the whole or any part thereof, or an agreement in writing to submit to arbitration an existing controversy arising out of such a contract, transaction, or refusal, shall be valid, irrevocable, and enforceable, save upon such grounds as exist at law or in equity for the revocation of any contract.

The Federal Arbitration Act is found in Appendix D.

Whether an arbitration agreement is enforceable under section 2 of the FAA depends on whether the written agreement appears in a contract evidencing a transaction that involves interstate commerce. In *Ex parte Ephraim,* the parties debate whether the arbitration clause in the employment contract was enforceable under section 2 of the Federal Arbitration Act.

Ex parte Ephraim
Supreme Court of Alabama
806 So.2d 352 (2001)

SEE, Justice.

Flora Ephraim sued her former employer, Tenet Healthcare Corporation, alleging a retaliatory discharge. See 25-5-11.1, Ala. Code 1975. The defendant moved for an order compelling Ephraim to arbitrate her claim. The circuit court granted the motion. Ephraim petitions for a writ of mandamus directing the circuit court to vacate its order compelling arbitration.

I
Ephraim alleges that on March 20, 1997, while she was working in the Transportation Department at Brookwood Medical Center, she suffered an on-the-job injury while lifting wet linens. Ephraim filed a workers' compensation claim against Tenet Healthcare Corporation (hereinafter "Tenet"), the corporation that owned Brookwood Medical Center. Ephraim underwent back surgery on June 5, 1999. According to Ephraim, Tenet refused to reimburse her for medical expenses related to the surgery and refused to pay her weekly benefits while she recovered from the surgery. She claims that when her physician released her to return to work, Tenet refused to reinstate her.

On April 1, 1996, Ephraim had received an Employee Handbook while attending a presentation at Brookwood Medical Center. Tenet drafted the Handbook, which sets forth Tenet's personnel policies and each employee's privileges and obligations. Ephraim signed an "Employee Acknowledgment Form," acknowledging that she had received of a copy of the Handbook. The Employee Acknowledgment Form reads, in pertinent part:

> I acknowledge that I have received a copy of the Tenet Employees Handbook and Standards of Conduct and that I understand that they contain important information about the company's general personnel policies and about my privileges and obligations as an employee. I further understand and acknowledge that I am governed by the contents of the Employee Handbook and Standards of Conduct and that I am expected to read, understand, familiarize myself with and comply with the policies contained in them. . . .
>
> In addition, I acknowledge that I have received a copy of the Tenet Fair Treatment Process brochure. *I hereby voluntarily agree to use the Company's Fair Treatment Process and to submit to final and binding arbitration any and all claims and disputes that are related in any way to my employment or the termination of my employment with Tenet.* I understand that final and binding arbitration will be the sole and exclusive remedy for any such claim or dispute against Tenet or its parent, subsidiary or affiliated companies or entities, and each of its and/or their employees, officers, directors or agents, and that, *by agreeing to use arbitration to resolve my dispute, both the Company and I agree to forgo any right we each may have had to a jury trial on issues covered by the Fair Treatment Process.* I also agree that such arbitration will be conducted before an experienced arbitrator chosen by me and the Company, and will be conducted under the Federal Arbitration Act and the procedural rules of the American Arbitration Association.
>
> I further acknowledge that in exchange for my agreement to arbitrate, the Company also agrees to submit all claims and disputes it may have with me to final and binding arbitration, and that the Company further agrees that if I submit a request for binding arbitration, my maximum out-of-pocket expenses for the arbitrator and the administrative costs of the AAA will be an amount equal to one day's pay (if I am an exempt employee) or eight times my hourly rate of pay (if I am a non-exempt employee), and that the Company will pay all of the remaining fees and administrative costs of the arbitrator and the AAA. I further acknowledge that this mutual agreement to arbitrate may not be modified or rescinded except by a writing signed by both me and the Company.

(Emphasis added.) As the fifth step in Tenet's "Fair Treatment Process," an employee has "the right to submit the problem or dispute to final and binding arbitration." (Employee Handbook at 68.)

On April 4, 2000, Ephraim sued Tenet, alleging that she had been wrongfully discharged in retaliation for filing a workers' compensation claim for her March 20, 1997, injury. See 25-5-11.1, Ala. Code 1975. On September 8, 2000, Tenet filed a motion to dismiss or, in the alternative, to compel arbitration, based on the arbitration agreement contained in the Employee Acknowledgment Form.

On September 20, 2000, Ephraim objected to arbitration, claiming (1) . . . ; (2) that her employment contract with Tenet did not substantially affect interstate commerce; (3) . . . .

On September 29, 2000, the trial court overruled Tenet's motion to dismiss. However, the trial court granted Tenet's motion to compel arbitration in accordance with the arbitration provisions in the Employee Acknowledgment Form.

On October 11, 2000, Ephraim moved the trial court for a reconsideration, which the trial court granted. On October 27, 2000, the trial court held a hearing on Tenet's motion to compel arbitration. In a November 3, 2000, order, the trial court again granted Tenet's motion to compel arbitration, stating, in pertinent part:

> This Court, relying upon *Beasley v. Brookwood Medical Center,* 712 So.2d 338 (Ala. 1998), grants the Motion to Compel Arbitration. The arbitration agreement in this case is identical to the arbitration agreement contained in the *Beasley* case. The Court notes that the Defendant in the *Beasley* case, Brookwood Medical Center, is now Tenet Healthcare Corporation. The Court in granting the Writ of Mandamus in *Beasley* stated it did so because the employee did not sign the arbitration agreement. In *Beasley,* however, Justice See stated that had the employee signed the employee acknowledgment form it would have created a binding obligation to arbitrate. In the instant case the employee signed the employee acknowledgment form and, therefore, a binding obligation to arbitrate was created.

Ephraim petitions for a writ of mandamus directing the trial court to vacate its order compelling the arbitration of her retaliatory-discharge claim against Tenet.

(continued)

(continued from previous page)

II

"A writ of mandamus is an extraordinary remedy, requiring the showing of: (1) a clear legal right in the petitioner to the order sought; (2) an imperative duty on the respondent to perform, accompanied by a refusal to do so; (3) the lack of another adequate remedy; and (4) the properly invoked jurisdiction of the court." *Ex parte Beasley,* 712 So.2d 338, 339 (Ala. 1998). A petition for the writ of mandamus is the generally accepted method for obtaining review when the trial court grants a motion to compel arbitration. *Ex parte Alexander,* 558 So.2d 364, 365 (Ala. 1990). (*But see* Rule 4(d), Ala. R.App. P., as amended by order dated May 10, 2001. That amendment, to be effective October 1, 2001, makes "[a]n order granting or denying a motion to compel arbitration" reviewable by appeal.)

Ephraim argues that the trial court erred in compelling her to arbitrate arbitration of her retaliatory-discharge claim against Tenet because, she says, Tenet produced no evidence demonstrating that its employment contract with Ephraim substantially affected interstate commerce—without a substantial effect on interstate commerce, she says, the arbitration agreement is not enforceable under the Federal Arbitration Act ("FAA").

The FAA provides:

> A written provision in any maritime transaction or a contract evidencing a transaction involving commerce to settle by arbitration a controversy thereafter arising out of such contract or transaction . . . shall be valid, irrevocable, and enforceable, save upon such grounds as exist at law or in equity for the revocation of any contract.

9 U.S.C. § 2 (emphasis added). "The [FAA] preempts contrary state law (specifically, contrary law based on Ala. Code 1975, § 8-1-41(3) and public policy) and renders enforceable a written predispute arbitration agreement but only if that agreement appears in a contract evidencing a transaction that 'involves' interstate commerce." *Southern United Fire Ins. Co. v. Knight,* 736 So.2d 582, 585-86 (Ala. 1999); *see TefcoFin. Co. v. Green,* [Ms. 1991402, March 16, 2001]———So.2d———(Ala. 2001).

"A 'party seeking to compel arbitration has the burden of proving the existence of a contract calling for arbitration and proving that that contract involves a transaction affecting interstate commerce.' " *Tefco Fin. Co. v. Green,*———So.2d at———(quoting *Ex parte Caver,* 742 So.2d 168, 172 n.4 (Ala. 1999)). " '[T]o prevail on an assertion of arbitrability, the moving party is required to produce some evidence which tends to establish its claim.' " *Jim Burke Auto., Inc. v. Beavers,* 674 So.2d 1260, 1265 (Ala. 1995) (opinion on application for rehearing) (quoting *In re American Freight Sys., Inc.,* 164 B.R. 341, 345 (D.Kan. 1994)).

To meet this burden, a party must show that the effects the contract has on interstate commerce are substantial. *United States v. Lopez,* 514 U.S. 549, 558-59, 115 S.Ct. 1624, 131 L.Ed.2d 626 (1995). In determining whether an economic transaction substantially affects interstate commerce, the Supreme Court considers the aggregate effects of the transaction on interstate commerce. *See United States v. Morrison,* 529 U.S. 598, 628, 120 S.Ct. 1740, 146 L.Ed.2d 658 (2000) (Souter, J., dissenting) (citing *Wickard v. Filburn,* 317 U.S. 111, 124-28, 63 S.Ct. 82, 87 L.Ed. 122 (1942), and *Hodel v. Virginia Surface Mining & Reclamation Ass'n,* 452 U.S. 264, 277, 101 S.Ct. 2352, 69 L.Ed.2d 1 (1981)); *see also Solid Waste Agency of Northern Cook County v. United States Army Corps of Eng'rs,* 531 U.S. 159, 173-74, 121 S.Ct. 675, 683-84, 148 L.Ed.2d 576 (2001) (citing Morrison); *Tefco,*———So.2d at———.

Tenet argues that it has met its burden. In support of its contention that the employment contract between Tenet and Ephraim substantially affected interstate commerce, Tenet has submitted the affidavit of Patsy Adams, the "human resources coordinator" for Brookwood Medical Center. Her affidavit states, in pertinent part:

> 3. Tenet Healthcare Corporation is the parent corporation of Brookwood Medical Center. Tenet Healthcare Corporation is headquartered in Santa Barbara, California and has its principal place of business in California. Tenet owns and operates 120 hospitals in many . . . states including California, Arizona, Arkansas,

South Carolina, Georgia, Tennessee, Florida, Alabama, Mississippi, Louisiana, Missouri, Indiana, and Texas.

4. At all times involved in this case, Brookwood Medical Center and Tenet have been engaged in interstate commerce. Brookwood is located within a few miles of three interstate highways, and routinely treats out-of-state patients, as well as patients from foreign countries. Further, medical costs of many of Brookwood's patients are paid through out-of-state and multi-state insurance carriers and employment plans.

5. Plaintiff, Flora Ephraim, is a resident of the State of Alabama and worked for Brookwood from 1975 to 1999.

6. In March of 1997, Ms. Ephraim alleges that she was injured on-the-job when she attempted to pick up a wet bag of linens.

7. At the time of her alleged injury, Ms. Ephraim worked in the Transportation Department as a transporter.

8. I am personally familiar with Ms. Ephraim's work and activities, which included transporting patients. Ms. Ephraim's work activities facilitated and affected Brookwood's business activities, including its interstate activities and patient care. As a Brookwood employee, Ms. Ephraim was covered by various federal laws and regulations, including Title VII of the 1964 Civil Rights Act, the Americans with Disabilities Act, the Fair Labor Standards Act and other laws which cover employers who are engaged in interstate commerce or an industry affecting interstate commerce.

9. Brookwood Hospital treats and cares for patients from several states throughout the United States and from several foreign countries. Ms. Ephraim was responsible for transporting these patients. Following their treatment at Brookwood, these out-of-state patients travel back to their homes outside of Alabama.

10. Tenet Healthcare paid Ms. Ephraim to transport patients, including patients from states other than Alabama.

11. In addition, Brookwood regularly purchases and receives goods and services from numerous out-of-state vendors and Ms. Ephraim regularly used these goods in her job.

. . .

18. Tenet Healthcare Corporation has distributed this Employee Handbook to its employees throughout the United States.

According to Tenet, then, it is engaged in "commerce" within the meaning of the FAA, based on its treating out-of-state patients, receiving reimbursements from out-of-state or multi-state insurance carriers, and regularly receiving goods and services from out-of-state vendors. (Respondent's Brief at 8.)

The materials before us, however, give no indication that Adams's affidavit was presented to the trial court before it ruled on Tenet's motion to compel arbitration. Adams's affidavit, which is included in the materials Tenet submitted to this Court in response to Ephraim's mandamus petition, was signed and dated January 9, 2001. The trial court had granted Tenet's motion to compel arbitration on September 29, 2000. On October 11, 2000, Ephraim had moved the trial court for a reconsideration, which the trial court granted. On October 27, 2000, the trial court had held a hearing on Tenet's motion to compel arbitration, and had again granted that motion on November 3, 2000. Ephraim's petition for mandamus relief was filed on January 9, 2001—the same day Adams's affidavit was signed and notarized. Therefore, the trial court, when granting Tenet's motion to compel arbitration, could not have considered this affidavit, which was executed over three months later. This Court does not review evidence presented for the first time on appeal. *See Ryan's Family Steak Houses, Inc., v. Regelin,* 735 So.2d 454, 457 n.1 (Ala. 1999) ("[T]he propriety of a ruling on a motion to compel arbitration, like the propriety of a ruling on a summary-judgment motion, must be tested by reviewing the pleadings and the evidence the trial court had before it when it ruled."). Accordingly, it appears from the record that, when it moved to compel arbitration, Tenet did not meet its burden of demonstrating that its employment contract with Ephraim had such an effect on interstate commerce that the FAA mandated arbitration of Ephraim's wrongful-discharge claim. The trial court, therefore, erred in compelling arbitration of Ephraim's claim.

(continued)

(continued from previous page)

Tenet asserts that this Court's decision in *Ex parte Beasley*, 712 So.2d 338 (Ala. 1998), requires the arbitration of Ephraim's claim because Ephraim signed the Employee Acknowledgment Form and that form contained an arbitration provision. In *Beasley*, a case involving the same defendant and identical Employee Handbook provisions, the plaintiff signed an acknowledgment form upon receiving a copy of the revised Employee Handbook; the acknowledgment form did not contain an arbitration clause. 712 So.2d at 341. This Court held that, absent the plaintiff's signature on a document that contains a valid arbitration clause, she could not be held to have agreed to arbitrate her employment-related claims against Brookwood. *Id.* Although Tenet correctly emphasizes that Ephraim signed an acknowledgment form that contained an arbitration provision, its reliance on *Beasley* is nevertheless misplaced, because the interstate-commerce issue was not raised by the parties in *Beasley*. Therefore, this Court's holding in *Beasley* does not speak to a situation in which, as in this case, the party moving to compel arbitration has failed to demonstrate that the contract at issue substantially affected interstate commerce.

Because Tenet did not present the trial court any evidence indicating that its employment contract with Ephraim substantially affected interstate commerce, the court should not have granted its motion to compel arbitration of Ephraim's wrongful-termination claim. Accordingly, we grant Ephraim's petition and issue a writ of mandamus directing the trial court to vacate its order granting Tenet's motion to compel arbitration.

PETITION GRANTED; WRIT ISSUED.

MOORE, C.J., and BROWN, HARWOOD, and STUART, JJ., concur.

In 1947, Congress enacted the Labor-Management Relations Act (LMRA), known as the Taft-Hartley Act, which established the National Labor Relations Board (NLRB) to arbitrate disputes alleging unfair labor practices.

Until the early 1970s, arbitration had its primary use in commercial transactions and labor agreements. The last quarter of the twentieth century witnessed the growth of arbitration well beyond those two areas to almost any area where parties have disputes.

Against the backdrop of the Federal Arbitration Act and the Uniform Arbitration Act, private arbitration operates under rules selected by the parties, or if the parties do not select the rules, the arbitration operates under rules selected by the arbitration service, the arbitrator, or the arbitration panel. For an example of the rules of an arbitration service, see The American Arbitration Association's Rules for Commercial Arbitration in Appendix F.

Problem 13-2

Should all disputes require the detail of the AAA's commercial arbitration rules found in Appendix F?

Problem 13-3

A group of female athletes and their parents have sued a local school board in federal court with violating title IX of the United States Code. The allegation is that girl's sports and boy's sports are treated unequally when it comes to the allocation of resources. Both the school board and the plaintiffs would like to resolve this dispute by private arbitration rather than continue the litigation. They have decided to draft their own rules for the arbitration.

1. Could the AAA commercial arbitration rules be used for this arbitration? Check Appendix F.
2. Which rules would you delete or modify?

The Private Arbitration Process

Figure 13-1 presents an overview of the private arbitration process.

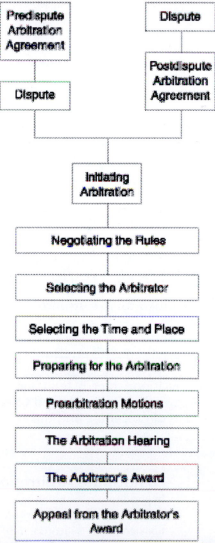

FIGURE 13-1 An Overview of the Private Arbitration Process

The Arbitration Agreement

For disputes to be resolved through private arbitration, the parties to the dispute must consent to the process. The parties may select private arbitration as their dispute resolution process either before or after the dispute arises.

Predispute Arbitration Agreement

A predispute arbitration clause may be agreed upon in a contract or separate arbitration agreement that binds the parties to arbitrate rather than litigate all disputes that arise under the contract. The agreement may specify the arbitrator or arbitration panel, the rules to be followed, and even the parameters of the arbitration award. Some predispute arbitration agreements, however, simply state the arbitration service. The details of the arbitration process are left to that service.

Example 13-1

The following are four examples of predispute arbitration provisions:

1. Any dispute arising out of or relating to this contract shall be settled by private arbitration administered by _____ under its arbitration rules, and any award rendered by the arbitrator or arbitration panel may be entered as a judgment in any court having jurisdiction.

2. Any controversy or claim arising out of or relating to this agreement or the breach of this agreement shall be settled by arbitration in accordance with the rules of the ___[name of the arbitration service]___.

3. Any controversy or claim arising out of or relating to this agreement, the relationship resulting in or from this agreement, or the breach of this agreement shall be settled by binding arbitration in accordance with the rules of ___[name the arbitration service]___. The arbitrator's award shall be final and binding, and judgment may be entered enforcing the award. The parties knowingly and voluntarily waive their right to a trial by judge or jury. In the event a party fails to comply with the arbitrator's award or unsuccessfully challenges the arbitrator's award, the other party is entitled to all costs incurred for having to compel arbitration or defend or enforce the award.

4. In a dispute arising out of or relating to this agreement, the parties will submit the controversy to binding arbitration. The arbitration panel shall be composed of ___[insert specific names or positions of people to comprise the arbitration panel]___, and shall be required to reach a consensus decision which is final and unappealable, except as provided by the Federal Arbitration Act. Each party is allowed to engage in documentary discovery prior to the arbitration. The rules of procedure and the arbitrator's award will conform to the laws of the State of _____.

Postdispute Arbitration Agreement

In postdispute arbitration agreements the parties to the dispute agree after the dispute arises to submit the dispute to private arbitration rather than litigation. The postdispute arbitration agreement is identical to the predispute arbitration agreement in its enforceability and procedures followed. The main difference is that the parties did not agree in advance to arbitrate disputes.

Example 13-2

The following are two examples of postdispute arbitration provisions.

1. We, _____ and _____, agree to submit the following dispute _____ [describe briefly] _____

   _____

   to private arbitration administered by _____ under its arbitration rules. We further agree that

   (1) this dispute shall be submitted to _____ [select one or three] arbitrator(s);
   (2) we will faithfully observe this agreement and the rules;
   (3) we will abide by and perform any award rendered by the arbitrator(s); and
   (4) a judgment of any court having jurisdiction may be entered on the award.

2. We agree to submit for binding arbitration the dispute involving ___[briefly explain the dispute being submitted to arbitration]___ and further agree that the above controversy shall be submitted to one (panel of three) arbitrator(s) selected from the panel of arbitrators provided by the _____ [arbitration service] _____.

   We knowingly and voluntarily waive our right to trial by judge or jury.
   We agree to observe this agreement and to abide by any award rendered by the arbitrator(s).
   Any dispute arising out of or relating to this agreement shall initially be submitted to non-binding arbitration to ___(name arbitration tribunal)___. If the parties do not agree with the arbitration award the parties may resolve this dispute by other means.

Initiating the Arbitration Process

The party filing the claim submits documents to the agreed-upon arbitrator, arbitration panel, or arbitration service stating the dispute to be resolved. By initiating the arbitration, the party filing the claim becomes the claimant. The documents submitted by the claimant set forth the nature of the dispute, the grounds for relief, and the amount of award demanded. The claimant also provides a copy of the arbitration agreement and any other relevant contracts to the dispute. At this time the claimant also pays all filing or adminis-tration fees required by the arbitrator, panel, or arbitration service.

The claimant gives notice to the other party that a claim has been filed by serving the other party with a copy of all documents filed. The party served becomes the respondent. The service of notice must adhere to the rules of the state in which the claim is to be arbitrated.

The respondent may admit or deny the claim, assert affirmative defenses, submit a counterclaim, or add other parties to the dispute. The respondent provides the claimant, any other parties involved in the arbitration process, and the arbitrator, panel, or arbitration ser-vice with all relevant documents and a written response to the claim. If the respondent believes the arbitration agreement is not enforceable, he or she may file a lawsuit seeking to stay the arbitration.

If litigation is pending before the aggrieved party asserts his or her contractual right to arbitrate, the parties can agree to dismiss the litigation or stay the litigation pending the outcome of the arbitration. Once the arbitration has been heard and an award entered, the parties must proceed before the same court to secure a judgment by confirmation of the award. One advantage the parties have by staying the litigation is access to the court. If the arbitration should somehow go awry (i.e., a party delays in selecting the arbitrator or arbitrators), the existing case allows the other party to immediately seek the aid of the court, particularly if the court has entered an agreed order directing the parties to arbitrate in furtherance of their earlier agreement. If no case is pending, the complaining party would need to file a new action to invoke the court's aid in enforcing the arbitration agreement.

The Respondent's Failure to Participate

If the respondent fails to answer the claim or participate in the arbitration hearing, the arbitrator or arbitration panel may enter a default award in the claimant's favor. A default award in arbitration is similar to a default judgment in litigation. A default award, however, is not automatic. The claimant must prove the claim through evidence, witness testimony, and affidavits. If the arbitrator or arbitration panel believes the claimant is entitled to a default award after the claimant's presentation, a binding award is entered. The default award has the same effect as an award issued after a hearing in which the respondent participated. A default award may be vacated if the respondent did not receive proper notice of the arbitration.

The Prehearing Activities

If the respondent does answer the claim, the parties must select the arbitrator or arbitration panel (if not named in the arbitration agreement), exchange information before the hearing, schedule the hearing and its location, and prepare for the hearing itself.

Selecting the Arbitrator or Arbitration Panel

The arbitrator or arbitration panel may be named in the arbitration agreement, may be selected under the rules of the named arbitration service, or by a method agreed upon by the parties in the arbitration agreement. If the arbitrator or arbitrators are selected under the rules of an arbitration service, the service either appoints the arbitrator or arbitrators or provides the parties with a list of prospective arbitrators that contains a biographical sketch of each candidate. The parties agree upon an arbitrator or arbitrators from the list. If a panel of three arbitrators is used, each party may select an arbitrator and these two arbitrators select a third arbitrator.

The number of arbitrators required for an arbitration varies from case to case, but is usually one or three. Regardless of the method used to select the arbitrator or arbitration panel, the goal is to have an arbitrator or panel that is neutral, impartial, unbiased, experienced in dispute resolution, and knowledgeable in the particular field in which the dispute arose.

Exchanging Information before the Hearing

Unlike litigation, where information between the parties is compelled to be disclosed through discovery proceedings, private arbitration does not require full disclosure. The parties may request certain information be disclosed, but normally disclosure cannot be demanded. The exchange of information depends upon the parties' arbitration agreement, the applicable statutes, and the rules of the arbitration service. In some instances, such as cases involving complex issues or if important documents to the dispute are in the exclusive possession of one party, a party may convince the arbitrator or the panel that discovery is necessary to resolve the dispute. The best method for parties to obtain information, however, is to issue subpoenas requiring third parties to bring documents to the arbitration hearing or to testify at the proceeding.

Scheduling the Time and Location for the Hearing

The scheduling of the arbitration hearing is made at a time that is convenient for the parties, their attorneys, the arbitrator or arbitrators, and key witnesses. The hearing is scheduled for a date after each party has had adequate time to prepare. The amount of time scheduled for the hearing depends on the complexity of the issues involved. The hearing may last half a day, one day, or several days. The location of the hearing is typically in or near the city closest to where the respondent works or lives. The hearing itself is typically located in a neutral site such as a hotel conference room or an arbitrator's office.

Problem 13-4

1. Based on the facts in Problem 13-3, when should the arbitration take place?
2. How much discovery is needed before the parties would be ready for the arbitration?
3. How much research is needed before the parties are ready for the arbitration?

Preparing for an Arbitration Hearing

Although an arbitration hearing is similar to litigation in many aspects, the arbitration hearing is much more informal and can proceed at a quicker pace. Preparing for the arbitration depends upon the rules that govern the procedure and presentation of evidence that were selected by the parties.

Preparing for an arbitration hearing requires the claimant's attorney to select the theory of the case, determine the significant issues, research the applicable law, and gather and arrange evidence for presentation.

The theory of the case is a short concise summary of the legal theories and evidence that support the claimant's case. This basically summarizes why the arbitrator or arbitration panel should rule in the party's favor.

One of the primary reasons arbitration is used as a dispute resolution method is because of the quick resolution of the dispute. Therefore, the parties must select only the primary issues in contention in order to take full advantage of the procedure. Minor, insignificant issues will tend to bog the proceedings down and defeat the purpose of a quick resolution.

The party must determine the best way to present the evidence to the arbitrator or arbitration panel. Certain methods of presentation by the parties may prove to be more effective in persuading the arbitrator or the arbitration panel to rule in that party's favor. The methods normally used to present evidence in arbitration include: witness testimony (including expert testimony, lay testimony, and testimony taken prior to the proceedings under oath), exhibits and documents, and stipulations and admissions made by the opposing party.

The best witnesses should be selected for the arbitration. The client may or may not be one of the best witnesses. The attorney should prepare various visual aids such as graphs, enlarged pictures, slides, and videos. This will help the arbitrator or the arbitration panel understand the case.

The respondent's attorney must determine the significant flaws in the claimant's case and gather and arrange its evidence for presentation. The respondent's attorney must also select and prepare any counterclaim that the respondent may want to assert.

The attorneys prepare a complete statement of the case as if it were a trial. Although the evidentiary rules and procedural rules usually will not apply as strictly as if this were a trial, the attorneys prepare their opening statements, their evidence, and their closing arguments. Since the arbitrator or arbitration panel will decide the outcome of the case, the attorneys prepare their closing arguments for the arbitrator or arbitration panel and do *not* prepare their closing arguments as if there were a jury. Passionate pleas such as those normally given to the jury serve little purpose and may even detract from the presentation.

Time may be at a premium in an arbitration hearing. Therefore, when preparing for the arbitration, the attorneys carefully prepare their opening statements, their evidence, and their closing arguments so they effectively use the time that will be allocated.

The attorneys also prepare their clients for the arbitration hearing. The clients must understand that neither they nor their attorneys have a role in the resolution of the dispute. A third party, the arbitrator or arbitration panel (and not a jury), will resolve the dispute and the resolution will be based on the law as it applies to the facts.

The parties must also understand that the claimant has the burden of proof on the claim and the respondent has the burden of proof on any counterclaim. Therefore, the claimant must establish both the facts and the law on the claim. Since the claimant and respondent are the repositories of the facts, it is incumbent upon them to assist their attorneys in the development of the facts.

In an arbitration hearing, as in litigation, the parties may be called to the witness stand and may be asked to testify. If the parties testify, they will be subject to cross-examination. They have no formal role at the arbitration hearing other than to be a witness and to caucus with their attorneys.

The Arbitration Hearing

The arbitration hearing consists of the opening remarks by the arbitrator or arbitration panel, the presentation of the case, and the arbitrator's or panel's award.

The arbitration proceeding begins with the arbitrator or arbitrators explaining to the parties the procedures of the hearing and answering any questions the parties may have. Each party, beginning with the claimant's attorney (unless the claimant is *pro se*) makes an opening statement to the arbitrator or to the panel explaining the client's view of the dispute.

After the opening statements, the claimant's attorney introduces evidence, examines witnesses, and submits documents that support the claim. The respondent's attorney has the opportunity to cross-examine the claimant's witnesses. After the claimant's attorney has presented his or her client's case, the respondent's attorney has the opportunity to introduce evidence, examine witnesses, and submit documents. The claimant's attorney has the opportunity to cross-examine the respondent's witnesses.

After the closing arguments, the arbitrator or arbitration panel advises the parties when a decision will be reached. The award made by the arbitrator or arbitration panel is final and legally enforceable, unless otherwise stipulated by the parties in the arbitration agreement. A simple one-page written description of the award is generally sent to each party and neither the arbitrator nor the panel provides reasons or explanations in support of the award unless the arbitration agreement so requires. The award may require the losing party to pay the costs of the arbitration unless the arbitration agreement provides otherwise.

Appeal of the Award

An arbitration award can seldom be appealed. Judicial review of the arbitration award is generally limited to the following:

The agreement to arbitrate was unenforceable.

The agreement to arbitrate was not followed.

Corruption, fraud, or misconduct was present during the arbitration.

The arbitrator or the arbitration panel exceeded its power.

The agreed-upon procedures were not followed during the arbitration hearing.

The parties were denied a fair and impartial hearing.

The statute of limitations barred the arbitrated claim.

Final Offer, Last Offer, or Baseball Arbitration

Final Offer (Last Offer or Baseball) Arbitration
Final offer arbitration follows the private arbitration process with the exception that in final offer arbitration, the parties agree that the arbitrator must select one of the parties' last offers.

A cost-effective impasse breaker is **final offer** or **last offer arbitration,** also known as **baseball arbitration.** Final offer arbitration occurs when the parties have reached an impasse in their negotiations but need to resolve the dispute and continue their relationship.

In final offer arbitration, the parties have a resolution at the end of the arbitration, the process minimizes the risks for each party, and the parties have some control over what the outcome will be.

In final offer arbitration, negotiations precede the arbitration. During these negotiations each party stakes positions and makes concessions. Each understands the other party's position and concessions. Since the parties have been negotiating, each knows the other's last counteroffer prior to the arbitration.

At the arbitration each party has only one opportunity to submit its last offer to the arbitrator. The arbitrator, after considering the evidence presented at the hearing, selects one of the final offers submitted by the parties. Since the parties have only one final offer, their final offers tend to be closer together because they know that an unreasonable offer will not be selected by the arbitrator. Thus the parties make their concessions in arriving at their final offer, rather than risk the arbitrator selecting the other party's final offer as the arbitrator's award. As the distance between the final offers is reduced, the risk of a significantly adverse decision by the arbitrator is also reduced. If the final offers have come within the settlement range, the arbitrator's choice is of no real consequence to the parties since they will be getting what, in effect, is a negotiated agreement.

Example 13-3

Rachel Normandy plays professional soccer for the San Francisco Gold Diggers. Her contract requires final offer arbitration if an impasse occurs during salary negotiations. Rachel's final offer was $250,000. The Gold Diggers's final offer was $150,000. The arbitrator's award may be either $150,000 or $250,000. The arbitrator may not award more than $250,000, less than $150,000, or something in between.

Problem 13-5

Javier Ortiz, the center fielder for the Washington Capitols, earned $2.5 million during this past baseball season. His contract was up for renegotiation and he was eligible for final offer arbitration. Ortiz had begun his negotiations by asking for $6.5 million. Management began its negotiations at $2.5 million. When the negotiations had reached an impasse, Ortiz was at $4.75 million and management was at $3 million. The parties entered into final offer arbitration.

1. Should Ortiz's final offer be $4.75 million or should he return to his $6.5 million offer?
2. What does Ortiz have to gain if he goes for $4.75 million?
3. What does Ortiz have to lose if he goes for $4.75 million?
4. What should Ortiz use as his arbitration offer? What would you like to know?

High/Low or Bounded Arbitration

High/Low (Bounded) Arbitration
High/low arbitration follows the private arbitration process with the exception that in high/low arbitration, the parties agree on the range of the outcome and the arbitrator's award must be in the range established by the parties.

A variation of final offer arbitration is **high/low** or **bounded arbitration.** At the parties' option, the high and low offers may or may not be disclosed to the arbitrator. By selecting high/low arbitration, the parties limit the boundaries of the arbitrator's award to one party's high and the other party's low. The arbitrator's award must come within these two numbers. By setting the boundaries, the claimant knows at the beginning of the arbitration that the arbitrator's award cannot exceed the high and will not be below the low. If the low is more than zero, the claimant knows that he or she is guaranteed to receive something.

If the arbitrator's award falls within the range, the award stands as issued. If, however, the award is above the high, the award will be rounded down to the high. If the award is less than the low, the award will be rounded up to the low.

Problem 13-6

Rachel Normandy plays professional soccer for the San Francisco Gold Diggers. Her contract requires high/low arbitration if an impasse occurs during salary negotiations. Rachel's final offer was $250,000. The Gold Diggers's final offer was $150,000.

1. If the arbitrator's award is $100,000, will it be adjusted and, if so, to what?
2. If the arbitrator's award is $150,000, will it be adjusted and, if so, to what?
3. If the arbitrator's award is $200,000, will it be adjusted and, if so, to what?
4. If the arbitrator's award is $250,000, will it be adjusted and, if so, to what?
5. If the arbitrator's award is $275,000, will it be adjusted and, if so, to what?

Ethical and Legal Issues

Private arbitration raises a number of ethical and legal issues. Is the issue arbitrable? Is the arbitrator really impartial? Does lack of a jury render private arbitration unconstitutional? Does mandatory arbitration deny a grievant access to a forum to seek redress of the grievance? Does the inability to withdraw from an arbitration that is perceived to be unfair render the process unfair? Does the lack of judicial review result in a flawed system?

Arbitrability
The issue of arbitrability considers whether the dispute is properly the subject of arbitration.

Substantive Arbitrability
Substantive arbitrability inquires whether the parties intended the issue or particular subject matter of the dispute to come within their arbitration agreement.

Arbitrability

The issue of **arbitrability** considers whether the dispute is properly the subject of arbitration. Arbitrability comes in two forms: substantive arbitrability and procedural arbitrability. **Substantive arbitrability** inquires whether the parties intended the issue or particular subject matter of the dispute to come within their arbitration agreement.

Example 13-4

Salsitz and D'Ugo executed letters of understanding whereby each agreed to invest $6,500 in Alternative Utility Services of IL., Inc. (AUS). Kreiss executed the letters of understanding as president of AUS. On the same day, Salsitz and D'Ugo each executed a document entitled "Incentive Stock Option Program." This latter document included a mandatory arbitration provision.

Several months later, Salsitz and D'Ugo requested the return of their investment and reimbursement of certain expenses they had incurred ($29,888). Kreiss returned their investment but did not reimburse them for their expenses.

When Salsitz and D'Ugo reasserted their claim for expenses, Kreiss demanded arbitration. Salsitz and D'Ugo assert their claim was nonarbitrable (substantive arbitrability) because their claim related to their letters of understanding (that did not have an arbitration provision) and not to the Incentive Stock Option Program (that did have an arbitration provision). *See Salsitz v. Kreiss,* 2001 WL 1105814 (Supreme Court of Illinois).

Procedural Arbitrability
Procedural arbitrability inquires whether the procedural requirements for arbitration, such as timeliness and specificity, have been met.

Procedural arbitrability inquires whether the procedural requirements for arbitration, such as timeliness and specificity, have been met.

Example 13-5

Louise Deschamps, the former administrator/office manager for Hermosa Outpatient Surgery Center, Inc., claimed to have been wrongfully terminated by Hermosa. Deschamps and Hermosa agreed to resolve their dispute by private arbitration. The arbitration agreement called for each party to submit confidential offers to the case manager for the arbitrator at least seven days prior to the commencement of the arbitration. After the arbitrator has issued her award, the case manager would give the confidential offers to the arbitrator who would adjust her award to the closer of the two confidential offers.

Deschamps delivered her confidential offer to the case manager four days, rather than seven days, before the arbitration was to commence. The case manager accepted the late delivery, the arbitration hearing was held, and the arbitrator's award was adjusted to Deschamps offer.

Hermosa contends that the arbitrator abused her authority by accepting Deschamps' late offer. This raises a question of procedural arbitrability. See *Deschamps v. Hermosa Outpatient Surgery Center, Inc.,* 2001 WL 1289172 (California Court of Appeals).

Impartiality

As with private mediation, private arbitration adds a "neutral" third party. But is this party always impartial? When a contract includes a predispute mandatory arbitration provision, the drafter of the contract is seeking a substantial advantage over the other contracting party. Such arbitration places an unsuspecting party at a disadvantage if a dispute arises. The party who promoted arbitration selects the arbitration service provider, the location, and the rules that govern the arbitration. The arbitration service provider looks to the party who drafted the predispute arbitration provision to continue to use its services. This creates, at the minimum, the appearance of bias and the potential for a lack of impartiality on the part of the arbitrator.

If private arbitration comes about after a dispute arises and is by consent of the parties (i.e., without a predispute mandatory arbitration provision), the parties jointly select the arbitrator or at least the service that provides the arbitrator or arbitration panel. If one party frequently uses the arbitrator, the members of the panel, or the arbitration service and the other party is either an infrequent user or a onetime user, the potential exists for the arbitrator or the members of the panel to favor the frequent user since being an arbitrator depends on the demand for one's services. Therefore, at least hypothetically, the arbitrator or members of the panel in a private arbitration may be less than totally impartial.

Denial of Trial by Jury

Does the fact that arbitration has no jury mean the process is less fair than litigation where, except in equitable matters, the opportunity for a jury may exist? The jury, while instructed on the law, may in fact deviate from the law when they feel "justice" demands it. The jury, although not instructed to do so, may act as the great leveler in the justice system. With the arbitrator being both the trier of fact and the trier of law, the process lacks the jury's influence on the fairness of the process.

The courts, however, when faced with this issue have not found the lack of a jury to be unconstitutional. In *GTFM, LLC. v. TKN Sales, Inc.,* the issue raised involves the constitutionality of the state statute (Minnesota Sales Representative Act) that mandated arbitration in certain industry disputes.

GTFM, LLC. v. TKN Sales, Inc.
United States Court of Appeals, Second Circuit
257 F.3d 235 (2001)

Before KEARSE, LEVAL, and SOTOMAYOR, Circuit Judges. Judge SOTOMAYOR concurs in a separate opinion.

KEARSE, Circuit Judge:

Defendant TKN Sales, Inc. ("TKN"), appeals from a final judgment of the United States District Court for the Southern District of New York, Barbara S. Jones, *Judge,* (1) declaring that, as applied to plaintiff GTFM, LLC. ("GTFM"), the requirement of the Minnesota Sales Representative Act, Minn. Stat. § 325E.37 (1995), that certain claims for violation of that statute be resolved only through binding arbitration denies GTFM a jury trial, in violation of the Seventh Amendment to the United States Constitution, and (2) permanently enjoining TKN from demanding arbitration of its current dispute with GTFM under the Minnesota statute. The district court ruled principally that TKN's statutory claims against GTFM were analogous to common-law claims for breach of contract and that the statute's requirement that they be submitted to binding arbitration is thus unconstitutional. TKN challenges that conclusion on appeal. For the reasons that follow, we conclude that the Minnesota statute does not violate GTFM's Seventh Amendment rights, and we reverse.

I. BACKGROUND

Although there is an underlying controversy between the parties, the facts material to this appeal are not in dispute. GTFM, a New York limited liability company headquartered in New York, is a manufacturer of apparel. TKN, a Minnesota corporation whose principal place of business is in Missouri, is an apparel distributor. In 1996, GTFM and TKN entered into an oral agreement for TKN to distribute one of GTFM's clothing lines to retailers in various locations, including Minnesota. TKN's compensation was to be in the form of commissions based on the quantity of goods it sold. In mid 1999, disputes arose between TKN and GTFM with respect to the terms and performance of the contract.

The Minnesota Sales Representative Act ("MSRA" or the "Act") applies to sales representative agreements, *i.e.,* agreements by which, *inter alia,* a manufacturer grants a sales representative the right to offer the manufacturer's goods for sale, where there is "a community of interest between the parties in the marketing of the goods at wholesale," Minn. Stat. § 325E.37, subd. 1(e). A sales representative, within the meaning of the Act, is one "who is compensated, in whole or in part, by commission," *id.* subd. 1(d), and who is a Minnesota resident, or whose principal place of business is in Minnesota, or whose geographic sales territory includes all or part of Minnesota, *see id.* subd. 6(a). As set forth in greater detail in Part II.B. below, the Act contains provisions governing, *inter alia,* the termination or renewal of such agreements and the prompt payment of commissions. The Act also provides that "[t]he sole remedy for a manufacturer . . . who alleges a violation of any provision of this section is to submit the matter to arbitration," Minn. Stat. § 325E.37, subd. 5(a), and that a sales representative has the option of either submitting a matter to arbitration or bringing

suit in court, *see id.* The arbitrator is given the power to, *inter alia,* reinstate the agreement, award damages, and grant other relief for frivolous claims or defenses. *See id.* subd. 5(b). The arbitrator's decision, though subject to judicial confirmation, is "final and binding." *Id.* subd. 5(c).

In August 1999, pursuant to MSRA 325E.37, subd. 5, TKN served on GTFM a demand for arbitration ("Arbitration Demand") to be conducted by the American Arbitration Association in Minneapolis, Minnesota, and a complaint ("Arbitration Complaint"). The demand described the nature of the dispute as "[w]rongful termination of independent sales representative agreement in violation of Minn. Stat. § 325E.37, Subdivision 2," and "[f]ailure to pay earned commissions in violation of Minn. Stat. § 325E.37, Subdivision 4 and Minn. Stat. § 181.145." (TKN Arbitration Demand dated August 24, 1999.) The Arbitration Complaint asserted the above claims for statutory violations, plus a common-law claim for breach of contract; it requested, *inter alia,* reinstatement of the sales representative agreement, damages in excess of $50,000 for each of TKN's three claims, and attorneys' fees. GTFM, after unsuccessfully seeking a stay of the proceedings and a transfer of the arbitration from Minneapolis to New York City, commenced the present action in the Southern District of New York.

GTFM's complaint challenged the constitutionality of MSRA on the ground that its provision for arbitration violates GTFM's right to a jury trial under the Seventh Amendment to the Constitution. GTFM premised federal jurisdiction on the existence of a federal question, to wit, MSRA's constitutionality, and on diversity of citizenship. Although GTFM's complaint contained allegations as to the merits of the underlying business dispute, its only requests for relief, other than the usual catchall phrase ("such other and further relief as to the court seems just and proper"), were for (1) a declaratory judgment that the Act as applied would violate its Seventh Amendment right to a jury trial, and (2) a permanent injunction against arbitration. GTFM moved for a preliminary injunction to halt the pending Minnesota arbitration; TKN cross-moved to dismiss GTFM's complaint. The district court, with the consent of the parties, treated GTFM's motion as one for

(continued)

(continued from previous page)
summary judgment, and proceeded directly to the merits of GTFM's attack on the Minnesota statute.

In an Opinion & Order dated April 7, 2000, 2000 WL 364871 ("Opinion"), relying principally on *Chauffeurs, Teamsters & Helpers Local 391 v. Terry*, 494 U.S. 558, 564, 110 S.Ct. 1339, 108 L.Ed.2d 519 (1990), and *Tull v. United States*, 481 U.S. 412, 417, 107 S.Ct. 1831, 95 L.Ed.2d 365 (1987), the district court ruled that GTFM is entitled to a jury trial because most of TKN's claims, including those asserted under MSRA, seek legal, as contrasted with equitable, relief. The court began by noting that

> [t]he Seventh Amendment preserves the right to a jury trial in "[s]uits at common law" in federal court. U.S. Const. amend. VII; *Tull v. United States*, 481 U.S. 412, 417, 107 S.Ct. 1831, 95 L.Ed.2d 365 (1987). The right to a jury trial "is of such importance and occupies so firm a place in our history and jurisprudence that any seeming curtailment of the right to a jury trial should be scrutinized with the utmost care." *Beacon Theatres, Inc. v. Westover*, 359 U.S. 500, 501, 79 S.Ct. 948, 3 L.Ed.2d 988 (1959) (internal quotation and citation omitted).
>
> The Seventh Amendment right to a jury trial attaches to suits in federal court in which legal rights and remedies, as distinguished from equitable rights and remedies, are to be determined. See *Chauffeurs, Teamsters & Helpers Local 391 v. Terry*, 494 U.S. 558, 564, 110 S.Ct. 1339, 108 L.Ed.2d 519 (1990); *Curtis v. Loether*, 415 U.S. 189, 193, 94 S.Ct. 1005, 39 L.Ed.2d 260 (1974); *Daisy Group, Ltd. v. Newport News, Inc.*, 999 F.Supp. 548, 550 (S.D.N.Y.1998). That is, the Seventh Amendment applies not only to common law causes of action that existed in the eighteenth century, "but also to 'actions brought to enforce statutory rights that are analogous to common-law causes of action.' " *Feltner v. Columbia Pictures Television, Inc.*, 523 U.S. 340, 348, 118 S.Ct. 1279, 140 L.Ed.2d 438 (1998) (quoting *Granfinanciera, S.A. v. Nordberg*, 492 U.S. 33, 42, 109 S.Ct. 2782, 106 L.Ed.2d 26 (1989)); *Tull*, 481 U.S. at 417, 107 S.Ct. 1831, 95 L.Ed.2d 365 (1987).

Opinion at 9–10, 2000 WL 364871 (footnote omitted). The court dismissed TKN's argument that the Seventh Amendment has not been incorporated into the Fourteenth Amendment and hence gives GTFM no right to avoid arbitration here, stating that

> [t]his argument—true as far as it goes—misses the mark. But for the MSRA's mandatory and binding arbitration system, TKN would have had to commence its action in either state or federal court, because it is undisputed that there was no agreement among the parties to arbitrate. Had TKN commenced this action in state court, there is no dispute that GTFM would have had the right to remove the matter to federal court under 28 U.S.C. § 1332. Once in federal court, GTFM would have the right to a jury trial.
>
> The fact that the MSRA, a state law, requires arbitration does nothing to change this conclusion. The right to a jury trial in federal court is clearly a question of federal law. *Simler v. Conner*, 372 U.S. 221, 222, 83 S.Ct. 609, 9 L.Ed.2d 691 (1963); *Kampa v. White Consolidated Industries, Inc.*, 115 F.3d 585, 587 (8th Cir. 1997). Federal law controls the issue, even in cases such as this, where the federal court would be enforcing a state-created right and "even when a state statute or state constitution would preclude a jury trial in state court." *Gipson v. KAS Snacktime Co.*, 83 F.3d 225, 230 (8th Cir. 1996) (citing *Byrd v. Blue Ridge Rural Elec. Co-op., Inc.*, 356 U.S. 525, 538–39, 78 S.Ct. 893, 2 L.Ed.2d 953 (1958)).

Opinion at 8 n.6, 2000 WL 364871.

The district court stated that TKN's common-law claim for breach of contract was one as to which GTFM clearly has a right to a jury trial. *See id.* at 11. It ruled that GTFM has the right to a jury trial as well on TKN's claim under 181.145 of the Minnesota statutes for unpaid commissions and lateness penalties because that claim seeks both a traditional legal remedy, as to which a jury trial right attaches, and civil penalties, *i.e.*, " '[r]emedies [that are] intended to punish culpable individuals, as opposed to those intended simply to extract compensation or restore the status quo,' " which traditionally " 'were issued by courts of law, not courts of equity,' " *id.* at 11 (quoting *Tull v. United States*, 481 U.S. at 422, 107 S.Ct. 1831).

As to TKN's claims that GTFM violated other provisions of MSRA, causes of action that did not exist at common law, the court stated, in pertinent part, as follows:

> To determine whether the right to a jury trial attaches to MSRA claims, the Court applies the two-prong *Tull* analysis, mindful that the second inquiry is the more important. *See*

Tull, 481 U.S. at 417–18, 107 S.Ct. 1831. As for the first inquiry—whether the nature of the issues involved [is] analogous to actions at common law—the MSRA provides a specialized remedy for a breach of contract claim involving sales representatives and supplies additional terms to sales representative agreements regarding notice and grounds for termination. An action brought pursuant to the MSRA, therefore, is premised on a breach of contract, including the terms added by the statute. "'The Seventh Amendment question depends on the nature of the *issue* to be tried rather than the character of the overall action.'" *Terry,* 494 U.S. at 569, 110 S.Ct. 1339 (quoting *Ross v. Bernhard,* 396 U.S. 531, 538, 90 S.Ct. 733, 24 L.Ed.2d 729 (1970) [emphasis in *Terry*]). Because TKN's MSRA claim presents the legal issue of breach of contract, the first prong of the *Tull* test would strongly suggest that GTFM is entitled to a jury trial. . . .

The second, and more important, *Tull* inquiry . . . resolves the issue. It requires the Court to examine the remedy sought and determine whether it is legal or equitable. *See Terry,* 494 U.S. at 570, 110 S.Ct. 1339. On its MSRA claim, TKN seeks contract damages, a civil penalty under Minn. Stat. § 181.145 and reinstatement of the contract. *See* Minn. Stat. § 325E.37(5)(b). As discussed above, contract damages and the civil penalty are clearly legal remedies.

Opinion at 12–13. The court noted that although reinstatement of the contract would be equitable relief, the joinder of that claim with legal claims did not eliminate GTFM's right to a jury trial on the legal claims. *See id.* at 13.

The court concluded that "because the MSRA's mandatory and binding arbitration system operates to deny GTFM its right to a jury trial, the MSRA is unconstitutional as applied to these facts." Opinion at 14 (footnote omitted). The court declared the MSRA provision for arbitration unconstitutional and permanently enjoined the Minnesota arbitration proceeding. This appeal followed. For the reasons that follow, we reverse.

II. DISCUSSION

The Seventh Amendment to the United States Constitution provides, in pertinent part, that "[i]n Suits at common law, where the value in controversy shall exceed twenty dollars, the right of trial by jury shall be preserved. . . ." U.S. Const. amend VII. The Federal Rules of Civil Procedure, governing cases in the federal courts, provide that "[t]he right of trial by jury as declared by the Seventh Amendment to the Constitution or as given by a statute of the United States shall be preserved to the parties inviolate." Fed.R.Civ.P. 38(a).

The Seventh Amendment has not, however, been applied to the States through the Fourteenth Amendment and hence does not require that jury trials be held in proceedings in State tribunals. *See, e.g., Gasperini v. Center for Humanities, Inc.,* 518 U.S. 415, 418, 116 S.Ct. 2211, 135 L.Ed.2d 659 (1996) ("Seventh Amendment . . . governs proceedings in federal court, but not in state court"); *Curtis v. Loether,* 415 U.S. 189, 192 n.6, 94 S.Ct. 1005, 39 L.Ed.2d 260 (1974) (Supreme Court "has not held that the right to jury trial in civil cases is an element of due process applicable to state courts through the Fourteenth Amendment"); *Walker v. Sauvinet,* 92 U.S. 90, 92, 23 L.Ed. 678 (1875) ("The States, so far as [the Fourteenth] amendment is concerned, are left to regulate trials in their own courts in their own way. A trial by jury . . . is not, therefore, a privilege or immunity of national citizenship, which the States are forbidden by the Fourteenth Amendment to abridge.").

The district court, as set out in Part I above, viewed the inapplicability of the Seventh Amendment to State proceedings as irrelevant because if TKN had sued GTFM in State court, "GTFM would have had the right to remove the matter to federal court under 28 U.S.C. § 1332," and "[o]nce in federal court, GTFM would have the right to a jury trial," because "[t]he right to a jury trial in federal court is clearly a question of federal law [,] *Simler v. Conner,* 372 U.S. 221, 222, 83 S.Ct. 609, 9 L.Ed.2d 691 (1963) (per curiam)," Opinion at 8 n.6; federal law requires a jury trial when the claims asserted and at least some of the remedies sought are legal rather than equitable, *see id.* at 9–10, 12–14. However, other than *Simler,* most of the cases relied on by the district court for the proposition that federal law is determinative are cases in which the jurisdiction of the district court was premised on the presence of federal questions. *See, e.g., Feltner v. Columbia Pictures Television, Inc.,* 523 U.S. 340, 118 S.Ct. 1279, 140 L.Ed.2d 438 (1998) (copyright infringement, 17 U.S.C. § 504(c)); *Chauffeurs, Teamsters & Helpers Local 391 v. Terry,* 494 U.S. 558, 110 S.Ct. 1339, 108 L.Ed.2d 519 (Labor Management

(continued)

(continued from previous page)

Reporting and Disclosure Act, 29 U.S.C. § 185); *Granfinanciera, S.A. v. Nordberg*, 492 U.S. 33, 109 S.Ct. 2782, 106 L.Ed.2d 26 (1989) (suit by bankruptcy trustee, *see* 11 U.S.C. 548(a)); *Tull v. United States*, 481 U.S. 412, 107 S.Ct. 1831, 95 L.Ed.2d 365 (1987) (Clean Water Act, 33 U.S.C. § 1319); *Curtis v. Loether*, 415 U.S. 189, 94 S.Ct. 1005, 39 L.Ed.2d 260 (1974) (Fair Housing Act, 42 U.S.C. § 3612); *Beacon Theatres, Inc. v. Westover*, 359 U.S. 500, 79 S.Ct. 948, 3 L.Ed.2d 988 (1959) (Sherman and Clayton Antitrust Laws, 15 U.S.C. §§ 1, 2, 15).

To be sure, *Simler v. Conner*, cited by the district court, was a diversity case; but the focus of that case was simply whether a lawyer's suit to recover fees from his client should be characterized as legal or equitable, and the precise question was whether the proper characterization was a matter of federal law or state law. With that focus in mind, the *Simler* Court stated that "the characterization of that state-created claim as legal or equitable for purposes of whether a right to jury trial is indicated must be made by recourse to federal law," 372 U.S. at 222, 83 S.Ct. 609; but *Simler* prefaced that statement with the observation that "[i]n diversity cases, of course, the substantive dimension of the claim asserted finds its source in state law," *id.*

A. Substantive State Limitations in Diversity Cases

When a federal court's jurisdiction is based on diversity of citizenship, "[w]e put to one side the considerations relevant in disposing of questions that arise when a federal court is adjudicating a claim based on a federal law," *Guaranty Trust Co. v. York*, 326 U.S. 99, 101, 65 S.Ct. 1464, 89 L.Ed. 2079 (1945), and we act as "only another court of the State," *id.* at 108, 65 S.Ct. 1464. In *Guaranty Trust*, the Court considered whether a federal court whose jurisdiction over a suit for breach of trust was based solely on diversity was required to honor a state statute of limitations. The Court stated that the answer depended on whether the state's statute governed merely the manner and means by which a plaintiff could recover or whether it was instead "a matter of substance" in the sense that the

federal court's disregard of the statute would "significantly affect the result of [the] litigation," causing that result to differ from the outcome that would be reached in state court. *Id.* at 109, 65 S.Ct. 1464. The Court stated that the intent of the decision in *Erie R. Co. v. Tompkins*, 304 U.S. 64, 58 S.Ct. 817, 82 L.Ed. 1188 (1938),

> was to insure that, in all cases where a federal court is exercising jurisdiction solely because of the diversity of citizenship of the parties, *the outcome of the litigation in the federal court should be substantially the same, so far as legal rules determine the outcome of a litigation, as it would be if tried in a State court.* . . .
>
> Plainly enough, a statute that would completely bar recovery in a suit if brought in a State court bears on a State-created right vitally and not merely formally or negligibly. As to consequences that so intimately affect recovery or non-recovery a federal court in a diversity case should follow State law.

Guaranty Trust, 326 U.S. at 109–10, 65 S.Ct. 1464 (emphasis added). The Court added that

> The operation of a double system of conflicting laws in the same State is plainly hostile to the reign of law. *Certainly, the fortuitous circumstance of residence out of a State of one of the parties to a litigation ought not to give rise to a discrimination against others equally concerned but locally resident.* The source of substantive rights enforced by a federal court under diversity jurisdiction, it cannot be said too often, is the law of the States. Whenever that law is authoritatively declared by a State, whether its voice be the legislature or its highest court, such law ought to govern in litigation founded on that law, whether the forum of application is a State or a federal court and whether the remedies be sought at law or may be had in equity.

Id. at 112, 65 S.Ct. 1464 (emphasis added).

These principles were applied to an arbitration question in *Bernhardt v. Polygraphic Co. of America*, 350 U.S. 198, 203, 76 S.Ct. 273, 100 L.Ed. 199 (1956), a contract action that raised the question of whether the federal court sitting in diversity was required to apply a Vermont statute that made an agreement to arbitrate revocable at any time before an arbitration award was actually made:

> We deal here with a right to recover that owes its existence to one of the States, not to the United States. The federal court enforces the state-created right by rules of procedure which it has acquired from the Federal Government and which therefore are not identical with those of the state courts. Yet, in spite of that difference in procedure, the federal court enforcing a state-created right in a diversity case is, as we said in *Guaranty Trust Co. v. York,* 326 U.S. 99, 108, 65 S.Ct. 1464, 89 L.Ed. 2079, in substance "only another court of the State."

Bernhardt, 350 U.S. at 202–03, 76 S.Ct. 273. The *Bernhardt* Court held that the State's requirements with respect to arbitration must be honored by the federal court because significant differences between arbitration and court adjudication create a very substantial potential for differences in outcome:

> If the federal court allows arbitration where the state court would disallow it, the outcome of litigation might depend on the courthouse where suit is brought. For *the remedy by arbitration, whatever its merits or shortcomings, substantially affects the cause of action created by the State.* The nature of the tribunal where suits are tried is an important part of the parcel of rights behind a cause of action. *The change from a court of law to an arbitration panel may make a radical difference in ultimate result.* Arbitration carries no right to trial by jury. . . . Arbitrators do not have the benefit of judicial instruction on the law; they need not give their reasons for their results; the record of their proceedings is not as complete as it is in a court trial; and judicial review of an award is more limited than judicial review of a trial. . . .

Bernhardt, 350 U.S. at 203, 76 S.Ct. 273 (emphases added). In addition,

> [w]hether the arbitrators misconstrued a contract is not open to judicial review. . . . Questions of fault or neglect are solely for the arbitrators' consideration. . . . Arbitrators are not bound by the rules of evidence. . . . They may draw on their personal knowledge in making an

award. . . . Absent agreement of the parties, a written transcript of the proceedings is unnecessary. . . . Swearing of witnesses may not be required. . . . And the arbitrators need not disclose the facts or reasons behind their award.

Id. at 203 n.4, 76 S.Ct. 273. The Court concluded that "[t]here would in our judgment be a resultant discrimination if the parties suing on a Vermont cause of action in the federal court were remitted to arbitration, while those suing in the Vermont court could not be." *Id.* at 204, 76 S.Ct. 273.

B. MSRA

Section 325E.37 of the Minnesota Sales Representative Act governs, *inter alia,* the termination or nonrenewal of sales representative agreements, "express or implied, whether oral or written," Minn. Stat. § 325E.37 subd. 1(e), between a manufacturer and a sales representative, *i.e.,* "a person who contracts with a principal to solicit wholesale orders and who is compensated, in whole or in part, by commission," *id.* subd. 1(d), if that person is a resident of or maintains his principal place of business in Minnesota, or his geographical sales territory includes all or part of Minnesota, *see id.* subd. 6(a). As a substantive matter, that section provides, *inter alia,* that

> (a) A manufacturer . . . may not terminate a sales representative agreement unless the person has good cause and:
> (1) that person has given written notice setting forth the reason(s) for the termination at least 90 days in advance of termination; and
> (2) the recipient of the notice fails to correct the reasons stated for termination in the notice within 60 days of receipt of the notice.
> (b) A notice of termination is effective immediately upon receipt where the alleged grounds for termination are the reasons set forth in subdivision 1, paragraph (b), clauses (1) to (6), hereof.

Id. subd. 2. The six clauses referred to provide that good cause includes, but is not limited to, the sales representative's

(continued)

(continued from previous page)

bankruptcy or insolvency; assignment of his assets for the benefit of creditors; voluntary abandonment of the business; conviction of, or a plea of guilty or no-contest to, a charge of violating any law relating to his business; failure to forward customer payments to the manufacturer; and any act that materially impairs the manufacturer's good will. *See id.* subd. 1(b). The Act similarly prohibits the manufacturer from failing to renew a sales representative agreement on less than 90 days' notice, unless there is good cause for nonrenewal. *See id.* subd. 3.

The Act also provides that if a sales representative agreement is terminated, "[p]ayment of commissions due the sales representative shall be paid in accordance with the terms of the sales representative agreement or, if not specified in the agreement, payments of commissions due the sales representative shall be paid in accordance with section 181.145." *Id.* subd. 4. Section 181.145 of the Minnesota statutes, which deals generally with the employment of persons "paid on the basis of commissions for sales," Minn. Stat. § 181.145 subd. 1, requires that a commission salesperson who is terminated be paid his earned commissions promptly, generally within three to ten working days, *see id.* subds. 2(b), (c), (d). Section 181.145 provides that if the manufacturer fails to make payment as promptly as subdivision 2 requires, a monetary penalty will be assessed, *see id.* subd. 3, and attorneys' fees are to be awarded to the sales representative, *see id.* subd. 4.

MSRA provides that a manufacturer claiming violation of any provision of 325E.37 must do so through arbitration, and that a sales representative seeking resolution of such a dispute has the option of proceeding through either arbitration or court action:

> The sole remedy for a manufacturer, wholesaler, assembler, or importer *who alleges a violation of any provision of this section is to submit the matter to arbitration.* A sales representative may also submit a matter to arbitration, or in the alternative, at the sales representative's option prior to the arbitration hearing, the sales representative may bring the sales representative's claims in a court of law, and in that event the claims of all parties must be resolved in that forum. . . . Each party to a sales representative agreement shall be bound by the arbitration.

Minn. Stat. § 325E.37 subd. 5(a) (emphasis added). The arbitrator has the power to grant a variety of monetary and equitable relief, *see id.* subd. 5(b); and subject to a court order of confirmation on motion of any party, "[t]he decision of any arbitration hearing under this subdivision is final and binding on the sales representative and the manufacturer," *id.* subd. 5(c). Thus, MSRA's provisions make it plain that a manufacturer has no right to pursue MSRA claims in court unless the sales representative has chosen the court as a forum, and that the sales representative has the option of insisting on arbitration.

We note that this adjudication scheme is consistent with Minnesota's general policy of favoring arbitration of commercial contracts. *Eden Land Corp. v. Minn-Kota Excavating, Inc.,* 302 Minn. 529, 530, 223 N.W.2d 658, 659 (1974) (per curiam) (Minnesota law "has consistently looked on arbitration as a proceeding favored in the law" (internal quotation marks omitted)); *Grover-Dimond Associates v. American Arbitration Association,* 297 Minn. 324, 327, 211 N.W.2d 787, 788 (1973) ("Clearly, it is the policy of this state . . . to encourage arbitration as a speedy, informal, and relatively inexpensive procedure for resolving controversies arising out of commercial transactions." (internal quotation marks omitted)). With respect to similar Minnesota statutes, the state's courts have noted that "[e]ven though resort to courts is authorized, the basic intent of [such] act[s] is to discourage litigation and to foster voluntary resolution of disputes." *Har-Mar Inc. v. Thorsen & Thorshov, Inc.,* 300 Minn. 149, 154, 218 N.W.2d 751, 754–55 (1974) (internal quotation marks omitted).

"A State may, of course, distribute the functions of its judicial machinery as it sees fit," *Byrd v. Blue Ridge Rural Elect. Cooperative, Inc.,* 356 U.S. 525, 536, 78 S.Ct. 893, 2 L.Ed.2d 953 (1958). With respect to sales representative agreements, MSRA explicitly gives the sales representative the right to choose arbitration and provides that arbitration is the manufacturer's "sole" remedy, unless the sales representative chooses to proceed in court. The district court in the present case stated that "*[h]ad TKN commenced this action in state court,* . . . GTFM would have had the right to remove the matter to federal court," and that "[o]nce in federal court, GTFM would have the right to a jury trial." Opinion at 8 n.6 (emphasis added). Given that MSRA does not purport to prohibit jury trial in a civil action in either federal or state court when the sales representative has elected to bring his claims in court, we agree with that observation. But the district court's factual premise is purely hypothetical; and, given the potentially outcome-affecting differences between arbitration and court adjudication discussed in *Bernhardt*, the mere fact that the parties are of diverse citizenship does not give the federal court the power to force TKN to proceed in court on a State-created cause of action as to which the State has given TKN the right to insist on arbitration.

We note also that GTFM concedes that "if both GTFM and TKN were citizens of Minnesota, or if the amount in controversy were less than $75,000, there would be no basis upon which the present action [*sic*— TKN's claims] could be heard by a federal court[, and that i]n such a case," GTFM would have no right to a jury trial, for "the Seventh Amendment would not apply." (GTFM brief on appeal at 9 n.8.) Thus, for the federal court to compel TKN to pursue its claims against GTFM in court rather than through arbitration would confer on GTFM, by reason of its foreign citizenship, a potentially outcome-affecting right that Minnesota citizens do not have. The Supreme Court has expressly stated that such a "discrimination" is a reason for the federal court, in diversity, to honor, not dishonor, a State's law. *Bernhardt*, 350 U.S. at 204, 76 S.Ct. 273; *Guaranty Trust*, 326 U.S. at 112, 65 S.Ct. 1464.

Finally, we note that the fact that TKN has included a common-law breach of contract claim in its Arbitration Complaint provides no basis for either revoking its statutory right to compel arbitration of its MSRA claims or finding a Seventh Amendment violation. The MSRA claims plainly are subject to arbitration. Moreover, it is hardly clear that MSRA does not envision the arbitration of related common-law claims as well. *See* Minn. Stat. § 325E.37 subd. 5(a) ("sales representative may also submit *a matter* to arbitration" (emphasis added).) The question of whether MSRA gives the arbitrator jurisdiction over TKN's common-law contract claim is a matter of state law. If the arbitrator has no jurisdiction over such claims,

and if they are pursued in court, GTFM will enjoy whatever right of jury trial the forum provides.

In sum, the Seventh Amendment, though guaranteeing the right to a jury trial for legal issues in cases tried in federal courts, does not apply to the States. The Minnesota Act gives a sales representative the right to pursue State-created claims against the manufacturer through arbitration. GTFM has no right under the Seventh Amendment to force a sales representative to pursue such claims in court rather than in arbitration.

CONCLUSION

We have considered all of GTFM's arguments in support of its Seventh Amendment claim and have found them to be without merit. The judgment of the district court is reversed, and the matter is remanded for entry of judgment dismissing the complaint.

SOTOMAYOR, Circuit Judge, concurring:
The district court held that GTFM is entitled to a jury because, in federal court, the right to a jury attaches in suits involving legal rights and remedies. The majority disagrees, reasoning, *inter alia*, that when a federal court sits in diversity, it applies state substantive law and that, under *Erie* and its progeny, arbitration is substantive rather than procedural. My problem with the reasoning of both the district court and the majority is that this action was not brought in federal court. Even more importantly, this action was not brought in *any* court.

The majority seems to accept the mistaken premise which led the district court into a discussion of what might happen in federal court, that, "[h]ad TKN commenced this action in state court, . . . GTFM would have had the right to remove the matter to federal court." District court opinion at 8 n.6. TKN, in fact, commenced this action in arbitration, *not* in court. TKN's decision to arbitrate its MSRA claims eliminated GTFM's right to defend itself in any court, to say nothing of an Article III court that is the gateway to the Seventh Amendment. Because the Minnesota legislature has placed an impenetrable barrier between the arbitration GTFM finds itself in and the court proceedings it wishes

(continued)

(continued from previous page)

that TKN had instead brought, this Seventh Amendment challenge easily fails.

At most, GTFM attempts to repackage under a Seventh Amendment label a more general assault on the authority of a state legislature to assign TKN's claims to a non-judicial forum for resolution by mandatory, binding arbitration. *See* Complaint § 1 ("This action involves the constitutionality of a Minnesota statute which requires a foreign corporation . . . to submit to binding arbitration, even though the foreign corporation never agreed to arbitrate."). Challenges of this sort have previously failed under other constitutional theories, and invoking the Seventh Amendment does not change matters. In disposing of one such challenge, the Supreme Court explained:

> The present statute substitutes a determination by arbitration for trial in court. . . . As appellant's objection to it is directed specifically to the power of the state to substitute the one remedy for the other, rather than to the constitutionality of the particular procedure prescribed or followed before the arbitrators, it suffices to say that the procedure by which rights may be enforced and wrongs remedied is peculiarly a subject of state regulation and control. The Fourteenth Amendment neither implies that all trials must be by jury, nor guarantees any particular form or method of state procedure. In the exercise of that power and to satisfy a public need, a state may choose the remedy best adapted, in the legislative judgment, to protect the interests concerned, provided its choice is not unreasonable or arbitrary, and the procedure it adopts satisfies the constitutional requirements of reasonable notice and opportunity to be heard.

Hardware Dealers' Mut. Fire Ins. Co. of Wis. v. Glidden Co., 284 U.S. 151, 158, 52 S.Ct. 69, 76 L.Ed. 214 (1931) (citation omitted) (rejecting due process and equal protection challenges to a Minnesota statute).

Instead of deciding this appeal solely along these lines, the majority addresses a situation, different from ours, in which GTFM would find itself in federal court based on diversity of citizenship defending an MSRA action commenced in arbitration. The majority concludes that because *Bernhardt v. Polygraphic Co. of Am.,* 350 U.S. 198, 76 S.Ct. 273, 100 L.Ed. 199 (1958), held that arbitration is substantive rather than procedural, a federal court does not have the "power to force TKN to proceed in court on a State-created cause of action as to which the State has given TKN the right to insist on arbitration." *Ante* at 244.

But GTFM has never sought to remove this action from arbitration to federal court, perhaps expecting that such an attempt would fail. *See* 28 U.S.C. § 1441(a) (permitting removal to federal district court from "any civil action brought in a State court"). Even if GTFM had requested removal and had succeeded, the federal courts would more likely find that they have no jurisdiction to hear the claim, rather than broaching the *Erie* question. *See, e.g., Beach v. Owens-Corning Fiberglas Corp.,* 728 F.2d 407, 409 (7th Cir. 1984) ("The Indiana law vesting exclusive jurisdiction over disputes between employees and their employers in the disputes board operates to close state court doors to the plaintiffs. The state's denial of a judicial remedy in this case is a denial of the substantive right asserted by the plaintiffs. . . . Accordingly, the state courts have no jurisdiction over the plaintiffs' claims, and the plaintiffs therefore have no claim to press in this federal action, which depends entirely upon state law.").

In denying GTFM's Seventh Amendment challenge to the MSRA, I would simply reaffirm that the Minnesota legislature was free to forgo a judicial forum in permitting resolution of TKN's claims through mandatory, binding arbitration. Once in arbitration, GTFM had no constitutional right to a jury.

Denial of Access to a Forum to Seek Redress of a Grievance

The following case of *Camacho v. Holiday Homes, Inc.* raises the issue whether an arbitration provision is unenforceable if the cost associated with the arbitration proceeding prohibits one of the parties from seeking redress of his or her grievance.

Camacho v. Holiday Homes, Inc.
United States District Court, W.D. Virginia
167 F.Supp.2d 892 (2001)

Memorandum Opinion

WILSON, Chief J.

Plaintiff Heidi R. Camacho ("Camacho"), proceeding *in forma pauperis*, brings this action against Defendant Holiday Homes, Inc. ("Holiday") for damages arising out of Camacho's purchase of a manufactured home under a retail installment contract. Camacho alleges violations of the Truth in Lending Act ("TILA"), 15 U.S.C. § 1640, Virginia's Uniform Commercial Code, and common law trespass. The court has jurisdiction pursuant to 15 U.S.C. § 1640 and 28 U.S.C §§ 1331, 1337. The court may exercise supplemental jurisdiction over the state law claims under 28 U.S.C. § 1367. This case is before the court on Holiday's motion to dismiss for lack of subject matter jurisdiction,[1] or, alternatively, to compel arbitration. Finding that jurisdiction over these claims is proper, and that Camacho has demonstrated that the contract's arbitration clause precludes Camacho from vindicating her statutory rights under the TILA because the arbitral forum is financially inaccessible to her, the court denies Holiday's motion.

[1]In support of its motion to dismiss, Holiday argues that this court lacks subject-matter jurisdiction because the arbitration clause contained in the contract Camacho signed encompasses all her claims and binds her to resolve them in an arbitral forum. The court disagrees. The threshold issue in this case is whether the arbitration clause is enforceable. That question is for the court. *Dean Witter Reynolds, Inc. v. Byrd,* 470 U.S. 213, 218 (1985). Accordingly, this court properly exercises subject-matter jurisdiction under 28 U.S.C § 1331 and 15 U.S.C. § 1640, and will deny Holiday's motion to dismiss.

I

Camacho executed a retail installment contract, effective March 31, 2000, with Holiday for the installment purchase of a new manufactured home for herself and her three young children. The contract was a pre-printed form provided by Holiday and contained an arbitration clause that provides, in pertinent part, as follows:

ARBITRATION OF DISPUTES AND WAIVER OF JURY TRIAL: a. Dispute Resolution. Any controversy or claim between or among you and me or our assignees arising out of or relating to the Contract or any agreements or instruments relating to or delivered in connection with this Contract, including any claim based on or arising from an alleged tort, shall, if requested by either you or me, be determined by arbitration, reference, or trial by judge as provided below. A controversy involving only a single claimant, or claimants who are related or asserting claims arising from a single transaction, shall be determined by arbitration as described below. Any other controversy shall be determined by judicial reference of the controversy to a referee appointed by the court or, if the court where the controversy is venued lacks the power to appoint a referee, by trial by a judge without a jury, as described below. **YOU AND I AGREE AND UNDERSTAND THAT WE ARE GIVING UP THE RIGHT TO TRIAL BY JURY, AND THERE SHALL BE NO JURY WHETHER THE CONTROVERSY OR CLAIM IS DECIDED BY ARBITRATION, BY JUDICIAL REFERENCE, OR BY TRIAL BY A JUDGE.**

(continued)

(continued from previous page)

The arbitration clause does not mention the costs of arbitration or which party is responsible for paying them. However, the contract provides that "[t]he Commercial Rules of the American Arbitration Association . . . apply" to any arbitration arising from the contract.

Camacho brought this suit on March 28, 2001, claiming that Holiday violated the TILA, the Virginia Uniform Commercial Code, and committed common law trespass. On the same day, the court granted Camacho's application to proceed *in forma pauperis,* thereby exempting her from the court's $150 filing fee. Camacho is the only claimant in this action. On May 25, 2001, Holiday moved to dismiss for lack of subject matter jurisdiction, or, alternatively, to compel arbitration. On August 1, 2001, Camacho filed a brief in opposition to Holiday's motions arguing, in part, that the arbitration provision is unconscionable because the excessive fees associated with the arbitration of her claims prohibit her from accessing the arbitral forum.

The parties stipulate to the following facts regarding the potential arbitration of their dispute. According to the Commercial Arbitration Rules of the American Arbitration Association ("AAA"), a party initiating a claim the size of Camacho's (between $75,000 and $150,000) must pay an initial filing fee of $1250, and, after a scheduling conference, a case fee of $750 before the case can proceed to an evidentiary hearing. If the initiating party ultimately prevails, it may be awarded those fees by the arbitrator in the final disposition of the case. The rules permit the initiating party to apply for a waiver, reduction, or deferral (complete or partial) of these administrative fees due to "extreme hardship." The AAA's accounting department determines which claimant should be afforded "extreme hardship" status. There are no formal standards that govern the accounting department's determination. In practice, the complete waiver of a fee is extremely rare; partial deferral is the usual response when hardship is established. The arbitrator may assess the losing party any deferred fee as part of the arbitrator's final award.

After a party initiates a claim with the AAA, the Commercial Arbitration Rules provide that the parties may not proceed until they pay the arbitrator's fee and expenses. Each party is responsible for half those costs. The arbitrator selected by the parties sets the arbitration fee, which typically ranges between $100 and $300 per hour, for a minimum of one full day for hearings, plus the arbitrator's additional preparation and research time before and after the hearing. There is only one qualified arbitrator in the Roanoke area. It is possible, therefore, that the arbitrator chosen by the parties would have to travel to hear their dispute. Arbitrators customarily charge their hourly rate for travel time. Thus, regardless of who pays the initial administrative fees, the arbitration will not proceed until both parties pay their half of the arbitrator's fees. Camacho suggests that the total amount of an arbitrator's fees will likely range between $1200 (assuming $100 hourly fees for one hearing plus time for preparation and resolution without travel or other expenses) and $8000 (assuming $300 hourly fees for 24 hours of hearings, preparation, resolution, and travel, plus accommodation expenses). Holiday does not dispute these figures.

On July 26, 2001, Camacho filed a declaration of her financial condition. Camacho indicates that she provides sole support for herself and her three children, ages 18, 13, and 10. Though she is entitled to child support amounting to $600 per year, she rarely, if ever, is able to collect those payments. She received no child support from February 2001 through at least July 2001. Camacho works as a waitress at a local restaurant where she earns an average weekly income, including tips, of $300. Camacho attends Virginia Western Community College part-time, taking two classes per semester towards an associates degree in sociology. These classes typically require 12 to 18 hours per week for preparation and attendance. Because of her financial hardship, Camacho receives a $1200 Pell grant or similar award per semester, which is insufficient to cover her tuition, books, travel and living expenses related to her education. She owes $14,125 in old student loans which have been deferred until she finishes school.

Camacho declares that due to her limited income, her family currently shares a house with another family. Camacho is not responsible for rent but pays for one half of the other household expenses. Her share of those expenses consist of the following monthly amounts: electricity, including heat and well pump, $60–75; telephone, $20; food, $430. Camacho claims that she is solely responsible for the following monthly expenses: daughter's drug prescriptions, $40; car payments, $260; car insurance for herself and her daughter, $128; gasoline, $100; and occasional expenses for clothes and other needs. Camacho also claims that she is paying her daughter's car payment, $140 per month, until her daughter gets a job. At the time of filing her declaration, she expected to spend about $300 for back-to-school clothes and supplies for her two youngest children, for whom she shops at thrift stores.

Camacho claims that she cannot afford health insurance, and that she currently owes Community Hospital $445. She owns nothing that would provide collateral for a loan. Her car is a 1997 Ford Taurus valued at $6000, on which she still owes about $5000. Camacho declares that she cannot afford to pay any significant costs associated with the adjudication of her dispute.

II

Typically, in determining whether federal statutory claims must be arbitrated, a court must resolve two issues. First, the court must determine whether the parties agreed to submit their present claims to arbitration. *Green Tree Financial Corp.-Alabama v. Randolph*, 531 U.S. 79, 90 (2000) (citing *Gilmer v. Interstate/Johnson Lane Corp.*, 500 U.S. 20, 31 (1991); *Mitsubishi Motors Corp. v. Soler Chrysler Plymouth, Inc.*, 473 U.S. 614, 626 (1985)). Second, the court must ask whether Congress intended to preclude a waiver of judicial remedies for the statutory rights at issue. *Id.* However, recent Supreme Court precedent requires that this court consider a third issue. In *Randolph*, the Court indicated that "the existence of large arbitration costs could preclude a litigant . . . from effectively vindicating her federal statutory rights in the arbitral forum." *Id.* Thus, a party seeking to avoid arbitration may "invalidate an arbitration agreement" by "showing the likelihood of incurring such [prohibitive] costs." *Id.* Once the likelihood of prohibitive costs are established, the onus is on the party seeking arbitration to provide contrary evidence. *Id.* at 92. Therefore, the court must determine whether Camacho has demonstrated that the arbitration clause at issue prevents her from effectively vindicating her rights under the TILA because the costs of

arbitration render that forum inaccessible to her. The court will consider Camacho's motion to compel arbitration by addressing these three issues, in turn.

First, the court finds that the parties agreed to arbitrate the claims currently before the court. Camacho asserts that the arbitration clause provides for elective rather than mandatory arbitration. She rests this argument entirely on the first sentence of the arbitration clause which provides that arbitration of any claim shall be determined by arbitration "if requested by you or me." In so doing, Camacho fails even to acknowledge the plain language of the very next sentence mandating that "[a] controversy involving only a single claimant . . . shall be determined by arbitration as described below." Camacho does not dispute that she voluntarily signed the contract containing the arbitration clause or that she is the only claimant in this action. However, she alleges in her complaint, though not in her brief opposing this motion, that Holiday did not provide her with an opportunity to read the contract before signing it. The failure to provide such an opportunity is of no consequence. It is well settled that a party to a written contract is responsible for "inform[ing][her]self of its contents before executing it, . . . and in the absence of fraud or overreaching [she] will not be allowed to impeach the effect of the instrument by showing that [she] was ignorant of its contents or failed to read it." *Corbett v. Bonney*, 121 S.E.2d 476, 480, 202 Va. 933, 938 (1961). Accordingly, the court finds that because Camacho is the only claimant in this action, the parties agreed that her claim would be resolved through arbitration.

Second, Camacho "bears the burden of establishing that Congress intended to preclude arbitration" of her TILA claims. *Randolph*, 531 U.S. 91–92 (citing *Gilmer*, 500 U.S. at 26; *Shearson/American Express Inc. v. McMahon*, 482 U.S. 220, 227 (1987)). Because Camacho does not raise the issue, the court assumes, without deciding, that Congress did not intend to preclude the arbitration of her claims under the TILA.

Third, the court finds that Camacho has adequately demonstrated that the arbitral forum provided for in the contract is financially inaccessible to her, and, therefore fails to ensure that she can vindicate her statutory rights

(continued)

(continued from previous page)

under the TILA.[2] At the outset, the court notes that in *Randolph,* the record did not contain any useful evidence regarding the cost of arbitration, and that the Court, therefore, refused to invalidate the arbitration agreement based on the mere "risk" that the plaintiff would "be required to bear prohibitive arbitration costs." *Randolph,* 531 U.S. at 90. Here, however, in contrast to the plaintiff in *Randolph,* Camacho has presented substantial evidence that the costs of arbitrating her claims would preclude her from vindicating her federal statutory rights.

The arbitration clause does not indicate directly which party will be responsible for the costs of initiating arbitration. Instead, it provides that "[t]he Commercial Rules of the American Arbitration Association ("AAA") . . . shall apply" to the arbitration of any claim. The parties stipulate that, under those rules, Camacho must pay an initial filing fee of $1250 to initiate her claim and a $750 case fee shortly thereafter.[3] Camacho could not recover those fees, unless she ultimately prevailed on her claim. Even if she prevailed, however, Camacho does not have $2000 to pay the fees in the first place, and she has no collateral with which she could obtain a sufficient loan. Though Camacho may apply for

fee deferral or reduction due to "extreme hardship," the parties stipulate that waiver of fees is extremely rare in practice. The AAA does not provide formal standards for granting hardship, and its accounting department actually determines who is afforded "extreme hardship" status.

However, even if the initial $2000 in administrative fees were waived or deferred, Mrs. Camacho has demonstrated that the additional costs of the arbitration process itself amount to an insurmountable financial barrier to her. To proceed in arbitration, Camacho would be responsible for paying one-half of the anticipated fee and expenses of the arbitrator. Since there is only one qualified arbitrator in the Roanoke area, it is possible that another arbitrator would have to travel to the Roanoke area to hear the parties' dispute. Camacho has shown that an arbitrator would require payment ranging from $600 (one-half the cost of the cheapest arbitrator for 12 hours and no expenses) to $4100 (one-half the cost of the most expensive arbitrator for 24 hours and $1000 travel and accommodation expenses).[4] The parties stipulate that these fees are not subject to waiver or deferral for "extreme hardship." In acknowledgment of Camacho's strained financial condition, this court found her unable to pay the $150 filing fee normally required to initiate the claim it now considers. In view of these facts, the court finds that Camacho's limited income affords no margin for expenses of the magnitude required to pay an arbitrator to consider her claim.

Accordingly, the court concludes that Camacho has successfully demonstrated that the arbitration clause precludes her from effectively vindicating the rights afforded her by the TILA because the arbitral forum is financially inaccessible to her. Holiday does not contend that the arbitral forum is not prohibitively expensive. Therefore, the court finds that the arbitration clause is unenforceable. In the event, however, that Holiday agreed to bear the costs associated with the arbitration, the court would entertain a motion to reconsider its ruling on that basis.

---

[2]Although Camacho claims that the arbitration clause is unenforceable because it is unconscionable, she relies heavily on *Randolph* to support her claim. Moreover, in urging the court to consider whether the arbitration agreement allowed Camacho to "vindicate [her] statutory rights in the arbitral forum," *Mitsubishi Motors,* 473 U.S. 614, 637 (1985), Camacho offers the court the standard appropriate for analysis of her claim under *Randolph. Randolph* did not evaluate the arbitration clause in issue under the equitable doctrine of unconscionability, but rather asked whether the plaintiff had established "that arbitration would be prohibitively expensive," 531 U.S. at 92, thereby precluding her from "effectively vindicating her federal statutory rights in the arbitral forum." *Id.* at 90. The Fourth Circuit has repeatedly indicated that the circumstances in which a court may find an arbitration agreement unconscionable are limited, and that arbitrators should generally decide whether arbitration procedures are fair. *See Hooters of America v. Phillips,* 173 F.3d 933, 940 (4th Cir. 1999); *Sydnor v. Conseco,* 246 F.3d 668, No. 00-2304, 2001 WL 223243 (4th Cir. March 7, 2001) (unpublished). Therefore, the court today declines to decide whether the arbitration clause is unconscionable, and instead analyzes it under the principles articulated by the Supreme Court in *Randolph.*

[3]To date, Holiday has neither initiated arbitration of the parties' dispute nor indicated that it would pay the fees necessary to do so.
[4]It is impossible to establish the exact amount Camacho would have to pay because the arbitrator sets the amount after the arbitration has been initiated.

III	Order
For the foregoing reasons, the court denies Holiday's motions. An appropriate order will enter this day.	In accordance with the Memorandum Opinion filed today, the Defendant's motion to dismiss, or, alternatively, to compel arbitration is DENIED.

Inability to Withdraw from the Process

Unlike negotiation and mediation where the parties may terminate the process, once the arbitration process begins, neither party has the power to terminate the process. Therefore, neither party has the power to terminate what he or she perceives to be an unfair process. The aggrieved party's only recourse is an appeal to the courts and this may prove unsuccessful if the appeal does not conform to one of the narrow issues that the courts will review.

Lack of Judicial Review

Can the outcome of private arbitration be incorrect? The parties in a private mediation may elect to give up their legal rights in exchange for an outcome that satisfies their personal or business needs and interests. The parties in a private arbitration give up their power to satisfy their needs and interests in exchange for the resolution of the dispute to be based on what they may think will be their legal rights. Unless the parties direct the arbitrator or the arbitration panel to follow the law, the arbitrator or panel may or may not follow the law. The arbitrator's or panel's award may be made on what was perceived as a reasonable outcome. Since arbitration seldom yields a written reasoned opinion for the award and therefore there is little if any precedent, predicting an outcome may be difficult at best. The arbitrator's or panel's award, regardless of its basis, will end the dispute, establish certainty as to the rights and duties of the parties, and permit the parties to move forward.

Finally, the arbitrator's or panel's award may not be legally correct. The arbitrator or panel may not be required to deliver a written reasoned opinion. The arbitrator or panel may only be required to state, orally or in writing, the decision and award. The parties may never know why the arbitrator or panel reached its decision. Even if the arbitrator or panel has issued a written reasoned opinion, the grounds for appeal to a court are extremely limited, so judicial oversight of private arbitration is limited as well.

In *Westerbeke Corporation v. Daihatsu Motor Co., Ltd*, Westerbeke purchased engines from other manufacturers to convert into engines that were suitable for operating in marine environments. Westerbeke entered into an exclusive long-term sales agreement with Daihatsu whereby Westerbeke would purchase engines to convert from Daihatsu. Westerbeke claimed that Daihatsu breached the agreement by failing to offer to negotiate the sale of a new engine to Westerbeke and instead entering into a sales contract with Briggs. The dispute was arbitrated and Westerbeke received the award. When Westerbeke sought confirmation of the arbitration award in the United States District Court for the Southern District of New York, the court faced the issue of scope of judicial review. A number of citations have been omitted from the court's opinion.

Westerbeke Corporation v. Daihatsu Motor Co., Ltd.
United States District Court, S.D. New York
162 F.Supp.2d 278 (2001)

DECISION AND ORDER

MARRERO, District Judge.

In October 1997, Plaintiff Westerbeke Corporation (hereinafter "Westerbeke") initiated arbitration proceedings for breach of contract against Daihatsu Motor Co., Ltd. (hereinafter "Daihatsu") with the American Arbitration Association. On November 6, 2000, Ira G. Greenberg, Esq. (hereinafter the "Arbitrator" or the "Tribunal"), sitting as the sole member of the panel, issued a Final Award in favor of Westerbeke in the amount of $4,202,255.00. Westerbeke filed an action to confirm the arbitration award in this Court, and Daihatsu has moved to vacate the same.

I. BACKGROUND

A. THE PARTIES AND THE COMPONENT SALES AGREEMENT

Westerbeke is a Delaware corporation with its principal place of business in Taunton, MA. Westerbeke engages in the production and marketing of generators, marine generators and marine propulsion engines. A large part of its business consists of purchasing "carcass" engines from other manufacturers and "marinizing" them for resale. Marinization consists of modifying carcass engines in order to make them suitable for operation in marine environments. Westerbeke's marine products are sold through a distribution network and also directly to builders of boats.

Daihatsu is a subsidiary of the Toyota Motor Company organized under the laws of Japan, with its principal operations in Osaka, Japan. Daihatsu manufactures engines and engine components.

In 1983, the parties commenced negotiations on a long-term sales agreement for the purchase by Westerbeke of Daihatsu's gasoline-powered carcass engines for eventual marinization and incorporation into Westerbeke's product line. Like many other long-term transna-

tional business ventures, the parties entered into complex and protracted negotiations on the proposed form and substance of the contractual relationship. The negotiations involved balancing the competing interests and priorities of the parties and memorializing their compromises in the form of a workable agreement.

Westerbeke was primarily concerned with present and future exclusivity. According to Westerbeke, the company expends substantial sums to marinize and then promote a line of engines. Its efforts could easily be undermined if the manufacturer of carcass engines routes its sales to another distributor piggybacking off the efforts already made by Westerbeke. Furthermore, manufacturers of engines continually discontinue old models and replace them with new ones. Naturally, continued access to the new product lines is critical to the viability of a long-term relationship, and Westerbeke sought to ensure a prospective approach to its agreement with Daihatsu.

Daihatsu, on the other hand, was naturally averse to long-term exclusivity. As a manufacturer, Daihatsu's interests lie in preserving its freedom to sell its engines and components in the most efficient and advantageous distribution channels. A long-term exclusive purchaser who fails to maintain minimum purchase quantities or neglects to market aggressively not only ensures its own failure, but also that of the component maker. In short, Daihatsu's concern was being tied to a "poor choice" for a distribution partner.

Ultimately, the parties balanced their competing interests and reached a compromise that culminated in the Component Sales Agreement (hereinafter the "CSA") entered into on May 1, 1985. The CSA provided for the present exclusivity that Westerbeke sought. For a period of six years, Daihatsu agreed to supply Westerbeke with certain contractually-defined engines on an exclusive basis in the United States and Canada. The CSA also contained an automatic renewal provision for successive two-year terms, and it appears from the record that the CSA was renewed twice for an additional four years.

With respect to Daihatsu's future engine models, however, exclusivity was not automatic. Article 3.2 of the CSA required that Daihatsu respect Westerbeke's right of first refusal during the first six months that Daihatsu wished to sell other "Engines," as defined by the CSA. The exclusivity provision of the CSA would only apply to the new engine if, during the six month term, Westerbeke and Daihatsu reached agreement on the material terms of sale for the new engines"specifications, prices, minimum purchase quantities, delivery terms, etc.".

B. DAIHATSU'S NEW E-070 ENGINE

In the early 1990s, Daihatsu was actively developing, and perhaps marketing, a new product line, the E-070 Engine. The new model was a water-cooled, three-cylinder gasoline engine. After a thorough review of the record, the Arbitrator found that the E-070 Engine was of the type that triggered Article 3.2 of the CSA, a finding of fact which was not clearly erroneous. (Interlocutory Award, *Westerbeke Corporation v. Daihatsu Motor Co. Ltd.*, AAA Case No. 13 T 153 01057 97, at 18 (Mar. 8, 1999) (hereinafter "Interlocutory Award")). Initially, it also appears that Daihatsu did not bring this new model to the attention of Westerbeke.

The parties are at odds as to why the E-070 Engine never became an "Engine" as defined by the CSA, subject to Westerbeke's right of exclusivity. Daihatsu contends that the E-070 Engine was never intended to be a marine product, a point which was contradicted to some extent by documents produced in the proceedings below. Daihatsu also explains that its decision not to pursue sales of the E-070 to Westerbeke was motivated by its growing dissatisfaction with Westerbeke's sales volume. Daihatsu's dissatisfaction was manifested in threats to terminate the exclusivity provisions of the CSA at least as early as 1990.

Westerbeke believes that Daihatsu's unwillingness to negotiate with respect to the E-070 Engine had nothing to do with either the target markets for the new model or the level of Westerbeke's purchases. Rather, Westerbeke contends that Daihatsu was secretly developing the E-070 Engine and negotiating with another North American distributor, the Briggs & Stratton Corporation (hereinafter "Briggs"), for exclusive rights to the new engine.

Around June 1993, Briggs issued a press release announcing a joint venture between it and Daihatsu for the purpose of marketing, selling, and servicing a new line of water-cooled engines in North America. Later that Summer, trade publications ran advertisements of the E-070 Engine which came to the attention of Westerbeke's President and Chief Executive Officer. This was the first time that Westerbeke had learned of Daihatsu's new engine.

In the ensuing months, representatives of Westerbeke contacted Daihatsu to communicate its belief that Daihatsu had breached the CSA. It appears from the record that the parties attempted to salvage some sort of working relationship, but those efforts never came to fruition. In October 1994, Daihatsu terminated the CSA by providing Westerbeke six months notice.

C. THE ENSUING ARBITRATION AND THE PRESENT PROCEEDINGS

The demise of the parties' working relationship resulted in several legal proceedings. In February 1997, Westerbeke filed an action in Norfolk Superior Court and a subsequent action in the United States District Court for the District of Massachusetts in March 1997. Westerbeke filed a separate action against Briggs for its role in the dispute between the parties. All of these actions were voluntarily dismissed or stayed when Westerbeke invoked Article 23 of the CSA, which requires all disputes to be resolved by arbitration pursuant to the Japan-American Trade Arbitration Agreement of September 16, 1952. Article 23 also stipulates New York as the situs of arbitration.

Accordingly, Westerbeke filed a claim with the American Arbitration Association in October 1997. The Arbitrator bifurcated proceedings into separate phases for liability and damages. At the close of the liability phase, the Arbitrator issued an Interlocutory Award which stated: "[t]he primary issue for decision is whether respondent Daihatsu Motor Company, Limited violated the contractual rights of claimant Westerbeke Corporation in *refusing to negotiate for the inclusion* of the E-070 engines as Engines within the meaning of the 1985 Component Sales Agreement between the two parties. The Tribunal holds that it did."

(continued)

(continued from previous page)

Notwithstanding this clear and unambiguous basis for liability enunciated in the Interlocutory Award, the Tribunal effectively replaced its liability analysis in the Final Award of damages: "[t]he appropriate analytical framework is that of a contract with condition precedent to the addition of a new Engine." The Arbitrator awarded Westerbeke over $4 million in damages, which included damages for lost profits that Westerbeke expected from hypothetical sales of the E-070 Engines.

Westerbeke now moves to confirm the award as Daihatsu has refused to recognize it. Westerbeke contends that the Tribunal's decision was proper in all respects and that Daihatsu has not advanced sufficient grounds to interfere with the Arbitrator's award. In any event, Westerbeke avers that Daihatsu should be precluded from judgment because it has not met its burden of production, which Westerbeke believes to require production of the complete record in the arbitration proceedings below.

For its part, Daihatsu moves to vacate the award on four principal grounds: (1) the Arbitrator manifestly disregarded controlling New York law on the award of expectancy damages for breach of a duty to negotiate; . . . ."

II. STANDARD OF REVIEW OF AN ARBITRATION AWARD

It is beyond dispute that an arbitration award is entitled to substantial deference and that a district court's review is narrowly circumscribed. *See Yusuf Ahmed Alghanim & Sons, W.L.L. v. Toys "R" Us, Inc.*, 126 F.3d 15, 23 (2d Cir. 1997) (citations omitted), *cert. denied*, 522 U.S. 1111, 118 S.Ct. 1042, 140 L.Ed.2d 107 (1998). As the Second Circuit has stated, "[a]n arbitrator's decision is entitled to substantial deference, and the arbitrator need only explicate his reasoning under the contract 'in terms that offer even a barely colorable justification for the outcome reached' in order to withstand judicial scrutiny." *In re Marine Pollution Serv., Inc.*, 857 F.2d 91, 94 (2d Cir. 1988) (quoting *Matter of Andros Compania Maritima, S.A. of Kissavos (Marc Rich & Co., A.G.)*, 579 F.2d 691, 704 (2d Cir. 1978)). The Second Circuit has also characterized a district court's review of an arbitration award as

a "summary proceeding that merely makes what is already a final arbitration award a judgment of the court." *Toys "R" Us*, 126 F.3d at 23 (citations omitted). The deference accorded to arbitration awards is particularly high in contract cases, where courts are generally reluctant to second guess an arbitrator's resolution of the parties' dispute. *Id.*

Informing the high standard of deference accorded to arbitration awards are the judicially-recognized advantages of arbitration as an alternative to litigation. One of those advantages is "a speedier, more economical and more effective enforcement of rights by way of arbitration than can be had by the tortuous course of litigation, especially in the City of New York." *Wilko v. Swan*, 346 U.S. 427, 439–40, 74 S.Ct. 182, 98 L.Ed. 168 (1953) (Frankfurter, J., *dissenting*), *overruled on other grounds*, *Rodriguez de Quijas v. Shearson/American Express, Inc.*, 490 U.S. 477, 109 S.Ct. 1917, 104 L.Ed.2d 526 (1989); *see also Folkways Music Publishers, Inc. v. Weiss*, 989 F.2d 108, 111 (2d Cir. 1993) ("[a]rbitration awards are subject to very limited review in order to avoid undermining the twin goals of arbitration, namely, settling disputes efficiently and avoiding long and expensive litigation.") (citations omitted).

Although the deference to which arbitration awards are entitled is substantial, the FAA itself and the common law in this Circuit do not perfunctorily insulate those awards from review. Section 10(a) of the FAA enumerates grounds for vacating arbitration awards in the event of fraud, corruption, procedural misconduct or abuse of powers.

Apart from the relevant provisions of the FAA, the Second Circuit has recognized an alternative ground for vacatur of an arbitration award when that award is made in "manifest disregard of the law." Manifest disregard of the law is a "judicially-created ground for vacating [an] arbitration award, which was introduced by the Supreme Court in *Wilko v. Swan*. . . . It is not to be found in the federal arbitration law." *Merrill Lynch, Pierce, Fenner & Smith, Inc. v. Bobker*, 808 F.2d 930, 933 (2d Cir. 1986). As the court explains, manifest disregard of the law is more than misunderstanding or error in the application of the law:

[t]he error must have been obvious and capable of being readily and instantly perceived by the average person qualified to serve as an arbitrator. Moreover, the term 'disregard' implies that the arbitrator appreciates the existence of a clearly governing legal principle but decides to ignore or pay no attention to it.

Id. (citations omitted); *see also Halligan v. Piper Jaffray, Inc.,* 148 F.3d 197, 202 (2d Cir. 1998), *cert. denied,* 526 U.S. 1034, 119 S.Ct. 1286, 143 L.Ed.2d 378 (1999); *Greenberg v. Bear Stearns & Co., Inc.,* No. 99 Civ. 358(JSM), 1999 WL 642859 (S.D.N.Y. 1999), *aff'd,* 220 F.3d 22 (2d Cir. 2000), *cert. denied,* 531 U.S. 1075, 121 S.Ct. 770, 148 L.Ed.2d 669 (2001).

Therefore, when reviewing an award for manifest disregard of the law, the relevant inquiry is "extremely limited," and even more narrowly circumscribed than the threshold standard for reviewing arbitration awards. *Merrill Lynch,* 808 F.2d at 934. In order to vacate an award on the ground of manifest disregard of the law, a court must find both that (1) the arbitrators knew of a governing legal principle yet refused to apply it or ignored it altogether, and (2) the law ignored by the arbitrators was well defined, explicit and clearly applicable to the case. *DiRussa v. Dean Witter Reynolds, Inc.,* 121 F.3d 818, 821 (2d Cir. 1997) (quotations and citations omitted), *cert. denied,* 522 U.S. 1049, 118 S.Ct. 695, 139 L.Ed.2d 639 (1998).

Despite the rigid confines of its review, the Court holds that the Arbitrator's award of expected profits in favor of Westerbeke was one of those "extremely limited" instances when the Tribunal manifestly disregarded the controlling law.

III. DISCUSSION

A. THE RIGHTS AND OBLIGATIONS IN ARTICLE 3.2 OF THE CSA

Beyond that, Westerbeke may only demand that Daihatsu "*negotiate* the open terms in good faith toward a final contract incorporating the agreed terms." *Id.* at 498 (emphasis supplied). By failing to approach Westerbeke in connection with its desire to sell the E-070 Engine in North America and by entering into the joint venture with Briggs, Daihatsu breached its duty to negotiate toward the inclusion of the new product into the CSA.

B. NEW YORK STATE LAW OF DAMAGES

Having determined that Article 3.2 reflects a duty to negotiate which Daihatsu breached, there remains the issue of the appropriate measure of damages flowing from that breach. Specifically, the parties disagree as to whether the award should include expectancy damages—anticipated profits that Westerbeke lost as a result of the breach. New York State law controls, as the parties agreed to a choice of law clause stipulating that "[t]his Agreement shall be construed in accordance with and governed by the laws of the State of New York." CSA, Article 27.7.

The appropriate measure of damages from breach of a preliminary agreement to negotiate was directly addressed by the Court of Appeals of New York in *Goodstein Construction Corp. v. City of New York,* 80 N.Y.2d 366, 590 N.Y.S.2d 425, 604 N.E.2d 1356 (1992). In *Goodstein,* plaintiff entered into a letter agreement with the City of New York " 'to exclusively negotiate the terms and conditions of a land disposition agreement.' " *Id.* at 1358. Any binding formal agreement was contingent upon obtaining the approval of relevant municipal agencies with jurisdiction over the proposed land disposition. *Id.* Plaintiff's prayer for relief included $800 million, all but $1 million of which consisted of anticipated profits lost from the terminated agreement. *Id.*

As a threshold matter, the court in *Goodstein* characterized the nature of the obligation at issue as a "preliminary agreement to negotiate." *Id.* at 1360. The court held that based upon the breach of the defendant's duty to negotiate, the appropriate measure of damages precludes recovery for plaintiff's expected profits. In particular, the court reasoned that

[t]o allow the profits that plaintiff might have made under the prospective LDA as the damages for breach of the exclusive negotiating agreements would be basing damages not on the exclusive negotiating agreements but on the prospective terms of a nonexistent contract which the City was fully at liberty to reject. It would, in effect, be

(continued)

(continued from previous page)

transforming an agreement to negotiate for a contract into the contract itself.

Id. at 1361. Similarly, awarding expectancy damages in this case, where the breach related only to an agreement to negotiate, would give Westerbeke full damages for breach of a contract which was never reached, a result which runs counter to the principle that courts and arbitrators alike should give primary effect to the intentions of the parties. By its terms, Article 3.2 of the CSA required the parties to reach agreement, at minimum, with respect to specifications, prices, purchase quantities and delivery terms. Only satisfaction of these conditions following negotiations would furnish a quantifiable basis upon which to ground a reasonable award of damages. As already indicated, no such negotiations or agreement occurred here.

The principle of damages in *Goodstein* is further refined by the Court of Appeals decision in *Kenford Co. v. County of Erie,* 67 N.Y.2d 257, 502 N.Y.S.2d 131, 493 N.E.2d 234 (1986) *(Kenford I); see also Kenford Co. v. County of Erie,* 73 N.Y.2d 312, 540 N.Y.S.2d 1, 537 N.E.2d 176 (1989) *(Kenford II).* In *Kenford I,* the plaintiff entered into a formal contract with the County of Erie for the construction and operation of a domed stadium. *Id.* 493 N.E.2d at 234. The County terminated the contract two years after formal acceptance when it became clear that the parties could not agree upon a mutually acceptable lease. *Id.* at 235. The court held that in order to award lost profits anticipated from the stadium venture, plaintiff was required to show (1) that the damages claimed were caused by the breach; (2) that the alleged damages are capable of determination with reasonable certainty; and (3) that the particular damages were fairly within the contemplation of the parties at the time the agreement was made. *Id.* The plaintiff was precluded from recovering lost profits as yet unrealized because proof of damages fell far short of the standard for reasonable certainty and because the court was not persuaded that liability for lost profits was in the contemplation of the parties at the time of the agreement.

The Court notes that the damages rules in *Goodstein* and *Kenford* have been firmly endorsed in several deci-

sions of this District. *See Schonfeld v. Hilliard,* 62 F.Supp. 2d 1062, 1078 (S.D.N.Y. 1999) ("[a]pplying those principles here, the purpose of entering the contracts was eventually to capture the profits projected under the business plans, but the [defendant's] anticipation of hypothetical profits does not translate into acceptance of full liability for such profits"), *aff'd in part, rev'd in part on other grounds,* 218 F.3d 164 (2d Cir. 2000); *Coastal Aviation, Inc. v. Commander Aircraft Co.,* 937 F.Supp. 1051, 1064 (S.D.N.Y. 1996), *aff'd,* 108 F.3d 1369 (2d Cir. 1997).

On this authority, the Court holds that the appropriate measure of Westerbeke's damages resulting from Daihatsu's breach of its agreement to negotiate with respect to the E-070 Engines precludes an award of Westerbeke's expected lost profits. Furthermore, the record fails to reflect that Westerbeke's lost profits from an unrealized agreement to include the E-070 Engines in the CSA was fairly in the contemplation of the parties when Article 3.2 took effect.

C. THE TRIBUNAL'S AWARD AND MANIFEST DISREGARD OF THE LAW

With respect to the determination of liability above, the Court and the Arbitrator are in complete agreement, at least until the issuance of the Final Award. In particular, the Interlocutory Award found that "[t]he primary issue for decision is whether respondent Daihatsu Motor Company, Limited violated the contractual rights of claimant Westerbeke Corporation in *refusing to negotiate* for the inclusion of the E-070 engines as Engines within the meaning of the 1985 Component Sales Agreement between the two parties. The Tribunal holds that it did." This is precisely the conclusion that this Court reached above, and the Court agrees with Daihatsu that this is the only basis of liability that the Arbitrator advanced in the Interlocutory Award.

Notwithstanding the Court's initial concurrence with the Interlocutory Award, the Arbitrator's Final Award takes an unusual and legally fatal turn. In the Final Award, the Arbitrator abandons the sole basis of liability as set forth in the Interlocutory Award and holds that "[t]he appropriate analytical framework is that of a contract with condition precedent to the addition of a new Engine. The condition precedent, by the terms of the CSA, is agreement on the stated terms." Reaching further, the Arbitrator proceeded to find a legally binding obligation on the part of Daihatsu to sell E-070 Engines on an exclusive basis to Westerbeke when no such agreement was ever reached because Daihatsu had never engaged in negotiations for inclusion of the new engines within the CSA. The Tribunal arrived at this result by examining and giving weight to documents extrinsic to any negotiation between the parties relating to the E-070 Engines and by concluding on this basis that "Daihatsu never pointed to any disagreement on a specific major term." In this manner, in this Court's estimation, the Final Award stretches beyond the limits of sound jurisprudence and in effect substitutes the Arbitrator's own judgment for the intentions of the parties.

The Tribunal's finding that there was, in effect, an agreement between the parties with regard to the new engines is particularly untenable in light of commercial realities. Agreements that leave open terms such as specifications, prices, and minimum purchase quantities defer to a later date legal commitment on the most substantial and material terms that comprise a contract. Furthermore, when these crucial conditions are left open, related and corollary issues are also left undecided by the parties.

After advancing this alternative theory of liability in the Final Award, the Arbitrator proceeded to award Westerbeke damages for its expected lost profits. This was done in recognition of and in contravention to the principles set forth in *Goodstein* and *Kenford I.*

Westerbeke urges this Court to confirm the Arbitrator's award on several grounds: (1) that *Goodstein* does not apply because it was a real estate case not decided in accordance with the New York Uniform Commercial Code (hereinafter "NY UCC"); (2) that the Tribunal correctly found a binding, fully-integrated contract with a condition precedent in light of N.Y. UCC §§ 2-204 and 2-305; and (3) that N.Y. UCC §§ 2-712 and 2-715 provide the statutory vehicle for awarding expectancy damages. None of these arguments justifies confirming the Arbitrator's award.

First, Westerbeke's attempt to explain away the applicability of *Goodstein* fails. Westerbeke avers that *Goodstein* does not apply to Article 3.2 of the CSA because that case involved a real estate transaction not subject to the N.Y. UCC and because *Goodstein* was subject to uncertainties such as municipal approvals not at issue here. In effect, Westerbeke asks this Court to draw a rigid line between the N.Y. UCC and the common law of contracts in order to award, without legal basis, expectancy damages. There is no case law to support such a rigid differentiation, and this Court declines Westerbeke's invitation to render inapplicable the relevant common law rule of damages to an entire category of cases purportedly governed exclusively by the N.Y. UCC.

In *Coastal Aviation,* the court confronted a similar argument from plaintiff that a contract for the sale of goods is not subject to the requirements of certainty and foreseeability set out in *Kenford I.* 937 F.Supp. at 1064 n.6 ("*Coastal* attempts to distinguish the instant case from *Kenford I* and its progeny by arguing that the instant case involves a contract for the sale of goods (and is therefore governed by the New York Uniform Commercial Code) rather than a contract for services (governed by the common law).". The court found plaintiff's argument unpersuasive: "*Coastal's* attempt to rigidly delineate UCC and common law principles is misplaced. . . . We conclude that rules of law under the UCC and the common law are not mutually exclusive. . . . Because there was no market yet for the 114Bs, the principles set forth in *Kenford I* and its progeny are directly applicable to this case." *Id.*

The Court concurs with *Coastal Aviation's* statement on the complementarity of the common law and the N.Y. UCC. The rules set forth in *Goodstein* and *Kenford I* do not stand apart from the N.Y. UCC, but rather, both serve to inform analyses under the other. Thus, the holding in *Goodstein* that expectancy damages are unavailable for the breach of an agreement to negotiate applies directly to the present dispute.

The Court's conclusion above also disposes of Westerbeke's second argument, that N.Y. UCC §§ 2-204 and 2-305 permit the finding that the agreement between the parties was a complete, fully-integrated contract with a condition precedent. The relevant portion of N.Y. UCC § 2-204 states: "[e]ven though one or more terms are left open a contract for sale does not fail for indefiniteness if

(continued)

(continued from previous page)

the parties have intended to make a contract and there is a reasonably certain basis for giving an appropriate remedy." NY UCC § 2-204(3). And N.Y. UCC § 2-305 merely stands for the proposition that the parties, if they so intend, may conclude a contract even though agreement on price is left open.

Neither of these two provisions supports Westerbeke's contention as to the existence here of a fully-integrated, binding contract and neither abrogates the common law rule in *Goodstein.* The two provisions merely restate the principle set forth in *Tribune,* that certain preliminary agreements . . . constitute complete, binding contracts capable of being enforced by courts notwithstanding incomplete agreement on all terms. Neither provision overrules the common law principle that other agreements that leave material terms open for negotiation can only give rise to a duty to negotiate. That Westerbeke and Daihatsu enjoyed a ten-year relationship that provided for exclusivity with respect to prior models is important to note, but does not change the fundamental character of Article 3.2 of the CSA. When a new engine was contemplated for distribution in North America, Article 3.2 merely obligated Daihatsu to negotiate in good faith toward agreement on new terms of sale for the new product.

Westerbeke's third argument that N.Y. UCC §§ 2-712 and 2-715 statutorily permit the award of expectancy damages also fails. Both of these provisions merely state the appropriate measure of damages if the seller breaches his obligation under a full, binding contract. As already noted, the underlying obligation at issue was not a legally binding contract, but an agreement to negotiate. Neither 2-712 nor 2-715 alters that conclusion.

In short, Westerbeke's grounds for sustaining the Arbitrator's decision fail. Accordingly, the Court holds that the Tribunal manifestly disregarded the law by abrogating the proper basis for liability set forth in the Inter-

locutory Award and substituting the theory of a contract with condition precedent in the Final Award. Furthermore, the award to Westerbeke of lost profits expected from the future sales E-070 Engines was made in manifest disregard to the applicable law on damages for breach of an agreement to negotiate.

Recognizing that courts reach the conclusion of manifest disregard of the law only in "extremely limited" instances, the Court underscores the following circumstances that support that finding here: (1) the Arbitrator obviously understood and appreciated the law on preliminary agreements because his Interlocutory Award correctly states the basis for liability, that is, breach of a duty to negotiate; (2) the Tribunal knew and appreciated the applicable law on damages because Daihatsu had brought the case law to its attention on numerous occasions and because the Tribunal attempted to address those cases in the Final Award. These findings support the conclusion that the applicable standard for vacating an arbitration award was crossed here, that is, that the Arbitrator ignored or refused to apply properly the law on both preliminary agreements and appropriate damages in fashioning his Final Award.

IV. CONCLUSION AND ORDER

For the foregoing reasons, it is hereby

ORDERED that Westerbeke's motion to confirm the arbitration award is denied; and it is further

ORDERED that Daihatsu's motion to vacate the arbitration award is granted, and the case is remanded to the Arbitration Tribunal for an appropriate determination of damages consistent with this Decision and Order; and it is finally

ORDERED that the Clerk of Court is directed to close this case.

SO ORDERED.

Prior to *Major League Baseball Players Association v. Garvey*, the major league baseball clubs established a settlement fund to compensate former players for damages suffered as a result of the club's collusion in the free-agent market. Steve Garvey, a former professional baseball player, sought to establish his claim for damages before the Baseball Players Association, the distributor of the fund. The Association denied Garvey's claim and an arbitrator confirmed the Association's decision. Garvey then brought action in a federal district court asking the court to vacate the arbitrator's decision. The case made its way up to the United States Supreme Court on the issue of the courts' role in reviewing arbitrators' decisions.

Major League Baseball Players Association v. Garvey
Supreme Court of the United States
121 S.Ct. 1724 (2001)

Justice Ginsburg concurred in part and concurred in judgment, and filed opinion.

Justice Stevens dissented, and filed opinion.

PER CURIAM.

The Court of Appeals for the Ninth Circuit here rejected an arbitrator's factual findings and then resolved the merits of the parties' dispute instead of remanding the case for further arbitration proceedings. Because the Court's determination conflicts with our cases limiting review of an arbitrator's award entered pursuant to an agreement between an employer and a labor organization and prescribing the appropriate remedy where vacation of the award is warranted, we grant the petition for a writ of certiorari and reverse. The motions for leave to file briefs *amicus curiae* of the National Academy of Arbitrators and the Office of the Commissioner of Baseball are granted.

In the late 1980's, petitioner Major League Baseball Players Association (Association) filed grievances against the Major League Baseball Clubs (Clubs), claiming the Clubs had colluded in the market for free-agent services after the 1985, 1986 and 1987 baseball seasons, in violation of the industry's collective-bargaining agreement. A free agent is a player who may contract with any Club, rather than one whose right to contract is restricted to a particular Club. In a series of decisions, arbitrators found collusion by the Clubs and damage to the players. The Association and Clubs subsequently entered into a Global Settlement Agreement (Agreement), pursuant to which the Clubs established a $280 million fund to be distributed to injured players. The Association also designed a "Framework" to evaluate the individual player's claims, and, applying that Framework, recommended distribution plans for claims relating to a particular season or seasons.

The Framework provided that players could seek an arbitrator's review of the distribution plan. The arbitrator would determine "only whether the approved Framework and the criteria set forth therein have been properly applied in the proposed Distribution Plan." *Garvey v. Roberts*, 203 F.3d 580, 583 (C.A.9 2000) (*Garvey I*). The Framework set forth factors to be considered in evaluating players' claims, as well as specific requirements for lost contract-extension claims. Such claims were cognizable " 'only in those cases where evidence exists that a specific offer of an extension was made by a club prior to collusion only to thereafter be withdrawn when the collusion scheme was initiated.' " *Id.* at 584.

Respondent Steve Garvey, a retired, highly regarded first baseman, submitted a claim for damages of approximately $3 million. He alleged that his contract with the San Diego Padres was not extended to the 1988 and 1989 seasons due to collusion. The Association rejected Garvey's claim in February 1996, because he presented no evidence that the Padres actually offered to extend his contract. Garvey objected, and an arbitration hearing was held. He testified that the Padres offered to extend his contract for the 1988 and 1989 seasons and then withdrew the offer after they began colluding with other teams. He presented a June 1996 letter from Ballard

(continued)

(continued from previous page)
Smith, Padres' President and CEO from 1979 to 1987, stating that, before the end of the 1985 season, Smith offered to extend Garvey's contract through the 1989 season, but that the Padres refused to negotiate with Garvey thereafter due to collusion.

The arbitrator denied Garvey's claim, after seeking additional documentation from the parties. In his award, he explained that " '[t]here exists . . . substantial doubt as to the credibility of the statements in the Smith letter.' " *Id.* at 586. He noted the "stark contradictions" between the 1996 letter and Smith's testimony in the earlier arbitration proceedings regarding collusion, where Smith, like other owners, denied collusion and stated that the Padres simply were not interested in extending Garvey's contract. *Ibid.* The arbitrator determined that, due to these contradictions, he " 'must reject [Smith's] more recent assertion that Garvey did not receive [a contract] extension' " due to collusion, and found that Garvey had not shown a specific offer of extension. *Ibid.* He concluded that:

> " '[t]he shadow cast over the credibility of the Smith testimony coupled with the absence of any other corroboration of the claim submitted by Garvey compels a finding that the Padres declined to extend his contract not because of the constraints of the collusion effort of the clubs but rather as a baseball judgment founded upon [Garvey's] age and recent injury history.' " *Ibid.*

Garvey moved in Federal District Court to vacate the arbitrator's award, alleging that the arbitrator violated the Framework by denying his claim. The District Court denied the motion. The Court of Appeals for the Ninth Circuit reversed by a divided vote. The court acknowledged that judicial review of an arbitrator's decision in a labor dispute is extremely limited. But it held that review of the merits of the arbitrator's award was warranted in this case, because the arbitrator " 'dispensed his own brand of industrial justice.' " *Id.* at 589. The court recognized that Smith's prior testimony with respect to collusion conflicted with the statements in his 1996 letter. But in the court's view, the arbitrator's refusal to credit Smith's

letter was "inexplicable" and "border[ed] on the irrational," because a panel of arbitrators, chaired by the arbitrator involved here, had previously concluded that the owners' prior testimony was false. *Id.* at 590. The court rejected the arbitrator's reliance on the absence of other corroborating evidence, attributing that fact to Smith and Garvey's direct negotiations. The court also found that the record provided "strong support" for the truthfulness of Smith's 1996 letter. *Id.* at 591–592. The Court of Appeals reversed and remanded with directions to vacate the award.

The District Court then remanded the case to the arbitration panel for further hearings, and Garvey appealed. The Court of Appeals, again by a divided vote, explained that *Garvey I* established that "the conclusion that Smith made Garvey an offer and subsequently withdrew it because of the collusion scheme was the only conclusion that the arbitrator could draw from the record in the proceedings." No. 00-56080, 2000 WL 1801383, at *1 (Dec. 7, 2000), judgt. order to be reported at 243 F.3d 547. (*Garvey II*). Noting that its prior instructions might have been unclear, the Court clarified that *Garvey I* "left only one possible result—the result our holding contemplated—an award in Garvey's favor." *Ibid.* The Court of Appeals reversed the District Court and directed that it remand the case to the arbitration panel with instructions to enter an award for Garvey in the amount he claimed.

The parties do not dispute that this case arises under § 01 of the Labor Management Relations Act, 1947, 61 Stat. 156, 29 U.S.C. § 185(a), as the controversy involves an assertion of rights under an agreement between an employer and a labor organization. Although Garvey's specific allegation is that the arbitrator violated the Framework for resolving players' claims for damages, that Framework was designed to facilitate payments to remedy the Clubs' breach of the collective-bargaining agreement. Garvey's right to be made whole is founded on that agreement.

Judicial review of a labor-arbitration decision pursuant to such an agreement is very limited. Courts are not authorized to review the arbitrator's decision on the merits despite allegations that the decision rests on factual errors or misinterprets the parties' agreement. *Paperworkers v.*

Misco, Inc., 484 U.S. 29, 36, 108 S.Ct. 364, 98 L.Ed.2d 286 (1987). We recently reiterated that if an " 'arbitrator is even arguably construing or applying the contract and acting within the scope of his authority,' the fact that 'a court is convinced he committed serious error does not suffice to overturn his decision.' " *Eastern Associated Coal Corp. v. Mine Workers*, 531 U.S. 57, 62, 121 S.Ct. 462, 148 L.Ed.2d 354 (2000) (quoting *Misco*, HYPERLINK "http://www.westlaw.com/Find/Default.wl?rs=dfa1.0&vr =2.0&DB=708&FindType=Y&SerialNum= 1987147170" at 38, 108 S.Ct. 364). It is only when the arbitrator strays from interpretation and application of the agreement and effectively "dispense[s] his own brand of industrial justice" that his decision may be unenforceable. *Steelworkers v. Enterprise Wheel & Car Corp.*, 363 U.S. 593, 597, 80 S.Ct. 1358, 4 L.Ed.2d 1424 (1960). When an arbitrator resolves disputes regarding the application of a contract, and no dishonesty is alleged, the arbitrator's "improvident, even silly, factfinding" does not provide a basis for a reviewing court to refuse to enforce the award. *Misco*, 484 U.S. at 39, 108 S.Ct. 364.

In discussing the courts' limited role in reviewing the merits of arbitration awards, we have stated that " 'courts . . . have no business weighing the merits of the grievance [or] considering whether there is equity in a particular claim.' " *Id.* at 37, 108 S.Ct. 364 (quoting *Steelworkers v. American Mfg. Co.*, 363 U.S. 564, 568, 80 S.Ct. 1343, 4 L.Ed.2d 1403 (1960)). When the judiciary does so, "it usurps a function which . . . is entrusted to the arbitration tribunal." *Id.* at 569, 80 S.Ct. 1343; see also *Enterprise Wheel & Car Corp., supra* at 599, 80 S.Ct. 1358 ("It is the arbitrator's construction [of the agreement] which was bargained for . . . "). Consistent with this limited role, we said in *Misco* that "[e]ven in the very rare instances when an arbitrator's procedural aberrations rise to the level of affirmative misconduct, as a rule the court must not foreclose further proceedings by settling the merits according to its own judgment of the appropriate result." 484 U.S. at 40–41, n.10, 108 S.Ct. 364. That step, we explained, "would improperly substitute a judicial determination for the arbitrator's decision that the parties bargained

for" in their agreement. *Ibid.* Instead, the court should "simply vacate the award, thus leaving open the possibility of further proceedings if they are permitted under the terms of the agreement." *Ibid.*

To be sure, the Court of Appeals here recited these principles, but its application of them is nothing short of baffling. The substance of the Court's discussion reveals that it overturned the arbitrator's decision because it disagreed with the arbitrator's factual findings, particularly those with respect to credibility. The Court of Appeals, it appears, would have credited Smith's 1996 letter, and found the arbitrator's refusal to do so at worst "irrational" and at best "bizarre." *Garvey I*, 203 F.3d at 590–591. But even "serious error" on the arbitrator's part does not justify overturning his decision, where, as here, he is construing a contract and acting within the scope of his authority. *Misco*, HYPERLINK "http://www.westlaw.com/Find/Default.wl?rs=dfa1.0&vr= 2.0&DB=708&FindType=Y&SerialNum=1987147170" at 38, 108 S.Ct. 364.

In *Garvey II*, the court clarified that *Garvey I* both rejected the arbitrator's findings and went further, resolving the merits of the parties' dispute based on the court's assessment of the record before the arbitrator. For that reason, the court found further arbitration proceedings inappropriate. But again, established law ordinarily precludes a court from resolving the merits of the parties' dispute on the basis of its own factual determinations, no matter how erroneous the arbitrator's decision. *Misco, supra* at 40, n.10, 108 S.Ct. 364; *see also American Mfg. Co.*, 363 U.S. at 568, 80 S.Ct. 1343. Even when the arbitrator's award may properly be vacated, the appropriate remedy is to remand the case for further arbitration proceedings. *Misco, supra* at 40, n.10, 108 S.Ct. 364. The dissent suggests that the remedy described in *Misco* is limited to cases where the arbitrator's errors are procedural. *Post*, at 1729 (opinion of STEVENS, J.) *Misco* did involve procedural issues, but our discussion regarding the appropriate remedy was not so limited. If a remand is appropriate *even* when the arbitrator's award has been set aside for "procedural aberrations" that constitute "affirmative misconduct," it follows that a remand ordinarily will be appropriate when the arbitrator

(continued)

(continued from previous page)

simply made factual findings that the reviewing court perceives as "irrational." The Court of Appeals usurped the arbitrator's role by resolving the dispute and barring further proceedings, a result at odds with this governing law.[1]

For the foregoing reasons, the Court of Appeals erred in reversing the order of the District Court denying the motion to vacate the arbitrator's award, and it erred further in directing that judgment be entered in Garvey's favor. The judgment of the Court of Appeals is reversed, and the case is remanded for further proceedings consistent with this opinion.

It is so ordered.

Justice GINSBURG, concurring in part and concurring in the judgment.

I agree with the Court that in *Garvey v. Roberts*, 203 F.3d 580 (C.A.9 2000) (*Garvey I*), the Ninth Circuit should not have disturbed the arbitrator's award. Correction of that error sets this case straight. I see no need to say more.

Justice STEVENS, dissenting.

It is well settled that an arbitrator "does not sit to dispense his own brand of industrial justice." *Steelworkers v. Enterprise Wheel & Car Corp.*, 363 U.S. 593, 597, 80 S.Ct. 1358, 4 L.Ed.2d 1424 (1960). We have also said

fairly definitively, albeit in dicta, that a court should remedy an arbitrator's "procedural aberrations" by vacating the award and remanding for further proceedings. *Paperworkers v. Misco, Inc.*, 484 U.S. 29, 40–41, n.10, 108 S.Ct. 364, 98 L.Ed.2d 286 (1987). Our cases, however, do not provide significant guidance as to what standards a federal court should use in assessing whether an arbitrator's behavior is so untethered to either the agreement of the parties or the factual record so as to constitute an attempt to "dispense his own brand of industrial justice." Nor, more importantly, do they tell us how, having made such a finding, courts should deal with "the extraordinary circumstance in which the arbitrator's own rulings make clear that, more than being simply erroneous, his finding is completely inexplicable and borders on the irrational." *Garvey v. Roberts*, 203 F.3d 580, 590 (C.A.9 2000) (case below). Because our caselaw is not sufficiently clear to allow me to conclude that the case below was wrongly decided—let alone to conclude that the decision was so wrong as to require the extraordinary remedy of a summary reversal—I dissent from the Court's disposition of this petition.

Without the benefit of briefing or argument, today the Court resolves two difficult questions. First, it decides that even if the Court of Appeals' appraisal of the merits is correct—that is to say, even if the arbitrator did dispense his own brand of justice untethered to the agreement of the parties, and even if the correct disposition of the matter is perfectly clear—the only course open to a reviewing court is to remand the matter for another arbitration. That conclusion is not compelled by any of our cases, nor by any analysis offered by the Court. As the issue is subject to serious arguments on both sides, the Court should have set this case for argument if it wanted to answer this remedial question.

Second, without reviewing the record or soliciting briefing, the Court concludes that, in any event, "no serious error on the arbitrator's part is apparent in this case." *Ante*, at 1729, n.2. At this stage in the proceedings, I simply cannot endorse that conclusion. After examining the record, obtaining briefing, and hearing oral argument,

---

[1]In any event, no serious error on the arbitrator's part is apparent in this case. The fact that an earlier panel of arbitrators rejected the owners' testimony as a whole does not compel the conclusion that the panel found Smith's specific statements with respect to Garvey to be false. The arbitrator's explanation for his decision indicates that he simply found Smith an unreliable witness and that, in the absence of corroborating evidence, he could only conclude that Garvey failed to show that the Padres had offered to extend his contract. The arbitrator's analysis may have been unpersuasive to the Court of Appeals, but his decision hardly qualifies as serious error, let alone irrational or inexplicable error. And, as we have said, any such error would not justify the actions taken by the court.

the Court of Appeals offered a reasoned explanation of its conclusion. *See* 203 F.3d at 589–592; also *id.* at 593–594 (Hawkins, J., concurring). Whether or not I would ultimately agree with the Ninth Circuit's analysis, I find the Court's willingness to reverse a factbound determination of the Court of Appeals without engaging that court's reasoning a troubling departure from our normal practice.[1]

Accordingly, I respectfully dissent.

[1]The Court's opinion is somewhat ambiguous as to its reasons for overturning the portion of the Court of Appeals' decision setting aside the arbitration. It is unclear whether the majority is saying that a court may never set aside an arbitration because of a factual error, no matter how perverse, or whether the Court merely holds that the error in this case was not sufficiently severe to allow a court to take that step. If it is the latter, the Court offers no explanation of what standards it is using or of its reasons for reaching that conclusion.

The Advantages and Disadvantages of Private Arbitration as a Dispute Resolution Process

Private arbitration has both advantages and disadvantages as a dispute resolution process. Unlike negotiation which may just happen, the decision to arbitrate requires actual consent and planning by both parties because a neutral third party or a neutral panel will participate in the process.

If the decision to arbitrate a future dispute is made by contract (predispute mandatory arbitration provision), the arrangement smacks of overreaching by the party who drafted the contract. These contracts are adhesion contracts and the party who agrees to arbitrate has little or no power to negotiate for the exclusion of the arbitration provision, even if he or she knew the implications of the provision. This issue has been litigated, with the courts generally upholding the predispute provision.

In those cases where parties negotiate whether to arbitrate and the decision to arbitrate is made after the dispute has arisen, that decision is based on personal and business needs and interests and not on the law. The parties weigh the gains attributable through arbitration against the hypothetical gains that another process might produce. What does a party gain by selecting private arbitration as the method of dispute resolution?

Private arbitration, as do negotiation and private mediation, offers the parties complete flexibility. They can arrange when the arbitration will begin, where the arbitration will be held, and how the arbitration will be conducted. They must agree upon the selection of the arbitrator or arbitrators and how the arbitrator or arbitrators will be compensated. They can select an arbitrator or arbitrators with specialized expertise. In short, they can negotiate all the details about the arbitration or they can leave the details to the arbitrator, the arbitration panel, or an arbitration service.

Private arbitration, although informal, is significantly more formal than private mediation. The arbitrator or panel controls the process, directs the presentation of evidence, and decides the outcome of the dispute.

Unlike negotiation and mediation, private arbitration guarantees the parties that the dispute will be resolved by the end of the process (unless the parties decided before the arbitration that the arbitrator's or panel's award would be advisory and nonbinding). In private arbitration, the arbitrator or panel not only provides the process but also, as the trier of both the facts and the law, makes the award that resolves the dispute. The arbitrator or panel decides how the dispute will be resolved. The Uniform Arbitration Act, the Federal Arbitration Act, and state arbitration statutes do not direct the arbitrator or panel to apply the law to the dispute. Rather, legislation is silent on this matter. The parties, however, may in their arbitration agreement specify the rules to be followed in resolving the dispute and the arbitrator is obligated to adhere to this directive. Without such a directive, the arbitrator or panel is not bound by the law or by precedent and will resolve the dispute according to his or her sense of justice. The parties, in their opening statements and summations, will advise the arbitrator or panel on how they believe the dispute should be resolved, but the ultimate decision is that of the arbitrator or panel.

The arbitrator or arbitration panel is required to render an award. Depending on the preestablished procedural rules for the arbitration, the award may be rendered at the close of the arbitration or at a later date. If at a later date, the time within which the award must be made is stated in the procedural rules for the arbitration. The award is generally made as a brief written statement with no supporting explanations or reasons.

A private arbitration may reduce transaction costs but the reduction often will not be dramatic when compared to litigation. The parties will still be represented by counsel, and discovery will still be performed. The parties, however, have an opportunity to control discovery and thus attempt to reduce discovery costs. The case will still be presented to a trier of fact and of law through the use of opening statements, direct and cross-examination of witnesses including expert witnesses, exhibits, and closing arguments. Adding to the transaction costs are the administrative costs of the private arbitration, which may exceed the court costs associated with litigation.

When selecting private arbitration, the parties weigh the necessity of having the dispute resolved now by arbitration against what might happen if the dispute is not resolved now by this process. This involves weighing arbitration against all the other ADR processes (inaction, acquiescence, self-help, ombuds, negotiation, private mediation, and private judging) and against litigation.

The parties selecting private arbitration control only the initiation of the process (including the procedural and substantive rules, and the number, qualifications, and identification of the arbitrators). Once appointed, the arbitrator or arbitration panel takes control of the process and of the outcome. Generally, the arbitration is private and confidential with no public airing of the dispute. If the dispute is resolved through arbitration, the parties will preserve the privacy of their records and documents to the outside world. Unless a party later decides not to comply with the arbitrator's or panel's decree, the resolution of the dispute is final.

Generally the party dissatisfied with the arbitrator's or panel's award has no ground to appeal to a court. Since the grounds for appeal are quite limited, the arbitration award is virtually unreviewable.

Parties who select private arbitration as their method of dispute resolution forego the opportunity to litigate. Only when the arbitration award is advisory can the parties litigate before a court. The fact that a claimant receives a favorable award from the arbitrator or panel does not necessarily mean that the respondent will comply. Enforcement of the decree may present a problem. The prevailing party may, however, confirm the arbitration award into a judgment. A confirmed award has the same effect as a judgment and the prevailing party may use any of the means available to enforce a judgment.

Finally, although the arbitration process will be less formal than that of litigation, the award in private arbitration will provide the parties with a win/lose outcome and do little to promote a continuing business relationship between the parties. Figure 13-2 is a summary of private arbitration.

AVAILABILITY	always available
PROCESS SELECTION	the parties select the process and decide whether they want to create the process or whether they would like the arbitrator or arbitration service to create the process the parties control the scheduling, and the arbitration can be scheduled before a case is filed or at any time after filing
THE PARTICIPANTS	the parties, their attorneys, the arbitrator or arbitration panel, and the necessary witnesses
PREPARATION	fashion the rules for the process and select the number of arbitrators, what expertise they must have, and who they will be the parties determine the parameters of discovery the parties must prepare their evidence and their opening statements and closing arguments as if the arbitration hearing were a bench trial
THE PROCESS	takes place in a private setting more formal than mediation but less formal than litigation, with each party having an opportunity to present his or her case to the arbitrator or the arbitration panel confidential and preserves the privacy of the parties' records and documents
FAIRNESS	if the parties are represented by counsel, the power imbalances may be reduced in some, but not all cases
THE OUTCOME	does not allow the parties to control the outcome of their dispute since the arbitrator or arbitration panel will resolve the dispute does not encourage creative resolutions since the solution should be based on the law the parties have no control over the outcome arbitrator's or arbitration panel's award is enforceable as a judgment and is subject to very limited judicial review
COSTS	the parties pay the arbitrator or arbitrators and any costs involved private arbitration will be more expensive than mediation but could be less expensive than litigation if discovery is limited and the hearing length shortened private arbitration generally will save appeal costs because most issues are not appealable
PRECEDENTIAL VALUE	generally establishes no binding precedent although nonbinding precedent by performance may be created between the parties
IMPACT ON FUTURE RELATIONSHIP	does not encourage future cooperation or reduce confrontation between the parties

FIGURE 13-2 Private Arbitration

Key Terms and Phrases

final offer, last offer, or baseball arbitration
high/low or bounded arbitration
private arbitration
procedural arbitrability
substantive arbitrability

Review Questions

True/False Questions

1. T F In private arbitration, the jury is the finder of fact and the judge is the finder of law.
2. T F In private arbitration, the parties must be represented by legal counsel.
3. T F In private arbitration, the outcome is based more on the needs and interests of the parties than the law.
4. T F In private arbitration, the parties negotiate the rules although the negotiation may consist of agreeing on an arbitration service.
5. T F Private arbitration leads to a win/win solution.
6. T F Private arbitration may be conducted before or after a complaint is filed with the court.
7. T F Private arbitration generally takes place over a period of time and may start and stop.
8. T F An effective arbitration is based on preparation.
9. T F Private arbitration is consensual and can be terminated by either party at any time.
10. T F An agreement to arbitration is enforceable as a contract.
11. T F An arbitration award may be entered as a judgment and is enforceable as any other judgment issued by a court.
12. T F During an arbitration, a dominant party may take advantage of a weaker party through psychological gamesmanship.
13. T F A court may find an agreement to arbitrate unenforceable if at the time of contracting one of the parties took an unconscionable advantage over the other, committed fraud or duress, or misrepresented material facts.
14. T F Arbitration gives the parties control over the outcome.
15. T F Arbitration is designed so one party wins and the other loses.
16. T F Arbitration awards are similar to court judgments in that they are appealable to a higher tribunal.

Fill-in-the-Blank Questions

1. _____ An arbitration where the arbitrator or arbitration panel must select either the claimant's or the respondent's offer.

2. _____ The arbitration where the arbitrator's or arbitration panel's award must not exceed the claimant's demand or be below the respondent's counteroffer.

3. _____ The decision of the arbitrator or arbitration panel.

Multiple-Choice Questions

1. Which of the following always participate in private arbitration as a dispute resolution process:
   (a) the aggrieved party
   (b) the other party to the dispute
   (c) a neutral third party
   (d) a jury
   (e) the attorney for the aggrieved party

2. Private arbitration is classified as:
   (a) unilateral action in dispute resolution
   (b) bilateral action in dispute resolution
   (c) third-party evaluation as a prelude to dispute resolution
   (d) third-party assistance in dispute resolution
   (e) third-party adjudication in dispute resolution

Short-Answer Questions

1. Cynthia Rogers has filed a sexual harassment complaint in federal court against her employer, Galaxy Realty Company. Galaxy has offered to settle this dispute through private arbitration and to pay all the costs for the arbitration, including Cynthia's attorney, if Cynthia would dismiss her claim in federal court.
   Should Cynthia accept Galaxy's offer to arbitrate?

2. Discuss the advantages and disadvantages of private arbitration as a dispute resolution process.

3. Is private mediation or private arbitration more popular in the United States and why?

4. Discuss how a predispute arbitration provision may place an individual consumer at a disadvantage against a merchant?

5. Discuss the role of the arbitrator in a private arbitration.

6. Discuss the role of the courts in reviewing arbitrators' decisions.

7. Discuss whether private arbitration or private mediation is the better dispute resolution process for domestic relations disputes such as custody, support, visitation, and property distribution.

Role-Play Exercises

Role-Play Exercise 13-1   Sports Law

Return to Role-Play Exercise 6-2 concerning sports law. Change the dispute resolution process from negotiation to private "baseball" arbitration by adding a three-member arbitration panel. This exercise will be conducted without attorneys and with the same representatives as in previous versions of this problem.

The Players: Agent for Darrell James, a pitcher for a major league baseball team
The general manager for the baseball team
Three members of the arbitration panel

If you are representing the claimant or the respondent, check Figure 6-1, Work Sheet for Dissecting the Content of a Negotiation, as you plan for the arbitration. Will this information be helpful in creating your arbitration plan? What should you tell the arbitration panel?

Role-Play Exercise 13-2   Racial Discrimination

Return to Role-Play Exercise 6-3 concerning racial discrimination. Change the dispute resolution process from negotiation to private arbitration by adding attorneys and a panel of arbitrators.

The Players: Mr. Jefferson
Mr. Jefferson's attorney
A vice president for Big Sky
Big Sky's attorney
Three arbitrators

CHAPTER 14

Court-Annexed Arbitration

As noted in Chapter 1, some forms of ADR that were traditionally public processes have become private processes as well, and some ADR processes that were traditionally private processes have become public processes. Arbitration, a traditionally private ADR process, is now used by some courts after the litigation process has been initiated.

The first court-annexed or court-ordered arbitration programs in federal district courts trace back to 1978 when the Northern District of California and the Eastern District of Pennsylvania began their programs. In the mid 1980s eight more districts added court-annexed arbitration programs to their dispute resolution processes. In 1988 Congress formally authorized the 10 district courts to continue their pilot programs and authorized an additional 10 districts to establish voluntary arbitration programs. See 28 U.S.C. §§ 651–658. By 1994, 12 districts had added voluntary arbitration programs and two of the original 10 mandatory programs had changed to voluntary programs (see Figure 14-1). Under the voluntary arbitration programs, the court's referral to arbitration required consent from all parties.

The latter half of the 1990s saw interest in court-annexed arbitration in federal court wane. By the end of the federal year 2000 (September 30), the number of districts having court-annexed arbitration programs had decreased to 10. And even within the 10, only 5 had referred 10 or more cases to arbitration during the preceding twelve months (see Figure 14-2).

About 20 states by statute or court rule have court-annexed arbitration. These states include California, Florida, Hawaii, Indiana, Pennsylvania, and Washington.

Mandatory Arbitration Programs	Voluntary Arbitration Programs	Additional Mandatory Arbitration Programs
Northern District of California (1978)	Eastern District of Washington (1988)	District of Rhode Island (1995)
Eastern District of Pennsylvania (1978)	Middle District of Georgia (1991)	
Middle District of Florida (1984)	Northern District of New York (1991)	
Western District of Michigan (1985)*	Northern District of Ohio (1991)**	
Western District of Missouri (1985)*	Western District of Pennsylvania (1991)	
District of New Jersey (1985)	District of Arizona (1992)	
Middle District of North Carolina (1985)	Southern District of California (1992)**	
Western District of Oklahoma (1985)	District of Idaho (1992)	
Western District of Texas (1985)	Western District of New York (1992)	
Eastern District of New York (1986)	Western District of Washington (1992)	
	District of Utah (1993)**	
	Northern District of Alabama (1994)	

* Changed to voluntary in 1992
** In these few voluntary arbitration districts, a judge could also order court-annexed arbitration on a case by case basis.

FIGURE 14-1 Federal Court-Annexed Arbitration Programs

United States District Court	Cases Filed	Cases Referred to Arbitration
Northern District of California	5,814	306
Middle District of Florida	7,017	590
Western District of Michigan	1,574	—
Western District of Missouri	1,633	1
District of New Jersey	6,485	2,098
Eastern District of New York	8,664	378
Middle District of North Carolina	1,288	—
Western District of Oklahoma	2,395	5
Eastern District of Pennsylvania	8,548	948
Western District of Texas	3,231	—
total	46,645	4,326

FIGURE 14-2 Civil Cases Referred to Arbitration by a Federal District Court during the 12-Month Period Ending September 30, 2000*

* data found in Table S-12, federal courts website *http://www.uscourts.gov/judbus2000/contents.html*

Problem 14-1

Does your state by statute or court rule authorize the use of court-annexed arbitration? Check your state court's website for its menu of ADR programs.

Court-Annexed Arbitration

Court-annexed arbitration provides the litigants with an abbreviated bench-type trial that is conducted without the formality required by the state or Federal Rules of Evidence and state or Federal Rules of Civil Procedure.

Court-annexed arbitration provides the litigants with an abbreviated bench-type trial (i.e., a trial without a jury) but with less formality when compared to a full trial before a judge. In court-annexed arbitration, the state or Federal Rules of Evidence and state or Federal Rules of Civil Procedure are relaxed.

Court-annexed arbitration is closely related to private arbitration; however, several crucial differences between the two exist. Private arbitration is voluntary. The parties select arbitration as their method of dispute resolution (although the private arbitration may have been selected predispute when the parties contracted) and may negotiate the rules for the arbitration and the time and setting for the arbitration hearing, and may select the arbitrator. In contrast, the remaining five active federal court-annexed arbitration programs are mandatory. If litigation has been filed in the federal court in one of these districts, the parties must participate in the arbitration process if the court determines the case falls within the scope of the court's arbitration program. The parties have no say in the rules that govern the arbitration because the rules are those published by the court in its local rules and they are universal in that they apply to all the arbitrations sponsored by the court.

Trial de novo

A trial de novo is a trial from the beginning and proceeds as if no court-annexed arbitration has taken place.

Private arbitration is binding, unless the parties have previously decided that the arbitrator's award should not be binding. The arbitrator's award is generally final and nonappealable with only a limited opportunity for judicial review. Court-annexed arbitration awards, on the other hand, are nonbinding. A party to the court-annexed arbitration has the power to disregard the award and ask the court for a trial de novo. A **trial de novo** is a trial from the beginning and proceeds as if no court-annexed arbitration had taken place. If the application for a trial de novo is not filed within the time frame specified by the court's local rules, the arbitrator's award becomes binding and is entered in the record as a final judgment.

The Court-Appointed List of Arbitrators

Court-annexed arbitration uses prescreened members of the local bar association as arbitrators. The court's local rules usually require an arbitrator to be a member of the state bar for a certain number of years, be admitted to practice before that court, and be approved by the chief judge of the district as a person competent to perform the duties of an arbitrator. An advisory committee consisting of members of the bar may assist the chief judge in screening applicants. These attorneys are selected for the court's arbitration panel because they are recognized by the court and their peers as experienced members of the practicing bar, have expertise in the subject matter, have judicial temperament, and have expressed a willingness to serve.

Once the screening has been completed, the chief judge certifies those persons who are eligible and qualified to serve as arbitrators in the court's arbitration program. The names of those attorneys certified are then placed on the court's list of available arbitrators. They are trained by the court and are appointed on a case-by-case basis.

The Court-Annexed Arbitration Process

The court-annexed arbitration process is governed by the court's local rules. The process has the following components:

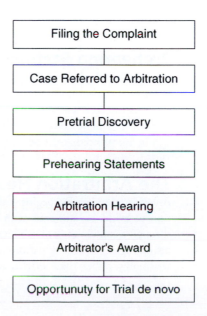

Filing the Complaint

Case Referred to Arbitration

Pretrial Discovery

Prehearing Statements

Arbitration Hearing

Arbitrator's Award

Opportunuty for Trial de novo

Filing of the Complaint and the Referral to Arbitration

After a complaint is filed with the Office of the Clerk of the Court, the case is evaluated against the criteria in the court's local rules to determine whether it comes within the court's arbitration program. Cases that come within the program's subject matter and jurisdictional amount are then assigned to the court-annexed arbitration program and the parties are notified.

As cases are scheduled for arbitration, a judge or the program's administrator selects an arbitrator from the court's list of arbitrators and assigns him or her to the arbitration. In some programs or in some cases, a panel of three arbitrators is assigned.

Pretrial Discovery and the Timing of the Arbitration Hearing

Under the court's local rules, the parties are required to complete all pretrial discovery prior to the arbitration hearing. Some courts resist extending the discovery deadlines. For example, in the United States District Court for New Jersey, where the largest number of court-annexed arbitration cases are being processed, the court takes the following position on delays in discovery:

> Unlike other cases, these dates [the pretrial discovery dates] will not be extended except where a new party has been joined recently or an *exceptional* reason is presented to the Judge or Magistrate Judge. Extended discovery and the final pretrial conference will be eliminated. This means that approximately one (1) month following the filing of the last answer plus a 120–day discovery period, or at such other date as set by the scheduling order, the case will be set for arbitration through the Arbitration Clerk.

United States District Court for the District of New Jersey, Appendix M, Guidelines for Arbitration, § 1, Case Management Responsibility of the Assigned District Judge. *http://www.pacer.njd.uscourts.gov/*

Prehearing Statements

Prior to the arbitration hearing, each litigant may be required to submit a prehearing statement to the arbitrator and the opposing party. The prehearing statement includes a statement of the facts and the party's position on damages, a list of expert and nonexpert witnesses who will be called to testify, and a list of all exhibits and documentary evidence that will be introduced at the hearing.

The Arbitration Hearing

An arbitration hearing begins with opening statements, followed by the summary presentation of evidence, and ends with closing arguments. The attorneys present their evidence through a combination of exhibits, affidavits, deposition transcripts, and expert reports. Live testimony of witnesses is permitted, if the credibility of a witness may be in issue. Live expert testimony, rather than written reports, is permitted when direct and cross-examination would help the arbitrator resolve critical differences of opinion between the experts. The sequence of events for an arbitration hearing is as follows:

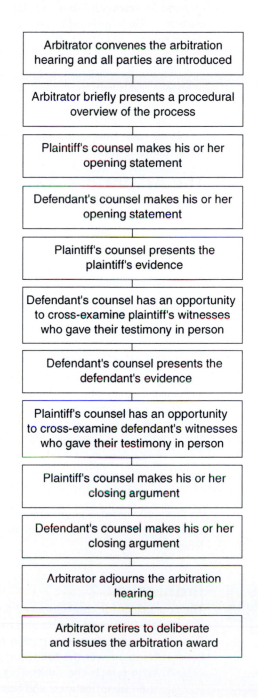

The court, by appointing the arbitrator, delegates to the arbitrator the power to control and regulate the scope and duration of the arbitration hearing. The arbitrator may begin the hearing in the absence of a party, rule on requests of counsel to excuse individual parties or corporate representatives from attending the arbitration hearing; rule on the admissibility of evidence, including the admissibility of testimonial, documentary, and demonstrative evidence; rule on objections to the evidence; limit the time for the presentation of evidence and the summary arguments by the parties; compel the presence of witnesses; swear in witnesses; and adjourn the arbitration hearing to a date certain to accommodate lengthy proceedings or an unavailable witness whom the arbitrator determines to be essential to the proceedings.

The arbitrator does not have the power to continue the hearing for an indefinite time or exercise civil or criminal contempt.

If the court rules so provide, a party may have the arbitration hearing recorded and a transcript made at his or her own expense.

The Arbitrator's Award

The arbitrator adjudicates the facts, selects the law that will apply to the facts, and applies the law to the facts. Following the arbitration hearing, the arbitrator issues an award. The actual award need not be limited to the jurisdictional limit (i.e., the court's local rule's monetary limit below which the case could be referred to arbitration). The arbitrator's award also may include interest and punitive damages, if appropriate.

After the arbitration hearing, the arbitrator files the award with the Clerk of the Court. The clerk's office dockets the fact that an award had been made although leaving out the details of the award. The clerk's office mails a copy of the award and the arbitrator's written basis for the award to the arbitrator and the attorneys.

Opportunity for a Trial de novo

The local court rules will specify the number of days a party has to reject the arbitrator's award and demand a trial de novo. Some courts provide parties 30 days in which to make the request.

If the case goes to a trial de novo, neither the fact that the case went to arbitration nor the amount of the award is admissible. Testimony given during an arbitration hearing is inadmissible unless it is used to impeach the credibility of a witness.

Comparing Court-Annexed Arbitration Programs

As previously noted, a court-annexed arbitration program is governed by statute or local court rule. Although the programs are similar from court to court and state to state, differences do exist.

Problem 14-2

The court rules for court-annexed arbitration of United States District Court for the Middle District of Florida and the United States District Court for the Northern District of California are located in Appendices G and H, respectively. Use these court rules to answer the following questions:

1. Who selects the arbitrators for the court's panel of arbitrators, what are their qualifications, and how are they trained to be arbitrators?

2. What categories of cases are assigned to arbitration?
3. What is the maximum monetary amount for arbitration?
4. What is the process for a case to be sent to arbitration?
5. Do the parties have any input on whether their case will go to arbitration?
6. How is the date for calendaring the arbitration hearing selected?
7. What are the rules for the hearing?
8. How long does the arbitrator have to make the award, what are the parameters for the award, and must the arbitrator provide his or her reasoning for making the award?
9. How long does a party have to request a trial de novo?

Problem 14-3

The Nevada Supreme Court authorizes court-annexed arbitration. The Court's rules are located at http://www.leg.state.nv.us/other/cr/Nar.html. Use these court rules to answer the following questions:

1. Who selects the arbitrators for the court's panel of arbitrators, what are their qualifications, and how are they trained to be arbitrators?
2. What categories of cases are assigned to arbitration?
3. What is the maximum monetary amount for arbitration?
4. What is the process for a case to be sent to arbitration?
5. Do the parties have any input on whether their case will go to arbitration?
6. How is the date for calendaring the arbitration hearing selected?
7. What are the rules for the hearing?
8. How long does the arbitrator have to make the award, what are the parameters for the award, and must the arbitrator provide his or her reasoning for making the award?
9. How long does a party have to request a trial de novo?
10. Compare your answers to your answers in Problem 14-2 for the United States District Court for the Middle District of Florida. Are your answers the same or different?

Problem 14-4

Hawaii has court-annexed arbitration by court rule. These court rules are located in Appendix I. Use these court rules to answer the following questions:

1. Who selects the arbitrators for the court's panel of arbitrators, what are their qualifications, and how are they trained to be arbitrators?
2. What categories of cases are assigned to arbitration?
3. What is the maximum monetary amount for arbitration?
4. What is the process for a case to be sent to arbitration?
5. Do the parties have any input on whether their case will go to arbitration?
6. How is the date for calendaring the arbitration hearing selected?
7. What are the rules for the hearing?
8. How long does the arbitrator have to make the award, what are the parameters for the award, and must the arbitrator provide his or her reasoning for making the award?

9. How long does a party have to request a trial de novo?
10. Compare your answers to your answers in Problem 14-3 for the state courts in Nevada. Are your answers the same or different?

Preparing for Court-Annexed Arbitration

Seldom will a party file a civil complaint *pro se.* A party who files a complaint *pro se* files on his or her own behalf and is not represented by an attorney. In cases where the complaint has not been filed *pro se,* the litigants' attorneys and the attorneys' paralegals will conduct the discovery for a court-annexed arbitration.

Court-annexed arbitration requires the same discovery as if the case were scheduled for trial. In fact, if the arbitrator's award is rejected and a trial de novo requested, the case will go to trial on the same discovery that was conducted for the arbitration. Therefore, the attorney and his or her paralegal should approach discovery as if the case were going to trial.

The preparation for arbitration requires an emphasis on exhibits, affidavits, deposition transcripts, and expert reports with a deemphasis on live witness testimony. Preparation should be made for a case before the arbitrator and not a case before a jury. Preparation also should be made for a presentation that will move more rapidly since the arbitration hearing will be substantially shorter in duration than a trial because of the abbreviated nature of the presentation and the reduced reliance on the state or Federal Rules of Evidence and state or Federal Rules of Civil Procedure.

Those present at the arbitration hearing include the arbitrator, the litigants, their attorneys and their attorneys' paralegals, and a limited number of witnesses who will testify. The litigants' role in the arbitration hearing is limited to sitting next to their attorneys at counsel table (and conferring with their attorneys) and testifying under oath if their live testimony is necessary. The litigants have no role in deciding the outcome of their case, with the exception of conferring with counsel on the facts and strategy.

The paralegals are present to assist their attorneys, much as they would do if the case were before a judge rather than before an arbitrator. The paralegals may have prepared many of the exhibits and may have organized the affidavits, deposition transcripts, and expert reports. The paralegals will assist their attorneys with managing these materials as the presentation of evidence unfolds.

The Advantages and Disadvantages of Court-Annexed Arbitration as a Dispute Resolution Process

Court-annexed arbitration may take place after a civil complaint has been filed in a state or federal district court that maintains such a program. This ADR process is touted as providing litigants with a prompt and less-expensive alternative to the traditional courtroom trial. Court-annexed arbitration also was designed to relieve the heavy burden of the court's constantly increasing caseload.

Court-annexed arbitration is more prompt than a full trial, especially if the trial is a jury trial. By eliminating the jury, voir dire, side bar discussions, instructions to the jury, and jury deliberation, a significant amount of trial time is saved. In preparation for arbitration, court rules can significantly reduce extensions on discovery deadlines inherent in a trial. By maintaining firm discovery deadlines for arbitration, the case can come to a hearing before it would come to trial. By replacing many of the live witnesses, including expert witnesses, with exhibits, affidavits, deposition transcripts, and expert reports, and by significantly reducing the formality required by the court's rules of evidence and civil procedure, an arbitration hearing can be completed in a fraction of the time needed to complete a courtroom trial before a trial court judge. By shifting the adjudicator from a trial court judge to a court-appointed arbitrator and by reducing the time required to complete the presentation of evidence, the hearing phase of the process can be completed with little or no interruption that was caused by the hearing officer being called away to deal with other matters. The court-appointed arbitrator can focus on the case being arbitrated rather than constantly having to shift focus to other matters on his or her calendar. By reducing the number of live witnesses thus reducing the hearing time and by eliminating the jury, the case would not require scheduling into a large courtroom. Also, by freeing the district court judge to hear other cases in his or her courtroom, arbitration with court-appointed arbitrators permits more cases to be heard at one time.

Court-annexed arbitration may or may not be less expensive in the long run when compared to a trial. The pretrial discovery may be comparable in expense. Pretrial discovery, whether for the arbitration hearing or for the trial, must be completed before the adjudication hearing. Arbitration saves attorneys' costs and some witness expenses because of the comparative durations of the hearings and the number of witnesses being presented at each. While there is some savings by taking a case through court-annexed arbitration, the key issue on expense is whether the arbitrator's award will be disregarded and a trial de novo requested. If the arbitration is followed by a trial, the total costs for arbitration plus litigation will exceed the costs for litigation alone. The potential for cost savings, reducing the time from filing to disposition of the case, and lessening the burden on the courts is lost if the arbitrator's award is rejected and a trial de novo requested.

Another disadvantage relates to the fact that arbitration and litigation are both adjudicative processes, requiring a neutral third party who resolves the dispute for the parties. In court-annexed arbitration, the plaintiff has filed a complaint in the trial court seeking a decision by a trial court judge. Instead, the plaintiff gets a decision by a colleague in the bar. The parties may view the arbitrator's award as less authoritative since their colleagues from the bar do not have a lifetime appointment or even a term appointment and do not render judicial decisions on a daily basis. Figure 14-3 is a summary of court-annexed arbitration.

AVAILABILITY	the litigation process must have been initiated and the court must have a court-annexed arbitration program
PROCESS SELECTION	by the court if the cases comes within the court's criteria for arbitration local court rules describe the rules for the process local court rules designate the number of arbitrators (one or three), what expertise they must have, what they will be paid, and how an attorney can become an arbitrator for the court the court's administrator will designate the arbitrator from the court's list of arbitrators the court controls the scheduling
THE PARTICIPANTS	the parties and their attorneys, the court-appointed arbitrator or arbitration panel, and any necessary witnesses
PREPARATION	the parties must prepare their evidence and their opening statements and closing arguments as if the arbitration hearing were a bench trial
THE PROCESS	takes place in a public setting more formal than mediation but less formal than litigation, with each party having an opportunity to present his or her case to the arbitrator or the arbitration panel does not preserve the privacy of the parties' records and documents
FAIRNESS	since the parties are represented by counsel, the power imbalances may be reduced in some, but not all, cases
THE OUTCOME	court-annexed arbitration does not allow the parties to control the outcome of their dispute since the arbitrator or arbitration panel will resolve the dispute does not encourage creative resolutions since the solution should be based on the law the parties have no control over the outcome at the end of the court-annexed arbitration, the dispute will be resolved although a party can seek a trial de novo arbitrator's or arbitration panel's award is enforceable as a judgment unless a party requests a trial de novo
COSTS	the parties pay according to the court's local rules court-annexed arbitration will be more expensive than mediation but could be less expensive than litigation if discovery is limited, the hearing length shortened, and the case does not proceed to a trial de novo
PRECEDENTIAL VALUE	generally establishes no binding precedent although nonbinding precedent by performance may be created between the parties
IMPACT ON FUTURE RELATIONSHIP	does not encourage future cooperation or reduce confrontation between the parties

FIGURE 14-3 Court-Annexed Arbitration

Key Terms and Phrases

court-annexed arbitration
trial de novo

Review Questions

True/False Questions

1. T F In court-annexed arbitration, the jury is the finder of fact and the judge is the finder of law.

2. T F In court-annexed arbitration, the parties must be represented by legal counsel.

3. T   F   In court-annexed arbitration, the outcome is based more on the needs and interests of the parties than the law.

4. T   F   In court-annexed arbitration, the parties negotiate the rules although the negotiation may consist of agreeing on an arbitration service.

5. T   F   Court-annexed arbitration leads to a win/win solution.

6. T   F   Court-annexed arbitration may be conducted before or after a complaint is filed with the court.

7. T   F   Court-annexed arbitration generally takes place over a period of time and may start and stop.

8. T   F   An effective court-annexed arbitration is based on preparation.

9. T   F   Court-annexed arbitration is consensual and can be terminated by either party at any time.

10. T   F   To initiate court-annexed arbitration, the parties petition the court to arbitrate rather than litigate the dispute.

11. T   F   Unless a party requests a trial de novo, the court-annexed arbitration award is entered as a judgment and is enforceable as any other judgment issued by a court.

12. T   F   During a court-annexed arbitration, a dominant party may take advantage of a weaker party through psychological gamesmanship.

13. T   F   Court-annexed arbitration gives the parties control over the outcome.

14. T   F   Court-annexed arbitration is designed so one party wins and the other loses.

15. T   F   Court-annexed arbitration awards are similar to court judgments in that they are appealable to a higher tribunal.

Fill-in-the-Blank Questions

1. _____ What a party requires when he or she rejects the arbitrator's award.

2. _____ Another name for court-annexed arbitration.

3. _____ The sources of authority for court-annexed arbitration.

Multiple-Choice Questions

1. Which of the following always participate in court-annexed arbitration as a dispute resolution process:
   (a) the aggrieved party
   (b) the other party to the dispute
   (c) a neutral third party
   (d) a jury
   (e) the attorney for the aggrieved party

2. Court-annexed arbitration is classified as:
   (a) unilateral action in dispute resolution
   (b) bilateral action in dispute resolution
   (c) third-party evaluation as a prelude to dispute resolution
   (d) third-party assistance in dispute resolution

(e) third-party adjudication in dispute resolution

Short-Answer Questions

1. Cynthia Rogers has filed a sexual harassment complaint in federal court against her employer, Galaxy Realty Company. Galaxy has offered to settle this dispute through private arbitration and to pay all the costs for the arbitration, including Cynthia's attorney, if Cynthia would dismiss her claim in federal court.

   Cynthia, after considering Galaxy's offer for private arbitration, has rejected it. After rejecting Galaxy's offer, Cynthia learned that the federal court in which her complaint was filed has court-annexed arbitration and that her case comes within the guidelines for arbitration and will more than likely be sent to court-annexed arbitration.

   Galaxy has renewed its offer for private arbitration. Should Cynthia now accept Galaxy's offer or would she be better off to let the court process proceed to court-annexed arbitration?

2. Discuss the advantages and disadvantages of court-annexed arbitration as a dispute resolution process.

3. Is court-sponsored mediation or court-annexed arbitration more popular in the United States and why?

4. Discuss the role of the arbitrator in a court-annexed arbitration.

5. Discuss the role of the courts in reviewing the arbitrator's decisions made during the arbitration and the arbitrator's award.

6. Discuss whether court-annexed arbitration or court-sponsored mediation is the better dispute resolution process for domestic relations disputes such as custody, support, visitation, and property distribution.

CHAPTER 15

Mediation-Arbitration

The Mediation-Arbitration (Med-Arb) Process

Mediation-Arbitration (Med-Arb)
In med-arb the parties agree that the process will begin as a private mediation and, if they are unable to reach a mediated agreement, the process shifts to private arbitration.

Mediation-arbitration (med-arb) is a combination of mediation and arbitration. In med-arb the parties agree that the process will begin as a private mediation and if they are unable to reach a mediated agreement, the process shifts to private arbitration. The arbitrator may, or may not, depending on the prior agreement of the parties, be the same person as the mediator. If the arbitrator is not the mediator, the process may be called "med then arb."

At the end of the process, the disputants will have a resolution for their dispute. They can either resolve their dispute themselves making a decision based on their needs and interests, or they can have a neutral third party resolve the dispute for them based on the law.

The Advantages and Disadvantages of Mediation-Arbitration as a Dispute Resolution Process

Mediation-arbitration has many of the advantages and disadvantages of both mediation and arbitration with a few exceptions. Unlike a process that is just private arbitration where the parties have no opportunity to resolve their own dispute, in med-arb the parties first have an opportunity to resolve their dispute through the first stage of the process, mediation. Also, unlike a process that is just private mediation where the dispute may not have been resolved when the process ends, in med-arb the second stage of the process, private arbitration, guarantees a resolution. See Figure 15-1 for a summary of the mediation-arbitration (med-arb) process.

Problem 15-1
What are the advantages of using the same person as both the mediator and the arbitrator?

Problem 15-2
1. Would using the same person as both the mediator and the arbitrator have a chilling effect on the mediation?
2. Could this chilling effect be reduced if the arbitrator gave only an advisory opinion rather than a binding award?
3. What would the process lose if the arbitrator gave only an advisory opinion rather than a binding award?

AVAILABILITY	always available
PROCESS SELECTION	the parties select the process and decide whether they want to create the process or whether they would like the mediator-arbitrator or mediation-arbitration provider to create the process
	the parties decide whether the mediator shall also be the arbitrator
	the parties choose the mediator and the number of arbitrators, what expertise they must have, and who they will be
	the parties control the scheduling and the mediation and arbitration processes can be scheduled before a case is filed or at any time after filing and can schedule the arbitration to immediately follow the mediation or to follow at some later date
THE PARTICIPANTS	the parties, their attorneys, the mediator, the arbitrator or arbitration panel (although the mediator may also be the arbitrator), and the necessary witnesses for the arbitration
PREPARATION	fashion the rules for the process and select the mediator and the number of arbitrators, what expertise they must have, and who they will be
	the parties determine the parameters of discovery
	the parties must prepare their evidence and their opening and closing statements as if the arbitration hearing were a bench trial
THE PROCESS	takes place in a private setting
	the mediation is less formal than the arbitration, with each party having an opportunity to discuss his or her perception of the dispute, his or her feelings, interests, and proposed solutions; the arbitration is less formal than litigation, with each party having an opportunity to present his or her case to the arbitrator or the arbitration panel
	confidential and preserves the privacy of the parties' records and documents
FAIRNESS	if the parties are represented by counsel, the power imbalances may be reduced in some, but not all cases
THE OUTCOME	the mediation allows the parties to control the outcome of their dispute since they resolve their own dispute; the arbitration does not allow the parties to control the outcome of their dispute since the arbitrator or arbitration panel will resolve the dispute
	mediation encourages creative resolutions since the solution is based primarily on the parties' needs and interests; arbitration does not encourage creative resolutions since the solution should be based on the law
	the dispute will be resolved by the end of the med-arb process
	a mediated settlement is enforceable as a contract; the arbitrator's or arbitration panel's award is enforceable as a judgment and is generally not subject to judicial review
COSTS	the parties pay the mediator and arbitrator or arbitrators and pay any costs involved
	med-arb will be more expensive than mediation but could be less expensive than litigation if discovery is limited and the hearing length shortened
	will save appeal costs
PRECEDENTIAL VALUE	generally establishes no binding precedent, although nonbinding precedent by performance may be created between the parties
IMPACT ON FUTURE RELATIONSHIP	the mediation will encourage future cooperation or will reduce confrontation between the parties; the arbitration will not encourage future cooperation or will not reduce confrontation between the parties

FIGURE 15-1 Mediation-Arbitration (Med-Arb)

Key Terms and Phrases

mediation-arbitration (med-arb)

Review Questions

True-False Questions

1. T F In med-arb, the jury is the finder of fact and the judge is the finder of law.
2. T F Med-arb is more of a case management tool than a dispute resolution process.
3. T F The parties can streamline issues and discovery at med-arb.
4. T F Med-arb gives the parties an objective evaluation of the case.
5. T F Med-arb is conducted by the judge who will try the case.
6. T F Med-arb is a court-sponsored program and occurs after the complaint has been filed and before trial.
7. T F Med-arb is generally held after discovery has been completed.
8. T F Med-arb is confidential and preserves the confidentiality of private records.
9. T F Med-arb is another name for a mini-trial.
10. T F Med-arb is better suited for issues of law than for questions of fact.

Fill-in-the-Blank Questions

1. _____ List four advantages of med-arb.

   _____

   _____

   _____

2. _____ List four disadvantages of med-arb.

   _____

   _____

   _____

Multiple-Choice Questions

1. Which of the following actively participates in med-arb:
   (a) the aggrieved party
   (b) the other party to the dispute
   (c) a neutral third party
   (d) a jury
   (e) the attorney for the aggrieved party

2. Med-arb is classified as:
   (a) unilateral action in dispute resolution
   (b) bilateral action in dispute resolution
   (c) third-party evaluation as a prelude to dispute resolution
   (d) third-party assistance in dispute resolution
   (e) third-party adjudication in dispute resolution

3. The primary functions of med-arb are:
   (a) to streamline discovery issues
   (b) to give the parties a setting to discuss settlement
   (c) to give the parties an objective evaluation of their case
   (d) to clear the court's docket
   (e) to have the case decided by a neutral third party

Short-Answer Question

The public school teachers who are members of Teachers Local 405 have been working without a contract for the past 16 months. Local 405 has attempted to negotiate a new contract with the school board for over two years but with little success. Local 405 has threatened to strike.

The school board has proposed med-arb. Should Local 405 accept the school board's offer?

CHAPTER 16

Litigation

Although litigation is generally not considered ADR, an *alternative* method of dispute resolution, its inclusion in this text is essential if comparisons are to be made between alternative methods and litigation. Therefore, for comparison purposes, some knowledge of litigation is necessary.

Litigation is the most complex of all forms of dispute resolution. The parties must follow the court's established rules of procedure and its rules of evidence. The process is filled with technical complaints, answers, motions, objections, rulings, depositions under oath, examination and cross-examination of witnesses under oath, jury instructions (if a jury has been seated), and trial briefs. The judge controls the process and rules as to the outcome. The outcome is based on the law and not on the needs and interests of the parties. The technical rules of procedure and rules of evidence play an extremely important role in the outcome.

After a judgment is rendered, there can be a motion for new trial, an appeal, appellate briefs, and possibly oral arguments before an appellate court. If the judgment of the trial court is reversed, the appellate court may order a new trial and the process begins anew.

Even when a complaint is filed to initiate the litigation process, most cases, more than 90 percent, are resolved before the litigation process has been completed. This means that initiating the litigation process is a vehicle to a negotiated or mediated settlement.

The Litigation Process

Before a lawsuit is initiated, a dispute must exist and one of the parties must feel, for whatever reason, that a court's intervention is necessary to resolve the dispute. In most cases, an aggrieved party seeks the advice of an attorney who thoroughly investigates the situation. In cases that could be before a small claims court and in a few other cases, a claimant may decide to pursue litigation without the assistance of an attorney and therefore proceeds *pro se.*

The attorney determines whether the law furnishes a remedy for this dispute. If the courts do not provide redress for the claimant's injury, a lawsuit would be a waste of time and money.

Even if the law does provide redress for the injury, the attorney must determine whether the claimant has a high enough probability of winning the lawsuit, and winning with sufficient recovery, to make the lawsuit worthwhile. Can the party who caused the injury, the witnesses, and the documents be found and brought into court? Whose witnesses and evidence are more likely to be believed? What defenses will be raised and how effective will they be?

Finally, the attorney considers whether good business sense dictates that a lawsuit not be pursued, even if the claimant could win. Is it worth the time, the effort, the actual expense, and the psychological trauma, to make litigation a viable method of dispute resolution? Will the party who would become the defendant be able to satisfy (i.e., to pay) the judgment? Will the publicity of a lawsuit damage the claimant's reputation or cause the claimant to lose goodwill? Should another form of dispute resolution be pursued (e.g., self-help, negotiation, ombuds, mediation, or arbitration) or should the claimant not pursue the matter at all (inaction or acquiescence)?

Figure 16-1 outlines the steps of a civil lawsuit from the claimant's point of view. Note the complexity of the process.

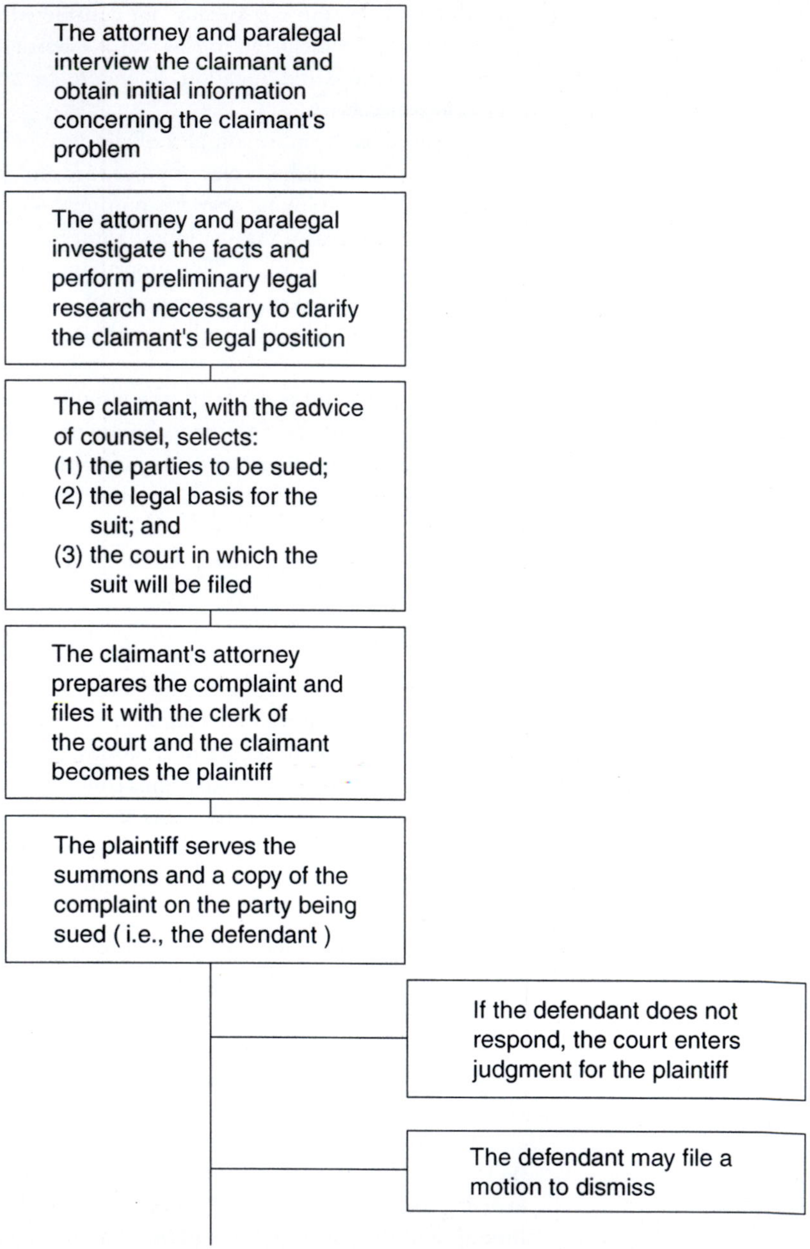

The attorney and paralegal interview the claimant and obtain initial information concerning the claimant's problem

The attorney and paralegal investigate the facts and perform preliminary legal research necessary to clarify the claimant's legal position

The claimant, with the advice of counsel, selects:
(1) the parties to be sued;
(2) the legal basis for the suit; and
(3) the court in which the suit will be filed

The claimant's attorney prepares the complaint and files it with the clerk of the court and the claimant becomes the plaintiff

The plaintiff serves the summons and a copy of the complaint on the party being sued (i.e., the defendant)

If the defendant does not respond, the court enters judgment for the plaintiff

The defendant may file a motion to dismiss

FIGURE 16-1 The Order of Events in Civil Litigation

If the court sustains the
defendant's motion to
dismiss, the court enters a
judgment for the defendant;
the plaintiff takes nothing
and pays the costs

The defendant files an answer:
(1) admitting to some of the
    plaintiff's allegations
    and denying others;
(2) asserting affirmative
    defenses;
(3) asserting counterclaims;
(4) asserting cross-claims

The plaintiff files a reply
to any counterclaim or other
new matter asserted in the
defendant's answer

The plaintiff and defendant
conduct discovery which
may involve:
(1) depositions;
(2) interrogatories;
(3) requests for admissions;
(4) orders for the production
    of documents and other
    items;
(5) requests for physical and
    mental examinations

Either the plaintiff, the
defendant, or both may file
a motion for summary judgment

FIGURE 16-1 *continued*

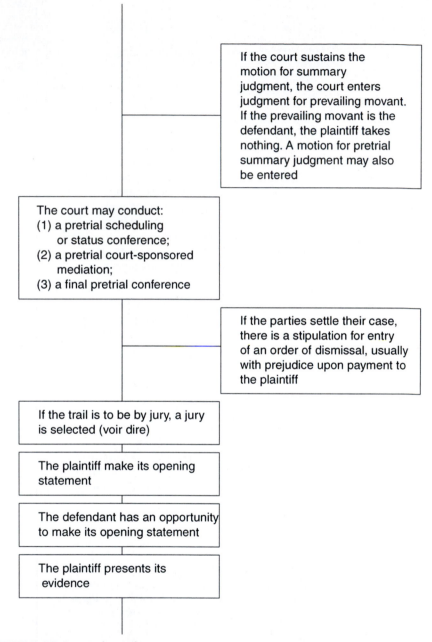

If the court sustains the motion for summary judgment, the court enters judgment for prevailing movant. If the prevailing movant is the defendant, the plaintiff takes nothing. A motion for pretrial summary judgment may also be entered

The court may conduct:
(1) a pretrial scheduling or status conference;
(2) a pretrial court-sponsored mediation;
(3) a final pretrial conference

If the parties settle their case, there is a stipulation for entry of an order of dismissal, usually with prejudice upon payment to the plaintiff

If the trail is to be by jury, a jury is selected (voir dire)

The plaintiff make its opening statement

The defendant has an opportunity to make its opening statement

The plaintiff presents its evidence

FIGURE 16-1 *continued*

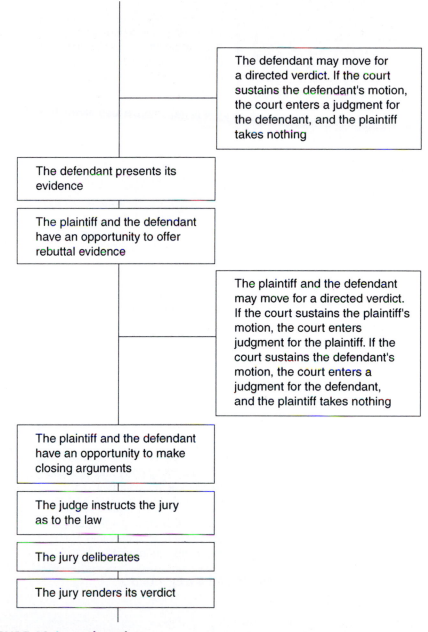

FIGURE 16-1 *continued*

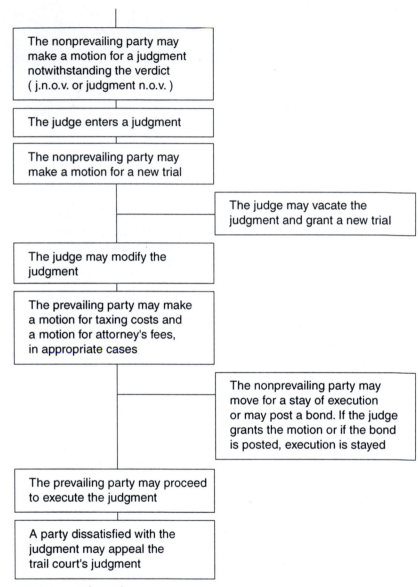

FIGURE 16-1 *continued*

Pretrial

In many ways, pretrial is more important to the outcome of the dispute than the trial. Certainly, pretrial decisions define the trial. Pretrial events include selecting the parties, the nature of the lawsuit and the court, the pleadings, discovery, pretrial motions including a motion for summary judgment, pretrial conferences, and pretrial court-sponsored mediation.

Selecting the Parties, the Nature of the Lawsuit, and the Court

The complainant must select the appropriate party or parties to sue. It is necessary to determine whether:

1. the claimant is a real party in interest; and
2. the claimant and the potential defendant have the legal capacity to sue and be sued.

The real-party-in-interest rules ensure that the person who will be named plaintiff is the person who possesses the substantive rights upon which the lawsuit will be based. If a lawsuit is not brought by a real party in interest, it may be dismissed unless a proper plaintiff is joined. The real-party-in-interest rules are intended to protect potential defendants from harassing and duplicative litigation.

The plaintiff must have "standing" to bring an action in a federal court. To have standing, the plaintiff must have suffered an actual injury. A hypothetical question does not give a person standing.

The parties (plaintiff and defendant) must have legal capacity to be qualified to appear as a named party in the lawsuit. The legal capacity rules deal with the status of the party and not the rights of the parties involved. Persons within certain classes (e.g., classes based on age or mental incapacity) may not be able to protect their own interests and therefore must have a legal representative in a lawsuit. Certain organizations (e.g., a nonresident corporation that is not registered to do business in a state) may not have standing to sue in a nonresident state.

Even if a party could be sued, the question of whether that party should be sued remains. A claimant may not want to sue a potential defendant because the parties have an ongoing family, business, or personal relationship or because litigation may not make economic sense. The claimant might find preparation of the case against this party expensive, or the party may not have the resources to satisfy a judgment, even if the claimant prevails.

Example 16-1

Anita Sorenson was injured in a one-vehicle accident that occurred as she was driving east on Highway 106. She was driving her friend's 1998 Ford Explorer that had been manufactured by the Ford Motor Company and sold by Davis Motors, a local Ford dealer.

Anita told the police that the accident occurred when she was "just driving along and all of a sudden I heard a loud bang and then felt a big bump. The Explorer left the road and rolled over. When I woke up the Explorer was in a ditch and I was hanging by my seat belt upside down."

Several weeks after the accident, Anita's friend, Randy Monroe, received a letter from Ford notifying all Explorer owners that 1998 Explorers were being recalled due to a problem with their Bridgestone/Firestone tires.

If Anita would like to sue, she must choose whether to sue Davis Motors (the retailer), Ford Motor Company (the manufacturer of the Explorer), Bridgestone/Firestone, Inc. (the manufacturer of the tire), Randy Monroe (her friend), or all four.

Problem 16-1

In Example 16-1, list the nonlegal advantages and disadvantages of choosing to sue only Davis Motors.

List the advantages and disadvantages of choosing to sue only Ford.

List the advantages and disadvantages of choosing to sue only Bridgestone/Firestone.

List the advantages and disadvantages of choosing to sue only Randy Monroe.

List the advantages and disadvantages of choosing to sue two, three, or all four at the same time.

The claimant must determine the nature of the lawsuit. On what legal theory could and should the claimant base his or her claim?

Example 16-2

Anita also must determine whether to sue for breach of an express warranty under the Uniform Commercial Code (UCC § 2–313), for breach of an implied warranty of merchantability under the Uniform Commercial Code (UCC § 2–314), in tort for products liability (Restatement (Second) of Torts § 402A), or in tort for negligence.

Each cause of action presents a number of obstacles, including the following. If Anita considers suing for breach of an express warranty, she must prove that Davis, or Ford, or Bridgestone/Firestone, or Randy made an express warranty to her and that any statements made about the safety of the Explorer were not mere puffing. She also has a problem that she was not a buyer and therefore she had no contract to purchase and any express warranty was not made directly to her.

If Anita considers suing Davis Motors (the retailer) for breach of an implied warranty of merchantability under the UCC, she may discover the warranty extended to Randy as the buyer but may not extend to her. Anita's problem is that she did not purchase the automobile from Davis Motors. It was purchased by Randy. Whether the warranty will extend to Anita will depend on whether the applicable state law requires the injured user of the product to be a member of the purchaser's household to be covered under the implied warranty. If the applicable state law requires this, Anita could not maintain an action against Davis Motors for breach of an implied warranty of merchantability.

If Anita considers suing Ford (the manufacturer of the Explorer) or Bridgestone/Firestone (the manufacturer of the tire) for breach of warranty under the UCC, she will discover that in addition to the problem that she had against Davis Motors, she will have an additional problem. The Uniform Commercial Code creates an implied warranty of merchantability that runs from the seller to the seller's buyer. The code is silent about whether the warranty runs from the seller's seller to the ultimate buyer. This has been left for state courts to develop as they deem necessary or appropriate.

If Anita considers suing Davis Motors in tort for products liability, she will discover that under the Restatement (Second) of Torts § 402A, a seller is strictly liable for a product sold in a defective condition which is unreasonably dangerous to the user or consumer. Anita may be able to show all of these requirements are met in her case. She may also be able to prove the elements necessary under § 402A for an action against Ford.

Jurisdiction
A court with jurisdicton over the subject matter has the power to decide the case in question.

The claimant must determine the appropriate court in which to file the lawsuit. The court must have **jurisdiction** over the subject matter, that is, it must have the power to decide this type of case.

Federal court jurisdiction is limited by the United States Constitution and federal statutes. The claimant who wants to file a lawsuit in a federal court must determine whether the federal court has jurisdiction. At times, federal courts and state courts have concurrent jurisdiction, that is, both courts are authorized to deal with the same subject matter, thereby giving the claimant a choice of courts.

Questions of subject matter jurisdiction for state courts typically are determined by reference to state constitutions and statutes. They authorize particular courts to entertain certain categories of controversies. In some instances, certain types of problems are assigned to specialized tribunals (e.g., probate, domestic relations, juvenile, workers compensation).

Jurisdiction over the subject matter cannot be waived by the parties.

Example 16-3

If Anita decides to file suit in her home state court, she will file the case in a court of general jurisdiction which has subject matter jurisdiction over claims for breach of implied warranty and strict liability. She will not file the case in a family, juvenile or probate court as each of these courts has jurisdiction over the specified area of law.

The court also must have jurisdiction over the parties. The court must have the constitutional and statutory power to require the defendant to appear. A state court has personal jurisdiction over all residents of that state. Long arm statutes give courts the authority to assume jurisdiction over some residents of other states. A defendant who would not be within the court's jurisdiction may consent to jurisdiction.

Example 16-4

Davis Motors is incorporated and conducts its business in the state in which Anita's lawsuit is being brought. The court in Anita's state has jurisdiction over Davis Motors because Davis, in effect, agreed to submit to the jurisdiction of the state when it was incorporated in that state and when it was doing business in that state.

The court may also have jurisdiction over Ford although Ford is not located in Anita's state. Ford is "doing business" in Anita's state and would, therefore, come under the long arm statute of Anita's state.

In addition to the court's having jurisdiction over the subject matter and jurisdiction over the person of the defendant, the lawsuit must be brought in a court having proper

Venue
Venue concerns the geographical location of the court—which county court in the state or which district court within the federal system is the appropriate location for the lawsuit.

venue. **Venue** concerns the geographical location of the court. It must be determined which county court in the state, or which district court within the federal system is the appropriate location for the lawsuit. Venue is designed to ensure that there is minimum inconvenience for the litigants and witnesses and that the case can be administered efficiently. The state and federal venue rules limit the plaintiff's choice of forum to ensure that the locality of the lawsuit has some logical relationship either to the parties or to the subject matter of the dispute. Proper venue can be waived by the defendant.

Example 16-5

If Anita lives in Amarillo, Texas, and is suing Ford which is located in Detroit, Michigan, she will file suit in either Texas or Michigan. If she chooses to sue in federal court in Texas, the United States District Court for the Northern District of Texas, rather than the United States District Court for the Eastern District of Michigan, will have venue since it is located in Amarillo and is most convenient to the plaintiff.

Problem 16-2

Ruby Chapman, while on vacation in Hawaii, bought a hula skirt from The Island Tourist Trap. The skirt was made by Grass Skirts, Inc., of New York City. After her vacation, Ruby returned to her home in Texas. Several months later, Ruby loaned the skirt to her niece, Carol, for a costume party. Carol wore the hula skirt all evening at the party where the guests were drinking alcoholic beverages and smoking cigarettes. Toward the end of the evening, Carol was sitting on the floor with friends when her skirt caught fire. The skirt was quickly consumed by the flames. Carol suffered burns on 40 percent of her body. Carol wants to recover for her medical expenses, physical injury, loss of income, and pain and suffering.

Based on the information in the preceding materials, comment on the following:
1. Who should Carol sue?
2. Should Carol sue on an implied warranty of merchantability under the Uniform Commercial Code, for products liability under the Restatement (Second) of Torts § 402A, or for negligence?
3. Which court has subject matter jurisdiction?
4. Which court has personal jurisdiction?
5. Which court has venue?

The Pleadings

Initiating a lawsuit does not guarantee that a case will go to trial. The case can be settled by the parties before trial or the court can dismiss the case before a trial on the facts.

Example 16-6

After Davis Motors found out that Anita was going to sue, it contacted Anita's attorney. Davis Motors' attorney met with Anita's attorney and offered to pay a settlement of $250,000. When Anita's attorney conveyed Davis's offer to her client, Anita informed her attorney that she wanted to accept the settlement offer from Davis. The attorneys finalized the agreement and Anita dismissed her case against Davis Motors.

   Anita's attorney was also contacted by Ford. Ford offered Anita $5,000 to settle. When Anita's attorney conveyed the Ford offer to Anita, she did not think this was a fair settlement and rejected it. The case against Ford was not dismissed, so it would continue on to trial.

Complaint (petition)
A complaint or petition is the document used to initiate a lawsuit.

The Plaintiff's Complaint or Petition   A **complaint** or **petition** is the document used to initiate a lawsuit. In federal court, the document is called a complaint and the Federal Rules of Civil Procedure for the United States district courts apply. The Federal Rules of Civil Procedure are found in 28 U.S.C.A. Appendix. Some state courts call the document a complaint while others call it a petition. The state's rules of civil procedure apply and can be found in the state statutes.

Problem 16-3
Find the rules of civil procedure for your state.

The following discussion will assume that the case has been filed in federal court. Thus, the Federal Rules of Civil Procedure apply.

   The complaint gives the party being sued (the defendant) written notice of the plaintiff's claims. The complaint must be simple, concise, and direct and contain a short and plain statement of the grounds for jurisdiction, a short and plain statement showing the plaintiff is entitled to relief, and a demand for the relief the plaintiff seeks. Although the Federal Rules of Civil Procedure do not require a technical form of complaint, the complaint must contain a caption setting forth the name of the court, the title of the action (including the names of all the parties), the file number, and a designation that it is a complaint. All averments (assertions) of the claim must be made in numbered paragraphs. The contents of each paragraph must be limited as far as practicable to a statement of a single set of circumstances. Each claim founded on a separate transaction or occurrence must be stated in a separate count (i.e., a separate numbered paragraph) whenever such a separation adds to the clarity of the presentation. Sample forms are contained in the Federal Rules of Civil Procedure.

   Once the complaint has been drafted, it must be signed by the attorney of record and filed with the clerk of the court. The clerk of the court will issue a **summons** (an official order to appear in court) and deliver it to the plaintiff or the plaintiff's attorney, who is then responsible for service of the summons and a copy of the complaint to the defendant.

Summons
A summons is an official order to appear in court.

   Under the Federal Rules service of process may be by a federal marshal or a person specially appointed to give service. Service may be accomplished in a variety of ways. If the defendant being served is an individual, service is made by delivering the complaint and summons to the individual personally; by leaving the complaint and summons at the individual's residence with someone of suitable age and discretion who resides there; or by leaving the complaint and summons with an agent authorized by appointment or by law to receive service of process. If the defendant being served is a corporation, partnership, or other unincorporated association, service is made by delivering a copy of the summons and the complaint to an officer, managing or general agent, or any other agent authorized by appointment or by law to receive service of process. If the agent is authorized by statute to receive service, the statute also may authorize mailing a copy of the summons and complaint to the defendant. Once the complaint and summons have been served, the process server must promptly make proof of service to the court.

The Defendant's Response   If the defendant does not respond to the summons within the time allowed (20 days in federal cases), the court may issue a default judgment against the defendant and in favor of the plaintiff. Generally, a defendant will consult an attorney and respond to the summons.

The defendant may respond to the summons by filing a motion to dismiss. This motion may challenge the court's jurisdiction over the subject matter, the court's jurisdiction over the person, the sufficiency of process, the sufficiency of service of process, the court's venue or allege failure to state a claim upon which relief can be granted or failure to join an indispensable party.

The motion to dismiss also may be a motion to dismiss for failure to state a cause of action. In some courts a motion to dismiss for failure to state a cause of action is called a *demurrer*. The term *demurrer* is no longer used in federal court. Through this motion to dismiss, the defendant asserts that even if the facts as alleged by the plaintiff in the complaint were accepted as true, the plaintiff has not stated a cause of action (i.e., has not stated a claim upon which the court could grant relief). If the court grants the defendant's motion to dismiss, the litigation ends without a trial.

Example 16-7

Anita decided to sue Ford for breach of an implied warranty of merchantability under the UCC § 2-314. Ford responds with a motion to dismiss for failure to state a cause of action. Ford asserts that Anita did not state a cause of action because state law requires that Anita be a member of the purchaser's household to be covered under the implied warranty of merchantability, and even if there was an implied warranty of merchantability, the implied warranty was from Davis Motors to Anita, and not from Ford to Anita. Therefore, even if all the facts which Anita alleged were true, Anita could not get relief from the court. The court could dismiss this claim against Ford.

Ford would want the court to dismiss the claim at this stage of the proceedings so that it would not have to prepare for and go to trial on the implied-warranty-of-merchantability issue. A dismissal would end that part of the case although the other cause of action for strict liability could continue.

Answer
Answer is the defendant's response to the plaintiff's complaint.

If the defendant has not made a motion to dismiss or if the defendant's motion to dismiss is denied, the defendant must file an answer. In the **answer,** the defendant must admit or deny the allegations made by the plaintiff in the complaint. The denial may be a general denial, specific denial, qualified denial, denial based on lack of sufficient information to form a belief as to the truth of the allegation, or a denial of allegations based on a good-faith belief they are false. The answer must be stated in short, plain terms.

In the answer, the defendant also must raise any affirmative defenses relevant to the case. Affirmative defenses must be pled in the answer to be raised at trial. The affirmative defenses include accord and satisfaction, arbitration and award, assumption of risk, contributory negligence, discharge in bankruptcy, duress, estoppel, failure of consideration, fraud, illegality, injury by fellow servant, laches, licenses, payment, release, res judicata, statute of frauds, statute of limitations, and waiver.

Example 16-8

In Anita's case against Ford, it has come to light that Anita had been at a party for several hours that evening and had consumed several glasses of wine. Ford pled misuse of product in the answer asserting that Anita's drinking before driving the automobile was the cause of the accident.

The defendant may, at the pleading stage, add parties (implead) to the lawsuit. This occurs when the defendant believes another party is liable to the defendant for the plaintiff's claim. This makes the original defendant the third-party plaintiff, and the new party is a third-party defendant.

Example 16-9

Ford believes that Plastico, Inc., which made the seatback adjustment mechanism, is liable to Ford if Anita adds Plastico to the lawsuit. Ford becomes a third-party plaintiff and Plastico is the third-party defendant.

Counterclaim
A counterclaim is the defendant's complaint and requires the plaintiff to respond to it in the same manner the defendant had to respond to the plaintiff's complaint.

Cross-claim
A cross-claim is a claim that one party to a lawsuit has against a coparty (e.g., a plaintiff against a coplaintiff or a defendant against a codefendant) that arises out of the same occurrence.

If the defendant has a claim against the plaintiff, particularly if the claim arises out of the occurrence over which the plaintiff is suing, the defendant may plead this claim as a counterclaim as part of the answer. This **counterclaim** is in essence a complaint by the defendant, and the plaintiff will have to respond to it (with a motion to dismiss and if unsuccessful, an answer) as if it were the original complaint.

A **cross-claim** is a claim that one party to a lawsuit has against a coparty (e.g., a plaintiff against a coplaintiff or a defendant against a codefendant), that arises out of the same occurrence. Thus, one plaintiff may become a defendant to another plaintiff, or a defendant may act as a plaintiff against another defendant.

Example 16-10

The original case included Anita, as plaintiff, and Davis Motors and Ford, as defendants. After Ford delivered the car to Davis Motors, Davis refused to pay the contract price. Ford adds a cross-claim against Davis Motors for breach of contract.

Example 16-11

In a counterclaim, Davis Motors has decided to sue Anita for intentional interference with a contractual obligation. Anita told her roommate, from whom she borrowed the car, to stop paying her car payments.

The defendant may wish to settle with the plaintiff rather than go to trial. The plaintiff and defendant, through their attorneys, may negotiate a settlement which includes the plaintiff's dismissal of the defendant with prejudice. A dismissal with prejudice means that the lawsuit cannot be refiled against the party who is dismissed. Although a dismissal with prejudice in fact operates as a release in connection with any issues that were brought or could have been brought in the lawsuit, many corporate defendants also insist on a *common law release*. This is a separate document that spells out specifically that the company is released from any and all causes of action that could arise out of the particular incident or set of circumstances giving rise to the lawsuit.

If during the settlement process, it appears that the merits of a case are doubtful or the continued prosecution of the case may be more expensive than the ultimate recovery, a plaintiff may agree to dismiss his or her lawsuit without prejudice. This means that the lawsuit can be refiled under the state saving statute. Such provisions vary from state to state. In some states, the state saving statute allows refiling within one year. When the plaintiff agrees to dismiss the lawsuit without prejudice, the defendant may, in turn, agree not to request costs or sanctions.

Settlement is available at all stages of the process.

Example 16-12

Once Anita's lawyer has agreed with Ford's lawyer to settle the case for $100,000, Anita agrees to dismiss Ford with prejudice and the attorneys prepare and file with the court a stipulation for dismissal with prejudice. If a common law release is executed, it is generally kept by the defendant, but is not filed. Anita cannot subsequently attempt to sue Ford based on any facts from this case.

The Plaintiff's Response to the Defendant's Answer   Any new matter raised may be answered by the adverse party. Whether a new matter raised in the answer is automatically taken as denied by the plaintiff depends on the particular practice in the locality. The tendency today, however, is to close the pleadings after the answer unless the answer raises a counterclaim. No pleading beyond a reply is required or permitted.

Discovery

Discovery is a pretrial process used to enable the litigants to prepare effectively for trial by obtaining knowledge about the dispute; to make the litigants take less-rigid positions with respect to the issues at the beginning of the lawsuit, before they have had the opportunity to obtain information; to narrow the issues before trial; to preserve testimony of witnesses who will not be available at trial; to eliminate surprise during litigation; and to prepare accurate, factual data to support a motion for summary judgment.

Discovery usually involves one or more of the following: taking depositions by oral examination or written questions; seeking written interrogatories; requesting admissions; seeking a court order for the production of documents and things; and requesting physical and mental examinations. Discovery is allowed as long as it is relevant to the pending action or appears to be reasonably calculated to lead to the discovery of admissible evidence.

Depositions   A **deposition** is the testimony of a prospective witness including a party to the lawsuit. A deposition may be conducted by oral examination or by written questions. The deposition is the only discovery device available to get information from nonparties.

A deposition will take place after proper notice is given and a subpoena is served if the deponent is a nonparty. Generally, objections to a deposition are not allowed. Rather, if the deponent or opposing party has objections to the deposition, the objection must be raised in a motion for a protective order. Unless the court actually issues a protective order canceling or restricting the deposition, the deposition proceeds. If a party or subpoenaed deponent refuses to allow his or her deposition to be taken, without first procuring a protective order of the court, the deponent is subject to sanctions.

In an oral deposition, the attorney for one party asks the other party or a nonparty witness questions under oath. The other attorney has an opportunity to cross-examine the person being deposed. The proceedings are recorded and transcribed by a court reporter. In a written deposition, a court reporter reads the questions to the person being deposed and records the answers. Written depositions, although available, are seldom used.

The deposition is useful in finding information relevant to the case, including the discovery of information that may lead to other witnesses and documents. The deposition also is useful in laying a basis for impeaching a witness who attempts to change his or her testimony at trial. In preparing for trial, each disputant will almost certainly be deposed because statements made by them during a deposition will be treated as an admission and can be used by the other party as evidence at the trial. In some circumstances, the depositions of nonparty witnesses who are unavailable at trial may be used in place of live testimony.

Written Interrogatories   **Interrogatories** are written questions to be answered in writing by a party to the lawsuit. Once the questions are answered, they are signed by the respondent under oath. Written interrogatories may be addressed only to a party to the lawsuit. Interrogatories are the least-expensive "formal" means of obtaining information. Unlike the deposition where the deposed's answers are more or less spontaneous, the answers to written interrogatories are not. Interrogatories may, however, require the person subject to the interrogatories to supply some information that cannot be answered spontaneously and thus may, depending on the information sought, be more valuable than a deposition. Some jurisdictions limit the number of interrogatory questions to 20 or 30.

Discovery
Discovery is a pretrial process used to enable the litigants to prepare effectively for trial.

Deposition
A deposition is the oral or written testimony of a prospective witness, including a party to the lawsuit.

Interrogatories
Interrogatories are written questions to be answered in writing by a party to a lawsuit.

Requests for Admissions Written requests for admissions serve to narrow disputed issues. A party can respond to requests for admission by:

1. admitting the truth of the matter;
2. denying the truth of the matter in whole or in part; or
3. stating reasons why he or she cannot admit or deny the truth of the matter.

If a party does not respond to the requests for admissions, the facts will be deemed admitted. Facts admitted are deemed conclusively established for purposes of the lawsuit.

Orders for the Production of Documents and Other Items The discovery of documents and other items provides access to tangible information relevant to the lawsuit.

Request for Physical and Mental Examinations The request for a physical or mental examination is allowed when the physical or mental condition of a party is at issue. In addition to the physical or mental condition of a party being in actual controversy, there must be a showing of good cause for the exam. The physical or mental examination will only be conducted by an order of the court.

Pretrial Motions—The Motion for Summary Judgment

The pretrial motions include a motion for summary judgment. A **motion for summary judgment** is a method for one party to prevail in an action without requiring the actual trial of the case. A motion for a *partial* summary judgment is a method for one party to prevail as to some issues of the case and thus simplify the lawsuit.

The motion for summary judgment is argued before a judge. Outside evidence is produced and the judge is not limited to the pleadings to make his or her decision. A motion for summary judgment will be granted if there is no dispute as to the material facts of the case and one litigant is entitled to judgment as a matter of law. The evidence will be viewed in the light most favorable to the opposing party, and the burden of proof is on the party seeking the motion. If the motion for summary judgment is granted, the court will enter a judgment for the party seeking the motion. If the prevailing movant is the defendant, the plaintiff takes nothing. When a motion for summary judgment is granted, a full trial is unnecessary. If the motion for summary judgment is granted, the losing party may appeal. If there is a dispute as to the material facts of the case, the motion for summary judgment cannot be granted and the case proceeds to trial.

Motion for Summary Judgment
A motion for summary judgment will be granted if there is no dispute as to the material facts of the case and one litigant is entitled to judgment as a matter of law.

Example 16-13

Davis Motors files a motion for summary judgment against Anita. There is no dispute that Anita's roommate was the purchaser of the car and that Anita was injured when the seat-back mechanism failed. The only issue is whether the UCC § 2-314 warranty covers Anita, who is a friend of the purchaser. The court applies the law that the warranty extends only to members of the purchaser's household and, therefore, Anita does not get the benefit of the warranty. The judge grants Davis Motors's motion for summary judgment because the material facts are not in dispute and the only question before the court was an issue of law.

Pretrial Conferences

The pretrial conference is held when the case becomes crystallized. Attorneys for both sides meet with the judge to decide and agree on which issues are in dispute. The conference helps to plan the course of the trial.

The objectives of the pretrial conference are: to expedite the disposition of the action; to establish early and continuing control so that the case will not be protracted due to lack of management; to discourage wasteful pretrial activities; to improve the quality of the trial through more thorough preparation; and, to facilitate the settlement of the case. There are three types of pretrial conferences: the scheduling (or status) conference, the pretrial court-sponsored mediation, and the final pretrial conference.

Pretrial Scheduling (Status) Conference   The pretrial scheduling conference gives the judge the opportunity to develop deadlines which limit the time to join other parties and amend the pleadings, to file and hear motions, and to complete discovery. The scheduling order also may include the date or dates for other pretrial conferences and trial.

The subjects discussed at a pretrial conference may include:

1. the formulation and simplification of the issues, including the elimination of frivolous claims or defenses;
2. the necessity or desirability of amendments to the pleadings;
3. the possibility of obtaining admissions of fact and documents which will avoid unnecessary proof, stipulations regarding the authenticity of documents, and advance rulings from the court on the admissibility of evidence;
4. the avoidance of unnecessary proof and of cumulative evidence;
5. the identification of witnesses and documents, the schedule for filing and exchanging pretrial briefs (if pretrial briefs are needed), and the date or dates for further conferences and for trial;
6. the advisability of referring matters to a magistrate judge or master;
7. the possibility of settlement or the use of extrajudicial procedures to resolve the dispute;
8. the form and substance of the pretrial order;
9. the disposition of pending motions;
10. the need for adopting special procedures for managing potentially difficult or protracted actions that may involve complex issues, multiple parties, difficult legal issues, or unusual proof problems; and
11. such other matters as may aid in the disposition of the action.

Pretrial Court-Sponsored Mediation   The pretrial court-sponsored mediation is conducted before a judge or court-appointed mediator and is held in private at the courthouse. The judge or mediator gives the litigants and their attorneys an opportunity to explore the factors that might lead to settlement. The factors may include: the strengths and weaknesses of each side; a disputant's ability to pay; the costs of litigation; the extent of the injury (and how sympathetic the injured party will look at trial); the legal aspects of the dispute; the "hometown" aspects of the case (whether a local litigant will have an advantage over an out-of-town litigant); the attractiveness of the parties and the witnesses to the jury; the fairness of the result; and the individual concerns of the parties. The proceedings are informal but structured by the judge or court-appointed mediator.

If settlement is achieved, a mutually acceptable binding agreement is attained. The agreement is the parties' agreement and not a resolution imposed by a third party. The agreement need not parallel the "legal" resolution of the dispute. If there is a settlement, the parties generally agree to a stipulation for entry of an order of dismissal, usually with prejudice. Occasionally, consent judgments are entered. If the parties choose, the settlement agreement may become a part of the judicial record. If settlement is not reached, the mediation can be used to streamline the issues for trial.

The Final Pretrial Conference   The final pretrial conference usually occurs anywhere from 30 days to 2 weeks prior to the actual trial date. This conference is designed to crystallize the issues, deal with evidentiary questions, eliminate duplication of testimony, and generally get the case ready for trial. At the final pretrial conference the court and the attorneys may also discuss jury instructions, issues of law, and factual questions. The court may decide motions *in limine* (motions to prevent certain evidence from being presented to the jury), may purge deposition transcripts, and may take care of any special circumstances or last-minute problems that may have arisen in the case.

The Trial

The trial will deal with two issues: questions of fact and issues of law. If the trial is before a jury, the jury will resolve questions of fact and the judge will resolve issues of law. If the trial is a nonjury trial (a "bench trial"), the judge will resolve both questions of fact and issues of law.

Example 16-14

Anita stated that "I was just driving along and all of a sudden the seat fell backward and I was looking at the roof of the car." The car then hit the median.

The defendants assert that Anita was driving recklessly, hit the median, and then the seat fell backward. The issue of whether the seat fell backward before or after Anita hit the median is a question of fact. As a question of fact, the jury will determine when the seat fell backward.

Ford wanted the judge to instruct the jury that if Anita was contributorily negligent, it would be a defense to Anita's strict liability cause of action against Ford. Anita contends that contributory negligence cannot be a defense to her strict liability cause of action against Ford. The issue of whether contributory negligence is, or is not, a defense is an issue of law. As an issue of law, the judge will determine whether the defense is applicable and, thus, whether the instruction should be given to the jury.

The Right to a Jury and Jury Selection (Voir Dire)

If the litigants have a right to a jury trial, prospective jurors must be questioned to determine their impartiality.

Right to a Jury Trial   In most actions for damages, the litigants have a right to have the facts tried by the jury. This right is guaranteed by the Seventh Amendment to the United States Constitution for actions in federal court and by state constitutional provisions for actions in state court. Either litigant may assert his or her right to a jury trial. If both litigants waive their right to a jury trial, the lawsuit will be tried before the judge and the judge will decide both questions of fact and issues of law.

Not all civil lawsuits can be tried to a jury. Historically, the early English courts were divided between common law courts and equity courts. The judges of the equity courts, called *chancellors,* operated the courts without juries and gave equitable remedies. These remedies included orders directing specific action (specific performance) or prohibiting specific action (injunction). Therefore, civil actions today brought for an equitable remedy will be tried by the judge without a jury.

Jury Selection   Jury selection varies depending on whether the court is a federal or state court. Jury selection also varies from jurisdiction to jurisdiction, court to court, and judge to judge. Selection of potential jurors has been made from voter registration, tax rolls, street directories, and driver license lists. Traditionally, a jury had 12 members and from one to six alternates. Today, many juries will be less than 12.

> **Voir Dire**
>
> Voir dire is the screening of the potential jurors by asking them questions to determine if any of them may have a bias or a prejudice which would affect their impartiality in the case.

Screening of the potential jurors is called **voir dire.** Voir dire may be conducted by the judge or by the attorneys, depending on the court. Voir dire consists of asking the prospective jurors questions to determine if any of the jurors may have a bias or a prejudice which would affect their impartiality in the case.

After the prospective jurors are questioned, the attorneys can challenge a prospective juror for cause. A challenge for cause is used when a prospective juror has shown signs of bias or prejudice that would preclude him or her from rendering a fair decision in the case. There is no limit on the number of jurors who can be excused for cause.

> **Preemptory Challenge**
>
> A preemptory challenge is an attorney's challenge of a prospective juror for no actual cause.

Each attorney may also challenge a prearranged number of prospective jurors for no actual cause. These challenges are known as **preemptory challenges.** The number of preemptory challenges is limited. In a preemptory challenge, the attorney does not have to give any reason why he or she wants the prospective juror dismissed. Preemptory challenges are used to remove a juror from the jury panel based on some personal reason or instinct of the attorney.

After the members of the jury are selected, they are sworn in by the judge or the judge's bailiff. The oath to jurors in a civil case in federal district court is:

> You, and each of you, do solemnly swear (affirm) that you will well and truly try the matters in issue now on trial and render a true verdict, according to the law and the evidence; So Help You God [under the penalties of perjury].

Opening Statements

After the jurors are sworn in, the opening statements afford the attorneys the opportunity to give their versions of what the case is about, what contentions will be made, and what evidence will be presented to support those contentions to the judge and the jury in a jury trial, or the judge in a nonjury trial. Since the plaintiff is the party who began the lawsuit, it is the plaintiff's attorney who makes the first opening statement. After the plaintiff's opening statement, the defendant's attorney has the option of making the defendant's opening statement at that time or of waiting until the plaintiff has presented its case and has rested (i.e., waiting until the beginning of the defendant's case).

Presentation of Evidence by the Plaintiff

Because the plaintiff is the party who brought the action, and since the plaintiff is the party with the burden of proof, the plaintiff is the first to present evidence. The plaintiff may present witnesses, one by one, and introduce documents and photographs. The plaintiff's attorney will call witnesses to the stand who will give testimony favorable to the plaintiff's case. The plaintiff's attorney will ask each witness a series of questions, a process known as *direct examination.* After the plaintiff's attorney has completed his or her direct examination of the witness he or she has called, the defendant's attorney may question the witness. This is called *cross-examination.* After cross-examination, the plaintiff's attorney may request to examine the witness again if he or she feels that it is necessary. This is called *redirect examination.* The defendant's attorney may request to reexamine the witness, a process known as *recross examination.* This process is repeated for each of the plaintiff's witnesses. After the plaintiff's attorney has completed his or her presentation of evidence, the plaintiff will rest his or her case.

If the case is in federal court, the admissibility of the evidence is governed by the Federal Rules of Evidence. If the case is in state court, the admissibility of the evidence is governed by the state's rules of evidence.

Problem 16-4

Locate the Federal Rules of Evidence and the rules of evidence for your state.

The attorneys have the responsibility for objecting to evidence that is thought to be inadmissible under the rules of evidence. As each objection is raised, it must be ruled upon by the judge before the trial can proceed. If the judge rules the evidence inadmissible, he or she will instruct the jury to disregard the evidence. Since the judge must make numerous instantaneous evidentiary rulings during a trial, the allegation that some of these rulings were erroneous often is raised on appeal by the nonprevailing party.

Documents, photographs, and other tangible items may be introduced into evidence either by their stipulation in advance of the trial or through witnesses.

Defendant's Motion for a Directed Verdict

After the plaintiff has rested his or her case, the defendant's attorney may move for a directed verdict. By making this motion the defendant contends that the plaintiff's evidence is not sufficient to support a judgment in the plaintiff's favor. A motion for a directed verdict will only be granted if the plaintiff has failed to introduce enough evidence for the jury to find in his or her favor. If no reasonable jury could find for the plaintiff on the facts of this case, the defendant's motion for a directed verdict will be granted. If the motion is granted there is no need for the defendant to present evidence and the judge will enter a verdict and judgment for the defendant. The plaintiff has the opportunity to appeal the judge's decision. If the judge denies the defendant's motion for a directed verdict, the defendant then proceeds with the presentation of his or her evidence.

Presentation of Evidence by the Defendant

Once the plaintiff has presented his or her case and the defendant's motion for a directed verdict has been denied, the defendant has an opportunity to present evidence. The defendant may present witnesses and introduce documents and photographs. The defendant's attorney will call to the stand witnesses who will give testimony favorable to the defendant's case. The defendant's attorney will ask each witness a series of questions on direct examination. After the defendant's attorney has completed his or her direct examination of the witness, the plaintiff's attorney may cross-examine the witness. After cross-examination, the defendant's attorney may request to examine the witness again on redirect examination. This process is repeated for each of the defendant's witnesses. After the defendant's attorney has presented evidence, the defendant will rest his or her case.

Rebuttal Evidence

After the defendant has rested his or her case, the plaintiff is entitled to offer rebuttal evidence to refute any evidence that has been presented by the defendant. The plaintiff's evidence is limited to that which contradicts the defendant's evidence. After the plaintiff has completed his or her presentation of rebuttal evidence, the defendant is entitled to offer rebuttal evidence. This evidence is limited to rebutting what the plaintiff brought forward in the plaintiff's rebuttal. This process may continue until both sides are satisfied.

Motion for a Directed Verdict

After all the evidence has been presented, either the plaintiff or defendant may make a motion for a directed verdict. If the motion is granted, the judge enters a verdict and judgment for the prevailing party and the trial is concluded. If the motion for a directed verdict is not granted, the case will be submitted to the jury for a determination of the questions of fact.

Closing Arguments

After the judge determines that the case will be submitted to the jury, the plaintiff's and defendant's attorneys will make closing arguments. A closing argument gives each party the opportunity to sum up the trial in a light most favorable to his or her client. The attorneys will review the evidence from their client's point of view and suggest how the jury should weigh certain evidence and resolve specific issues. The attorneys cannot use their final arguments to introduce new evidence or to discuss evidence that has been excluded as inadmissible.

Because the plaintiff has the burden of proof, the plaintiff's attorney will make the first closing argument. The defendant's attorney will follow with his or her closing argument. After the defendant's closing argument, the plaintiff's attorney has an opportunity for a rebuttal.

Jury Instructions

Prior to closing arguments, the judge will invite the plaintiff's and defendant's attorneys to submit proposed instructions that each would like the judge to give to the jury. The judge will consider these instructions and select from among these, and his or her own, instructions to give to the jury. After the closing arguments have been completed, the judge will issue instructions to the jury. In these instructions, the judge will summarize the facts and the issues of the case. The judge will determine the applicable law and will tell the jury about the law on which their decision must be based. The judge will instruct the jury that they must apply the law given to them to the facts presented by the parties. The judge informs the jury whether the plaintiff or defendant has the burden of persuasion for each question of fact and may give the jury general information on determining the credibility of witnesses. In a civil case, the burden of persuasion will ordinarily require that the party prove his or her contention by a preponderance of the evidence. On most issues, the plaintiff will carry the burden of persuasion but on some affirmative defenses, such as contributory negligence, the defendant may carry the burden.

If the judge refuses to submit a proposed instruction to the jury or gives an instruction which a party believes should not be submitted, the nonprevailing party may assert the refusal to submit or may assert the erroneous submission as error when seeking an appeal.

Jury Deliberations and Verdict

Upon receiving the judge's instructions, the jury will retire and deliberate in private. Once the jury begins deliberations, no one is allowed in or out of the jury deliberation room. The jury begins its deliberations by selecting a foreman or forewoman, who will be its spokesperson. During the deliberations the jury may ask the judge to repeat the instructions or to read the testimony of a witness. In some cases, juries reach their verdicts quickly. In others, juries may deliberate for days or weeks. In some long cases, jurors may go home each evening. In others, where there is a risk that the jury will be contaminated by mingling with nonjurors, jurors will be sequestered in a local hotel until they reach their verdict.

Although jury verdicts in civil cases were traditionally required to be unanimous, many states permit a verdict to be entered with less than a unanimous vote. In federal court, the parties can consent to a nonunanimous verdict.

Juries may give, depending on the judge's instructions, a general verdict, a general verdict with interrogatories, or a special verdict. The general verdict, the most common, requires the jury to decide who prevails and, if the prevailing party is the claimant, the amount of damages. The general verdict with interrogatories requires the jury to go beyond the mere recitation of who prevails and, if the prevailing party is the claimant, the amount of damages. The jury must answer several key questions that are designed to test whether it understood the issues. If the answers to the interrogatories are inconsistent with the general verdict, the answers to the interrogatories control the judge's entering of the judgment. The special verdict requires the jury to answer questions relating to all the factual issues in the case without instructions as to their legal effect. After the jury answers the questions, the judge applies the law to the jury's answers and determines whether the plaintiff or defendant prevails.

Once the verdict is reached, the jury returns to the courtroom. The verdict is read in open court and in the presence of the parties. The members of the jury may be polled individually to determine whether the verdict as read is their verdict. Once the verdict is read, the jury is dismissed.

Motion for a Judgment Notwithstanding the Verdict (JNOV)

Motion for a Judgment Notwithstanding the Verdict

The motion for a judgment n.o.v. is a request to the judge to set aside the jury's verdict and to enter judgment for the party making the motion.

The litigant who was adversely affected by the jury's verdict may make a **motion for a judgment notwithstanding the verdict** (judgment n.o.v.), which requests the judge to set aside the jury's verdict and to enter judgment for the party making the motion. This motion requires the judge to determine whether the jury was reasonable. If the judge determines that the jury acted unreasonably in reaching its verdict (a reasonable jury—based on the evidence presented—could have found only for the party making the motion for the judgment n.o.v.), the judge will grant the motion.

The Judgment

The judgment is the final determination of the trial. The judgment of the trial court may be the final determination of the lawsuit if an appeal is not taken. The judgment may be rendered when the defendant does not file an answer or does not enter an appearance (default judgment); a motion to dismiss, a motion for summary judgment, or a motion for judgment notwithstanding the verdict (judgment *non obstante veredicto,* j.n.o.v., or judgment n.o.v.) has been granted; the jury returns a verdict; or the judge renders findings of fact and conclusions of law in a nonjury trial.

When the plaintiff prevails, the judgment may take the form of a money award (money judgment), a declaration of rights between the parties (declaratory judgment), the recovery of specific real or personal property (specific performance), or an order requiring or prohibiting the defendant to do something (specific performance or injunction). When the defendant prevails, the judgment will provide that the plaintiff takes nothing by his or her complaint. If the defendant has prevailed on a counterclaim against the plaintiff, the defendant may recover a judgment.

The prevailing party may be awarded costs, as provided by statute, and certain out-of-pocket expenses (such as the clerk's fee and witnesses' mileage). If costs are awarded, they are included in the judgment. Unless authorized by statute or contract, attorney's fees are not recoverable as costs. Each litigant, therefore, must pay for his or her own attorney.

Motion for a New Trial

After the judge enters the judgment on the verdict, the nonprevailing party may make a motion for a new trial. A **motion for a new trial** asks the judge to grant a new trial because of an error committed during the trial. A motion for a new trial also may be granted on the basis of newly discovered evidence, errors of law, misconduct by a party, attorney or juror, excessive damages awarded, or a jury verdict against the clear weight of the evidence. If a motion for a new trial is not granted, the judgment entered on the jury's verdict stands.

Execution of the Judgment

Even though a judgment may order a defendant to pay money, most defendants do not come to court with checkbooks in hand. The plaintiff may have to collect the money owed through a process known as *execution.* The plaintiff asks the court to issue a writ of execution which commands an officer, usually the sheriff, to seize the defendant's property. The property will then be sold at a public sale and the proceeds will be used to satisfy the plaintiff's judgment.

If the plaintiff's relief is in the form of an equitable remedy (a decree rather than a judgment) such as specific performance (the defendant is ordered to do something) or an injunction (the defendant is ordered not to do something), the decree operates against the defendant's person (in personam) rather than against the defendant's property (in rem). If the defendant does not comply with the court's order, the court may hold the defendant in contempt and subject the defendant to a fine or imprisonment.

The nonprevailing party may move to stay execution or post a supersedeas bond while the decision is being appealed. A supersedeas bond is a bond which will cover all damages caused to the prevailing party by the delay should the nonprevailing party lose again on appeal. If the nonprevailing party has posted the supersedeas bond or if the trial court grants the motion to stay execution, the prevailing party cannot execute the judgment during the appeal.

Appeals

An appeal is available when a litigant believes that the trial court has made a mistake. Grounds for appeal are usually errors in trial procedure or errors in substantive law. Certain procedural rules must be followed when filing an appeal.

A nonprevailing party may appeal to an appellate court from a judgment. In some cases, an appeal of certain orders may be taken prior to judgment if such an appeal is imperative. This is known as an *appeal of an interlocutory order*. In these cases, the trial must be suspended while the appeal is pending. Judicial systems differ as to their tolerance of appeals from interlocutory orders. The federal court system generally requires the appeal to be of a final judgment. Some states may be more lenient in their treatment of appeals from interlocutory orders.

Example 16-15

Anita filed a complaint against Ford for breach of contract. In response to Anita's complaint, Ford filed a motion to dismiss on the ground Anita had not stated a cause of action. The trial judge entered an order denying Ford's motion to dismiss.

If Anita had filed her complaint in federal court, Ford could not appeal the decision of the trial court judge to the court of appeals until after the case was tried and a final judgment rendered. If, however, Anita had filed her complaint in a state court that permitted the appeal of interlocutory orders, Ford may have had the opportunity to appeal the trial court's denial of its motion to dismiss before proceeding with the remainder of the trial.

Filing the Appeal

The record on appeal will contain the pleadings (complaint and answer), a trial transcript (the court reporter's verbatim record of the trial), and the relevant orders and rulings. The litigants submit written briefs with arguments on why the case should or should not be reversed.

The Scope of Review

The scope of review determines what the appellate court will consider when reviewing the trial court's decision. The appellate court will seldom review a question of fact. The trier of fact, whether it was the jury or the judge, personally observed the demeanor of the witnesses and, therefore, was in a better position than appellate judges reading the cold record to make findings as to facts.

The appellate court will review rulings of law by the trial judge. The scope of review, however, will not lead to a reversal of the judgment if the error was nonprejudicial (i.e., the error did not substantially affect the outcome of the case).

Oral Arguments

In addition to the submission of written briefs, the attorneys for the litigants may have an opportunity to personally appear before the appellate court and make a short oral presentation of their salient contentions to the court. The personal appearances give the members of the court an opportunity to question the attorneys as to their contentions. Although oral arguments were once common occurrences, many appellate courts have restricted the number of cases that will be orally argued.

The Decision

The appellate court may affirm, reverse, or modify the judgment of the trial court. If the appellate court reverses the judgment of the trial court, it may order that judgment be entered for the appellant (the party appealing the judgment of the trial court), or it may remand the case back to the trial court for a new trial or for other proceedings which are not inconsistent with its decision.

The appellate court's decision often is accompanied by a written opinion. One appellate judge will usually appear as the author of the court's opinion, although the other appellate judges who heard the case may concur in the opinion. At times, the judge who authors the opinion will accept suggestions by the other judges to enable them to concur with the opinion. Judges who cannot concur with the court's opinion may write separate concurring opinions and dissenting opinions, thus explaining why they could not concur in the court's opinion. The written opinions of the appellate courts set forth the reasons for their decisions, provide guidance to the trial court judges, and promote greater predictability so attorneys can better advise their clients in the future.

A Second Appeal

All American judicial systems provide for one appeal from the trial court. Some jurisdictions are designed with two levels of appellate courts. The first review will usually be taken to the intermediate court by an appeal. The party who did not prevail before the intermediate court may seek a review by the highest court. This review may not be demanded as of right. Rather, the nonprevailing party may file a petition for a writ of certiorari. The highest court has the discretion to refuse to grant the writ of certiorari and thus never consider the merits of the case. If the highest court grants the writ of certiorari, it will then consider the merits of the case.

Example 16-16

In the federal court system, the trial court is the United States District Court. The nonprevailing party may appeal the judgment of the United States District Court to the United States Court of Appeals, the intermediate court. The party who does not prevail before the United States Court of Appeals may file a petition for a writ of certiorari with the United States Supreme Court, the highest court. The Supreme Court has the discretion to grant the writ and subsequently consider the merits of the case or deny the writ without any consideration of the merits of the case.

Problem 16-5

Consider the judicial system of your state.
1. Does it have one or two levels of appellate courts?
2. If your state system has two levels of appellate courts, can the party who does not prevail before the intermediate appellate court appeal to the highest court or must the party file a petition for a writ of certiorari?

Res judicata
Res judicata bars a party from commencing a new lawsuit based on the same facts and against the same parties as a previous lawsuit when the subject matter of the case has been finally decided between the parties in the first lawsuit and the time for appeal or further appeal has expired.

Collateral Estoppel
Collateral estoppel prevents the relitigation of an issue in any lawsuit brought after the issue has been litigated in a previous suit.

When the time for appeal or further appeal has expired, the judgment is final and cannot be contested and a party cannot commence a new lawsuit based on the same facts against any of the same parties. The subject matter of the case is finally decided between the parties. This is known as **res judicata,** "a thing decided." Res judicata is also called *claim preclusion.*

Collateral estoppel, also called *issue preclusion,* is another doctrine that deals with the binding effect of judgments. Collateral estoppel prevents the relitigation of an issue in any lawsuit brought after the issue has been litigated in a previous suit.

The Advantages and Disadvantages of Litigation as a Dispute Resolution Process

Litigation, as is the case with arbitration, adds a third-party neutral to the dispute resolution process. As with arbitration, the litigants lose control over the outcome and do not resolve their own dispute. Depending on the nature of the dispute, the third party may be a judge and a jury rather than just a judge. The judge controls the pretrial conferences and the presentation of evidence at trial. If the case is before a jury, the jury will decide questions of fact while the judge will decide issues of law.

Unlike court-sponsored mediation and court-annexed arbitration, the parties know that at the end of the court process (i.e., the trial), the judge will issue a ruling (judgment or decree) that resolves their dispute. The parties also know that the judge's ruling will resolve the dispute according to the law, independent of the parties' needs and interests. The parties also know that although the dispute will be resolved at the end of the process, the process may not end with the trial but may involve an appeal and possibly a second trial with possibly even a second appeal.

When selecting litigation, a claimant must carefully consider the strength of his or her legal claim. If a claimant's legal position is not very strong, or if the evidence needed to present this claim is unavailable, litigation may not be well suited to the dispute. On the other hand, if a careful assessment of the law and the facts would lead a claimant to believe that there is a high degree of probability of success at trial, the filing of a complaint may be the appropriate course of action.

Filing a complaint for a trial before a court does not necessarily mean that the case will be resolved by a court through a judgment or decree. Most cases, well over 90 percent, are resolved before a judgment or decree is ever rendered. Filing a complaint has proven to be a tactical weapon to stimulate serious negotiation and mediation. Also, if a court has a court-annexed arbitration program, the filing of a complaint may be designed to take advantage of that program.

If a case does proceed through trial to judgment or decree, the judge's ruling may be important to establish precedent. Examples include a case with a constitutional issue, a case establishing new boundaries for a cause of action such as products liability, or a case challenging an archaic definition of mental incapacity in a breach of contract action. Bad precedent, however, may be worse than no precedent at all. The judge's ruling may also be important to force action where a party is reluctant to act, even though it might be the right thing to do. For example, a public official may refuse to make an unpopular, but legally necessary decision for fear of not being reelected. By having the judge make the unpopular decision, the public official can say to his or her constituents, "the judge made me do it."

The plaintiff knows that at trial, both parties will be given an opportunity to present their cases to the trier of fact and to the trier of law and that the playing field will be level because what will matter at the conclusion of the trial will be whether the plaintiff has proved his or her cause of action by a preponderance of the evidence. A trial also gives the plaintiff's grievance public exposure since the trial will be open to the public, including the press.

The plaintiff must consider that whoever "loses" at the trial court may appeal to a higher court, thereby increasing the already substantial transaction costs. The plaintiff also must consider that even if he or she "wins," the defendant may not voluntarily "pay up" and the judgment will need to be enforced. The plaintiff also must consider whether the defendant has the resources to pay the judgment. If not, the plaintiff achieves a hollow victory. Figure 16-2 is a summary of litigation as a dispute resolution process.

AVAILABILITY	always available
PROCESS SELECTION	one party controls whether the dispute will be litigated and where the dispute will be litigated statutes and court rules describe the rules of evidence and procedure for the process the court controls the scheduling
THE PARTICIPANTS	the parties, and their attorneys (unless *pro se*), the judge, the jury (unless the case is a bench trial), and any necessary witnesses the parties do not select the judge
PREPARATION	the parties must prepare their evidence and their opening and closing statements
THE PROCESS	takes place in a public setting more formal than arbitration, with each party having an opportunity to present his or her case to the judge and jury or to the judge does not preserve the privacy of the parties' records and documents the process from the time the complaint is filed until the final appellate decision is written generally takes longer than any other dispute resolution process
FAIRNESS	since the parties are represented by counsel (unless *pro se*), the power imbalances may be reduced in some, but not all cases
THE OUTCOME	does not allow the parties to control the outcome of their dispute since the judge and jury or the judge will resolve the dispute does not encourage creative resolutions since the solution should be based on the law the parties have no control over the outcome at the end of the trial, the dispute will be resolved, although a party can seek a new trial or may appeal to a higher court the judgment may or may not be performed by the losing party, although the prevailing party may execute the judgment thus using the judicial system to collect on its judgment
COSTS	pretrial discovery can be costly a party may be assessed court costs by the judge generally the most expensive dispute resolution process, although in some cases, costs and attorney's fees may be assessed to the losing party
PRECEDENTIAL VALUE	establishes binding precedent if the case produces a published opinion
IMPACT ON FUTURE RELATIONSHIP	does not encourage future cooperation or reduce confrontation between the parties

FIGURE 16-2 Litigation

Key Terms and Phrases

answer
collateral estoppel
complaint or petition
counterclaim
cross-claim
deposition
discovery
interrogatories
judgment n.o.v.

jurisdiction
motion for a new trial
motion for summary judgment
preemptory challenge
res judicata
summons
venue
voir dire

Review Questions

True/False Questions

1. T F In litigation, the jury is the finder of fact and the judge is the finder of law, unless the trial is a bench trial.
2. T F In litigation, the parties must be represented by legal counsel.
3. T F In litigation, the outcome is based more on the needs and interests of the parties than the law.
4. T F In litigation, the parties negotiate the rules.
5. T F Litigation leads to a win/win solution.
6. T F Litigation may be conducted before or after a complaint is filed with the court.
7. T F Litigation may take place over a period of days, weeks, or months and may start and stop.
8. T F Effective representation at trial is based on preparation.
9. T F Litigation is consensual and can be terminated by either party at any time.
10. T F To initiate litigation, the parties petition the court to hear their dispute.
11. T F Unless the judge grants a motion for judgment n.o.v. or a motion for a new trial, the verdict is entered as a judgment and enforceable through a writ of execution.
12. T F During litigation, a dominant party may easily take advantage of a weaker party through psychological gamesmanship.
13. T F Litigation gives the parties control over the outcome.
14. T F Litigation is designed so one party wins and the other loses.
15. T F A judgment may be appealed to a higher tribunal on issues of law.

Fill-in-the-Blank Questions

1. _____ The jury's decision.
2. _____ The motion that asks the judge not to follow the jury's decision.
3. _____ The motion that asks the judge to end the trial after the plaintiff has presented his or her evidence.
4. _____ The motion that asserts reversible errors were made during the trial.
5. _____ The challenges to a prospective juror that are made without cause.
6. _____ The questioning of prospective jurors before the jury is empaneled.
7. _____ The questioning of the plaintiff's witnesses by the defendant's attorney.

8. _____ Bars a party from commencing a new lawsuit based on the same facts, against the same parties as a previous lawsuit when the subject matter of the case has been finally decided between the parties in the first lawsuit and the time for appeal or further appeal has expired.

Multiple-Choice Questions

1. Which of the following may participate in the litigation process:
   (a) the aggrieved party
   (b) the other party to the dispute
   (c) a neutral third party
   (d) a jury
   (e) the attorney for the aggrieved party
2. Litigation is classified as:
   (a) unilateral action in dispute resolution
   (b) bilateral action in dispute resolution
   (c) third-party evaluation as a prelude to dispute resolution
   (d) third-party assistance in dispute resolution
   (e) third-party adjudication in dispute resolution
3. Which of the following is the most complicated dispute resolution process?
   (a) inaction
   (b) self-help
   (c) negotiation
   (d) private mediation
   (e) litigation

Short-Answer Questions

1. Over the summer, the Hillborough School Board has ordered each of its schools to prominently display the Ten Commandments. A group of parents believes that such a display is a violation of the separation of church and state under the First and Fourteenth Amendments to the United States Constitution.

   Should these parents file a complaint in federal court or should this issue be resolved by some other method of dispute resolution?
2. Discuss the advantages and disadvantages of litigation as a dispute resolution process.
3. Is private mediation or litigation more popular in the United States and why?
4. Discuss the role of the judge in litigation.
5. Discuss the role of the courts in reviewing a trial court's judgment.
6. Discuss whether court-sponsored mediation or litigation is the better dispute resolution process for domestic relations disputes such as custody, support, visitation, and property distribution.

CHAPTER 17

Private Judging

Private Judging ("Rent-a-Judge")
A neutral third party who is not a sitting judge is selected to conduct a private trial between the parties.

Private judging is a dispute resolution process in which a neutral third party who is not a sitting judge (i.e., retired or former judge, law professor, or practicing or retired attorney) is selected to conduct a private trial between the parties. Private judging may be created as a matter of contract between the parties or may be authorized by law (i.e., constitution, statute, or court rule). If private judging is created by contract, the private judge is selected by the parties. If private judging is created by law, the private judge is appointed by a court at the parties' request. In either case, the private judge is compensated by the parties. The private judge appointed by the parties (as per their contract) does not have the powers of a sitting judge and his or her decision cannot be appealed to a court. The private judge appointed by a court has the same powers as a sitting judge and the parties have the right to appeal as if the decision were rendered by a sitting judge.

Private Judging as a Matter of Contract

Private judging may be selected by the parties as their dispute resolution process. The agreement to use this process is a matter of contract law. By contracting for private judging, the parties keep the resolution of their dispute out of the public forum.

The Process

As with private mediation and private arbitration, the parties design their own process or select an ADR service to design the process for them. If the parties design their own process they control the selection of the private judge, how the private judge will be paid, the extent of discovery, when and where the trial will be held, how long the trial will last, and whether the private judge will follow the procedures and rules of evidence as if the case were being litigated before a sitting judge in a public courtroom or whether these rules will be relaxed.

Although most private judging is before a judge without a jury, since the process is a matter of contract between the parties, they could agree to a trial with or without a jury.

The parties could limit the outcome so the plaintiff could recover no more than a set amount or no less than a set amount. They could decide whether the judge's decision is binding or advisory. They could decide whether the judge will render a decision at the close of the case or will have a period of time to deliberate. They could decide whether the judge will merely issue the judgment or whether the judgment will be accompanied by a written, reasoned opinion.

If the parties, when developing the rules for the trial, agree that the judge's decision will be binding, the judge's decision stands without review. Since this form of private judging is by contract, the parties have no recourse to a court in the event a party believes the judge committed error during the trial in determining the applicable law or in applying the law to the facts.

Advantages and Disadvantages of the Contractual Form of Private Judging as a Dispute Resolution Process

Private judging is an adjudication and at the end of the process, the trial, the dispute is resolved. By selecting private judging, the parties give up control over the outcome and place control in the hands of a neutral third person, the private judge. In return, the parties receive a prompt resolution of their dispute.

Private judging gives the parties control over when the trial takes place, thus eliminating the long wait at the courthouse and the uncertainty of the exact date of trial. Attorneys can prepare once for trial without having to prepare again because of delays in the judge's docket or unavailability of courtrooms. Witnesses can have certainty about when they will be needed to testify. Private judging also limits the duration of trial because the private judge can remain focused on the case being tried rather than balancing the case at trial with other judicial duties. Some of these costs savings can partially offset the cost of the private judge, the ADR service (if one is employed), and the courtroom.

The timing of the outcome of the dispute is predictable because the parties have no avenue of appeal. The decision of the private judge, whether it is right or wrong, is final. The outcome of the dispute is not delayed by appeals and new trials. This provides the parties with a date certain when the dispute will be resolved.

Private judging gives the parties control over the selection of the private judge. The parties can decide to select a private judge with specific expertise if the case warrants such a selection.

Private judging is private both in process and in outcome. The dispute is not of public record and unless the parties reveal the outcome, it remains private. The outcome does not establish precedent.

It is one thing to receive a favorable judgment and another to satisfy or get paid on that judgment. If the case were decided by a public court, the court's judgment could be enforceable through a writ of execution. A writ of execution is an order, usually issued by the clerk of the court, directing the sheriff to seize and sell the defendant's nonexempt property. The proceeds from the sheriff's sale defray the administrative expenses accompanying the seizure and sale and pay the plaintiff to satisfy the judgment.

Since this form of private judging is a contractual process, the use of the court system to collect a judgment is unavailable. If a party does not perform according to the judgment, the prevailing party may treat the other party's failure as a breach of contract and pursue a breach of contract action. Figure 17-1 presents an overview of private judging by contract as a dispute resolution process.

Private Judging as Authorized by Law

About half of the 50 states, by constitution, statute, or court rule, have authorized the courts to appoint private judges to conduct trials at the parties' request. California and New York lead all other states in the use of private judging. Some federal courts have also authorized the appointment of private judges.

Reference Proceedings
Reference proceedings is the private judging process when a case is referred to a private judge by the court.

This private judging process is known as **reference proceedings.** *Reference* means referred as when a case is referred to a private judge by the court. In some states the private judge is known as a *temporary judge* or a *judge pro tem.* Some refer to the private judge as a *rent-a-judge.*

Example 17-1

In California private judging is authorized by constitution and further developed by statute and court rule. See Appendix J.

Problem 17-1

Does your state by constitution, statute, or court rule provide for private judging? Check for the concept *private judge*. If you have no luck, check under its other names, such as *temporary judge, judge pro tem,* and *rent-a-judge* or check under the procedure's name (reference procedure). Your search may be expedited by Westlaw or Lexis. The website of your highest court or state bar association may provide assistance.

———————

The private judge who is appointed by a public court will have the same powers as a sitting judge and the parties have the right to appeal the private judge's decision to the public court.

The Process

The process begins when a party files a complaint in the office of a clerk of the court. As the litigation process unfolds, the parties ask the judge overseeing the case to appoint a private judge to hear the case. If the judge agrees, he or she will confer with the parties to select the private judge. The private judge may be appointed by the sitting judge or by order of the court, depending on the court's protocol. Upon appointment, the private judge becomes a temporary judge of the court. Once the private judge is appointed, he or she will assume the management and trial of the case, although the judge who appointed the private judge may retain oversight supervision.

Since the private judge is acting as a temporary judge of the court, the trial before a private judge will follow the procedural and evidentiary rules of the court that appointed him or her. If the case is one that could be tried before a jury, the parties may select a jury trial. Some procedural and evidentiary deviations may be permitted. For example, the parties may agree to limit discovery, to stipulate the facts that are not in issue, to define the issues as they choose, to alter the order of proof, to restructure the damage phase of the trial, to set limits on the type and amount of the damages that may be awarded, to permit evidence to be admitted by means that would not be admissible in court (e.g., by telephone or by affidavit), and to permit evidence to be admitted that would otherwise be inadmissible in court (e.g., hearsay).

At the conclusion of the trial, an aggrieved party has the right to appeal the decision of the private judge to either the trial court or to an appellate court, depending on the rules of the jurisdiction.

Advantages and Disadvantages of Court-Appointed Private Judging as a Dispute Resolution Process

Many of the advantages and disadvantages of private judging by contract also apply to private judging as authorized by law. The parties are able to select a private judge who has the qualifications and experience to match the case. The parties pay for the private judge, for the ADR service that manages the process and provides the private judge, if one is used, and for the use of the courtroom, thus increasing transaction costs.

The trial will proceed when originally scheduled and will not be continued to accommodate the court's busy schedule, thus reducing attorney and witness time and transaction costs associated with those expenses.

Private judging as authorized by law may not provide the same finality as would private judging by contract. In the latter, the parties have no right to appeal and therefore the decision of the private judge is final. In private judging as authorized by law, the aggrieved party may appeal the private judge's decision to a public court.

Private judging as authorized by law may or may not provide the parties with a private process and confidentiality. The trial before the private judge may be private and confidential but if one of the parties appeals the decision of the private judge to a public court, the process is no longer private and the dispute is no longer confidential. Figure 17-2 presents an overview of private judging by court reference as a dispute resolution process.

The Social Implications of Private Judging

Private judging, especially reference proceedings, has drawn significant criticism. Some assert that private judging inhibits reform of the public dispute resolution system by providing alternatives to the wealthy while not being available to those with less wealth. Since the wealthy can bypass congested courthouses and expedite their trial date, as well as select a judge with case-specific expertise, they lose their interest in reforming the existing litigation system. The supporters for private judging point out that private judging is not necessarily available only to the wealthy because it is used primarily for personal injury and domestic relations disputes. In fact private judging may save money for those with less wealth because of the efficiency of the process. The efficiency of the process may also lead to the less wealthy plaintiff recovering money from the defendant sooner rather than later. Finally, the advocates note that the court reform movement is very much alive and has not been hindered by private judging.

Some critics point to the growing number of judges who leave the bench through early retirement or just leave the bench and enter the dispute resolution market offering their services as private judges. Certainly, the control over one's own schedule, the offer of a less frenetic day, and the attraction of more money, may lure some highly experienced judges from the bench. Some sitting judges who must run for reelection or retention may even find the thought of not having his or her name on a ballot alluring. The supporters of private judging assert that judges leave the bench or retire early due to health, family concerns, and burnout from the daily stress of the work and are not motivated to leave the bench for the rewards of private judging.

Some critics theorize that even though private judges are "neutral," the fact that they operate for profit may mean that they may tend to favor the litigants who are more likely to use their services again over the litigants who are onetime users. In addition to this profit motive argument, critics express concern about whether private judges are sensitive to disclosure issues and the appearance of impropriety that arise when the same private judges are employed by the same attorneys, law firms, or litigants. Advocates of private judging argue that court rules can be drafted to address the neutrality and disclosure issues.

Problem 17-2

1. Do you find merit in the critics' or the advocates' contentions?
2. Does the following court rule (California Rules of Court rule 244(c)) address some of the issues raised by the critics?

    (c) Disqualification   A request for disqualification of a privately compensated temporary judge shall be determined as provided in Code of Civil Procedure sections 170.1, 170.2, 170.3, 170.4 and 170.5. A privately compensated temporary judge, as soon as practicable, shall disclose to the parties any potential ground for disqualification under the provisions of Code of Civil Procedure section 170.1, and any facts that might reasonably cause a party to entertain a doubt that the temporary judge would be able to be impartial. A temporary judge who has been privately compensated in any other proceeding in the past 18 months as a judge, referee, arbitrator, mediator, or settlement facilitator by a party, attorney, or law firm in the instant case shall disclose the number and nature of other proceedings before the first hearing.

3. Should private judging, at least reference judging, be prohibited or severely limited?

Problem 17-3

Do the criticisms aimed at private judging also apply to private mediation and private arbitration, or is there a reason why private judging is being singled out?

AVAILABILITY	always available
PROCESS SELECTION	the parties select the process and decide whether they want to create the process or whether they would like the private judge or ADR service to create the process the parties control the scheduling and the private trial can be scheduled before a case is filed or at any time after filing the dispute will be resolved much more quickly than litigation in the courts because the parties will not need to wait for a trial date
THE PARTICIPANTS	the parties, their attorneys, the private judge, a jury if the parties so decide, and the necessary witnesses
PREPARATION	the parties fashion the rules for the process and select the private judge or ADR service the parties determine the parameters for discovery the parties prepare their evidence and their opening and closing statements as if the private trial were a trial in court
THE PROCESS	takes place in a private setting more formal than mediation but less formal than litigation in the court, with each party having an opportunity to present his or her case to the judge and jury if a jury is present confidential and preserves the privacy of the parties' records and documents
FAIRNESS	since the parties are represented by counsel, the power imbalances may be reduced in some, but not all, cases
THE OUTCOME	does not allow the parties to control the outcome of their dispute since the judge and jury or the judge will resolve the dispute does not encourage creative resolutions since the solution is based on the law the parties have no control over the outcome the decision is enforceable as a contract and is not subject to judicial review
COSTS	the parties pay the judge and jurors and any costs involved could be more or less expensive than litigation depending on whether discovery is limited and the hearing length shortened and whether the other costs associated with the process do not exceed these savings will save appeal costs
PRECEDENTIAL VALUE	establishes no binding precedent, although nonbinding precedent by performance may be created between the parties
IMPACT ON FUTURE RELATIONSHIP	does not encourage future cooperation or reduce confrontation between the parties

FIGURE 17-1   Private Judging by Contract

AVAILABILITY	depends on the court
PROCESS SELECTION	the litigants request the court to refer their case to a private judge the parties control the scheduling the dispute will be resolved much more quickly than litigation in the courts because the parties will not need to wait for a trial date
THE PARTICIPANTS	the parties, their attorneys, the private judge, a jury if the parties so decide, and the necessary witnesses
PREPARATION	the process follows the evidentiary and procedural rules of the court with some adjustment the parties and the private judge determine the parameters for discovery the parties prepare their evidence and their opening and closing statements as if the private trial were a trial in court
THE PROCESS	takes place in a private setting more formal than mediation but less formal than litigation in the court, with each party having an opportunity to present his or her case to the judge and jury, if a jury is present confidential and preserves the privacy of the parties' records and documents
FAIRNESS	since the parties are represented by counsel, the power imbalances may be reduced in some, but not all cases
THE OUTCOME	does not allow the parties to control the outcome of their dispute since the judge and jury or the judge will resolve the dispute does not encourage creative resolutions since the solution is based on the law the parties have no control over the outcome the decision is enforceable as a judgment and is not subject to judicial review
COSTS	the parties pay the judge and jurors and any costs involved could be more or less expensive than litigation depending on whether discovery is limited, the hearing length shortened, an appeal is taken, and the other costs associated with the process do not exceed these savings
PRECEDENTIAL VALUE	if the process calls for a written judicial opinion, the judge's opinion will not be published and therefore will not establish binding precedent
IMPACT ON FUTURE RELATIONSHIP	does not encourage future cooperation or reduce confrontation between the parties

FIGURE 17-2 Private Judging by Court Reference

Key Terms and Phrases

private judging
reference proceedings

Review Questions

True/False Questions

1. T F In private judging, the jury is the finder of fact and the judge is the finder of law, provided the private judging does not take the form of a bench trial.
2. T F In private judging, the parties will be represented by legal counsel.
3. T F In private judging, the outcome is based more on the needs and interests of the parties than the law.
4. T F In private judging, the parties have input in the rules.
5. T F Private judging leads to a win/win solution.
6. T F Private judging may be conducted before or after a complaint is filed with the court.
7. T F Private judging generally takes place over a period of time and may start and stop.
8. T F Effective representation in private judging is based on preparation.
9. T F Private judging is consensual and can be terminated by either party at any time.
10. T F During private judging, a dominant party may take advantage of a weaker party through psychological gamesmanship.
11. T F Private judging gives the parties control over the outcome.
12. T F Private judging is designed so one party wins and the other loses.
13. T F A private judge will write a reasoned opinion at the end of the trial.
14. T F Private judging may never take place after one party has filed a complaint with the clerk of the court.
15. T F All judgments rendered by a private judge may be appealed to the court.

Fill-in-the-Blank Questions

1. _____ Private judging that takes place without court involvement.
2. _____ Private judging that takes place with court involvement.
3. _____ Several names for a private judge.
   _____

Multiple-Choice Questions

1. Which of the following always participate in private judging:
   (a) the aggrieved party
   (b) the other party to the dispute
   (c) a neutral third party
   (d) a jury
   (e) the attorney for the aggrieved party

2. Private judging is classified as:
   (a) unilateral action in dispute resolution
   (b) bilateral action in dispute resolution
   (c) third-party evaluation as a prelude to dispute resolution
   (d) third-party assistance in dispute resolution
   (e) third-party adjudication in dispute resolution

Short-Answer Questions

1. The Red Rock Electric Company has a requirements contract with the Appalachian Coal Company. Under this requirements contract, Red Rock has promised to purchase all of its coal from Appalachian for five years at "two percent less than the market price." After the first shipment, a dispute arose between the parties as to what "two percent less than the market price" meant. Red Rock contends that the "market price" pertains to what Appalachian is charging others. Appalachian contends that the "market price" is what all sellers charge. Naturally, Appalachian will be charging Red Rock more under the Appalachian interpretation than under the Red Rock interpretation.

   Would private judging be an appropriate method of dispute resolution for this dispute?

2. Contrast private judging by contract with private judging by reference.

3. Is private judging detrimental to the legal system?

PART SEVEN

Selecting a Dispute Resolution Strategy

Introduction

Part VII, the final part of this text, focuses on developing a dispute resolution strategy from among the array of processes introduced in Part I and studied in detail in Parts II through VI. Part VII consists of two chapters: Chapter 18, "Selecting a Dispute Resolution Process before the Dispute Arises"; and Chapter 19, "Selecting a Dispute Resolution Strategy after the Dispute Arises."

Chapter 18 focuses on those disputes that arise from the nonperformance or misperformance of contractual duties where the parties at the time of contracting selected a dispute resolution process to govern future disputes. In these situations, the dispute resolution process was included as a term in their contract. Chapter 18 describes the dispute resolution provisions that can be drafted into a contract, the advantages and disadvantages that arise when such a dispute resolution is included in a contract, and whether these predispute provisions are enforceable in court. This chapter also investigates other contract provisions that have an impact on the subsequent selection of a dispute resolution process.

Chapter 19 explores the creation of a dispute resolution strategy after the dispute arises. Postdispute selection returns to the array of methods of dispute resolution presented in Chapter 1 and reviews the attributes of each process. Chapter 19 then discusses the creation of a dispute resolution strategy that may consist of one process or a series of processes linked together in a strategically significant way. Chapter 19 concludes with a discussion of the execution of the dispute resolution plan.

CHAPTER 18

Selecting a Dispute Resolution Process before the Dispute Arises

Written contracts may include substantially more than the subject matter of the agreement. They may include a dispute resolution provision. Traditionally, when parties designate a dispute resolution process, they specify arbitration. Recently, however, some parties have designated mediation rather than arbitration in order to keep control over the outcome of any future dispute.

This chapter discusses both the predispute arbitration and mediation provisions. This chapter also examines other contract provisions that, without designating a dispute resolution process, influence a party's selection of a dispute resolution process.

Predispute Arbitration Provision

Predispute Arbitration Provision

A predispute arbitration provision requires the parties to arbitrate all disputes that arise under their contract.

A **predispute arbitration provision** requires the parties to arbitrate all disputes that arise under their contract. The parties are precluded from litigating their dispute and must use arbitration if their dispute is to be resolved by adjudication.

Predispute arbitration provisions are described in Chapter 13, Private Arbitration. For tips in drafting predispute arbitration provisions, see *Drafting Dispute Resolution Clauses—A Practical Guide*, by the American Arbitration Association, *http://www.adr.org/rules/guides/clausebook.html#Arbitration*.

As discussed in Chapter 13, incorporation of a mandatory arbitration provision into a written contract is generally the work of only one of the parties. Often the arbitration provision appears in a form contract (i.e., preprinted contract) that is presented to the other party on a take-it or leave-it basis.

The drafters include mandatory arbitration because arbitration favors the drafters. They have an advantage as frequent users of the arbitration process and the arbitration service while the other parties (i.e., the claimants) are generally at a disadvantage as onetime users.

A mandatory arbitration clause may cause a number of claimants to think twice before pursuing their claims. Rather than get involved in private arbitration, a process that they know little about, they may instead choose inaction as their method of dispute resolution.

A mandatory arbitration provision reduces the claimant's options. The claimant with a small claim may lose the option of taking his or her dispute to small claims court or to a neighborhood mediation center. And when reading the terms of the contract, the claimant may find that the other party's costs and attorney's fees may be assessed to him or her if he or she loses at arbitration. Therefore, the claimant may find it easier to walk away (inaction) or acquiesce if the other party makes a demand.

Contract of Adhesion (Adhesion Contract)

A contract whereby one party imposes his or her will upon the other party with take-it or leave-it terms.

Unconscionable Contract Provision

An unconscionable contract provision is a provision, that at the time of contract formation, was imposed by one of the contract parties that is unreasonably favorable to that party and the other party lacked a meaningful choice to accept or reject it.

Fraud in the Inducement

Fraud in the inducement (different than fraud in the factum) is a false representation or concealment of fact, that should have been disclosed, that deceives and is intended to deceive another party to the contract.

Predispute arbitration provisions have been challenged as contracts of adhesion. A **contract of adhesion (adhesion contract)** is a contract whereby one party imposes his or her will on the other party. Generally the courts have recognized that these contracts are indeed contracts of adhesion because one party controls the terms of the contract and the terms are offered on a take-it or leave-it basis. The courts, however, have ruled that even though a predispute arbitration clause makes a contract a contract of adhesion, the contract is still enforceable. Only when a predispute arbitration provision was **unconscionable** (a provision, that at the time of contract formation, was imposed by one of the contract parties that is unreasonably favorable to that party and the other party lacked a meaningful choice to accept or reject it) or was created by **fraud in the inducement** (a false representation or concealment of fact, that should have been disclosed, that deceives and is intended

Duress
Duress is the use of any wrongful act or threat to influence a party to contract.

Unenforceable Contract Provision
An unenforceable contract provision is a contract provision that the court will not implement.

to deceive another party to the contract) or was entered into under **duress** (the use of any wrongful act or threat to influence a party to contract) is the provision **unenforceable** (a contract provision that the court will not implement).

In *Green Tree Financial Corp.-Alabama v. Randolph*, Randolph, the buyer of a mobile home, brought a class action in the United States District Court for the Middle District of Alabama against Green Tree Financial, the lender that financed the sale, asserting claims under the Truth in Lending Act (TILA) and the Equal Credit Opportunity Act (ECOA). The District Court granted Green Tree's motion to compel arbitration and dismissed Randolph's claims with prejudice. Randolph appealed to the United States Court of Appeals for the Eleventh Circuit. The Court of Appeals reversed the District Court and remanded the case for trial. Green Tree's writ for certiorari was granted by the United States Supreme Court. The Court considered two issues: (1) whether the District Court's order compelling arbitration and dismissing Randolph's underlying claims was a "final decision with respect to an arbitration" within the meaning of the Federal Arbitration Act (FAA), and therefore immediately appealable; and (2) whether the arbitration agreement that did not mention arbitration costs and fees was not *per se* unenforceable because it fails to affirmatively protect a party from potentially steep arbitration costs. Chief Justice Rehnquist delivered the opinion of the Court and was joined by all members of the Court on the "final decision" issue. He was joined by Justices O'Connor, Scalia, Kennedy, and Thomas on the arbitration agreement issue. Justice Ginsburg filed an opinion concurring on the "final decision" issue and dissenting on the arbitration agreement issue. She was joined by Justices Stevens and Souter. Justice Breyer joined this opinion on part of the arbitration agreement issue.

Consider why the Federal Arbitration Act applied to this transaction (see note 1). Also consider the differences between the majority and dissent on the arbitration agreement issue.

Green Tree Financial Corp.-Alabama v. Randolph
531 U.S. 79, 121 S.Ct. 513 (2000)

178 F.3d 1149, affirmed in part and reversed in part.

Chief Justice Rehnquist delivered the opinion of the Court.

In this case we first address whether an order compelling arbitration and dismissing a party's underlying claims is a "final decision with respect to an arbitration" within the meaning of § 16(a)(3) of the Federal Arbitration Act, 9 U.S.C. § 16(a)(3), and thus is immediately appealable pursuant to that Act. Because we decide that question in the affirmative, we also address the question whether an arbitra-

tion agreement that does not mention arbitration costs and fees is unenforceable because it fails to affirmatively protect a party from potentially steep arbitration costs. We conclude that an arbitration agreement's silence with respect to such matters does not render the agreement unenforceable.

I

Respondent Larketta Randolph purchased a mobile home from Better Cents Home Builders, Inc., in Opelika, Alabama. She financed this purchase through petitioners Green Tree Financial Corporation and its wholly owned subsidiary, Green Tree Financial Corp.-

Alabama. Petitioners' Manufactured Home Retail Installment Contract and Security Agreement required that Randolph buy Vendor's Single Interest insurance, which protects the vendor or lienholder against the costs of repossession in the event of default. The agreement also provided that all disputes arising from, or relating to, the contract, whether arising under case law or statutory law, would be resolved by binding arbitration.[1]

Randolph later sued petitioners, alleging that they violated the Truth in Lending Act (TILA), 15 U.S.C. § 1601 *et seq.*, by failing to disclose as a finance charge the Vendor's Single Interest insurance requirement. She later amended her complaint to add a claim that petitioners violated the Equal Credit Opportunity Act, 15 U.S.C. § 1691-1691f, by requiring her to arbitrate her statutory causes of action. She brought this action on behalf of a

---

[1]The arbitration provision states in pertinent part: "All disputes, claims, or controversies arising from or relating to this Contract or the relationships which result from this Contract, or the validity of this arbitration clause or the entire contract, shall be resolved by binding arbitration by one arbitrator selected by Assignee with consent of Buyer(s). This arbitration Contract is made pursuant to a transaction in interstate commerce, and shall be governed by the Federal Arbitration Act at 9 U.S.C. § 17. Judgment upon the award rendered may be entered in any court having jurisdiction. The parties agree and understand that they choose arbitration instead of litigation to resolve disputes. The parties understand that they have a right or opportunity to litigate disputes through a court, but that they prefer to resolve their disputes through arbitration, except as provided herein. THE PARTIES VOLUNTARILY AND KNOWINGLY WAIVE ANY RIGHT THEY HAVE TO A JURY TRIAL EITHER PURSUANT TO ARBITRATION UNDER THIS CLAUSE OR PURSUANT TO A COURT ACTION BY ASSIGNEE (AS PROVIDED HEREIN). The parties agree and understand that all disputes arising under case law, statutory law, and all other laws, including, but not limited to, all contract, tort, and property disputes, will be subject to binding arbitration in accord with this Contract. The parties agree and understand that the arbitrator shall have all powers provided by the law and the Contract." Joint Lodging 37.

similarly situated class. In lieu of an answer, petitioners filed a motion to compel arbitration, to stay the action, or, in the alternative, to dismiss. The District Court granted petitioners' motion to compel arbitration, denied the motion to stay, and dismissed Randolph's claims with prejudice. The District Court also denied her request to certify a class. 991 F.Supp. 1410 (M.D.Ala. 1997). She requested reconsideration, asserting that she lacked the resources to arbitrate, and as a result, would have to forgo her claims against petitioners. See Plaintiff's Motion for Reconsideration, Record Doc. No. 53, p. 9. The District Court denied reconsideration. 991 F.Supp. at 1425-1426. Randolph appealed.

The Court of Appeals for the Eleventh Circuit first held that it had jurisdiction to review the District Court's order because that order was a final decision. 178 F.3d 1149 (1999). The Court of Appeals looked to § 16 of the Federal Arbitration Act (FAA), 9 U.S.C. § 16, which governs appeal from a district court's arbitration order, and specifically § 16(a)(3), which allows appeal from "a final decision with respect to an arbitration that is subject to this title." The court determined that a final, appealable order within the meaning of the FAA is one that disposes of all the issues framed by the litigation, leaving nothing to be done but execute the order. The Court of Appeals found the District Court's order within that definition.

The court then determined that the arbitration agreement failed to provide the minimum guarantees that respondent could vindicate her statutory rights under the TILA. Critical to this determination was the court's observation that the arbitration agreement was silent with respect to payment of filing fees, arbitrators' costs, and other arbitration expenses. On that basis, the court held that the agreement to arbitrate posed a risk that respondent's ability to vindicate her statutory rights would be undone by "steep" arbitration costs, and therefore was unenforceable. We granted certiorari, 529 U.S. 1052, 120 S.Ct. 1552, 146 L.Ed.2d 458 (2000), and we now affirm the Court of Appeals with respect to the first conclusion, and reverse it with respect to the second.

(continued)

(continued from previous page)

II

Section 16 of the Federal Arbitration Act, enacted in 1988, governs appellate review of arbitration orders. 9 U.S.C. § 16. It provides:

(a) An appeal may be taken from—
    (1) an order—
        (A) refusing a stay of any action under section 3 of this title,
        (B) denying a petition under section 4 of this title to order arbitration to proceed,
        (C) denying an application under section 206 of this title to compel arbitration,
        (D) confirming or denying confirmation of an award or partial award, or
        (E) modifying, correcting, or vacating an award;
    (2) an interlocutory order granting, continuing, or modifying an injunction against an arbitration that is subject to this title; or
    (3) a final decision with respect to an arbitration that is subject to this title.
(b) Except as otherwise provided in section 1292(b) of title 28, an appeal may not be taken from an interlocutory order—
    (1) granting a stay of any action under section 3 of this title;
    (2) directing arbitration to proceed under section 4 of this title;
    (3) compelling arbitration under section 206 of this title; or
    (4) refusing to enjoin an arbitration that is subject to this title.

The District Court's order directed that arbitration proceed and dismissed respondent's claims for relief. The question before us, then, is whether that order can be appealed as "a final decision with respect to an arbitration" within the meaning of § 16(a)(3). Petitioners urge us to hold that it cannot. They rely, in part, on the FAA's policy favoring arbitration agreements and its goal of "mov[ing] the parties to an arbitrable dispute out of court and into arbitration as quickly and easily as possi-

ble." *Moses H. Cone Memorial Hospital v. Mercury Constr. Corp.*, 460 U.S. 1, 22, 103 S.Ct. 927, 74 L.Ed.2d 765 (1983). In accordance with that purpose, petitioners point out, § 16 generally permits immediate appeal of orders hostile to arbitration, whether the orders are final or interlocutory, but bars appeal of interlocutory orders favorable to arbitration.

Section 16(a)(3), however, preserves immediate appeal of any "final decision with respect to an arbitration," regardless of whether the decision is favorable or hostile to arbitration. And as petitioners and respondent agree, the term "final decision" has a well-developed and longstanding meaning. It is a decision that "'ends the litigation on the merits and leaves nothing more for the court to do but execute the judgment.'" *Digital Equipment Corp. v. Desktop Direct, Inc.*, 511 U.S. 863, 867, 114 S.Ct. 1992, 128 L.Ed.2d 842 (1994), and *Coopers & Lybrand v. Livesay*, 437 U.S. 463, 98 S.Ct. 2454, 57 L.Ed.2d 351 (1978) (both quoting *Catlin v. United States*, 324 U.S. 229, 233, 65 S.Ct. 631, 89 L.Ed. 911 (1945). *See also St. Louis, I.M. & S.R. Co. v. Southern Express Co.*, 108 U.S. 24, 28-29, 2 S.Ct. 6, 27 L.Ed. 638 (1883). Because the FAA does not define "a final decision with respect to an arbitration" or otherwise suggest that the ordinary meaning of "final decision" should not apply, we accord the term its well-established meaning. *See Evans v. United States*, 504 U.S. 255, 259-260, 112 S.Ct. 1881, 110 L.Ed.2d 57 (1992).

The District Court's order directed that the dispute be resolved by arbitration and dismissed respondent's claims with prejudice, leaving the court nothing to do but execute the judgment. That order plainly disposed of the entire case on the merits and left no part of it pending before the court. The FAA does permit parties to arbitration agreements to bring a separate proceeding in a district court to enter judgment on an arbitration award once it is made (or to vacate or modify it), but the existence of that remedy does not vitiate the finality of the District Court's resolution of the claims in the instant proceeding. 9 U.S.C. §§ 9, 10, 11. The District Court's order was therefore "a final decision with respect to an arbitration" within the meaning of § 16(a)(3), and an appeal may be taken.[2] *See Sears, Roebuck & Co. v. Mackey*, 351 U.S. 427, 431, 76 S.Ct. 895, 100 L.Ed. 1297 (1956) (explaining that had the District Court dismissed all the claims in an action, its decision would be final and appealable); *Catlin, supra*, at 236, 65 S.Ct. 631 (noting that had petitioners' motion to dismiss been granted and a judgment of dismissal entered, "clearly there would have been an end of the litigation and appeal would lie . . . ").

Petitioners contend that the phrase "final decision" does not include an order compelling arbitration and dismissing the other claims in the action, when that order occurs in an "embedded" proceeding, such as this one. Brief for Petitioners 26. "Embedded" proceedings are simply those actions involving both a request for arbitration and other claims for relief. "Independent" proceedings, by contrast, are actions in which a request to order arbitration is the sole issue before the court. Those Courts of Appeals attaching significance to this distinction hold that an order compelling arbitration in an "independent" proceeding is final within the meaning of § 16(a)(3), but that such an order in an "embedded" proceeding is not, even if the district court dismisses the remaining claims.[3]

Petitioners contend that the distinction between independent and embedded proceedings and its consequences for finality were so firmly established at the time of § 16's enactment that we should assume Congress meant to incorporate them into § 16(a)(3). See Brief for Petitioners 23-26.

We disagree. It does not appear that, at the time of § 16(a)(3)'s enactment, the rules of finality were firmly established in cases like this one, where the District Court both ordered arbitration and dismissed the remaining claims.[4] We also note that at that time, Courts of Appeals did not have a uniform approach to finality with respect to orders directing arbitration in "embedded" proceedings.[5] The term "final decision," by contrast, enjoys a consistent and longstanding interpretation.

---

[2]Had the district court entered a stay instead of a dismissal in this case, that order would not be appealable. 9 U.S.C. § 16(b)(1). The question whether the district court should have taken that course is not before us, and we do not address it.

[3]The majority of courts of appeals have so opined, contrary to the instant decision of the Court of Appeals for the Eleventh Circuit. *See, e.g., Seacoast Motor of Salisbury, Inc. v. Chrysler Corp.*, 143 F.3d 626, 628-629 (C.A.1 1998); *Altman Nursing, Inc. v. Clay Capital Corp.*, 84 F.3d 769, 771 (C.A.5 1996); *Napleton v. General Motors Corp.*, 138 F.3d 1209, 1212 (C.A.7 1998); *Gammaro v. Thorp Consumer Discount Co.*, 15 F.3d 93, 95 (C.A.8 1994); *McCarthy v. Providential Corp.*, 122 F.3d 1242, 1244 (C.A.9 1997). *But see Arnold v. Arnold Corp.—Printed Communications for Business*, 920 F.2d 1269, 1276 (C.A.6 1990) (order compelling arbitration in an "embedded" proceeding treated as a final judgment when the district court dismissed the action in deference to arbitration and had nothing left to do but execute the judgment); *Arijo v. Prudential Insurance Co. of America*, 72 F.3d 793, 797 (C.A.10 1995) (same).

[4]*Seacoast Motors of Salisbury, Inc., supra*, at 628 (noting in 1998 that the Court had not before addressed the question whether a district court order directing arbitration and dismissing the proceedings was a "final decision" within the meaning of § 16(a)(3); *Napleton, supra*, at 1212 (noting in 1998 that the appeal at issue adds an "unfamiliar ingredient" because the district court ordered arbitration and dismissed the proceedings).

[5]*Cincinnati Gas & Elec. Co. v. Benjamin F. Shaw Co.*, 706 F.2d 155, 158 (C.A.6 1983) (rejecting the argument that because a declaratory judgment and other relief was sought in suit where arbitration was ordered, order to arbitrate should not be appealable); *Howard Elec. and Mechanical Co. v. Frank Friscoe Co.*, 754 F.2d 847, 849 (C.A.9 1985) (plaintiff brought suit for work performed under contract and then sought arbitration; order compelling arbitration held appealable). *Cf. In re Hops Antitrust Litigation*, 832 F.2d 470, 472-473 (C.A.8 1987) (district court order requiring arbitration of some claims before it is not a final appealable order because other matters remained pending before the court); *County of Durham v. Richards & Assocs., Inc.*, 742 F.2d 811, 813, n.3 (C.A.4 1984) (noting that a number of courts of appeals have held that an order compelling arbitration may be appealed even when it is entered in the course of a dispute over the underlying claim). *See generally* 15B C. Wright, A. Miller, & E. Cooper, *Federal Practice and Procedure* § 3914.17, pp. 19-25 (1992).

(continued)

(continued from previous page)

Certainly the plain language of the statutory text does not suggest that Congress intended to incorporate the rather complex independent/embedded distinction, and its consequences for finality, into § 16(a)(3). We therefore conclude that where, as here, the District Court has ordered the parties to proceed to arbitration, and dismissed all the claims before it, that decision is "final" within the meaning of § 16(a)(3), and therefore appealable.

III

We now turn to the question whether Randolph's agreement to arbitrate is unenforceable because it says nothing about the costs of arbitration, and thus fails to provide her protection from potentially substantial costs of pursuing her federal statutory claims in the arbitral forum. Section 2 of the FAA provides that "[a] written provision in any maritime transaction or a contract evidencing a transaction involving commerce to settle by arbitration a controversy thereafter arising out of such contract . . . shall be valid, irrevocable, and enforceable, save upon such grounds as exist at law or in equity for the revocation of any contract." 9 U.S.C. § 2. In considering whether respondent's agreement to arbitrate is unenforceable, we are mindful of the FAA's purpose "to reverse the longstanding judicial hostility to arbitration agreements . . . and to place arbitration agreements upon the same footing as other contracts." *Gilmer v. Interstate/Johnson Lane Corp.*, 500 U.S. 20, 24, 111 S.Ct. 1647, 114 L.Ed.2d 26 (1991).

In light of that purpose, we have recognized that federal statutory claims can be appropriately resolved through arbitration, and we have enforced agreements to arbitrate that involve such claims. *See, e.g., Rodriguez de Quijas v. Shearson/American Express, Inc.*, 490 U.S. 477, 109 S.Ct. 1917, 104 L.Ed.2d 526 (1989) (Securities Act of 1933); *Shearson/American Express, Inc. v. McMahan*, 482 U.S. 220, 170 S.Ct. 2332, 96 L.Ed.2d 185 (1987) (Securities Exchange Act of 1934 and Racketeer Influenced and Corrupt Organizations Act); *Mitsubishi Motors Corp. v. Soler Chrysler-Plymouth, Inc.*, 473 U.S. 614, 105 S.Ct. 3346, 87 L.Ed.2d 444 (1985) (Sherman Act). We have likewise rejected generalized attacks on arbitration that rest on "suspicion of arbitration as a method of weakening the protections afforded in the substantive law to would-be complainants." *Rodriguez de Quijas, supra* at 481, 109 S.Ct. 1917. These cases demonstrate that even claims arising under a statute designed to further important social policies may be arbitrated because "'so long as the prospective litigant effectively may vindicate [his or her] statutory cause of action in the arbitral forum,'" the statute serves its functions. *See Gilmer, supra* at 28, 111 S.Ct. 1647 (quoting *Mitsubishi, supra* at 637, 105 S.Ct. 3346).

In determining whether statutory claims may be arbitrated, we first ask whether the parties agreed to submit their claims to arbitration, and then ask whether Congress has evinced an intention to preclude a waiver of judicial remedies for the statutory rights at issue. *See Gilmer, supra* at 26, 111 S.Ct. 1647 (quoting *Mitsubishi, supra* at 628, 105 S.Ct. 3346). In this case, it is undisputed that the parties agreed to arbitrate all claims relating to their contract, including claims involving statutory rights. Nor does Randolph contend that the TILA evinces an intention to preclude a waiver of judicial remedies. She contends instead that the arbitration agreement's silence with respect to costs and fees creates a "risk" that she will be required to bear prohibitive arbitration costs if she pursues her claims in an arbitral forum, and thereby forces her to forgo any claims she may have against petitioners. Therefore, she argues, she is unable to vindicate her statutory rights in arbitration. See Brief for Respondent 29–30.

It may well be that the existence of large arbitration costs could preclude a litigant such as Randolph from effectively vindicating her federal statutory rights in the arbitral forum. But the record does not show that Randolph will bear such costs if she goes to arbitration. Indeed, it contains hardly any information on the matter.[6] As the Court of Appeals recognized, "we lack . . . information about how claimants fare under Green Tree's arbitration clause." 178 F.3d at 1158. The record reveals only the arbitration agreement's silence on the subject, and that fact alone is plainly insufficient to render it unenforceable. The "risk" that Randolph will be saddled with prohibitive costs is too

[6]In Randolph's motion for reconsideration in the district court, she asserted that "[a]rbitration costs are high" and that she did not have the resources to arbitrate. But she failed to support this assertion. She first acknowledged that petitioners had not designated a particular arbitration association or arbitrator to resolve their dispute. Her subsequent discussion of costs relied entirely on unfounded assumptions. She stated that "[f]or the purposes of this discussion, we will assume filing with the [American Arbitration Association], the filing fee is $500 for claims under $10,000 and this does not include the cost of the arbitrator or administrative fees." Randolph relied on, and attached as an exhibit, what appears to be informational material from the American Arbitration Association that does not discuss the amount of filing fees. She then noted: "[The American Arbitration Association] further cites $700 per day as the average arbitrator's fee." For this proposition she cited an article in the *Daily Labor Report*, February 15, 1996, published by the Bureau of National Affairs, entitled "Labor Lawyers at ABA Session Debate Role of American Arbitration Association." Plaintiff's Motion for Reconsideration, Record Doc. No. 53, pp. 8-9. The article contains a stray statement by an association executive that the average arbitral fee is $700 per day. Randolph plainly failed to make any factual showing that the American Arbitration Association would conduct the arbitration, or that, if it did, she would be charged the filing fee or arbitrator's fee that she identified. These unsupported statements provide no basis on which to ascertain the actual costs and fees to which she would be subject in arbitration. In this Court, Randolph's brief lists fees incurred in cases involving other arbitrations as reflected in opinions of other courts of appeals, while petitioners' counsel states that arbitration fees are frequently waived by petitioners. None of this information affords a sufficient basis for concluding that Randolph would in fact have incurred substantial costs in the event her claim went to arbitration.

speculative to justify the invalidation of an arbitration agreement. To invalidate the agreement on that basis would undermine the "liberal federal policy favoring arbitration agreements." *Moses H. Cone Memorial Hospital*, 460 U.S. at 24, 103 S.Ct. 927. It would also conflict with our prior holdings that the party resisting arbitration bears the burden of proving that the claims at issue are unsuitable for arbitration. *See Gilmer, supra* at 26, 111 S.Ct. 1647; *McMahon, supra* at 227, 107 S.Ct. 2332. We have held that the party seeking to avoid arbitration bears the burden of establishing that Congress intended to preclude arbitration of the statutory claims at issue. *See Gilmer, supra; McMahon, supra*. Similarly, we believe that where, as here, a party seeks to invalidate an arbitration agreement on the ground that arbitration would be prohibitively expensive, that party bears the burden of showing the likelihood of incurring such costs. Randolph did not meet that burden. How detailed the showing of prohibitive expense must be before the party seeking arbitration must come forward with contrary evidence is a matter we need not discuss; for in this case neither during discovery nor when the case was presented on the merits was there any timely showing at all on the point. The Court of Appeals therefore erred in deciding that the arbitration agreement's silence with respect to costs and fees rendered it unenforceable.

The judgment of the Court of Appeals is affirmed in part and reversed in part.

It is so ordered.

Justice Ginsburg, with whom Justice Stevens and Justice Souter join, and with whom Justice Breyer joins as to Parts I and III, concurring in part and dissenting in part.

I

I join Part II of the Court's opinion, which holds that the District Court's order, dismissing all the claims before it, was a "final," and therefore immediately appealable, decision. *Ante*, at 518-521. On the matter the Court

(continued)

(continued from previous page)

errs in Part III, ante, at 521-523—allocation of the costs of arbitration—I would not rule definitively. Instead, I would vacate the Eleventh Circuit's decision, which dispositively declared the arbitration clause unenforceable, and remand the case for closer consideration of the arbitral forum's accessibility.

II

The Court today deals with a "who pays" question, specifically, who pays for the arbitral forum. The Court holds that Larketta Randolph bears the burden of demonstrating that the arbitral forum is financially inaccessible to her. Essentially, the Court requires a party, situated as Randolph is, either to submit to arbitration without knowing who will pay for the forum or to demonstrate up front that the costs, if imposed on her, will be prohibitive. *Ante*, at 522-523. As I see it, the case in its current posture is not ripe for such a disposition.

The Court recognizes that "the existence of large arbitration costs could preclude a litigant such as Randolph from effectively vindicating her federal statutory rights in the arbitral forum." *Ante*, at 522. But, the Court next determines, "the party resisting arbitration bears the burden of proving that the claims at issue are unsuitable for arbitration" and "Randolph did not meet that burden." *Ante*, at 522. In so ruling, the Court blends two discrete inquiries: First, is the arbitral forum *adequate* to adjudicate the claims at issue; second, is that forum *accessible* to the party resisting arbitration.

Our past decisions deal with the first question, the *adequacy* of the arbitral forum to adjudicate various statutory claims. *See, e.g., Gilmer v. Interstate/Johnson Lane Corp.*, 500 U.S. 20, 111 S.Ct. 1647, 114 L.Ed.2d 26 (1991) (Age Discrimination in Employment Act claims are amenable to arbitration); *Shearson/American Express, Inc. v. McMahon*, 482 U.S. 220, 107 S.Ct. 2332, 96 L.Ed.2d 185 (1987) (Claims under Racketeer Influenced and Corrupt Organizations Act and Securities Exchange Act are amenable to arbitration). These decisions hold that the party resisting arbitration bears the burden of establishing the inadequacy of the arbitral forum for adjudication of claims of a particular genre. *See Gilmer*, 500 U.S. at 26, 111 S.Ct. 1647; *McMahon*, 482 U.S. at 227, 107 S.Ct. 2332. It does not follow like the night the day, however, that the party resisting arbitration should also bear the burden of showing that the arbitral forum would be financially inaccessible to her.

The arbitration agreement at issue is contained in a form contract drawn by a commercial party and presented to an individual consumer on a take-it or leave-it basis. The case on which the Court dominantly relies, *Gilmer*, also involved a nonnegotiated arbitration clause. But the "who pays" question presented in this case did not arise in *Gilmer*. Under the rules that governed in *Gilmer*—those of the New York Stock Exchange—it was the standard practice for securities industry parties, arbitrating employment disputes, to pay all of the arbitrators' fees. *See Cole v. Burns Int'l Security Servs.*, 105 F.3d 1465, 1483 (C.A.D.C. 1997). Regarding that practice, the Court of Appeals for the District of Columbia Circuit recently commented:

> [I]n *Gilmer* the Supreme Court endorsed a system of arbitration in which employees are not required to pay for the arbitrator assigned to hear their statutory claims. There is no reason to think that the Court would have approved arbitration in the absence of this arrangement. Indeed, we are unaware of any situation in American jurisprudence in which a beneficiary of a federal statute has been required to pay for the services of the judge assigned to hear her or his case." *Id.* at 1484.

III

The form contract in this case provides no indication of the rules under which arbitration will proceed or the costs a consumer is likely to incur in arbitration.[7]

[7]In Alabama, as in most states, courts interpret a contract's silence (about arbitration fees and costs) according to "usage or custom." *Green Tree Financial Corp. of Ala. v. Wampler*, 749 So.2d 409, 415 (Ala. 1999); *see also* Restatement (Second) of Contracts § 204, Comment *d* (1979) (where an essential term is missing, "the court should supply a term which comports with community standards of fairness and policy"). *Cf. First Options of Chicago, Inc. v. Kaplan*, 514 U.S. 938, 944, 115 S.Ct. 1920, 131 L.Ed.2d 985 (1995) (courts should generally apply state contract law principles when deciding whether parties agreed to arbitrate a certain matter); *Mastrobuono v. Shearson Lehman Hutton, Inc.*, 514 U.S. 52, 62-64, and n.9, 115 S.Ct. 1212, 131 L.Ed.2d 76 (1995) (interpreting arbitration clause according to New York and Illinois law).

Green Tree, drafter of the contract, could have filled the void by specifying, for instance, that arbitration would be governed by the rules of the American Arbitration Association (AAA). Under the AAA's Consumer Arbitration Rules, consumers in small-claims arbitration incur no filing fee and pay only $125 of the total fees charged by the arbitrator. All other fees and costs are to be paid by the business party. Brief for American Arbitration Association as *Amicus Curiae* 15-16. Other national arbitration organizations have developed similar models for fair cost and fee allocation.[8] It may be that in this case, as in *Gilmer* there is a standard practice on arbitrators' fees and expenses, one that fills the blank space in the arbitration agreement. Counsel for Green Tree offered a hint in that direction. See Tr. of Oral Arg. 26 ("Green Tree does pay [arbitration] costs in a lot of instances . . . "). But there is no reliable indication in this record that Randolph's claim will be arbitrated under any consumer-protective fee arrangement.

As a repeat player in the arbitration required by its form contract, Green Tree has superior information about the cost to consumers of pursuing arbitration. *Cf. Raleigh v. Illinois Dept. of Revenue*, 530 U.S. 15, 21, 120 S.Ct. 1951, 147 L.Ed.2d 13 (2000) ("the very fact that the burden of proof has often been placed on the taxpayer [to disprove tax liability] . . . reflects several compelling rationales . . . [including] the taxpayer's readier access to the relevant information"); 9 J. Wigmore, Evidence § 2486 (J. Chadbourn rev. ed. 1981) (where fairness so requires, burden of proof of a particular fact may be assigned to "party who presumably has peculiar means of knowledge" of the fact); Restatement (Second) of Contracts § 206 (1979) ("In choosing among the reasonable meanings of . . . [an] agreement or a term thereof, that meaning is generally preferred which operates against the [drafting] party . . . ."). In these circumstances,

it is hardly clear that Randolph should bear the burden of demonstrating up front the arbitral forum's inaccessibility, or that she should be required to submit to arbitration without knowing how much it will cost her.

As I see it, the Court has reached out prematurely to resolve the matter in the lender's favor. If Green Tree's practice under the form contract with retail installment sales purchasers resembles that of the employer in *Gilmer*, Randolph would be insulated from prohibitive costs. And if the arbitral forum were in this case financially accessible to Randolph, there would be no occasion to reach the decision today rendered by the Court. Before writing a term into the form contract, as the District of Columbia Circuit did, *see Cole*, 105 F.3d at 1485[9] or leaving cost allocation initially to each arbitrator, as the Court does, I would remand for clarification of Green Tree's practice.

The Court's opinion, if I comprehend it correctly, does not prevent Randolph from returning to court, postarbitration, if she then has a complaint about cost allocation. If that is so, the issue reduces to when, not whether, she can be spared from payment of excessive costs. Neither certainty nor judicial economy is served by leaving that issue unsettled until the end of the line.

For the reasons stated, I dissent from the Court's reversal of the Eleventh Circuit's decision on the cost question. I would instead vacate and remand for further consideration of the accessibility of the arbitral forum to Randolph.[10]

---

[8] They include National Arbitration Forum provisions that limit small-claims consumer costs to between $49 and $175 and a National Consumer Disputes Advisory Committee protocol recommending that consumer costs be limited to a reasonable amount. National Arbitration Forum, Code of Procedure, App. C, Fee Schedule (July 1, 2000); National Consumer Disputes Advisory Committee, Consumer Due Process Protocol, Principle 6, Comment (Apr. 17, 1998), http://www.adr.org/education/education/consumer_protocol.html.

[9] The Court interpreted a form contract to arbitrate employment disputes, silent as to costs, to require the employer "to pay all of the arbitrator's fees necessary for a full and fair resolution of [the discharged employee's] statutory claims." 105 F.3d at 1485.

[10] Randolph alternatively urges affirmance on the ground that the arbitration agreement is unenforceable because it precludes pursuit of her statutory claim as a class action. *But cf. Johnson v. West Suburban Bank*, 225 F.3d 366 (C.A.3 2000) (holding arbitration clause in short-term loan agreement enforceable even though it may render class action to pursue statutory claims unavailable). The class-action issue was properly raised in the District Court and the Court of Appeals. I do not read the Court's opinion to preclude resolution of that question now by the Eleventh Circuit. Nothing Randolph has so far done in seeking protection against prohibitive costs forfeits her right to a judicial determination whether her claim may proceed either in court or arbitration as a class action.

Predispute Mediation Provision

Predispute Mediation Provision
A predispute mediation provision requires the parties to participate in mediation for all disputes that arise under their contract.

With the increased popularity of private mediation, some drafters have altered their form contracts to require private mediation rather than private arbitration. A **predispute mediation provision** binds the parties to participate in private mediation to attempt to resolve all disputes that arise under the contract. Thus the parties are precluded from pursuing an adjudication form of dispute resolution (arbitration, litigation in the court, private judging) until they have participated in mediation.

Example 18-1

The following illustrates a predispute mediation provision:

Any dispute arising out of this contract that cannot be settled by negotiation shall be submitted to mediation administered by _____.

For tips in drafting predispute mediation provisions, see *Drafting Dispute Resolution Clauses—A Practical Guide*, the American Arbitration Association, *http://www.adr.org/rules/guides/clausebook.html#Mediation*.

By preselecting mediation rather than arbitration, the drafters have negated some of the one-sidedness of mandatory arbitration. Either party may end the mediation process at any time and for any reason. The parties are on more of an equal footing during the mediation. In mediation the parties retain their power to resolve their own dispute rather than empowering an arbitrator or judge to decide for them. Mediation, however, does not guarantee resolution at the end of the process. The parties may be unable to resolve their own dispute and may ultimately find it necessary to pursue an adjudication form of dispute resolution.

The Subtle Impact of Nondispute Resolution Provisions on the Selection of a Dispute Resolution Process

A mandatory predispute arbitration or mediation provision appears in a written contract as an obvious selection of a method of dispute resolution. The provision stands by itself for all to see. Those who have not taken the time to read their contracts are still held to their terms because under normal circumstances the failure to read the contract is not a defense.

A number of other contract provisions have a more subtle impact on developing a dispute resolution strategy. They often significantly influence a party's conduct. The following explores a few of these provisions.

Liquidated Damages
Damages included in the contract by the parties that will be due in the event of breach.

Liquidated Damages

A contract may include a liquidated damages provision. **Liquidated damages** are damages included in the contract by the parties that will be due in the event of breach.

Example 18-2

A liquidated damages provision may take the following form:

If the time of completion extends beyond March 15, 2003, liquidated damages will be incurred at the rate of $2,000/day.

If the Lessor terminates the Lessee's lease before the expiration of the lease term, the Lessor shall pay the Lessee the total cost of the Lessee's improvements to the leased property, multiplied by the number of months remaining in the lease, divided by the total number of months of the lease.

If the Buyer cancels the contract prior to the Seller shipping the goods, the Seller shall retain the Buyer's 5 percent deposit.

Not all provisions that purport to be liquidated damages are enforceable in the courts. When the breaching party challenges such a provision, the court will evaluate whether the provision is in fact a liquidated damages provision or merely a penalty. Provisions that are classified as penalties are unenforceable. The nonbreaching party then must prove his or her damages as if the liquidated damages provision were not in the contract.

A provision is a liquidated damages provision and not a penalty if:

1. at the time of contract formation the damages in the event of a breach will be impossible or very difficult to estimate accurately;
2. there was a reasonable endeavor by the parties to fix a fair compensation; and
3. the amount stipulated bears a reasonable relation to probable damages and is not disproportionate to any damages reasonably anticipated.

A liquidated damages/penalty provision may have a substantial impact on a party's performance. A party who is contemplating breach may think twice before breaching. He or she may not want to face the consequences of the liquidated damages provision or test whether the provision is in fact a penalty and therefore unenforceable in court.

Problem 18-1

You have signed a one-year lease for an apartment located on the lower East Side of Manhattan. The rent is $2,500 a month. You have given the landlord two months' rent as a deposit. After living in this apartment for six months, you now have an opportunity to lease a larger apartment nearby for less rent.

1. Should you break the lease (i.e., breach the contract) if your deposit will be returned and your only liability will be to pay the landlord for any actual losses caused by your breach? Actual losses would include the cost to repair and repaint your apartment prior to leasing it to another, the costs to advertise to find another lessee, and the rent lost during the time the apartment is vacant.
2. What impact would the following lease provision have on your decision?

    Termination of this lease by Tenant for any reason whatsoever will result in Landlord's retaining the total deposit in liquidation of damages resulting from Tenant's breach.

3. If you breach the lease, should you test in court whether the provision is unenforceable as a penalty provision or should you acquiesce and let the landlord retain the deposit according to the lease provision?

Now assume the lease contains the following provision in addition to the two months' rent provision:

Tenant waives the right to legal action to recover the deposit.

1. What impact does this provision have on your decision to terminate the lease?
2. What impact does this provision have on your decision to let the landlord retain your deposit?
3. Should a court enforce this provision?
4. Would your decisions change if the deposit had been only $500?

Security Agreement
An agreement to use collateral to guarantee payment of an obligation.

Secured Transaction
A transaction in which the buyer gives the seller a security interest in specified collateral thus giving the seller the right to repossess the collateral in the event the buyer defaults in payment.

Security Interest
The seller's right to repossess specified collateral in the event the buyer defaults in payment.

Repossession

When a buyer purchases an item from a seller on credit and signs a contract promising to pay, the seller only has the buyer's written word that he or she will pay for the item purchased. The seller may need additional guarantees to ensure that the buyer will in fact do what he or she is obligated to do. The seller may require the buyer to put the item purchased up as collateral to guarantee the obligation to pay. This agreement to use collateral to guarantee payment is known as a **security agreement** and the transaction is known as a **secured transaction**. The buyer gives the seller a **security interest** in the collateral which means the buyer gives the seller the right to repossess the collateral in the event the buyer defaults in payment.

Example 18-3

A security agreement could take the following form:

_____, the Buyer, hereby granted to _____, the Seller, a security interest in _____.

The Seller reserves title in the goods until the Buyer has paid for the goods in full.

In the event the Buyer defaults in a payment, the Seller may repossess _____.

If a buyer breaches the underlying sales contract and does not pay, the seller may exercise self-help and repossess the item sold. The seller may then resell the item and recover at least some of the money owed. The buyer remains liable to the seller for any deficiency (i.e., money still owed).

Problem 18-2

Bernie Shapiro purchased a new Ford Explorer from Butterfield Motors. He paid 20 percent down, financed the balance with Butterfield, and gave Butterfield a security interest in the Explorer. The security interest provides that if Bernie defaults in the payment of his loan, Butterfield could repossess the Explorer, sell it, and apply the proceeds of the sale to pay down the outstanding balance.

1. How does the inclusion of this right to repossess affect the buyer's conduct?
2. Will Bernie pay Butterfield before he pays other loans that are not secured?
3. If a Firestone tire on the Explorer fails while Bernie is driving and the Explorer rolls over, must Bernie still pay Butterfield?
4. What happens to the insurance proceeds from the accident?
5. What happens to any settlement Bernie receives from the Ford Motor Company, Butterfield Motors, and Bridgestone/Firestone?
6. Does Butterfield have an interest in these proceeds because it had a security interest in the Explorer?
7. Does the security interest impact on Bernie's choice of methods of dispute resolution?

The buyer may buy an item from one party and borrow the money to pay for this item from a third party, such as a bank or credit union. The third party may require a security interest in the item before it lends the money to the buyer.

Problem 18-3

Bernie Shapiro purchased a new Ford Explorer from Butterfield Motors. He borrowed the purchase price from First Bank and gave First Bank a security interest in the Explorer. The security interest provides that if Bernie defaults in the payment of his loan, the bank could repossess the Explorer, sell it, and apply the proceeds of the sale to the pay down the loan.

1. How does the inclusion of this right to repossess affect the buyer's conduct, that is, will Bernie pay First Bank before he pays other loans that are not secured?
2. If a Firestone tire on the Explorer fails while Bernie is driving and the Explorer rolls over, must Bernie still pay the Bank?
3. What happens to the insurance proceeds from the accident?
4. What happens to any settlement Bernie receives from the Ford Motor Company, Butterfield Motors, and Bridgestone/Firestone?
5. Does the Bank have an interest in these proceeds because it had a security interest in the Explorer?
6. Does the security interest impact on Bernie's choice of methods of dispute resolution?

Secured transactions do not require a sale. A party may borrow money and use items that he or she already has as collateral for the loan. This often occurs in business where an individual, partnership, or corporation uses its inventory, equipment, or accounts receivable (i.e., promises to pay that others have given it) as collateral for a loan.

Example 18-4

A security agreement could take the following form:

_____, the debtor, hereby granted to _____, the creditor, a security interest in _____.

In the event the Borrower defaults in a payment, the Lender may repossess _____.

When the collateral is real estate, the transaction is called a *real estate mortgage*. The real estate is used as collateral for a loan or sale where the sale price is yet to be paid.

Problem 18-4

You have $2,100 in bills but only $1,300 to pay them with. Arrange your bills in the order in which you will pay them.

doctor for medical bills	$300
bank for car payments	$500
lessor for apartment rent	$600
gas and electric company	$125
bank for student loan	$200
cable TV company	$ 30
mobile phone company	$ 60
home phone company	$ 30
credit card company	$200
money borrowed from a family member	$ 55

1. Which bills will not be paid this month?
2. What is your creditor's remedy if you do not pay that bill?
3. Does this enter into your decision to pay that bill?

Costs and Attorney's Fees

The allocation of costs (i.e., filing fees, service of process, jury fees, and court officer charges, but not attorney's fees) and attorney's fees may play a significant role when a party selects a dispute resolution process. When selecting a dispute resolution process, parties are concerned not only with their own costs and attorney's fees but also with whether they might be obligated to reimburse the other party for his or her costs and attorney's fees in the event the other side prevails in an adjudicative process.

Some processes such as inaction, acquiescence, self-help, and ombuds have minimal costs and may require little, if any, assistance of counsel. Negotiation and mediation may or may not have some costs and may or may not require the assistance of counsel. Others such as arbitration, litigation in the courts, and private judging involve significant costs and attorney's fees. In an adjudication process, costs and attorney's fees will be allocated by the presiding officer according to the forum's procedures or according to the parties' agreement.

In private arbitration or private judging, the parties could allocate the costs and attorney's fees when contracting to enter into one of these processes.

If the dispute arises out of a contract, the parties may have allocated costs and attorney's fees in their contract.

Example 18-5

A contract to borrow money could have the following provision:

For value received, the undersigned, jointly and severally, guarantee unconditionally prompt payment of this promissory note when due, whether at maturity, by acceleration, or otherwise. The undersigned shall pay all costs and expenses, including attorney's fees, incurred in the collection of this promissory note and in the enforcement of this guaranty.

Problem 18-5

You have contracted with Sun Valley Construction Company for the construction of a new home. The contract price is $400,000. The contract provides:

If litigation arises from this contract, the party obtaining a favorable judgment in such litigation may recover his or her attorney's fees from the opposing party.

When you signed the contract, the contractor promised to complete your home in four months. It is now six months and the construction is only 80 percent complete. You have paid the contractor 75 percent of the contract price ($300,000). The contract specifies that another $50,000 is due in three days.

1.   Should you withhold payment?
2.   Does the attorney's fees provision in the contract affect your decision?

If the contract does not include a provision for costs, most courts will allocate costs to the losing party. Some states, however, authorize their courts to apportion costs between the parties if the case is not decided on all the issues presented.

Unlike costs, the nonbreaching party in a breach of contract action generally cannot recover its attorney's fees from the other party, even after receiving a favorable judgment. This rule has two general exceptions: (1) attorney's fees can be recovered if suit is brought under a statute allowing the nonbreaching party to recover attorney's fees; and (2) attorney's fees can be recovered if the contract provides for their recovery.

If the dispute did not arise out of contract, a state statute may authorize the court to allocate costs and attorney's fees.

Example 18-6

The statute could read:

A judgment, decree or appealable order may provide for costs, attorney's fees and interest or any of these items, but it need not include them.

Problem 18-6

Check the statutes of your state for provisions as to the court's allocation of costs and attorney's fees.

What impact would these statutes have on a party's selection of a dispute resolution strategy?

Confession of Judgment
Confessions of judgment, also known as a *cognovit*, permits a contracting party to have a judgment entered by the court without the need to proceed through trial.

Confession of Judgment

A contract may include a provision whereby a party confesses judgment in the event of a future breach. A **confession of judgment** permits a party to have a judgment entered by the court without the need to proceed through trial.

Example 18-7

A confession of judgment may occur in a loan transaction.

For value received, the undersigned guarantees unconditionally prompt payment of this instrument when due, whether at maturity, by acceleration, or otherwise. The undersigned shall pay all costs and expenses, including attorney's fees, incurred in the collection of this instrument. No renewal or extension of the instrument, no release or surrender of any security for the instrument, nor release of any person, primarily or secondarily liable on the instrument, no delay in the enforcement of the payment of the instrument, and no delay or omission in exercising any right or power under the instrument shall affect the liability of the undersigned. The liability of the undersigned on this guaranty shall be direct and not conditional or contingent on the pursuit of any remedies against any collateral held as security for the payment of this instrument. The undersigned expressly waive presentment, protest, demand, notice of dishonor or default, notice of acceptance of this guaranty, and notice of any kind with respect to this instrument or the performance of the obligations under the instrument. The undersigned consent to be bound by all the terms and provisions of this instrument, including the authority to confess judgment.

Problem 18-7

What impact could a contract provision that provides for a confession of judgment have on a party's selection of a dispute resolution strategy?

Choice of Law
Choice of law is the determination of which law applies when more than one state is involved in a transaction, where conflicting laws exist within a state, or where federal law may preempt state law.

Choice of Law

Choice of law is the determination of which law applies when more than one state is involved in a transaction, where conflicting laws exist within a state, or where federal law may preempt state law. For the purposes of this text, the focus is on which state's law applies when the laws of different states conflict. The contracting parties may provide the answer. When the contract was formed, the parties may have chosen the state whose laws would apply to the transaction.

Example 18-8

A choice-of-law provision may take the following form:

This agreement shall be governed by the laws of the State of _____.

The validity, interpretation, construction, and enforcement of this agreement shall be governed by the laws of the State of _____.

Not all choice-of-law provisions are enforced by the courts. Although the courts give deference to parties' choice of applicable law, deference is not without limitations. For example, a court will not give deference to a choice-of-law provision if: (1) the chosen state has no substantial relationship to the parties or to the transactions; or (2) the result obtained from the applicability of the law of the chosen state would be contrary to the forum state's (i.e., the state where the litigation is taking place) public policy.

If the parties have not selected the state or have made an ineffective selection, the applicable law is found in the forum state's choice-of-law rules. Determining the choice-of-law rule is often a complex question. States do not share a uniform solution.

Problem 18-8

On September 1, the River Valley School District, a California school district, invited bids for a new elementary school from general contractors. On September 3, the Begay Construction Company, a general contractor from California, invited subcontractors to bid on the heating and air conditioning system for the school. On September 5, the Quality Heating and Air Company, a Nevada corporation, submitted its bid to Begay for $2,000,000. On September 7, Begay used Quality's bid in calculating its bid to the school district. On September 8, the school district accepted Begay's bid for the construction of the school.

Before Begay could notify Quality that it accepted Quality's bid for the heating and air conditioning, Quality notified Begay that it was revoking its bid.

Begay was then forced to hire Ace Heating and Air to do the heating and air conditioning at $2,500,000.

A number of years ago the California Supreme Court was faced with a similar situation and created an implied option contract to negate the subcontractor's power to revoke its offer, thus giving the general contractor an opportunity to accept the subcontractor's bid (offer) and form a contract. The result was that by refusing to work for the contract price, the subcontractor was in breach and was required to pay the general contractor the difference between what the general contractor was required to pay another subcontractor and the original subcontractor's contract price.

Nevada has never ruled on this issue, so in Nevada the current law would permit the subcontractor to revoke its bid (offer) and no contract would be formed. Therefore, the subcontractor would not be liable to the general contractor in a breach of contract action.

What impact could a choice-of-law provision that required the court to use the law of California have on Quality's selection of a dispute resolution strategy?

Choice of Forum
Choice of forum provision determines which state's courts may hear a dispute.

Choice of Forum

Choice of forum is the determination of which court will hear any dispute that may arise as a contract is being performed.

Example 18-9

> The following are examples of a choice-of-forum provision:
>
> All disputes arising from this contract shall be decided by the courts of North Carolina.
>
> The courts of North Carolina shall have exclusive jurisdiction to hear any and all disputes arising out of this contract.

A choice-of-forum provision does not guarantee that all future disputes will be heard only by the courts in the named state. A plaintiff may file an action in a state other than the state named in the contract. It is then incumbent upon the defendant to ask the court to enforce the choice-of-forum provision and transfer the action to the forum named in the contract.

Courts will transfer the action to the named forum only if the forum selection provision: (1) does not violate the public policy of the named forum; (2) is not unjust and unreasonable; (3) is free from fraud, undue influence and unequal bargaining power that subverts the party's free will at the time of contracting; and (4) is intended as the exclusive forum and not merely as a suggested forum for the resolution of these disputes.

 ## Problem 18-9

Amy Olson, a successful stock broker in State A, was hired by Bull & Bear, a brokerage company in State B. The contract required Amy to move from State A to State B. The employment contract provided:

> The courts of State B shall have exclusive jurisdiction to hear any and all disputes arising out of this contract.

Shortly after Amy quit her job in State A and moved to State B, she received an e-mail from Bull & Bear stating that because of the conditions in the market, her services would no longer be needed.

State A has a court-sponsored mediation program. State B has a court-annexed arbitration program.

Does where the case will be litigated, if the dispute resolution process comes down to litigation, influence Amy's selection of a dispute resolution strategy?

Remember that choice of forum is different from choice of law. Choice of forum relates to the place; choice of law relates to the substantive rules that will be applied to resolve the dispute. If appropriate, a court in State A could use the law of State B and a court in State B could use the law of State A.

Key Terms and Phrases

choice of forum
choice of law
confession of judgment
contract of adhesion
duress
fraud
liquidated damages

predispute arbitration provision
predispute mediation provision
secured transaction
security agreement
security interest
unconscionable
unenforceable contract provision

Review Questions

True/False Questions

1. T   F   Predispute arbitration provisions are generally unenforceable.
2. T   F   Predispute mediation provisions negate some of the one-sidedness inherent in predispute arbitration provisions.
3. T   F   Predispute arbitration provisions are contracts of adhesion because they are offered on a take-it or leave-it basis.
4. T   F   Predispute arbitration provisions are generally not unconscionable.
5. T   F   A party's selection of dispute resolution processes is often altered by terms in the contract other than mandatory arbitration or mediation.

Fill-in-the-Blank Questions

1. _____   List two dispute resolution processes
   _____   that can be drafted into a contract.
2. _____   List five contract provisions (in addition to
   _____   mandatory arbitration and mandatory mediation)
   _____   that may impact on a party's selection of dispute
   _____   resolution processes.
   _____

Multiple-Choice Questions

1. Which of the following may be included in contracts to preselect a dispute resolution process?
   (a) mandatory litigation provision
   (b) mandatory arbitration provision
   (c) mandatory negotiation provision
   (d) mandatory mediation provision
   (e) mandatory private judging provision

2. A predispute arbitration provision may be unenforceable if a court finds it was:
   (a) a contract of adhesion
   (b) unconscionable
   (c) entered into under fraud
   (d) entered into under duress
   (e) not in bold print

3. Which of the following contract provisions substantially influence a party's selection of dispute resolution processes?
   (a) choice of law
   (b) liquidated damages
   (c) time and place of delivery
   (d) confession of judgment
   (e) warranty

Short-Answer Questions

1. Assume you have purchased a tractor for your family farm on credit from Seller. The contract that you signed contains the following:

Sale of Personal Property

1. Buyer agrees by acceptance of the goods listed above to pay off invoices within 30 days and to pay a service charge of 1½ percent per month, which is an annual percentage rate of 18 percent on all overdue balances.
2. Buyer further agrees that in the event suit is necessary to recover payment of the purchase price, the site of venue will be __[Seller's]__ County.
3. Buyer further agrees to pay Seller's attorney's fees and costs including attorney's fees to appeal.
4. In consideration of this extension of credit, Seller has a lien on all product and property of Buyer in Buyer's possession, including the goods purchased by this contract, until payment of this bill in full.
5. The sale of these goods is governed by California law.
6. Seller warrants the goods for 90 days from the date of delivery in lieu of any further express or implied warranties.
7. Seller's liability for any damages claimed by Buyer is limited to the purchase price of the goods sold.

After you used the tractor for six months, the tractor developed transmission problems. You have informed the seller but the seller's response is that the problem is yours since the express warranty has expired. You still owe the seller about half of the purchase price.

What provisions in the contract limit the array of processes that you could use when you develop your dispute resolution strategy?

How do these provisions limit your strategy? What would your strategy have been without these provisions? What would your strategy be with these provisions?

2. Rather than purchase the tractor, you leased it for one year. The contract that you signed contains the following:

Lease of Personal Property

1. PARTIES. This agreement is made on _____ between _____, the lessor, and _____, the lessee.
2. LEASE OF EQUIPMENT.   The lessor leases to lessee the following equipment:

   _____

   _____

   _____

   for the period of _____ months beginning on _____
   and ending on _____.
3. DELIVERY AND RETURN OF PROPERTY.   The lessor promises to deliver the equipment to _____, at _____. At the end of the lease term, the lessee promises to return the equipment to lessor at the place from where equipment was shipped and in as good a condition as existed when the equipment was received by the lessee, with the exception of reasonable wear and tear.
4. RENT.   The lessee promises to pay the lessee $_____ in monthly rentals of $_____ as rent for the use of the equipment. Each installment shall be due on the first of the month.
5. RESERVATION OF TITLE.   The equipment shall remain the personal property of the lessor and the title to this equipment shall not pass to the lessee.
6. REPOSSESSION.   If the lessee sells, assigns, or attempts to sell or assign the equipment or any interest in the equipment, or if the lessee defaults in any promises under this lease, the lessor may immediately and without notice take possession of equipment wherever found and remove and keep or dispose of the equipment and any unpaid rentals shall become due and payable at once.
7. LOCATION AND USE. The lessee promises to use the equipment only in _____ (location of use) and promises not to remove the equipment from the place _____ (location of equipment) at any time except when returning it to the lessor or except as may be permitted by the lessor in writing.
8. INDEMNIFICATION OF THE LESSOR.   The lessee promises to hold the lessor harmless against any and all losses or damage to equipment by fire, flood, explosion, tornado, or theft and the lessee promises to assume all liability to any person arising from the location, condition, or use of the equipment, and promises to indemnify the lessor for all liability, claim, and demand arising from the location, condition, or use of equipment whether in operation or not, and growing out of any cause, and from every other liability, claim and demand whatever during the term of this lease or arising while the equipment is in the possession of the lessee. The lessee also promises to reimburse the lessor promptly for all personal property taxes levied against the equipment and paid by the lessor.
9. TIME OF ESSENCE.   Time is the essence of this agreement.
10. NO ASSIGNMENT.   Neither this lease nor any right or interest under this lease shall be assigned by the lessee.
11. CHOICE OF LAW.   This lease and agreement shall be deemed to have been executed and entered into in the State of _____ and shall be construed, enforced, and performed in accordance with the laws of that state.

12. EXCLUSION OF ORAL STATEMENTS. This writing contains all of the agreements of the parties. No oral or other statements shall be binding on either the lessor or lessee.

13. GUARANTY. All parts of this equipment are guaranteed against defective parts or workmanship for a period of ninety (90) days from date of delivery and any parts returned by the lessee to factory freight prepaid will be replaced by the lessor free of charge if found defective.

By _____   By _____

  Lessor   Lessee

_____   _____

  Title   Title

After you used the tractor for six months, it developed transmission problems. You have informed the lessor but the lessor's response is that the problem is yours since the 90-day express warranty has expired. You still have six months remaining on the lease.

What provisions in the contract limit the array of processes that you could use when you develop your dispute resolution strategy?

How do these provisions limit your strategy? What would your strategy have been without these provisions? What would your strategy be with these provisions?

CHAPTER 19

Selecting a Dispute Resolution Strategy after the Dispute Arises

In most cases, the dispute resolution strategy must be developed after the dispute arises. This chapter considers postdispute strategy development when either the disputing parties were not contracting parties or, if they were, they did not include a mandatory dispute resolution provision in their contract.

Creating a Strategy for Resolving the Dispute

Creating a strategy for resolving a dispute requires the informed and cooperative efforts of the attorney, the paralegal, and the client. Each must fully understand his or her role in the development of the strategy and in its execution. The attorney gathers the facts, researches the law, develops a number of strategies for the client to evaluate, and counsels the client. The paralegal assists the attorney in gathering the facts, researching the law, and developing the strategies for presentment to the client. The client provides the attorney and paralegal with the facts, evaluates the various strategies presented by the attorney, and ultimately selects the strategy to be followed.

This information will help the paralegal understand the strategy development process and the tasks that may be assigned to him or her. A party who is represented by an attorney will find the following information helpful as he or she works with the attorney in developing a dispute resolution strategy. A party who is not represented by an attorney will find the following information helpful as well in planning a strategy.

The following interview/counseling model focuses on gathering information from the client (i.e., facts, feelings, needs and interests, and goals) and establishing the attorney/client relationship at the interview. Neither the law nor the dispute resolution processes are discussed at the interview unless it is essential that immediate action be taken.

After the interview, the attorney, with the assistance of his or her paralegal, uses the information gathered at the interview to investigate the facts, research the law, and create an array of dispute resolution processes.

At the counseling session the attorney further explores the client's feelings, needs and interests, and goals. It is at the counseling session that the attorney advises the client of the strengths and weaknesses of the client's case (legal and practical) and the advantages and disadvantages of various dispute resolution processes as they relate to the client's problem, and together they design a dispute resolution strategy.

Preparing to Discuss Dispute Resolution Processes at the Counseling Session

An effective counseling session requires careful planning by the attorney and paralegal. One goal for the counseling session is to expand the client's horizons beyond litigation. Alternative processes may offer a client time and cost reduction, control over the process, and control over the outcome of the dispute. Some processes build bridges between parties so they may repair dysfunctional relationships and enhance the opportunity for long-term cooperation. Some provide the parties with an opportunity to fashion solutions that would not be available had the dispute been resolved in court. In short, alternative processes may produce a better result in less time and at a lower cost.

Precounseling planning requires the attorney and paralegal to develop an extensive written list of alternative processes for the client to consider. Before the list is prepared, a number of questions must be answered.

- What are the key factual and legal issues of this dispute?
- What would be the likelihood of success on each key factual and legal issue?
- Have the parties previously agreed to a method of dispute resolution such as arbitration?
- Is that agreement enforceable?
- Who would have jurisdiction over this dispute?
- If the dispute is litigated, would state or federal court provide the better forum?
- Which would provide a better outcome for your client?
- Is this dispute within the jurisdiction of that forum?
- If the dispute is litigated, does the court sponsor mediation or order arbitration as part of the litigation process?
- Is this dispute one that the court would order to mediation or arbitration?
- In addition to court-related dispute resolution (litigation, court-sponsored mediation, court-annexed arbitration), what other methods of dispute resolution would be available to address these issues?
- What are the reputations of opposing client and counsel?
- Do they have reputations in negotiation, mediation, arbitration, and litigation?

Once these questions are answered, the list of alternative processes is developed. The list ranges from those processes that the attorney and paralegal believe the client would select to those the client would reject. The processes span from those where the client could take unilateral action to those where a third party resolves the dispute. The processes include court-sponsored and private processes. The processes are not to be limited to those that the client suggested during the interview.

Example 19-1

Marybelle Washington was injured in an automobile accident. The list of alternative processes could include:

litigation (negligence action)
private arbitration
court-sponsored mediation (assuming the court has such a program)
negotiation
inaction (walk away and do nothing)

Once the list of alternative processes is developed, each process is considered, one by one, for its positive and negative consequences as they relate to the client.

Example 19-2

Returning to Marybelle Washington and her automobile accident from Example 19-1, one dispute resolution process could involve filing a negligence action against the driver of the other vehicle. Litigation would have the following consequences for Marybelle:

- Litigation requires money to pay for fees and expenses.
- Litigation involves a substantial time commitment on behalf of the client.
- Litigation takes time to complete.
- Litigation involves depositions of Marybelle and her family.
- Litigation involves testimony and cross-examination at trial for Marybelle and her family.
- Litigation opens the dispute to the public.
- In litigation, the parties empower the judge (and jury) to resolve the dispute for them.
- Litigation carries a likelihood of success of about _____ percent.
- If litigation yields a favorable judgment, then the damages may be in the _____ to _____ range.
- Litigation may involve some difficulty in collecting the judgment due to an appeal, the defendant being judgment proof, or the defendant's lack of cooperation.
- Filing a complaint could stimulate settlement discussions.

Next the acceptability or unacceptability of each consequence is formulated into questions that examine the client's interests and needs.

Example 19-3

Using the consequences from Example 19-2, the following questions examine how Marybelle feels about each. These questions include:

- How much is Marybelle willing and able to spend trying to recover money from the other party? [Relates to: "Litigation requires money to pay for fees and expenses."]
- How much time is Marybelle willing and able to devote to resolving this problem? [Relates to: "Litigation involves a substantial time commitment on behalf of the client."]
- How long is Marybelle willing to wait for a final outcome? [Relates to: "Litigation takes time to complete."]
- How does Marybelle feel about having her family involved in the resolution of this dispute? [Relates to: "Litigation involves testimony and cross-examination at trial for Marybelle and her family."]
- Would Marybelle prefer to have this dispute resolved in public or in private? [Relates to: "Litigation opens the dispute to the public."]
- Would Marybelle rather have a third party resolve this dispute instead of trying to work it out herself? [Relates to: "In litigation, the parties empower the judge (and jury) to resolve the dispute for the parties."]

(continued)

(continued from previous page)

- Would Marybelle prefer to pursue the resolution of this dispute vigorously rather than not pursue it even though there was a good possibility that she would not recover anything in the end? [Relates to: "Litigation carries a likelihood of success of about _____ percent" and "If litigation yields a favorable judgment, then the damages may be in the _____ to _____ range" and "Litigation may involve some difficulty in collecting the judgment due to an appeal, the defendant being judgment proof, or the defendant's lack of cooperation."]

Problem 19-1

Read the following facts and prepare your list of alternative processes, consequences, and questions for the counseling session. Note that the facts are divided into two categories: (1) those that the client, Amy Yamauchi, revealed to the attorney and paralegal when she told her story to them (i.e., in response to the attorney's question "begin from the beginning, take your time, and tell me about your problem in as much detail as you can"); and (2) those that she revealed to them when questioned by the attorney.

I

The following facts were revealed to the attorney and paralegal when Amy told her story:

She is married. -
She chose not to bring her husband to the initial interview.
She is employed as an assistant buyer for a national department store.
Her husband is employed as a high school science teacher and assistant track coach.
She has a B.A. in economics and her husband has a B.S. in science.

About five years ago, Amy became pregnant for the first time. A cesarean section was performed but the baby was dead at birth. Dr. Sheila Smith performed the cesarean.

The next year Amy, pregnant with her second child, consulted Dr. Anthony Harding. A normal, healthy baby was delivered by cesarean section seven months later. Dr. Harding performed the cesarean.

The next year, Amy became pregnant for a third time, and again Dr. Harding supervised her prenatal care.

Sometime during the birth, Amy and Dr. Harding discussed the possibility of sterilization. Dr. Harding told Amy that a future pregnancy would imperil her health.

After performing Amy's third cesarean, Dr. Harding performed a tubal ligation on Amy.

Prior to performing the tubal ligation, Amy was told by Dr. Harding that she would not be having any more children.

A year later, Amy became pregnant (fourth pregnancy) and delivered her third healthy child by an uneventful cesarean section.

II

The following facts were revealed to the attorney and paralegal after the attorney probed for additional information:

Toward the end of Amy's first pregnancy, she developed a dangerous condition known as eclampsia. [Eclampsia is the occurrence of one or more convulsions, not attributable to other cerebral conditions such as epilepsy or cerebral hemorrhage, in a patient with preeclampsia. Preeclampsia is the development of hypertension due to pregnancy.] As a consequence, Amy experienced a series of severe convulsions necessitating the premature delivery of her child by Caesarean section to save her life and the life of the baby.

Prior to tubal ligation (10 to 15 minutes before she was wheeled into the delivery room for the cesarean delivery and tubal ligation), Amy signed a form entitled "Consent." She believes that she still has a copy of it in her medical records but does not remember what it says. Amy also believes that she has other papers that may relate to her hospitalization in that file as well.

Amy believes that no one told her what the form said. Amy did not read the form prior to signing it.

Amy believes that she was given the form within an hour of going into surgery.

Prior to the delivery of her third child, Amy told Dr. Harding that she did not want any more children. She believes that she told Dr. Harding that she did not want more children because she had "lost a lot of blood" and "couldn't afford any more children."

Amy believes that Dr. Harding did not discuss with her the fact that women usually do not have more than three cesareans.

When Dr. Harding and Amy discussed her options to pregnancies, he told her there were three options: sterilization, oral contraception, and the use of an intrauterine device (IUD). Amy believes that Dr. Harding never mentioned the possibility of vasectomy.

Amy believes that Dr. Harding did not discuss the various methods of performing a tubal ligation. She claims that she has never heard of the Madlener technique, the Pomerroy technique, the Irving methods, the Uchida method, the Aldridge method, and the Erlich method. Amy does not know which method Dr. Harding used on her.

Amy claims that Dr. Harding did not discuss the fact that she might still become pregnant even though she had a tubal ligation.

Dispute Resolution as a Strategy

After the client's needs and interests are explored, the client's responses are related back to the consequences and the consequences back to the dispute resolution processes. This gives the client an understanding of which process (or processes) comes closest to his or her needs and interests. The processes that most closely meet the client's needs and interests are then assembled into a dispute resolution strategy. The strategy may be simple involving one dispute resolution process. For example, the client may not pursue the dispute (inaction), the dispute is resolved, and no further action is required.

Often one method of dispute resolution will not prove adequate. A sequence of methods must be developed. The counseling session provides an excellent opportunity for developing this strategy. For example, the action plan may require the attorney to negotiate with opposing counsel or with the opposing party if he or she is unrepresented by counsel. Negotiation may or may not resolve the dispute. If not, the action plan is further implemented. The attorney may seek to have the dispute mediated or arbitrated or may initiate litigation by filing a complaint (or petition). If the opposing party agrees to mediation, the mediation may or may not result in an agreement. If an agreement is reached, the dispute is resolved. If the parties cannot reach an agreement, then the action plan is further implemented. This may involve the initiation of litigation or an initiative toward arbitration.

The route to the resolution of a dispute follows no magic avenue. The initiation of litigation may be used to gain the other party's attention or to gain access to court-sponsored ADR. The initiation of litigation, on the other hand, may not be desirable because it may harden the opposing party's position and may make ADR less effective. Even when litigation has been initiated, it does not preclude the parties from continuing to negotiate or from pursuing private mediation or private arbitration. Initiating litigation may even require the parties to participate in court-sponsored mediation (settlement conference) or court-annexed arbitration before they can try their case before a public judge.

Even after the trial court has rendered a judgment, the parties can use an alternative dispute resolution process to resolve the dispute while their case is on appeal or even after all appeals have been exhausted. The various methods of dispute resolution continue to be available until the dispute has been ultimately resolved.

Example 19-4

Returning to Marybelle Washington and her automobile accident from Examples 19-1, 19-2, and 19-3, the list of alternative strategies could include:

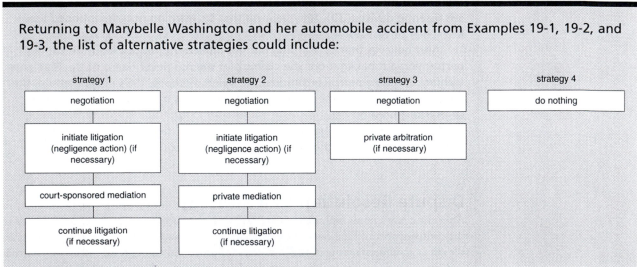

The following examples illustrate how a strategy is developed for addressing the process aspect for resolving the dispute.

Example 19-5

ABC Towing Company entered into a contract with the Sunrise Restaurant to tow cars illegally parked in Sunrise's parking lot. Under the contract, ABC was to receive $50 from Sunrise for each car towed. A dispute arose between ABC and Sunrise whether the contract required Sunrise to pay $50 per car even if the owner paid $50. ABC sought legal counsel to resolve its problem.

ABC's attorney and the attorney's paralegal knew that based on the facts of this dispute, the case, if litigated, would be before the state court. In addition, they knew that this state court had court-ordered mediation and court-ordered arbitration, and this case would be a candidate for both processes. They also knew that the contract did not provide for mandatory arbitration.

At the counseling session, the following strategy is developed:

1. ABC would attempt to negotiate a resolution of the dispute with Sunrise prior to filing a complaint. If negotiations were successful, the dispute would be resolved without any judicial intervention.
2. If negotiations were not successful, ABC's attorney would file a complaint to get Sunrise's attention.
3. The complaint would be followed by further negotiations, this time between ABC's attorney and Sunrise's attorney. If negotiations were successful, the dispute would be resolved and the complaint would be dismissed.
4. If the negotiations were not successful, ABC's attorney would ask the court to order a judicially sponsored mediation. If the mediation was successful, the dispute would be resolved and the complaint would be dismissed.
5. If the mediation was not successful, the court would order the parties to a court-sponsored arbitration because the case came within the court rules for mandatory court-annexed arbitration. At the close of the arbitration, if the parties accepted the arbitrator's decree, the dispute would be resolved and the arbitrator's decree entered as a judgment.
6. If one party did not accept the arbitrator's decree, a trial de novo would be held. At trial, the jury, if one were present, would decide questions of fact, and the judge would decide issues of law. The jury would render a verdict and the judge would issue the judgment. If neither party appealed, the dispute would be resolved.
7. If one party decided to appeal, the appellate court would either reverse or affirm the judgment of the trial court. If the appellate court affirmed the judgment, the dispute would be resolved.
8. If the appellate court reversed the judgment of the trial court, the case might be returned to the trial court for a new trial, depending on the reason for the reversal.

(continued)

(continued from previous page)

The material in Figure 19-1 diagrams the strategy for Example 19-5:

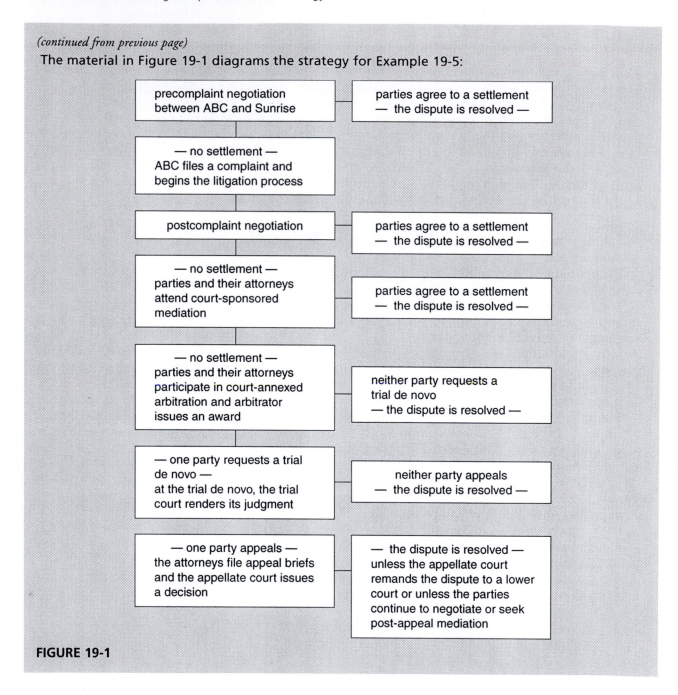

precomplaint negotiation between ABC and Sunrise	parties agree to a settlement — the dispute is resolved —
— no settlement — ABC files a complaint and begins the litigation process	
postcomplaint negotiation	parties agree to a settlement — the dispute is resolved —
— no settlement — parties and their attorneys attend court-sponsored mediation	parties agree to a settlement — the dispute is resolved —
— no settlement — parties and their attorneys participate in court-annexed arbitration and arbitrator issues an award	neither party requests a trial de novo — the dispute is resolved —
— one party requests a trial de novo — at the trial de novo, the trial court renders its judgment	neither party appeals — the dispute is resolved —
— one party appeals — the attorneys file appeal briefs and the appellate court issues a decision	— the dispute is resolved — unless the appellate court remands the dispute to a lower court or unless the parties continue to negotiate or seek post-appeal mediation

FIGURE 19-1

Example 19-6

Same facts as in Example 19-5 except at the counseling session, ABC and its attorney and the paralegal developed the following strategy:

1. ABC would attempt to negotiate a resolution of the dispute with Sunrise. If negotiation is successful, the dispute is resolved.
2. If negotiation is not successful, ABC suggests private mediation. If Sunrise refuses to mediate, ABC terminates the contract.
3. If Sunrise agrees to private mediation, the parties select a mediator. If mediation is successful, the dispute is resolved.
4. If the mediation is not successful, ABC terminates its contract with Sunrise.

Figure 19-2 diagrams the strategy:

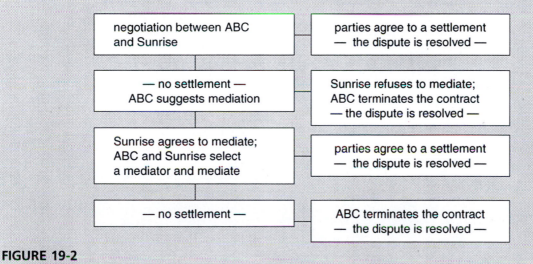

FIGURE 19-2

Example 19-7

Same facts as in Example 19-5 except at the counseling session, ABC, its attorney, and the paralegal developed the following strategy:

1. ABC would attempt to negotiate a resolution of the dispute and the dispute is resolved.
2. If negotiation is not successful, ABC suggests private arbitration. If Sunrise refuses to arbitrate, ABC terminates the contract.
3. If Sunrise agrees to private arbitration, the parties select an arbitrator. ABC and Sunrise make their presentations of fact and law before the arbitrator. If the arbitrator rules in ABC's favor, Sunrise returns any duplicate payments.
4. If the arbitrator rules in Sunrise's favor, ABC terminates its contract with Sunrise.

Figure 19-3 diagrams the strategy:

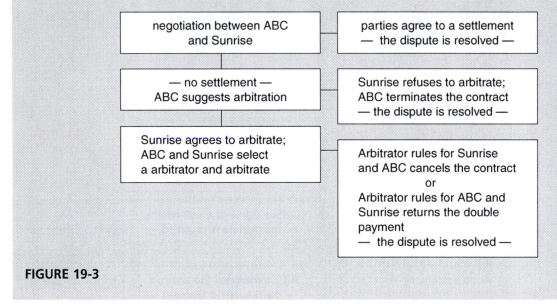

FIGURE 19-3

 ## Problem 19-2

Based on the facts in Example 19-5, do you prefer the strategy in Example 19-5, 19-6, or 19-7? Why?

Assisting the Decision-Making Process with Visual Aids

People process information and make decisions differently. Some make decisions based on intuition; others are more analytical. Some are more visual; others are more auditory. For those who like to view the written word, visual aids may assist them in their decision making.

One simple form of visual aid involves standard typing paper and a computer. Each alternative has its own page, and the consequences for that alternative are listed on that page.

Example 19-8

Figure 19-4 is a sample visual aid illustrating the consequences that arise if the client pursues a negligence action.

- Public process
- Slow and lengthy (discovery, trial, and possible appeal)
- Third party resolves the dispute
- Decision is based on the law as it applies to the facts
- Requires substantial personal time
- Significant transaction costs
- Substantial discovery—including depositions and interrogatories
- May involve family members, friends, and professional associates
- Testimonies and cross-examination in open court
- Adversarial process—Chance of success _____%
- If successful, range of recovery $ _____ to $_____
- Judgment may be difficult to collect
- Filing the complaint could stimulate settlement discussions and lead to receiving something

FIGURE 19-4 File a Negligence Action with the Court (for the Claimant)

Assessing the Client's Level of Acceptable Risk

A party is exposed to different levels of acceptable risk depending on the dispute resolution process. **Risk** involves the probability of losing and the probability of the amount of loss. The "walk away" version of inaction carries no risk since the party who walks away knows the outcome when the decision to walk away is made. The "wait and see" version of inaction carries more risk because the other party may not walk away from the dispute but rather may pursue a more favorable resolution. Negotiation and mediation carry little risk because each party has the power to reject a proposed solution.

Arbitration, litigation, and private judging are adversarial processes. Since the arbitrator or judge pronounces a winner and a loser, both the plaintiff and the defendant risk losing as well as winning. The risks of winning or losing change as the life of the case evolves.

Assessing these risks is important when evaluating a case for arbitration or litigation and for settlement purposes. One method for assessing these risks is through a decision tree. A **decision tree** is a diagram of branching lines with each point of branching representing an issue that requires a pair of opposite conclusions. (See Figure 19-5.)

In developing a decision tree, all the issues must be identified, then organized in the sequence in which they would be considered and resolved. What are the first, the second, the third issues to be resolved? Each issue is then evaluated and assigned a percentage that relates to the likelihood that this issue will be resolved for a particular party. So it becomes: what is the likelihood that the plaintiff will prevail on the first issue? What is the likelihood that the plaintiff will prevail on the second issue? What is the likelihood that the plaintiff will prevail on the third issue? Once each issue is identified, sequenced, and evaluated, the likelihood of prevailing on the first issue is multiplied by the likelihood of prevailing on the second. This result is multiplied by the likelihood of prevailing on the third. The final number is the plaintiff's likelihood of prevailing in the lawsuit.

Risk
Risk involves the probability of loss and the amount of loss.

Decision Tree
A decision tree is a diagram of branching lines with each point of branching representing an issue that requires a pair of opposite conclusions.

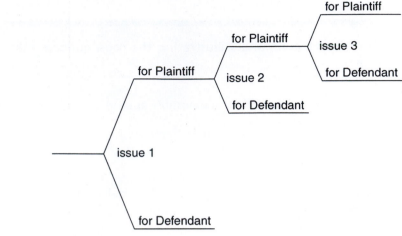

FIGURE 19-5 Decision Tree

Example 19-9

Assume a case with three issues. Also assume that each issue could only have two answers—one for the plaintiff and the other for the defendant. Assume the plaintiff has a 50 percent chance to prevail on the first issue, a 70 percent chance on the second issue, and a 40 percent chance on the third issue.

Issue	Prevailing Party	Chance (%)	
One	*Plaintiff*	*50%*	*.50*
	Defendant	*50%*	*.50*
Two	*Plaintiff*	*70%*	*.70*
	Defendant	*30%*	*.30*
Three	*Plaintiff*	*40%*	*.40*
	Defendant	*60%*	*.60*

The plaintiff must win on all three issues to prevail in this case. The defendant must win on only one issue to prevail. The plaintiff's likelihood for winning all three issues is the plaintiff's likelihood on the first issue, multiplied by the plaintiff's likelihood on the second issue, multiplied by the plaintiff's likelihood on the third issue or $.50 \times .70 \times .40 = .18$ or 18 percent. Thus, the plaintiff has only an 18 percent likelihood to prevail in this case.

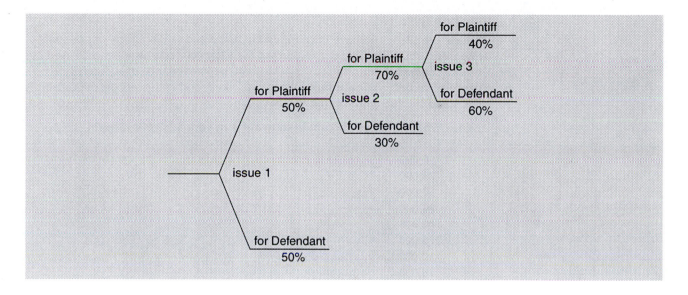

The current value of $100,000 is $100,000. The current value of a 100 percent chance to win $100,000 is $100,000. The current value of a 70 percent chance to win $100,000 is $70,000. When faced with a choice, some people would rather take less than $70,000 now rather than take a 70 percent chance to win $100,000. Others would want more than $70,000 now rather than a 70 percent chance to win $100,000. Some people are willing to assume more risk than others.

Problem 19-3

Mary Brown has two clients: Agnes Adams and Benjamin Yarnell. Both have been involved in automobile accidents and have suffered personal injury.

Agnes has been offered $300,000 to settle her case. Mary has told Agnes that she has a 40 percent chance to receive a $1,000,000 judgment. Based on this information, Mary has accepted the settlement offer.

Benjamin has also been offered $300,000 to settle his case. Mary has told Benjamin that he has a 30 percent chance to receive a $1,000,000 judgment. Based on this information, Benjamin has rejected the settlement offer.

Who was more of a gambler, Agnes or Benjamin?

Who would accept a high level of risk?

Care must be taken not to equate the attorney's or paralegal's level of acceptable risk with the client's level of acceptable risk. The problem is the client's problem and therefore it is the client's level of acceptable risk that is important. The attorney, paralegal, and client may not share the same level of acceptable risk.

Problem 19-4

You are the client and have been injured in a slip and fall in a local upper-scale restaurant. You have sued the restaurant for $250,000. You have been advised by your attorney that your claim at trial has a 40 percent chance of success. By *chance of success*, your attorney means your likelihood of success on the cause of action and the full amount that you have pled.

1. What would you accept in settlement of your $250,000 claim?

   $ 0
        10,000
        25,000
        50,000
        75,000
       100,000
       125,000
       150,000
       175,000
       200,000
       225,000
       250,000

2. What factors led you to select this amount?

Problem 19-5

You are the client and have been injured in a slip and fall in a local mom & pop hamburger restaurant. You have sued the restaurant for $25,000. You have been advised by your attorney that your claim at trial has a 40 percent chance of success. By *chance of success*, your attorney means your likelihood of success on the cause of action and the full amount that you have pled.

1. What would you accept in settlement of your $25,000 claim?

   $ 0
         1,000
         2,500
         5,000
         7,500
        10,000
        12,500
        15,000
        17,500
        20,000
        22,500
        25,000

2.   What factors led you to select this amount?

Now multiply your answers by 10. Is this the same amount that you selected for the previous problem? If not, why?

Problem 19-6

1.   If you are the client, what chance of success at trial (from the following per-centages) would you want in order to accept an offer for $50,000 for your $250,000 claim?

   10%
   20%
   30%
   40%
   50%
   60%
   70%
   80%
   90%
   100%

2.   Why did your select this percentage?
3.   Would your answer have been different if the settlement offer had been $150,000?
4.   Why?

Is a Nonjudicial Solution Always Appropriate?

Precedential Value
An judicial opinion has precedential value when it serves as the rule for future cases that are similar.

Do some disputes mandate a judicial solution? Published judicial opinions offer precedential value. An opinion has **precedential value** when it serves as the rule for future cases that are similar. With the exception of a few states, for example, New York and Pennsylvania, most state trial courts, however, do not have their opinions published. Even in those states where trial court opinions are published, only a few find their way into print. In federal court, however, trial court opinions can be published, but whether an opinion is submitted for publication is discretionary with the judge. Therefore, a party may need to appeal for an opinion to be published that will establish precedent.

Some cases do establish precedent that will be important for others in a similar situation.

Example 19-10

Recently the farmers upstream built a dam so they could divert water for irrigation. The dam, in effect, severely reduced the water supply downstream, so downstream dairy farmers have no water for their herds. The water rights issue is an issue that should be litigated so all upstream and downstream users of the water know their rights.

Problem 19-7

What are three issues that should be litigated so precedent is established? You may find it helpful to check out some recent court opinions and consider whether they needed to be litigated so precedent could be established.

Preparing for the Process

Some processes are driven by the facts, the law, and how the law applies to the facts. Others are driven by the needs and interests of the parties. The process naturally determines to what extent the law and the facts must be prepared.

The documents and other evidence that must be prepared for a dispute resolution process vary from process to process. In addition to what should be prepared, the party also must consider how these documents and other evidence can be made as effective as possible.

Clients have different roles depending on the dispute resolution process. For example, if the dispute involves a corporation, the level and number of participants will vary depending on what expertise and decision-making authority is needed for the process.

When a party is represented by an attorney, the party may or may not participate in the dispute resolution process. A party who participates in the process must understand his or her role and be fully prepared for that role.

Initiating the Dispute Resolution Plan

After the counseling session has ended and the dispute resolution strategy has been determined, it is now time to implement the plan. Some processes (e.g., inaction, acquiescence, self-help, ombuds, and litigation) can be implemented by one party. Others (i.e., negotiation, private mediation, private arbitration, and private judging) require both parties. The timing for the implementation of the dispute resolution plan often has a substantial impact on the final result.

Selecting the Best Timing for a Dispute Resolution Process

To maximize a dispute resolution process, the party must capitalize on the best timing for the process. A private dispute resolution process can take place before or after a complaint is filed. In determining when to proceed with a dispute resolution process, it is important to know what needs to be done in a case before the process will be meaningful.

- What facts must be known, how long will it take to gather these facts, and how (or by whom) will these facts be gathered?
- Does the process focus on the law or will it be driven by the needs and interests of the parties?
- How much law must be known, and how long will it take to find the law and apply it to the facts?
- Is this dispute better settled before initiating litigation, or is the litigation critical to the process?

There is no perfect timing for initiating a dispute resolution process. The timing is a matter of personal preference. Some parties like to have litigation pending to encourage settlement discussion, whether through negotiation or mediation. Others view pending litigation as counterproductive to settlement discussions because it makes the parties more defensive, adds to the costs of resolution, and creates a court-ordered schedule for resolving the dispute. Some like to have discovery concluded so they know all the facts. Others prefer to have limited discovery, thus either saving a client time and money if the case settles or gaining "free" discovery during the settlement discussions if the case does not settle. Some like to have dispositive motions such as motions for summary judgment pending during settlement discussions. Others prefer to have all dispositive motions resolved by the court before tendering or addressing a settlement offer. Some like the uncertainty of pending dispositive motions; others do not.

Selling a Dispute Resolution Process to the Other Party

When one party has selected a dispute resolution strategy, it may be necessary to sell a process to the other party. Some dispute resolution processes such as inaction, acquiescence, self-help, early neutral evaluation, ombuds, court-sponsored mediation, court-annexed arbitration, and litigation can be initiated without the assent of the other party. Other processes such as negotiation, private mediation, private arbitration, and private judging require the cooperation of the other party. For these processes, the party or his or her attorney must sell the other party on the process.

All disputes are two-sided. Both parties have their own perceptions as to what occurred and why. To sell another party on a dispute resolution process, it becomes essential to consider what that party would gain or lose by going through that process. The local judges or the members of the practicing bar who believe in alternative methods of dispute resolution can be powerful allies when dealing with a reluctant party. Some issues to consider include:

- What will the other party gain by using a dispute resolution process?
- Is the other party eager to relinquish control over the process by which the dispute is resolved or over the outcome of the dispute?
- Is the other party interested in a legal or a needs-based solution?
- Does the other party need "his or her day in court" or at least an opportunity to tell his or her story to a judge figure?
- Is the other party interested in curtailing costs?
- Will the other party gain by having a speedy resolution of the dispute?
- Is the other party interested in a private resolution?
- Will the court encourage an alternative process if the issue is raised in conference before the judge?

Creating the Dispute Resolution Documents

Some dispute resolution processes, such as inaction, acquiescence, self-help, and ombuds, require few, if any, documents to initiate the process. Others require substantial documentation. Litigation requires the aggrieved party to file a complaint with the clerk of the court. This may lead to court-sponsored mediation which will require a brief position document stating the facts of the case, the issues that are to be litigated, and a history of settlement discussion. Filing a complaint also may lead to court-annexed arbitration, which will require a more law-oriented document for the arbitrator or arbitration panel. This document will be similar to a bench brief submitted to the trial judge and may provide the arbitrator or the arbitration panel with a statement of the facts, the issues, and the application of the law to the facts. If the parties have selected private mediation or private arbitration, they must contract to enter the process and prepare the documents that these processes require.

Key Terms and Phrases

decision tree
precedential value
risk

Review Questions

True/False Questions

1. T F The attorney decides on the dispute resolution strategy for the client.
2. T F The client may not share the attorney's or paralegal's level of risk aversion.
3. T F A decision tree may help evaluate the present value of a case.
4. T F The settlement value of a case may change from day to day.
5. T F The counseling session generally is a part of the interview session.
6. T F The dispute resolution strategy is static and does not provide for contingencies.
7. T F Litigation is more often than not a tool for getting the parties to the bargaining table.
8. T F The dispute resolution strategy may continue beyond trial and appeal.
9. T F The timing of a dispute resolution process is critical to the success of that process.
10. T F At some time or other and in some way or other, all disputes will come to a resolution.

Fill-in-the-Blank Questions

1. _____ List the three steps in preparing for the counseling
   _____ session.
   _____

Multiple Choice Questions

1. Which three of the following five dispute resolution methods are the most commonly used?
   (a) litigation
   (b) private judging
   (c) private mediation
   (d) ombuds
   (e) court-annexed arbitration
2. Which three of the following five dispute resolution methods are the most commonly used?
   (a) self-help
   (b) negotiation
   (c) litigation
   (d) summary jury trial
   (e) inaction

Short-Answer Questions

1. Distinguish between what happens at the interview from what happens at the counseling session.
2. Discuss the advantages and disadvantages of bifurcating the interview from the counseling session.
3. Discuss preparations for the counseling session.
4. What is a decision tree, and how does it work in evaluating the present value of a case? Does the decision tree approach give an accurate evaluation of the present value of a case? Is there a better method?
5. Should the client's tolerance to risk be assessed at the counseling session and, if so, why? How can this be accomplished?
6. What is the difference between selecting a dispute resolution process and a dispute resolution strategy? What are the advantages of having a predetermined strategy rather than just a preselected process?

Role-Play Exercises

For each of the following role-play exercises, the following facts were gathered by the attorney and the paralegal at the interview with the client. Prior to the counseling session, develop the following:

1. A list of the legal and nonlegal information that must be researched or gathered before the counseling session;
2. A list of the additional facts that must be obtained from the client during the counseling session;
3. An array of dispute resolution processes to present the client, a list of consequences associated with each process, and a series of questions designed to explore the client's needs and interests as they relate to the consequences and ultimately to the dispute resolution processes; and
4. Visual aids for the counseling session. At the counseling session, use this information to help the client develop a dispute resolution strategy.

Role-Play Exercise 19-1   The Abused and Neglected Child

The Players: Nina Perea, the client
               The attorney
               The paralegal

Nina Perea related the following story during her interview. Nina, age 17, was born in Honduras. Her mother is Marlene Perea. Her father is Honduran and his whereabouts are unknown. Marlene left Honduras when Nina was 2 years old and had returned to visit her only once in 15 years. Nina's great-grandmother raised her in Honduras. Nina did not want to leave Honduras, but her mother forced her to come to the United States and her great-grandmother told her she had to obey her mother. Her uncle brought her to the United States.

Nina has a 6-year-old half-sister, Mirna. Mirna's mother is Marlene Perea and her father is Phillip Aster. Mirna was instructed by her mother to tell the AFDC social worker that Phillip Aster was not her father. Because Mirna complied and told the social worker Phillip is not her father, Marlene received AFDC money, even though Phillip worked and owned a shop, was Mirna's father, and had been with Marlene for more than 6 years.

Several months after Nina arrived in the United States, her mother took her to a laundromat, where her mother accepted money from a 40-year-old man. The man took Nina to a hotel and forced her to have sex with him. The man gave her $150 and told her to give it to her mother.

When Nina got home, her mother found the money and took it. She then woke up Nina's stepfather and the two of them left to buy drugs. When they returned they smoked a black, chunky substance they called opium.

Nina saw her mother use drugs approximately 10 times, although she had not seen any drugs other than opium. Her mother sometimes used drugs when Nina's stepfather was not present and had also used drugs in the presence of Nina's half-sister, Mirna.

Nina also stated that her mother was an alcoholic and drank eight beers a day and more on weekends.

Phillip Aster's brother also lived with them. Nina had seen both her stepfather and his brother use opium.

When her mother wanted Nina to go away with the man again, Nina refused and ran away. Her mother became angry, beat her, and kicked her out of the house, calling her stupid. Nina stated she did not trust her mother and that if her mother loved her she would not have made her go and have sex with a stranger for money.

After Nina left her mother's house, she met someone who helped her get to an Immigration Department office, because she wanted to return to Honduras. A police officer interviewed her at the Immigration Department office and then transferred her to the Sheriff's Department. Nina told the police her mother forced her to have sexual relations with a man in exchange for money. Nina is now in custody at the juvenile center.

Role-Play Exercise 19-2   The Eviction

The Players: Dorothy Williams, the client
               Terry Gibson, the client
               The attorney
               The paralegal

Damian Fox owns and manages a 12-unit house on Pine Street. Fox contracted with Dorothy Williams and Terry Gibson by means of a document entitled, "Apartment Sharing and Room Rental Lease Agreement" to rent one of the apartments to them on a weekly basis beginning in March. The agreement described Fox as the "landlord" and Williams and Gibson as "tenants."

The apartment consisted of one furnished room with a bed, dresser, cabinet, table, television, couch, refrigerator, and telephone. Fox provided a set of sheets, a pillow, a blanket, and a comforter, but Williams and Gibson were responsible for laundering the linens and obtaining any other linens they needed. No bathroom, running water, or kitchen facilities were supplied in the room, so Williams and Gibson shared a common bathroom and kitchen area with the other tenants on their floor. The kitchen area consisted of a microwave, toaster oven, and coffee machine, but the toaster oven and coffee machine were not always available. These common areas were cleaned and maintained by Fox, but Williams and Gibson were responsible for cleaning their room. The weekly rental included heat, electricity, cable television service, and local phone service. Although the rooms are rented on a weekly basis, Fox stated he attempts to rent to tenants who will stay for longer periods. A Certificate of Occupancy issued by the City's Department of Building Inspection approved the property for residence as a "lodging house."

By December, Williams and Gibson had fallen behind in their rent. Fox obtained a writ of possession utilizing the forcible entry and detainer procedure under state statute. Before Fox executed the writ, however, he reached an agreement with Williams and Gibson whereby Williams and Gibson were permitted to remain in the room, but agreed to continue paying their weekly rent with additional payments for the back rent due. By September of the following year, although Williams and Gibson had made some additional payments, they had also missed other payments and had fallen even further behind in the rent payments. Fox attempted to execute the writ of possession he had obtained the previous December, but Williams and Gibson were granted an injunction by the district court preventing Fox from executing on the writ, the court concluding that because rent was paid and accepted after the writ was issued, a new tenancy had been created.

One evening in October, without prior notice, Fox padlocked the door to Williams and Gibson's room while they were out. Included among the possessions that could not be accessed were Gibson's epilepsy medication and his identification to refill the prescription for the medication. As a result of being unable to access his medication, Gibson went to the emergency room twice within the next week for treatment of epileptic seizures.

Williams and Gibson would like injunctive relief and damages for, among other allegations, illegal eviction and intentional and negligent infliction of emotional distress. Fox has said that he wanted the rent due and incidental charges.

After the interview with Williams and Gibson, the attorney and paralegal have discovered that there is an issue with Fox's contention that his property qualified as a lodging house. If this is true, then Williams and Gibson may recover on their claim of illegal eviction. Williams would like to recover $1,000 damages for her claim of intentional infliction of emotional distress, and Gibson would like to recover $5,000 damages for intentional infliction of emotional distress. Fox wants $300 for unpaid back rent.

Role Play Exercise 19-3   Child Support

The Players: Gene McWhorter, the client
The attorney
The paralegal

Five years ago, Gene and Bernice McWhorter were divorced. Gene was a self-employed trucker. Two children had been born of the marriage—Warren, who is 10, and Kimberly, who is 8. Under their divorce decree, custody was awarded to Bernice, and Gene was ordered to pay child support in the amount of $465 per month.

Bernice wants Gene to increase his child support. After including gambling winnings but not his gambling losses (about $1,000 a month), Gene's yearly and monthly income for the past three years was:

Year	Yearly Income	Monthly Income
one	$ 34,306	$ 2,858
two	$ 82,737	$ 6,894
three	$ 58,000	$ 4,833

Gene's average monthly income for the three-year period was $4,862. Based on this averaging, Bernice believes that Gene's monthly child-support payments should be increased to $1,017 per month.

Gene does not want his child support payments to be increased. If they are, he wants his gambling losses to be included in the calculation of his income. He also does not want the increase in payments, if there are any, to be retroactive.

Role Play Exercise 19-4   Emotional Distress

The Players: Marvin Stanley, the client
Gina Stanley, the client
The attorney
The paralegal

Marvin and Gina Stanley are husband and wife and the natural parents of Bertie Stanley. About 7:25 P.M. on an August evening three years ago, Marvin and Gina were driving their SUV, followed closely by their son Bertie, who was driving a late model pickup truck. Due solely to the negligence of Chandler O'Neil, O'Neil's vehicle collided with Bertie's pickup, causing serious bodily injury to Bertie, including a broken collarbone, broken femur, cuts, and abrasions.

Marvin and Gina Stanley were not involved in the collision, nor did their Expedition SUV sustain any impact or damage as a result. They did, however, observe the accident and quickly turned back to witness the immediate aftermath of the accident, including the serious bodily injuries sustained by their son Bertie. Although Marvin and Gina sustained no physical injury, Reliable Insurance Exchange agreed that they sustained emotional distress as a direct result of observing the serious injuries sustained by Bertie.

Mr. O'Neil was insured by Global Indemnity Company. His policy was subject to limits of $25,000 per person and $50,000 per occurrence. Global settled the claims against O'Neil through payments to the Stanley family, exhausting the policy limits. Reliable Insurance Exchange consented to the settlement.

Through Reliable, Gina Stanley had insured the SUV in which she and her husband were riding at the time of their son's accident. Subject to the stated terms of the policy, Reliable agreed to provide underinsured motorist coverage (UIM) to Marvin and Gina Stanley.

Marvin Stanley has made a claim under Reliable's UIM coverage for $20,000 as compensation for the emotional damage he suffered as a result of witnessing his son's accident and its immediate aftermath. Gina Stanley has asserted a similar claim seeking emotional distress damages in the amount of $47,000.

Reliable has denied the emotional distress claims on the grounds that the emotional distress suffered by the Stanleys falls outside the scope of "bodily injury" as described in the UIM coverage. All claims for UIM coverage asserted by Bertie Stanley have been settled and released by separate agreement of the parties.

Appendix A

The Ombudsman Association

Code of Ethics

copyright 1985 by The Ombudsman Association

The ombudsman, as a designated neutral, has the responsibility of maintaining strict confidentiality concerning matters that are brought to his/her attention unless given permission to do otherwise. The only exceptions, at the sole discretion of the ombudsman, are where there appears to be imminent threat of serious harm.

The ombudsman must take all reasonable steps to protect any records and files pertaining to confidential discussions from inspection by all other persons, including management.

The ombudsman should not testify in any formal judicial or administrative hearing about concerns brought to his/her attention.

When making recommendations, the ombudsman has the responsibility to suggest actions or policies that will be equitable to all parties.

Standards of Practice

copyright 1985 by The Ombudsman Association

The mission of the organizational ombudsman is to provide a confidential, neutral and informal process which facilitates fair and equitable resolutions to concerns that arise in the organization. In performing this mission, the ombudsman serves as an information and communication resource, upward feedback channel, advisor, dispute resolution expert and change agent.

While serving this role:

1. We adhere to The Ombudsman Association Code of Ethics.
2. We base our practice on confidentiality.

   2.1. An ombudsman should not use the names of individuals or mention their employers without express permission.
   2.2. During the problem-solving process an ombudsman may make known information as long as the identity of the individual contacting the office is not compromised.
   2.3. Any data that we prepare should be scrutinized carefully to safeguard the identity of each individual whose concerns are represented.
   2.4. Publicity about our office conveys the confidential nature of our work.
3. We assert that there is a *privilege* with respect to communications with the ombudsman and we resist testifying in any formal process inside or outside the organization.

   3.1 Communications between an ombudsman and others (made while the ombudsman is serving in that capacity) are considered privileged. Others cannot waive this privilege.
   3.2. We do not serve in any additional function in the organization which would undermine the privileged nature of our work (such as compliance officer, arbitrator, etc.)
   3.3. An ombudsman keeps no case records on behalf of the organization. If an ombudsman finds case notes necessary to manage the work, the ombudsman should establish and follow a consistent and standard practice for the destruction of any such written notes.
   3.4. When necessary, the ombudsman's office will seek judicial protection for staff and records of the office. It may be necessary to seek representation by separate legal counsel to protect the privilege of the office.
4. We exercise discretion whether to act upon a concern of an individual contacting the office. An ombudsman may initiate action on a problem he or she perceives directly.
5. We are designated neutrals and remain independent of ordinary line and staff structures. We serve no additional

role (within an organization where we serve an ombudsman) which would comprise this neutrality.

5.1 An ombudsman strives for objectivity and impartiality.

5.2 The ombudsman has a responsibility to consider the concerns of all parties known to be involved in a dispute.

5.3. We do not serve as advocates for any person in a dispute within an organization; however, we do advocate for fair processes and their fair administration.

5.4. We help develop a range of responsible options to resolve problems and facilitate discussion to identify the best options. When possible, we help people develop new ways to solve problems themselves.

5.5. An ombudsman should exercise discretion before entering into any additional affiliations, roles or actions that may impact the neutrality of the function within the organization.

5.6. We do not make binding decisions, mandate policies or adjudicate issues for the organization.

6. We remain an informal and off-the-record recourse. Formal investigations—for the purpose of adjudication—should be done by others. In the event that an ombudsman accepts a request to conduct a formal investigation, a memo should be written to file noting this action as an exception to the ombudsman role. Such investigations should not be considered privileged.

6.1. We do not act as agent for the organization and we do not accept notice on behalf of the organization. We do always refer individuals to the appropriate place where formal notice can be made.

6.2. Individuals should not be required to meet with an ombudsman. All interactions with the ombudsman should be voluntary.

7. We foster communication about the philosophy and function of the ombudsman's office with the people we serve.

8. We provide feedback on trends, issues, policies and practices without breaching confidentiality or anonymity. We identify new problems and we provide support for responsible systems change.

9. We keep professionally current and competent by pursuing continuing education and training relevant to the ombudsman profession.

10. We will endeavor to be worthy of the trust placed in us.

Glossary

copyright 1985 by The Ombudsman Association

Confidential   Confidential describes communications, or a source of communications, which are intended to be held in secret. In an ombudsman's work confidentiality is often accomplished by providing anonymity to the source of communications. When the source of a communication is kept secret or private, this is known as an anonymous communication.

Independent   An ombudsman functions independent of the management. The ombudsman reporting relationship is with highest authority in an organization.

Neutrality   We do not serve as advocates for any person in a dispute within an organization, however, we do advocate for fair processes and their fair administration.

When making recommendations, the ombudsman has the responsibility to suggest actions or policies that will be equitable to all parties.

Privilege   Privilege is a legal term which describes a relationship which the law protects from forced disclosure. Traditional privileges are client/lawyer, doctor/patient, priest/penitent, husband/wife. An ombudsman privilege differs from these other forms of privilege because the office holds the privilege and it cannot be waived by others. The privilege is necessary to preserve the process that allows people to come forward to resolve their concerns in a confidential setting without the risk of reprisal.

Appendix B

Uniform Mediation Act

SECTION 1. TITLE.
This [Act] may be cited as the Uniform Mediation Act.

SECTION 2. DEFINITIONS. In this [Act]:
(1) "Mediation" means a process in which a mediator facilitates communication and negotiation between parties to assist them in reaching a voluntary agreement regarding their dispute.

(2) "Mediation communication" means a statement, whether oral or in a record or verbal or nonverbal, that occurs during a mediation or is made for purposes of considering, conducting, participating in, initiating, continuing, or reconvening a mediation or retaining a mediator.

(3) "Mediator" means an individual who conducts a mediation.

(4) "Nonparty participant" means a person, other than a party or mediator, that participates in a mediation.

(5) "Mediation party" means a person that participates in a mediation and whose agreement is necessary to resolve the dispute.

(6) "Person" means an individual, corporation, business trust, estate, trust, partnership, limited liability company, association, joint venture, government; governmental subdivision, agency, or instrumentality; public corporation, or any other legal or commercial entity.

(7) "Proceeding" means:
(A) a judicial, administrative, arbitral, or other adjudicative process, including related pre-hearing and post-hearing motions, conferences, and discovery; or
(B) a legislative hearing or similar process.

(8) "Record" means information that is inscribed on a tangible medium or that is stored in an electronic or other medium and is retrievable in perceivable form.

(9) "Sign" means:
(A) to execute or adopt a tangible symbol with the present intent to authenticate a record; or
(B) to attach or logically associate an electronic symbol, sound, or process to or with a record with the present intent to authenticate a record.

SECTION 3. SCOPE.
(a) Except as otherwise provided in subsection (b) or (c), this [Act] applies to a mediation in which:
(1) the mediation parties are required to mediate by statute or court or administrative agency rule or referred to mediation by a court, administrative agency, or arbitrator;
(2) the mediation parties and the mediator agree to mediate in a record that demonstrates an expectation that mediation communications will be privileged against disclosure; or
(3) the mediation parties use as a mediator an individual who holds himself or herself out as a mediator, or the mediation is provided by a person that holds itself out as providing mediation.

(b) The [Act] does not apply to a mediation:
(1) relating to the establishment, negotiation, administration, or termination of a collective bargaining relationship;
(2) relating to a dispute that is pending under or is part of the processes established by a collective bargaining agreement, except that the [Act] applies to a mediation arising out of a dispute that has been filed with an administrative agency or court;
(3) conducted by a judge who might make a ruling on the case; or
(4) conducted under the auspices of:
(A) a primary or secondary school if all the parties are students or
(B) a correctional institution for youths if all the parties are residents of that institution.

(c) If the parties agree in advance in a signed record or a record of proceeding so reflects, that all or part of a mediation is not privileged, the privileges under Sections 4 through 6 do not apply to the mediation or part agreed upon. However, Sections 4 through 6 apply to a mediation communication made by a person that has not received actual notice of the agreement before the communication is made.

SECTION 4. PRIVILEGE AGAINST DISCLOSURE; ADMISSIBILITY; DISCOVERY.

(a) Except as otherwise provided in Section 6, a mediation communication is privileged as provided in subsection (b) and is not subject to discovery or admissible in evidence in a proceeding unless waived or precluded as provided by Section 5.

(b) In a proceeding, the following privileges apply:
   (1) A mediation party may refuse to disclose, and may prevent any other person from disclosing, a mediation communication.
   (2) A mediator may refuse to disclose a mediation communication, and may prevent any other person from disclosing a mediation communication of the mediator.
   (3) A nonparty participant may refuse to disclose, and may prevent any other person from disclosing, a mediation communication of the nonparty participant.

(c) Evidence or information that is otherwise admissible or subject to discovery does not become inadmissible or protected from discovery solely by reason of its disclosure or use in a mediation.

SECTION 5. WAIVER AND PRECLUSION OF PRIVILEGE.

(a) A privilege under Section 4 may be waived in a record or orally during a proceeding if it is expressly waived by all parties to the mediation and:
   (1) in the case of the privilege of a mediator, it is expressly waived by the mediator; and
   (2) in the case of the privilege of a nonparty participant, it is expressly waived by the nonparty participant.

(b) A person that discloses or makes a representation about a mediation communication which prejudices another person in a proceeding is precluded from asserting a privilege under Section 4, but only to the extent neces-

sary for the person prejudiced to respond to the representation or disclosure.

(c) A person that intentionally uses a mediation to plan, attempt to commit or commit a crime, or to conceal an ongoing crime or ongoing criminal activity is precluded from asserting a privilege under Section 4.

SECTION 6. EXCEPTIONS TO PRIVILEGE.

(a) There is no privilege under Section 4 for a mediation communication that is:
   (1) in an agreement evidenced by a record signed by all parties to the agreement;
   (2) available to the public under [insert statutory reference to open records act] or made during a session of a mediation which is open, or is required by law to be open, to the public;
   (3) a threat or statement of a plan to inflict bodily injury or commit a crime of violence;
   (4) intentionally used to plan a crime, attempt to commit a crime, or to conceal an ongoing crime or ongoing criminal activity;
   (5) sought or offered to prove or disprove a claim or complaint of professional misconduct or malpractice filed against a mediator;
   (6) except as otherwise provided in subsection (c), sought or offered to prove or disprove a claim or complaint of professional misconduct or malpractice filed against a mediation party, nonparty participant, or representative of a party based on conduct occurring during a mediation; or
   (7) sought or offered to prove or disprove abuse, neglect, abandonment, or exploitation in a proceeding in which a child or adult protective services agency is a party, unless the
   [Alternative A: [State to insert, for example, child or adult protection] case is referred by a court to mediation and a public agency participates.]
   [Alternative B: public agency participates in the [State to insert, for example, child or adult protection] mediation].

(b) There is no privilege under Section 4 if a court, administrative agency, or arbitrator finds, after a hearing in camera, that the party seeking discovery or the proponent of the evidence has shown that the evidence is not otherwise available, that there is a need for the evidence that substantially outweighs the interest in protecting confidentiality, and that the mediation communication is sought or offered in:

(1) a court proceeding involving a felony [or misdemeanor]; or

(2) except as otherwise provided in subsection (c), a proceeding to prove a claim to rescind or reform or a defense to avoid liability on a contract arising out of the mediation.

(c) A mediator may not be compelled to provide evidence of a mediation communication referred to in subsection (a)(6) or (b)(2).

(d) If a mediation communication is not privileged under subsection (a) or (b), only the portion of the communication necessary for the application of the exception from nondisclosure may be admitted. Admission of evidence under subsection (a) or (b) does not render the evidence, or any other mediation communication, discoverable or admissible for any other purpose.

SECTION 7. PROHIBITED MEDIATOR REPORTS.

(a) Except as required in subsection (b), a mediator may not make a report, assessment, evaluation, recommendation, finding, or other communication regarding a mediation to a court, administrative agency, or other authority that may make a ruling on the dispute that is the subject of the mediation.

(b) A mediator may disclose:

(1) whether the mediation occurred or has terminated, whether a settlement was reached, and attendance;

(2) a mediation communication as permitted under Section 6; or

(3) a mediation communication evidencing abuse, neglect, abandonment, or exploitation of an individual to a public agency responsible for protecting individuals against such mistreatment.

(c) A communication made in violation of subsection (a) may not be considered by a court, administrative agency, or arbitrator.

SECTION 8. CONFIDENTIALITY.

Unless subject to the [insert statutory references to open meetings act and open records act], mediation communications are confidential to the extent agreed by the parties or provided by other law or rule of this State.

SECTION 9. MEDIATOR'S DISCLOSURE OF CONFLICTS OF INTEREST; BACKGROUND.

(a) Before accepting a mediation, an individual who is requested to serve as a mediator shall:

(1) make an inquiry that is reasonable under the circumstances to determine whether there are any known facts that a reasonable individual would consider likely to affect the impartiality of the mediator, including a financial or personal interest in the outcome of the mediation and an existing or past relationship with a mediation party or foreseeable participant in the mediation; and

(2) disclose any such known fact to the mediation parties as soon as is practical before accepting a mediation.

(b) If a mediator learns any fact described in subsection (a)(1) after accepting a mediation, the mediator shall disclose it as soon as is practicable.

(c) At the request of a mediation party, an individual who is requested to serve as a mediator shall disclose the mediator's qualifications to mediate a dispute.

(d) A person that violates subsection [(a) or (b)][(a), (b), or (g)] is precluded by the violation from asserting a privilege under Section 4.

(e) Subsections (a), (b), [and] (c), [and] [(g)] do not apply to an individual acting as a judge.

(f) This [Act] does not require that a mediator have a special qualification by background or profession.

[(g) A mediator must be impartial, unless after disclosure of the facts required in subsections (a) and (b) to be disclosed, the parties agree otherwise.]

SECTION 10. PARTICIPATION IN MEDIATION.

An attorney may represent, or other individual designated by a party may accompany the party to, and participate in a mediation. A waiver of representation or participation given before the mediation may be rescinded.

SECTION 11. RELATION TO ELECTRONIC SIGNATURES IN GLOBAL AND NATIONAL COMMERCE ACT.

This [Act] modifies, limits, or supersedes the federal Electronic Signatures in Global and National Commerce Act, 15 U.S.C. Section 7001 et seq., but this [Act] does not modify, limit, or supersede Section 101(c) of that Act or authorize electronic delivery of any of the notices described in Section 103(b) of that Act.

SECTION 12. UNIFORMITY OF APPLICATION AND CONSTRUCTION.

In applying and construing this [Act], consideration must be given to the need to promote uniformity of the law with respect to its subject matter among States that enact it.

SECTION 13. SEVERABILITY CLAUSE.

If any provision of this [Act] or its application to any person or circumstance is held invalid, the invalidity does not affect other provisions or applications of this [Act] which can be given effect without the invalid provision or application, and to this end the provisions of this [Act] are severable.

SECTION 14. EFFECTIVE DATE.

This [Act] takes effect . . . .

SECTION 15. REPEALS.

The following acts and parts of acts are hereby repealed:

(1)
(2)
(3)

SECTION 16. APPLICATION TO EXISTING AGREEMENTS OR REFERRALS.

(a) This [Act] governs a mediation pursuant to a referral or an agreement to mediate made on or after [the effective date of this [Act]].

(b) On or after [a delayed date], this [Act] governs an agreement to mediate whenever made.

Appendix C

44.101 Definitions.

As used in this chapter:

(1) . . . .

(2) "Mediation" means a process whereby a neutral third person called a mediator acts to encourage and facilitate the resolution of a dispute between two or more parties. It is an informal and nonadversarial process with the objective of helping the disputing parties reach a mutually acceptable and voluntary agreement. In mediation, decision making authority rests with the parties. The role of the mediator includes, but is not limited to, assisting the parties in identifying issues, fostering joint problem solving, and exploring settlement alternatives. "Mediation" includes:

(a) "Appellate court mediation," which means mediation that occurs during the pendency of an appeal of a civil case.

(b) "Circuit court mediation," which means mediation of civil cases, other than family matters, in circuit court. If a party is represented by counsel, the counsel of record must appear unless stipulated to by the parties or otherwise ordered by the court.

(c) "County court mediation," which means mediation of civil cases within the jurisdiction of county courts, including small claims. Negotiations in county court mediation are primarily conducted by the parties. Counsel for each party may participate. However, presence of counsel is not required.

(d) "Family mediation" which means mediation of family matters, including married and unmarried persons, before and after judgments involving dissolution of marriage; property division; shared or sole parental responsibility; or child support, custody, and visitation involving emotional or financial considerations not usually present in other circuit civil cases. Negotiations in family mediation are primarily conducted by the parties. Counsel for each party may attend the mediation conference and privately communicate with their clients. However, presence of counsel is not required, and, in the discretion of the mediator, and with the agreement of the parties, mediation may proceed in the absence of counsel unless otherwise ordered by the court.

(e) "Dependency or in need of services mediation," which means mediation of dependency, child in need of services, or family in need of services matters. Negotiations in dependency or in need of services mediation are primarily conducted by the parties. Counsel for each party may attend the mediation conference and privately communicate with their clients. However, presence of counsel is not required and, in the discretion of the mediator and with the agreement of the parties, mediation may proceed in the absence of counsel unless otherwise ordered by the court.

44.102 Court-Ordered Mediation.

(1) Court-ordered mediation shall be conducted according to rules of practice and procedure adopted by the Supreme Court.

(2) A court, under rules adopted by the Supreme Court:

(a) Must, upon request of one party, refer to mediation any filed civil action for monetary damages, provided the requesting party is willing and able to pay the costs of the mediation or the costs can be equitably divided between the parties, unless:

1. The action is a landlord and tenant dispute that does not include a claim for personal injury.

2. The action is filed for the purpose of collecting a debt.

3. The action is a claim of medical malpractice.
4. The action is governed by the Florida Small Claims Rules.
5. The court determines that the action is proper for referral to nonbinding arbitration under this chapter.
6. The parties have agreed to binding arbitration.
7. The parties have agreed to an expedited trial pursuant to § 45.075.
8. The parties have agreed to voluntary trial resolution pursuant to § 44.104.

(b) May refer to mediation all or any part of a filed civil action for which mediation is not required under this section.

(c) In circuits in which a family mediation program has been established and upon a court finding of a dispute, shall refer to mediation all or part of custody, visitation, or other parental responsibility issues as defined in § 61.13. Upon motion or request of a party, a court shall not refer any case to mediation if it finds there has been a history of domestic violence that would compromise the mediation process.

(d) In circuits in which a dependency or in need of services mediation program has been established, may refer to mediation all or any portion of a matter relating to dependency or to a child in need of services or a family in need of services.

(3) Each party involved in a court-ordered mediation proceeding has a privilege to refuse to disclose, and to prevent any person present at the proceeding from disclosing, communications made during such proceeding. All oral or written communications in a mediation proceeding, other than an executed settlement agreement, shall be exempt from the requirements of chapter 119 and shall be confidential and inadmissible as evidence in any subsequent legal proceeding, unless all parties agree otherwise.

(4) There shall be no privilege and no restriction on any disclosure of communications made confidential in subsection (3) in relation to disciplinary proceedings filed against mediators pursuant to § 44.106 and court rules, to the extent the communication is used for the purposes of such proceedings. In such cases, the disclosure of an otherwise privileged communication shall be used only for the internal use of the body conducting the investigation. Prior to the release of any disciplinary files to the public, all references to otherwise privileged communications shall be deleted from the record. When an otherwise confidential communication is used in a mediator disciplinary proceeding, such communication shall be inadmissible as evidence in any subsequent legal proceeding. "Subsequent legal proceeding" means any legal proceeding between the parties to the mediation which follows the court-ordered mediation.

(5) The chief judge of each judicial circuit shall maintain a list of mediators who have been certified by the Supreme Court and who have registered for appointment in that circuit.

(a) Whenever possible, qualified individuals who have volunteered their time to serve as mediators shall be appointed. If a mediation program is funded pursuant to § 44.108, volunteer mediators shall be entitled to reimbursement pursuant to § 112.061 for all actual expenses necessitated by service as a mediator.

(b) Nonvolunteer mediators shall be compensated according to rules adopted by the Supreme Court. If a mediation program is funded pursuant to § 44.108, a mediator may be compensated by the county or by the parties. When a party has been declared indigent or insolvent, that party's pro rata share of a mediator's compensation shall be paid by the county at the rate set by administrative order of the chief judge of the circuit.

(6) (a) When an action is referred to mediation by court order, the time periods for responding to an offer of settlement pursuant to § 45.061, or to an offer or demand for judgment pursuant to § 768.79, respectively, shall be tolled until:
   1. An impasse has been declared by the mediator; or
   2. The mediator has reported to the court that no agreement was reached.

(b) Sections 45.061 and 768.79 notwithstanding, an offer of settlement or an offer or demand for judgment may be made at any time after an impasse has been declared by the mediator, or the mediator has reported that no agreement was reached. An offer is deemed rejected as of commencement of trial.

44.106 Standards and procedures for mediators and arbitrators; fees.

The Supreme Court shall establish minimum standards and procedures for qualifications, certification, professional conduct, discipline, and training for mediators and arbitrators who are appointed pursuant to this chapter. The Supreme Court is authorized to set fees to be charged to applicants for certification and renewal of certification. The revenues generated from these fees shall be used to offset the costs of administration of the certification process. The Supreme Court may appoint or employ such personnel as are necessary to assist the court in exercising its powers and performing its duties under this chapter.

44.107 Immunity for arbitrators and mediators.

An arbitrator appointed under § 44.103 or § 44.104 or a mediator appointed under § 44.102 shall have judicial immunity in the same manner and to the same extent as a judge. A person appointed under § 44.106 to assist the Supreme Court in performing its disciplinary function shall have absolute immunity from liability arising from the performance of that person's duties while acting within the scope of that person's appointed function.

Appendix D

Federal Arbitration Act

United States Code title 9

Chapter 1. General Provisions

Section 1. "Maritime Transactions" and "Commerce" Defined; Exceptions to Operation of Title

"Maritime transaction," as herein defined, means charter parties, bills of lading of water carriers, agreements relating to wharfage, supplies furnished vessels or repairs to vessels, collisions, or any other matters in foreign commerce which, if the subject of controversy, would be embraced within admiralty jurisdiction; "commerce," as herein defined, means commerce among the several States or with foreign nations, or in any Territory of the United States or in the District of Columbia, or between any such Territory and another, or between any such Territory and any State or foreign nation, or between the District of Columbia and any State or Territory or foreign nation, but nothing herein contained shall apply to contracts of employment of seamen, railroad employees, or any other class of workers engaged in foreign or interstate commerce.

Section 2. Validity, Irrevocability, and Enforcement of Agreements to Arbitrate

A written provision in any maritime transaction or a contract evidencing a transaction involving commerce to settle by arbitration a controversy thereafter arising out of such contract or transaction, or the refusal to perform the whole or any part thereof, or an agreement in writing to submit to arbitration an existing controversy arising out of such a contract, transaction, or refusal, shall be valid, irrevocable, and enforceable, save upon such grounds as exist at law or in equity for the revocation of any contract.

Section 3. Stay of Proceedings Where Issue Therein Referable to Arbitration

If any suit or proceeding be brought in any of the courts of the United States upon any issue referable to arbitration under an agreement in writing for such arbitration, the court in which such suit is pending, upon being satisfied that the issue involved in such suit or proceeding is referable to arbitration under such an agreement, shall on application of one of the parties stay the trial of the action until such arbitration has been had in accordance with the terms of the agreement, providing the applicant for the stay is not in default in proceeding with such arbitration.

Section 4. Failure to Arbitrate under Agreement; Petition to United States Court Having Jurisdiction for Order to Compel Arbitration; Notice and Service Thereof; Hearing and Determination

A party aggrieved by the alleged failure, neglect, or refusal of another to arbitrate under a written agreement for arbitration may petition any United States district court which, save for such agreement, would have jurisdiction under Title 28, in a civil action or in admiralty of the subject matter of a suit arising out of the controversy between the parties, for an order directing that such arbitration proceed in the manner provided for in such agreement. Five days' notice in writing of such application shall be served upon the party in default. Service thereof shall be made in the manner provided by the Federal Rules of Civil Procedure. The court shall hear the parties, and upon being satisfied that the making of the agreement for arbitration or the failure to comply therewith is not in issue, the court shall make an order directing the parties to proceed to arbitration in accordance with the terms of the agreement. The hearing and proceedings, under such agreement, shall be within the district in which the petition for an order directing such arbitration is filed. If the making of the arbitration agreement or the failure, neglect, or refusal to perform the same be in issue, the court shall proceed summarily to the trial thereof. If no jury trial be demanded by the party alleged to be in default, or if the matter in dispute is within admiralty jurisdiction, the court shall hear and determine such issue. Where such an issue is raised, the party alleged to be in default may, except in cases of admiralty, on or before the return day of the notice of application, demand a jury trial of such issue, and upon such demand the court shall make an order referring the issue or issues to a jury in the manner provided by the Federal Rules of Civil Procedure, or may specially call a jury for that purpose. If the jury find that no agreement in writing for arbitration was made or that there is no default in proceeding thereunder, the proceeding shall be dismissed. If the jury find that an agreement for arbitration was made in writing and that there is a default in proceeding thereunder, the court shall make an order summarily directing the parties to proceed with the arbitration in accordance with the terms thereof.

Section 5. Appointment of Arbitrators or Umpire

If in the agreement provision be made for a method of naming or appointing an arbitrator or arbitrators or an umpire, such method shall be followed; but if no method be provided therein, or if a method be provided and any party thereto shall fail to avail himself of such method, or if for any other reason there shall be a lapse in the naming of an arbitrator or arbitrators or umpire, or in filling a vacancy, then upon the application of either party to the controversy the court shall designate and appoint an arbitrator or arbitrators or umpire, as the case may require, who shall act under the said agreement with the same force and effect as if he or they had been specifically named therein; and unless otherwise provided in the agreement the arbitration shall be by a single arbitrator.

Section 6. Application Heard as Motion

Any application to the court hereunder shall be made and heard in the manner provided by law for the making and hearing of motions, except as otherwise herein expressly provided.

Section 7. Witnesses before Arbitrators; Fees; Compelling Attendance

The arbitrators selected either as prescribed in this title or otherwise, or a majority of them, may summon in writing any person to attend before them or any of them as a witness and in a proper case to bring with him or them any book, record, document, or paper which may be deemed material as evidence in the case. The fees for such attendance shall be the same as the fees of witnesses before masters of the United States courts. Said summons shall issue in the name of the arbitrator or arbitrators, or a majority of them, and shall be signed by the arbitrators, or a majority of them, and shall be directed to the said person and shall be served in the same manner as subpoenas to appear and testify before the court; if any person or persons so summoned to testify shall refuse or neglect to obey said summons, upon petition the United States district court for the district in which such arbitrators, or a majority of them, are sitting may compel the attendance of such person or persons before said arbitrator or arbitrators, or punish said person or persons for contempt in the same manner provided by law for securing the attendance of witnesses or their punishment for neglect or refusal to attend in the courts of the United States.

Section 8. Proceedings Begun by Libel in Admiralty and Seizure of Vessel or Property

If the basis of jurisdiction be a cause of action otherwise justiciable in admiralty, then, notwithstanding anything herein to the contrary, the party claiming to be aggrieved may begin his proceeding hereunder by seizure of the vessel or other property of the other party according to the usual course of admiralty proceedings, and the court shall then have jurisdiction to direct the parties to proceed with the arbitration and shall retain jurisdiction to enter its decree upon the award.

Section 9. Award of Arbitrators; Confirmation; Jurisdiction; Procedure

If the parties in their agreement have agreed that a judgment of the court shall be entered upon the award made pursuant to the arbitration, and shall specify the court, then at any time within one year after the award is made any party to the arbitration may apply to the court so specified for an order confirming the award, and thereupon the court must grant such an order unless the award is vacated, modified, or corrected as prescribed in sections 10 and 11 of this title. If no court is specified in the agreement of the parties, then such application may be made to the United States court in and for the district within which such award was made. Notice of the application shall be served upon the adverse party, and thereupon the court shall have jurisdiction of such party as though he had appeared generally in the proceeding. If the adverse party is a resident of the district within which the award was made, such service shall be made upon the adverse party or his attorney as prescribed by law for service of notice of motion in an action in the same court. If the adverse party shall be a nonresident, then the notice of the application shall be served by the marshal of any district within which the adverse party may be found in like manner as other process of the court.

Section 10. Same; Vacation; Grounds; Rehearing

a. In any of the following cases the United States court in and for the district wherein the award was made may make an order vacating the award upon the application of any party to the arbitration
   1. Where the award was procured by corruption, fraud, or undue means.
   2. Where there was evident partiality or corruption in the arbitrators, or either of them.
   3. Where the arbitrators were guilty of misconduct in refusing to postpone the hearing, upon sufficient cause shown, or in refusing to hear evidence pertinent and material to the controversy; or of any other misbehavior by which the rights of any party have been prejudiced.
   4. Where the arbitrators exceeded their powers, or so imperfectly executed them that a mutual, final, and definite award upon the subject matter submitted was not made.
   5. Where an award is vacated and the time within which the agreement required the award to be made has not expired the court may, in its discretion, direct a rehearing by the arbitrators.
b. The United States district court for the district wherein an award was made that was issued pursuant to section 590 of title 5 may make an order vacating the award upon the application of a person, other than a party to the arbitration, who is adversely affected or aggrieved by the award, if the use of arbitration or the award is clearly inconsistent with the factors set forth in section 582 of title 5.

Section 11. Same; Modification or Correction; Grounds; Order

In either of the following cases the United States court in and for the district wherein the award was made may make an order modifying or correcting the award upon the application of any party to the arbitration—

a. Where there was an evident material miscalculation of figures or an evident material mistake in the description of any person, thing, or property referred to in the award.

b. Where the arbitrators have awarded upon a matter not submitted to them, unless it is a matter not affecting the merits of the decision upon the matter submitted.
c. Where the award is imperfect in matter of form not affecting the merits of the controversy.

The order may modify and correct the award, so as to effect the intent thereof and promote justice between the parties.

Section 12. Notice of Motions to Vacate or Modify; Service; Stay of Proceedings

Notice of a motion to vacate, modify, or correct an award must be served upon the adverse party or his attorney within three months after the award is filed or delivered. If the adverse party is a resident of the district within which the award was made, such service shall be made upon the adverse party or his attorney as prescribed by law for service of notice of motion in an action in the same court. If the adverse party shall be a nonresident then the notice of the application shall be served by the marshal of any district within which the adverse party may be found in like manner as other process of the court. For the purposes of the motion any judge who might make an order to stay the proceedings in an action brought in the same court may make an order, to be served with the notice of motion, staying the proceedings of the adverse party to enforce the award.

Section 13. Papers Filed with Order on Motions; Judgment; Docketing; Force and Effect; Enforcement

The party moving for an order confirming, modifying, or correcting an award shall, at the time such order is filed with the clerk for the entry of judgment thereon, also file the following papers with the clerk:

a. The agreement; the selection or appointment, if any, of an additional arbitrator or umpire; and each written extension of the time, if any, within which to make the award.
b. The award.
c. Each notice, affidavit, or other paper used upon an application to confirm, modify, or correct the award, and a copy of each order of the court upon such an application.

The judgment shall be docketed as if it was rendered in an action.

The judgment so entered shall have the same force and effect, in all respects, as, and be subject to all the provisions of law relating to, a judgment in an action; and it may be enforced as if it had been rendered in an action in the court in which it is entered.

Section 14. Contracts Not Affected
This title shall not apply to contracts made prior to January 1, 1926.

Section 15. Inapplicability of the Act of State Doctrine
Enforcement of arbitral agreements, confirmation of arbitral awards, and execution upon judgments based on orders confirming such awards shall not be refused on the basis of the Act of State doctrine.

Section 16. Appeals
a. An appeal may be taken from
    1. an order—
        A. refusing a stay of any action under section 3 of this title,
        B. denying a petition under section 4 of this title to order arbitration to proceed,
        C. denying an application under section 206 of this title to compel arbitration,
        D. confirming or denying confirmation of an award or partial award, or
        E. modifying, correcting, or vacating an award;
    2. an interlocutory order granting, continuing, or modifying an injunction against an arbitration that is subject to this title; or
    3. a final decision with respect to an arbitration that is subject to this title.
b. Except as otherwise provided in section 1292(b) of title 28, an appeal may not be taken from an interlocutory order—
    1. granting a stay of any action under section 3 of this title;
    2. directing arbitration to proceed under section 4 of this title;
    3. compelling arbitration under section 206 of this title; or
    4. refusing to enjoin an arbitration that is subject to this title.

Appendix E

Uniform Arbitration Act

SECTION 1. DEFINITIONS.

In this [Act]:

(1) "Arbitration organization" means an association, agency, board, commission, or other entity that is neutral and initiates, sponsors, or administers an arbitration proceeding or is involved in the appointment of an arbitrator.

(2) "Arbitrator" means an individual appointed to render an award, alone or with others, in a controversy that is subject to an agreement to arbitrate.

(3) "Court" means [a court of competent jurisdiction in this State].

(4) "Knowledge" means actual knowledge.

(5) "Person" means an individual, corporation, business trust, estate, trust, partnership, limited liability company, association, joint venture, government; governmental subdivision, agency, or instrumentality; public corporation; or any other legal or commercial entity.

(6) "Record" means information that is inscribed on a tangible medium or that is stored in an electronic or other medium and is retrievable in perceivable form.

SECTION 2. NOTICE.

(a) Except as otherwise provided in this [Act], a person gives notice to another person by taking action that is reasonably necessary to inform the other person in ordinary course, whether or not the other person acquires knowledge of the notice.

(b) A person has notice if the person has knowledge of the notice or has received notice.

(c) A person receives notice when it comes to the person's attention or the notice is delivered at the person's place of residence or place of business, or at another location held out by the person as a place of delivery of such communications.

SECTION 3. WHEN [ACT] APPLIES.

(a) This [Act] governs an agreement to arbitrate made on or after [the effective date of this [Act]].

(b) This [Act] governs an agreement to arbitrate made before [the effective date of this [Act]] if all the parties to the agreement or to the arbitration proceeding so agree in a record.

(c) On or after [a delayed date], this [Act] governs an agreement to arbitrate whenever made.

SECTION 4. EFFECT OF AGREEMENT TO ARBITRATE; NONWAIVABLE PROVISIONS.

(a) Except as otherwise provided in subsections (b) and (c), a party to an agreement to arbitrate or to an arbitration proceeding may waive or, the parties may vary the effect of, the requirements of this [Act] to the extent permitted by law.

(b) Before a controversy arises that is subject to an agreement to arbitrate, a party to the agreement may not:

    (1) waive or agree to vary the effect of the requirements of Section 5(a), 6(a), 8, 17(a), 17(b), 26, or 28;

    (2) agree to unreasonably restrict the right under Section 9 to notice of the initiation of an arbitration proceeding;

    (3) agree to unreasonably restrict the right under Section 12 to disclosure of any facts by a neutral arbitrator; or

    (4) waive the right under Section 16 of a party to an agreement to arbitrate to be represented by a lawyer at any proceeding or hearing under this [Act], but an employer and a labor organization may waive the right to representation by a lawyer in a labor arbitration.

(c) A party to an agreement to arbitrate or arbitration proceeding may not waive, or the parties may not vary the effect of, the requirements of this section or Section 3(a) or (c), 7, 14, 18, 20(d) or (e), 22, 23, 24, 25(a) or (b), 29, 30, 31, or 32.

SECTION 5. [APPLICATION] FOR JUDICIAL RELIEF.

(a) Except as otherwise provided in Section 28, an [application] for judicial relief under this [Act] must be made by [motion] to the court and heard in the manner provided by law or rule of court for making and hearing [motions].

(b) Unless a civil action involving the agreement to arbitrate is pending, notice of an initial [motion] to the court under this [Act] must be served in the manner provided by law for the service of a summons in a civil action. Otherwise, notice of the motion must be given in the manner provided by law or rule of court for serving [motions] in pending cases.

SECTION 6. VALIDITY OF AGREEMENT TO ARBITRATE.

(a) An agreement contained in a record to submit to arbitration any existing or subsequent controversy arising between the parties to the agreement is valid, enforceable, and irrevocable except upon a ground that exists at law or in equity for the revocation of a contract.

(b) The court shall decide whether an agreement to arbitrate exists or a controversy is subject to an agreement to arbitrate.

(c) An arbitrator shall decide whether a condition precedent to arbitrability has been fulfilled and whether a contract containing a valid agreement to arbitrate is enforceable.

(d) If a party to a judicial proceeding challenges the existence of, or claims that a controversy is not subject to, an agreement to arbitrate, the arbitration proceeding may continue pending final resolution of the issue by the court, unless the court otherwise orders.

SECTION 7. [MOTION] TO COMPEL OR STAY ARBITRATION.

(a) On [motion] of a person showing an agreement to arbitrate and alleging another person's refusal to arbitrate pursuant to the agreement:
   (1) if the refusing party does not appear or does not oppose the [motion], the court shall order the parties to arbitrate; and
   (2) if the refusing party opposes the [motion], the court shall proceed summarily to decide the issue and order the parties to arbitrate unless it finds that there is no enforceable agreement to arbitrate.

(b) On [motion] of a person alleging that an arbitration proceeding has been initiated or threatened but that there is no agreement to arbitrate, the court shall proceed summarily to decide the issue. If the court finds that there is an enforceable agreement to arbitrate, it shall order the parties to arbitrate.

(c) If the court finds that there is no enforceable agreement, it may not pursuant to subsection (a) or (b) order the parties to arbitrate.

(d) The court may not refuse to order arbitration because the claim subject to arbitration lacks merit or grounds for the claim have not been established.

(e) If a proceeding involving a claim referable to arbitration under an alleged agreement to arbitrate is pending in court, a [motion] under this section must be made in that court. Otherwise a [motion] under this section may be made in any court as provided in Section 27.

(f) If a party makes a [motion] to the court to order arbitration, the court on just terms shall stay any judicial proceeding that involves a claim alleged to be subject to the arbitration until the court renders a final decision under this section.

(g) If the court orders arbitration, the court on just terms shall stay any judicial proceeding that involves a claim subject to the arbitration. If a claim subject to the arbitration is severable, the court may limit the stay to that claim.

SECTION 8. PROVISIONAL REMEDIES.

(a) Before an arbitrator is appointed and is authorized and able to act, the court, upon [motion] of a party to an arbitration proceeding and for good cause shown, may enter an order for provisional remedies to protect the effectiveness of the arbitration proceeding to the same extent and under the same conditions as if the controversy were the subject of a civil action.

(b) After an arbitrator is appointed and is authorized and able to act:
   (1) the arbitrator may issue such orders for provisional remedies, including interim awards, as the arbitrator finds necessary to protect the effectiveness of the arbitration proceeding and to promote the fair and expeditious resolution of the controversy, to the same extent and under the same conditions as if the controversy were the subject of a civil action and

(2) a party to an arbitration proceeding may move the court for a provisional remedy only if the matter is urgent and the arbitrator is not able to act timely or the arbitrator cannot provide an adequate remedy.

(c) A party does not waive a right of arbitration by making a [motion] under subsection (a) or (b).

SECTION 9. INITIATION OF ARBITRATION.

(a) A person initiates an arbitration proceeding by giving notice in a record to the other parties to the agreement to arbitrate in the agreed manner between the parties or, in the absence of agreement, by certified or registered mail, return receipt requested and obtained, or by service as authorized for the commencement of a civil action. The notice must describe the nature of the controversy and the remedy sought.

(b) Unless a person objects for lack or insufficiency of notice under Section 15(c) not later than the beginning of the arbitration hearing, the person by appearing at the hearing waives any objection to lack of or insufficiency of notice.

SECTION 10. CONSOLIDATION OF SEPARATE ARBITRATION PROCEEDINGS.

(a) Except as otherwise provided in subsection (c), upon [motion] of a party to an agreement to arbitrate or to an arbitration proceeding, the court may order consolidation of separate arbitration proceedings as to all or some of the claims if:

(1) there are separate agreements to arbitrate or separate arbitration proceedings between the same persons or one of them is a party to a separate agreement to arbitrate or a separate arbitration proceeding with a third person;

(2) the claims subject to the agreements to arbitrate arise in substantial part from the same transaction or series of related transactions;

(3) the existence of a common issue of law or fact creates the possibility of conflicting decisions in the separate arbitration proceedings; and

(4) prejudice resulting from a failure to consolidate is not outweighed by the risk of undue delay or prejudice to the rights of or hardship to parties opposing consolidation.

(b) The court may order consolidation of separate arbitration proceedings as to some claims and allow other claims to be resolved in separate arbitration proceedings.

(c) The court may not order consolidation of the claims of a party to an agreement to arbitrate if the agreement prohibits consolidation.

SECTION 11. APPOINTMENT OF ARBITRATOR; SERVICE AS A NEUTRAL ARBITRATOR.

(a) If the parties to an agreement to arbitrate agree on a method for appointing an arbitrator, that method must be followed, unless the method fails. If the parties have not agreed on a method, the agreed method fails, or an arbitrator appointed fails or is unable to act and a successor has not been appointed, the court, on [motion] of a party to the arbitration proceeding, shall appoint the arbitrator. An arbitrator so appointed has all the powers of an arbitrator designated in the agreement to arbitrate or appointed pursuant to the agreed method.

(b) An individual who has a known, direct, and material interest in the outcome of the arbitration proceeding or a known, existing, and substantial relationship with a party may not serve as an arbitrator required by an agreement to be neutral.

SECTION 12. DISCLOSURE BY ARBITRATOR.

(a) Before accepting appointment, an individual who is requested to serve as an arbitrator, after making a reasonable inquiry, shall disclose to all parties to the agreement to arbitrate and arbitration proceeding and to any other arbitrators any known facts that a reasonable person would consider likely to affect the impartiality of the arbitrator in the arbitration proceeding, including:

(1) a financial or personal interest in the outcome of the arbitration proceeding; and

(2) an existing or past relationship with any of the parties to the agreement to arbitrate or the arbitration proceeding, their counsel or representatives, a witness, or another arbitrators.

(b) An arbitrator has a continuing obligation to disclose to all parties to the agreement to arbitrate and arbitration proceeding and to any other arbitrators any facts that the arbitrator learns after accepting appointment which a reasonable person would consider likely to affect the impartiality of the arbitrator.

(c) If an arbitrator discloses a fact required by subsection (a) or (b) to be disclosed and a party timely objects to the appointment or continued service of the arbitrator based upon the fact disclosed, the objection may be a ground under Section 23(a)(2) for vacating an award made by the arbitrator.

(d) If the arbitrator did not disclose a fact as required by subsection (a) or (b), upon timely objection by a party, the court under Section 23(a)(2) may vacate an award.

(e) An arbitrator appointed as a neutral arbitrator who does not disclose a known, direct, and material interest in the outcome of the arbitration proceeding or a known, existing, and substantial relationship with a party is presumed to act with evident partiality under Section 23(a)(2).

(f) If the parties to an arbitration proceeding agree to the procedures of an arbitration organization or any other procedures for challenges to arbitrators before an award is made, substantial compliance with those procedures is a condition precedent to a [motion] to vacate an award on that ground under Section 23(a)(2).

SECTION 13. ACTION BY MAJORITY.

If there is more than one arbitrator, the powers of an arbitrator must be exercised by a majority of the arbitrators, but all of them shall conduct the hearing under Section 15(c).

SECTION 14. IMMUNITY OF ARBITRATOR; COMPETENCY TO TESTIFY; ATTORNEY'S FEES AND COSTS.

(a) An arbitrator or an arbitration organization acting in that capacity is immune from civil liability to the same extent as a judge of a court of this State acting in a judicial capacity.

(b) The immunity afforded by this section supplements any immunity under other law.

(c) The failure of an arbitrator to make a disclosure required by Section 12 does not cause any loss of immunity under this section.

(d) In a judicial, administrative, or similar proceeding, an arbitrator or representative of an arbitration organization is not competent to testify, and may not be required to produce records as to any statement, conduct, decision, or ruling occurring during the arbitration proceeding, to the same extent as a judge of a court of this State acting in a judicial capacity. This subsection does not apply:

(1) to the extent necessary to determine the claim of an arbitrator, arbitration organization, or representative of the arbitration organization against a party to the arbitration proceeding; or

(2) to a hearing on a [motion] to vacate an award under Section 23(a)(1) or (2) if the [movant] establishes prima facie that a ground for vacating the award exists.

(e) If a person commences a civil action against an arbitrator, arbitration organization, or representative of an arbitration organization arising from the services of the arbitrator, organization, or representative or if a person seeks to compel an arbitrator or a representative of an arbitration organization to testify or produce records in violation of subsection (d), and the court decides that the arbitrator, arbitration organization, or representative of an arbitration organization is immune from civil liability or that the arbitrator or representative of the organization is not competent to testify, the court shall award to the arbitrator, organization, or representative reasonable attorney's fees and other reasonable expenses of litigation.

SECTION 15. ARBITRATION PROCESS.

(a) An arbitrator may conduct an arbitration in such manner as the arbitrator considers appropriate for a fair and expeditious disposition of the proceeding. The authority conferred upon the arbitrator includes the power to hold conferences with the parties to the arbitration proceeding before the hearing and, among other matters, determine the admissibility, relevance, materiality and weight of any evidence.

(b) An arbitrator may decide a request for summary disposition of a claim or particular issue:

(1) if all interested parties agree; or

(2) upon request of one party to the arbitration proceeding if that party gives notice to all other parties to the proceeding, and the other parties have a reasonable opportunity to respond.

(c) If an arbitrator orders a hearing, the arbitrator shall set a time and place and give notice of the hearing not less than five days before the hearing begins. Unless a party to the arbitration proceeding makes an objection to lack or insufficiency of notice not later than the beginning of the hearing, the party's appearance at the hearing waives the objection. Upon request of a party to the arbitration proceeding and for good cause shown, or upon the arbitrator's own initiative, the arbitrator may adjourn the hearing from time to time as necessary but may not postpone the hearing to a time later than that fixed by the agreement to arbitrate for making the award unless the parties to the arbitration proceeding consent to a later date. The arbitrator may hear and decide the controversy upon the evidence produced although a party who was duly notified of the arbitration proceeding did not appear. The court, on request, may direct the arbitrator to conduct the hearing promptly and render a timely decision.

(d) At a hearing under subsection (c), a party to the arbitration proceeding has a right to be heard, to present evidence material to the controversy, and to cross-examine witnesses appearing at the hearing.

(e) If an arbitrator ceases or is unable to act during the arbitration proceeding, a replacement arbitrator must be appointed in accordance with Section 11 to continue the proceeding and to resolve the controversy.

SECTION 16. REPRESENTATION BY LAWYER.

A party to an arbitration proceeding may be represented by a lawyer.

SECTION 17. WITNESSES; SUBPOENAS; DEPOSITIONS; DISCOVERY.

(a) An arbitrator may issue a subpoena for the attendance of a witness and for the production of records and other evidence at any hearing and may administer oaths. A subpoena must be served in the manner for service of subpoenas in a civil action and, upon [motion] to the court by a party to the arbitration proceeding or the arbitrator, enforced in the manner for enforcement of subpoenas in a civil action.

(b) In order to make the proceedings fair, expeditious, and cost effective, upon request of a party to or a witness in an arbitration proceeding, an arbitrator may permit a deposition of any witness to be taken for use as evidence at the hearing, including a witness who cannot be subpoenaed for or is unable to attend a hearing. The arbitrator shall determine the conditions under which the deposition is taken.

(c) An arbitrator may permit such discovery as the arbitrator decides is appropriate in the circumstances, taking into account the needs of the parties to the arbitration proceeding and other affected persons and the desirability of making the proceeding fair, expeditious, and cost effective.

(d) If an arbitrator permits discovery under subsection (c), the arbitrator may order a party to the arbitration proceeding to comply with the arbitrator's discovery-related orders, issue subpoenas for the attendance of a witness and for the production of records and other evidence at a discovery proceeding, and take action against a noncomplying party to the extent a court could if the controversy were the subject of a civil action in this State.

(e) An arbitrator may issue a protective order to prevent the disclosure of privileged information, confidential information, trade secrets, and other information protected from disclosure to the extent a court could if the controversy were the subject of a civil action in this State.

(f) All laws compelling a person under subpoena to testify and all fees for attending a judicial proceeding, a deposition, or a discovery proceeding as a witness apply to an arbitration proceeding as if the controversy were the subject of a civil action in this State.

(g) The court may enforce a subpoena or discovery-related order for the attendance of a witness within this State and for the production of records and other evidence issued by an arbitrator in connection with an arbitration proceeding in another State upon conditions determined by the court so as to make the arbitration proceeding fair, expeditious, and cost effective. A subpoena or discovery-related order issued by an arbitrator in another State must be served in the manner provided by law for service of subpoenas in a civil action in this State and, upon [motion] to the court by a party to the arbitration proceeding or the arbitrator, enforced in the manner provided by law for enforcement of subpoenas in a civil action in this State.

SECTION 18. JUDICIAL ENFORCEMENT OF PREAWARD RULING BY ARBITRATOR.

If an arbitrator makes a preaward ruling in favor of a party to the arbitration proceeding, the party may request the arbitrator to incorporate the ruling into an award under Section 19. A prevailing party may make a [motion] to the court for an expedited order to confirm the award under Section 22, in which case the court shall summarily decide the [motion]. The court shall issue an order to confirm the award unless the court vacates, modifies, or corrects the award under Section 23 or 24.

SECTION 19. AWARD.

(a) An arbitrator shall make a record of an award. The record must be signed or otherwise authenticated by any arbitrator who concurs with the award. The arbitrator or the arbitration organization shall give notice of the award, including a copy of the award, to each party to the arbitration proceeding.

(b) An award must be made within the time specified by the agreement to arbitrate or, if not specified therein, within the time ordered by the court. The court may extend or the parties to the arbitration proceeding may agree in a record to extend the time. The court or the parties may do so within or after the time specified or ordered. A party waives any objection that an award was not timely made unless the party gives notice of the objection to the arbitrator before receiving notice of the award.

SECTION 20. CHANGE OF AWARD BY ARBITRATOR.

(a) On [motion] to an arbitrator by a party to an arbitration proceeding, the arbitrator may modify or correct an award:

   (1) upon a ground stated in Section 24(a)(1) or (3);

   (2) because the arbitrator has not made a final and definite award upon a claim submitted by the parties to the arbitration proceeding; or

   (3) to clarify the award.

(b) A [motion] under subsection (a) must be made and notice given to all parties within 20 days after the movant receives notice of the award.

(c) A party to the arbitration proceeding must give notice of any objection to the [motion] within 10 days after receipt of the notice.

(d) If a [motion] to the court is pending under Section 22, 23, or 24, the court may submit the claim to the arbitrator to consider whether to modify or correct the award:

   (1) upon a ground stated in Section 24(a)(1) or (3);

   (2) because the arbitrator has not made a final and definite award upon a claim submitted by the parties to the arbitration proceeding; or

   (3) to clarify the award.

(e) An award modified or corrected pursuant to this section is subject to Sections 19(a), 22, 23, and 24.

SECTION 21. REMEDIES; FEES AND EXPENSES OF ARBITRATION PROCEEDING.

(a) An arbitrator may award punitive damages or other exemplary relief if such an award is authorized by law in a civil action involving the same claim and the evidence produced at the hearing justifies the award under the legal standards otherwise applicable to the claim.

(b) An arbitrator may award reasonable attorney's fees and other reasonable expenses of arbitration if such an award is authorized by law in a civil action involving the same claim or by the agreement of the parties to the arbitration proceeding.

(c) As to all remedies other than those authorized by subsections (a) and (b), an arbitrator may order such remedies as the arbitrator considers just and appropriate under the circumstances of the arbitration proceeding. The fact that such a remedy could not or would not be granted by the court is not a ground for refusing to confirm an award under Section 22 or for vacating an award under Section 23.

(d) An arbitrator's expenses and fees, together with other expenses, must be paid as provided in the award.

(e) If an arbitrator awards punitive damages or other exemplary relief under subsection (a), the arbitrator shall specify in the award the basis in fact justifying and the basis in law authorizing the award and state separately the amount of the punitive damages or other exemplary relief.

SECTION 22. CONFIRMATION OF AWARD.

After a party to an arbitration proceeding receives notice of an award, the party may make a [motion] to the court for an order confirming the award at which time the court shall issue a confirming order unless the award is modified or corrected pursuant to Section 20 or 24 or is vacated pursuant to Section 23.

SECTION 23. VACATING AWARD.

(a) Upon [motion] to the court by a party to an arbitration proceeding, the court shall vacate an award made in the arbitration proceeding if:

   (1) the award was procured by corruption, fraud, or other undue means;

   (2) there was:

(A) evident partiality by an arbitrator appointed as a neutral arbitrator;

(B) corruption by an arbitrator; or

(C) misconduct by an arbitrator prejudicing the rights of a party to the arbitration proceeding;

(3) an arbitrator refused to postpone the hearing upon showing of sufficient cause for postponement, refused to consider evidence material to the controversy, or otherwise conducted the hearing contrary to Section 15, so as to prejudice substantially the rights of a party to the arbitration proceeding;

(4) an arbitrator exceeded the arbitrator's powers;

(5) there was no agreement to arbitrate, unless the person participated in the arbitration proceeding without raising the objection under Section 15(c) not later than the beginning of the arbitration hearing; or

(6) the arbitration was conducted without proper notice of the initiation of an arbitration as required in Section 9 so as to prejudice substantially the rights of a party to the arbitration proceeding.

(b) A [motion] under this section must be filed within 90 days after the [movant] receives notice of the award pursuant to Section 19 or within 90 days after the [movant] receives notice of a modified or corrected award pursuant to Section 20, unless the [movant] alleges that the award was procured by corruption, fraud, or other undue means, in which case the [motion] must be made within 90 days after the ground is known or by the exercise of reasonable care would have been known by the [movant].

(c) If the court vacates an award on a ground other than that set forth in subsection (a)(5), it may order a rehearing. If the award is vacated on a ground stated in subsection (a)(1) or (2), the rehearing must be before a new arbitrator. If the award is vacated on a ground stated in subsection (a)(3), (4), or (6), the rehearing may be before the arbitrator who made the award or the arbitrator's successor. The arbitrator must render the decision in the rehearing within the same time as that provided in Section 19(b) for an award.

(d) If the court denies a [motion] to vacate an award, it shall confirm the award unless a [motion] to modify or correct the award is pending.

SECTION 24. MODIFICATION OR CORRECTION OF AWARD.

(a) Upon [motion] made within 90 days after the [movant] receives notice of the award pursuant to Section 19 or within 90 days after the [movant] receives notice of a modified or corrected award pursuant to Section 20, the court shall modify or correct the award if:

(1) there was an evident mathematical miscalculation or an evident mistake in the description of a person, thing, or property referred to in the award;

(2) the arbitrator has made an award on a claim not submitted to the arbitrator and the award may be corrected without affecting the merits of the decision upon the claims submitted; or

(3) the award is imperfect in a matter of form not affecting the merits of the decision on the claims submitted.

(b) If a [motion] made under subsection (a) is granted, the court shall modify or correct and confirm the award as modified or corrected. Otherwise, unless a motion to vacate is pending, the court shall confirm the award.

(c) A [motion] to modify or correct an award pursuant to this section may be joined with a [motion] to vacate the award.

SECTION 25. JUDGMENT ON AWARD; ATTORNEY'S FEES AND LITIGATION EXPENSES.

(a) Upon granting an order confirming, vacating without directing a rehearing, modifying, or correcting an award, the court shall enter a judgment in conformity therewith. The judgment may be recorded, docketed, and enforced as any other judgment in a civil action.

(b) A court may allow reasonable costs of the [motion] and subsequent judicial proceedings.

(c) On [application] of a prevailing party to a contested judicial proceeding under Section 22, 23, or 24, the court may add reasonable attorney's fees and other reasonable expenses of litigation incurred in a judicial proceeding after the award is made to a judgment confirming, vacating without directing a rehearing, modifying, or correcting an award.

SECTION 26. JURISDICTION.

(a) A court of this State having jurisdiction over the controversy and the parties may enforce an agreement to arbitrate.

(b) An agreement to arbitrate providing for arbitration in this State confers exclusive jurisdiction on the court to enter judgment on an award under this [Act].

SECTION 27. VENUE.

A [motion] pursuant to Section 5 must be made in the court of the [county] in which the agreement to arbitrate specifies the arbitration hearing is to be held or, if the hearing has been held, in the court of the [county] in which it was held. Otherwise, the [motion] may be made in the court of any [county] in which an adverse party resides or has a place of business or, if no adverse party has a residence or place of business in this State, in the court of any [county] in this State. All subsequent [motions] must be made in the court hearing the initial [motion] unless the court otherwise directs.

SECTION 28. APPEALS.

(a) An appeal may be taken from:
  (1) an order denying a [motion] to compel arbitration;
  (2) an order granting a [motion] to stay arbitration;
  (3) an order confirming or denying confirmation of an award;
  (4) an order modifying or correcting an award;
  (5) an order vacating an award without directing a rehearing; or
  (6) a final judgment entered pursuant to this [Act].
(b) An appeal under this section must be taken as from an order or a judgment in a civil action.

SECTION 29. UNIFORMITY OF APPLICATION AND CONSTRUCTION.

In applying and construing this uniform act, consideration must be given to the need to promote uniformity of the law with respect to its subject matter among States that enact it.

SECTION 30. RELATIONSHIP TO ELECTRONIC SIGNATURES IN GLOBAL AND NATIONAL COMMERCE ACT.

The provisions of this Act governing the legal effect, validity, and enforceability of electronic records or electronic signatures, and of contracts performed with the use of such records or signatures conform to the requirements of Section 102 of the Electronic Signatures in Global and National Commerce Act.

SECTION 31. EFFECTIVE DATE.

This [Act] takes effect on [effective date].

SECTION 32. REPEAL.

Effective on [delayed date should be the same as that in Section 3(c)], the [Uniform Arbitration Act] is repealed.

SECTION 33. SAVINGS CLAUSE.

This [Act] does not affect an action or proceeding commenced or right accrued before this [Act] takes effect. Subject to Section 3 of this [Act], an arbitration agreement made before the effective date of this [Act] is governed by the [Uniform Arbitration Act].

Appendix F

Excerpt from The American Arbitration Association's Commercial Dispute Resolution Procedures (Arbitration Rules)— as Amended and Effective on September 1, 2000

copyright 2001 by the American Arbitration Association

R-1 Agreement of Parties*

The parties shall be deemed to have made these rules a part of their arbitration agreement whenever they have provided for arbitration by the American Arbitration Association (hereinafter AAA) under its Commercial Arbitration Rules or for arbitration by the AAA of a domestic commercial dispute without specifying particular rules. These rules and any amendment of them shall apply in the form in effect at the time the demand for arbitration or submission agreement is received by the AAA. The parties, by written agreement, may vary the procedures set forth in these rules.

*A dispute arising out of a contract, agreement or plan between a consumer and a business, which involves claims of $10,000.00 or less, will be administered in accordance with the AAA's Arbitration Rules for the Resolution of Consumer-Related Disputes, unless the parties agree otherwise after the commencement of the arbitration. Consumers are not prohibited from seeking relief in a small claims court for disputes or claims within the scope of its jurisdiction, even in consumer arbitration cases filed by the business.

R-2 AAA and Delegation of Duties

When parties agree to arbitrate under these rules, or when they provide for arbitration by the AAA and an arbitration is initiated under these rules, they thereby authorize the AAA to administer the arbitration. The authority and duties of the AAA are prescribed in the agreement of the parties and in these rules, and may be carried out through such of the AAA's representatives as it may direct. The AAA may, in its discretion, assign the administration of an arbitration to any of its offices.

R-3 National Panel of Arbitrators

The AAA shall establish and maintain a National Panel of Commercial Arbitrators and shall appoint arbitrators as provided in these rules. The term "arbitrator" in these rules refers to the arbitration panel, whether composed of one or more arbitrators and whether the arbitrators are neutral or party-appointed.

R-4 Initiation under an Arbitration Provision in a Contract

(a) Arbitration under an arbitration provision in a contract shall be initiated in the following manner:

   i. The initiating party (the "claimant") shall, within the time period, if any, specified in the contract(s), give to the other party (the "respondent") written notice of its intention to arbitrate (the "demand"), which demand shall contain a statement setting forth the nature of the dispute, the names and addresses of all other parties, the amount involved, if any, the remedy sought, and the hearing locale requested.

   ii. The claimant shall file at any office of the AAA two copies of the demand and two copies of the arbitration provisions of the contract, together with the appropriate filing fee as provided in the schedule included with these rules.

   iii. The AAA shall confirm notice of such filing to the parties.

(b) A respondent may file an answering statement in duplicate with the AAA within 15 days after confirmation of notice of filing of the demand is sent by the AAA. The respondent shall, at the time of any such filing, send a copy of the answering statement to the claimant. If a counterclaim is asserted, it shall contain a statement setting forth the nature of the counterclaim, the amount involved, if any, and the remedy sought. If a counterclaim is made, the party making the counterclaim shall forward to the AAA with the answering statement the appropriate fee provided in the schedule included with these rules.

(c) If no answering statement is filed within the stated time, respondent will be deemed to deny the claim. Failure to file an answering statement shall not operate to delay the arbitration.

(d) When filing any statement pursuant to this section, the parties are encouraged to provide descriptions of their claims in sufficient detail to make the circumstances of the dispute clear to the arbitrator.

R-5 Initiation under a Submission

Parties to any existing dispute may commence an arbitration under these rules by filing at any office of the AAA two copies of a written submission to arbitrate under these rules, signed by the parties. It shall contain a statement of the nature of the dispute, the names and addresses of all parties, any claims and counterclaims, the amount involved, if any, the remedy sought, and the hearing locale requested, together with the appropriate filing fee as provided in the schedule included with these rules. Unless the parties state otherwise in the submission, all claims and counterclaims will be deemed to be denied by the other party.

R-6 Changes of Claim

After filing of a claim, if either party desires to make any new or different claim or counterclaim, it shall be made in writing and filed with the AAA. The party asserting such a claim or counterclaim shall provide a copy to the other party, who shall have 15 days from the date of such transmission within which to file an answering statement with the AAA. After the arbitrator is appointed, however, no new or different claim may be submitted except with the arbitrator's consent.

R-7 Applicable Procedures

Unless the parties or the AAA in its discretion determines otherwise, the Expedited Procedures shall be applied in any case where no disclosed claim or counterclaim exceeds $75,000, exclusive of interest and arbitration costs. Parties may also agree to use the Expedited Procedures in cases involving claims in excess of $75,000. The Expedited Procedures shall be applied as described in Sections E-1 through E-10 of these rules, in addition to any other portion of these rules that is not in conflict with the Expedited Procedures. All other cases shall be administered in accordance with Sections R-1 through R-56 of these rules.

R-8 Jurisdiction

(a) The arbitrator shall have the power to rule on his or her own jurisdiction, including any objections with respect to the existence, scope or validity of the arbitration agreement.

(b) The arbitrator shall have the power to determine the existence or validity of a contract of which an arbitration clause forms a part. Such an arbitration clause shall be treated as an agreement independent of the other terms of the contract. A decision by the arbitrator that the contract is null and void shall not for that reason alone render invalid the arbitration clause.

(c) A party must object to the jurisdiction of the arbitrator or to the arbitrability of a claim or counterclaim no later than the filing of the answering statement to the claim or counterclaim that gives rise to the objection. The arbitrator may rule on such objections as a preliminary matter or as part of the final award.

R-9 Mediation

At any stage of the proceedings, the parties may agree to conduct a mediation conference under the Commercial Mediation Rules in order to facilitate settlement. The mediator shall not be an arbitrator appointed to the case. Where the parties to a pending arbitration agree to mediate under the AAA's rules, no additional administrative fee is required to initiate the mediation.

R-10 Administrative Conference

At the request of any party or upon the AAA's own initiative, the AAA may conduct an administrative conference, in person or by telephone, with the parties and/or their representatives. The conference may address such issues as arbitrator selection, potential mediation of the dispute, potential exchange of information, a timetable for hearings and any other administrative matters. There is no administrative fee for this service.

R-11 Fixing of Locale

The parties may mutually agree on the locale where the arbitration is to be held. If any party requests that the hearing be held in a specific locale and the other party files no objection thereto within 15 days after notice of the request has been sent to it by the AAA, the locale shall be the one requested. If a party objects to the locale requested by the other party, the AAA shall have the power to determine the locale, and its decision shall be final and binding.

R-12 Qualifications of an Arbitrator

(a) Any neutral arbitrator appointed pursuant to Section R-13, R-14, R-15, or E-5, or selected by mutual choice of the parties or their appointees, shall be subject to disqualification for the reasons specified in Section R-19. If the parties specifically so agree in writing, the arbitrator shall not be subject to disqualification for those reasons.

(b) Unless the parties agree otherwise, an arbitrator selected unilaterally by one party is a party-appointed arbitrator and is not subject to disqualification pursuant to Section R-19.

R-13 Appointment from Panel

If the parties have not appointed an arbitrator and have not provided any other method of appointment, the arbitrator shall be appointed in the following manner:

(a) Immediately after the filing of the submission or the answering statement or the expiration of the time within which the answering statement is to be filed, the AAA shall send simultaneously to each party to the dispute an identical list of names of persons chosen from the panel. The parties are encouraged to agree to an arbitrator from the submitted list and to advise the AAA of their agreement.

(b) If the parties are unable to agree upon an arbitrator, each party to the dispute shall have 15 days from the transmittal date in which to strike names objected to, number the remaining names in order of preference, and

return the list to the AAA. If a party does not return the list within the time specified, all persons named therein shall be deemed acceptable. From among the persons who have been approved on both lists, and in accordance with the designated order of mutual preference, the AAA shall invite the acceptance of an arbitrator to serve. If the parties fail to agree on any of the persons named, or if acceptable arbitrators are unable to act, or if for any other reason the appointment cannot be made from the submitted lists, the AAA shall have the power to make the appointment from among other members of the panel without the submission of additional lists.

(c) Unless the parties have agreed otherwise no later than 15 days after the commencement of an arbitration, if the notice of arbitration names two or more claimants or two or more respondents, the AAA shall appoint all the arbitrators.

R-14 Direct Appointment by a Party

(a) If the agreement of the parties names an arbitrator or specifies a method of appointing an arbitrator, that designation or method shall be followed. The notice of appointment, with the name and address of the arbitrator, shall be filed with the AAA by the appointing party. Upon the request of any appointing party, the AAA shall submit a list of members of the panel from which the party may, if it so desires, make the appointment.

(b) If the agreement specifies a period of time within which an arbitrator shall be appointed and any party fails to make the appointment within that period, the AAA shall make the appointment.

(c) If no period of time is specified in the agreement, the AAA shall notify the party to make the appointment. If within 15 days after such notice has been sent, an arbitrator has not been appointed by a party, the AAA shall make the appointment.

R-15 Appointment of Neutral Arbitrator by Party-Appointed Arbitrators or Parties

(a) If the parties have selected party-appointed arbitrators, or if such arbitrators have been appointed as provided in Section R-14, and the parties have authorized them to appoint a neutral arbitrator within a specified time and no appointment is made within that time or any agreed extension, the AAA may appoint a neutral arbitrator, who shall act as chairperson.

(b) If no period of time is specified for appointment of the neutral arbitrator and the party-appointed arbitrators or the parties do not make the appointment within 15 days from the date of the appointment of the last party-appointed arbitrator, the AAA may appoint the neutral arbitrator, who shall act as chairperson.

(c) If the parties have agreed that their party-appointed arbitrators shall appoint the neutral arbitrator from the panel, the AAA shall furnish to the party-appointed arbitrators, in the manner provided in Section R-13, a list selected from the panel, and the appointment of the neutral arbitrator shall be made as provided in that section.

R-16 Nationality of Arbitrator

Where the parties are nationals or residents of different countries, the AAA, at the request of any party or on its own initiative, may appoint as a neutral arbitrator a national of a country other than that of any of the parties. The request must be made prior to the time set for the appointment of the arbitrator as agreed by the parties or set by these rules.

R-17 Number of Arbitrators

If the arbitration agreement does not specify the number of arbitrators, the dispute shall be heard and determined by one arbitrator, unless the AAA, in its discretion, directs that three arbitrators be appointed. The parties may request three arbitrators in their demand or answer, which request the AAA will consider in exercising its discretion regarding the number of arbitrators appointed to the dispute.

R-18 Notice to Arbitrator of Appointment

Notice of the appointment of the neutral arbitrator, whether appointed mutually by the parties or by the AAA, shall be sent to the arbitrator by the AAA, together with a copy of these rules, and the signed acceptance of the arbitrator shall be filed with the AAA prior to the opening of the first hearing.

R-19 Disclosure and Challenge Procedure

(a) Any person appointed as a neutral arbitrator shall disclose to the AAA any circumstance likely to affect impartiality or independence, including any bias or any financial or personal interest in the result of the arbitration or any past or present relationship with the parties or their representatives. Upon receipt of such information from the arbitrator or another source, the AAA shall commu-nicate the information to the parties and, if it deems it appropriate to do so, to the arbitrator and others.

(b) Upon objection of a party to the continued service of a neutral arbitrator, the AAA shall determine whether the arbitrator should be disqualified and shall inform the parties of its decision, which shall be conclusive.

R-20 Communication with Arbitrator

(a) No party and no one acting on behalf of any party shall communicate unilaterally concerning the arbitration with a neutral arbitrator or a candidate for neutral arbitrator. Unless the parties agree otherwise or the arbitrator so directs, any communication from the parties to a neutral arbitrator shall be sent to the AAA for transmittal to the arbitrator.

(b) The parties or the arbitrators may also agree that once the panel has been constituted, no party and no one acting on behalf of any party shall communicate unilaterally concerning the arbitration with any party-appointed arbitrator.

R-21 Vacancies

(a) If for any reason an arbitrator is unable to perform the duties of the office, the AAA may, on proof satisfactory to it, declare the office vacant. Vacancies shall be filled in accordance with the applicable provisions of these rules.

(b) In the event of a vacancy in a panel of neutral arbitrators after the hearings have commenced, the remaining arbitrator or arbitrators may continue with the hearing and determination of the controversy, unless the parties agree otherwise.

(c) In the event of the appointment of a substitute arbitrator, the panel of arbitrators shall determine in its sole discretion whether it is necessary to repeat all or part of any prior hearings.

R-22 Preliminary Hearing

(a) At the request of any party or at the discretion of the arbitrator or the AAA, the arbitrator may schedule as soon as practicable a preliminary hearing with the parties and/or their representatives. The preliminary hearing may be conducted by telephone at the arbitrator's discretion. There is no case service fee for the first preliminary hearing.

(b) During the preliminary hearing, the parties and the arbitrator should discuss the future conduct of the case, including clarification of the issues and claims, a schedule for the hearings and any other preliminary matters.

R-23 Exchange of Information

(a) At the request of any party or at the discretion of the arbitrator, consistent with the expedited nature of arbitration, the arbitrator may direct (i) the production of documents and other information, and (ii) the identification of any witnesses to be called.

(b) At least five (5) business days prior to the hearing, the parties shall exchange copies of all exhibits they intend to submit at the hearing.

(c) The arbitrator is authorized to resolve any disputes concerning the exchange of information.

R-24 Date, Time, and Place of Hearing

The arbitrator shall set the date, time, and place for each hearing. The parties shall respond to requests for hearing dates in a timely manner, be cooperative in scheduling the earliest practicable date, and adhere to the established hearing schedule. The AAA shall send a notice of hearing to the parties at least 10 days in advance of the hearing date, unless otherwise agreed by the parties.

R-25 Attendance at Hearings

The arbitrator and the AAA shall maintain the privacy of the hearings unless the law provides to the contrary. Any person having a direct interest in the arbitration is entitled to attend hearings. The arbitrator shall otherwise have the power to require the exclusion of any witness, other than a party or other essential person, during the testimony of any other witness. It shall be discretionary with the arbitrator to determine the propriety of the attendance of any other person other than a party and its representatives.

R-26 Representation

Any party may be represented by counsel or other authorized representative. A party intending to be so represented shall notify the other party and the AAA of the name and address of the representative at least three days prior to the date set for the hearing at which that person is first to appear. When such a representative initiates an arbitration or responds for a party, notice is deemed to have been given.

R-27 Oaths

Before proceeding with the first hearing, each arbitrator may take an oath of office and, if required by law, shall do so. The arbitrator may require witnesses to testify under oath administered by any duly qualified person and, if it is required by law or requested by any party, shall do so.

R-28 Stenographic Record

Any party desiring a stenographic record shall make arrangements directly with a stenographer and shall notify the other parties of these arrangements at least three days in advance of the hearing. The requesting party or parties shall pay the cost of the record. If the transcript is agreed by the parties, or determined by the arbitrator to be the official record of the proceeding, it must be provided to the arbitrator and made available to the other parties for inspection, at a date, time, and place determined by the arbitrator.

R-29 Interpreters

Any party wishing an interpreter shall make all arrangements directly with the interpreter and shall assume the costs of the service.

R-30 Postponements

The arbitrator may postpone any hearing upon agreement of the parties, upon request of a party for good cause shown, or upon the arbitrator's own initiative.

R-31 Arbitration in the Absence of a Party or Representative

Unless the law provides to the contrary, the arbitration may proceed in the absence of any party or representative who, after due notice, fails to be present or fails to obtain a postponement. An award shall not be made solely on the default of a party. The arbitrator shall require the party who is present to submit such evidence as the arbitrator may require for the making of an award.

R-32 Conduct of Proceedings

(a) The claimant shall present evidence to support its claim. The respondent shall then present evidence to support its defense. Witnesses for each party shall also submit to questions from the arbitrator and the adverse party. The arbitrator has the discretion to vary this procedure, provided that the parties are treated with equality and that each party has the right to be heard and is given a fair opportunity to present its case.

(b) The arbitrator, exercising his or her discretion, shall conduct the proceedings with a view to expediting the resolution of the dispute and may direct the order of proof, bifurcate proceedings and direct the parties to focus their presentations on issues the decision of which could dispose of all or part of the case.

(c) The parties may agree to waive oral hearings in any case.

R-33 Evidence

(a) The parties may offer such evidence as is relevant and material to the dispute and shall produce such evidence as the arbitrator may deem necessary to an understanding and determination of the dispute. Conformity to legal rules of evidence shall not be necessary. All evidence shall be taken in the presence of all of the arbitrators and all of the parties, except where any of the parties is absent, in default or has waived the right to be present.

(b) The arbitrator shall determine the admissibility, relevance, and materiality of the evidence offered and may exclude evidence deemed by the arbitrator to be cumulative or irrelevant.

(c) The arbitrator shall take into account applicable principles of legal privilege, such as those involving the confidentiality of communications between a lawyer and client.

(d) An arbitrator or other person authorized by law to subpoena witnesses or documents may do so upon the request of any party or independently.

R-34 Evidence by Affidavit and Posthearing Filing of Documents or Other Evidence

(a) The arbitrator may receive and consider the evidence of witnesses by declaration or affidavit, but shall give it only such weight as the arbitrator deems it entitled to after consideration of any objection made to its admission.

(b) If the parties agree or the arbitrator directs that documents or other evidence be submitted to the arbitrator after the hearing, the documents or other evidence shall be filed with the AAA for transmission to the arbitrator. All parties shall be afforded an opportunity to examine and respond to such documents or other evidence.

R-35 Inspection or Investigation

An arbitrator finding it necessary to make an inspection or investigation in connection with the arbitration shall direct the AAA to so advise the parties. The arbitrator shall set the date and time and the AAA shall notify the parties. Any party who so desires may be present at such an inspection or investigation. In the event that one or all parties are not present at the inspection or investigation, the arbitrator shall make an

oral or written report to the parties and afford them an opportunity to comment.

R-36 Interim Measures

(a) The arbitrator may take whatever interim measures he or she deems necessary, including injunctive relief and measures for the protection or conservation of property and disposition of perishable goods.

(b) Such interim measures may take the form of an interim award, and the arbitrator may require security for the costs of such measures.

(c) A request for interim measures addressed by a party to a judicial authority shall not be deemed incompatible with the agreement to arbitrate or a waiver of the right to arbitrate.

R-37 Closing of Hearing

The arbitrator shall specifically inquire of all parties whether they have any further proofs to offer or witnesses to be heard. Upon receiving negative replies or if satisfied that the record is complete, the arbitrator shall declare the hearing closed. If briefs are to be filed, the hearing shall be declared closed as of the final date set by the arbitrator for the receipt of briefs. If documents are to be filed as provided in Section R-34 and the date set for their receipt is later than that set for the receipt of briefs, the later date shall be the closing date of the hearing. The time limit within which the arbitrator is required to make the award shall commence, in the absence of other agreements by the parties, upon the closing of the hearing.

R-38 Reopening of Hearing

The hearing may be reopened on the arbitrator's initiative, or upon application of a party, at any time before the award is made. If reopening the hearing would prevent the making of the award within the specific time agreed on by the parties in the contract(s) out of which the controversy has arisen, the matter may not be reopened unless the parties agree on an extension of time. When no specific date is fixed in the contract, the arbitrator may reopen the hearing and shall have 30 days from the closing of the reopened hearing within which to make an award.

R-39 Waiver of Rules

Any party who proceeds with the arbitration after knowledge that any provision or requirement of these rules has not been complied with and who fails to state an objection in writing shall be deemed to have waived the right to object.

R-40 Extensions of Time

The parties may modify any period of time by mutual agreement. The AAA or the arbitrator may for good cause extend any period of time established by these rules, except the time for making the award. The AAA shall notify the parties of any extension.

R-41 Serving of Notice

(a) Any papers, notices, or process necessary or proper for the initiation or continuation of an arbitration under these rules, for any court action in connection therewith, or for the entry of judgment on any award made under these rules may be served on a party by mail addressed to the party, or its representative at the last known address or by personal service, in or outside the state where the arbitration is to be held, provided that reasonable opportunity to be heard with regard to the dispute is or has been granted to the party.

(b) The AAA, the arbitrator and the parties may also use overnight delivery or electronic facsimile transmission (fax), to give the notices required by these rules. Where all parties and the arbitrator agree, notices may be transmitted by electronic mail (E-mail), or other methods of communication.

(c) Unless otherwise instructed by the AAA or by the arbitrator, any documents submitted by any party to the AAA or to the arbitrator shall simultaneously be provided to the other party or parties to the arbitration.

R-42 Majority Decision

When the panel consists of more than one arbitrator, unless required by law or by the arbitration agreement, a majority of the arbitrators must make all decisions.

R-43 Time of Award

The award shall be made promptly by the arbitrator and, unless otherwise agreed by the parties or specified by law, no later than 30 days from the date of closing the hearing, or, if oral hearings have been waived, from the date of the AAA's transmittal of the final statements and proofs to the arbitrator.

R-44 Form of Award

(a) Any award shall be in writing and signed by a majority of the arbitrators. It shall be executed in the manner required by law.

(b) The arbitrator need not render a reasoned award unless the parties request such an award in writing prior to appointment of the arbitrator or unless the arbitrator determines that a reasoned award is appropriate.

R-45 Scope of Award

(a) The arbitrator may grant any remedy or relief that the arbitrator deems just and equitable and within the scope of the agreement of the parties, including, but not limited to, specific performance of a contract.

(b) In addition to a final award, the arbitrator may make other decisions, including interim, interlocutory, or partial rulings, orders, and awards. In any interim, interlocutory, or partial award, the arbitrator may assess and apportion the fees, expenses, and compensation related to such award as the arbitrator determines is appropriate.

(c) In the final award, the arbitrator shall assess the fees, expenses, and compensation provided in Sections R-51, R-52, and R-53. The arbitrator may apportion such fees, expenses, and compensation among the parties in such amounts as the arbitrator determines is appropriate.

(d) The award of the arbitrator(s) may include: (a) interest at such rate and from such date as the arbitrator(s) may deem appropriate; and (b) an award of attorneys' fees if all parties have requested such an award or it is authorized by law or their arbitration agreement.

R-46 Award upon Settlement

If the parties settle their dispute during the course of the arbitration and if the parties so request, the arbitrator may set forth the terms of the settlement in a "consent award."

R-47 Delivery of Award to Parties

Parties shall accept as notice and delivery of the award the placing of the award or a true copy thereof in the mail addressed to the parties or their representatives at the last known addresses, personal or electronic service of the award, or the filing of the award in any other manner that is permitted by law.

R-48 Modification of Award

Within 20 days after the transmittal of an award, any party, upon notice to the other parties, may request the arbitrator, through the AAA, to correct any clerical, typographical, or computational errors in the award. The arbitrator is not empowered to redetermine the merits of any claim already decided. The other parties shall be given 10 days to respond to the request. The arbitrator shall dispose of the request within 20 days after transmittal by the AAA to the arbitrator of the request and any response thereto.

R-49 Release of Documents for Judicial Proceedings
The AAA shall, upon the written request of a party, furnish to the party, at the party's expense, certified copies of any papers in the AAA's possession that may be required in judicial proceedings relating to the arbitration.

R-50 Applications to Court and Exclusion of Liability
(a) No judicial proceeding by a party relating to the subject matter of the arbitration shall be deemed a waiver of the party's right to arbitrate.
(b) Neither the AAA nor any arbitrator in a proceeding under these rules is a necessary party in judicial proceedings relating to the arbitration.
(c) Parties to an arbitration under these rules shall be deemed to have consented that judgment upon the arbitration award may be entered in any federal or state court having jurisdiction thereof.
(d) Neither the AAA nor any arbitrator shall be liable to any party for any act or omission in connection with any arbitration conducted under these rules.

R-51 Administrative Fees
As a not-for-profit organization, the AAA shall prescribe an initial filing fee and a case service fee to compensate it for the cost of providing administrative services. The fees in effect when the fee or charge is incurred shall be applicable.

The filing fee shall be advanced by the party or parties making a claim or counterclaim, subject to final apportionment by the arbitrator in the award.

The AAA may, in the event of extreme hardship on the part of any party, defer or reduce the administrative fees.

R-52 Expenses
The expenses of witnesses for either side shall be paid by the party producing such witnesses. All other expenses of the arbitration, including required travel and other expenses of the arbitrator, AAA representatives, and any witness and the cost of any proof produced at the direct request of the arbitrator, shall be borne equally by the parties, unless they agree otherwise or unless the arbitrator in the award assesses such expenses or any part thereof against any specified party or parties.

R-53 Neutral Arbitrator's Compensation
(a) Unless the parties agree otherwise, members of the National Panel of Commercial Arbitrators appointed as neutrals on cases administered under the Expedited Procedures with claims not exceeding $10,000, will customarily serve without compensation for the first day of service. Thereafter, arbitrators shall receive compensation as set forth herein.
(b) Arbitrators shall be compensated at a rate consistent with the arbitrator's stated rate of compensation, beginning with the first day of hearing in all cases with claims exceeding $10,000.
(c) If there is disagreement concerning the terms of compensation, an appropriate rate shall be established with the arbitrator by the AAA and confirmed to the parties.
(d) Any arrangement for the compensation of a neutral arbitrator shall be made through the AAA and not directly between the parties and the arbitrator.

R-54 Deposits
The AAA may require the parties to deposit in advance of any hearings such sums of money as it deems necessary to cover the expense of the arbitration, including the arbitrator's fee, if any, and shall render an accounting to the parties and return any unexpended balance at the conclusion of the case.

R-55 Interpretation and Application of Rules
The arbitrator shall interpret and apply these rules insofar as they relate to the arbitrator's powers and duties. When there is more than one arbitrator and a difference arises among them concerning the meaning or application of these rules, it shall be decided by a majority vote. If that is not possible, either an arbitrator or a party may refer the question to the AAA for final decision. All other rules shall be interpreted and applied by the AAA.

R-56 Suspension for Nonpayment
If arbitrator compensation or administrative charges have not been paid in full, the AAA may so inform the parties in order that one of them may advance the required payment. If such payments are not made, the arbitrator may order the suspension or termination of the proceedings. If no arbitrator has yet been appointed, the AAA may suspend the proceedings.

Appendix G

Rules of the United States District Court for the Middle District of Florida

Court-Annexed Arbitration

Rule 8.01. Statement of Purpose; Certification of Arbitrators

(a) It is the purpose of the Court, through adoption and implementation of this rule, to provide an alternative mechanism for the resolution of civil disputes (a Court annexed, mandatory arbitration procedure) leading to an early disposition of many civil cases with resultant savings in time and costs to the litigants and to the Court, but without sacrificing the quality of justice to be rendered or the right of the litigants to a full trial de novo on demand.

(b) The Chief Judge shall certify those persons who are eligible and qualified to serve as arbitrators under this rule, in such numbers as he shall deem appropriate, and shall have complete discretion and authority to thereafter withdraw the certification of any arbitrator at any time. Separate lists of certified arbitrators shall be maintained in the Jacksonville-Ocala, Orlando, and Tampa-Ft. Myers Divisions of the Court, respectively.

(c) An individual may be certified to serve as an arbitrator under this rule if: (1) he has been for at least five years a member of the Florida Bar; (2) he is admitted to practice before this Court; and (3) he is determined by the Chief Judge to be competent to perform the duties of an arbitrator. An advisory committee or committees comprised of members of the bar in each Division of the Court, respectively, may be constituted to assist the Chief Judge in screening applicants and aiding in the formulation and application of standards for selecting arbitrators.

(d) Each individual certified as an arbitrator shall take the oath or affirmation prescribed by 28 U.S.C. Section 453 before serving as an arbitrator. Current lists of all persons certified as arbitrators in each Division of the Court, respectively, shall be maintained in the office of the Clerk as a public document. Depending upon the availability of funds from the Administrative Office of the United States Courts, or other appropriate agency, arbitrators shall be compensated for their services in such amounts and in such manner as the Chief Judge shall specify from time to time by standing order; and no arbitrator shall charge or accept for his services any fee or reimbursement from any other source whatever absent written approval of the Court given in advance of any such payment. Any member of the bar who is certified and designated as an arbitrator pursuant to these rules shall not for that reason be disqualified from appearing and acting as counsel in any other case pending before the Court.

Rule 8.02. Definition of Cases to be Arbitrated

(a) Any civil action shall be referred by the Clerk to arbitration in accordance with this rule if:

   (1) The United States is a party; and

      (A) The action is of a type that the Attorney General has provided by regulation may be submitted to arbitration; or

      (B) The action consists of a claim for money damages not in excess of $150,000, exclusive of interest and costs (and the Court determines in its discretion that any non-monetary claims are insubstantial), and is brought pursuant to the Miller Act, 40 U.S.C. Section 270(a) et seq., or the Federal Tort Claims Act, 28 U.S.C. Sections 1346(b) and 2671 et seq.

      (C) The action is not based on an alleged violation of a right secured by the Constitution of the United States, and jurisdiction is not based in whole or in part on 28 U.S.C. Section 1343.

   (2) The United States is not a party; and

      (A) The action consists of a claim or claims for money damages not in excess of $150,000, individually, exclusive of punitive damages, interest, costs and attorneys fees (and the Court determines in its discretion that any non-monetary claims are insubstantial), and is brought pursuant to

(i) 28 U.S.C. Section 1331 and the Jones Act, 46 U.S.C. Section 688, or the FELA, 45 U.S.C. Section 51;

(ii) 28 U.S.C. Sections 1331 or 1332 arising out of a negotiable instrument or a contract; or

(iii) 28 U.S.C. Sections 1332 or 1333 and Rule 9(h), Fed.R.Civ.P., to recover for personal injuries or property damage.

(B) The action is not based on an alleged violation of a right secured by the Constitution of the United States, and jurisdiction is not based in whole or in part on 28 U.S.C. Section 1343.

(3) The parties consent to arbitration as provided in this rule with respect to any case not within the provisions of subsections (a)(1) and (2) above, and agree to pay a reasonable fee to the arbitrator(s). The written consent to arbitration shall include a statement of understanding that

(A) Consent to arbitration is freely and knowingly obtained; and

(B) No party or attorney can be prejudiced for refusing to participate in arbitration by consent.

(4) For the purpose of making a determination concerning the dollar amount of unstated or unliquidated claims incident to the application of subsection (a) of this Rule, claims for damages shall be presumed in all cases to be less than $150,000 exclusive of punitive damages, interest, costs and attorney's fees, unless counsel asserting the claim certifies in writing before the case is referred by the Clerk for arbitration that to the best of his knowledge and beliefs, in good faith, the damages recoverable exceed $150,000 exclusive of punitive damages, interest, costs and attorney's fees.

(5) Notwithstanding the amount alleged or stated in a party's pleading relating to liquidated claims, and despite a party's good faith certification concerning the amount recoverable with regard to unliquidated claims, the Court may in any appropriate case at any time disregard such allegation or such certificate and require arbitration if satisfied that recoverable damages do not in fact exceed $150,000 exclusive of punitive damages, interest, costs and attorney's fees, or that arbitration may promote prompt and just disposition of the cause. Conversely, any civil action subject to arbitration pursuant to this rule may be exempt or withdrawn from arbitration by the presiding Judge at any time, before or after reference, upon a determination for any reason that the case is not suitable for arbitration.

(b) Mediation may be substituted for arbitration by the presiding Judge in any civil action subject to arbitration pursuant to this rule upon a determination for any reason that the case is susceptible to resolution through mediation.

Rule 8.03. Referral to Arbitration

(a) In any civil action subject to arbitration pursuant to Rule 8.02, the Clerk shall notify the parties within twenty (20) days after the case is at issue that the action is being referred to arbitration in accordance with these rules. Within twenty (20) days thereafter, by written notice to the Clerk, the parties may select by agreement not more than three certified arbitrators to conduct the arbitration proceedings. Upon the expiration of such twenty (20) day period and in the absence of timely notice of such agreement, the Clerk shall promptly select at random a panel of three certified arbitrators to whom the case will be referred for arbitration, one of whom will be designated at random as chairman of the panel. Not more than one member or associate of a firm or association of attorneys shall be appointed to the same panel of arbitrators.

(b) Any person selected as an arbitrator may be disqualified for bias or prejudice as provided in 28 U.S.C. Section 144, and shall disqualify himself in any action in which he would be required to do so if he were a justice, judge, or magistrate governed by 28 U.S.C. Section 455.

Rule 8.04. Arbitration Hearing

(a) Immediately upon selection and designation of the arbitrators pursuant to Rule 8.03, the Clerk shall communicate with the parties and the arbitrators in an effort to ascertain a mutually convenient date for a hearing, and shall then schedule and give notice of the date and time of the arbitration hearing which shall be held in space to be provided in the United States Courthouse. The hearing shall be scheduled within ninety (90) days from the date of the selection and designation of the arbitrators on at least twenty (20) days notice to the parties. Any continuance of the hearing beyond that ninety (90) day period may be allowed only by order of the Court for good cause shown.

(b) The arbitration hearing may proceed in the absence of a party who, after due notice, fails to be present; but an award of damages shall not be based solely upon the absence of a party.

(c) At least ten (10) days prior to the arbitration hearing each party shall furnish to every other party a list of witnesses, if any, and copies (or photographs) of all exhibits to be offered at the hearing. The arbitrators may refuse to consider any witness or exhibit which has not been so disclosed.

(d) Individual parties or authorized representatives of corporate parties shall attend the arbitration hearing unless excused in advance by the arbitrators for good cause shown. The hearing shall be conducted informally; the Federal Rules of Evidence shall be a guide, but shall not be binding. It is contemplated by the Court that the presentation of testimony shall be kept to a minimum, and that cases shall be presented to the arbitrators primarily through the statements and arguments of counsel.

(e) Any party may have a recording and transcript made of the arbitration hearing at his expense.

Rule 8.05. Arbitration Award and Judgment

(a) The award of the arbitrators shall be filed with the Clerk within ten (10) days following the hearing, and the Clerk shall give immediate notice to the parties. The award shall state the result reached by the arbitrators without necessity of factual findings or legal conclusions. A majority determination shall control the award. The amount of the award, if any, shall not be limited to the sum stated in Rule 8.02 if the arbitrators determine that an award in excess of that amount is just and is in keeping with the evidence and the law.

(b) At the end of thirty (30) days after the filing of the arbitrator's award the Clerk shall enter judgment on the award if no timely demand for trial de novo has been made pursuant to Rule 8.06. If the parties have previously stipulated in writing that the award shall be final and binding, the Clerk shall enter judgment on the award when filed.

(c) The contents of any arbitration award shall not be made known to any judge who might be assigned to the case—(1) Except as necessary for the Court to determine whether to assess costs or attorney fees under 28 U.S.C. Section 655, (2) Until the District Court has entered final judgment in the action or the action has been otherwise terminated, or (3) Except for purposes of preparing the report required by Section 903b of the Judicial Improvements and Access to Justice Act.

Rule 8.06. Trial de Novo

(a) Within thirty (30) days after the filing of the arbitration award with the Clerk, any party may demand a trial de novo in the District Court. Written notification of such a demand shall be filed with the Clerk and a copy shall be served by the moving party upon all other parties. Unless permitted by the Court to proceed in forma pauperis, the party demanding trial de novo, other than the United States or its agencies or officers, shall deposit with the Clerk an amount equal to the cost of the Arbitrators' fees.

(b) Upon a demand for a trial de novo the action shall be placed on the calendar of the Court and treated for all purposes as if it had not been referred to arbitration, and any right of trial by jury shall be preserved inviolate.

(c) At the trial de novo the Court shall not admit evidence that there has been an arbitration proceeding, the nature or amount of the award, or any other matter concerning the conduct of the arbitration proceeding, except that testimony given at an arbitration hearing may be used for any purpose otherwise permitted by the Federal Rules of Evidence, or the Federal Rules of Civil Procedure.

(d) If the party who demands a trial de novo fails to obtain a judgment in the District Court which is more favorable to him than the arbitration award, exclusive of interest and costs, that party shall be assessed the amount of the arbitration fees and the deposit made with the demand for trial de novo shall be transferred to the Treasury of the United States. If the judgment is more favorable, or if the case is disposed of before the trial de novo is conducted, such deposit shall be returned to the party who made it. The Court may order a return of the deposited sum to the party demanding trial de novo if it determines that the demand was made for good cause.

(e) No penalty for demanding a trial de novo, other than that provided in these rules, shall be assessed by the Court.

Appendix H

Local Rules of the United States District Court for the Northern District of California

4. Non-Binding Arbitration

4-01. Description.
Arbitration under this local rule is an adjudicative process in which an arbitrator or a panel of three arbitrators issues a nonbinding judgment ("award") on the merits after an expedited, adversarial hearing. Either party may reject the nonbinding award and request a trial *de novo*. An arbitration occurs earlier in the life of a case than a trial and is less formal and less expensive. Because testimony is taken under oath and is subject to cross-examination, arbitration can be especially useful in cases that turn on credibility of witnesses. Arbitrators do not facilitate settlement discussions.

4-02. Automatic Referral to Arbitration.
(a) Eligible Cases. Pursuant to 28 U.S.C. § 654, any of the following civil actions seeking only money damages in an amount not exceeding $150,000, exclusive of punitive damages, interest, costs and attorney fees, and which do not allege violations of civil or constitutional rights, may be referred automatically by the Clerk to the arbitration program at filing:
   (1) When United States is Not a Party. Actions founded on diversity of citizenship (28 U.S.C. § 1332), federal question (28 U.S.C. § 1331), admiralty or maritime jurisdiction (28 U.S.C. § 1333), and which arise under a contract or written instrument or out of personal injury or property damage.
   (2) When United States is a Party. Actions which arise under the Federal Tort Claims Act (28 U.S.C. § 2671, et seq.); the Longshoremen's and Harbor Workers Act (33 U.S.C. § 901, et seq.); the Miller Act (40 U.S.C. § 270b), when the United States has no monetary interest in the claim; or the Suits in Admiralty Act (46 U.S.C. § 741, et seq., § 781 et seq.) which involve no general average.
(b) Determination of Monetary Claim.
   (1) Separate Certification. In all cases otherwise subject to arbitration under this rule, the Court shall presume the damages claim to be for less than $150,000, exclusive of punitive damages, interest, costs and attorney fees, unless counsel asserting the claim files a separate certification that the damages reasonably recoverable exceed $150,000, exclusive of punitive damages, interest, costs and attorney fees. Any such certification must be filed by plaintiff within 30 days after the case was filed in this Court or by defendant at the time of filing a counterclaim or cross-claim.
   (2) Determination. Notwithstanding the amount of damages alleged in a party's pleading or certification under ADR L.R. 4-2(b)(1), the assigned Judge may, acting *sua sponte* or in response to a motion under Civil L.R. 7, and after affording the parties an opportunity to be heard, require arbitration if satisfied that recoverable damages cannot reasonably exceed $150,000, exclusive of punitive damages, interest, costs and attorney fees.
(c) Relief from Automatic Referral.
   (1) Selection of Different ADR Process. The assigned Judge will exempt a case from arbitration upon the filing, no later than 60 days after the case was filed, or within 20 days after the defendant's first appearance, of a stipulation and proposed order, under ADR L.R. 2-3(b), to mediation, ENE, or private ADR.
   (2) Exemption. The assigned Judge may, *sua sponte* or on motion by any party under Civil L.R. 7 brought within 20 days after the moving party's first appearance, exempt any case from arbitration if the objectives of arbitration would not be realized because:
      (a) The case involves complex or novel legal issues;
      (b) Legal issues predominate over factual issues; or
      (c) For other good cause shown.

4-03. Referral by Stipulation.

A case that does not meet the criteria for automatic referral to arbitration at filing as set forth in ADR L.R. 4-2 may be referred to arbitration by order of the assigned Judge only upon the written consent of all parties. Consent must be given freely and knowingly and no party or attorney in any such case may be prejudiced for refusing to consent to participate in arbitration. If consent is given by fewer than all parties, no Judge to whom the case might be assigned shall be advised of the identity of any party or attorney who elected not to consent to arbitration.

4-04. Arbitrators.

(a) Selection. After entry of an order referring the case to arbitration, and after the expiration of time for filing a motion under ADR L.R. 4-2(c) to exempt the case from arbitration, the Clerk shall promptly furnish to each party a list of ten arbitrators randomly selected from the Court's panel. The parties shall then confer in the following manner to select a single arbitrator or, if all parties so request in writing, a panel of three arbitrators:

(1) Striking Names. Each side shall be entitled to strike two names from the list, plaintiff(s) to strike the first name, defendant(s) the next, then plaintiff(s) and then defendant(s).

(2) Ranking Names. The parties shall then select the arbitrator or panel from the remaining six names by alternately selecting one name; defendant(s) to make the first choice, plaintiff(s) the next, and continuing in this fashion.

(3) Submitting List. Within ten days of receipt of the original list of ten names, the parties shall list the six names in the order selected and submit them to the Clerk. If the parties fail to submit such a list within the prescribed time, the Clerk shall select an arbitrator at random from the original list of ten names.

(4) Notification by Clerk. The Clerk shall promptly notify the person or persons whose names appear as the parties' first choice or choices of their selection, or, if the parties have not chosen, the person(s) the Clerk has selected. If any person so selected is unable or unwilling to serve, the Clerk shall notify the person whose name appears next on the list. If the Clerk is unable to select an arbitrator or constitute a panel of arbitrators from the six selections, the process of selection under this Rule shall be repeated.

When the requisite number of arbitrators has agreed to serve, the Clerk shall promptly send written notice of the selections to the arbitrator(s) and to the parties. The rules governing conflicts of interest and the procedure for objecting to an arbitrator are set forth in ADR L.R. 2-5(d). When a panel of three arbitrators is selected, the Clerk shall designate the person to serve as the panel's presiding arbitrator.

(b) Compensation. Arbitrators shall be paid by the Court $250 per day or portion of each day of hearing in which they serve as a single arbitrator or $150 for each day or portion of each day in which they serve as a member of a panel of three. No party may offer or give the arbitrator(s) any gift.

(c) Payment and Reimbursement. When filing an award, arbitrators shall submit a voucher on the form prescribed by the Clerk for payment of compensation and for reimbursement of any reasonable transportation expenses necessarily incurred in the performance of duties under this Rule. No reimbursement will be made for any other expenses.

4-05. Timing and Scheduling the Hearing.

(a) Scheduling by Arbitrator. Promptly after being appointed to a case, the arbitrator(s) shall arrange for the pre-session phone conference under ADR L.R. 4-8 and, after consulting with all parties, shall fix the date and place for the arbitration not less than 10 days after the phone conference and within the deadline fixed by the assigned judge, or if no such deadline is fixed, within 70 days after the phone conference. Counsel shall respond promptly to and cooperate fully with the arbitrator(s) with respect to scheduling the pre-session phone conference and the arbitration hearing. The hearing date shall not be continued or vacated except for emergencies as established in writing and approved by the assigned Judge. If the case is resolved before the hearing date, or if due to an emergency a participant cannot attend the arbitration, counsel shall notify the arbitrator and the ADR Unit immediately upon learning of such settlement or emergency.

(b) Place and Time. The hearing may be held at any location within the Northern District of California selected by the arbitrator(s), including a room at a federal courthouse, if available. In selecting the location, the arbitrator(s) shall consider the convenience of the parties and witnesses. Unless the parties agree otherwise, the hearing shall be held during normal business hours.

4-06. Ex Parte Contact Prohibited.
Except with respect to scheduling matters, there shall be no *ex parte* communications between parties or counsel and an arbitrator.

4-07. Written Arbitration Statements.
(a) Time for Submission. No later than 10 calendar days before the arbitration session, each party shall submit directly to the arbitrator(s), and shall serve on all other parties, a written arbitration statement.
(b) Prohibition against Filing. The statements shall not be filed and the assigned Judge shall not have access to them.
(c) Content of Statement. The statements shall be concise and shall:
(1) Summarize the claims and defenses;
(2) Identify the significant contested factual and legal issues, citing authority on the questions of law;
(3) Identify proposed witnesses; and
(4) Identify, by name and title or status, the person(s) with decision-making authority, who, in addition to counsel, will attend the arbitration as representative(s) of the party.
(d) Modification of Requirement by Arbitrator(s). After jointly consulting counsel for all parties, the arbitrator(s) may modify or dispense with the requirements for the written arbitration statements.

4-08. Telephone Conference Before Arbitration.
The arbitrator(s) shall schedule a brief joint telephone conference with counsel before the arbitration to discuss matters such as the scheduling of the arbitration, the procedures to be followed, whether supplemental written material should be submitted, which witnesses will attend, how testimony will be presented, including expert testimony, and whether and how the arbitration will be recorded.

4-09. Attendance at Arbitration.
(a) Parties. Each party shall attend the arbitration hearing unless excused under paragraph (d), below. This requirement reflects the Court's view that principal values of arbitration include affording litigants an opportunity to articulate their positions and to hear, first hand, both their opponent's version of the matters in dispute and a neutral assessment of the merits of the case.
(1) Corporation or Other Entity. A party other than a natural person (e.g., a corporation or an association) satisfies this attendance requirement if represented by a person (other than outside counsel) who is knowledgeable about the facts of the case.
(2) Government Entity. A party that is a government or governmental agency, in addition to counsel, shall send a representative knowledgeable about the facts of the case and the governmental unit's position. If the action is brought by the government on behalf of one or more individuals, at least one such individual also shall attend.
(b) Counsel. Each party shall be accompanied at the arbitration session by the lawyer who will be primarily responsible for handling the trial of the matter.
(c) Request to be Excused. A person who is required to attend an arbitration hearing may be excused from attending in person only after a showing that personal attendance would impose an extraordinary or otherwise unjustifiable hardship. A person seeking to be excused must submit, no fewer than 15 days before the date set for the arbitration, a letter to the ADR Magistrate Judge, simultaneously copying the ADR Unit, all other counsel and the arbitrator(s). The letter shall:
(1) Set forth with specificity all considerations that support the request;
(2) State realistically the amount in controversy in the case;
(3) Indicate whether the other party or parties join in or object to the request; and
(4) Be accompanied by a proposed order.
(d) Participation by Telephone. A person excused from attending an arbitration in person shall be available to participate by telephone.

4-10. Authority of Arbitrators and Procedures at Arbitration.
(a) Authority of Arbitrators. Subject to the provisions of these ADR local rules, arbitrators shall be authorized to:
(1) Administer oaths and affirmations;
(2) Make reasonable rulings as are necessary for the fair and efficient conduct of the hearing; and
(3) Make awards.

(b) Prohibition on Facilitating Settlement Discussions. Arbitrators are not authorized to facilitate settlement discussions. If the parties desire assistance with settlement, the parties or arbitrator(s) may request that the case be referred to mediation, ENE, or a settlement conference.

(c) Presumption against Bifurcation. Except in extraordinary circumstances, the arbitrator(s) shall not bifurcate the arbitration.

(d) Quorum. Where a panel of three arbitrators has been named, any two members of a panel shall constitute a quorum, but the concurrence of a majority of the entire panel shall be required for any action or decision by the panel, unless the parties stipulate otherwise.

(e) Testimony.
　(1) Subpoenas. Attendance of witnesses and production of documents may be compelled in accordance with FRCivP 45.
　(2) Oath and Cross-examination. All testimony shall be taken under oath or affirmation and shall be subject to such reasonable cross-examination as the circumstances warrant.
　(3) Evidence. In receiving evidence, the arbitrator(s) shall be guided by the Federal Rules of Evidence, but shall not thereby be precluded from receiving evidence which the arbitrator(s) consider(s) relevant and trustworthy and which is not privileged.

(f) Transcript or Recording. A party may cause a transcript or recording of the proceedings to be made but shall provide a copy to any other party who requests it and who agrees to pay the reasonable costs of having a copy made.

(g) Default of Party. The unexcused absence of a party shall not be a ground for continuance, but damages shall be awarded against an absent party only upon presentation of proof thereof satisfactory to the arbitrator(s).

4-11. Award and Judgment.

(a) Form of Award. An award shall be made after an arbitration under this Rule. Such an award shall state clearly and concisely the name or names of the prevailing party or parties and the party or parties against which it is rendered, and the precise amount of money, if any, awarded. It shall be in writing and (unless the parties stipulate otherwise) be signed by the arbitrator or by at least two members of a panel. No arbitrator shall participate in the award without having attended the hearing.

Costs within the meaning of FRCivP 54 and Civil L.R. 54 may be assessed by the arbitrator(s) as part of an arbitration award.

(b) Filing and Serving the Award. Within 10 days after the arbitration hearing is concluded, the arbitrator(s) shall file the award with the Clerk in an unsealed envelope with a cover sheet stating: "Arbitration Award to be filed under seal pursuant to ADR L.R. 4-11—not to be forwarded to the Assigned Judge." The cover sheet also shall list the case caption, case number and name(s) of the arbitrator, but shall not specify the content of the award. The Clerk shall promptly serve copies of the arbitration award on the parties. In addition, immediately after receiving a copy of the arbitration award, the party that prevailed in the arbitration shall serve a copy of the award on the other parties and shall promptly file proof of said service under Civil L.R. 5, but shall not attach a copy of the award.

(c) Sealing of Award. Each filed arbitration award shall promptly be sealed by the Clerk. The award shall not be disclosed to any Judge who might be assigned to the case until the Court has entered final judgment in the action or the action has been otherwise terminated, except as necessary to assess costs or prepare the report required by Section 903(b) of the Judicial Improvements and Access to Justice Act.

(d) Entry of Judgment on Award. If no party has filed a demand for trial *de novo* (or a notice of appeal, which shall be treated as a demand for trial *de novo*) within 30 days of notice of the filing of the arbitration award, the Clerk shall enter judgment on the arbitration award in accordance with FRCivP 58. A judgment so entered shall be subject to the same provisions of law and shall have the same force and effect as a judgment of the Court in a civil action, except that the judgment shall not be subject to review in any other court by appeal or otherwise.

4-12. Trial De Novo.

(a) Time for Demand. If any party files and serves a demand for trial *de novo* within 30 days of notice of the filing of the arbitration award, no judgment thereon shall be entered by the Clerk and the action shall proceed in the normal manner before the assigned Judge. Failure to file and serve a demand for trial *de novo* within this 30-day period waives the right to trial *de novo*.

(b) Limitation on Admission of Evidence. At the trial *de novo* the Court shall not admit any evidence indicating that there has been an arbitration proceeding, the nature or amount of any award, or any other matter concerning the conduct of the arbitration proceeding, unless:
  (1) The evidence would otherwise be admissible in the trial under the Federal Rules of Evidence, or
  (2) The parties have otherwise stipulated.
(c) Award Not to be Attached. A party filing a demand for a trial *de novo* shall not attach the arbitration award.

4-13. Stipulation to Binding Arbitration.
At any time before the arbitration hearing, the parties may stipulate in writing to waive their rights to request a trial *de novo* pursuant to ADR L.R. 4-12. Such stipulation shall be submitted to the assigned Judge for approval and shall be filed. In the event of such stipulation, judgment shall be entered on the arbitration award pursuant to ADR L.R. 4-11(d).

4-14. Federal Arbitration Act Presumptively Inapplicable.
Nothing in these ADR Local Rules limits any party's right to agree to arbitrate any dispute, regardless of the amount, pursuant to Title 9, United States Code, or any other provision of law.

Appendix I

Hawaii Arbitration Rules

Rule 1. THE COURT ANNEXED ARBITRATION PROGRAM.

The Court Annexed Arbitration Program (the Program) is a mandatory, non-binding arbitration program, as hereinafter described, for certain civil cases in the State of Hawaii.

Rule 2. INTENT OF PROGRAM AND APPLICATION OF RULES.

(A) The purpose of the Program is to provide a simplified procedure for obtaining a prompt and equitable resolution of certain civil matters to be designated by the Judicial Arbitration Commission.

(B) These rules shall not be applicable to arbitration by private agreement or to other forms of arbitration under existing statutes, policies and procedures.

(C) These arbitration rules are not intended, nor should they be construed, to address every issue which may arise during the arbitration process. The intent of these rules is to give considerable discretion to the arbitrator, the Arbitration Administrator, the Arbitration Judge, and the Judicial Arbitration Commission. Arbitration hearings are intended to be informal, expeditious and consistent with the purposes and intent of these rules.

Rule 3. THE ARBITRATION JUDGE.

(A) The Arbitration Judge for the Program in each judicial circuit shall be a Circuit Court Judge who shall be appointed by the Chief Justice. The Arbitration Judge may delegate his or her powers and duties under these rules to another Circuit Court Judge as may be needed for the efficient operation of the Program.

(B) The Arbitration Judge shall determine all disputed issues under these rules as hereinafter set forth, including, but not limited to, all disputed issues concerning the arbitrability of cases and the qualifications and acts of arbitrators.

Rule 4. THE JUDICIAL ARBITRATION COMMISSION.

(A) The Chief Justice shall establish a Judicial Arbitration Commission which will have the responsibility to develop, monitor, maintain, supervise and evaluate the Program for the State of Hawaii.

(B) The Judicial Arbitration Commission shall include the Arbitration Judges of each judicial circuit and a representative to be designated by the President of the Hawaii State Bar Association. The chairperson shall be designated by the Chief Justice. Additional members shall be appointed at the discretion of the Chief Justice. The Chief Justice may also appoint advisors to the Judicial Arbitration Commission, who shall not have the right to vote.

(C) The Judicial Arbitration Commission shall be responsible for the selection and training of arbitrators.

(D) The Judicial Arbitration Commission shall be responsible for the supervision and evaluation of the Arbitration Administrator in each judicial circuit.

(E) The Judicial Arbitration Commission shall interpret these rules prior to the appointment of an arbitrator in any case under the Program.

(F) The Judicial Arbitration Commission may recommend the adoption or amendment of rules and regulations to the Supreme Court for the implementation and administration of the Program.

Rule 5. THE ARBITRATION ADMINISTRATOR.

The Arbitration Administrator for the Program in each judicial circuit shall be appointed by the Chief Justice and shall be responsible for the operation and management of the Program, as hereinafter set forth.

Rule 6. MATTERS SUBJECT TO ARBITRATION.

(A) All tort cases having a probable jury award value, not reduced by the issue of liability and not in excess of One Hundred Fifty Thousand Dollars ($150,000.00), exclusive of interest and costs, may be accepted into the Program at the discretion of the Judicial Arbitration Commission.

(B) Any other civil case, regardless of the monetary value or the amount in controversy, may be submitted to the Program upon the agreement of all parties and the approval of the Arbitration Judge.

(C) Parties to cases submitted or ordered to the Program may agree at any time to be bound by any arbitration ruling or award.

(D) The Arbitration Judge may accept into, or remove from, the Program any action where good cause for acceptance or removal is found. The Court's decision in this regard is non-reviewable.

Rule 7. RELATIONSHIP TO CIRCUIT COURT JURISDICTION AND RULES; FORM OF DOCUMENTS.

(A) Cases filed in, or removed to, the Circuit Court shall remain under the jurisdiction of that court for all phases of the proceedings, including arbitration.

(B) Except for the authority to act or interpret these rules expressly given to the arbitrator, the Arbitration Administrator, the Judicial Arbitration Commission, or the Arbitration Judge, all issues shall be determined by the Circuit Court with jurisdiction.

(C) Before a case is submitted or ordered to the Program, and after a Notice of Appeal and Request for Trial *De Novo* is filed, all applicable rules of the Circuit Court and of civil procedure apply. After a case is submitted or ordered to the Program, and before a Notice of Appeal and Request for Trial *De Novo* is filed, or until the case is removed from the Program, these rules apply.

(D) The calculation of time and the requirements of service of pleadings and documents under these rules shall be the same as under the Hawaii Rules of Civil Procedure, except that service under these rules by the Arbitration Administrator may be made by facsimile transmission.

(E) Circuit Court Rule 12(q), and all rules of court or of civil procedure requiring the filing of pleadings, remain in effect notwithstanding the fact that a case is under the Program.

(F) All dispositive motions shall be made to the Circuit Court as required by law or rule notwithstanding the fact that a case is under the Program.

(G) All documents required to be utilized or filed under these rules shall be in a form designated by the Arbitration Judge.

(H) Once a case is submitted or ordered to the Program all parties subsequently joined in the action shall be parties to the arbitration unless dismissed by the Arbitration Judge.

Rule 8. DETERMINATION OF ARBITRABILITY.

(A) The court shall view all tort cases as arbitration eligible and automatically "in" the Program unless plaintiff certifies that his or her case has a value in excess of the jurisdictional amount of the Program which is $150,000. Plaintiff shall file a request for exemption at the time of filing and such a request shall include a summary of facts which support plaintiff's contentions.

(B) Where exemptions from arbitration have been requested, the Arbitration Administrator shall review the contentions, facts and evidence available and determine eligibility. The Arbitration Administrator may upon request require that a party submit additional facts which support the party's contentions. Any objection(s) to his decision must be filed with the Arbitration Judge within ten (10) days from the date the decision is served, with service to opposing counsel.

(C) Subsequent to the filing of the complaint, any party who believes a case should be removed from, admitted or readmitted to the Program, shall file a request to remove, admit or readmit, with the Arbitration Judge. Such a request shall include a summary of the facts which support their contentions, with service to opposing party.

(D) The Arbitration Judge shall make all final determinations regarding the arbitrability of a case when that issue is disputed by any party, and may hold a conference on the issue of arbitrability at his discretion.

(E) The Arbitration Judge may, at his discretion, impose sanctions of reasonable costs and attorney's fees against any party who without good cause or justification attempts to remove a case from the Program.

Rule 9. ASSIGNMENT TO ARBITRATOR.

(A) Parties may select and stipulate to a private arbitrator(s), who is an arbitrator not on the panel of the Program, or one who is on the panel but who has agreed to serve on a private basis. Such stipulation must be made within twenty (20) days after the appearance of defense counsel and must include a statement signed by the arbitrator(s) expressing his or her express willingness to arbitrate under the rules and procedures of the Court Annexed Arbitration Program and a duly signed arbitrator's oath.

(B) Any and all fees or expenses related to the use of a private arbitrator(s) shall be borne by the parties.

(C) Unless the Arbitration Administrator is notified of a stipulation for a private arbitrator(s) within the above twenty (20) day period, one (1) arbitrator will be assigned. If the assigned arbitrator is disqualified, another arbitrator shall be assigned.

(D) Any party may object, for good cause, to the assigned arbitrator. Said objection shall be in writing and received by the Arbitration Administrator within ten (10) days from the date of the assignment of the arbitrator. Appeals of the decision of the Arbitration Administrator must be filed with the Arbitration Judge within ten (10) days from the date the decision is served, with service to opposing counsel.

(E) Where an arbitrator is assigned to a case and subsequent thereto, additional party(s) are added, said party(s) may object to the arbitrator assigned to the case within ten (10) days from the party(s)' appearance. Objection(s) must be in writing stating specific grounds and filed with the Arbitration Administrator, who will review the objection(s) and render a decision. This decision may be appealed to the Arbitration Judge.

(F) The above described method of selection of an arbitrator shall be followed in all the Judicial Circuits.

Rule 10. QUALIFICATIONS OF ARBITRATORS.

(A) The Judicial Arbitration Commission shall create and maintain a panel of arbitrators consisting of attorneys licensed to practice in the State of Hawaii and, in its discretion, qualified non-attorneys.

(B) Attorneys serving as arbitrators shall have substantial experience in civil litigation, and shall have been licensed to practice law in the State of Hawaii for a period of five (5) years, or can provide the Judicial Arbitration Commission with proof of equivalent qualifying experience.

(C) Arbitrators shall be required to complete an orientation and training program following their selection to the panel and other additional training sessions or classes scheduled by the Judicial Arbitration Commission or Arbitration Administrator.

(D) Arbitrators shall be sworn or affirmed by the Chief Justice or his designee to uphold these rules of the Program, the laws of the State of Hawaii, and the Code of Ethics of the American Arbitration Association.

(E) An arbitrator who would be disqualified for any reason that would disqualify a judge under the Code of Judicial Conduct shall immediately resign or be withdrawn as an arbitrator.

(F) Any issue concerning the qualification of a person to serve as an arbitrator on the panel of arbitrators shall be referred to the Judicial Arbitration Commission for a final, non-reviewable determination.

Rule 11. AUTHORITY OF ARBITRATORS.

(A) Arbitrators shall have the general powers of a court and may hear cases in accordance with established rules of evidence and procedure, liberally construed to promote justice and the expeditious resolution of disputes. These include, but are not limited to, the power:

(1) To administer oaths or affirmations to witnesses;

(2) To relax all applicable rules of evidence and procedure to effectuate a speedy and economical resolution of the case without sacrificing a party's right to a full and fair hearing on the merits;

(3) To decide procedural issues arising before or during the arbitration hearing, except issues relating to his or her qualifications as an arbitrator,

(4) To invite or order, with reasonable notice, the parties to submit pre-hearing or post-hearing briefs;

(5) To examine, after notice to the parties, any site or object relevant to the case;

(6) To issue subpoenas for the attendance of witnesses or production of documentary evidence;

(7) To determine the place, time and procedure to hear all matters;

(8) To interpret these rules in all proceedings before him or her;

(9) To find witnesses or parties in contempt and to impose sanctions as provided by the laws of the State of Hawaii; and

(10) To attempt, with the consent of all parties in writing, to aid in the settlement of the case.

(B) Any challenge to the authority or the act of an arbitrator shall be made to the Arbitration Administrator who will make a ruling on the issue in due course. An appeal from the ruling of the Arbitration Administrator may be made within ten (10) days from the date of said ruling to the Arbitration Judge, who shall have the non-reviewable power to uphold, overturn or modify the ruling of the Arbitration Administrator, including the power to stay any proceeding.

Rule 12. STIPULATIONS.

Any stipulation between the parties relating to the conduct of the arbitration proceeding, or any factual matter therein, shall be in writing and signed by the counsel or parties, and filed with the arbitrator.

Rule 13. RESTRICTIONS ON COMMUNICATIONS.

(A) Neither counsel nor parties may communicate directly with the arbitrator regarding the merits of the case, except in the presence of, or with reasonable notice to, all of the other parties.

(B) No disclosure of any offer or demand of settlement made by any party shall be made to the arbitrator prior to the filing of an award without the agreement of all other parties.

Rule 14. DISCOVERY.

(A) Once a case is submitted or ordered to the Program, the extent to which discovery is allowed, if at all, is at the sole discretion of the arbitrator, except as provided in section (B) of this rule. Types of discovery shall be those permitted by the Hawaii Rules of Civil Procedure, but these may be modified in the discretion of the arbitrator to save time and expense.

(B) A party may at anytime: (1) serve on other parties the standard form interrogatories and requests for production of documents, which the Judicial Arbitration Commission has approved; and (2) conduct, by agreement, additional formal or informal discovery. Any dispute arising out of the discovery permitted by this section (B) shall be determined by the arbitrator upon his or her assignments.

Rule 15. SCHEDULING OF HEARINGS; PRE-HEARING CONFERENCES.

(A) All arbitrations shall take place and all awards filed no later than nine (9) months from the date of service of the complaint to all defendants, or the Order of Arbitration by the Arbitration Judge, unless said time is modified by the Arbitration Judge pursuant to this rule. Arbitrators shall set the time and date of the hearing within this period.

(B) The arbitration hearing date may be advanced or continued by the arbitrator for good cause upon written request from either party; however, a request for a continuance of the hearing beyond the above nine (9) month period may not be granted by the arbitrator until said arbitrator obtains an extension of the above nine (9) month period. Any request for extension of the above nine (9) month period must be made in writing to the Arbitration Judge by the arbitrator.

(C) Consolidated actions shall be heard on the date assigned to the latest case involved.

(D) Arbitrators and/or the Arbitration Administrator may, at their discretion, conduct pre-arbitration hearings or conferences. However, arbitrators shall conduct a prehearing conference within thirty (30) days from the date a case is assigned to an arbitrator.

(E) The arbitrator shall give immediate written notification to the Arbitration Administrator of any change of the arbitration date, any settlement or change of counsel.

Rule 16. PREHEARING STATEMENT.

(A) At least thirty (30) days prior to the date of the arbitration hearing, each party shall file with the arbitrator and serve upon all other parties a Prehearing Statement. The Prehearing Statement shall state that the party submitting the statement will be ready to proceed with the hearing upon completion of the inspection and/or copying permitted in section (B) of this rule. The statement shall also contain, wherever applicable, the following information:

(1) Information about the party submitting the statement, including, at minimum:

  (i) The name, address, telephone number, age, marital status and occupation of such party;

  (ii) The name, address, telephone number, and place of registration, if such party is a general or limited partnership; or

  (iii) The name, address, telephone number, and place of incorporation, if such party is a corporation.

(2) A statement of the facts which the party submitting the statement reasonably believes will be established at the hearing by such party;

(3) The name, address, telephone number and field of expertise of each expert, including all doctors, whom the party submitting the statement intends to call as a witness or use in any other manner at the hearing, and copies of their reports;

(4) The name, address and telephone number of all other witnesses the party submitting the statement intends to call at the hearing;

(5) A statement of the party's position on general damages;

(6) A statement of the party's position on special damages and an itemized list of all special damages claimed or disputed by such party; and

(7) A list of exhibits and documentary evidence anticipated to be introduced at the hearing by the party submitting the statement.

(B) Each party shall provide copies of all exhibits and documentary evidence to the arbitrator and upon request shall make all exhibits and documentary evidence available for inspection and copying by other parties, at least twenty (20) days prior to the date of the hearing.

(C) A party failing to comply with this rule, or failing to comply with any discovery order, may not present at the hearing a witness or exhibit required to be disclosed or made available, except with the permission of the arbitrator.

(D) Each party shall furnish the arbitrator at least twenty (20) days prior to the arbitration hearing copies of any pleadings and other documents contained in the court file which that party deems relevant.

Rule 17. CONDUCT OF THE HEARING.

(A) The arbitrator shall have complete discretion over the mode and order of presenting evidence and the conduct of the hearing.

(B) No transcription or recording shall be permitted of the arbitration proceedings.

Rule 18. ARBITRATION IN THE ABSENCE OF A PARTY.

An arbitration may proceed in the absence of any party who, after due notice, fails to be present or fails to obtain a continuance. The arbitrator shall require the party present to submit such evidence as he or she may require for the making of an award, and may offer the absent party an opportunity to appear at a subsequent hearing.

Rule 19. FORM AND CONTENT OF AWARD.

(A) Awards by the arbitrator shall be in writing, signed and on forms prescribed by the Judicial Arbitration Commission.

(B) The arbitrator shall determine all issues raised by the pleadings that are subject to arbitration under the Program, including a determination of comparative negligence, if any, damages, if any, and costs. The amount of damages that can be awarded is not limited to the jurisdictional amount for arbitration.

(C) Findings of Fact and Conclusions of Law are not required.

(D) After an award is made, the arbitrator shall return all exhibits to the parties who offered them during the hearing.

Rule 20. FILING OF AWARD.

(A) Within seven (7) days after the conclusion of the arbitration hearing, or thirty (30) days after the receipt of the final authorized memoranda of counsel, the arbitrator shall file the award with the Arbitration Administrator, who shall then serve copies of said award to the attorneys of record. Application by the arbitrator to the Arbitration Administrator must be made for an extension of these time periods.

(B) The arbitrator may file with the Arbitration Administrator an amended award to correct an obvious error in the award if done within the seven day period for filing an award. Subsequent to this time, application must be made to the Arbitration Administrator. Any amended award shall be served upon the attorneys of record by the Arbitration Administrator.

(C) This rule does not authorize the use of an amended award to change the arbitrator's decision on the merits. An amended award may only modify an award in order to correct an inadvertent miscalculation or description, or to adjust the award in a matter of form rather than substance. Any modification of substance can only be made upon application to the Arbitration Judge.

Rule 21. JUDGMENT ON AWARD.

If, after twenty (20) days after the award is served upon the parties, no party has filed a written Notice of Appeal and Request for Trial *De Novo,* the clerk of the court shall, upon notification by the Arbitration Administrator, enter the arbitration award as a final judgment of the court. This period may be extended by written stipulation, filed within twenty (20) days after service of the award upon the parties, to a period no more than forty (40) days after the award is served upon the parties. Said award shall have the same force and effect as a final judgment of the court in the civil action, but may not be appealed.

Rule 22. REQUEST FOR TRIAL *DE NOVO.*

(A) Within twenty (20) days after the award is served upon the parties, any party may file with the clerk of the court and serve on the other parties and the Arbitration Administrator a written Notice of Appeal and Request for Trial *De Novo* of the action. This period may be extended to a period of no more than forty (40) days after the award is served upon the parties, by stipulation signed by all parties remaining in the action and filed with the Arbitration Administrator within twenty (20) days after service of the award upon the parties.

(B) After the filing and service of the written Notice of Appeal and Request for Trial *De Novo,* the case shall be set for trial pursuant to applicable court rules.

(C) If the action is triable by right to a jury, and a jury was not originally demanded but is demanded within ten (10) days of service of the Notice of Appeal and Request for Trial *De Novo* by a party having the right of trial by jury, the trial *de novo* shall include a jury, and a jury trial fee shall be paid as provided by law.

(D) After a written Notice of Appeal and Request for Trial *De Novo* has been filed and served, it may not be withdrawn except by stipulation of all remaining parties or by order of the Arbitration Judge. The Arbitration Judge shall not allow withdrawal of a Notice of Appeal and Request for Trial *De Novo* over objection of any non-appealing party but may order that an objecting party be deemed an appealing party for purposes of these rules. The Arbitration Judge in allowing a withdrawal may do so upon such terms and conditions as the Court deems proper, including an order that the appealing party pay the attorneys' fees and costs incurred by non-appealing parties after service of the Notice of Appeal and Request for Trial *De Novo.* In the event a Notice of Appeal and Request for Trial *De Novo* is withdrawn pursuant to this rule and no other Notice of Appeal and Request for Trial *De Novo* remains, judgment shall be entered in accordance with Rule 21.

Rule 23. PROCEDURES AT TRIAL *DE NOVO.*

(A) The clerk shall seal any arbitration award if a trial *de novo* is requested. The jury will not be informed of the arbitration proceeding, the award, or about any other aspect of the arbitration proceeding. The sealed arbitration award shall not be opened until after the verdict is received and filed in a jury trial, or until after the judge has rendered a decision in a court trial.

(B) All discovery permitted during the course of the arbitration proceedings shall be admissible in the trial *de novo* subject to all applicable rules of civil procedure and evidence. The court in the trial *de novo* shall insure that any reference to the arbitration proceeding is omitted from any discovery taken therein and sought to be introduced at the trial *de novo.*

(C) No statements or testimony made in the course of the arbitration hearing shall be admissible in evidence for any purpose in the trial *de novo.*

Rule 24. SCHEDULING OF THE TRIAL *DE NOVO.*

Every case transferred to the Program shall maintain the approximate position on the civil trial docket as if the case had not been so transferred, unless at the discretion of the court, the docket position is modified.

Rule 25. THE PREVAILING PARTY IN THE TRIAL *DE NOVO;* COSTS.

(A) The "Prevailing Party" in a trial *de novo* is the party who (1) appealed and improved upon the arbitration award by 30% or more, or (2) did not appeal and the appealing party failed to improve upon the arbitration award by 30% or more. For the purpose of this rule, "improve" or "improved" means to increase the award for a plaintiff or to decrease the award for the defendant.

(B) The "Prevailing Party" under these rules, as defined above, is deemed the prevailing party under any statute or rule of court. As such, the prevailing party is entitled to costs of trial and all other remedies as provided by law, unless the Court otherwise directs.

Rule 26. SANCTIONS FOR FAILING TO PREVAIL IN THE TRIAL *DE NOVO*.

(A) After the verdict is received and filed, or the court's decision rendered in a trial *de novo,* the trial court may, in its discretion, impose sanctions, as set forth below, against the non-prevailing party whose appeal resulted in the trial *de novo.*

(B) The sanctions available to the court are as follows:

    (1) Reasonable costs and fees (other than attorneys' fees) actually incurred by the party but not otherwise taxable under the law, including but not limited to, expert witness fees, travel costs, and deposition costs;

    (2) Costs of jurors;

    (3) Attorneys' fees not to exceed $15,000;

(C) Sanctions imposed against a plaintiff will be deducted from any judgment rendered at trial. If the plaintiff does not receive a judgment in his or her favor or the judgment is insufficient to pay the sanctions, the plaintiff will pay the amount of the deficiency. Sanctions imposed against a defendant will be added to any judgment rendered at trial.

(D) In determining sanctions, if any, the Court shall consider all the facts and circumstances of the case and the intent and purpose of the Program in the State of Hawaii.

Rule 27. EFFECTIVE DATE.

These rules become effective as of February 15, 1986 for the circuit court of the first circuit; as of October 1, 1987 for the circuit court of the third circuit; as of October 15, 1987 for the circuit court of the second circuit; and as of November 1, 1987 for the circuit court of the fifth circuit.

Rule 28. SANCTIONS FOR FAILURE TO MEANINGFULLY PARTICIPATE IN ARBITRATION HEARING.

The Arbitration Judge, on the motion of any party filed and served within thirty (30) days after the arbitration award is served upon the parties by the Arbitration Administrator, shall have the power to award sanctions against any party or attorney for failure to participate in the arbitration hearing in a meaningful manner. Sanctions may include costs, expert fees and attorneys' fees reasonably incurred by all other parties for the arbitration hearing and in the prosecution of the motion for sanctions. These sanctions are independent of sanctions under Rule 26. The court may hold hearings as deemed appropriate. If the court determines that the motion was brought without good cause, it may award costs and attorney fees against the movant.

Rule 29. MASTER MEDIATOR PILOT PROJECT.

(A) Effective Date. Effective April 1, 1995, the Master Mediator Pilot Project (hereinafter "MPP") is established to promote the settlement of cases in the program.

(B) Eligibility. All cases in the program are eligible to participate in the MPP.

(C) Participation in MPP. Upon the agreement of all parties a mediator may be utilized. If all parties do not agree to mediation but at least one party chooses to use a mediator and pay the mediator's fees, all parties must participate in the mediation. In either case, the first mediation session shall commence no later than seven (7) days before the arbitration hearing.

(D) Selection of Master Mediator. Parties may select a mediator, by agreement, from the mediator panel list created and maintained by the Judicial Arbitration Commission. If the parties do not agree on a mediator, the Arbitration Administrator shall randomly make the selection from the mediator panel list.

(E) Authority of Mediator. The primary goal of a mediator is to settle the case. Upon the agreement of all parties, the mediator may also engage in case management functions, including but not limited to, identifying issues and areas of agreement, formulating a discovery plan, setting limitations on discovery, if any, and allocating discovery expense.

(F) Fees. Actual mediation time shall be limited initially to three (3) hours, at a cost of $500.00. If the duration of the mediation is less than three (3) hours, the mediator shall still receive the entire $500.00 fee. If only one party chooses to use a mediator, that party shall pay the entire $500.00. If more than one party chooses to use a mediator, those parties shall pay the $500.00 on a *pro rata* basis, or as otherwise agreed to by such parties. Upon the agreement of all parties, the mediation may be extended beyond the initial three (3) hours. The parties and the mediator shall determine the fee for any such extension. The parties shall deal directly with the mediator in all matters relating to fees and payment thereof. The Office of the Arbitration Administrator shall not participate in any fee arrangements, collections, or disputes.

(G) Expiration Date. The MPP will expire on April 1, 2000, unless extended or made permanent by order of the Supreme Court of Hawaii. Cases in which a party or the parties have elected mediation in accordance with section (C) of this rule and notified the Arbitration Administrator of such election in writing by March 31, 2000, shall be completed in accordance with this Rule 29.

Appendix J

Private Judging—California Constitution, Statute, and Court Rule

California Constitution art. VI

Section 21. Temporary Judges

On stipulation of the parties' litigant the court may order a cause to be tried by a temporary judge who is a member of the State Bar, sworn and empowered to act until final determination of the cause.

California Code of Civil Procedure

Section 638. Appointment of Referee; Agreement of Parties

A referee may be appointed upon the agreement of the parties filed with the clerk, or judge, or entered in the minutes or in the docket, or upon the motion of a party to a written contract or lease that provides that any controversy arising therefrom shall be heard by a referee if the court finds a reference agreement exists between the parties:

(a) To hear and determine any or all of the issues in an action or proceeding, whether of fact or of law, and to report a statement of decision thereon.

(b) To ascertain a fact necessary to enable the court to determine an action or proceeding.

(c) In any matter in which a referee is appointed pursuant to this section, a copy of the order shall be forwarded to the office of the presiding judge. The Judicial Council shall, by rule, collect information on the use of these referees. . . .

California Rules of Court

Rule 244. Temporary Judge—Stipulation, Order, Oath, Assignment, Compensation, and Other Matters

(a) Stipulation

Except as provided in rule 1727, the stipulation of the parties that a case may be tried by a temporary judge shall be in writing and shall state the name and office address of the member of the State Bar agreed upon. It shall be submitted for approval to the presiding judge or to the supervising judge of a branch court. This subdivision does not apply to the selection of a court commissioner to act as a temporary judge.

(b) Order and Oath

The order designating the temporary judge shall be endorsed upon the stipulation, which shall then be filed. The temporary judge shall take and subscribe the oath of office, which shall be attached to the stipulation and order of designation, and the case shall then be assigned to the temporary judge for trial. After the oath is filed, the temporary judge may proceed with the hearing, trial, and determination of the case.

A filed oath and order, until revoked, may be used in any case in which the parties stipulate to the designated temporary judge. The stipulation shall specify the filing date of the oath and order.

This subdivision does not apply to the selection of a court commissioner to act as a temporary judge.

(c) Disqualification

A request for disqualification of a privately compensated temporary judge shall be determined as provided in Code of Civil Procedure sections 170.1, 170.2, 170.3, 170.4 and 170.5. A privately compensated temporary judge, as soon as practicable, shall disclose to the parties any potential ground for disqualification under the provisions of Code of Civil Procedure section 170.1, and any facts that might reasonably cause a party to entertain a doubt that the temporary judge would be able to be impartial. A temporary judge who has been privately compensated in any other proceeding in the past 18 months as a judge, referee, arbitrator, mediator, or settlement facilitator by a party, attorney, or law firm in the instant case shall disclose the number and nature of other proceedings before the first hearing.

(d) Use of Court Facilities, Court Personnel, and Summoned Jurors

A party who has elected to use the services of a privately compensated temporary judge is deemed to have elected to proceed outside the courthouse, and court facilities, court personnel, or summoned jurors shall not be used, except upon a finding by the presiding judge that the use would further the interests of justice. For all matters pending before privately compensated temporary judges, the clerk shall post a notice indicating the case name and number as well as the telephone number of a person to contact to arrange for attendance at any proceeding that would be open to the public if held in a courthouse.

(e) Order for Appropriate Hearing Site

The presiding judge or supervising judge, on request of any person or on the judge's own motion, may order that a case before a privately compensated temporary judge must be heard at a site easily accessible to the public and appropriate for seating those who have made known their plan to attend hearings. The request shall be by letter with reasons stated and shall be accompanied by a declaration that a copy of the request was mailed to each party, to the temporary judge, and to the clerk for placement in the file. The order may require that notice of trial or of other proceedings be given to the requesting party directly. An order for an appropriate hearing site shall not be grounds for withdrawal of a stipulation.

(f) Motion to Withdraw Stipulation or to Seal Records; Complaint for Intervention

A motion to withdraw a stipulation for the appointment of a temporary judge shall be supported by a declaration of facts establishing good cause for permitting the party to withdraw the stipulation, and shall be heard by the presiding judge or a judge designated by the presiding judge. A declaration that a ruling is based on error of fact or law does not establish good cause for withdrawing a stipulation. Notice of the motion shall be served and filed, and the moving party shall mail or deliver a copy to the temporary judge. If the motion is granted, the case shall be transferred to the trial court docket.

A motion to seal records in a cause before a privately compensated temporary judge shall be served and filed and shall be heard by the presiding judge or a judge designated by the presiding judge. The moving party shall mail or deliver a copy of the motion to the temporary judge and to any person or organization who has requested that the case be heard at an appropriate hearing site.

A motion for leave to file a complaint for intervention in a cause before a privately compensated temporary judge shall be served and filed, and shall be assigned for hearing as a law and motion matter. The party seeking intervention shall mail or deliver a copy of the motion to the temporary judge. If intervention is allowed, the case shall be returned to the trial court docket unless all parties stipulate in the manner prescribed in subdivision (a) to proceed before the temporary judge.

(g) Compensation

Temporary judges shall serve without compensation, unless the parties agree in writing on a rate of compensation to be paid by the parties, and that rate shall be allowed. This provision does not apply to juvenile dependency and delinquency proceedings in which the compensation of the referee is established by the county board of supervisors.

Rule 244.1. Reference by Agreement

(a) Reference Pursuant to Code of Civil Procedure Section 638

A written agreement for an order directing a reference pursuant to section 638 of the Code of Civil Procedure shall be presented with a proposed order to the judge to which the case is assigned, or to the presiding judge or supervising judge if the case has not been assigned. The proposed order shall state the name and business address of the proposed referee and bear the proposed referee's signature indicating consent to serve. The written agreement and order shall clearly state whether the scope of the reference covers all issues or is limited to specified issues.

(b) Objections to the Appointment

An agreement for an order directing a reference does not constitute a waiver of grounds for objection to the appointment under section 641 of the Code of Civil Procedure, but any objection shall be made with reasonable diligence. The referee shall disclose as soon as practicable any facts that might be grounds for disqualification. A referee who has been privately compensated in any other proceeding in the past 18 months as a judge, referee, arbitrator, mediator, or settlement facilitator by a party, attorney, or law firm in the instant case shall disclose the number and nature of other proceedings before the first hearing. Any objection to the appointment of a person as a referee shall be in writing and shall be filed and served upon all parties and the referee.

(c) Use of Court Facilities and Court Personnel

A party who has elected to use the services of a privately compensated referee pursuant to section 638 of the

Code of Civil Procedure is deemed to have elected to proceed outside the courthouse; therefore, court facilities and court personnel shall not be used, except upon a finding by the presiding judge that the use would further the interests of justice. For all matters pending before privately compensated referees, the clerk shall post a notice indicating the case name and number as well as the telephone number of a person to contact to arrange for attendance at any proceeding that would be open to the public if held in a courthouse.

(d) Order for Appropriate Hearing Site

The presiding judge or supervising judge, on request of any person or on the judge's own motion, may order that a case before a privately compensated referee must be heard at a site easily accessible to the public and appropriate for seating those who have made known their plan to attend hearings. The request shall be by letter with reasons stated and shall be accompanied by a declaration that a copy of the request was mailed to each party, to the referee, and to the clerk for placement in the file. The order may require that notice of trial or of other proceedings be given to the requesting party directly. An order for an appropriate hearing site shall not be grounds for withdrawal of a stipulation.

(e) Motion to Withdraw Stipulation or to Seal Records; Complaint for Intervention

A motion to withdraw a stipulation for the appointment of a referee shall be supported by a declaration of facts establishing good cause for permitting the party to withdraw the stipulation, and shall be heard by the presiding judge or a judge designated by the presiding judge. A declaration that a ruling is based on an error of fact or law does not establish good cause for withdrawing a stipulation. Notice of the motion shall be served and filed, and the moving party shall mail or deliver a copy to the referee. If the motion is granted, the case shall be transferred to the trial court docket.

A motion to seal records in a cause before a privately compensated referee shall be served and filed and shall be heard by the presiding judge or a judge designated by the presiding judge. The moving party shall mail or deliver a copy of the motion to the referee and to any person or organization who has requested that the case take place at an appropriate hearing site.

A motion for leave to file a complaint for intervention in a cause before a privately compensated referee

shall be served and filed, and shall be assigned for hearing as a law and motion matter. The party seeking intervention shall mail or deliver a copy of the motion to the referee. If intervention is allowed, the case shall be returned to the trial court docket unless all parties stipulate in the manner prescribed in subdivision (a) to proceed before the referee.

Rule 244.2. Reference by Order

(a) Reference Pursuant to Code of Civil Procedure Section 639

A motion by a party for the appointment of a referee pursuant to section 639 of the Code of Civil Procedure shall be served and filed and shall be heard in the department to which the case is assigned or, if the case has not been assigned, in the department in which law and motion matters are heard. The motion shall specify the scope of the requested reference. In determining whether a reference shall be made, the court, if requested to do so, shall balance the economic hardship to the litigants against the need for the reference. An order appointing a referee under section 639, whether based on a motion of a party or on the court's own motion, shall specify the reasons for the reference, the scope of the reference, and any conditions on the reference, including any limitation on the referee's total fees or hourly fee as well as the terms of the obligation of each party to pay the referee. When the issue of economic hardship is raised before the commencement of the referee's services, the court shall determine a fair and reasonable apportionment of reference costs. The court may modify its order as to the apportionment and may consider a recommendation by the referee as a factor in determining any modification.

(b) Selecting the Referee

In selecting the referee, the court shall accept nominations from the parties and provide a sufficient number of names so that the parties may choose the referee by agreement or elimination. The parties may waive his procedure by a waiver noted in the minutes. The name of the referee shall be stated in the order of reference.

(c) Objection to Reference

Participation in the selection procedure under subdivision (b) does not constitute a waiver of grounds for objection to the appointment under section 641 of the Code of Civil Procedure, or objection to the rate or apportionment of compensation of the referee, but any objection shall be made with reasonable diligence. It is the duty of a referee to disclose as soon as practicable any facts that are known by the referee that might be grounds for disqualification. A referee who has been privately compensated in any other proceeding in the past 18 months as a judge, referee, arbitrator, mediator, or settlement facilitator, by a party, attorney, or law firm in the instant case, shall disclose the number and nature of such other proceedings, including the name of any party, attorney, and law firm that appeared in the previous case and is appearing in the instant case. Any objection to the appointment of a person as a referee shall be in writing and shall be filed and served upon all parties and the referee.

(d) Use of Court Facilities

A reference ordered pursuant to section 639 of the Code of Civil Procedure shall entitle the parties to the use of court facilities and court personnel to the extent provided in the order of reference. The proceedings may be held in a private facility, but if so, the private facility shall be open to the public upon request of any person.

(e) Discovery Referees

An order of reference under section 639(e) of the Code of Civil Procedure to assist in the resolution of a discovery dispute shall:

(1) Grant the referee the authority to set the date, time, and place for all hearings determined by the referee to be necessary, to direct the issuance of subpoenas, to preside over hearings, to take evidence, and to rule on objections, motions, and other requests made during the course of the hearing.

(2) Require the referee to submit a written report to the parties and to the court within 20 days after the completion of the hearing, with a proposed order and any recommendation for the imposition of sanctions.

(3) Require that objections to the report shall be served and filed no later than 15 calendar days after the report is mailed to counsel, that any party who objects to the report shall serve and file notice of a request for a hearing, and that copies of the objections and any responses shall be served upon the referee.

(4) State that the court may seek the recommendation of the referee as to an allocation of referee's fees.

(5) Address other matters as necessary.

Glossary

Acquiescence Acquiescence, as a dispute resolution process, occurs when one party gives up and accedes to the demands of the other. When parties select acquiescence as their method of dispute resolution, they also select the substantive resolution of their dispute.

Adhesion Contract (Contract of Adhesion) An adhesion contract is formed when one party imposes take-it or leave-it terms upon the other party.

Adjudication In adjudication, the disputing parties come before a neutral third party, they relate the nature of their dispute to the third party, and the third party resolves the dispute. The parties do not resolve their own dispute. The third party adjudicates or judges the dispute. Adjudication processes include arbitration, mediation-arbitration, litigation, and private judging.

Advocate Ombuds An advocate ombuds advocates on behalf of those who seek the advocate ombuds's services and is not an ombuds in the traditional sense since an ombuds is the designation for a neutral and impartial third party.

Answer Answer is the defendant's response to the plaintiff's complaint. In the answer, the defendant must admit or deny the allegations made by the plaintiff in the complaint. The denial may be a general denial, specific denial, qualified denial, denial based on lack of sufficient information to form a belief as to the truth of the allegation, or a denial of allegations based on a good faith belief that they are false. In the answer, the defendant also must raise any affirmative defenses relevant to the case such as accord and satisfaction, arbitration and award, assumption of risk, contributory negligence, discharge in bankruptcy, duress, estoppel, failure of consideration, fraud, illegality, injury by fellow servant, laches, license, payment, release, res judicata, statute of frauds, statute of limitations, and waiver.

Arbitration In arbitration, the disputing parties come before a neutral third party (an arbitrator) or a panel of neutral third parties (an arbitration panel), they relate the nature of their dispute to the arbitrator or the arbitration panel, and the arbitrator or arbitration panel resolves the dispute. The parties do not resolve their own dispute. Since the arbitrator or the arbitration panel resolves the dispute, the parties have lost control over the outcome of their dispute.

Baseball Arbitration *See* final offer arbitration.

Bilateral Action In a bilateral dispute resolution action, the two parties to the dispute are involved in the process and both, together, resolve the dispute. A bilateral action is negotiation.

Bounded Arbitration *See* high/low arbitration.

Choice of Forum Choice of forum is the determination of which court will hear any dispute.

Choice of Law Choice of law is the determination of which law applies when more than one state is involved in a transaction, where conflicting laws exist within a state, or where federal law may preempt state law.

Classical Ombuds The classical ombuds involves a public official appointed to address issues raised by members of the general public, usually concerning actions or policies of the governmental entity or individuals within those entities.

Collateral Estoppel Collateral estoppel, also known as *issue preclusion*, deals with the binding effect of judgments and prevents the relitigation of an issue in any lawsuit brought after the issue has been litigated in a previous suit.

Complaint A complaint or petition is the document used to initiate a lawsuit. Whether the document is called a complaint or petition depends on the jurisdiction in which the document is filed.

Confession of Judgment Confession of judgment, also known as a *cognovit*, permits the party to a contract who receives the confession of judgment to have a judgment entered in court without the need to proceed through trial.

Conflict of Interest A conflict of interest exists when the neutral third party (ombuds, mediator, arbitrator, or judge) and one of the disputing parties have potentially incompatible interests.

Contract of Adhesion   *See* adhesion contract.

Counterclaim   A counterclaim is the defendant's complaint and requires the plaintiff to respond to it in the same manner the defendant had to respond to the plaintiff's complaint.

Court-Annexed Arbitration   Court-annexed arbitration (court-sponsored or court-ordered arbitration) provides the litigants with an abbreviated (i.e., summary presentation of the evidence with a limited number of witnesses) bench-type trial (i.e., a trial without a jury) that is conducted without the formality required by the state or Federal Rules of Evidence and state or Federal Rules of Civil Procedure. If a case came within the local court rules for arbitration, the litigants would be required to arbitrate their dispute before a court-appointed arbitrator before they would have the opportunity to present their case before a judge. The parties could accept the arbitrator's award or proceed to a trial de novo before the court.

Court-Sponsored Mediation (or **Settlement Conference**) In a court-sponsored mediation, often called a *settlement conference,* the litigants participate in mediation before they have an opportunity to try their dispute in court. The mediation is conducted by a neutral third party (judge, magistrate judge, or court-appointed settlement judge) and is held in private at the courthouse. The neutral party may or may not have been selected because of his or her specialized subject expertise.

Cross-claim   A cross-claim is a claim that one party to a lawsuit has against a coparty (e.g., a plaintiff against a coplaintiff or a defendant against a codefendant) that arises out of the same occurrence. Thus, one plaintiff may become a defendant to another plaintiff or a defendant may act as a plaintiff against another defendant.

Decision Tree   A decision tree is a diagram of branching lines with each point of branching representing an issue that requires a pair of opposite conclusions. A simple decision tree would have one issue and two conclusions. A decision tree could be visualized as a fork in the road: one fork goes to the left; the other fork goes to the right. A more complicated decision tree would have two issues. The one fork goes to the left; the other goes to the right. The fork that went to the left now has a fork: one to the left and the other to the right.

Deposition   A deposition is the testimony of a prospective witness, including a party to the lawsuit. A deposition may be conducted orally or by written questions.

Discovery   Discovery is a pretrial process used to enable the litigants to prepare effectively for trial by obtaining knowledge about the dispute; to make the litigants take less-rigid positions with respect to the issues at the beginning of the lawsuit, before they have had the opportunity to obtain information; to narrow the issues before trial; to preserve testimony of witnesses who will not be available at trial; to eliminate surprise during litigation; and to prepare accurate, factual data to support a motion for summary judgment. Discovery usually involves one or more of the following: taking depositions by oral examination or written questions; seeking written interrogatories; requesting admissions; seeking a court order for the production of documents and other evidence; and requesting physical and mental examinations.

Duress   Duress is the use of any wrongful act or threat to influence a party to enter into a contract.

Early Neutral Evaluation (ENE)   Early neutral evaluation (ENE) involves an early case assessment by a member of the bar who has experience in the substantive area of the dispute. This evaluation by a neutral third party provides the parties and their attorneys with the opportunity to visualize the case from a third party's perspective. By having this preview of what might happen at trial, the parties have a clearer understanding of the settlement value of their dispute.

Facilitative Mediation   In a facilitative mediation, the mediator refrains from suggesting solutions, but does assist the parties in focusing on the nature of their problem, their interests, and an array of resolutions they suggest for their dispute. Not all mediators are facilitative mediators. Some mediators evaluate the problem and suggest solutions as they assist the parties in working through the process. Even if the mediator suggests solutions, the parties ultimately must resolve their own dispute.

Final Offer Arbitration (Last Offer or Baseball Arbitration)   Final offer arbitration, also known as *baseball arbitration* because it is used to resolve salary disputes in major league baseball, is another variation of private arbitration. Final offer arbitration follows the private arbitration process with the exception that in final offer arbitration, the parties agree that the arbitrator must select one of the parties' last offer. The arbitrator has no leeway and may not make an award more than, less than, or in between the parties' last offers.

Forum State The forum state is the state where the lawsuit is filed.

Fraud (Fraud in the Factum) Fraud in the factum relates to the very character or essence of the proposed contract.

Fraud (Fraud in the Inducement) Fraud in the inducement is a false representation or concealment of fact, that should have been disclosed, that deceives and is intended to deceive another party to enter into the contract.

High/Low (Bounded Arbitration) High/Low arbitration, also known as *bounded arbitration,* is a variation of private arbitration. High/low arbitration follows the private arbitration process with the exception that in high/low arbitration, the parties agree on the range of the outcome. The arbitrator's award must be in the range established by the parties. The arbitrator's award may be neither more than nor less than this preagreed amount.

Impartiality Impartiality is a lack of bias or prejudice on the part of the neutral third person (ombuds, mediator, arbitrator, or judge) in favor of one party over the other.

Inaction Inaction is one party's voluntary withdrawal from the dispute. Since a dispute requires at least two participants, if one party does not pursue the other, the dispute is resolved.

Interest-Based Negotiation The parties negotiate by defining their problems, identifying interests, and creating a range of solutions.

Interrogatories Interrogatories are written questions to be answered in writing by a party to a lawsuit. Once the questions are answered, they are signed by the respondent under oath. Written interrogatories may be addressed only to a party to the lawsuit.

Jurisdiction A court with jurisdiction over the subject matter has the power to decide the case before it.

Last Offer Arbitration *See* final offer arbitration.

Legal Assistant *See* paralegal.

Liquidated Damages Damages specified in the contract by the parties that will be due in the event of breach.

Litigation Litigation is initiated by one of the parties before a public forum (i.e., the governmentally created, managed, and financed court). The party who initiates the process becomes the plaintiff. The other party involuntarily becomes the defendant. The procedural and evidentiary rules of the court apply to this dispute and to these parties as well as to all disputes and all parties coming before this court. The parties have no say in the applicable rules of procedure, the rules of evidence, the scheduling of trial, or the selection of the judge.

Mediation In mediation, the third party is a neutral and is invited to direct the process.

Mediation-Arbitration (Med-Arb) Med-Arb is a combination of mediation and arbitration. In med-arb the parties agree that the process will begin as a private mediation and, if they are unable to reach a mediated agreement, the process shifts to private arbitration.

Mini-Trial A mini-trial is an abbreviated nonbinding trial held before a three-person panel (one corporate officer with settlement authority from each corporation and a neutral third party) and is followed by the corporate officers negotiating a settlement. If the corporate officers invite the neutral third party to participate, the process becomes a mediation.

Motion for a Directed Verdict The defendant's attorney may make a motion for a directed verdict after the plaintiff has rested his or her case. By making this motion the defendant contends that the plaintiff's evidence is not sufficient to support a judgment in the plaintiff's favor (i.e., the plaintiff has not established a prima facie case).

Once all the evidence has been presented, either the plaintiff or defendant may make a motion for a directed verdict. If the motion is granted, the judge enters a verdict and judgment for the prevailing party and the trial is concluded. If the motion for a directed verdict is not granted, the case will be submitted to the jury for a determination of the questions of fact.

Motion for a Judgment Notwithstanding the Verdict The motion for a judgment n.o.v. is a request to the judge to set aside the jury's verdict and to enter judgment for the party making the motion. This motion requires the judge to determine whether the jury was reasonable. If the judge determines that the jury acted unreasonably in reaching its verdict (a reasonable jury—based on the evidence presented—could have found only for the party making the motion for the judgment n.o.v.), the judge will grant the motion.

Motion for a New Trial   A motion for a new trial asks the judge to grant a new trial because of an error committed during the trial. A motion for a new trial also may be granted on the basis of newly discovered evidence, errors of law, misconduct by a party, attorney, or juror, excessive damages awarded, or a jury verdict against the clear weight of the evidence. If a motion for a new trial is not granted, the judgment entered on the jury's verdict stands.

Motion for Summary Judgment   A motion for summary judgment is a method for one party to prevail in an action without requiring the actual trial of the case. A motion for a *partial* summary judgment is a method for one party to prevail as to some issues of the case and thus simplify the lawsuit. A motion for summary judgment will be granted if there is no dispute as to the material facts of the case and one litigant is entitled to judgment as a matter of law.

Negotiation   Negotiation is a private, voluntary, consensual dispute resolution process involving the two disputing parties (or their representatives) as they attempt to resolve their dispute. Unlike inaction, acquiescence, and self-help where a party acts unilaterally, the parties in negotiation must work together to resolve their dispute.

Ombuds   *See* advocate ombuds, classical ombuds and organizational ombuds.

Organizational Ombuds   An organizational ombuds may be in either the public or private sector of the community and ordinarily addresses problems presented by members, employees, or contractors of the entity, or students in an academic institution, concerning the actions of individuals within the entity or policies of the entity.

Paralegal (Legal Assistant)   The American Bar Association defines a paralegal or legal assistant as "a person qualified by education, training or work experience who is employed or retained by a lawyer, law office, corporation, governmental agency or other entity who performs specifically designated substantive legal work for which a lawyer is responsible."

Parol Evidence Rule   A substantive rule of contract law whereby a term not included in the final writing (the integration) is determined to be or not to be a term of the contract.

Petition   *See* complaint.

Position-Based Negotiation   The parties begin negotiating by stating their respective solution to the problem and attempt to convince the other party to accept their stated solution.

Precedential Value   An judicial opinion has precedential value when it serves as the rule for future cases that are similar.

Predispute Arbitration Provision   A predispute arbitration provision requires the parties to arbitrate all disputes that arise under their contract. The parties are precluded from litigating their dispute and must use arbitration if their dispute is to be resolved by adjudication.

Predispute Mediation Provision   A predispute mediation provision requires the parties to participate in mediation for all disputes that arise under their contract. If the parties are unable to resolve their dispute through mediation, they may move to another form of dispute resolution.

Preemptory Challenge   A preemptory challenge is an attorney's challenge of a prospective juror for no actual cause. The number of preemptory challenges is limited and decided prior to the commencement of trial. In a preemptory challenge, the attorney does not have to give any reason why he or she wants the prospective juror dismissed. Preemptory challenges are used to remove a juror from the jury panel based on some personal reason or instinct of the attorney.

Private Arbitration   In private arbitration, the parties agree to arbitrate their dispute either before the dispute arises or after the dispute has arisen. The parties select the arbitrator, arbitration panel, or arbitration service provider and pay for the process. In private mediation, the arbitrator or arbitration panel hears the evidence and then resolves the dispute for the parties.

Private Judging ("Rent-a-Judge")   Private judging is a dispute resolution process where a neutral third party who is not a sitting judge (i.e., retired or former judge, law professor, or practicing or retired attorney) is selected to conduct a private trial between the parties. Private judging may be by contract or by court referral.

Private Judging by Contract   In private judging by contract, both parties agree on the process. The parties must negotiate the procedural and evidentiary rules as well as the extent of pretrial discovery, whether the trial will be before a judge and jury or only a judge, who will be the judge (and jurors), who will pay the judge (and jurors) and how much, where and when the trial will be held, how long the trial will last, and whether the decision will be advisory or binding. In private judging, the parties' attorneys choreograph the presentation of facts and law and the third party or parties (the judge or the jury and judge) resolve the dispute. The dispute is resolved according to "the law" and the decision is binding unless the parties have decided otherwise. If binding, the decision may not be appealed to a public tribunal.

Private Judging by Court Referral   Private judging by court referral, also known as a *referenced procedure,* takes place after one of the parties has initiated litigation by filing a complaint before a court. As the case is proceeding down the litigation track, the litigants decide that they may not want to wait for trial before the court. Rather than wait, they may ask the judge to refer the case to a private judge. About half of the states have laws that permit the courts to appoint a private judge if requested by the parties.

Private Mediation   In private mediation, a neutral third party facilitates the discussion between the parties in an attempt to help the parties resolve their dispute. The mediator controls the process and the parties negotiate through the mediator. The mediator does not resolve the dispute. The parties must agree on the resolution of the dispute. When parties select mediation as their method of dispute resolution, they become involved in a process that will most likely require compromise.

Privileged Communication   A privileged communication is information given by one party to another that is not permitted by law to be divulged by the party receiving it. The privilege is the privilege of the party conferring the information and not the party who receives it.

Procedural Arbitrability   Procedural arbitrability inquires whether the procedural requirements for arbitration, such as timeliness and specificity, have been met.

Pro se   A party who files a complaint *pro se* files on his or her own behalf and is not represented by an attorney.

Public Litigation   *See* litigation.

Quid pro quo   Quid pro quo is the exchange of one thing for another. In the law of contracts, one party promises to entice the other party to promise. One promise is the quid pro quo for the other promise.

Reference Proceedings   Reference proceedings is the private judging process when a case is referred to a private judge by the court.

Rent-a-Judge   *See* private judging.

Res judicata   Res judicata, also known as *claim preclusion,* bars a party from commencing a new lawsuit based on the same facts and against the same parties as a previous lawsuit when the subject matter of the case has been finally decided between the parties in the first lawsuit and the time for appeal or further appeal has expired. The judgment is final and cannot be contested.

Risk   Risk involves the probability of loss and the amount of loss. Acceptable risk is the probability that an aggrieved party will not recover (or not recover as much as he or she expected to recover) or the probability that the other party will be required to pay (or pay more than he or she expected to pay).

Secured Transaction   The transaction in which the buyer (or borrower) gives the seller (or lender) a security interest in specified collateral thus giving the seller the right to repossess the collateral in the event the buyer (or borrower) defaults in payment.

Security Agreement   A security agreement is an agreement to use collateral to guarantee payment of an obligation.

Security Interest   The right the buyer (or borrower) gives the seller (or lender) to repossess specified collateral in the event the buyer (or borrower) defaults in payment.

Self-Help   Under self-help, as a dispute resolution process, an aggrieved party may pursue relief without the assistance of the courts. Often, the self-help relief occurs when a contract has been breached.

Settlement Conference   *See* court-sponsored mediation.

Substantive Arbitrability　Substantive arbitrability inquires whether the parties intended the issue or particular subject matter of the dispute to come within their arbitration agreement.

Summary Jury Trial　A summary jury trial is an abbreviated trial, usually before a mock jury. The evidentiary presentations are shortened so the jury receives enough of the flavor of the case upon which to render a mock verdict. The summary jury trial gives the litigants and their attorneys an opportunity to preview what might be the result if the case proceeds to trial. The parties and their attorneys can use this information to pursue settlement discussions.

Summons　A summons is an official order to appear in court.

Third-Party Adjudication　In a third-party dispute resolution adjudication, three parties are involved in the process (the two disputing parties and a neutral third party), and the neutral third party, not the disputing parties, resolves the dispute. Third-party adjudication includes arbitration, mediation-arbitration, litigation, and private judging.

Third-Party Assistance　In a third-party dispute resolution assistance, three parties are involved in the process (the two disputing parties and a neutral third party), and the disputants, not the neutral third party, resolve the dispute. Third-party assistance includes ombuds, mediation, and mini-trial.

Third-Party Evaluation　In a third-party dispute resolution evaluation, three parties are involved in the process (the two disputing parties [and their attorneys] and a neutral third party). The third party listens to the attorneys' discussion of the case and then provides the parties with an evaluation as to the strengths and weaknesses of the case. The third party neither resolves the dispute nor assists the parties in resolving their dispute.

Third-party evaluation includes early neutral evaluation and summary jury trial.

Trial de novo　A trial de novo after an award in a court-annexed arbitration is a trial from the beginning and takes place as if no court-annexed arbitration has taken place.

Unconscionable Contract Provision　An unconscionable contract provision is a provision that, at the time of contract formation, was imposed by one of the contracting parties that is unreasonably favorable to that party and the other party lacked a meaningful choice to accept or reject it.

Unenforceable Contract Provision　An unenforceable contract provision is a contract provision that the court will not implement.

Unilateral Action　In a unilateral dispute resolution action, only one party is involved in the selection of the process, has an active role in the process, and determines the resolution of the dispute. Unilateral action includes inaction, acquiescence, and self-help.

Venue　Venue concerns the geographical location of the court. It must be determined which county court in the state or which district court within the federal system is the appropriate location for the lawsuit. Venue is designed to ensure that there is minimum inconvenience for the litigants and witnesses and that the case can be administered efficiently.

Voir Dire　*Voir dire* is the screening of the potential jurors by the judge or by the attorneys, depending on the court. *Voir dire* consists of asking the prospective jurors questions to determine if any of the jurors may have a bias or a prejudice which would affect their impartiality in the case.

Writ of Execution　A writ of execution is an order, usually issued by the clerk of the court, directing the sheriff to seize and sell the defendant's nonexempt property.

Index